The way to build aircraft or do

anything else worthwhile is to think out

quietly every detail, analyze every situation

that may possibly occur, and, when you

have it all worked out in practical sequence

in your mind, raise heaven and earth

and never stop until you have produced the

thing you started to make.

—GLENN L. MARTIN, 1918

Raise Heaven and Earth

*The Story of
Martin Marietta People
and Their
Pioneering Achievements*

WILLIAM B. HARWOOD

SIMON & SCHUSTER
NEW YORK   LONDON   TORONTO   SYDNEY   TOKYO   SINGAPORE

SIMON & SCHUSTER
Rockefeller Center
1230 Avenue of the Americas
New York, New York 10020

Designed by Barbara Marks
Manufactured in the United States of America

10   9   8   7   6   5   4   3   2   1

Library of Congress Cataloging-in-Publication Data

Harwood, William B., date
    Raise heaven and earth : the story of Martin Marietta people and
their pioneering achievements / William B. Harwood.
       p.   cm.
    Includes bibliographical references.
    1. Martin Marietta Corporation—History.   2. Aeronautics—United
States—History.   3. Martin, Glenn L. (Glenn Luther), 1886–1955.
I. Title.
TL568.M37H37   1993   93-30509   CIP
338.7'6291'0973—dc20

ISBN: 0-671-74998-6

This book is for the tens upon tens of thousands of extraordinary Martin Marietta people who have known the satisfaction of "raising heaven and earth" and for those yet too young to know . . .

. . . and for Ellen and Janet, Bob, Frank, Sarah, Jessica, Andrew, and Emma, but most especially for Ruth, to whom this book is dedicated; she has shared the life—as surely as if she wore the badge—as friend, critic, fan, and my loving wife.

Contents

■

CONTENTS

Preface

■

From the flat cornfields of Kansas and the steep palisades of New York's Delaware River Valley grew two enterprising men—Glenn Luther Martin and Grover Martin Hermann. Entirely dissimilar in backgrounds, except for small-town beginnings and the times in which they lived, they were remarkably alike in style, focus, determination, and the ability to shape their own destinies. One was a self-taught visionary, a pioneer aviation genius; the other a merchant entrepreneur. Although there is no record that they ever met, both built and peopled industrial enterprises that one day would merge. Each in his own way was a mastermind, endowed with the creative intelligence to take technology and direct it into a project or system.

This is not just their story but the story of tens upon tens of thousands who worked with them in the companies they created and in the corporation that emerged—the oldest aerospace enterprise in America, if not the world. It is the story of kindred people drawn together, as the title suggests, by more than their common vocation; of the remarkable times and some of the extraordinary pioneering achievements their lives witnessed and helped mold. It does not attempt to be a history in the purest sense, although the narrative chronicles much that was historic in the century-plus it encompasses,

1886 to 1993, and particularly in the eighty-four years of its principal focus, 1909 through 1993. The intent from the outset has been to report—more than to create—to collect, connect, and record in one place as many riches of fact and lore as could be contained comfortably in one volume.

Long a dream of many, this book owes its life to a spark lit in 1988 when Griffin B. Bell, former attorney general of the United States and a member of Martin Marietta's board of directors, suggested to the chairman, "We really ought to have a history," and the chairman turned to the author and said, "Let's do it!" It would take two years before the project could begin and three more to research and write it.

Much of the early material and dialogue was taken from *To Ride the Wind*, a biography of Glenn L. Martin written by a friend and former company colleague of many years, the late C. Henry Still, and published in 1964 by Julian Messner, Inc., a division of Simon & Schuster, which granted permission for its use here. Hank Still's book drew heavily, as does this one, on an undated company publication, *Box Kites to Bombers*, circa 1950. A third resource was the extensive collection of Glenn L. Martin papers in the Library of Congress, including hundreds of newspaper stories and pictures meticulously clipped and mounted in scrapbooks. The simultaneous discovery deep in some old Martin Marietta files of photographic reductions of those same scrapbook pages made detailed study possible as well as photocopying of some of the pictures reproduced herein. Credit for this material, however, is given to the Library of Congress collection.

The author acknowledges with thanks the many generous interviews granted by those identified in the text. Thanks also to an almost equal number who contributed indirectly through material they supplied or wrote, or through articles reporting their participation in dramatic events of the past. Those unnamed in the text are acknowledged in Notes and Other Sources. Thanks also for the encouragement and support of Tom Pownall, who said, "Let's do it," and Norm Augustine, whose enthusiasm and thoughtful reading contributed significantly to this book.

Three others lent significant effort, patience, and encouragement to the author. Elliott H. Miller, colleague and friend for nearly thirty-five years, expanded an excellent slide-show history he previously had created into a useful timeline for this book. His knowledge and wisdom in picture selection and editing were invaluable, as was his careful manuscript reading, which suggested the title. Hal Gettings, another friend and fellow worker for many years before he retired, edited the Appendix, including research on eighty-four years of patent history which had been carefully organized and computerized by the late Jean Adams of the company's legal staff. And finally, Donna Price, whose dedication and hard work on the mechanical preparation of the manuscript and other material is gratefully acknowledged. Donna transcribed every word of the more than two hundred hours of recorded interviews, and her knowledge and impressive facility with the computer efficiently converted hundreds of pages of rudimentary word processing into a presentable final manuscript.

Without these contributions, the author never would have been able to *Raise Heaven and Earth*.

—W. B. HARWOOD
December 1993

Introduction

∎

This is a book I had hoped to write myself, not only because I enjoy writing but because there is an engaging story to be told. It is a story of some of the greatest technological challenges in the history of mankind, of great triumphs and of occasional disappointments. But above all it is a story of people, of a group of people so incredibly lucky as to have lived and worked during that sliver of time when humans first broke free from this earth and learned to fly—and fly they did, all the way to outer space. Along the way they helped create fabulous inventions, from devices that enable one to see in the dark and skis made of revolutionary new materials to missiles that can shoot down a bullet and giant aircraft that fight forest fires. In so doing they helped win wars and preserve the peace. They participated in missions to six of the seven planets visited by U.S. spacecraft in the past quarter century and built the first robot to land safely on a planet other than Earth. In the process, they helped found an entire new industry that one day would employ more than a million people. In short, they made a difference.

This is *their* story, and although in truth it was intended just for the enjoyment of the Martin Marietta family (now expanded to include two entire new teams of individuals of great accomplishment, one tracing its proud heritage all the way back to Thomas A. Edison, and the other to the creation of Sandia National Laboratories half a century ago), it is an inspiring story for every American who is intrigued by great challenges and even greater victories.

It was only when Bill Harwood decided to retire from his position as Martin Marietta's vice president of public relations that I abandoned my dream of telling this story myself. The opportunity to have Bill author the company's history was simply too great an opportunity to pass, given his more than thirty-one years of service to Martin Marietta, his deep insight into the company and its people, and his extraordinary writing talents. Further, and sadly, many of those who had helped make the earlier portions of this story a reality were fast reaching advanced age, making it all the more imperative that their recollections be promptly gathered and recorded.

But the motive in writing this book was not simply to tell a tale too good to risk losing, although that in itself is probably an adequate justification. More important, it was to provide a means of reminding those who carry on the torch what it was and what it is that makes Martin Marietta a great organization. All companies have personalities, just as people do, and hopefully the character of Martin Marietta will be thought of as the product of uncompromising integrity and an intense commitment to "mission success"—in short, a group of decent people performing quality work.

The aerospace industry, which can conveniently be viewed as including a related portion of the electronics industry and might therefore be dubbed the "aerotronics" industry, is in many respects unique. As a fairly young industry it still enjoys a strong pioneering spirit. Attacking great challenges, such as traveling to the Moon or the planets, is an everyday affair among its participants, some of whom actually *do* have to be "rocket scientists." Further, the laws of nature are a wonderfully fair and uncompromising judge to those who seek to challenge the leading edges of the state of knowledge.

The aerotronics industry is a demanding and unforgiving one. You either win the Titan competition or you lose it—*all* of it, forever—often after years of intense preparation and heavy investment of talent and money. When you launch a Space Shuttle, it either succeeds gloriously or, on occasion, fails tragically. Thus, the emotional highs experienced by those in this industry are truly sky high, and the lows plumb the depths. Over time a certain camaraderie has evolved among the practitioners of the aerospace art, nurtured at least in part by the occasional attacks from critics who in peacetime would refer to what we consider the arsenal of democracy as the "military-industrial complex," or worse. It is not unlike soldier

Tommy in Kipling's poem: "It's Tommy this, an' Tommy that, an' 'Chuck 'im out, the brute!' But it's 'Savior of 'is country' when the guns begin to shoot."[1]

And when the guns begin to shoot, as they all too often have this century, the aerotronics industry invariably has proven equal to the challenge. In World War II our predecessors at the Glenn L. Martin Company built close to ten thousand military aircraft, from long-range bombers to giant seaplanes. Martin planes also played prominent roles over Korea and Vietnam. During the most recent conflict in the Persian Gulf, the first round fired by the allies was produced by Martin Marietta as were a dozen other systems used in Operation Desert Storm. The Patriot missile probably changed the course of history by enabling Israel to remain aloof from offensive combat even when sorely provoked, thereby preserving the solidarity of the allied coalition.

Ironically, a few years earlier Martin Marietta had been called upon to fight a war of its own in response to a 1982 hostile takeover attempt—the corporate equivalent of a street fight but without the dignity. After the initial salvo, *each* company found itself owning a majority of the other, creating a dilemma unprecedented in the annals of corporate combat and one that only the media or a corporate lawyer could have enjoyed. Eventually escaping with both its dignity and its freedom, Martin Marietta set out to restore its financial health by shedding its peripheral businesses—but hanging on to its core aggregates and aerospace interests. The resulting corporation's products literally range from rocks to rockets, or to be more inclusive and quote from the text, from "pebbles to perigees."

In a sense this is a story not of a company but of an entire industry, with many of its origins traceable to Glenn L. Martin. His early employees went on to found companies with such distinguished aviation names as Douglas, McDonnell, Vought, Brewster, Consolidated (now General Dynamics), and North American Aviation (now Rockwell).

Seventy-seven years elapsed from the time of the famous flight of Orville Wright, who later became Glenn Martin's partner, until the first flight of America's Space Shuttle, fueled by the giant Martin Marietta–built External Tank. That tank is so large that if laid on its side, its cavernous interior would accommodate the Wrights' first flight, both in length and altitude.

During its eighty-four years, 1909–93, the company was led by only five chief executive officers, but with the exception of Glenn Martin himself, this is the story of the people in the shops, in the laboratories, on the design boards, on the flight lines, and at the launch pads. These are the people of Martin Marietta who made the company what it is today, an institution in which all can unabashedly take great pride.

As this book lifts off the presses, yet another chapter in the history of Martin Marietta is being written in the operating centers and offices of the corporation in thirty-nine states and seventeen other countries. This is the combination of General Electric Aerospace and Martin Marietta, creating the largest aerospace/electronics—aerotronics, if you will—company in the world. Augmented by the recent addition of Sandia National Laboratories, which Martin Marietta operates for the Department of Energy, the resulting organization of nearly one hundred thousand employees is the fortieth largest company in America by sales, with a total backlog of some $25 billion. This is not to suggest that this new company can escape being severely tested as America once again seeks to display its love of peace by disarming itself, much as it has done on four previous occasions in this century alone. It would seem overly fortuitous that in this closing decade of the second millennium the history of human behavior would suddenly reverse itself and become peaceful. Therefore, the men and women of Martin Marietta will continue their commitment to national security even as they move into altogether different markets to build a new Martin Marietta that is rich in technological diversity.

In 1909 when Glenn Martin built and flew his first aeroplane, it is unlikely that even he could have foreseen the giant China Clippers that in less than three decades would fly large groups of passengers in living-room comfort across the Pacific Ocean. It seems equally unlikely that the pilots of those giant flying ships could have foreseen the Manned Maneuvering Unit, which in five more decades would enable earthlings to become "human satellites." And today the employees of the new Martin Marietta are working to astonish the world with even grander accomplishments in the next fourscore and four years . . . and more.

As John F. Kennedy said of the space program, "We do these things not because they are easy but because they are hard." Who can guess what yet-to-be-invented products will emerge from the dedication, talent, and perseverance of this extraordinary team of people?

NORMAN R. AUGUSTINE
Chairman and Chief Executive Officer
Martin Marietta Corporation
Bethesda, Maryland, 1993

PART I

Beginnings
1886–1913

◼

CHAPTER 1

Bedsheets, Box Kites, and Biplanes

■

Winter comes early and stays late in Macksburg, Iowa. By mid-January, five or six feet of hard-packed snow is not uncommon. Cattle stay close to the barn, and farmers have to spread feed where snow won't cover it. The winter of 1886 was one of the worst, with temperatures 25 degrees below zero. So it was not surprising that Araminta Martin, in the eighth month of her second pregnancy, dreamed of spring and an early delivery.

The Martins had been married three years: Araminta DeLong was a stern schoolmarm who brooked little nonsense in her Afton, Iowa, classroom, and Clarence Y. Martin was a not-too-successful hardware salesman not particularly known for hardheadedness. No one was surprised when the strong-willed Minta persuaded Clarence to marry and begin their new life together in Macksburg. It was there that their first child, a daughter named Della, was born two years later. She was nearly two years old that cold Christmas season of 1885 when Minta Martin had her remarkable dream. Excitedly, Minta woke her husband to describe it. There she was, she told him, floating effortlessly through the sky, high above the streets of Macksburg.

"I was actually flying, Clarence. It was wonderful," she exclaimed. "I wish I could teach everyone to do it." Prophetic vision? How could she know that the son she bore several weeks later, on

January 16, 1886, would indeed fly and would enable her and thousands of others to one day soar through the heavens? Minta named her son Glenn Luther Martin and from that day on dedicated her life to him, to the decided detriment of her husband and daughter. In fact, the daughter would later be committed to a mental institution and all but disappear from the family's life.[1]

Glenn was two when the family packed up and moved to southwest Kansas and what they hoped would be a brighter economic future. Clarence, with Minta's persistent prodding, had decided the future in hardware was farther west, where he could sell machinery and implements to farmers. The long train trip across Kansas's rolling fields of grain encouraged their resolve, that is, until the train pulled into Liberal, their chosen destination. It was flat, dry, and hot, and tumbleweed rolled along the streets, driven by a wind that seemed never to cease, and that was too warm to offer relief.

Clarence Martin opened his new hardware store on Liberal's Main Street, and the family settled into a modest house farther down the street. It would be their home for the next six years. Liberal would also be the foundation of young Glenn's earliest fascination with the wind and all things that flew. The Martins would spend a total of seventeen years in Kansas, until Glenn's mid-teens. In Liberal he discovered the wind and learned to control it. Already a bright little fellow, Glenn benefited greatly from his schoolteacher mother.

C. Y. Martin's hardware store, Liberal, Kansas, 1890

She not only doted on him but encouraged him in every mental and creative activity. It was no surprise to her, nor was she cross with her precocious son, when he took a bedsheet from the clothesline and tied it to a makeshift mast he had only that morning rigged to his wagon.

There are no hills in Liberal, Kansas; it is as flat as the American Midwest gets. Its prevailing breezes are strong, sometimes gusty, but most often sustained. So it was not too much for even one so young to conceive that the wind could drive a wagon rigged with a sail. And drive it it did, straight down Liberal's Main Street, startling passersby and spooking a team of horses tied by a customer outside Clarence Martin's hardware store. The snapping of the bedsheet would have been enough to cause the horses to bolt. The grinding racket of the iron wagon wheels plus the whoops of delight from young Glenn guaranteed the result for which Clarence Martin reprimanded his son that evening at the dinner table. The elder Martin had expected his wife's support, at least in his scolding for the use of the bedsheet, but Minta was amused and more than a little proud of her young son.

"Wait a minute, Clarence. He didn't intend any harm." Minta's voice was soft but firm. "As for that worn bedsheet, it was ready to fall apart. Besides," she said, "there is little enough for a boy to do in this town. I think it's good that he was able to rig that sail by himself."

"You're going to spoil the boy, Minta," he admonished his wife. "I've said it before. But if you keep on taking his side in everything, he'll run wild with all those crazy ideas of his." And there the matter rested—until the next time. Unbeknownst to her husband, Minta Martin had heard the clamor on Main Street that afternoon and had rushed to the front door in time to see her exuberant son sail by in the strangest contraption she had ever seen.

"Look! Look, Mother" he shouted. "I'm flying." It was the spring of 1890. Glenn Martin was four.[2]

■

IN THAT SAME YEAR THERE was a clamor of another sort halfway across the country in the sleepy little Delaware River village of Callicoon, New York. The wailing of a newborn baby boy announced the arrival on July 21 of Grover Martin Hermann, the second child of Mary Elizabeth and Martin Hermann, a hardworking and relatively well-established lumberman. They named him Grover Martin Hermann, his first name from his mother's family and his middle name

Hermann lumber mill, Grover and Dad

from his father and grandfather before him. (There was no connection with the Martins of Kansas).

As the birds fly, Callicoon is about twelve hundred miles east of Liberal and less than one-tenth the size. Callicoon had no more than eight hundred people then, as it does today. Like Liberal, it had been Indian country, inhabited by both the Iroquois and the Algonquins before the first settlers arrived in 1607. When the Dutch sailed up the Hudson River and explored its tributaries, they called the area "Kollikon" for the wild turkey they hunted through its hemlock and pine forests. Literally translated "cackling hen," the word was later anglicized to Callicoon.

Like the Martins of Kansas, the Hermanns were of German descent. They were part of a great influx of immigrant farmers driven from their homeland in the mid-1800s by the oppressive, militaristic regime of Bismarck. By hard work and austere living they transformed a densely forested, rocky land into one of the most productive farming regions of the upper Delaware Valley. Besides farming, the other industries of the area were logging and tanning. The tallest pine trees, cut for masts, were floated downriver as far south as the shipyards of Philadelphia. The plentiful hemlocks supplied lumber, and their bark fed the tanneries.[3]

Grover's father, Martin, was one of eleven children. As the first son, he broke the farming tradition at the age of twelve when he had to help provide for his large family after his father's death. Martin

Hermann's Garage, Callicoon, N.Y.

Hermann was good with his hands. So while his older sisters and younger brothers took over the farm chores, he became a carpenter and eventually established his own woodworking and building business. The year Grover was born, his father erected a saw mill and later added a hardware store. His business was eventually expanded to a repair shop and one of America's earliest automobile dealerships.

■

BY THE TIME GLENN MARTIN entered first grade, he was already exhibiting a mental agility and capacity well advanced for a boy of six. Thanks to his mother's home tutoring and her ambition for him, he had mastered primary skills in reading and arithmetic. Every morning's breakfast included a mother-son game that progressively climbed the multiplication tables. On his walks to and from school and whenever he was out of the house on his own, Glenn increasingly sought the solitude and beauty of the cornfields and the banks of the Cimmaron River, where he could watch the birds, especially the waterfowl migrating north. He developed a love for bird life that carried through his lifetime and even influenced some of his future aircraft designs. He studied the shape of the birds' wings, their habits, their landings and takeoffs. He was particularly fascinated by geese. He watched them skim low above the surface of the river, lowering their legs at the last moment for splashdown. On takeoff, their rapid threshing along the surface until airborne also captured the boy's imagination.

In addition to migrating geese, spring brought another airborne ritual that appealed to Glenn. Practically all the youngsters in Liberal built and flew their own kites. Now that he was six, Glenn was able to join in this activity, and he had his own ideas of what a kite should be. It was indeed a different kite that he took to the field that first time. Most kites looked alike—brown wrapping paper glued over string that was stretched across the four points of two crossed sticks. All had long tails, which despite the weight increased stability in the strong Kansas winds. Not Glenn's. His was a box kite. By trial and error he had discovered that warped wood struts and wrinkled paper caused uneven flight patterns. By reducing and tightening the paper area and lengthening the exposed sticks, Glenn produced a narrow box, almost as tall as he was. Both ends were covered with paper, and the exposed sticks of the midsection offered little resistance to the wind. It brought laughs from the older kids when he carried it onto the field.

"What kind of a kite is that?" teased Joe Rankin, a third grader who was the undisputed kite-flying champion. His kite was five feet tall and had a tail nearly twenty feet long. "Bet it won't get off the ground," he challenged. Glenn didn't have any money, but he was willing to bet that his box kite would fly and that it would fly higher than Joe's or anyone else's.[4]

The contest was joined, each agreeing to use only two hundred feet of string, which was all Glenn had. Each chose an assistant to hold his kite off the ground and let out about fifty feet of string. Joe went first. As he ran quickly into the breeze, his kite lumbered into the air and climbed slowly. When his turn came, Glenn didn't run at all. He merely snapped the string taut, and the box kite leaped from the assistant's hands and danced gracefully toward the sky. It climbed almost straight above their heads. The more string Joe Rankin let out, the farther out his kite flew, but it climbed only slightly higher. Glenn's climbed straight up and clearly was the high flyer, all the boys agreed. Joe Rankin looked at the younger boy with new respect as he reeled in his kite.

"How much will you take for it?" he asked. Glenn paused before answering. He hadn't considered selling it. "Well, the string cost quite a lot, and I worked a long time on the kite itself," he replied.

"How much?" Joe pressed. "How much?" Glenn hadn't expected this turn to the contest. He would either keep his kite or get a lot for it. "Twenty-five cents," he blurted out, sure that he would retain ownership.

"I'll take it," Joe replied, flipping a quarter at the surprised Glenn, who couldn't believe his good fortune. He seldom had a whole quarter at one time. Others crowded around, asking if he would build them box kites, too. Most didn't have a quarter but offered a nickel down and a nickel a week.

Glenn L. Martin was in business at the age of six, manufacturing "air craft" on the installment plan. The year was 1892. His factory was the floor of his mother's kitchen where, with her usual indulgence and encouragement, he soon was turning out three kites a day. Neither boy nor mother could possibly have foreseen that the pattern of his entire life—producing superior products based on his own instincts and skills—had been set at this tender age. Equally ordained was that he would do so with her ever-present encouragement, guidance, and sponsorship.

By the time he was eight, like most youngsters that age, Glenn was put to work helping his father. The elder Martin had purchased a ghost town across the river, and Glenn's chore was helping to salvage the lumber after the buildings were demolished. One of the hired hands lost an entire wagonload to Cimmaron River quicksand, but not Glenn. With his customary thoroughness and foresight, the boy tested the path he intended to follow, walking barefoot through the shallow water before leading across the team and wagon filled with lumber.

In 1894, Glenn's father decided that neither the retail hardware business nor the secondhand lumber business was going any place in Liberal. He took a job as a traveling salesman for a manufacturer of hardware and implements, and the family moved again, this time to the larger town of Salina in north central Kansas. Traveling afforded Clarence an opportunity for new acquaintances and companionship he did not enjoy at home, where he was either unable or unwilling to share in the close mother-son relationship. The bond between mother and son grew stronger with the father's long absences from home in his new job.

Glenn's slender build, combined with weak eyes that caused him to wear glasses, hindered his competitiveness in rough-and-tumble sports. But he was no sissy. Fiercely competitive and with a well-hidden streak of daring that became a trademark in later years, Glenn proved himself in track. He became an outstanding foot racer and roller skater, and a strong member of the local roller hockey team. On ice skates he dazzled pond regulars with his skill and grace, frequently riding the wind by using the flaps of his coat as sails.

Glenn excelled in all subjects in school, thanks to the extra tutoring at home. But he still found time to pursue other interests. He was fascinated by tools, machinery, and all things mechanical, and by age twelve had built an electric motor. In his second year of high school, he got a job in Dave Methven's bicycle shop where he discovered how good he was with his hands. Wheels, chains, and gears—things to take apart and put together—came naturally to him. He figured out a way to put a sail on a bike to make it go with the breeze, without pedaling. And his eagerness and faithfulness to the job impressed his employer. The job at the bicycle shop lasted through his high school years, which were also the final years of the century. With the advent of the automobile and the arrival of the first one in Salina, Methven's bike shop became an auto agency.

■

THE AUTOMOBILE WAS ALSO BECOMING a large factor in the life of a growing Grover Hermann, who turned ten the first year of the new century. He also stopped being the baby of the family when his mother gave birth to twin sons, Edwin and Edgar. Life was not unpleasant for the son of a relatively well-to-do logger, lumberman, and hardware dealer. Already the largest employer in that part of Sullivan County, Grover's father had just obtained dealership rights for Buick automobiles.

By the time he was twelve, Grover spent many of his nonschool hours running errands or just hanging around the Hermann lumber mill, especially the carpentry shop. He wasn't particularly interested in the business until his father added the auto agency. There began the makings of an entrepreneur and the shaping of business talents that would become more evident with age. There also commenced an attraction to fancy, expensive cars that he would exhibit throughout his life.

■

AN ATTRACTION TO AUTOMOBILES AND to all things mechanical was mirrored in the life of Glenn Martin, both as boy and man. For sixteen-year-old Glenn in Salina, Kansas, the chance to tinker with internal combustion engines was pure heaven. He became immersed in engines and autos and how they worked. Keeping them working was the trick of those early days of the industry, and Glenn soon earned a reputation as a first-class mechanic and troubleshooter. He frequently went to the rescue of novice auto owners stalled in their cars on back-country roads.

Fresh out of Salina High School, he enrolled in a two-year business course at Kansas Wesleyan University. If he was to succeed in business, he told his mother, he needed to combine his mechanical skills with a knowledge of good business practices. For a young man who was to gain most of his technical knowledge from books, newspapers, and periodicals, communications left much to be desired in the early 1900s, particularly news of the world conveyed by the popular press of the day. America's first attempts at flight, for example, drew scant press attention in most parts of the country. Some of them went entirely unreported in Salina. Dr. Samuel Pierpont Langley's dismal failure on the Potomac River in 1903 and the Wright Brothers' first flight in Kitty Hawk on December 17 of the same year were events unknown to Glenn Martin at the time.

It was two years later that he rushed home, excitedly waving a newspaper with the story and a picture of a Wright airplane flight of twenty-and-a-half miles. The photo showed an airplane that looked like one of his box kites, only bigger and with an engine.

"Just imagine being able to fly, to actually leave the earth," he told his parents. "I'm going to build one of these and fly it myself one day."

"Yes, I'm sure you will," Minta Martin agreed. The year was 1905. Glenn Martin was nineteen.[5]

In the winter of that same year, Glenn's mother became seriously ill following one cold after another, and her doctor suggested the family find a milder climate. Clarence was genuinely concerned for his wife, and perhaps he also reasoned that a move farther west and south would offer more business opportunities for him. They decided on California, and the family boarded a train for Los Angeles. The City of Angels was indeed a growing community, but it appeared to have an abundance of hardware stores. The Martins decided to keep going, thirty miles farther south to the smaller city of Santa Ana. With a population of ten thousand, it looked like a pleasant, up-to-date community, surrounded by prosperous farms.

No sooner had the family settled into a house on Minter Street than Glenn found a job in a Santa Ana garage. It also happened to be the agency for the new and very popular Maxwell automobile. He worked hard and long, banking almost all the money he earned. In the space of a year Glenn managed to save $700. With that and a loan

Glenn in Liberal, circa 1900

he persuaded the bank president to give him, he opened his own automobile garage and new car agency. He hired a good local mechanic by the name of Roy Beall and talked his father into joining him as a partner and salesman for the Ford and Maxwell cars they had been franchised to sell. The young man's industriousness during that first year in Santa Ana impressed and pleased his father, who was happy to become a junior partner. After all, he was a salesman, the work was fun, and he had few responsibilities. Best of all, the elder Martin had plenty of time for his first love—fishing.

Doubling as a mechanic and salesman, Glenn was the driving force behind the fledgling venture that earned a $4,000 profit its first year, 1906, and gave the Martins their first real taste of prosperity.

■

BACK EAST, YOUNG GROVER HERMANN was sixteen. His father had purchased his first raft of logs, one of the few great sights to behold on the Delaware River. The Hermann lumber mill was booming, but the supply of wood was getting scarce as forests around Callicoon gave way to farming. In order to assure a supply of raw material, Grover's father entered into agreements with loggers farther up the river. He bought their felled trees, delivered to the riverbank where they would be ganged in huge log rafts to be floated downstream to the Hermann mill.

Grover vividly remembered the arrival of that first raft. It was huge—tens of thousands of logs boxed together. Smaller rafts, or colts, each twenty by eighty feet, were lashed together to form larger rafts. The raftsmen were a hearty bunch, generally big and rugged. When the logs reached their destination—Hermann's mill at the mouth of Callicoon Creek or farther downriver at Port Jervis, Newburgh, or even Trenton—the raftsmen were paid. Then, carrying their ropes and axes, they began the long journey back. It was not unusual for the raftsmen to walk the entire distance, with frequent stops along the way in the taverns that dotted the river. Heavy drinking and brawling were common.

The Delaware River and the Indian lore of its beautiful valley did much to shape young Hermann. As a middle child, Grover was pretty much a loner. His older sister, Lulu, was six years his senior, and his twin brothers were ten years younger. He had cousins by the score—sixty of them by actual count—but he was not especially close to these children of his ten uncles and aunts, even to those of them near his own age.

CHAPTER 2

Realizing the Dream

■

In the first year the Martin family lived in Santa Ana, Glenn's sister Della was committed to an institution, after having been declared a "religious fanatic and mentally ill."[1] For the twenty-two years she lived in Iowa and Kansas, there was little or no record of Della's existence; nor would there be for the next fifty-one years that she remained institutionalized.

As he became more successful, Glenn set about establishing his persona. He worked on it as diligently and as thoughtfully as he did everything else. His daily attire was a dark suit, a white shirt with a celluloid collar, a conservative tie, and a bowler hat. Combined with his slenderness and eyeglasses, Glenn was the model of a dignified and reliable businessman. No one in Santa Ana had known him as a boy, and he established his look with a clear vision of what was to come.

Beneath that conservative and somewhat cultivated appearance, however, lived the daredevil, adventurous spirit that would mark his future. He did not choose to reveal that side to the conservative bankers and other town leaders he would one day need. But when he was out of the office, Glenn could not hide his love for speed and power. At every opportunity he put each new automobile model through its paces. On early morning test drives, before most of the citizenry was awake, Glenn would push a car to maximum speed, then slam on the brakes to tax his control or to feel it dizzily spin when the pavement was wet.

Accounts differ of another early morning occasion when he reportedly demonstrated the ruggedness of one car by driving it up the courthouse steps. Some say it was a motorcycle. It could have been either because he was also noted for high-speed runs and stunts on a motorcycle. According to one historian, he set a record by racing his motorcycle the twenty-five miles from Santa Ana to San Juan Capistrano in twenty-six minutes.[2] His reputation for derring-do, while deserved, was occasionally self-promoted. One local resident recalled a favorite trick of Martin's: Making sure he had an audience, he would "accidentally" nudge off his cap while riding his motorcycle down the street, then circle around and pick it up without stopping.

As his auto agency prospered and the new cars became speedier, Glenn salted away his savings and eagerly scanned every newspaper he could find for stories from the East about the Wright Brothers or another Glenn, named Curtiss, who was also building and experimenting with airplanes. Finally, one afternoon in 1907, Glenn coaxed Roy Beall from his usual position flat on his back under a Maxwell and took his chief mechanic for a ride outside of town. Leaving the road, Glenn steered into McFadden's pasture where a small crowd had gathered around a strange contraption they could just barely see. Beall had never seen one, but Glenn knew it was an aeroplane, forced down that morning with engine trouble, according to the local newspaper. They both marveled that it consisted of nothing more than sticks, wire, cloth, and what appeared to be bicycle wheels. The engine was substantial enough, but apparently it wasn't working, from the perplexed look of the pilot tending its repair.

"As long as I can remember, I've always wanted to build one," Glenn told his companion. "How long do you think it would take us?"[3] They were back in the car headed for town before the full import of Glenn's question hit Roy Beall. He was a practical, simple man. He knew, of course, that aeroplanes existed, but only as dangerous playthings. Yet here was his boss, a level-headed man he admired and liked, talking about building one.

"Remember every detail you saw," Glenn told him. "I'll be over after supper so we can draw up some plans while our memories are fresh." He dropped Roy at the garage and sped off. Roy happened to bump into Clarence and told him what they had seen at the pasture and about Glenn's remarks. Clarence's disbelief and mounting anger led to another father-son confrontation at supper. Clarence was fuming. Such a cockamamy idea, and just when he thought the boy had straightened out.

"Now listen to me," he told his son at one point. "I know you're twenty-one, your own boss, and a good businessman, but you're not too old to take some advice. I don't see the sense of throwing away all you've got by messing around with those flying machines. It's the quickest way I know for somebody to get killed or hurt."

"I won't get hurt," Glenn reassured his father. "Besides, it will take a long time to build a machine like that. We'll make one part at a time right in the garage. Roy can help me in his spare time. There'll be plenty of time to learn how to run it safely."

Minta had been listening, her eyes darting from one face to the other. Then she spoke: "Maybe Glenn's right," she said. "He just might make a better flying machine than they have now. It seems, Clarence, that we should encourage him a little." Clarence knew that when mother and son agreed, he didn't stand a chance. He protested once more, this time on the folly of wasting money on such a foolhardy scheme, before he stormed out of the room and the house, slamming the door as he left.

"Don't worry," Minta told Glenn. "If you think you're right, go ahead. Just promise me that you'll be careful." Smiling his promise, Glenn left the house, already late for his meeting with Roy. He found his mechanic busily sketching on a large piece of butcher paper spread over the kitchen table. Roy had drawn a fairly accurate plan of the biplane they had seen in the pasture. Glenn unfolded a sketch he had brought with him and compared it to Roy's. Instead of two wings, Glenn had drawn only one. And the engine was mounted on the front instead of behind the wing like the one in the pasture.

Glenn called his version a monoplane. He told Roy that although they probably would be better off copying the plane they had seen or the Wrights' biplane, he did not want to infringe on any rights they might have. Besides, one wing was better, he reasoned. It would save weight and offer less resistance to the air. Glenn had confided on their way back to town that afternoon that he had been reading everything he could find on aeroplanes. With a single wing, he told Roy, they could make it bigger and get all the necessary lift. The two worked late into the night, the mechanic in Roy as caught up in the design as Glenn. They calculated sizes and shapes, structural stress points, and parts that needed to be stronger. Neither man

First plane, 1908

had any engineering education, but both were naturally gifted when it came to design and mechanics. At one point they turned to a book on bridge building to help them with problems of stress.

Both arrived early at the Martin garage the next morning. They took a secondhand Ford engine and began building the plane around it. Parts they had sketched the night before took shape in the garage. Days stretched into weeks and months. Ribs of spruce were steamed and shaped for the wing and tail, then covered with a fine muslin sewn by Roy Beall's wife. A third participant in the project was Charles Day, the mechanics instructor from the Santa Ana YMCA. Day had come up with the idea of laminating strips of wood for the propeller to save weight. He then carved it himself from the laminated block he had created.

The more time that was devoted to "Glenn's contraption," the more Clarence disapproved. Finally he asked his son what it was costing. Glenn couldn't bring himself to tell his father the true amount, so he passed the question off with "Not much, Dad." He was troubled by his own deceit and his father's continued opposition to the project. Despite his convictions, the young man was still sensitive to the opinion of others, particularly his father and Roy, his willing but doubting collaborator. Perhaps they were right, he thought as he looked over the framework of his delicate craft with its white wing panels. Much of the work was good, but some was pure guesswork. Maybe it wouldn't fly. Maybe he would appear a fool in front of the whole town. But he couldn't stop now. They had come too far and had invested much more than he had dared tell his father. And so the plane was finished and taken out to McFadden's pasture early on a warm July morning in 1907. Neither Roy Beall nor Charlie Day shared Glenn's enthusiasm for the plane. They had been carried along by his sheer drive and persuasive personality, but neither envied him the dubious distinction of flying it.

Although it was barely dawn, a small crowd of spectators collected in the pasture and stood at what they considered a safe distance from the strange-looking craft and the trio preparing it for flight. Most recognized Glenn, impeccably dressed as always, as the bespectacled owner of Martin's Garage and motorcar agency. But their attention was focused on his unlikely-looking contraption. The single wing was attached to what resembled a piece of steel scaffolding. Suspended within it was an engine from a Ford motorcar to which was attached the wooden propeller. Extending back from the scaffoldlike structure was a triangular framework, which ended in the tail. Both wing and tail were built of curved wooden ribs and straight spars. They were covered with white muslin that had been varnished.

When the three agreed that everything was ready, Glenn climbed into the seat under the wing, just behind the Ford motor. Day removed the stepladder they had used to inspect the wing and tail surfaces. Roy went to the nose and grasped the propeller. With a nod from Glenn, he pulled the prop through half a revolution, then pulled again. The engine caught after only four revolutions, coughing alive with a loud barking clatter. Sitting directly behind the now wildly spinning propeller, Glenn was caught in a strong blast of air and had to pull his hat down tightly to keep it from blowing off. Carefully but firmly he advanced the throttle, and the plane moved forward under its own power. He taxied the vibrating plane the full length of the bumpy pasture before turning and taxiing back to his waiting friends.

"Are you going to take her up?" Roy shouted above the roar of the engine.

"No," Glenn shouted back. "I'm going to learn to run on the ground first. Look out, I'm going around again."

On his fourth trip around the field, at the far end, the engine coughed, sputtered, and died. Rather than wait for Roy to come the full length of the pasture to help him, Glenn jumped out and spun the prop himself. The engine caught on the first pull, and the pilotless plane began to roll. Glenn dropped to the ground to avoid the whirling propeller, which sliced the crown of his hat, barely missing his scalp. Rolling free of the wheels, he jumped to his feet and tried to climb back into the open seat. Failing that, he lunged for the throttle but succeeded only in jarring it further open. The engine roared to nearly full power, and it was all Glenn could do to hold on to the framework. He was afraid to let go, fearful that the pilotless plane would wreak havoc, perhaps on the crowd gathered at the other end of the field.

He couldn't stop the plane, but he did influence its path. It dragged him in ever tighter circles until a wheel collapsed, causing the wing to dip into the ground and break. Then the frame crumpled, the prop splintered, and the entire craft tore itself to pieces around its still chugging engine and its would-be pilot. Although scratched and bruised, Glenn was not seriously hurt. Emotionally, he was crushed. And as he headed back to Santa Ana in an ambulance summoned by someone in the crowd, he shouted a loud "damn," the only oath anyone can ever remember hearing him utter.

His cuts and bruises healed faster than his feelings, but soon he was at it again. He built at least three gliders that same year and tried them out on nearby hills. He retrieved Roy Beall's sketch of the biplane they had seen, and he wrote to the Wrights, asking if that concept—two wings with a pusher engine—infringed on their work. The letter was well received by the brothers who had already sued Glenn Curtiss for patent infringement. Orville Wright wrote a cordial reply stating that he and his brother had "no objection to your building a plane according to the design you have outlined to us." He expressed a sincere interest and offered Glenn every encouragement.[4]

It was the start of a long and enduring friendship between Orville Wright and Glenn Martin, a relationship based on shared interests and mutual respect. The Wright letter spurred Glenn to proceed with his plans. As a result of his first failure, however, he became more secretive and tight-lipped. But it was impossible to keep tongues from wagging when he rented, for $12 a month, the abandoned Southern Methodist Church building, just a block and a half from the garage. Its stained-glass windows prevented the curious from peeking in, affording all the privacy he wanted. It was one of the few buildings in Santa Ana with unobstructed space large enough to build the entire aeroplane he had in mind.

At first the church saw little action. Parts were made at the Martin Garage, then stored in the church basement for later assembly. Glenn went about his regular daily business, perhaps with a bit more zeal, selling an extra Ford or Maxwell when he needed money

First "factory," Santa Ana church

for wood, glue, wire, or muslin. As parts accumulated, Glenn worked not only full days at the auto agency but late each night at the church. So did Roy Beall and occasionally Charles Day, who had been recruited again for the propeller and other detail work.

Even Minta Martin, who had urged her son to try again after his first plane was wrecked, worried about the late hours he was keeping. One night she wandered over to the church and found him alone. Trying to hold a lantern and work on the engine at the same time, he had not heard her enter.

"Here, son," she said. "Let me hold that." From that night on, Minta Martin was part and parcel of the project, and it was not unusual for Santa Anans out late at night to see mother and son driving home after midnight in his Maxwell roadster.

Thirteen months after they began, the plane was finished. Structural weight had been eliminated wherever possible. Wing spars and struts were built of spruce. Bamboo was used in the tail boom and supports for the front elevators because of its strength and lightness. Wings and control surfaces were covered with a fine muslin. The plane was then painted with a special varnish that not only closed the pores in the mesh but strengthened the fabric. A light copper crankcase had been fashioned by Roy Beall to replace the heavy iron one on the engine. A Charles Day–carved laminated propeller was mounted on the engine, which was placed behind the pilot so that it would literally push the plane. There were three control systems: A hand-operated wheel and lever controlled two cables, and Glenn manipulated a third by moving his shoulders. Total weight was an amazingly light 1,150 pounds.

Finally ready to take the field, Glenn and his compatriots faced the problem of getting the plane out of the church. Historical accounts differ. The most romantic relates how, under the guise of enlarging the vestibule, they knocked out the entire front wall of the church, albeit with the owner's permission. But according to Roy Beall, in an interview many years later, they simply removed the wings and took the plane though the front doors.[5]

Even though they had picked midnight to avoid attention, a sizable crowd had gathered to watch. A procession of vehicles followed Glenn's Ford roadster as it towed the fragile plane to a preselected bean field a few miles outside town. The forty-foot wings barely cleared the brush lining the roadway. The midnight hour had been chosen not so much because of Glenn's penchant for secrecy but to avoid traffic on the roads. Horses were still skittish around automobiles, and Glenn figured his great white bird would cause runaways if he moved it in daylight. The 160-acre field Glenn had selected was part of a fifteen-thousand-acre ranch belonging to James Irvine, who was to become one of young Martin's enthusiastic admirers, supporters, and early passengers.

After a thorough check of all surfaces and structures to make certain the trip from town had not damaged anything, Glenn, Roy, and Charlie Day settled down to await the dawn. Sleep was out of the question, but the three men did relax for a couple of hours. At the first light of day, the engine was started. Sputtering at first in the morning dampness, it quickly settled into an even roar, and the plane was pointed into the wind. Seated in front of the wings, below the engine, Glenn flexed the controls and relived all the practice hours of taxiing and flight he had simulated in the church during the year the plane was being built.

His stomach was in knots. He hadn't eaten since lunch the day before. The time was now, he told himself. Everything had been checked. A glance to the left told him Roy Beall was ready on that wingtip. To the right, Charlie Day held the other wing. Glenn gave them a nod and slowly advanced the throttle. The engine responded loudly, and the plane began to roll. As he continued to push the throttle, the engine roar became deafening and the plane increased its bumpy path across the field. His feeling of nausea gave way to vivid alertness. From the corners of his eyes, he saw Roy and Charlie

Airborne, 1909

running to keep up, still holding on to the wings. An added advance of the throttle, and the speeding, lurching plane outdistanced its wing walkers. Plane and pilot were now racing across the ground. The wind whipped Glenn's face even as he felt it swell under the wings.

"Now!" he whispered. "Now!" And at the very moment it seemed the plane would shake apart, the noise and violent motion suddenly ceased. In a rare moment of peace he was airborne. Glenn was ecstatic. He did not know whether to cry or shout for joy. Fleetingly, he recalled the birds he had watched by the hour as a boy back in Liberal. Then the disciplined, deliberate Glenn Martin regained mental control. Resisting the temptation to fly farther and higher, he immediately reversed throttle and put the plane back down on the ground.

He had done it. He had flown. The date was August 1, 1909.

Glenn Luther Martin at age twenty-three had joined the elite handful of pioneers who had dreamed of flying and had done so. Moreover, he had done it in a plane of his own design, built with his own hands. He had been airborne no more than eight feet above the ground and had flown a distance of one hundred feet, less than the wingspan of planes he would later build. The entire flight, in both distance and height, could have taken place inside the huge fuel tank his company would one day build for the Space Shuttle. But he had flown. The height and distance were no more than he had planned. It was enough for this first time.

Turning the plane carefully, Glenn taxied back to where Roy, Charlie, and the crowd of townsfolk were excitedly shouting and waving their hats. Climbing out, Glenn walked around the plane and gently touched it here and there, as much to reassure himself that it was real as to steady himself and mask his feeling of absolute giddiness. His companions grabbed and shook his hand and pounded him on the back.

"We did it," he said quietly.

"You bet we did!" Roy exclaimed. "You flew, Glenn! You actually flew!" Roy wanted to celebrate. Day wanted to go into town and spread the news.

"Not me," Glenn told them. "I'm going home and sleep about twenty hours." As he turned to climb into the roadster, he added, "Be back here tomorrow at sunrise. We'll start some real flying." When he reached home, he paused in the kitchen doorway just long enough to announce to his still-breakfasting parents: "We got it off the ground. It flew." And without waiting for their reply, he climbed the steps and went to bed.

CHAPTER 3

Pioneering Days

■

E very day for the next two months the trio arrived at the field
at dawn and spent most of the day there. Little by little
Glenn taught himself to fly. Through a combination of
methodical experimentation, imagination, and dogged determination, he literally inched into the sky, always putting the plane back on
the ground within the confines of the bean field. It was October
before he pulled far enough back on the controls to clear the fence
at the far end. And that was quite a performance for the little 15-
horsepower engine. Its maximum speed was forty-two miles per hour;
it would stall at thirty-eight—a very slim flying margin.

Nothing would do but to upgrade the engine, and Glenn found
a 4-cylinder, 30-horsepower Elbridge, which doubled the plane's
power without an equivalent gain in weight. The performance improvement was dramatic. He was able to fly farther, faster, and
higher, including lazy gliding turns over the field, and return to his
point of takeoff.

And so it went that autumn of 1909. Glenn's mother and father
frequently went to the field to watch their son fly. Even Clarence had
newfound respect for his son's exploits. Not so everyone in town.
Many shook their heads at the "wild turn" young Martin had taken.
But even though they generally disapproved, the skeptics came out

to watch and wait for what some considered the inevitable. It got to the point where Glenn and Roy built a booth and sold tickets for ten cents apiece to one and all, including those who ghoulishly waited to see him break his neck.

Glenn mostly ignored the criticism of skeptics and others he considered dimwitted or badly informed. But one morning at the breakfast table his mother handed him a note she had received from Dr. H. H. Sutherland, their family doctor. Scrawled in longhand with several spelling errors and addressed to Minta, it read:

> For Heaven's sake, if you have any influence with that Wild-eye, Hallucinated, Vissionary [sic] young man, call him off before he is killed. Have him devote his energies to substantial, feasable and profitable persuits leaving Dreaming to the Professional Dreamers.[1]

The note stung Glenn. It bothered him considerably that a learned man like Dr. Sutherland could be so narrow-minded. Surely he of all people should have some understanding of what Glenn was trying to do.

"He thinks I'm crazy," Glenn told his mother. "They all think I'm crazy." Absentmindedly fingering a bruise that was swelling on his arm from a particularly rough landing the day before, Glenn slumped in his chair. He reflected on Dr. Sutherland's note, on his own slow progress, on how far he lagged behind the Wrights and Glenn Curtis. Almost weekly reports in the local paper told of their exploits. Couldn't Dr. Sutherland and others see the potential for such machines? They could carry the mail or cargo or maybe even passengers someday. Didn't this educated man know that the Army was even considering the aeroplane for military purposes? The possibilities were unlimited.

"They're all wrong! Just plain wrong!" Glenn told his mother with some vehemence. His momentary doubt had passed. Minta Martin smiled. "Don't worry about Dr. Sutherland," she said. "I'll tell him a thing or two. I believe there is a great deal of sense in what you believe and do. Time will tell who is right."[2]

Once more by being the patient, uncritical sounding board, Minta Martin had encouraged her genius son at a moment of doubt and uncertainty. But the critics and doubters were not all close to home. Among the scores of papers, periodicals, and trade publications Glenn devoured in the coming months, this comment from the trade paper *Flying Machines: Construction and Operation* caught his eye:

In the opinion of competent experts, it is idle to look for a commercial future for the flying machine. There is, and always will be, a limit to its carrying capacity, which will prohibit its employment for passenger or freight purposes in a wholesale or general way.[3]

One of the authors of the article was Octave Chanute, the Chicago civil engineer–turned–glider-pilot. The article further bolstered Glenn's resolve to disprove these naysayers.

Another publication Glenn read religiously was *Aero, America's Aviation Weekly*. It brought him the exploits of Ralph Johnstone of Kansas City, who set a high altitude record of 9,714 feet over New York City in a Wright biplane; of Maurice Tabuteau, who set a distance record of 290 miles in Europe; of another, a "Bud" Mars of Norfolk, Virginia, who flew a Curtiss plane in a race with a horse.

But it was a guest editorial by Johnstone, one of the most daring of the early stunt fliers, that most impressed Glenn:

> There are two kinds of aviators. There are Wilbur and Orville Wright. They have developed these machines, and they have flown in them many times, but neither of them will ever break any records in them. They are the creators of the machines. I am in another class. I find these aeroplanes ready to be used for my purpose, just as I found the bicycle. I couldn't invent either a bicycle or an aeroplane, but I can use them and use them better than the men who made them. Moreover, I can go on and on in discovering new methods of controlling and handling them because I have the vaudeville performer's instinct.[4]

Glenn took note of the distinction. He concluded that a blend of the two types might be more appropriate. He also determined that in adopting a bit of the vaudevillian, in order to help promote the aeroplane and the promise of aviation, he would not emulate Johnstone's desire to push the machine beyond its endurance. Be daring, yes, and a showman, but not foolhardy. Johnstone went on in the article to comment that whether he would be killed or not was largely a matter of improvement in the construction of aeroplanes:

> I am convinced that within a few years they will be built so stoutly that a man will be taking no more chances in them than on a bicycle. . . . At this time, however, it's a case of

taking chances every time a man tried any stunts in them. . . . Someday I will do the loop-the-loop in the air, and that will be a thing worth seeing.[5]

Ralph Johnstone never accomplished the loop-the-loop. On November 17, 1910, in an attempt to perform that maneuver over Denver, Colorado, a strut snapped, the wing crumpled, and Johnstone fell to his death with the plane before an air show crowd of thousands. It was one of the most spectacular accidents in the young history of American aviation.

For the remainder of the year and for much of 1911, Glenn continued to hone his skills as an aviator and to develop his aeroplane into a more efficient and predictable flying machine. The 30-horsepower Elbridge engine not only gave him the most trouble, but it was limiting the scope of his flying. Between master mechanic Roy Beall and himself, they had managed to adapt it to a flight task its ground-bound designer had never contemplated. But after a year, its limitations were all too obvious, and they replaced it with a Curtiss "O" engine rated at 70 horsepower, more than twice the power previously available. Now able to fly higher, faster, and farther, it wasn't long before Glenn L. Martin made the pages of *Aero*:

> Glenn L. Martin of Santa Ana is proving himself of late to be a very promising young aviator. Recently he made a cross-country flight of five miles. The flight extended 2½ miles into the country and return.[6]

Even the *Los Angeles Times* took notice of the "birdman" in its own backyard with a cautiously qualified report:

> A young man named Glenn Martin is alleged to have been seen flying his homemade aeroplane at the mesa close to Santa Ana, California.[7]

There followed local exhibitions, for an admission fee, first on the Irvine ranch field, then at county fairs throughout the area, and one all the way downstate in Brawley in the Imperial Valley, not far from the Mexican border. The offer to fly both days of that exhibition was $1,200, but the most Glenn could take home was $750 when his plane ran into one grounding mishap after another. The Brawley meet did provide him with invaluable experience and a primary lesson in aerodynamics. The heat-charged, dry air of the Imperial

Valley, although below sea level, provided less lift for the wings and less bite for the propeller. He did fly, but it was nearly sundown on the second and last day, after breaking one prop in a collision with a fence and a number of other frustrating attempts to get his plane off the ground.

He took home more prize money in December 1910 with some fancy flying in the Los Angeles Air Meet at Dominguez Field. There he flew rings around the other California pilots and rubbed elbows with pilots such as Lincoln Beachey and Navy Commander H. C. Richardson, both well-known pupils of Glenn Curtiss.

More important than the added revenue were the acquaintances Glenn made with a number of the wealthy young sportsmen interested in owning their own planes and learning to fly. He returned to Santa Ana and told his mother of his resolve to build and sell airplanes. Then he discovered that his reputation for being an upstanding Santa Ana businessman, known for good service and as a dealer of outstanding automobiles, did him little good at the local bank. When he attempted to arrange a loan to finance his planned

Glenns—Curtiss and Martin

Early pusher biplane

new business manufacturing aeroplanes, the bank president was among the skeptics who doubted their future. "Too risky" was his assessment in turning down Glenn's application for a loan. Glenn's disappointment was short-lived. His mother suggested he raise the money himself by performing in more air shows. She handed him a magazine listing every fair in California and helped him send out dozens of letters offering an aerial display.

The response was enthusiastic. Soon Glenn was barnstorming up and down the state—$1,500 for this meet, $3,000 for another. He earned $2,000 from the city of San Francisco for flying a letter across the bay to the mayor of Oakland. Except for barest living expenses, Glenn sent all the money home to his mother, who doled it out to Roy Beall and Charles Day. Acting on Glenn's instruction before he began the barnstorming tour, Beall and Day had rented a vacant peach cannery building on East First Street, only a few blocks from the church where they had put together the first plane. In the cannery they began assembling the ingredients of what would be Glenn's first airplane factory.

Minta Martin was right. There was plenty of money to be raised by aerial demonstrations. At the same time, Glenn was making quite a name for himself and the aeroplane. What's more, he was loving every minute of it. As his schedule and popularity increased, Glenn gave up his celluloid collar, business suit, and bowler hat for a showman's garb. Complete from head to toe, it included a black leather jacket, riding britches, black puttees, and a black helmet with goggles. Tall, slim, and suntanned, Glenn cut a dashing figure that soon earned him the nickname "The Flying Dude." At first he objected. Such a name would not help in his effort to give aviation a sound business appeal. But he soon gave up and adopted the moniker in his own promotional materials.

Promotion was the name of the game. He delivered newspapers from Fresno to Madera, a distance of eighteen miles. He carried the first airmail from Dominguez to Compton and dropped a baseball into a catcher's mitt, among other aerial capers. Martin's accuracy in dropping the baseballs was not in question, but Hap Hogan, the catcher and manager of the Vernon baseball team, was not able to hold any of the twelve balls Glenn dropped from an altitude of five hundred feet. Hogan, somewhat sheepish about the experience, ex-

G.L.M. at controls

plained that the motion of the aeroplane gave the ball a curve that was downright impossible to hold. If it had hit him, it probably would have broken his arm, Hogan told the *Los Angeles Herald,* and catching the ball was mere chance because of the curve.

Along with his fame, Glenn's associations grew—with Beachey and Glenn Curtiss as well as other noted pilots of the day, Phil Parmalee, Cliff Turpin, and Howard Gill. Among the aviation enthusiasts were men of considerable financial means, including James Irvine, the rancher, and Frank Garbutt, millionaire oilman and sportsman. They became friends and supporters. He met Charles Willard, who would later join his company as chief engineer, and Grover Bell, whose younger brother, Lawrence D. Bell, would also come to work for him as general manager of his Los Angeles plant.

One of Glenn's avid fans was an Iowa circus clown and tumbler named Joe E. Brown, who would later move to Hollywood and become a famous motion-picture comedian. Glenn gave him rides in his plane and flying lessons in exchange for Brown's teaching him tumbling. The two became lifelong friends.

In between air shows, Glenn returned to Santa Ana to supervise the fledgling business his flying engagements were financing. On August 9, 1911, Glenn became only the second American flier to be recognized internationally when he was awarded Expert Aviator's Certificate No. 2 by the Aero Club of America, the U.S. branch of the Federation Aeronautique Internationale. The first certificate had been given to Glenn Curtiss.

By the fall of 1911, Glenn was twenty-five years old and had seven people on his payroll, including Charles Day as chief designer at $20 a week and Charles Willard, the pilot Glenn had met while barnstorming, who was also a Harvard-educated engineer. Others were Gene Savage, a man named Stevens, and Minta, of course. His chief mechanic by then was Lawrence G. Stern, who had been hired when Roy Beall returned to the auto agency to work with Clarence Martin after deciding his first love was the automobile, not the aeroplane.[8]

CHAPTER 4

Fledgling Businesses

■

F all in Callicoon, New York, generally sets in by late September. It is a beautiful time of year, with the woods painted in reds, oranges, yellows, and browns. And 1911 marked the twenty-first fall of young Grover Hermann's life. By then he had determined to leave Callicoon, but he had not yet found the means or the vehicle. Until he did, he was working in his father's automobile agency, which was not all that bad.

Grover Martin Hermann did not have the mechanical genius of Glenn Luther Martin, but they did share the same natural sense of, and zest for, marketing and promotion. So when the elder Hermann added to his many businesses a line of custom Buick trucks and multipassenger touring cars, Grover's interest picked up considerably. Being a master woodworker, Martin Herman was actually building the bodies of the cars on Buick chassis supplied by General Motors. And Grover was chief salesman, promoter, and demonstrator. One of these vehicles, called a "buckboard" car, was actually a flatbed truck with four wooden benches capable of seating sixteen people. It was described in the sales literature as a "Model 16 Chase Truck with 16-passenger Racer Body built by Martin Hermann." It was never clear, as the *Sullivan County Democrat* opined, why anyone would need or want sixteen passengers in a racer.[1]

The other speciality vehicle built by the Hermanns was a bit more snazzy. Simply referred to as a twelve-passenger Buick, it had four leather-upholstered seats, open sides, and a rigid but surreylike roof. It was equally unclear what the market was for these cars. Perhaps they were used to haul the city folk from the summer trains that came into Callicoon Station and other stops along the Delaware River to posh resorts scattered throughout Sullivan County and the Catskills.

That same fall of 1911, only five days after Glenn was honored with Expert Aviator Certificate No. 2, Grover Hermann and the town of Callicoon saw their first airplane. A Curtiss biplane, it was piloted by Jimmy Ward, one of the intrepid aviators entered in a New York–to–San Francisco competition for a $50,000 prize offered by newspaper magnate William Randolph Hearst. Grover's younger brother, Edwin, was only eleven at the time but clearly recalled the event eighty years later. The pilot had actually stayed at their uncle Peter Hermann's house when mechanical difficulties and bad weather delayed his departure for two days. According to the front-page story in the *Democrat* on September 19, 1911, it was an exciting time:

> Early Wednesday morning it was reported about town that Ward would fly over Callicoon and the populace immediately got busy and everything was aeroplane from then on.... When one of Ward's mechanicians came on the milk train to look up a landing place the inhabitants took up the cry of aeroplane and since then everybody has a "bug" on aviation....

Grover at wheel, with Dad, in 16-passenger "racer"

Ward's flight from Middletown to Callicoon, a distance of 68 miles, was accomplished in 63 minutes and was one of the most daring known to aviation. . . . It was a sight never to be forgotten to see a human being in that frail flyer circling above one's head in absolute control of the most ingenious thing ever credited to man's ingenuity.[2]

Jimmy Ward and Glenn Martin would meet and even fly together two and a half years later. But Ward's flight in and out of Callicoon that day impressed Grover Hermann to the extent that in later years his company acquired its own private plane, which took him everywhere he went.

■

HISTORY AND LORE DISAGREE ON whether Glenn Martin's first manufacturing effort in 1911 at Santa Ana was the formal beginning of what would become the Glenn L. Martin Company. No one would have questioned that it was a going business, but there is no record that it was formally incorporated until later. In slightly more than a year, however, the number of airplanes on private order exceeded the space required to build them. Partially completed planes crowded the Santa Ana cannery floor. Newly covered and doped wing panels were stacked along the walls. Engines rested on blocks, waiting to be installed. Tools and half-finished parts were everywhere.

Two of the planes in assembly were designated Model 12, and when Glenn returned to the exhibition circuit, it was in one of the Model 12s. By then he had hired Roy Knabenshue, a dirigible pilot of some repute, to manage his exhibitions and act as publicist. Knabenshue booked him all the way east to Texas and north through Kansas and Iowa, including shows in Glenn's former hometowns of Salina and Liberal. He even performed in Saskatoon, Canada. The plane, with its 75-horsepower Curtiss engine, was easily his best. The tour also was the best financially, netting Glenn $12,000 after expenses.

He returned to Santa Ana with two projects foremost in his mind. The first involved the Signal Corps, which was responsible for the Army's aviation interest. It had a lone Wright aeroplane from 1908 until March 1911, when it ordered five more. Glenn was convinced the aeroplane had a brilliant military future as a platform not only for bombing but for artillery observation and for reconnaissance. He wanted some of that business to supplement the single

Martin Propeller shop, Santa Ana

orders he was filling for wealthy sportsmen. He had just hired Larry Bell as his shop foreman, and one of the first jobs he handed the aggressive young Bell, who would one day form his own company, was to help stage an aerial display that would back up Glenn's convictions about the future of military aviation. The demonstration was to include a night attack on a mock fort. Complete with crisscrossing searchlights from ships offshore, Glenn and his friend Lincoln Beachey piloted "attacking" planes that dropped "bombs" (bags of flour). At the same time, Bell, on the ground, set off explosions of black powder that simulated bomb bursts and added to the realism.

Thanks to Roy Knabenshue's priming, Los Angeles newspapers took due note of the January 25 event. There was no immediate indication of the Army's reaction, but the demonstration enhanced Glenn's reputation and was the first of a string of events that would make 1912 an auspicious year for the young aviator.

Glenn had long contemplated another goal that was realized later that year. The Pacific Ocean, practically on his doorstep, had been a constant challenge and source of frustration, always intimidating and ever present, given California's long coastline. It was

Launching early hydroplane

time, he told himself, to do something about it. He and Charlie Day fashioned a large pontoon which they mounted directly under the center of the wing on Model 12, right below the pilot's seat. And by the spring of 1912 he began testing the new hydroplane on the waters of Newport Bay. Taxiing only at first, to get the feel of it, Glenn gradually worked up in a space of weeks to water takeoffs and landings.

Roy Knabenshue was also busy, making certain the press knew that Glenn Martin was about to do something important on the water. This was not to be just a flight over water. Up to that time the world record for flight over water was held by Frenchman Louis Blériot, who had crossed the English Channel, a distance of approximately twenty miles. In America, the goal for would-be record setters over water was the ninety-five miles between Key West and Cuba. But it continued to daunt all who attempted it. Glenn's target was Catalina Island, slightly more than thirty miles offshore.

He scheduled the flight for the month of May in anticipation of nice spring weather and calm seas, but the appointed day, May 10, 1912, dawned under heavy clouds. Roy urged Glenn to postpone, arguing that he could lose his way above the clouds. So did Charlie Day and Larry Bell, both of whom had accompanied him to Balboa, where the plane was berthed. They thought the cloud cover made the trip too dangerous. But Glenn was ready. His mind was made up. A few clouds were not going to stop him.

"I'll take my heading from Newport dock," he told them. "It bears directly on the harbor at Avalon. Don't worry. I'll be back before you know it."

Glenn's parents had been sitting in the car and did not hear the discussion. When it became apparent that he was preparing to go, they came to the waterside. Minta helped her son slip an inflated bicycle inner tube around his neck and under one arm. Clarence shook his son's hand and wished him luck. As he climbed into the plane, Glenn remembered his gold watch and chain. He handed it to Charlie Day, asking him to "take care of this in case I go for a swim." Day had to give the propeller only one spin before the engine caught and roared into a smooth rhythm. Two of Glenn's employees from the factory waded into the water to turn the plane into the wind.

Shortly past noon he gunned the engine and was in the air after a takeoff run of only one hundred feet. Waving to those below, he made a climbing turn and headed southwest out over the ocean toward Catalina's Avalon Harbor. He broke out of the clouds at four thousand feet unable to see the ocean below but fixed on a compass heading of 240 degrees, a course that should take him to the island. Glenn figured he had a slight head wind but could only guess the relationship to his sixty-mile-an-hour airspeed.

After thirty minutes, judging that he must be about there, he started a slow descent through the clouds. White caps were his first glimpse of the surface, then bobbing boats of the Avalon fishing fleet. He was dead-on Catalina Island's Avalon Harbor. Thirty-seven minutes after taking off, he landed on the waters of Avalon Bay and taxied to shore.

The sound of his plane circling overhead had brought the population out of the hotels and shops and onto the beach. Two young men splashed into the surf eager to assist his mooring. Unaware of its fragile construction, they allowed the plane to grind onto the gravelly beach before Glenn could wave them off.

He jumped out to find a sizable hole torn in the front edge of the pontoon. Fortunately, the welcoming crowd of conventioning shriners and Mayor Ernst Windle also included Skip Charles, a visiting yachtsman. He offered to patch the pontoon, and while repairs were being made, Glenn was swept up by the throng crowding the beach. He was the toast of Catalina Island, or at least of Avalon, as reported in the *Los Angeles Examiner:*

The crowd surged about him, wrung his hand, and pounded him on the back. They danced about him and gave him cheer after cheer. They led him across the street and made him eat until he could eat no more. Avalon belonged to Glenn Martin.[3]

Even before the return trip, Glenn L. Martin, at the age of twenty-six, was assured a spot in aviation history. He had set a world distance record for hydroplanes.

Repairs to the pontoon and refueling took longer than he expected. Someone in the crowd offered a water pitcher, which Glenn used to pour fuel into the engine. But it was a slow process, and it was five o'clock in the afternoon before he had the plane back in the bay ready for takeoff. Cautiously, he advanced the throttle, and the plane picked up speed, its pontoon slapping dangerously at the crest of each swell. At the very moment of liftoff, a violent shock vibrated through the plane. The patch on the pontoon had apparently torn loose. Glenn carefully gained altitude and safety from the buffeting water. But what would happen on landing? He decided to worry about that after he found Newport Beach. Skies were clear for the return trip, and Glenn confirmed his direction when he overtook the steamer Cabrillo about halfway to the mainland.

For those waiting for him at Balboa, it had been an anxious afternoon, nearly six hours, until they spotted his speck in the sky and heard the sound of his engine. As Glenn circled above them, first Minta, then Charlie Day spotted the hole in the pontoon. Day had already ripped off his coat and was wading out as Glenn eased the plane, nose-high, onto the water. He touched down as close to shore as he dared in hopes of reaching shallow water before the pontoon filled and pulled the plane under. All those barnstorming months of precision landings to a predesignated spot paid off. The plane came to rest with only the lower wing awash just as Day splashed up shoulder-deep in the water.

"Charlie!" Glenn shouted. "What have you done with my watch?" Sheepishly, Day reached in his pocket and pulled out the soaked watch. Even Glenn laughed. It was the day's sole casualty. A day that had seen him set a second world record, the longest round-trip flight over water, sixty-six miles in less than eighty minutes of flying time. This time he made the front pages of more than the Los Angeles and Santa Ana papers.

But Glenn was not about to rest on his laurels. Selling airplanes one at a time did not produce sufficient cash flow for his fledgling business. His barnstorming fees remained the factory's chief source of income. So long as there was money to be made on the airshow circuit, he intended to continue getting it. Before returning to the tour, however, one of the first things he did, with considerable attention from the local press, was to fly his first passenger. That honor fell to none other than his mother, of course, who had been his champion and chief backer for as long as he could remember. Minta Martin was forty-eight when she made her first flight, and she went about it like the trooper she was—silk scarf holding her hat to her head and rubber bands confining her long flowing skirts. There being only one seat, she shared it with Glenn. Her feet dangled beneath the wing as she held firmly to a strut, with no safety belt or protection from the wind.

"I'll never have a thrill like that again," she said, all smiles on landing. "There's nothing like it. Flying is a thrilling experience."

The flight with his mother unexpectedly opened an entirely new opportunity when nearby Hollywood recognized the promotional value of having starlets carried aloft. This would eventually provide a new source of income and invaluable publicity opportunities. Meanwhile, back on the show trail, Glenn continued to please the crowds with his first-time-ever stunts. He dropped a bouquet into a May queen's lap, dropped advertising leaflets for a retail store, organized an aerial coyote hunt, and took part in an actual manhunt by plane for two escaped criminals (who, incidentally, got away).

In answer to a report in the *Santa Ana Blade* of July 6, 1912, that he might move his factory to Denver in order to be nearer the commercial market for aeroplanes, Glenn allowed that a move to Chicago was a possibility.[4]

However, on his next trip home, resolved to do something about the overcrowded cannery, he and Charlie Day took a day off to look for larger quarters. They found a suitable building in Los Angeles and over a period of months moved the Santa Ana business to the new shop. In a lengthy front-page story, obviously leaked in advance of the event by an "informed source," the *Santa Ana Register* reported on August 12, 1912:

> With a company organized to back him, Glenn L. Martin
> is to go into the aviation business on a far bigger scale than
> ever before. That company has been organized, articles of
> incorporation signed, and everything under way for the

Los Angeles plant, 1912

biggest aeroplane factory business on the Pacific Coast. . . .
It is capitalized at $100,000, of which all of the stock is
issued.

Martin's factory, now located on Tenth Street near
Main Street, Los Angeles, goes into the control of the new
company. . . . The place where the factory will be permanently located has not been determined. Martin has a
preference for Santa Ana, but conditions may arise that
will make it necessary to locate elsewhere.[5]

Eight days later, on August 24, 1912, the Glenn L. Martin Company of Los Angeles was formally incorporated, according to records
in the Sacramento office of the California secretary of state. Directors were Glenn; C. Y. Martin, his father; W. A. Zimmerman, a Santa
Ana banker; William Loftus of Whittier, the oil millionaire; and W. S.
Collins, Los Angeles developer and principal owner of Balboa Island,
according to the *Register*. Glenn was twenty-six.

■

A LITTLE MORE THAN A year after Glenn Martin incorporated the
company bearing his name on the West Coast, a continent away

Grover Hermann found his ticket out of Callicoon, New York. It came in the person of Charles Phelan, a traveling roofing salesman who was a periodic visitor to Callicoon. On this occasion he was repairing the roof on the Hermann lumber mill. Phelan and young Hermann were about the same age and hit it off pretty well. Grover was more than a little envious of his entrepreneurial friend, so when Phelan mentioned that he was looking for a partner to help develop and market paint from a formula he owned, Grover jumped at the chance.

He persuaded his father to advance him $5,000 to invest with Phelan, and the pair bid farewell to Callicoon and took the next train to New York City. There they opened an office, leased a plant across the river in Jersey City, and began doing business as the American Asphalt Paint Company. Neither partner being superstitious, they formally incorporated the company on December 13, 1913. Their sole product was an asphalt-based paint they called Gilsonite. Two decades later the business would become the American-Marietta Company, one of the first true conglomerates, and it would eventually make Grover Hermann a multimillionaire. He was twenty-three at the time of its modest beginning.

Hermann and partner Phelan entrain to New York City

PART II

Spawning Years

1913–28

CHAPTER 5

Birth of an Industry

■

Glenn Martin attracted more than a little attention to aerocraft and to the yet-to-be-born field of aviation with his three quite remarkable feats of 1912: his mock bombing demonstration, his record overwater flight, and the first flight with his mother as a passenger. He could not at that time have known—although, visionary that he was, he may have dreamed—that these three achievements would specifically herald aerial advances that would be the greatest of his lifetime: flying boats that would carry passengers across the Pacific and flying fortresses that would bomb an enemy into submission.

The flight with his mother brought instant reaction and unexpected benefits in income and notoriety from the nearby entertainment industry in Hollywood. Press agents, producers, and movie company moguls, all of them ever on the outlook for promotional opportunities, came knocking on the Martin door. One of the first was Valeska Suratt, vaudevillian and star of the musical comedy *The Kiss Waltz*. She hired Glenn to fly her over Los Angeles. Upon landing, as Glenn helped her climb out of the plane, she wrapped her arms around him and planted a tremendous kiss squarely on his lips for the benefit of the assembled crowd of fellow actors and actresses, photographers and assorted press agents. Glenn was "the most sur-

Celebrated kisser Valeska Surratt

prised man in all of East Newport," according to the *Los Angeles Express*. He was also mortified. Shy as he was where women were concerned, he was certain the picture would do little to help him earn the support of the conservative banking and business communities, which he sorely needed to finance his fledgling enterprise. A number of years later, in answer to an interviewer who asked what he feared the most, Glenn would answer "women" and tell the story of Valeska Suratt's surprise kiss.

The highly celebrated kiss did generate additional opportunities. The picture was on the front page virtually across the country, combining as it did the newfound glamour of Hollywood stars with the public's fascination with the wonders of the new flying machines and the "intrepid birdmen" who operated them. It landed Glenn a flying role in a full-fledged motion picture and, more important, an introduction to Georgia "Tiny" Broadwick, an equally intrepid parachute jumper.

The famous kiss-punctuated flight with actress Valeska Suratt actually marked the opening on November 20, 1912, of Glenn L. Martin's Aviation School at East Newport. Over the next half-dozen years he introduced many to the wonders of flying and taught a number of them to be pilots, at $500 per course. Among the most prominent students of the Martin School was William Edward Boeing, a wealthy Seattle lumberman and aviation enthusiast. Boeing, who also bought a Martin airplane, later went on to start his own manufacturing business, the Boeing Aircraft Company, which eventually became the world's largest manufacturer of commercial airliners.

Other notables who were anxious to share in the excitement and publicity of flying with the "birdman" or "gullman," two terms of growing press use and popularity, included Roald Amundsen, the Norwegian explorer who had been the first man on dogsled to reach the South Pole only slightly more than a year before. Amundsen now basked in publicity by flying with Glenn over the snow-covered peaks of the Sierra Madre.

The intrepid aviator also took his mother and father for a Thanksgiving Day flight, the first for Clarence Martin, to the front-page acclaim of the *Los Angeles Record* on November 29, 1913. In that bylined story, writer Estelle Lawton Lindsey skillfully summarized the contrasting parental relationships, particularly Minta Martin's strong influence on the twenty-seven years of Glenn's life and career to that point:[1]

> "Oh, we had a delightful ride," said Mrs. Martin fervently. "Great! Simply *immense!*" added Mr. Martin enthusiastically. "Weren't you afraid—not the least little bit?" I teased.
>
> The parents of Glenn Martin, famous aviator and aeroplane manufacturer, looked at me and shook their heads simultaneously. We three were sitting in the cozy living room of the Martin cottage in Santa Ana, and the old folks were telling me of the Thanksgiving ride their son had taken them in his new four-passenger biplane the day before my visit.
>
> Glenn Martin, leaving his Los Angeles factory, had swooped down on his parents from the blue sky, eaten with relish the turkey and cranberry sauce prepared by his capable mother, then sailed away with the parental pair to Long Beach.
>
> "The whole town came out to see us start," said Mrs. Martin, who, by the way, insists on being written down Mrs. Minta Martin, although her husband's initials are 'C. Y.' . . .
>
> "Yes," beamed 'C. Y.,' "it was as good as a circus. The photographers were all there from the papers and everybody cheered. There's a picture of the machine we

rode in. When we got to Long Beach, it seemed half the town came to see us land. I never *have* had such a good time before."

With the memory of a laughing remark I had heard on the street: "The old man used to be afraid of the game and sidestepped all Glenn's offers of a ride, but he got over it by and by as Glenn continued to ride and return alive," I repeated my question.

"Afraid?" echoed Mr. Martin with high scorn. "Not a bit of it. We were 1,500 feet in the air most of the time and, don't you know, there wasn't a bit of feeling of *altitude.* There wasn't any jolting and no uneasiness such as comes from fast riding in an automobile, just a splendid exhilaration like a bird soaring."

"A kind of cushiony sensation," added his placid wife, from whom the son inherits his splendid nerve. "I have been up before with Glenn. I wondered at first whether or not I would be dizzy or seasick, but just as soon as I saw how steady the biplane was beneath me I began to look around and enjoy myself. Yesterday you could see the whole country laid out just like a map. When I saw how plain everything looked I knew the government would just *have* to have a fleet of aeroplanes. Glenn had always figured on this and said he would make money, but his father discouraged him something awful."

"Of course I did," admitted the jolly-looking little gentleman who deals in automobiles. "We were in the automobile business—a good business too. Glenn was a peach of a salesman. Of course I didn't want him to quit and go into business that had nothing to it but a list of casualties."

"But you are reconciled now?" I asked.

"Of course; Glenn's made a business out of that foolishness. How could I know the boy would get rich and famous with the nonsense he was always projecting with?"

"You see," explained Mrs. Martin, "Papa always thought Glenn just *ought* to follow his footsteps in business. But I never was the least bit uneasy about the boy. He talked all his plans over with me and I understood that he was *sensing* what he ought to do. He was always tinkering with machines when he was little. Even when he wore dresses he could drive a nail as good as most carpenters.

He always liked things that would fly—the way he did *love* to make kites on my kitchen floor, no place was quite as good as my kitchen floor.

"When he got a little older he went hunting and spent hours watching big birds fly, studying how they rose, lit, and sailed. In those days nobody thought that humans would ever fly, but Glenn rigged up wings for his shoulders and learned to tack and sail before the wind. He used the wings in his skating—we lived back east then and he adored ice skating."

"He had kind of bird sense," added Father Martin.

"And a steady nerve, too, Papa; that's why he has been able to do all he has done. A man must learn to control himself first of all; then he can control others. A person who loses control of himself has no business in an aeroplane; he has no business anywhere; he should be under someone."

"Did you ever lose control of yourself in your life?" I demanded when the even voice had ceased. "I don't think I ever did," said Mrs. Martin placidly.

Glenn (rear) flies mother and dad, 1913

As with his barnstorming, "this hippodrome stuff," as Glenn himself called it in later years, had a practical purpose, for which his meeting with Tiny Broadwick was proof. Among other convictions held by Glenn was a belief that potential investors viewed flying as a risky investment because they felt it was an unsafe activity. Many aviators in the early stunt days died young, and each aerial fatality was chronicled in the press in all its gory detail. Glenn had been working on a device that would be to the airplane what the life vest was to boats, a way of getting out safely in times of distress. In fact, he held the original patent on the free-fall parachute.

Tiny Broadwick, a diminutive daredevil at four feet, eight inches, had been demonstrating a similar device and had already established a considerable reputation for parachuting from hot-air balloons before thrilled fair crowds. In Glenn's mind, the principal drawback to Tiny's quite large and bulky parachute was that it and its opener-drawstrings were attached to the balloon basket. The parachute was pulled through an opening in the basket when Tiny jumped, a somewhat limiting arrangement should something happen to the craft. Glenn had been working on a much more compact device, one that could be worn by the aviator independent of the aircraft.

Tiny and her foster father, Charles,[2] who folded and packed her chutes, made excellent teammates with Glenn. Quite apart from the exhibition crowds and swelling gate receipts, Glenn and the Broadwicks were developing a technology that would save countless lives and bring a very practical level of credibility to flying. He and Charles Broadwick came up with a parachute that Tiny could open by pulling a release cord. Then Glenn rigged a special "trapseat," a drop seat of sorts, on which Tiny could sit alongside the fuselage of his T-model. Her eleven-pound parachute was contained in a canvas bag directly behind her seat.

On June 20, 1913, Glenn and Tiny took off, and at an altitude of one thousand feet above Los Angeles' Griffith Park, Tiny dropped in one of the early public parachute demonstrations from a plane. It may even have been the first jump with a "free-fall" parachute.[3] The press took considerable notice, for the first time reporting it as more than just another aerial stunt. The *Los Angeles Tribune* reported:

> As the parachute sped down from the great height, aviator Martin with consummate skill drove his monster airplane hither and thither, around and about the falling bit of silk and its precious freight of record-making girlhood.[4]

THOUSANDS THRILLED BY AVIATORS
QUICK CLIMBING IS FEATURE OF DAY

Dominguez Field airshow

The true significance of the event as a development in the still-infant field of aviation was not recognized until the following year. In the meantime, Glenn and Tiny "performed" from one end of California to the other.

After they returned home, they repeated the jump over Los Angeles on January 10, 1914, this time before an audience of Army officers and the especially invited press. The latter invitation produced editorial praise in the *Los Angeles Times*:

> We may be permitted to hope that no longer shall the demons of the air pluck sacrificial victims from the bird-men. One of the greatest triumphs of aviation since the sons of man learned to fly came at the Griffith Aviation Field last Friday when a brave girl stepped from the bi-plane of Glenn Martin as one jumps from a table at play. Martin had staked a courageous human life in his game with death, and won by a device of silk and cord, woven under his direction and according to plans of his own.[5]

Brigadier General Robert Wankowski, one of the Army observers, was quoted as saying, "There is no question in my mind but that aviation would have a much smaller list of victims had the life vest been used before."

Whether that parachute jump actually influenced the Army to seek a new training plane at about the same time, it could not have hurt. No less than a dozen Army fliers had been killed in 1913 alone at the Army's North Island facility near San Diego. Most of them were killed when their planes' pusher engines broke loose in training accidents and crushed the pilots. The Army was left with only twelve pilots and eleven of the old planes built by Wright, Curtiss, and Burgess, all of them flimsy and hard to control.

The Signal Corps sent Grover C. Loening, an aeronautical engineer, to outline the problem to the few manufacturers of aircraft. On his visit to Martin's Los Angeles plant, Loening specified a reliable two-seat aircraft with dual controls for instructor and student, a nose-mounted engine with tractor blade instead of a pusher propeller, a plane that could climb eight hundred feet in ten minutes and with a top speed of fifty-eight miles per hour and a low of thirty-six miles per hour.

"Do you think you can do it?" he asked Martin.

Glenn, scarcely able to hide a smile, turned to Charles Willard, his chief engineer, who replied, "That depends on how soon the finished plane must be delivered." Neither Glenn nor Willard let on that in the Martin hangar at Griffith Park stood just such a plane, and it was virtually finished. It was a souped-up two-seater they had been working on for Tiny's parachute jumps. Practically all of the Army's requirements were already built in. All it lacked was a second set of controls. Loening said the Army needed delivery in six weeks, or it would have to shut down North Island.

"And there's one more thing," he added. "We don't have any money on hand, but if this plane you have in mind works, we'll get it." Glenn's eyes sparkled as he told the Army engineer, "We'll do it. I think we can chance it."[6]

Six weeks later the Martin company's first delivery to the Army rolled out of the hangar. It was the Model TT, for Tractor Trainer, aviation's first specially designated training plane. Its performance in subsequent flight tests exceeded the Army's expectations. Fourteen more were delivered in 1914, including a version with armor plate around the cockpit and engine.

The mortality rate at North Island dropped dramatically. Only one pilot was lost of the twenty-nine who trained in the Martin TT during the first six months it was in service, and Loening later told Glenn the Army did three or four times more flying per pupil than ever before. It was neither coincidence nor luck of timing that put the TT in Army hands so readily. Glenn had long believed in and preached the military promise of the airplane. It was only a matter of time, he figured, before the Army would need an airplane like his.

Now he had received an order and delivered military airplanes to the Army. Moreover, they performed spectacularly. He had achieved mission success on the first attempt.

It was ironic that San Diego's North Island and the Army's new Martin TT trainer would figure in Glenn's only serious accident. Although he cracked up more than one early airplane, Glenn had never been seriously hurt. But in 1914 while staging bombing tests with an Army flier, Captain I. E. Goodier, Jr., over North Island, the TT "fell ninety feet to the ground"[7] while making a slow-speed turn. According to one report, an Army doctor thought Glenn was dead. He was unconscious but was revived at the insistence of his chief mechanic. Both pilots were rushed to the hospital, but neither was seriously hurt. Glenn suffered a concussion and multiple bruises and Captain Goodier a broken leg. The fact that the plane was a tractor type, with the engine in front, probably saved both men's lives.

Many years later, Glenn's mother recalled visiting him in the hospital where he was recuperating from the accident. The nurse, meaning to be kind, said, "Well, Mrs. Martin, you can find comfort in one thing: The poor boy will never fly again."

"I'm sure he'll fly again the minute he gets out of this hospital," Minta Martin recalled telling the nurse. And of course he did.[8]

CHAPTER 6

Grim Visages
of Aerial Warfare

■

T he Army order for the training plane was a huge step for
the fledgling Martin company and the most significant
manufacturing contract in the infant industry. It would not
be the last time that the company Glenn Martin built produced an
advanced design *before* the customer realized the need.

It was a hydroplane version of the TT, designated the TT-S, with
a pontoon replacing the landing wheels and tandem cockpits each
seating two abreast, that Glenn and Tiny took to Chicago for a highly
successful and profitable exhibition. There Glenn introduced the
aircraft as the Great Lakes Tourer, a four-passenger "aeroyacht," he
called it.

They were invited to put on their "act" before Commodore
Robert E. Peary, who had just returned from the North Pole. Tiny
jumped successfully, floating down as planned to a wet landing in the
waters of Lake Michigan. A boat picked her up and delivered all
ninety soaking pounds of her to the reviewing stand, where Glenn
had already joined the governor and the commodore. It was a huge
success, and Glenn spent the next week taking wealthy ladies and
gentlemen who could afford his fee for a thrilling flight over Lake
Michigan.

The TT was also the plane Glenn flew for the Army's first

Glenn and friends in four-seater

official bombardment experiments at San Diego. Although the demonstrations went quite well, the Army's assessment was classified, and Glenn never heard the result. A very public event occurred at about the same time, however. A dispatch in the Los Angeles papers from the rebellion-torn city of Guaymas, Mexico, told of the French stunt pilot Didier Masson flying low over the city in a Martin plane, which "loosed bombs [that] fell in the principal streets, causing some loss of life and much damage."[1] Glenn knew nothing of it. He was unaware until he read it in the newspaper that one of his planes had been involved. But he was not surprised that the plane had the capability. It was demonstrated proof of his contention that the aircraft had tremendous military potential.

Although clearly not involved, Glenn later testified before a federal grand jury probing an alleged conspiracy to smuggle an airplane out of the country to Mexican Constitutionalists. As reported in the *Tucson Citizen,* Martin said he was ignorant of any such plan. Masson had been trying to purchase a plane for six months, Glenn told the paper, but couldn't come up with the money. The Frenchman worked for a time as an instructor in the Martin flying school, and when he finally arranged for payment, the plane was shipped to Tucson, per Masson's instructions, Glenn said.

Another paper, the *Los Angeles Tribune,* reported that the federal inquiry concerned a conspiracy to smuggle a plane that had been purchased (presumably for Masson) by Van M. Griffith, secretary of the Aero Club of Southern California. Whatever the case, the Mexican incident was the world's first report of a fixed-wing aircraft dropping bombs in an actual conflict. Previous aerial bombardments had been from balloons.

With clouds of war forming in Europe, the bombing in Mexico and Glenn's aerial bombing demonstration for the Army were events well-suited to the times and to the future of the airplane.

With the Army contract for the TT training planes, production in the Martin aircraft factory literally took off. The open-framework, box-kite construction of his original planes and of even the Model 12 that made the Catalina crossing had given way to an enclosed body, or "fuselage," although that French term would not be applied until more than a year later. Bamboo and cypress were replaced with steel, and not just ordinary steel but a vanadium steel of much greater strength and higher resistance to crystallization.

More than one hundred people were employed at the Los Angeles plant. The company also maintained a hangar at the adjoining Griffith Field (site of today's Los Angeles International Airport), a hydroplane base at Dark Slough, near Gardena, which was also the location of the flying school, and a research and test facility on Balboa Island.

There followed in rapid order a succession of different airplanes. The multipassenger GMP (Glenn Martin Passenger), or "aerial cruiser," could carry four to eight passengers at seventy-five miles per hour and operated on the water with twin pontoons. It was a considerable advance over the earlier, single-pontooned Great Lakes Tourer. The Navy took interest and suggested naming it the OWL for "On Water and Land," perhaps the military's very first acronym but one that did not stick. "A queer craft . . . that looks much like a hammerhead shark, carries the wings of a dragonfly, and shoots on the water like a flying fish," is the way the *Los Angeles Examiner* described the plane.[2]

In addition to the TT, the Martin company produced three other trainer aircraft at the time. The Model-T carried instructor and student side-by-side. The Model-S was a tandem-seat, single-float seaplane trainer, and the Model-R was an advanced trainer-observation

Model-R aerial scout with motorcycle

plane capable of a number of equipment changes depending on the need. One version carried a motorcycle that could be dropped by parachute along with its rider on a separate chute or could be landed and mounted by the pilot or another observer for ground scouting.

An armor-clad biplane, the TA-1, was rolled out of the factory with attendant publicity. Sheathed in metal plate around the cockpit and engine, the plane had transparent wings to make it more difficult to detect at high altitudes—perhaps the world's first stealth aircraft. The *Los Angeles Sunday Tribune* immediately dubbed it the "scoutship of the future, a terror alike for land or sea."[3]

And then there was the "aeroplane destroyer,"[4] Glenn's own name for what was purported to be the first pursuit plane, a single-passenger, pusher-engine craft with a gun mounted in the nose. It was only a Winchester rifle, but a mounted gun it was. Somewhat of a throwback, the plane revived the pusher-engine mounted behind the pilot rather than an in-front tractor engine, which would have prohibited the pilot from firing the gun. Having demonstrated aerial bombing, he now created the concept of a plane that would bring down the bomber. Although fighter aircraft would never become a Martin product line, it did illustrate Glenn's sagacity for things to come. (Incidentally, the same Jimmy Ward who had impressed

AEROPLANE DESTROYER BUILT FOR WAR

Martin and Ward in the "Aeroplane Destroyer"

Grover Hermann in Callicoon, New York, back in 1911 flew with Glenn Martin three years later as a gunner to help demonstrate the aeroplane destroyer.)

On August 7, 1914, three days after German armies began rolling into Belgium, a reporter asked, "Mr. Martin, of what use is your 'aeroplane destroyer' to a neutral America?" The young president of the "largest aircraft factory in America" made this lengthy and prophetic reply that appeared in the *Los Angeles Evening Herald*:

> The aeroplane will practically decide the war in Europe. Veritable flying death will smash armies, wreck mammoth battleships, and bring the whole world to a vivid realization of the awful possibilities of a few men and a few swift winging aerial demons. For the old-time war tactics are no more. The generals who realize this quickest and fight first with the flying death will win.
>
> Aeroplanes darting with cyclonic speed will demoralize armies and navies and leave the earth forces terror stricken. . . . Aviators, each with only one life to give for his country, will . . . grapple with the enemy's aeroplanes thousands of feet in midair. . . .

Three distinct types of airplanes will be used:

First, there is the reconnoitering machine, flying 75 miles an hour, carrying two men, one the pilot, the other the observer [who] operates the wireless apparatus, making notes of the country, of the enemy's position, strength, and other data, wirelessing the more important facts to his general back there with the waiting army. . . .

Second is the flying death machine, carrying two men and 600 to 800 pounds of explosive bombs. This type of machine has a speed of from 45 to 75 miles an hour.

The third class of aeroplane is one that is extremely light, with a speed of from 60 to 100 miles an hour, carrying two men and no added weight save fuel and light rapid-fire guns. The duty of these planes is the most dangerous of all—they must protect the scout planes against the enemy's aeroplanes.[5]

Glenn Martin's vision of air power was not the outpouring of a belligerent personality, nor did it reflect a desire to go to war. Rather, it was the concern of an uncommonly prescient twenty-eight-year-old hoping that his country would wake up to the realities of the age and the technical advances being made in aviation across the sea. His concerns were both for the effect of aviation upon the war and the effect of a war on aviation.[6] His predictions were only partially realized in World War I, but they proved accurate in practically every detail in later years and subsequent wars.

One month before war broke out, Glenn was given a singular honor by his peers in aviation. The Aero Club of America awarded him its coveted Medal of Merit for "outstanding development of aviation." It was no small honor. In the short span of only five years, almost to the day since his first flight, Glenn L. Martin had gained fame and fortune of a sort, but most important he had a reputation for producing reliable products expeditiously.

He took his mother with him to New York. At the formal dinner at which the award was presented, she wore a long satin gown and sat at the speaker's table with him. Both Glenn and his mother were proud of the honor he was receiving, and his head and heart were full of things he wanted to say. But his innate shyness overcame him when he rose to thunderous applause to accept the medal.

"Ladies and gentlemen, thank you for this great honor" was all he said.[7]

CHAPTER 7

A Wright Merger
That Was Wrong

■

When they returned home, Glenn continued to worry
and personally work the financial, personnel, and public relations ends of the business despite the varied and
full production coming out of the factory. There was always tomorrow when current contracts would run out. But first he had a major
personnel problem to solve. Charles Willard, his chief engineer, left
the company to go to work for the Signal Corps. Although the Army's action in wooing Willard away from the Martin Company was a
positive sign of the growing importance of aviation, it left Glenn
without one of his major players. Willard's heading design and Larry
Bell's running production had been a formidable team, proof of
Glenn's frequently quoted axiom: "I was always smart enough to
surround myself with men who knew more than I did."[1]

He was about to do it again. With his usual thoroughness, Glenn
wrote to Jerome Hunsaker at the Massachusetts Institute of Technology, asking his recommendation for a replacement for Willard. Hunsaker was one of the country's leading, if not the leading, aviation
theorists and academicians of the day, having established a curricu-
lum in aeronautical engineering at MIT. Hunsaker recommended
one of his former students, Donald Wills Douglas, who was then
working for the Navy. Glenn met and interviewed Douglas in a Los

Martin engineer
Donald Douglas (left).

Angeles hotel and hired him on the spot despite his youth (he was twenty-three) and appearance (he looked even younger). It was a fortuitous association. Young Douglas brought the first formal engineering to the enterprise, and he and Larry Bell forged an engineering-manufacturing working relationship that was every bit as strong as the Willard-Bell team.

In later memoirs Douglas, as well as some others who had worked for Glenn Martin, tended to turn up their formally trained engineering noses at his lack of formal education. Douglas used to delight in telling people how the early Martin company had no real engineering until he came aboard and how Glenn Martin would jump up and down on the wing of a new airplane to test its tolerance to stress. Such criticism failed to take into account that in those early days Glenn—like Glenn Curtiss and the Wrights—had more aeronautical smarts in the seat of his pants than an entire roomful of college-trained engineers.

Although Douglas and Martin were complete opposites in personality and training, the young engineer from MIT did recognize the innate talents and natural abilities of the self-taught genius who was his new boss. "He was not an engineer, but he had good instinctive ideas," Douglas was quoted later in life. "Glenn's greatest strength was that he was amazingly well coordinated physically. Most of the fellows who flew in those early days had to be. The airplanes were not very stable or controllable. But you could see it in Glenn in other ways—he was a marvelous bowler, billiard player, and duck shot."[2]

The personnel problem behind him, Glenn next completed an arrangement that would assure his company's financial health for

Glenn takes society belles aeroyachting

the immediate future. He persuaded his good friend and wealthy supporter Frank Garbutt to put up financing sufficient to enable Glenn to buy out his original partners. Comfortable that in essence he now owned the business exclusively, Glenn took off for Chicago to drum up business for his $8,500-per-copy "aeroyacht" by taking socialite friends of farm machinery millionaire Harold F. McCormick on aerial tours off McCormick's lakefront estate. All of the guests wore bathing suits, with the comely ladies "donning cork coats [life vests] for the flights," according to the *Los Angeles Times*, which covered the activities. Glenn and his competitor and friend Glenn Curtiss spent a weekend ferrying the young ladies and their escorts over and on Lake Michigan.

McCormick, who had already learned to fly and owned a Curtiss hydroplane, added a Martin aeroyacht to his collection. A similar aeroyachting party for society ladies of Coronado, California, was reported by the *San Diego Union*,[3] which included references to a rumored romance between Glenn and Catherine Irvine, the daughter of his good friend and supporter, rancher James Irvine.

Glenn's lifelong reserve toward women was apparently due to a number of circumstances that combined in his intensely focused life to eliminate distractions. One, he never forgot his mother's admonition to him as a boy that women would take too much time, attention, and money. Two, his thoughts and his days were filled with airplanes. And three, he was painfully shy when it came to girls.

Catherine Irvine was an exception. Glenn and Catherine did indeed have a real and lasting friendship with genuine affection.[4] It began in his early flight days in the Irvine bean field outside Santa Ana. Catherine was in almost daily attendance, fascinated by the handsome young man and his daring exploits. They became good friends, and Glenn even drove Catherine home on occasion.

One day he missed her presence. Learning that she was ill, he drove into town, bought an armful of flowers, and loaded them into his plane. He took off and buzzed the Irvine ranch house at treetop level. When the startled girl came to her window, he dove his plane straight at her, pulling up sharply as he tossed the flowers all over the roof and front yard of the Irvine house. Landing in a nearby lane, Glenn then went to the house and delivered the single remaining blossom to Catherine in person. Although their friendship never matured to marriage, it was warm and affectionate and endured throughout their lives. With one possible exception later in life, Catherine may have been the lone woman Minta Martin ever approved of for her son. When the subject of marriage came up, Glenn always had a ready answer. "I just can't find the nerve to ask any man for the hand of his daughter. It would be too easy for him to point out that I might make her a widow the day after the wedding."[5]

Throughout his professional life, Glenn was constantly in the company of beautiful women. One of the earliest and most celebrated occasions, even more noted than the famous Valeska Suratt kiss, was in 1914 when he agreed to play a role with his aeroplane for $700 a day in a Hollywood extravaganza. The movie was *The Girl of Yesterday,* and Glenn was cast opposite "America's Sweetheart," Mary

Rancher Irvine and Glenn

Flying Mary Pickford

Pickford. It was only one of many films in which Glenn and his aeroplane were to play, but it certainly was his starring role. In addition to the $4,900 he earned for two weeks' work, he got the girl in the movie, and he gained another lifelong friend in Mary Pickford. The movie, which was shot early in 1915, was a relaxing interlude for Glenn after a momentous but strenuous twelve months that saw his star soar. It also marked the beginning of a period of considerable difficulty and frustration, although his fortunes would continue to climb for much of the rest of the year.

Although Martin-built planes continued to attract attention in and out of the United States government, Uncle Sam was buying very few, thanks primarily to a strong automobile industry that convinced the government it had the only capacity for mass production. An even greater militating factor against the Martin company and the handful of other domestic aeroplane builders was the government's argument, supported by the auto moguls, that the United States should build only airplanes of foreign design, which were considered more advanced and more proven in operation.

Had it not been for the Dutch, the inevitable decline would have set in sooner for Glenn's booming Los Angeles aircraft company. Although orders for Army trainers kept the plant busy, the United States was not ordering any military planes, convinced that the fighting across the Atlantic was a foreign conflict in which it did not want to become entangled. On the other hand, the British and the Dutch were involved and were actively pursuing all sources of military equipment, including airplanes. Queen Wilhelmina's Netherlands government sent a young East Indies aviator, Lieutenant H. Ter Poorten, to visit the Los Angeles factory and evaluate the Martin airplanes. Ter Poorten liked the two airplanes Glenn built for him so much that he persuaded his government to order twenty more.

The Glenn L. Martin Company had its first foreign order, and more important, the contract marked the beginning of a long line of bombing aircraft that would make the words "Martin" and "bomber" virtually synonymous.

Despite its aversion to foreign entanglements, official Washington was beginning to reassess its position not only regarding involvement but as to the role of aircraft in a potential conflict. Those in charge of preparing America concluded that no American airplane design could compete with European planes. Therefore, it would be necessary to adapt a European design to American manufacturing methods and tooling, principally those already in place in the American automobile industry. Both Martin's chief engineer, Donald Douglas, and Glenn would eventually be involved in the process. Glenn would be summoned to Washington, although not on a permanent basis, when Secretary of War Newton D. Baker appointed him a member of the newly formed War Aviation Board. Although the appointment was a personal tribute to Glenn and was in recognition of the growing importance of the young industry and its reputable leaders, it was apparent from the start that the board would be dominated by the members from the auto industry. Lacking authority and a clear-cut charter of its mission, the board proved to be only time-consuming and ineffectual.

While in Washington, Glenn was approached by a group of eastern financiers about a possible merger with the Wright Company. Actually a syndication of capitalists, the group had set its sights on what it considered the inevitable involvement of America in the European war and the need for aircraft, engines, and other equipment. The proposition put to Glenn was that he merge his company with the Wright Company but that he continue to produce aircraft under his own name at the Los Angeles factory.

The proposed Wright-Martin Aircraft Corporation would be capitalized for $10 million (about $100 million in 1993 dollars), a staggering sum in August 1916. Its primary market would be the United States government—specifically, a recently passed Army appropriations bill that included $13,281,666 for the "purchase, manufacture, maintenance, operation, and repair of airships and other aerial equipment." Additionally, $3.5 million was earmarked for naval aviation.[6] The only competition to the powerful new Wright-Martin enterprise would be Glenn Curtiss's company. Curtiss had already absorbed the Burgess Company of Marblehead, Massachusetts, the fourth in size and smallest of the U.S. aircraft manufacturers at that time.

The proposed merger immediately appealed to Glenn, who could see the day rapidly approaching when his production lines would be nearly empty, the Dutch contract completed, and the few Army planes he had on order completed and delivered. Glenn Curtiss had most of the Army's business. The idea also appealed to him because of the union with Orville Wright, a friend he admired tremendously. Overlooked was the fact that Orville was little involved other than to lend his name. He had earlier sold his patents and the use of his name to the same financial interests who were now proposing the Wright-Martin merger. Orville's only connection to the new company that would bear his name was as a $25,000-a-year consultant.

The agreement stipulated, at Glenn's insistence, that the Los Angeles plant would continue to operate as the Glenn L. Martin Company, in effect operating as a subsidiary of the larger corporate entity. The name was not formally changed to Wright-Martin until November 19, 1917, and the arrangement preserved intact the company's claim to being the oldest airframe manufacturing concern in the United States. In addition to the Martin plant in Los Angeles and the Wright plant in Dayton, Ohio, the new corporation included the Simplex Automobile Company and the Standard Aircraft Company.

Thus was born a giant enterprise, headquartered in New York City and combining two of the three most prominent names in aviation. Glenn Martin was named vice president in charge of aircraft production. The chairman, Edgard M. Hager, was a stranger to the business, a cement manufacturer brought in presumably on the theory that a good manager can manage anything. Ironically, as a result of another merger forty-five years later, the manufacture of cement became a major element of a vastly larger Martin Marietta Corporation.

The United States had entered the war four months earlier, in April 1917, and there were airplanes to be built. But all was not to be as advertised for the new Wright-Martin Company. The Aircraft Production Board, dominated by leaders in the automotive industry, decided the one-a-day production of trainers by the Martin plant was insufficient. It would be better if it made engines. The new management complied by directing that the Martin plant confine its business to the manufacture of Wright-Cyclone engines. Glenn did not approve; after all, he was a manufacturer of aircraft, not engines.

Later in that first year, another management decision further rankled him. Production of 451 SJ-1 trainers, a contract acquired with the Standard Aircraft Company, was to be split between the

Wright plant in Dayton, Ohio, and the Martin Plant in Los Angeles. Ironically, the plane had been designed by Glenn's early Santa Ana colleague, Charles Day. Not long after, the new owners sent an engineer by the name of Chance Milton Vought to Los Angeles to work for Glenn as chief engineer, replacing Donald Douglas, who was called to New York for reassignment. Vought, an aviator like Glenn, had been with Simplex when it was absorbed into the new Wright-Martin merger. Glenn had nothing against Vought, but he had not been consulted on the reassignment and didn't like it. Neither did Douglas, who promptly resigned and took a job in Washington with the Signal Corps as chief civilian engineer. His primary task would be to help in the selection of the foreign aircraft that were to be produced in America.[7]

It was the third and final unsettling event for Glenn. Combined with the realization that he, like Orville Wright, was little more than a figurehead in the new company, he made up his mind to get out. He turned once again to the ever-supportive Frank Garbutt, who introduced him to a wealthy Ohio industrialist, Alva Bradley, probably better known as the owner of the major league Cleveland Indians baseball team. Bradley immediately saw the potential for attracting this nationally essential industry to his state. He met with several other Cleveland industrial heavyweights and arranged the financing necessary for Glenn to form a new company, but the backers insisted that the plant be located in Ohio. In the summer of 1917, Glenn withdrew his Glenn L. Martin company from the Wright-Martin Corporation. Less than a year after its auspicious beginning, the Wright-Martin venture was doomed to collapse and collapse it did a short time later.

CHAPTER 8

Cleveland and
The First Great Bomber

■

On September 19, 1917, a relocated Glenn L. Martin Company was incorporated under the laws of the State of Ohio. Incorporators in addition to Glenn and Alva Bradley were eighteen prominent Clevelanders. Some of the city's industrial elite, they were led by Charles E. Thompson, aviation buff and at that time head of Steel Products Company, which later became Thompson Products Company. Others were S. Livingston Mather and brothers W. G. and A. S. Mather of Pickens & Mather fame. It was Thompson who some thirty years later bankrolled a couple of Californians to form Ramo-Wooldridge Corporation, which later merged with Thompson Products to form Thompson-Ramo-Wooldridge, eventually becoming simply TRW, Inc.

Fred Crawford, an assistant to Thompson, credits Thompson, more than Bradley, with luring Glenn Martin to Cleveland. It may be that Thompson was the largest investor because at the outset, at least, he was listed as the company's president, with Glenn as vice president. At any rate, Crawford, who was once described by *Fortune* as "the only human thing around Thompson Products that runs faster than a turbine wheel, hotter than a valve head, and noisier than a drop forge," was there at the time. Celebrating the first birthday of his second century with a reminiscent interview in *Air & Space* magazine in 1992, Crawford remembered it this way:

Cleveland factory, 1918

Charles Thompson had decided that airplanes were the coming thing, so we had bought a cow pasture out in east Cleveland and built a hangar—it wasn't very big, but it was a hangar. But nobody in Cleveland knew a goddamned thing about airplanes. So my boss called Glenn Martin . . . and said he'd like to have him come to town so they could talk.

One day he said to me, "Get in the car, we're going to meet an interesting man." We got in the car, an old Winton—with a Victorian top of all things—and went down to the station, and Glenn Martin got off the train. I can see him now, big, tall, serious fella, skinny, with glasses.

We drove out to the Mayfield Country Club and had lunch on the porch and propositioned Martin to come and run this plant. He was interested, but he said he had to go home to arrange his affairs and get his mother.[1]

By December of the next to the last year of the Great War, Glenn and a few dozen of his close associates did move to Cleveland, but to a new, temporary factory with thirteen thousand square feet of floor space on Chestnut Avenue near Ninth Street, not the cow pasture hangar that Crawford recalled. Key employees who made the move with him from California included Larry Bell, Eric Springer, C. A. Van Dusen, George Strompl, Henry Guerin, Ross Elkins, George Borst, and Elmer Harts.

The move was not without its personal trauma for the Martin family. Glenn's father Clarence had no interest in going. Although no longer the critic and foot dragger as far as Glenn's aviation ex-

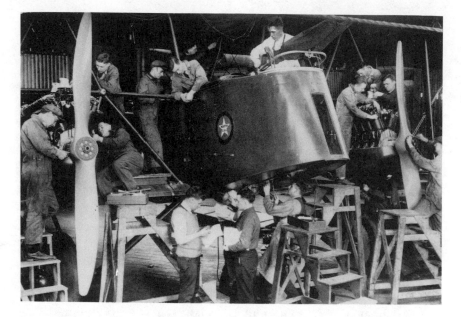

First real bomber, MB-1

ploits were concerned, he simply was not interested in starting over, particularly in a cold northern place like Cleveland. Glenn's mother Minta would make the move, of course, but later, after her son had established the business and located suitable living quarters.

One of Glenn's first actions after moving to Cleveland was to woo Donald Douglas back to the fold. Also joining the team as a designer and chief draftsman was J. H. "Dutch" Kindelberger.

Their first design in the new plant was for a sleek, fast, twin-engine biplane bomber. Designated the MB-1, for Martin Bomber No. 1, it would stamp Martin's identification indelibly on that type of aircraft for decades. It was revolutionary in design compared to any aircraft then in production, and Glenn hurried off to Washington with drawings of the plane tucked under his arm. But the Aircraft Production Board was not interested. New designs were not wanted, they told him. America was building only proven European designs.

Glenn returned to Cleveland and ordered the MB-1 built anyway. His disappointment in not being able to sell the new plane was matched by another personal setback. Up until this time Glenn Martin had personally flown most of the planes his factory turned out. But with wartime contracts and production lines anticipated, his financial backers reasoned it was time for the head man to stop risking his own neck. It ill-befit the president and guiding light of the country's leading aircraft manufacturing firm to be flying tricky new military aircraft, his bankers and insurance men argued. They were determined to make it a formal condition of their continued support. They sent a young representative of the bank's insurance division, a Mr. Hartwell, to break the news to Glenn Martin. Hartwell had scheduled an appointment for a Tuesday but showed up a day earlier, and Glenn agreed to see him. Hesitantly, the young banking executive told the stern-faced chief executive, "You represent a valuable property to the investors in your company, Mr. Martin. Two million dollars, to be precise."

"What exactly is on your mind, Mr. Hartwell?" Glenn asked.

"You are not to fly anymore," Hartwell blurted out. "The investors feel it is too risky, that your place is in the office, not in an airplane." Glenn interrupted with a deprecating wave of his hand, but Hartwell continued. "If you refuse, the investors will withdraw."

Without speaking, Glenn stood, removed his glasses, and slowly polished them with his handkerchief. Fixing Hartwell with a cold gaze, he spoke softly but with contempt in his voice.

"Very well, Mr. Hartwell. I will do as they say. We must do all we can to protect that money, mustn't we?" He rewarded his visitor with a frozen smile, then pointed to the calendar on his desk. "Actually, you were not supposed to visit me until tomorrow. Isn't that right, Mr. Hartwell?"

"Well, yes," the young man stammered. "It's just that I was in the neighborhood, and I—"

Glenn interrupted: "Well, then, let's just suppose that our meeting took place on schedule, that I won't hear about all this until tomorrow."

"I don't know . . ." The young man hesitated again, but Glenn was already ushering him out the door. "Agreed, Mr. Hartwell?"

"I guess so." Hartwell shrugged. "I wasn't supposed to be here until tomorrow."

"Splendid! Good day, Mr. Hartwell." Glenn closed his office door on the departing banker. He buzzed his secretary and told her he would be gone for the rest of the day. He walked briskly through the factory to the runway side, changed into his black flying gear, climbed into his private Model TT, taxied it out, and took off. For an hour he skylarked over Lake Erie, well away from the city and anyone who might be watching at the plant. He put the plane through every maneuver it would take, soaring up through the clouds, zigzagging between towering cumulus, rolling, diving, generally enjoying himself as he remembered earlier days when life was simpler and change less rapid. He would never be able to bring it back. In the dozen years he had been flying, aviation had changed drastically, and so had he.

In a graceful, lazy turn, Glenn headed the plane back to Cleveland. He landed at the plant, stepped out on the tarmac, and walked away without a backward glance. At the age of thirty-seven, the Flying Dude became the Grounded Falcon, as his colleagues and friends came to call him, though never to his face. He continued to ride in airplanes for the remainder of his life, but the man who had built his own plane and taught himself to fly it, and who became one of the most famous of early aviators, never again piloted an aircraft.[2]

Business once again consumed him. The MB-1 became the forerunner of an improved version, designated the MB-2. By the end of the year the Aircraft Production Board was under attack from Congress. Its ambitious plans and promises to turn out one hundred thousand aircraft in two years on automobile mass production assembly lines had to date produced not a single aircraft. On January 17, 1918, Glenn Martin was summoned to Washington by the same board that earlier had turned a deaf ear to his new design. This time it handed him his first wartime contract for twenty of the bombers.

Powered by two 400-horsepower Liberty engines, the biplane became known as the MB-2 Liberty bomber. The design was far more advanced than anything else flying. With a wingspan of seventy-two feet, the plane's size was further exaggerated by twin rudders and a unique landing gear of four main wheels attached to a single shaft. The MB-2 carried a crew of four and more than a ton-and-a-half of bombs at a remarkably fast speed of 125 miles per hour. Pilot and copilot sat side by side in an open cockpit, and the gunner-bombardier rode in the nose where he manned one of the four machine guns. The rear gunner sat aft of the wings. It was almost the same airplane that no one would even look at in 1917, the plane "that was to make the words 'Martin' and 'bomber' all but synonymous."[3]

Less than a month after signing the MB-2 contract, ground was broken at 16800 St. Clair Avenue for the permanent Cleveland plant. The seventy-one-acre site not only enjoyed proximity to the Nickel Plate Railroad, it allowed for two flying courses, a thirty-two-hundred-foot east-west runway and a fifteen-hundred-foot north-south strip. Construction was completed in April, equipment was installed, and on May 1 the MB-2 work begun in the temporary location was moved by the one hundred eighty employees to the new sixty thousand-square-foot facility.

In August the newly relocated Glenn L. Martin Company of Cleveland delivered the first of its MB-2 bombers to the Army Signal Corps. It had taken only seven months from contract signing, a production record that did not go unnoticed in Washington or in the automotive capital of Detroit. When a Cleveland reporter sought an interview, Glenn told him:

> The way to build aircraft or do anything else worthwhile is to think out quietly every detail, analyze every situation that may possibly occur, and when you have it all worked out in practical sequence in your mind, raise heaven and earth, and never stop until you have produced the thing you started to make.[4]

That's exactly what he had done, raised heaven and earth, as well as the attention of the Aircraft Production Board. In enunciating his philosophy to the Cleveland reporter, Glenn established perhaps unknowingly the raison d'être of his company. He had laid out a pattern for a corporate culture that would permeate the enterprise long after he was gone; half a century later, his management heirs would call it *mission success*.

It was amid the production swirl of a second world war that Glenn recalled the remarkable achievement of 1918 quite simply: "I

Bell, Springer, Martin, Douglas, and MB-2

had the ablest and most experienced men in the industry to help me." Indeed he had. Five of his "ablest" eventually went on to head their own great companies in an industrial production effort without equal. Included were Larry Bell, the factory manager, who would one day form Bell Aircraft. The chief engineer in Cleveland was Don Douglas, who not many years later started Douglas Aircraft. An engineer in the original cadre that moved with Glenn from Los Angeles was C. A. Van Dusen, who later became general manager and president of Brewster Aeronautical. And one of the draftsmen in the Martin plant was Dutch Kindelberger, one of the founders and later chairman and president of North American Aviation, the predecessor of Rockwell International.

After Martin's pullout had doomed the Wright-Martin venture, Chance Vought also left. He joined forces in 1917 with Birdseye B. Lewis to form the Lewis & Vought Corporation on New York's Long Island, which in 1922 became the Chance Vought Corporation. After a merger in 1929 with Sikorsky, Boeing, and Pratt & Whitney, forming United Aircraft and Transportation Corporation, Vought died of blood poisoning in 1930. Thirty-one-years later, in 1961, his company was joined with Ling and Temco to form Ling-Temco-Vought Corporation, which became LTV Corporation in 1965.[5] Those five protégés of Glenn L. Martin, plus a sixth, James Smith McDonnell, Jr., who would join the Martin team a decade and a half later in Baltimore, were truly the fledglings on whose wings the United States aviation and space industry took flight.

There were others, of course, whose young lives were influenced by this remarkable aviation pioneer. Most notable in the early days was Bill Boeing, whose curiosity about flight was nurtured in Glenn's flying school. Another was David Lewis, who worked as a young engineer for Martin in the 1930s, followed McDonnell when he founded his own company, and then went on to become chairman of General Dynamics Corporation from 1970 to 1985. Edward G. Uhl, who rose from boy engineer to vice president and general manager of a major Martin facility, later headed Fairchild Aircraft. Another young engineer, Joel Jacobson, left Martin's employ in 1951 to form Aircraft Armaments, Inc. (later to become AAI), a major supplier of aerospace subcomponents. Still another who left Martin to start his own business but also left the industry was Howard Head, an engineer in the Baltimore plant and a skiing enthusiast. Head envisioned another use for the honeycomb structure Martin developed to save weight while maintaining strength in metal airplane skins. In 1950 Head set up his own company to manufacture skis of honeycomb construction, and the firm bearing his name became a foremost American maker of sporting equipment and accessories. And there were others.[6]

The flight test of the first MB-2 was accelerated because Martin was anxious to get the fantastic new plane into action. After just two weeks it was pronounced ready for Army inspection. Glenn, Donald Douglas, and test pilot Eric Springer packed suitcases and took off for McCook Field, two hundred miles southwest, at Dayton. They had not taken the time to notify the Army that they were coming, and when the armored giant of a flying machine swooped in and landed at McCook, its occupants were arrested and guards were stationed around the aircraft. Officials of the Aircraft Production Board were suspicious of the radically different-looking craft. They considered it dangerous and allowed no one to fly it.

Finally, after considerable pleading of its merits by Glenn himself, the Army allowed Captain "Shorty" Schroeder, one of the great military pilots of the day, to take the big plane up. In an hour's time he gave the MB-2 every performance test he could think of, and the plane answered all his questions. It literally came through with flying colors. The Army had a plane that would be its standard bomber for many years.

With MB-1 and the MB-2 the company moved into its second decade with what could really be called production lines. In the first year of the Cleveland factory, gross sales of $397,409 netted the Glenn L. Martin company an extremely modest profit of $7,333, slightly less than 2 percent.

The initial order for fifty of the MB-1s had been scaled back to sixteen aircraft by the time the war ended in November, but the Martin plant was still humming, and in January 1919 it received a second Army contract for twenty of the improved MB-2 bombers. Sales, which along with earnings had doubled by the end of 1918, soared to nearly $1.5 million by the end of 1921, with a profit of $102,566, a very respectable 7 percent.

Although the Cleveland money men who had lured Glenn to Ohio and had bankrolled the new Martin company lost their patriotic interest when the war ended, Glenn was ready for the next step. He arranged to buy them out for $481,740, which he did on February 25, 1920. Guardian Trust Co. owned the land, plant, and equipment, and leased it to the company. Glenn had the option to buy it back for the same price after five years. Once more he was master of his own fate. He urged Douglas, Bell, and his other colleagues to hold tight despite end-of-war jitters about contracts being cut. "We'll come out all right. A great future lies ahead of us," he told them. Already on the drawing boards were designs for commercial offshoots of the MB-2. One was a mail plane, designated the MP; another was a twelve-passenger commercial transport, designated the M12P. It was actually an easy transition from the last of the MB-1 bombers, which the Army had asked Martin to convert to a military transport. A third variation, and perhaps the most significant, was the MBT, a torpedo bomber. Two were produced for the U.S. Navy, the first Martin sales to that customer and the forerunners of a long series of reliable Martin naval aircraft and a business arrangement that extended into the middle of the century.

Midway in 1919 the Army asked for two hundred more MB-2s. But the delirium in the Cleveland factory was short-lived when the government decided it needed to consider the rest of the aircraft industry. Actually, there were no competitors to the MB-2. It was accepted as the standard, but competitive bids were asked of other contractors who might build the Martin plane as a second source. No such contracts were let, but neither did the new Martin order materialize. The country was settling down to a peacetime economy, and the original twenty planes were all the pared-back budget would allow.

The first of the big mail planes was rolled out in the spring. Again the customer was the Army. The twin-engine plane could carry fifteen hundred pounds of mail in five compartments, each equipped with a trap door so the mail could be parachuted at specific drop stations. Six of these planes went into regular service between New York and Chicago.

The M12P never materialized as the twelve-passenger commercial transport Glenn envisioned, chiefly because there was no flying public to speak of. Hundreds of unemployed aviators back from the war took to barnstorming and stunting in poorly maintained war-surplus planes that could be purchased as cheaply as a used car. Before long they were "falling out of the skies like ducks in a Maryland December," as one chronicler put it later.[7]

Public enthusiasm was chilled. Even the well-publicized feat of two Army fliers, Colonel R. S. Hartz and Lieutenant Ernest E. Harmon, who piloted a Martin bomber 9,283 miles, completely around the perimeter of the United States, landing one hundred times in thirty-one states, failed to thaw the chill and demonstrate the airplane as safe transportation. That would have to wait for Lindbergh's Atlantic jaunt in 1927.

In an interview with the *The Plain Dealer*, February 2, 1919, Glenn was quoted as follows:

> There are still those who scoff at the idea of commercial application of the airplane, in spite of the remarkable development the war has brought. I mean operation in competition with other carriers—railroads and automobiles—at a profit. A most important and valuable application not yet encouraged is the carrying of passengers.
>
> The first immediate commercial application will be transporting aerial mail. Too much stress cannot be put upon the importance of every city in the United States having in close proximity to its centers an aerial landing terminal. Inventors are at work on navigation instruments. I believe the solution will come through a development of the radio compass and radio communication.[8]

Unable to realize his premature dreams for commercial aviation, Glenn concentrated on military markets, which in those years included the U.S. Mail. His one modified bomber, with comfortable seats in a windowed cabin, was used by the Army to fly the McCook baseball team to its scheduled games. In addition to bombers, the mail planes, and limited Army use of the airplane for transport, Glenn continued to focus on his conviction that the airplane was the mightiest military weapon.

CHAPTER 9

Vindication and Establishment

■

By 1921 the Air Corps had freed itself from the Signal Corps and had become a full-fledged arm of the Army. Glenn found an ally in Brigadier General William "Billy" Mitchell, the fiery, outspoken assistant chief of the new Army Air Service. The two men were opposites in personality; Mitchell voluble, energetically forceful, and somewhat rash, while Glenn was quiet, cautious, and reticent. But they were one in their conviction about air power, and Martin's powerful new bomber was just what the general was waiting for. On his frequent trips to Washington, Glenn talked at length with Billy Mitchell, and the formal customer-contractor relationship blossomed into a friendship built on mutual respect and trust as well as their single vision.

General Mitchell, in testimony earlier before the House Appropriations Committee, had startled the congressmen by saying the airplane had "obsoleted" the battleship. He was supporting a budget request of $60 million for the Air Service, about the cost of one and a half battleships. He had strongly contended for some time and vocally championed his belief that airplanes could sink surface ships, and he told the committee he could build a thousand airplanes for the cost of one battleship. Mitchell testified:

The air will prevail over the water in a very short time. An army fights on land, a navy on water, but an air force over both. We can tell you definitely now that we can either destroy or sink any ship in existence today. All we want to do is have you gentlemen watch us attack a battleship.[1]

Fanned by the national press that sensed a great story, the controversy swirled hotter and hotter until a test was authorized by Navy Secretary Josephus Daniels and Secretary of War Newton D. Baker. General Mitchell was told to put his airplane where his mouth was, and he selected the Martin bomber to prove the point. He had flown the plane and knew its bomb-carrying capability. The targets selected for the test were four German war prizes, combat ships given to the United States when remnants of the German imperial navy were divided among the allies. In addition to the submarine U-117, which only a few years before had preyed on American shipping, the targets were to include a destroyer, the G-102, the light cruiser *Frankfort,* and the mighty *Ostfriesland,* the battleship that had fought in the

Billy Mitchell as colonel

Martin bomber and battleship

Battle of Jutland (a 22,800-ton behemoth, it was generally considered unsinkable). Five days were scheduled for the tests, beginning on June 12 and continuing on July 13, 18, 20, and 21. The four ships were arrayed 75 miles at sea off the Virginia capes, and a virtual circus atmosphere prevailed.

Glenn Martin, probably the least disinterested of anyone in the country, did not even attend the preliminary rounds when three Navy planes dropped twelve relatively small 163-pound bombs to sink the submarine in only sixteen minutes. Nor was he there when the destroyer was sent to the bottom in nineteen minutes after being pummeled with 300-pounders dropped by a wave of Martin bombers, led by General Mitchell.

Glenn's friend and frequent correspondent, L. D. Gardner, publisher of *Aviation Magazine and Aircraft Journal*, wrote to him about those tests and urged him to attend the next round, which would involve the heavier ships. "The tests were better than anyone could expect," Gardner wrote. "There were 13 Martin bombers, each carrying four 300-pound bombs, [and] the accuracy with which they dropped these bombs from 4,000 feet was startling. It was the greatest test that has ever been made in this country. I think it would be well for you to come to some of these bombing tests, particularly the ones on the 18th and 20th of July."[2] Glenn replied to Gardner that he intended to see the upcoming tests and wondered if it would be proper to take his mother, to which Gardner hurriedly wrote back discouraging Minta Martin's attendance as "not at all appropriate."

The final tests with the *Osfriesland* were scheduled for two days, July 20 and 21. The heavy cruiser *Frankfort* had gone down two days earlier, dispatched in thirty-five minutes by three Martin bombers dropping eleven bombs. For the final test, the military wanted to see the effect of various sizes of bombs. On the first day, Navy F-5s, Marine DeHavilands, and the Army's Martin bombers showered 230-pound, 520-pound, and 600-pound bombs on the battleship with little more damage than the tattering of the *Osfriesland*'s superstructure.

For the main event the next day, a blazing July sun beat down on the assembly of high-ranking Navy and War Department officials, news correspondents, and other spectators, including Glenn, crowding the decks of the naval transport *Henderson*. At the appointed hour, seven Martin bombers appeared out of the sun, intending to deliver the coup de grace. "Seven puny Davids against an especially able-looking Goliath," wrote one correspondent.[3] What the witnesses did not know was the size of the bombs in David's slings. General

Mitchell and Glenn had had the Martin bombers especially outfitted to carry a newly developed one-ton bomb. Mitchell also had instructed his pilots to try for near-misses so that the explosive force and water pressure would combine to cave in the sides of the battleship. The MB-2s dropped four of them in the water directly alongside the *Ostfriesland* and a fifth squarely on her deck; the other two bombs fell some distance away from the ship. When the flashes and explosions and towering geysers of water cleared, the unsinkable battleship could be seen sinking stern-first. Her bow reared from the water, exposing a jagged hole, and then the once great ship rolled on her side and slipped beneath the waves. The entire spectacle lasted only twenty-one minutes.

Army and Navy officers, newsmen, and others observing the awesome demonstration of aerial supremacy were stunned, with two possible exceptions. One of those not surprised was in the sky piloting the lead Martin bomber. The other, watching from the rail of the *Henderson,* was the visionary who gave his name to the planes, Glenn Martin. Seven years before, in August 1914, he had predicted in a newspaper interview that airplanes would sink battleships.

Reaction to the tests was immediate. "A bomb was fired today that will be heard around the world," said Major General Clarence C. Williams, the Army's chief of ordnance. "We must put planes on battleships and get aircraft carriers immediately," proclaimed Rear Admiral William A. Moffett, who within the year would become the first chief of the newly organized Navy Bureau of Aeronautics. While both comments portended a brilliant future for the Martin company and its founder, Admiral Moffett's resolve had the most immediate impact on the company.

In the next ten years the Martin company produced more than four hundred aircraft for the U.S. Navy alone in a dozen different configurations, from observation planes to scouts, torpedo bombers, dive-bombers, and patrol bombers. Ironically, it would be a decade before the company built a new combat plane for the Army Air Corps even though it had been the Army's Billy Mitchell who had demonstrated aerial supremacy with the ship bombings.

Even before the battleship bombing success of the MB-2 and despite the championing Billy Mitchell gave the Martin plane and the tactic of aerial bombardment, the Army decided in the spring of 1921 to seek a second production source for the plane. The contract with Martin for twenty aircraft would be its last; subsequent production of thirty-five planes would go to L.W.F. Company of Long Island. The Army later contracted for fifty more MB-2s from Glenn Curtiss's

MB-2 over Washington

company. It would not be the last time that the firm building the better mousetrap saw its creation second-sourced to a lower bidder.

In another letter to his friend and frequent correspondent Lester Gardner, Glenn predicted that both L.W.F and Curtiss would lose their respective shirts at the prices they had agreed to build the MB-2. He was right. Curtiss, who had bid $18,000 per plane, lost a quarter million dollars on his contract, and Willard's firm went bankrupt trying to build the MB-2 for $23,000 apiece. Glenn's original contract for twenty planes had been for $1,003,737, or just a little more than $50,000 per plane. At that figure he made a profit, which was why he was in business, after all.

The philosophical and intellectual kinship between Billy Mitchell and Glenn Martin continued through the 1920s even though the customer-contractor relationship languished. Before the battleship sinking, Mitchell had written in a 1919 memorandum:

> Adequate aerial defense can only be assured by the development of an aeronautical industry in peacetime devoted largely to commercial manufacture which can be diverted immediately when hostilities are threatened to the quantity production of military planes.[4]

And Glenn Martin in 1920 had written a guest editorial in the *The Plain Dealer* on the importance of maintaining in peacetime a "robust industrial base" for aircraft and other items of weaponry:

> It is immediately evident that the industrial strength of the United States must be at the war strength all the time, as production of aircraft cannot be developed under one year from any given date. Therefore the government must stimulate and aid in the application of aircraft industrially, and also aid in foreign trade, furnishing sufficient outlet for industrial aviation and guaranteeing a continuity of production at the required rate.[5]

Both men were years ahead of the public thinking of the day, in and out of the government. Their concerns would be readdressed in the 1940s by President Eisenhower.[6]

Admiral Moffett's urgency to equip the Navy with all manner of aircraft resulted in multiple experimental projects with various manufacturers. Martin was in the fore of this work, and its first new Navy planes were built under contracts awarded in April 1922, nine months after the sinking of the warships. The first was for the M20-1 observation plane, three of which were ordered. The second contract called for six of another observation plane, designated the MO-1. Although not a true amphibian, the MO could be outfitted with wheels or floats, but more important, it could be catapulted from battleships. Previous Navy catapult craft had been rather small. The MO was the first of considerable size.

The MO-1 was also the first all-metal seaplane. A monoplane with a high cantilever wing, it was powered by a 375-horsepower Curtiss D-12 engine and could carry a crew of three. The Navy was very excited by the new Martin plane and ordered thirty more three months after the first one flew. Less than a year later Martin rolled out the N2M-1, a new type of Navy trainer. It was followed a year later by a midget observation plane, designed to be carried by submarines. Admiral Moffett and the Navy Bureau of Aeronautics were missing no bets.

Having outfitted the major surface ships with observer aircraft, it was decided to give eyes to the submariners as well. The MS-1, Martin submarine observation plane, was indeed a rare bird. Just seven and a half feet tall, the pontoon plane was seventeen feet in length and had a removable wing eighteen feet in length. A three-cylinder radial engine carried it to a speed of one hundred miles per hour. There were many smiles when the huge hangar doors of the Cleveland plant opened on April 17, 1923, and out scooted the tiny plane. The test pilot, "Ducky" Pond, after climbing into the cockpit, "grinned appreciatively as he all but pulled the plane on over himself."[7] And when it took off, watching Clevelanders had to laugh at the comparison when a giant MB-2 flew by. It looked much like a hawk next to a sparrow.

In operation, the newest Navy observation plane landed in its pontoon mode on the water. The submarine surfaced beneath it, lifting the plane high and dry on its deck. The wings were removed and stored with the plane in a special watertight container on the deck of the submarine. After its undersea mission, the sub surfaced again, unpacked its plane, then partially submerged to float it for launch. The Navy bought six of the MS-1s.

Of far more importance than the sub-mounted mini-scout was the development of torpedo bombing and the Navy's requirement for an airplane specifically designed for that mission. Martin won the competition and a contract for thirty-five planes, which were designated the SC-1. Sleek and straddle-legged, the SC-1 carried a torpedo between its specially designed landing gear. The first plane rolled off the assembly line seven months after the contract was awarded, and famed test pilot Cy Caldwell[8] put it through its paces. The Navy was so pleased with the SC-1 that it ordered forty more of an improved version, the SC-2, before the production run was half completed on the SC-1. Meanwhile, drawings were already on the board for the TM models, a three-purpose airplane the Navy considered suitable as torpedo craft, bomber, or scout. Beginning with the T3M-1, the Navy purchased 230 of this type of airplane in seven different versions from 1927 to 1930.

General Billy Mitchell, who remained relentless in his advocacy of air power and a separate Air Force, was court-martialed in 1925 and convicted for defiance of his superiors. Rather than accept a five-year suspension from the Army, he resigned his commission. He died in 1935 at age fifty-six, only a few years before events presaging World War II confirmed many of his beliefs and before Congress overturned his court martial and erased the sentence from his record.

CHAPTER 10

The Public Takes Flight

■

The second half of the decade in Cleveland was also a settling and maturing period both for Glenn personally and for his company. His mother had joined him, and they were settled in an imposing house on nearly three acres of Erie lakefront. The graciousness and grand level of their living had come about rather gradually as Glenn's business fortunes had improved. Glenn's position in the Cleveland community and in the aircraft industry called for nothing less. The city had prospered as a result of the Martin plant, and its young president was a sought-after leader and prominent member of the community. He became a director of the Cleveland Chamber of Commerce and was twice elected president of the East End Managers Association.

Glenn's fondness for sporty cars led to bigger, more luxurious vehicles as his fortunes increased. He bought the first of what would be a series of Stutz automobiles, a rather swank black Biarritz model. Although Glenn frequently entertained business and community leaders in the lakefront house, with his mother as hostess, neither of them considered their living standards luxurious. To their way of thinking, they led a simple, even frugal existence, although some would describe it otherwise.

One of the favorite stories about the "old man" bantered

Glenn (right) and favorite Stutz

around the Cleveland plant was told by a maintenance mechanic called to the Martin home one day to fix a plumbing problem. Although it would be strictly forbidden in the ethical climate of the nineties, it was not uncommon in those days for employers to dispatch employees from the plant when repairs were needed on the boss's house or grounds. The repair took most of the day, and noticing the lateness of the hour, Glenn's mother invited the repairman to stay for dinner. Despite his protestations that he was not dressed for dinner at the boss's house, Minta insisted that he stay and ordered him upstairs to clean up. Seated at the glistening mahogany table, set with fine china and gleaming silverware in the grand dining room of the lakefront house, the president of the company, his hostess mother, and the nervous but scrubbed maintenance man were served dinner by a uniformed maid. The fare was creamed chipped beef on toast with a baked potato. "I probably would have had a better meal at home" was the punchline of the mechanic's story that later became a legend throughout the Cleveland plant.

Another visitor was Glenn's father Clarence. He described the imposing house, its furnishings and servants as "too big and fancy." At the same time he acknowledged that it fit Minta's design for her famous son. He declined Glenn's sincere invitation and wish that he join them, being content with running Martin Garage and Auto Agency back in Santa Ana. Clarence told his son it gave him a place "where I can sit without being run over,"[1] with plenty of peace and quiet and enough time to enjoy his favorite pastimes, hunting and fishing.

At about this time in his life, Glenn came closer to love and marriage than he ever had before or ever would again. The circumstances are best told by his biographer, Henry Still, in *To Ride the Wind:*

> Though Minta continued to guard her son against what she called "feminine wiles," particularly now that Glenn as a handsome bachelor in his mid-thirties was regarded as a "good catch," a sizable crack appeared in the armor she had welded about him.
>
> Glenn fell in love. Her name was Jacqueline, a vivacious, beautiful, and petite girl with glorious dark eyes and a tinkling laugh. She was the first girl he had known since Catherine Irvine who was interested in the things he did and laughed delightedly when he told her of his early adventures as a barnstorming pilot.
>
> On their second date, Glenn took her home to meet his mother. Minta, quick to sense the seriousness of her son's attachment, accepted Jackie graciously. Then, too, she enjoyed the freshness and gaiety of youth that Jackie brought into the big house. If this was the girl who would make Glenn truly happy—for Minta had never seen him as glowing and at ease in the company of a woman before—then it would be all right. Wisely, Minta neither encouraged nor discouraged the friendship; it would have to run its natural course.
>
> Glenn literally showered attention upon Jackie—he took her to dinner and to the theater, for long, fast drives in the country and along the lakeshore. In her company he was able to unbend and even to join in her infectious laughter. The austere businessman gave way to the awkward boy in love.[2]

One night Glenn drove Jackie down to the Erie shore, parked in a secluded spot, and proposed, according to the account. Jackie professed great friendship for him but told him she did not love him. Rebuffed in his proposal, Glenn drove the young lady home. They parted friends, and after she later married an employee of the company and became the mother of four, Glenn made it his business to keep in touch and even send small gifts to the children. His concern for the family continued even after Jacqueline's husband left his employ. Although he frequently sought the company of beautiful women throughout the remainder of his life, there is no record that Glenn ever again made himself vulnerable to a woman, placing his complete trust only in Minta Martin.

Limited as he was in his desire for, and sense of, "family," Glenn ran his airplane factory and treated his employees like a stern but loving father, again aided and abetted by his attentive mother. Minta was a frequent visitor to the plant, sometimes even touring the assembly lines with her son. On one visit, after visiting the rest room for women workers, Minta stormed into her son's office indignant at the meager furnishings she had found. There was nothing but a bare cot, she told him; and no place for them to sit and rest for a moment. Employees should not be encouraged to hang around the rest rooms, Glenn told his mother. It wastes time and money. But the strong-willed Minta was not to be thwarted. Within a few days the bare cot was fitted with a brightly flowered slipcover, and other accessories were added at the direction of the president's mother.

Glenn was to have another personal and professional disappointment soon after his marriage rejection. Donald Douglas decided it was time to leave and form his own aircraft company, and he persuaded Dutch Kindelberger to go with him. Glenn was naturally reluctant to see them go, but the parting was amicable and the three stayed friends, albeit competitors, throughout their careers. To replace Douglas, Glenn hired Lessiter Milburn, a talented engineer and designer well known for his use of metal in the manufacture of aircraft.

Many advances were occurring in the manufacture of airplanes, all aimed at lighter weight with greater strength, providing more speed, endurance, and safety. All-metal construction and the monoplane with a single low wing were major developments, as was the lighter-weight, air-cooled engine. It improved weight-to-power ratios while increasing horsepower. The shape of propellers, struts, and the wing itself changed. But it took one attention-riveting human development to give the airplane public confidence and acceptance.

Glenn was in Newark, New Jersey, on business May 20–21, 1927, when the news of Charles A. Lindbergh's solo flight across the Atlantic hit the newspapers and airwaves. It was all he could do to go about his business, so engrossed was he in progress reports of the flight on the radio. His imagination soared. He could put himself in the cockpit with Lindbergh. He purchased a map so that he could track reports of the flight's progress. Preparing to check out of his hotel on Saturday to catch a noon train back to Cleveland, Glenn could not tear himself away until the announcement came at 5:30 in the afternoon: "Lindbergh has landed at Paris."

Two others who later became part of the Martin team were even closer observers of Lindbergh's history-making takeoff. One was a boy of twelve who washed planes and did other odd chores around Long Island's Roosevelt Field at the time Lindbergh was preparing for his flight. Lindbergh had befriended a stray kitten, and when it came time to climb into his plane, he turned to the waiting group and said, "Here, Billy, you take the kitten. I can't take it with me." That Billy was William B. Bergen, who grew up to work for Glenn Martin and one day become president of the company.

In the same small gathering seeing Lindy off was C. B. Allen, a young reporter assigned to cover the event for the *New York Herald*. He did not know the Bergen boy, nor did Allen know that one day he also would work for The Martin Company as a special assistant to Bergen as president.[3]

Glenn with Lindbergh

An exuberant Glenn returned home convinced that Lindbergh's feat would trigger public acceptance of flight, and indeed it came almost overnight. The public fell in love with "Lucky Lindy." The year before, only 5,782 passengers were carried in airplanes in the United States. That number more than doubled, to 12,594, by the end of the year of Lindbergh's flight and more than quadrupled in 1928, when 52,934 people rode airplanes as passengers.

That number didn't include the county fairgoers who paid $5 for a ten-minute ride in airplanes piloted by thousands of weekend barnstormers, such as nineteen-year-old F. G. "Gene" Foster. After graduating from high school in Crestline, Ohio, and attending Ohio Wesleyan for a semester, he took a job at Cincinnati's Lunken Airport, washing down and fueling airplanes in exchange for flying lessons. A relative of his wife Virginia worked at the Martin plant in Cleveland, and it wasn't long before Gene also applied and was added to a work force numbering close to one thousand in 1928. It was the beginning of a Martin production career that would run for forty-six years.[4]

Gene Foster started in ground testing on the T3M-1, the first of that distinguished line of planes, and then on the T4M-1, a seaplane version of the torpedo bomber. The company produced 125 of the 3s, which were so popular with the Navy that Martin was asked to build a follow-up, the T4M, that could be carrier-based. Gene also worked on these planes, and 102 of them were built for use on the first aircraft carriers in the fleet, the *Lexington* and the *Saratoga*.

Then came the XT5M-1 and XT6M-1 experimental torpedo bombers that would lead eventually to the Navy's BM series of dive bombers that Martin produced in later years. Although the plant was filled with Navy planes, there was little new Army business beyond the mail planes and the much-heralded Martin MB-2, which continued to break new frontiers of flight. A special MB-2 refitted with General Electric turbosuperchargers, carried Army parachutist Captain A. W. Stevens to 24,206 feet, a new parachute jump record. That was in June 1922. Two months later Lieutenant Leigh Wade piloted the same plane to 23,350 feet, a new altitude record for an airplane carrying three passengers.

The overcrowded factory made it apparent that more manufacturing space was needed. The Navy would soon want larger planes based on the water. Lindbergh's flight and the American public's rapidly growing acceptance of airplane travel convinced Glenn that there soon would be bigger markets.

Cleveland was planning a municipal airport, something Glenn

had championed for several years, and city fathers, anxious to keep the nation's leading aircraft manufacturer in their city, offered Glenn land adjoining the proposed airport for a new factory. But he had additional concerns other than airport access. Navy interest in sea-based aircraft made it imperative that a new plant have not only airport access but year-round open water. Lake Erie was frequently ice-clogged in winter months. It would not be easy for Glenn to leave a city where fortune had smiled so favorably on him. Except for 1924, when sales and earnings of the Martin Company were almost halved, sales were comfortably in excess of $2 million for each succeeding year of the decade. They reached $2,494,506 in 1928, when the company earned $406,201, an astounding profit of 16 percent. No matter. Glenn knew he had to move if he wanted to grow, and so the search began for a new plant location.

PART III

Golden Years

1929–36

■

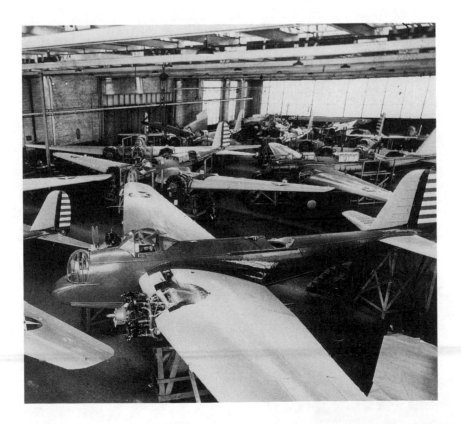

CHAPTER 11

Baltimore,
as in Middle River

■

E ven after resigning himself to the move from Cleveland, Glenn was careful and deliberate in planning the next step. He sent Charles Van Dusen, his business manager, to the East Coast to look for a proper location. Anywhere from Philadelphia south through Florida would make sense, they reasoned. The choice of Baltimore seemed ideal. It was a manufacturing town, large enough to offer a stable and affordable work force. It was a major seaport and rail terminal and only forty miles from the nation's capital, the seat of most of Martin's customers. The climate was moderate, and ample land was available with year-round access to the virtually unlimited waters of the Chesapeake Bay and its tributaries.

Glenn began a dialogue with Baltimore planners and other officials. The initial response was enthusiastic. With apparent open arms, city officials indicated a willingness, even an eagerness, to build a municipal airport to serve a prospective Martin plant. Lengthy correspondence passed back and forth between Cleveland and Baltimore. Proposed legislation and bond issues that would provide for a new airport were reviewed and revised. Finally, Baltimore offered free, with a few strings, a fifty-acre site for the factory. Anything more was available for a price.

Glenn was not exactly overwhelmed. In a personal appearance before the Baltimore City Council, he explained that fifty acres would hardly accommodate a plant the size he planned with its own airstrip. At minimum, he said, one hundred acres would be needed. Looking around the table, Glenn saw nothing but stone faces, not a single hint of real interest or encouragement. Rising quickly from the table, he thanked them for their time and excused himself on the pretext of catching a train. It was the end of negotiations with the City of Baltimore. And the city's officialdom never really got over the fact that they had let what was to become one of the largest industrial enterprises in the country slip from the city's tax rolls and out of their jurisdiction. It remained a sore point for years. Many held a thinly veiled grudge against the "idiosyncratic" Glenn Martin for not building within the Baltimore city limits.

However, Theodore Roosevelt McKeldin, the boy orator who later became the city's multiterm mayor and eventually governor of Maryland, never hesitated to lay the blame on city fathers. McKeldin was secretary to Baltimore Mayor William F. Broening at the time of the negotiations with Martin and therefore was in a position to know. In later years McKeldin frankly and frequently stated that Mayor Broening and the city council were myopic in their greed by attempting to squeeze every nickel they could get out of the potential corporate newcomer. They had little vision of the enormous potential such an enterprise would bring to the city in jobs, taxes, and other revenue.

It was not the end for Glenn, however. Instead of catching a train back to Cleveland, he hired a car and set out to explore the surrounding countryside, principally the shoreline regions lying immediately east and northeast of the city's limits in Baltimore County. It was a leisurely return to nature for the man who had grown up watching the birds and waterfowl in Kansas. He took his time, spending the weekend wandering in and out of the sheltered coves and inlets that laced the shores of the creeks and rivers emptying into the upper reaches of the Chesapeake. About twelve miles outside of Baltimore he stopped in a clearing that faced east with broad inlets of water cutting into the land at a half dozen spots. There was plenty of open land for a factory and a large airport at the water's edge, and the main line of the Pennsylvania Railroad was close at hand.

Returning to Cleveland, Glenn excitedly described the place called Middle River to his mother. It was large enough to build a plant that could accommodate the biggest airplane he could imagine, he said, with water enough to launch a seaplane a block long.

What's more, he told her, he intended to purchase a "big and beautiful" farm. Minta Martin had not seen her son so animated since before his rejected proposal of marriage. As always, she listened attentively, then encouraged him to act quickly and quietly to acquire the land before public knowledge of his interest drove up the prices.

The next day he dispatched William A. Crenning, assistant secretary of the company and a confidant, to Maryland where he was to look over the land and see about acquiring a thousand or so acres. Glenn had marked the site with a large dot on a road map. Like his boss, Crenning had a fondness for hunting and fishing, so he took on the guise of representing a group of New York sportsmen interested in the two-square-mile tract of land for a hunting and fishing club. He rented a room in the area and for two months lived, hunted, and fished with the residents of Middle River. What he learned was not encouraging. The property was owned by forty-five different individuals, and it took him an additional two months to acquire the majority of it, piece by piece, reporting his progress almost daily to Cleveland. At the end of that time Crenning had succeeded in acquiring all but one parcel, the largest piece. Its owner was a crotchety old fisherman who wasn't interested in parting with his homestead at any price.

Nervous that rumors already circulating about his land purchases might get back to Cleveland and his employer, and under considerable pressure from Glenn himself to get the job finished, Crenning made yet another call on the holdout landowner. To his surprise the fisherman was willing to discuss a possible sale. He apparently had talked with his neighbors about the high prices "those crazy New York fellers" were paying. Admitting that he didn't know what Crenning was up to, he said he might be willing to sell if Crenning was still willing to pay what had already been proffered. To Crenning's delight the old man offered to "shake on it." Crenning finally had a deal.

Papers were signed the next day, and the story was out. The Glenn L. Martin Company would build a giant new plant and an airfield complete with hangars on 1,260 acres near Middle River, Maryland, a dozen miles from the heart of Baltimore. The time was opportune. Glenn had already arranged to sell the Cleveland plant to the Great Lakes Aircraft Corporation. The formal papers were signed in October 1928.

He took one other step, perhaps to solidify his standing and reputation in what was to become his new home in Maryland. Louis

Chevrolet, an acquaintance through a mutual friend, at that time had a small company that produced 4-cylinder aircraft engines in Baltimore. Chevrolet had been in the group of wealthy sports car enthusiasts with Caleb Bragg who had bought one of Glenn's early planes and for a time had worked for him. Chevrolet had already sold his name to General Motors and was more than willing to sell a 90 percent interest in his Chevrolet Aircraft Company to Glenn for $175,000.[1]

That was in November, and on December 5, 1928, a new Glenn L. Martin Company was incorporated in Maryland, replacing the Ohio company of the same name, although it would be the fall of 1929 before a new plant was built and occupied. The company financed itself on a common stock basis and was provided with $4 million in capital by a syndication of banks. Glenn was the lone stockholder with 12,000 shares, to be increased to 475,000 shares within the coming year in anticipation of a public offering.

Louis Chevrolet became a vice president of the newly formed Martin company and apparently continued as general manager of the engine company principally owned by Martin and operated as a subsidiary of the Martin company. Although history is unclear about what role Chevrolet actually played in the management, he apparently did stay around at least a few years. His name would later appear, along with that of a brother, Charles Chevrolet, on a Martin-owned 1932 patent for a "rotor fuel pump."

Meanwhile, early in 1929, the Glenn L. Martin Company rented a warehouse at Canton in southeast Baltimore, and initial work and several hundred employees were transferred there from the Cleveland plant. "We were all one big family, a happy bunch,"[2] recalled Gene Foster, who with his wife Virginia was in that initial cadre of employees who made the move from Cleveland to Baltimore. "It was a new opportunity. They just said anyone who wanted to move to Baltimore would be welcome." Baltimore was a conservative bastion in 1929, a manufacturing, blue-collar town to be sure, but a community of quiet wealth and considerable tradition. Many of the first families, descendants of colonial times, resided and kept horses in the countryside where they "rode to the hounds."

"Baltimore had its blue laws, and if you wanted to go to a movie on Sunday, you had to drive to Washington," Gene Foster said. "Even the restaurants were closed on Sunday, and the blue-nosed politicians who were the city fathers didn't want to change anything." Baltimoreans were, in the Fosters' view, a bit more hidebound than Clevelanders. Glenn Martin's arrival in staid old Baltimore had about the same impact as a cannonball fired from Fort McHenry into a noontime crowd at Charles and Baltimore streets. The shovels had barely begun clearing land for his factory at Middle River when the famous aviator and aircraft manufacturer was invited to speak to the Baltimore Association of Commerce, an august luncheon assemblage of businessmen and city leaders.

Several in his audience chortled when he predicted the new plant at Middle River would be employing ten thousand people within ten years. Glenn suppressed an angry retort. His predictions had met ridicule and disbelief before. He finished his prepared remarks, and afterward, when the luncheon chairman apologized for the interruption, Glenn questioned his host's own belief in the employment forecast.

"After all, you've only been employing twelve hundred in Cleveland," he told Glenn. "I doubt whether there are ten thousand working in the entire aircraft industry in all of the United States." Glenn's rejoinder was an offer to place a memorandum of their conversation in his safe, for opening in ten years, at which time "we will see who was right and who was wrong." He would not have to produce that memorandum to prove his point a decade later. The buildup for worldwide conflagration swelled Martin's employment rolls to the predicted ten thousand by 1939 and to more than five times that number a few years later at the peak of World War II production.

The skeleton work force gathered in Canton was busy maintaining continuity of engineering, tooling, and procurement for the projects already under contract and the projects appearing on the drawing boards. The company had leased several small buildings and the old Colgate warehouse, which had previously stored brown sugar. "You could smell it a mile away," Gene Foster remembered. But employees rapidly became accustomed to the sweet smell, and airplane production actually took place in the temporary quarters.

Chief among the work moved to Baltimore were plans for the Navy's PM-1 seaplanes—P for patrol, M for Martin, and 1 for what would become the first in a long series of flying boats manufactured in the new Maryland plant. Already in production was the twin-engine BM-1, a rugged metal-and-fabric biplane that was the world's first successful dive-bomber.

BM-1 work begun in Cleveland was carried on in the Canton facility, where hiring also began in anticipation of the move to permanent quarters. Phil Goebel was one of the first brought aboard in Maryland, and his hiring was almost an accident. Phil played the

First Middle River plant, 1929

saxophone and was on his way to a jam session when a friend who worked for Martin at Canton asked him if he wanted a job.

"I wasn't particularly interested in working," Phil said. "I was into music. But I asked where, and the fellow said 'The Glenn L. Martin Company, down at the Canton warehouse near Thompson's SeaGirt House.'[3] I'd never heard of the outfit, but my friend said they made airplanes, and if I'd come down, he'd give me a job. So I went the next day, and they hired me."

He started at twenty-five cents an hour and worked forty-four hours a week with a half day on Saturday. The weekend was overtime at seventy-five cents an hour and included lunch on the company. "I was making more money playing music, but the work was steady, the people were nice, and I could still play the sax on the side," Phil said. In addition to providing mail service and other similar duties, he specifically was assigned to "Mr. Martin," who had a desk in the corner of the warehouse. "He sorta latched on to me. I was his 'gofer,'" Phil said.

"Mr. Martin had a Stutz Bearcat, a 16-cylinder beauty, with tan snakeskin upholstery and leather panels on the doors," Phil recalled. "On Saturdays, when only about a dozen or so of us worked, Mr. Martin would give me the keys to the Stutz and send me over to Thompson's to pick up lunch. He liked seafood, and I'd generally get crab imperial or crabcakes . . . whatever the folks wanted."[4]

The wooden-frame buildings at Canton served as the company's only quarters in Baltimore while the Middle River plant was under construction and until the first employees moved there on October 7, 1929. Phil Goebel was among them. So were Frank Vitek, and Gene and Ginny Foster, and within the month the entire work force of fifteen hundred was in place.

The architect's plan submitted to the company for the Middle River plant had been ambitious. It included an immense factory composed of three adjoining structures, an airport, hangars, and ancillary buildings. Approximately two hundred acres were set aside for the plant, with one thousand reserved for the airport. Glenn Martin considered the architectural concept "a master plan for the future," but he wisely authorized only one building initially. The eventual Middle River facility grew with remarkable likeness to that original plan, the first building becoming known in later years as "A" Building of Plant I.

A large high-bay structure, the new plant contained three hundred thousand square feet of unobstructed floor space. It was the most modern facility money could buy in 1929 and spacious enough to accommodate the largest seaplanes then imaginable. It came complete with woodblock floors, hand laid block by block on concrete subflooring. "They were about two and three-quarter inches thick,"

Wood-block floors

Frank Vitek remembered, "and were more comfortable for workers to stand on. That's why Mr. Martin put them in. They were warmer, too."[5]

The Middle River plant was not just a wonder to Baltimoreans, it was the largest unobstructed space under roof in the country. Locals referred to it not by its formal name, the "Glenn L. Martin Company" or even "the Martin company," but rather by the simple possessive, "Martin's," as if it were Glenn's place. It reflected a vernacular habit peculiar to Baltimore, where the department stores Hutzler Brothers, Hochschild Kohn, and Stewart & Co. were known simply as Hutzler's, Hochschild's, and Stewart's, and two other local firms, Panzer Pickles and Utz Potato Chips, were known familiarly as Panzer's and Utz's.

Financing for that first building came to $1.5 million, a remarkable sum fortunately committed by lenders and spent by contractors prior to that autumn's crash. The stock market's "Black Tuesday" came just three weeks after the plant opened.

The first aircraft to emerge was the BM-1, designed to survive the stress of pulling out of an almost vertical dive with a thousand-pound bomb slung under its fuselage. No mean feat, the plane did just that successfully for the many years it was deployed with the fleet. But many hours of hazardous test flying were required to perfect the BM. It took the life of Navy test pilot Ed Ritchie and nearly cut off the career of William "Ken" Ebel, probably Martin's best-known engineering test pilot and a future vice president of engineering. Unable to pull out of a dive, Ebel came within a few hundred feet of the ground before he was able to fight his way out of the cockpit and barely pop his parachute. Broken ribs were his only injury, and true to tradition, he jumped into another plane and immediately went back up, albeit with another pilot, just to make certain he hadn't lost his nerve.

Ken Ebel's parachute jump was responsible, at least in part, for recruiting to the company one of its production legends, Francis O. "Fuzz" Furman. It was an odd quirk of fate, which Fuzz would recall many years later. In the early thirties, Fuzz was a machinist stationed at the Anacostia Naval Air Station in Washington. On a visit to the Patuxent River Naval Test Station in southern Maryland, Fuzz helped a friend whose job was packing parachutes. Unbeknownst to Furman, his name was put in the parachute, in keeping with the custom of identifying the packer with the chute packed. That parachute saved Ken Ebel's life when he bailed out of the BM-1 in 1931. On a subsequent visit to Patuxent, Ebel went looking for Furman to thank

Veteran test pilot Ken Ebel

him for packing the chute properly. Fuzz's friend directed Ebel to Anacostia, and he eventually found Fuzz, thanked him, and offered him a job.

Despite the accidents, Martin and the Navy went on to perfect dive-bombing techniques with the BM-1 and its immediate modification, the BM-2. These planes ushered in a new era of aerial warfare copied to perfection by the Germans less than a decade later. A more-than-casual observer of the Navy dive-bombing demonstration at the National Air Races in Cleveland that year was Ernst Udet, Germany's World War I ace, who would later head Hitler's Luftwaffe. After watching the impressive Martin dive-bombers, Udet returned to Germany to champion development of the infamous Stuka JU-88 dive-bomber used so effectively in the Nazi drive across Poland on the eve of World War II.[6]

The next new plane to come off the Middle River production line in the early thirties, also for the Navy, was the PM-1. Twin engines were mounted between its two wings, which with a span of one hundred feet made the seaplane a giant of its day. The PM-1 could

PBM patrol bomber, 1930

patrol more than a thousand miles of ocean with a sizable bombload. "Enemy bombers can tear up a runway and stop land-based flying," Glenn was quoted as saying at the time, "but if a bomb explodes in the water of a seaplane base, the crater closes up again." The Navy evidently agreed, ordering seventy-seven of the flying patrol boats in a variety of configurations in 1930 and 1931. One experimental version, the XP2M-1, was a monoplane with a third engine mounted on top in the center of the wing. It was not retained in subsequent models, although the PM-2s and the P3Ms were twin-engine monoplanes. Three of the PM-1s were sold, with Uncle Sam's blessing, to the Brazilian Navy.

Not adverse to being lucky, and also smart, Glenn Martin had to move fast to save himself and the country's "most modern aircraft factory" in the wake of the stock market crash and the depression that followed. Sales dipped to $625,296, on which he turned a thin profit of $30,447 in 1929. His plan for a public stock offering had to be shelved, and the plant and virtually everything in it, including parts and supplies, were mortgaged in exchange for $2,730,000 in operating funds derived from the sale of $3 million worth of five-year, 6 percent convertible gold notes having a face value of 91 percent. "The bank owned everything," Frank Vitek remembered. "All the items in the storeroom were under seal . . . nuts, bolts, parts, all kinds of supplies . . . everything. We had to get special permission to check anything out, even pieces we were putting into the planes."[7]

Even an advanced thinker like Glenn Martin could not have been expected to foresee the depths of the depression ahead. His company's sales, which had nearly quadrupled to $2,227,056 and produced earnings of $73,924 in 1930, rose to $2,928,884 the next year, mostly on contracts for dive-bombers and the PM series of flying boats. But profits disappeared, and the company recorded a loss of $46,145 in 1931. It was the beginning of a five-year profit drought, with little better than a breakeven 1932 and posted losses of $140,341 in 1933, $59,849 in 1934, and a whopping $318,364 in 1935.

Even had he seen the financial peril ahead, Glenn's mindset early in 1931 would have prevented him from exercising caution. At forty-five years of age, he had been singularly honored by being invited to deliver the nineteenth Wilbur Wright Lecture before the Royal Aeronautical Society in London. Flush with success, he returned to the States intent, both in head and heart, on proceeding immediately with plans already on the drawing board for two new aircraft—one a revolutionary Army bomber that would outfly the fastest fighter planes, and the other a giant commercial flying boat. The first would be the B-10, and the second, the China Clipper.

CHAPTER 12

A Collier Trophy
and the China Clipper

■

The last of the Navy P3Ms was delivered in May, and the final PM2s were rolling out of the factory when Glenn received an invitation from Juan Trippe, the young head of Pan American Airways, to bid on a new plane. Trippe had begun mail service between Key West and Cuba in 1927, had expanded it to Puerto Rico and the Panama Canal Zone a year later, and in 1931 was looking for better aircraft to fly expanding routes into South America and the Pacific.

The letter seeking bids was dated June 26, 1931. It called for a "multimotored flying boat, having a cruising range of 2,500 miles and providing accommodations for a crew of four with at least 300 pounds of air mail and 12 passengers."[1] Both Lessiter Milburn, Martin's chief engineer, and Van Dusen, the business manager, calculated that the four engines required would have to be of unprecedented size. Specification of hundreds of other technical innovations called for heavy investment by the winning bidder. Both men advised against submitting a proposal. Glenn took less than a week before deciding to overrule their advice and go after the contract. He advised Pan American on July 2, "We will submit a proposal addressed to Mr. Charles A. Lindbergh, chairman of your Technical Committee, on or before August 15."

Martin's proposal was submitted on time, but subsequent negotiations took months. Van Dusen and plant manager Harry Vollmer produced eight versions of the contract, each time cutting and revising to counter a stiff Pan Am negotiating team. Two million dollars was Martin's final figure to produce three of the giant flying boats. Pan Am offered no more than $1.5 million, a figure Glenn finally accepted despite Van Dusen's warnings that it would bankrupt the company. He predicted a loss of between $700,000 and $900,000 on the contract.

Only one other aircraft firm submitted a bid: Igor Sikorsky proposed a smaller seaplane, the S-42, about half the size of the Martin entry. The Sikorsky plane would cost considerably less and could be built in less time, so Pan Am's Juan Trippe agreed to purchase ten of them for use on shorter Caribbean and South American routes. Trippe also planned to use one of the Sikorsky S-42s to survey the Pacific route while he waited for delivery of the longer-range Martin planes. All were to be called Clipper in honor of the tall-masted Yankee sailing ships that had once coursed the world's oceans. The name sat well with Baltimoreans, who had long identified their shipbuilding city as a mother port for the old sailing clippers.

Almost simultaneously with the Pan Am approval, the company was building at its own expense the M-139, which became the XB-907 prototype for the Army's new B-10 bomber competition. When the plane lost the Air Corps fly-off to a faster Boeing entry, Glenn was devastated. By contrast, Van Dusen and Milburn this time urged him to modify the plane and try again.

But Glenn was despondent. Not only had the Pan Am negotiations and the B-10 competition coincided, they had exacerbated a physical and mental exhaustion that had overtaken him. He had been unprepared for the myriad of management trials brought on by the depression, and the intensity of simultaneously birthing two radically new airplanes had taken its toll. Glenn had simply driven himself too hard. His mother had been established in Washington's luxury Kennedy-Warren Apartments while their Baltimore house was being built. Although it provided a convenient overnight accommodation on his frequent customer trips to Washington, her absence deprived him of the routine comforts of home, including three square meals a day and adequate rest and relaxation from the hectic factory pace. To avoid the daily eighty-mile Washington round-trip, Glenn spent weeknights in Baltimore. He took all his meals in the plant cafeteria, dining almost exclusively on canned peaches, crack-

B-10 production line in Baltimore

ers, and milk, to the amazement and consternation of employees who watched his physical decline.

When the Martin XB-907 lost the B-10 competition to a Boeing plane that was 20 miles per hour faster, the dejected Glenn had no enthusiasm for his colleagues' postmortem. True, their entry had reached a top speed of 165 miles per hour, far faster than any earlier bomber, including the MB-2, but the competition was over. They had lost, he told them. He hardly heard their entreaties that a longer wing and more powerful engines would enable the plane to fly rings around the Boeing craft.

Milburn and Van Dusen were shocked at Glenn's uncharacteristic lack of fight. Completely absent were his trademark traits—stubbornness, determination, and tightness with a dollar. How could he give up so easily the sizable investment in time and dollars that had already been put into this plane of his dreams? Finally, and with great weariness, he gave in. His doctor was treating him for anemia and an ulcer, and had told him he must rest. "Very well. I'll leave it up to you," he told Milburn and Van Dusen. "My mother and I will take a vacation for a little while. But while you're at it, take those bomb racks out from under the wing and put them inside the fuselage."[2]

Modifications to the prototype took about two months. A longer wing, 70 feet, from which protruded more powerful twin engines, was mounted in the middle of a fattened fuselage, giving the plane its nickname, "the Flying Whale." Bomb racks were inside as Glenn had suggested. The modified YB-10 dazzled Army evaluators at its Wright Field demonstration in October 1932. It could climb to ten thousand feet with two thousand pounds of bombs. Its top speed of 207 miles per hour not only was 22 miles per hour faster than the Boeing B-9, but it could outrun the fastest pursuit plane then in service. It was the fastest bomber in the world and America's first large all-metal monoplane; previous bombers, most of them biplanes, had tubular steel framework covered by fabric. The plane had a range of fourteen hundred miles and the first enclosed rotating turret for the machine gunner, a development that would be widely copied in the industry and was the forerunner of the first power-operated turret, also a Martin development, later in the decade.

The Army immediately ordered fourteen of the YB-10s, and the news wired to Glenn was like an elixir. Well rested, he returned home to congratulate his team and learn the depth of the Air Corps's interest in the new plane. The initial order was soon followed by modifications—the YB-10A, the YB-12, and the YB-14, a total of thirty-four additional aircraft—before the Army placed its large production order for 103 planes of the final B-10B configuration. But perhaps even more personally satisfying to Glenn than the new business was notification that he had been chosen to receive the 1932 Robert J. Collier Trophy, aviation's highest award for the greatest achievement in aviation in America during the preceding year. It was for the B-10, of course.

The award ceremony for the Collier Trophy was scheduled for May 31, 1933, and when that day dawned, Glenn was so excited, he would not trust himself to drive. His chauffeur-driven Stutz (the snakeskin-upholstered Bearcat had been exchanged for a more dignified Stutz Biarritz with specially ordered maroon Bedouin leather interior) stopped at Washington's Kennedy-Warren to pick up his mother, then proceeded down Connecticut Avenue to Dupont Circle, south on Sixteenth Street to St. John's, the "church of presidents," at the corner of H Street, around Lafayette Park to Pennsylvania Avenue, and into the driveway of the White House.

A receptionist met them at the door and ushered them to the Oval Office. There a beaming Franklin Delano Roosevelt waited behind his massive desk. Members of the selection committee from the National Aeronautical Society, the Secretary of the Army, newspaper representatives, and others were gathered for the ceremony. With introductions completed, the president of the United States turned to Glenn Martin and said, "When a man is selected to receive the Collier Trophy for the year's outstanding contribution to aviation, he is receiving, in effect, the thanks of the entire nation as well as the aviation industry." Then, turning to Minta Martin, the president added, "Mrs. Martin, we in America share your pride in the achievements of your son."[3]

Ill at ease as he was on such public occasions, Glenn managed a stiff and reserved recitation of remarks he had memorized: "Since 1909, there has never been a sensation more soul-satisfying than the first flight of a new design; no field of endeavor half so fascinating as the challenge of each new secret of flight." Then, remembering the perseverance and insistence of Lessiter Milburn and Charles Van Dusen when he had been ready to give up, Glenn added, "Credit for the B-10 bomber belongs to everyone who worked on the design and who helped to rivet it together. It is on their behalf that I accept this honor."

It was the first of six such occasions when his company would have its name inscribed on the nation's most prestigious aviation trophy for technological achievement. Three months earlier, Glenn had flown to Salina, where Kansas Wesleyan conferred the honorary degree of doctor of engineering on its 1903 business course alumnus.

As if to underline the importance of the Collier recognition, the Army embarked the following year on an unprecedented aerial mission with the B-10. Led by Lieutenant Colonel Henry H. Arnold, a flight of ten B-10s left Washington's Bolling Field on July 18, 1934, for a six-day photographic mapping mission to Alaska. Using Fairbanks as a base, the planes photographed more than two hundred thousand square miles of previously unmapped territory, including new aerial routes to Russia and across the Arctic Circle. Only one mishap marred the entire operation: One of the planes made a forced landing and sank on August 3 in Cook's Bay off Anchorage. No one was injured, and the sturdily built B-10 was pulled out of the water; within a week it was flying again. The "air power wonder of its day" was the accolade of Colonel Arnold, later to become General "Hap" Arnold of World War II fame and a postwar chief of Army air forces.

As close to his heart as the B-10 became, Glenn Martin's crowning achievement, at least in his view, was the fruition of the Cleveland newspaper interview of 1919 and his 1931 Wright Memorial Lecture in London, in which he envisioned international commerce whereby huge airplanes ferried passengers across the seas. Perhaps it was the ultimate escape from his landlocked upbringing in the heart of Kansas, or possibly it was a continuation of his first encounter with the Pacific when he flew from the California mainland to Catalina Island. Whatever the reason, the China Clipper would bring it all to life.

The mighty flying boat, designated M-130 within the company for the 130th model of Martin design, had been under construction in the Middle River factory since the contract signing two years before. Actually three Pan American Clippers were taking shape, and they were truly leviathans. The wing spanned 130 feet and was set high above a stocky but graceful boatlike fuselage that was 90 feet long. For its intended transpacific service, the Clipper would carry a crew of six, plus eighteen passengers in the comfort of sleeping quarters, a dining lounge, and other amenities. On short flights it could carry forty-eight passengers. Four 850-horsepower Pratt & Whitney Twin Wasp engines gave the China Clipper a range of four thousand miles at an average speed of 130 miles per hour. It held enough fuel to fly from San Francisco to Hawaii and still have ample reserves. With a gross takeoff weight of fifty-two thousand pounds, there were more than a few craftsmen in the plant who wondered whether the big boat would actually fly.

China Clipper on launching dolly

No such doubts were held in engineering, particularly by a recently hired young project engineer by the name of James McDonnell. He had come aboard in the spring of 1933 and would spend five years with Martin before leaving to establish his own aircraft manufacturing company. Although he had had nothing to do with the design or manufacture of the M-130, Jim McDonnell was as attentive as any of the hundreds gathered at Middle River to see her rolled gently down the ramp into Frog Mortar Creek. There the crew boarded, and Ken Ebel revved up the powerful engines to taxi out to the mouth of Middle River and into the Chesapeake Bay for its first flight trial. With him as copilot were L. D. McCarthy, the project engineer, and Benny Zelubowsky, the foreman of Experimental, acting as flight engineer.

Both Glenn and Minta Martin watched from an automobile parked at the water's edge. A reporter asked if he had any doubts about the great ship flying. Pointing to a flock of ducks skimming low over the water, Glenn smiled and said, "They don't worry about flying."

After a series of gentle turns in the water to test the plane's hydrodynamics, Ebel opened the throttles. The whale of a plane surged forward, raised easily "on the step," then lifted majestically out of the water and flew thirty feet above the surface for a short distance until Ebel eased it back onto the water. As with Glenn's first flight back in 1909, and as with most initial flights, proof of the craft's aerodynamics was all that was sought the first time in the air.

Pan Am accepted the first Martin flying boat and designated it the "China Clipper" on October 9, 1935, two weeks before Trippe was to receive the airmail contract he sought from the federal government to justify the Pacific route as profitable. More than a month and a half of nearly round-the-clock flight testing followed with both Martin and Pan American crews. On November 2, the M-130 made a practice run from Miami to Puerto Rico and return, a distance of twenty-four hundred miles, the same range it would span from San Francisco to Honolulu on the intended first leg of its planned transpacific service. Six days later the China Clipper left Middle River for the last time.

A Pan Am crew under the command of Captain Edwin Musick, a veteran Pan American pilot who had surveyed the Pacific route earlier in a Sikorsky S-42, flew the Martin Clipper to Acapulco, Mexico, and then to San Francisco. He also would be the captain of a very senior crew of seven on November 22 for the China Clipper's first scheduled flight across the Pacific. On the appointed day, according to Terry Gwynn-Jones's account in his book, *Wings Across the Pacific:*

> Twenty-five thousand people crammed the shore around Alameda for the departure of the China Clipper. Thousands more waited along the San Francisco waterfront to watch the flying boat depart across the bay. Nowhere along the route was the departure of the first service anticipated with more excitement than in Honolulu which, like much of the world, listened on the special international radio hookup. . . .
>
> As the celebrations to mark the China Clipper's departure from Alameda got underway, Hawaii prepared to celebrate. As if the gods were sending a spectacular acknowledgement of the event, the active volcano Mokuaweoweo erupted, sending smoke and sparks towering over Hawaii Island.
>
> On the flag-draped pier at Alameda, Postmaster General [James] Farley read a message from President Roosevelt. "This is a century of progress that is without parallel, and it is our just pride that America and Americans have played no minor part in the blazing of new trails," it said in part. Moments later a stagecoach, the mail carrier of earlier days, delivered 110,000 letters for the China Clipper service. Weighing 1,897 pounds, they represented Pan American's first Pacific payload.
>
> Stepping up to the microphone, Juan Trippe soberly addressed the crew lining the jetty alongside their Clipper. "Captain Musick, you have your sailing orders. Cast off and depart for Manila in accordance therewith." As the band struck up "The Star-Spangled Banner," the great gleaming flying boat taxied out into the bay.[4]

Within minutes the big plane lifted out of the water, circled the harbor, flew under the still-unfinished Bay Bridge, and headed out to sea. Listening to its departure by radio at the White House, President Roosevelt was quoted, "I thrill to the wonder of it all."

Among the thousands on shore was Glenn Martin, who would be described two years later in a *Saturday Evening Post* cover story as "a cool unmelted Icarus in a braided business suit." Recalling the first flight of the China Clipper, the magazine said of Martin, "His cult is transoceanic flight. . . . He has probed that glittering mystery off and on since he piloted his laboring frail 'pusher' over a spur of the sea to Catalina.''

The magazine quoted Glenn in reflection: "I thought then that if I could fly across part of the ocean, the time most surely [would] come when we could fly across all of it."

Actually, the takeoff had not gone entirely as planned. According to the *Wings Across the Pacific* account, Second Engineering Officer Victor Wright recalled the details thirteen years later in an anniversary article for the *Alameda Times Star:*

> After leaving the waterfront ramp, Captain Musick circled on the water a few times to warm up the engines and then headed up the bay toward the looping wires of the San Francisco–Oakland bridge, then being built. As we left, a convoy of escorting planes closed in behind us. It had been our intention to fly over the bridge, but Musick quickly saw that with the engine cowl flaps open he wouldn't be able to get enough speed to clear the wires, so he nosed the Clipper down at the last moment and went under the bridge cables, threading his way through the dangling construction wires. We all ducked and held our breath until we were in the clear. I think the little planes must have been as surprised as we were, but they all followed us right through.[5]

In addition to Captain Musick and Wright, the Pan Am log of that first flight of the China Clipper listed two other senior pilots: Capt. R. O. D. Sullivan, flying as first officer, and George King, a second officer by airline rank, flying as junior pilot. Wilson Jarboe was the radio officer, and another Wright, initials C. D., was the first engineering officer. The navigator was Fred Noonan, whose path through the annals of aviation history would be Martin-touched once more two years later as Amelia Earhart's navigator on her ill-starred, round-the-world flight attempt and disappearance in the Pacific.[6]

The manifest on that first flight—in addition to the mail, fifty-eight bags containing 110,865 letters—included a shipment of twenty-five canaries and twenty-five pounds of birdseed consigned to tiny Wake Island, which at that time was populated by only a small military contingent and a Pan Am ground crew.

The China Clipper proceeded to Hawaii without incident. Overnight in Honolulu it off-loaded its mail, took on new cargo, includ-

China Clipper in Hawaii and commemorative airmail stamp

ing fresh fruit and Thanksgiving turkeys for Pan Am employees working on Midway and Wake, plus fourteen Pan Am relief workers destined for those two islands. They became the first unofficial passengers on the new transpacific service. Next day, the China Clipper flew to Midway Island, the following day to Wake, then to Guam, finally arriving in Manila on the November 29, seven days and eight thousand two hundred miles from its initial liftoff in California.

Fifty years later, on the anniversary of the China Clipper's first flight, Peter Behr would write in *The Washington Post* that for its time the flight across the Pacific "was as audacious and extravagant as space flight today."

Two more Martin M-130s, the Hawaii Clipper and the Philippine Clipper, joined the Pan Am fleet by October 21, 1936, when the first routine luxury passenger service was inaugurated. Passengers paid $799 one way to be pampered by male flight attendants while eating haute cuisine off the finest "bone china and sterling silverware, set on spotless linen."[7] They had all the comforts of luxury ocean liner service while reducing the time for such a voyage from several weeks to just six days. Although the airfare was stiff (more than $7,500 in 1993 dollars), the sixty hours of actual time in the air seemed a reasonably leisurely pace spread over six days, compared with the jet-lagging rigors of a twelve-hour nonstop flight in the 1990s.

The Philippine Clipper had the distinction of making a special flight from Manila to Hong Kong to mark the awarding of landing rights in the British crown colony. That flight also fulfilled Juan Trippe's promise of California-to-the-Orient service, and he and Mrs. Trippe were among the passengers. Service on Pan Am's Martin Clippers became synonymous with "first class" during the six years they crisscrossed the Pacific.

During those same years, the Japanese were becoming more expansive as tensions grew in the Pacific. The Japanese had already invaded China and were making hostile overtures on the Dutch East Indies. Pan Am's Trippe had originally proposed his transpacific route from America to China because he saw the ease of obtaining landing rights and other concessions on United States–held island territories. The U.S. Navy, under whose jurisdiction the islands fell, had little trouble recognizing the benefit of ready-made commercial servicing and communications facilities as well as the benefits of U.S. citizens settling in the islands. A commercial air route across the Pacific would be a logical extension of the country's strategic interest in that part of the world. The Clippers' island-hopping transpacific route, from California to Hawaii, to Midway, to Wake, to Guam, to the Philippines, and then on to Hong Kong and Macao, carried America's presence to China's front door. While not apparent to civilian America, the military implications were readily perceived from the Japanese side of the ocean.

Early in 1938, Japan formally asked, through the U.S. ambassador in Tokyo, that the Clipper flights into Macao be stopped to avoid possible incidents with military aircraft that were enforcing Japan's blockade of the China coast. Although the United States rejected the request on the ground that it violated international freedom of the seas, Pan Am did limit the Clipper activity in and out of Macao to times when that area of the China Sea was free of military activity. There had also been vague rumors of sabotage aimed at the Clippers. In one earlier reported but unpublicized incident, the FBI interrupted two Japanese who were in the act of miscalibrating the radio-direction finder two days before the China Clipper's maiden flight from Alameda in 1935. But rumors of sabotage had subsided by the early summer of 1938.

On July 23, the China Clipper was inbound to the States from Hong Kong, the Philippine Clipper was already en route to the Far East, and the Hawaii Clipper lifted off from San Francisco Bay at 3:00 P.M., headed for the Orient. The Hawaii Clipper had completed 4,700 flawless hours on thirty-five Pacific round-trips, and on this day,

Flight 229 appeared to be another routine flight. The first four legs of the trip, from Alameda to Honolulu, to Midway, to Wake, and to Guam, were completely routine.

As had its sister ships, the Hawaii Clipper had every backup system and safety device known at the time, installed by Martin when the planes were built at Middle River. Six watertight compartments divided the seaplane's ninety-foot hull so that if damaged and forced down at sea, any two compartments would keep the twenty-six-ton flying boat afloat. Only two months before, the Hawaii Clipper and her sister ships had been refitted with brand-new, upgraded, 950-horsepower Pratt & Whitney engines and new Hamilton hydromatic propellers. Any two engines could keep the Clipper flying. There were two main radios and a third small emergency set complete with trailing antenna, plus an auxiliary generator, rubber rafts, provisions, shotguns, fishing tackle and bait, all stored in an emergency locker.

On July 29, at eleven minutes after noon, the Hawaii Clipper operating as Pan Am Flight 229 disappeared without a trace after radioing its position of latitude 12 degrees 27 minutes north, longitude 130 degrees 40 minutes east, between Guam and Manila. Radio operator William McCarthy had sent that position report and was preparing to receive a responding weather report from the island of Panay, the closest radio base to the Clipper's position, when communication ceased. Not one shred of evidence has ever been uncovered about what happened to the second Martin-built Clipper, its crew, or its fourteen passengers. An extensive surface and air search that lasted a week found not a single clue: no debris, no oil slick, absolutely nothing.

Four possible explanations were proposed at the time for what happened to the Hawaii Clipper: (1) it was destroyed by a terrible electrical storm, (2) mechanical or structural failure caused the giant plane to break up instantly, (3) it was sabotaged by a timed explosive device placed aboard before it left Guam, or (4) it was shot down by marauding Japanese fighters. "When explored, [those explanations] distort known facts and do not fit with what we really know about the flight and the subsequent seven-day search," according to Ronald Jackson in his intriguing book, *China Clipper*, which suggests rather forcefully a fifth possibility—hijacking.

Hijacking is the only one that makes sense, Jackson insists. The Pan Am Hawaii Clipper, Jackson asserts, was hijacked by the Japanese for two very logical reasons. First, the Japanese wanted to intercept one of the passengers, Wah Sun Choy, a Jersey City restaurateur and chairman of the Chinese War Relief Committee in America, who reportedly was carrying between $2 million and $3 million in American currency, which he was to turn over to Chiang Kai-shek's embattled Chinese Nationalists in Chungking. Second, they wanted the Martin Clipper intact so they could copy its technology and incorporate it into their new Emily flying boat, then in the second month of its design.

The Martin Clipper was, without debate then or now, the world's finest, most advanced seaplane. Jackson postulates that the known facts about the Hawaii Clipper's progress from Guam to Manila are so well documented that there was only one minute, between 12:11 and 12:12 P.M., on July 29, 1938, during which whatever happened occurred instantly and permanently.

Still two hours from the Philippine coast, radio operator McCarthy reported the Clipper's position, weather, health of the crew and passengers, and general condition of the plane. One minute later, Panay radio was unsuccessful in raising the Hawaii Clipper. Nor was it ever heard from again. Extensive search operations of the plane's well-documented location failed to turn up any evidence. There had been earlier sabotage attempts on the Clippers, and Jackson conjectures that two Japanese naval officers stowed away in the plane's cargo hold during its overnight in Guam, appeared on deck in midflight, and took over the Clipper, directing it south to the Japanese secret seadrome at Koror in the western Palau Islands.

Further proof of his theory, Jackson wrote, was the Japanese seaplane Emily. Similar in size and profile, it had an interior floor plan identical to the Martin Clipper and enough other overlapping engineering features to "strongly suggest that the Martin Clippers played a developmental role in the Emily's design." Jackson concluded:

> The Hawaii Clipper did not fly into a typhoon or a swarm of Japanese fighters; instead it flew into a web of Pacific politics, a force more powerful than any aboard realized. Though hijacking cannot be conclusively proven without a confession or demonstrable evidence, once the pieces of the political puzzle are assembled and combined with the physical facts surrounding the loss, hijacking is the most credible explanation of the Clipper's fate.[8]

Even the Hawaii Clipper's accident report leaves open this possibility; the book quotes in part:

No authentic trace of the airplane ever has been found and ... as a result, those who investigated its disappearance are unable to ascribe any probable cause for the disaster that is presumed to have overtaken the big flying boat. Pending the discovery of some concrete evidence as to the fate of the Hawaii Clipper, the investigation remains in an open status.[9]

Whatever the circumstances, the public of that day had little knowledge. The Martin Clippers had already done much to dispel public fear of flying and to establish the romance of travel by flying boat. Although average Americans would never get to fly on the China Clipper or its sister ships, they were made well aware of the luxury and charm of the experience through news articles and pictures, motion-picture newsreels, and a major Hollywood movie of the day, *China Clipper,* starring Humphrey Bogart.

Pearl Harbor put an end to commercial Pacific service by the Martin Clippers, and World War II's development of land-based airplanes with ocean-spanning ranges made inevitable the demise of the graceful queens of sea and air. The last eastbound Clipper flight before war broke out was delayed in its November departure from Manila in order to board the special Japanese envoy Saburo Kurusu on his way to the United States. He was in Washington when the bombs fell on Hawaii's Pearl Harbor.

CHAPTER 13

A *"Century of Progress"*
in Paint

■

From its modest Jersey City beginnings in 1913, the American Asphalt Paint Company prospered over the next two decades. Grover Hermann, with the $5,000 seed stake advanced by his father, and Charles Phelan, with his proprietary formula for asphalt paints and sealants, had parlayed their partnership into a burgeoning paint business approaching a million dollars by the early 1930s.

The original plant had produced heavy-duty paints containing a small amount of asphalt; they were sold under the trade name Valdura, a Hermann-contrived contraction of "valuable" and "durable." The color line was limited to red, green, and black until 1916, when the partners acquired a second plant at Lincoln, New Jersey, that produced aluminum paint, and all Jersey City operations were moved west to Lincoln. By then, roofing compounds and sealants, also asphalt-based, had become an equally important product line. The company operated for the next fourteen years, gradually expanding its sales and distribution reach.

In 1917, for reasons that remain obscure, the company's legal structure was replaced with a co-partnership that lasted until 1930. That was the year the enterprise was reincorporated in Illinois after the purchase of an abandoned piano plant in Kankakee, Illinois. It

First Hermann asphalt paint plant

was converted into a modern manufacturing facility for paint and varnish, and company offices were established in downtown Chicago. Product distribution became truly nationwide, with sales extending all the way to the West Coast through a branch office in San Francisco.

While much of the nation wallowed in depression, success seemed to beget success for the American Asphalt Paint Company. Sales were brisk, and the business expanded again with the acquisition of the Waterproof Paint and Varnish Company of Watertown, Massachusetts, in July 1931. Then tragedy struck the very next month. Charles Phelan, on vacation in Wyoming's Yellowstone National Park, was killed when he lost control of his automobile on a dirt road. It was a bitter shock to the surviving partner. Not only had the two men worked well as a team, they were genuinely good friends.

Saddened as he was by the untimely loss of his longtime friend and associate, Grover did not let his grief blur his focus or lessen his drive to expand the business. Twenty years before, when the two young men formed their original partnership, each had taken out an insurance policy on the other's life. As beneficiary of the Phelan policy, Grover used the insurance proceeds to purchase his partner's share of the business, including the asphalt paint formula, from Phelan's widow. Now he was the sole proprietor of the business, and he put his sales prowess and plans for expansion into even higher gear.

In 1932 he acquired the Chi-Namel Company of Cleveland and Florida, and made what would be the biggest sale of his life. It came

Chicago World's Fair

just two months before the election of Franklin Delano Roosevelt as the thirty-second president of the United States. Grover Hermann promoted his company into a contract to paint virtually all of the buildings for the Chicago World's Fair. At the time it was the largest single paint contract ever awarded. It called for American Asphalt Paint Company not only to supply the paints but to apply them. The job required 350 painters a day to apply Valdura Asphalt Aluminum base paint as a protective coat to carry the newly constructed buildings over the Chicago winter of 1932. Then came a rainbow of colorful finish coats of Valdura Aluminum and Valdura Oil paints in preparation for the fair's opening on May 27, 1933. The painting covered more than 10.5 million square feet of surface, the equivalent of 218 football fields. Included were 314,000 square feet of corrugated metal fence, more than 1.2 million square feet of metal siding in the sky ride alone, and nearly three thousand tons of steel construction of all kinds, plus buildings of other materials and every description.

Change was in the wind, not just in Chicago but throughout the land, when FDR took office in 1933, and the World's Fair that summer would mark a significant turning point for the American Asphalt Paint Company in its twentieth anniversary year. The fair was billed as "A Century of Progress," and the company made the most of the job, publishing a fancy, embossed, multicolor guide to the exposition and each of its major exhibits. The brochure also described the huge task of painting the fair and concluded with a testimonial promoting a world of color, paint in general, and Valdura paints specifically. "Color and protection" was the theme, and the pitch ended with this all-encompassing claim: "We produce paints to protect the bridge against corrosion, coatings to keep the roof from leaking, compounds to resist severe acid attack, and quality preparations to preserve, beautify, and extend the usefulness of metal, wood, and other surfaces subject to rust or decay."[1]

Twenty-eight colors selected to beautify and protect the fair "created an expanse of beauty never seen anywhere," trumpeted the booklet. "Even many of the interior murals created by world-famous artists were painted with Valdura oils," said the brochure, which placed the quantity of finishing coats alone at twenty-five thousand gallons. "Truly, this 'Century of Progress' was the world's greatest paint task," the booklet concluded. After the fair closed, its general manager, Lenox R. Lohr, agreed with that modest assessment in a letter to Grover Hermann:

> With the closing of the exposition I wish to express to you our appreciation of your company's part in making it the colorful and brilliant panorama which has attracted so many millions of visitors during the past summer. When the painting of both the interiors and exteriors of our own buildings was assigned to your company, the color palette adopted was not an easy one to match in actual production. Notwithstanding, you did a most creditable piece of work, not only in color matching, but in production and application.[2]

Within two years of the company's commercial triumph at the World's Fair, Hermann enlarged the enterprise and set it on a firm course for the next quarter century. The opportunity came in 1935 with the acquisition, for $90,000 in cash and an exchange of stock, of

The Marietta Paint & Color Company of Marietta, Ohio. It was an old, well-established company that dated from 1896, whose founder, C. J. LaVallee, had died just the previous year. Grover had become acquainted, whether by coincidence or design, with LaVallee's son and successor, G. A. LaVallee, early in 1935. The *Marietta* [Ohio] *Times* wrote many years later:

> As the acquaintance between the president of the Marietta Company and Hermann ripened, they decided that great advantages to both companies could result if they were put together. Accordingly, on September 1, 1935, through an exchange of stock (and cash) the American Asphalt Paint Company became a substantial stockholder in The Marietta Paint & Color Company, and LaVallee likewise became a stockholder in the American Asphalt Paint Company.[3]

Irving J. Johnson was there and vividly remembers the pivotal Marietta merger. He had been hired by Mr. Hermann earlier in 1935 as comptroller of the company on the recommendation of Ernst & Ernst, the company's accounting firm. "Before the Marietta deal, we scraped the bucket to do a million dollars in sales," Johnson said. "Now we were a full-line paint manufacturer with regular commercial trade sales, industrial paints and sealants, and special automotive finishes. They [Marietta] had come to us with a loss, but we came up with a profit of $4,000 the next year, and we never had a loss year after that."[4]

The balance of the Marietta stock was acquired in 1937, and in 1940 the parent company, American Asphalt Paint Company, formally changed its name to American-Marietta Company.

As comptroller and because of his accounting skills, Irving Johnson generally accompanied Mr. Hermann when he went to look at a company in which he had become interested. "He had an uncanny ability for finding them," Johnson said. "He was uncanny in a lot of ways. I think he read the death notices wherever he traveled. I know he did in the case of two paint and varnish companies we acquired. Mr. Hermann and I were visiting an office in New York, and there on our host's desk was a death notice of this man who owned two paint and varnish companies. The next week, Mr. Hermann was in Kansas City meeting the widow."

Hermann would later describe his own technique in evaluating a potential acquisition as mostly personal. "It was my habit to make

Hermann and sports roadster

up my mind quickly without much fuss," he said. "If a company interested me, I'd visit the premises, look around, and size up the character of the people and the tidiness of the housekeeping. These are the important things, the things the business-analysis approach all too often misses. I came to know many wonderful people in my travels—families that generation upon generation had provided the business underpinnings of their communities; gentle, decent people, fine Americans you've never heard of—and I can say, with all the companies we acquired, that we never had any unpleasant surprises."[5]

◼

THE NEXT DECADE, ENCOMPASSING WORLD War II, produced a flurry of fifteen new acquisitions for Grover Hermann's newly named company, mostly in paint: Keystone Asphalt Products of Chicago, 1940; Ferbert-Schorndorfer of Cleveland, 1942; Sewall Paint and Varnish of Kansas City and Dallas, Texas, 1944; Ottawa Paint Works Limited of Canada, Schorn Paint of Seattle, and Leon Finch of Los Angeles, all in 1945; Pacific Chemical of Los Angeles, Adhesive Products of Seattle, and Charles R. Long, Jr., Company of Louisville, all in 1946; and five more companies in 1947: Chlorine Solutions of Los Angeles, Berry Brothers, Inc., of Detroit and Ottawa, Jolley Paint and Glass Service, Inc., of Seattle, Indiana Wallpaper Company of Indianapolis, and Lac Chemicals, Inc., of Culver City, California.

None of the newly acquired firms was huge in size. Two of them had annual sales exceeding a million dollars each, five ranged from one-half to three-quarters of a million dollars, and the remainder were smaller, most of them much smaller. They required very little outlay of cash, according to Irving Johnson. In most cases the acquired company was purchased with stock, and in virtually every case it kept its name and management, continuing to operate as before except now it was a division of the new parent firm. With additional investment provided for research and expansion and little management interference as long as growth occurred, by and large the new members of the corporate family were a happy bunch. Sales close to $3 million in 1940 would more than quadruple during the war years due to the increased need for paints and finishes of all kinds and an aggressive, if not spectacular, program of acquiring additional small companies.

Grover Hermann's rate of acquiring new companies accelerated after World War II. Associates used to say he roamed the country with a pocketful of blank checks and a briefcase stuffed with American-Marietta common stock looking for companies to purchase.

CHAPTER 14

Bankruptcy's Brink and Baseball Bats

■

While Grover Hermann and his American-Marietta Company were enjoying new business and increasing prosperity, Glenn Martin and his Baltimore aircraft plant were on the brink of bankruptcy. It was ironic. Unprecedented fame had come to the company through its trophy-winning B-10 bomber and the wondrous China Clippers. The company was the premier aircraft production firm in the country, without peer in reputation because of its two famous airplanes. But Van Dusen's warning to Glenn that accepting the Clipper contract at Pan Am's unrealistically low price would bankrupt the company was close to becoming an uncomfortable reality.

Martin's principal bank, the Baltimore Trust Company, had itself gone bankrupt a year earlier. The bank had been a major investor in the Middle River plant, and its failure cost Martin $398,900 in deposits tied up without interest for several years. That loss combined with the predicted overrun loss of $789,303 for building the three Pan Am Clippers brought the company to the brink of bankruptcy. Unable to retire $2.5 million of five-year gold notes that had been issued when the new plant was built in 1929, Glenn turned to the government's Reconstruction Finance Corporation. The RFC lent the company $1.5 million, which together with some rigorous belt-tightening tided the company over until the Army's principal contract for 103 of the B-10 bombers came through.

All the bad news was not financial. Four months before the China Clipper inaugurated Pacific service, and in the midst of the company's economic woes, Glenn and his mother suffered a personal loss. Clarence Martin died in his seventy-eighth year in Santa Ana, where his son had become famous and where the elder Martin had elected to live out his days enjoying the "good life," as he put it. He had chosen to stay in California where he could hunt and fish, in preference to the busyness of the aviation business his son and wife pursued when they moved, first to Cleveland and eventually to Baltimore. Notified that his father was seriously ill, Glenn immediately flew to be with him, but he arrived a few hours after C. Y. Martin passed away early on the first day of June 1935.

Although father and son had never been as close as mother and son, Clarence's death left its mark on Glenn. It was almost as if at age forty-eight he became aware of his own mortality. He reflected at length on what might have been had he and his father been closer. Not long after, he purchased a large parcel of land near Chestertown on Maryland's Eastern Shore. On part of it he established a wildlife refuge at Green Oaks and simultaneously plunged himself with fervor into the wildlife conservation movement. Of particular interest was Ducks Unlimited, at that time primarily a Canadian-based organization, which he generously funded and helped expand into the United States. It had been Clarence Martin who gave the young boy in Kansas his first gun and taught him how to shoot it. His interest in wildlife, seemingly rekindled by his father's death, may have been the only thing in Glenn's life that was not influenced by his mother.

Although the Martin farm property adjoining the wildlife preserve became well known for its duck-shooting blinds and the important customer-guests entertained there, no shooting was allowed at the Green Oaks refuge. There, with the zeal he put into all new ventures, Glenn threw himself into the study of waterfowl and their migratory habits. He became an authority on the subject and known worldwide for his advocacy and support of Ducks Unlimited programs.

Financial problems continued to nag him and his company all through 1935 despite the public acclaim resulting from first flights of the B-10 bomber and the Pan Am Clipper. Matters were brought forcefully to Glenn's attention one payday morning when a Baltimore bank telephoned the company's treasurer, M. G. Shook, seeking assurance that forthcoming company deposits would be sufficient

Phil Goebel (center) with Marco Rod and Gun Club pals

to cover paychecks of Martin employees. Glenn instructed Shook to reassure the bank that the company would stand behind each and every check and not to panic. He expected an inflow of cash within a few weeks. Then he dictated a notice to all salaried employees asking them to bear with management and forgo their salaries until financial relief arrived.

Frank Vitek and his wife Helen remembered the notice vividly. Sent out with the "M.G.S." initials of the company treasurer, it explained the necessity of postponing a new stock offering "due to the prevailing general weakness of the stock market." Then it went on to say it would be "necessary for the company to postpone from day to day its salary payroll" and requested the "continued cooperation of every employee during this period, with the assurance that full payment will be made as soon as possible." It was more than a month before "full payment" of the back salaries could be made. "They were tough times, but we all understood," said Vitek.[1]

As was frequently his custom when troubled by events he could not master, Glenn left the plant. He got behind the wheel of his new Bentley and drove west toward Baltimore. In Dundalk, not far from Logan Field (later renamed Harbor Field), he stopped before a two-story brick building with a freshly painted sign identifying it as the General Aviation Manufacturing Corporation, a newly created firm headed by his old friend and onetime employee Dutch Kindelberger. Nine years younger than Glenn, he had also been a pilot, and the two had remained good friends. Kindelberger had started work as a draftsman for Martin in Cleveland after the World War I armistice ended his Army flying. He spent five years with Martin and about eight with Douglas before North American Aviation, Inc., wooed him to Baltimore. At that time essentially a holding company, North American had several years earlier acquired from General Motors Corporation its holdings in Fokker Aircraft. When North American merged the Fokker assets with Berliner-Joyce Aircraft in Berliner's Dundalk plant, Kindelberger became president and general manager of the new subsidiary.

The visit gave Glenn the opportunity to welcome his old colleague to town and at the same time talk with someone who knew the money problems he and the industry were facing. The two men discussed the general state of American aviation. Kindelberger noted that the worse conditions became, the more competitors entered the field, a reference to a former colleague of both, Larry Bell, who on July 10 of that year had opened Bell Aircraft Corporation in Buffalo, New York. Then Kindelberger told Glenn his plans for moving his own company to California, where he would have "room to roll an airplane out the door and not have to make a policy decision whether or not it should be equipped with wheels or floats." A year later he did just that.[2]

Kindelberger laughingly suggested that Glenn no longer had to worry about things like that and probably had forgotten how difficult it was to get a new company started. Glenn decided against discussing his own cash flow problems with Kindelberger, instead advising his friend to concentrate on seaplanes, which Glenn was convinced would be the passenger air transportation of the future. Seaplanes were very much in the future of the Glenn L. Martin Company for a good many years. But except for the Clippers, they were military planes, not the type of planes that played a role in the future of air transportation. For the Martin Company's immediate future, new business came first from the Army and from foreign governments for a land-based plane, the B-10, which would eventually stop the company's financial hemorrhaging. That business base set the stage for a cycle of seaplanes and other Navy aircraft that ran for twenty years.

Getting to that point was tough. Los Angeles had been a hand-to-mouth existence, as were the first couple of years in Cleveland. But the 1920s in Cleveland were largely a financial success story. With the exception of 1924, the company had turned a profit from 1920 through 1928. Although modest profits continued for the first two years in Baltimore, losses began piling up almost simultaneously with the move. For the first seven Baltimore years, 1929 through 1935 inclusive, project losses totaled $2,237,250, including the Clipper overrun.

More than $1.4 million was absorbed during those same years in experimental and development costs necessary to introduce the large all-metal flying boats and land planes never before attempted by the company. Eventually, after seven years of red ink, Martin's fortunes shifted dramatically in 1936, principally because of orders for the B-10. Sales soared by 350 percent, from $1,756,756 in 1935 to $6,219,744, and there was a turnaround of a million dollars plus in earnings, from a negative $318,364 to a very positive profit of $732,652, a handsome return of nearly 12 percent on sales.[3]

The Army order for 103 B-10s was generously supplemented by foreign buys. One of Martin's earliest customers back in Los Angeles, the government of the Dutch East Indies, was once again a primary source of sales, its numerous purchases ultimately exceeding the largest U.S. order. Much as the BM-2 had been a decade before, the Martin B-10 became the standard by which all other bomber designs were judged worldwide for the next decade. In addition to the 151 sold to the U.S. Army Air Corps, the company sold 191 additional B-10s abroad. In the years leading up to World War II, the Dutch purchased 120, Argentina 35, Turkey 20, China 9, Siam 6, and one was sold to Amtorg, the American trading company for the Soviet Union, which also purchased one complete set of parts.

As business improved and management of the growing company became less and less his sole purview, Glenn devoted more time to outside interests. He designed and had installed on his Eastern Shore farm a steam-heated duck blind so that in winter he could observe the ducks and geese at close range and in relative comfort. It included a mirrored front intended to confuse the waterfowl into believing the image was an extension of the water, thereby encouraging them to swim right up to the blind. He also installed elaborate recording devices to capture their sounds. By rebroadcasting the bird calls through a tiny speaker installed in a decoy, he was able to lure more flocks for close study.

The experiment in recording duck calls actually led Glenn to invest personally in a recording company, which lost money. He also supplied the financial backing for an all-girl orchestra, which failed, and toyed briefly with the development of a high explosive, briefly called GLMite until it made less than a loud pop on its first field test.

Among many such outside interests, he even leased some years later property and facilities near Murfreesboro, Arkansas, containing what was advertised as the only diamond mine in America. Glenn presumably believed, as had others before him, including Henry Ford, that the property might be the source of industrial diamonds, whose supply was tightly controlled worldwide by the South African DeBeers mining syndicate. There is no record that Martin's interest in the Arkansas venture ever produced diamonds in a quantity or quality sufficient to justify his investment. It was reported that because of lax security, "rough diamonds were peddled around the Pike County Courthouse square during the entire time Martin operated the mine."[4] His estate later sold the property, which today is operated as the Crater of Diamonds State Park, a tourist attraction where, for one dollar, you can keep whatever you might dig up.

Throughout the eleven years in Cleveland and at least until the mid-1930s in Baltimore—before employment levels began to soar—Glenn's presence and personal stamp were very much on his company and the people who worked for him. There was a sense of family, expressed in many ways other than in the multiple sets of relatives employed. Although the man's dress and formal manner gave the appearance of reserved aloofness, his employees were occasionally treated to glimpses of a warm, caring person, even friendly at times. Even during the low points of economic misfortune, he was known to lend a helping hand financially to employees in dire straits. Whether with a personal interest-free loan, an outright gift, or a paid hospital bill, "Mr. Martin" quietly took care of them.

Both Phil Goebel and Joe Ciekot, who joined the company in 1933 and put in thirty-three years (with a break of about nine years following World War II when he built houses for returning veterans), remembered the "ol' man" helping people through medical emergencies. Both also recalled that on his frequent walks through the plant, "Mr. Martin remembered everybody by first names."[5]

"He knew mine," Joe said, "because my sister Genevieve had introduced us. We were out on the baseball field, and he was sitting in the stands with his mother and a beautiful blond lady who I guess was his girlfriend at the time. From then on, whenever he'd come through the plant, he'd say, 'Hi, Joe. How're you doing?' and so forth." Genevieve Ciekot, who later became Mrs. Frank Jones, was a star on the Martin women's basketball team, the Bomberettes. All of the athletes on various company teams received special attention, and Glenn particularly knew the stars.

The Bomberettes and the men's baseball team, the Bombers, were Glenn's special pride. The Bombers were an uncommonly good baseball team that regularly won against industrial league competitors and could outhit and outpitch some of the professional teams of the day. Glenn recruited the best players and gave them jobs. He was on a first-name basis with Calvin Griffith, owner of the American League Washington Senators, and his team frequently played exhibition games in Griffith Stadium.

His company's own ballpark, located at the front of the Middle River property, on the corner of Eastern Avenue and Wilson Point Road, was generally considered the finest amateur baseball park in the country. Company engineers surveyed the site and sampled prevailing winds for more than a year before Glenn approved the location of home plate. Special soil was brought in for the pitcher's mound. The grandstand was covered by a section of aircraft wing, providing shade and shelter to spectators, chief among them the president of the company and occasionally his mother. Glenn rarely missed a home game and frequently followed the team on its road trips, always taking the wives of the players out to dinner in whatever town they were playing.

"The girls loved him," Franklin A. Gibson recalled. "He always looked like a million bucks in those suits with the four buttons and the fancy cuffs and lapels."[6] Gibson, who pitched for the Bombers and managed the team for several years, said, "Mr. Martin was always so courteous and nice to the ladies." He never cursed and didn't smoke or chew or drink, but he was the perfect host and very generous to the players and their wives. Even at the ball games, Glenn was always fully attired in a suit and tie, and most often with a hat, Gibson remembered.

If the ladies admired Mr. Martin, he returned the admiration, particularly to those who played basketball. The Bomberettes won the Maryland title and the national industrial league championships, and Genevieve Ciekot then toured South America with an all-star team. Two other well-known members of the Martin Bomberettes were the twin Vance sisters, Marge and Marie. They had gone to work in the plant three weeks after Pearl Harbor, on December 20, 1941. "They used to call Middle River 'Boystown' before we started," said Marge Katonka (née Vance). "We were the first women hired other than secretaries."[7] Marge went to work in production planning, and Marie was in the inspection department. And contrary to the popular belief that Mr. Martin hired them all just for his teams, the Vance sisters actually organized the original women's basketball team. It was in 1944, Marge recalled, that she and her sister and Ruth Thalhimer, who worked in the engineering lab, began playing.

"There were six of us who would pile into Ruth's car after work and drive over to Clifton Park to practice. Ruth knew all the teachers in town and got us into a league. We used to pay fifty cents apiece to pay for the lights when we practiced in the gym at Clifton Park Junior High School," she said. They didn't have uniforms, but they developed a pretty good team and were beating most of the other teams in the league. Word of their prowess got back to the plant, and one evening Glenn Martin showed up at the gym.

"He asked us if we knew who he was," Marge recalled. "Of course we did because he was frequently in the plant, and we had all seen pictures of him. He was really nice looking, a handsome man. He asked if we would like to play for the company, and from that moment on we did. He bought us complete uniforms, new basketballs, the works. It was great!" Marge said. "We traveled up and down the coast, everybody flying but me and Marie. We weren't fliers, and Mr. Martin would let us take the train."

The very next year, the Martin Bomberettes won the East Coast championship of the Amateur Athletic Union (AAU). Marge said the first person hired for her playing skills didn't come aboard until 1949. She was Wilma Jackson, the six-foot-one high scorer of a Kingsport, Tennessee, industrial league team. "She was a good pivot," Marge said, "and Mr. Martin sent me down to Tennessee to recruit her. She agreed to come to Baltimore for an interview, and Mr. Martin and Dan W. Siemon hired her on the spot." The Vance sisters were the shortest members of the team, Marge at five feet eight and Marie at five feet seven, "so Mr. Martin had special shoes made for us which actually gave us a lift of about two inches." The Bombererettes went on to the national AAU tournament twice, making the semifinals both times, at St. Joseph's, Missouri, in 1949 and again in 1950 at Dallas.

Marie Vance worked for Martin's eleven years; in 1948 she married William Hamilton (who worked in contracts from 1938 to 1944). Sister Marge married Frank Katonka (of research and development from 1938 to 1945) in 1946; she retired from the company in 1988 after forty-seven years. All but three of those years she worked in the same department, production planning, where she succeeded her boss as general supervisor in 1981. In her last year with the company, Marge Katonka was honored with the Baltimore operation's coveted Martin Cup "for management of production requirements and planning." Next to playing basketball for Mr. Martin, she said, receiving the award was the "happiest night of my life." But her best memory of all those years with the company, she said fondly, was Glenn Martin, "the most marvelous man I ever met aside from my husband."

Genevieve Ciekot said Mr. Martin "came to every one of our games. He even had a miniature basketball court on a board with small figures that he would maneuver to show us new plays he had dreamed up."[8] As with baseball, there is no evidence that Glenn Martin ever played basketball, but he was a keen student of the game and an enthusiastic fan.

In addition to Joe and Genevieve Ciekot, seven other members of their family eventually worked at the Martin Company: their father James; brother Casimir, better known as Johnny; sisters Sophie, Victoria, and Frances; Joe's wife Dot and her mother, Ida Stone. Between them the Ciekot family worked a total of more than sixty years at "Martin's."

Baseball and basketball were not the only sports. Glenn Martin turned to employee recreation with the same zeal he had shown for fancy cars. In fact, the athletic teams at the Baltimore plant seemingly took the place of the powerful and sporty Stutz automobiles and the Bentleys Glenn enjoyed driving himself. They were replaced

Playmaking for the "Bomberettes"

in the late 1930s by standard black limousines, chauffeur-driven. He hired a retired Army colonel and well-known sports figure named Charles W. Swan to be athletic director and head of a company recreation department. When Swan retired, he was succeeded by a former All-American football player from Pittsburgh, Ralph "Doc" McLaren, a practicing dentist before Glenn hired him to take over recreation.

Under Swan's and then McLaren's leadership, the teams proliferated, particularly during the early years of World War II as employment grew. Glenn considered them good morale boosters, essential to company esprit and the war effort. There were men's and women's softball teams, skeet-shooting clubs, wrestling teams, bowling, swimming, hunting, and fishing, even a Bible study group. For practically any sport or recreational activity you could name, the company had a team and subsidized its play. Glenn also founded the All-American Amateur Baseball Association at Johnstown, Pennsylvania, in 1955.

When the baseball team was first formed, it was known simply as Production Third Shift, and foremen and supervisors had to have a good reason or answer to Mr. Martin for denying team members time away from their jobs for practice. Frank Gibson, who pitched for the Bombers for three years and managed them a few more, was hired in 1939 as a drop hammer operator. A southpaw, he had pitched for an opposing industrial team and was noted for his remarkable control and the very few walks he gave up. He applied for a job, was hired, and was immediately enlisted to pitch for the team.

Gibson said the Martin ballpark was the finest in the country. "It had a drainage system under the field that cost a quarter million dollars. It could rain at twelve o'clock, and at two o'clock you could play ball. Home games were rarely rained out," he remembered. "They'd wait until the very last minute before Mr. Martin would allow them to call a game."[9]

When he started pitching for the Bombers, Gibson recalled, "I was sneaky fast—not a ninety-mile-an-hour pitcher, but I was sneaky fast—and could move the ball around. There was this catcher in the Army who played for us, used to come up from Fort Meade. He was warming me up, and he noticed my control. 'You got that type of control all the time?' he asked me. I said, 'Yes. I can put it pretty well where I want it.' He said, 'You listen to me,' and where he put his glove, I would put the ball. I think I allowed only one hit that game."

Frank Gibson also pitched two no-hitters, "twenty-seven up and

Glenn with "Bombers" in Griffith Stadium

twenty-seven down," as he remembered them, against Carroll Park and Chase (two Maryland community teams) before he exchanged his pitching glove for the manager's cap. He was also a remarkable hitter, especially for a pitcher, maintaining a .300 batting average.

He said Glenn only missed games when he was out of town, "and then he'd send me telegrams wanting to know who I was starting." After one home game that the Bombers won 12 to 1, Martin called Gibson into his office the next morning to complain about the one run the opposing team scored. " 'Dagnabit, Frank,' he said to me. . . . He never cussed. I never heard Mr. Martin cuss in his life. . . . 'Dagnabit, Frank, why did you let them get that one run?' The old man really liked to win, and win all the way. He didn't want to give up any score."

After another game, one that they lost by one run, Gibson said Mr. Martin came down on the field after the final pitch and began to chew him out: " 'Dagnabit, Frank, you left Cliff [pitcher Cliff Davis] in there too long. You shouldn't have given up that run.' Hell, the run scored on a couple of errors, or something. It wasn't the pitcher's fault. So I told him, 'Well, dang it, Mr. Martin, if you don't want me to manage the club, get somebody else. I quit!' 'No, no, no,' he said and let it go at that and walked away. I thought, man, I'm in trouble. I'm going to get fired the next day. But he never did, and he never mentioned it again. I think he liked me standing up to him, for talking back to him."

Dick Weber was another player recruited to the company for his baseball skills but also, as a degreed college graduate, for his potential administrative skills after his playing days on the baseball diamond. As such, he represented something of a transition in the company's recruitment of athletic talent. Weber was also a pitcher. His seventeen wins and only one loss during his last three years in college stood as a Rutgers University record for thirty-eight years. He was good enough to be signed by the Philadelphia Phillies, who assigned him to their Class D team at Bradford, Pennsylvania. But an opportunity to finish Rutgers on an academic scholarship intervened. Upon graduation in 1949 he was visited by Martin's Doc McLaren, who invited him to Baltimore for an interview with the head honcho himself.

Weber remembered being interviewed by Martin. Weber was sitting in his big office in the same chair where, Glenn told him, Edward V. "Eddie" Rickenbacker had sat only a few days before, talking about the twin-engine Martin 2-0-2 airliner, some of which Eastern Airlines purchased. After Weber began playing for the Bombers, he said, he would get morning-after critiques of his pitching relayed from Mr. Martin through manager Frank Gibson. "Tell Weber to move over about two inches on the rubber, and his curve ball will catch the corner of the plate instead of missing it" was the president's advice to his pitcher. On another occasion, Dick remem-

Fans Calvin Griffith and Martin

bered, they "lost a ball game to one of the very good industrial league teams in town, the one Al Kaline played with. We lost on a couple of Texas leaguers that just dropped in. Next day at practice, Frank was drilling us on hitting Texas-leaguers, on direct orders from Mr. Martin. That's the way the man's mind worked. He was a serious student of the game," Weber concluded.[10]

"He didn't know a thing about the game firsthand from playing it," Frank Gibson said with a laugh, "but man, there wasn't a thing he missed as a student of the game and number one fan."

His especially designed aerodynamic baseball bats were a case in point. To a man, all of Glenn's former ballplayers remember the famous Martin bats, which he had lathed to his own specifications in the plant model shop out of a special black ash wood imported from a swamp in South Carolina. He theorized that the Louisville Slugger and other commercially available bats of the day were not optimally aerodynamic and that he could produce a bat that not only would cut through the air with less resistance but would power the ball farther.

"They were heavier than sin," Gibson recalled, and only the biggest players could swing them effectively. Even the biggest players didn't use them by choice, but Mr. Martin encouraged their use. Dick Weber said the shape of the bats was hard to describe: "sorta like an airplane propeller, more oval than round." Harry George remembered the shape vividly and the meticulous care that was taken forming the bats to Mr. Martin's specification. An ardent professional baseball fan himself when he joined the company in 1936 right out of Baltimore Polytechnic Institute, George was fascinated with the bat episode.

"Mr. Martin, being the aerodynamic genius that he was, thought he could apply some of that expertise to the design of a bat," George recalled. "He had all kinds of sketches that he took down to the plant woodshop showing the cross-section of a bat. From the handle up about fifteen inches he felt the bat should not be round but oval, similar to an airfoil in shape, so that when the batter swung, he encountered less air resistance. We had all our lathes tied up at night making these bats. The guys in the model shop would hand-whittle the oval part because the lathe couldn't shape it.

"Mr. Martin would come down and inspect the progress, holding his pieces of paper with the airfoil shape up against a bat. 'Yes, it looks all right' or 'Shave some more off there' or whatever he would say. I guess he made three or four dozen bats, and he had the Bombers use them."[11]

Gibson told the story of one game when he was managing. Clifton Park was ahead by two runs in the ninth, and the Bombers had two men on base, with big Ed Slifker due to bat. The opposing manager "pulled his pitcher and put in Lefty Burns, one helluva good southpaw, to pitch to Ed." Slifker, who Gibson said was a brawny 245-pounder, was a lefty also and didn't like to bat against left-handed pitchers.

"I was coaching third," Gibson said, "and Ed holds up the bat . . . he always used a Martin bat . . . as if to say, 'Who's going to bat for me?' He got chicken. So I run up to home plate and say, 'Gimme the damn bat, you chicken,' and I pinch-hit myself for him. 'Gibson batting for Slifker,' I hollered to the ump. Then I hit the first pitch for a home run, using Ed's big, heavy bat. I'm just a little 165-pounder, but Ed made me so mad I got extra strength, I guess. Maybe that heavy bat had something to do with it, too," Gibson said with a chuckle.

George remembered another time when one of the Martin bats was given to Frank Pavlacheck, a catcher for the Buffalo Bisons, who were in town to play the Baltimore Orioles in an International League game. It was the first time one of the bats had been used in a professional game. "The first time Pavlacheck came to bat, he hit a home run with the Martin bat," George said. "That's a positive fact. . . . He hit a home run, and the next morning the papers were full of it. It was a big thing, and Mr. Martin was delighted, of course."

Although the bat design didn't endure, George said it had one very practical feature for a batter: "The way the bat was shaped, you were always sure to be gripping it properly so that the end grain was hitting the ball. In orienting the bat so that the narrow part of the oval was facing the pitcher, you were sure to have the sweet part with the grain contacting the ball. If the grain's the other way, you crack the bat. So from that standpoint, it was pretty good."

In the two years that Frank Gibson managed the team, the Bombers played eighty-eight games and won eighty-four of them, including the All-American semipro tournament in Griffith Stadium. Some of those who played with him or for him, in addition to Ed Slifker and Dick Weber, were Les Messenger, Johnny Bullington, Norm Lopez, YoYo Miller, Charlie Lauenstein, Blooper Bellew, and Norm Brady, all of them members of the 1943 team that compiled a season record of forty-nine wins, fourteen losses, and one tie.

Slifker spent thirty-nine years with the company, retiring in Orlando in 1968. Dick Weber worked forty-one years in Baltimore, Denver, and at Bethesda before retiring in 1991 as vice president of human relations in Colorado. Another old-time ballplayer was Ruck Davids, also a pretty fair pitcher, who retired as building manager at the corporation's Bethesda headquarters in 1984 after thirty-five years with the company.

Gibson still lives with his wife, Anne, on Fuselage Drive, the main street of Aero Acres, one of the Middle River housing projects built by Glenn Martin for his employees during World War II. They raised five children during his thirty-five-and-a-half years at Martin's. His wife worked there for twelve. Both have only the fondest memories of the place and of the man who gave it his name. "We loved Mr. Martin," Gibson summed it up.

The stories of Glenn Martin and his baseball team are legend. Bobby F. Leonard, who started with the company in 1956 in the security department at Middle River, remembered two that the late Cecil Tennant—who in the thirties and forties was a sergeant on the guard force at Middle River—used to tell. The two stories, he swore, were the truth, both testaments to "Mr. Martin's" frugality and close attention to detail. For the home games Mr. Martin attended, he would personally assign Sergeant Tennant to police the area for foul balls. Tennant was to recover fouls hit into the stands and those hit outside the park—in fact, any and all balls that weren't fielded. At the end of the game Mr. Martin would check the number of balls Tennant had recovered to make certain it jibed with the number of foul balls he had counted during the game.

Another story involved the company's 106-foot motor yacht, the *Glenmar,* a sumptuous eighty-five-ton cruiser purchased by Glenn in 1937 from acquaintance and fellow Cleveland industrialist Laurence Fisher, the head of Fisher Body Company. The boat, if one deigned to call it a boat, had three staterooms, each with a private toilet and shower, a paneled dining room that could seat ten in luxurious comfort, a sunroom, a spacious awninged deck, a motor launch, and two dinghies. Permanently staffed by a captain and crew of four, the *Glenmar* was purchased ostensibly as an observation boat for seaplane trials in the Chesapeake and was used for that purpose.

For much of its company life, however, the yacht was moored to the dock on Frog Mortar Creek, just off the "D" Building seaplane ramp. On its decks Glenn frequently entertained guests visiting the plant. On one such occasion he had scheduled lunch for noon. The cafeteria manager, Jafus A. Belue, Jr., better known as Mr. Belue, was noted throughout the East for his gourmet kitchen. He had sent over hot soup and a huge tray of luscious sandwiches, and Sergeant Tennant had been detailed to stand guard for the occasion. Twelve o'clock came and went without a sign of the company president or his guests. By one o'clock Cecil Tennant was getting hungry and becoming uneasy with the prospect of missing lunch if his special assignment should keep him past the cafeteria's closing time. So he carefully lifted a corner of the heavy linen napkin covering the silver platter and helped himself to one of Mr. Belue's delicious chicken salad sandwiches. He was especially careful to re-cover the platter and leave it looking as he had found it. Eventually Mr. Martin arrived, and no sooner had he seated his guests than he called the dumbfounded Tennant over to the side of the dining room and reprimanded him for eating one of the sandwiches. "I know you did, Sergeant," Tennant was fond of quoting Martin, "because there are crumbs on your shirt and on the deck."[12]

Martin at controls, 1912.

Comedian Joe E. Brown and Martin, 1911.

Martin Aeroplane chases auto, 1911.

Los Angeles pontoon department, 1912.

1911 pusher-type biplane.

Catalina welcoming, May 10, 1912.

Glenn flies with mother, 1912.

8

Tiny Broadwick and Martin, 1914.

Bell, Martin, Springer, Douglas, 1914.

9

10

Great Lakes Tourer, 1913.

Transportable Mail Plane,
MB-2 varietal, 1919

FDR presents Collier Trophy, 1933

B-10B bomber, 1932.

14

Mary Pickford with Martin, 1915.

15

China Clipper over San Francisco, 1935.

16

PBM-5 Mariner, 1944.

17

Mars seaplanes as firefighters, 1993.

18

Three famous Martin planes: Marauder, Maryland, Mariner.

B-26 hits D-Day target.

19

20

B-29 *Enola Gay*, which bombed Hiroshima.

21

Evelyn Short at 1943 reunion
of Charlie Day, Martin.

22

P4M Mercator patrol plane, 1946.

23

AM-1 Mauler dive bombers on carrier, 1946.

2-0-2 commercial airliner.

25

4-0-4 commercial airliner.

26

XB-48 six-jet bomber.

27

Souvenir plate of Martin aircraft.

28

Visions of 125-ton commercial seaplane in 1946 advertisement.

PART IV

The Clouds
of War
1937–45

■

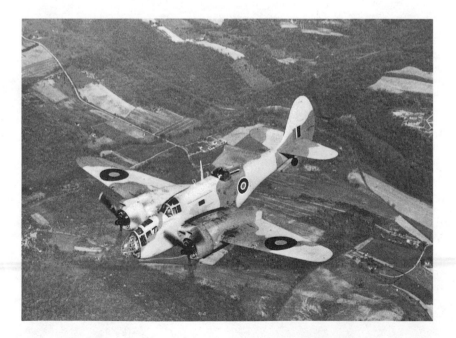

CHAPTER 15

Four Corners of
the World

■

All was not all fun and games, of course. The company's
recreational activities served their purpose for employee
morale, management strongly believed, but the responsibility of producing fighting machines for the United States and for a
number of its foreign friends and allies was a major business. From
the man whose name was on the door to those bending the metal
and bucking rivets in the shop, it was a mission taken very seriously.
The Middle River plant was alive with airplanes from the mid-1930s
on. B-10 bombers rolled off the production line for half a dozen
customers scattered around the globe, and Martin's reputation and
workmanship went with the planes, as did support personnel.

Francis O. "Fuzz" Furman and Gene Foster helped build and
test the B-10 bombers, and then both became field representatives
for Martin, accompanying the airplane to customers in the Orient.
Gene went to China in 1937, and Fuzz was sent to Java later the same
year in support of the Dutch East Indies purchase. Foster had worked
in ground testing on the B-10s as well as on the earliest seaplanes
built in Baltimore. He was flight test engineer for each of the Pan Am
Clippers, assisting the airline's crews and flying with them during
initial checkout flights and final acceptance before he was assigned
to field support on the B-10. When the first six bombers were deliv-

ered in February 1937 to the Chinese in Shanghai, Foster and Harry Rowland, who was vice president of sales, went with them.

"They were the export version of the B-10B, designated the 139W, and were the first of the B-10s to have self-sealing fuel tanks," a Martin invention, Foster said. "We had to assemble the planes, which had been shipped by boat, ground-test them, and then flight-test them. We did this out of a military airport just outside Shanghai. We also made demonstration flights to Peking and out of Tientsin until the Japanese began shelling and bombing Shanghai.

"This went on for a couple of months until one day Japanese marines in three cars tried to shoot their way into the field," Foster said. "They killed the first bunch of Chinese who tried to stop them and wounded some at the second checkpoint. But then the Chinese killed them all."[1]

Foster said the Japanese later claimed that incident as the reason they went to war with China. "Heck, they'd already started the war," he said. "We had watched them drop a bomb on a main intersection in Shanghai; it killed hundreds of people." It was right after the Japanese incident that Foster said he and Rowland decided to get out. "I was staying at the Park Hotel on Bubbling Well Road, right across from the racetrack in the middle of the international community. About four o'clock in the morning I had this call from Major Lee, one of the Chinese officers working with us. He wanted the 'compass,' which is what he called the automatic pilot. It was a separate box, one for each plane, which I always kept with me," Foster said. "I never let them have the box until we were ready to fly, but he said he had to have it right away. So we knew they were getting out, and I gave them the boxes. We never saw or heard of those airplanes again." Foster rather doubted that the six B-10s fell into Japanese hands because, he said, the Chinese were determined to leave the Japanese nothing but "scorched earth."

Gene Foster escaped from China on the last passenger ship to get out, but only after a harrowing nighttime run through machine-gun fire from both sides of the Whangpoo River on his way to the liner *President Lincoln* anchored fifteen miles offshore. "The river was filled with the bloated bodies of dead soldiers and horses," he said, and three of his fellow passengers in the open, bargelike lighter were wounded by Japanese fire. The *Lincoln* carried him to Hong Kong and then to Manila, where three additional China-bound B-10s, still in their shipping crates, had been diverted due to heavy Japanese submarine activity in the South China Sea. In Manila, Foster arranged for the planes to be sent via a neutral British shipping line to

Haiphong and Hanoi in French Indochina and then on to Chinese forces on the Yangtze river in Yunnan Province. His Martin responsibilities to the Chinese completed, Foster was lucky enough to hop a ride back to the States on Pan Am's Hawaii Clipper. The Martin Seaplane, coincidentally, was flown by some of the same Pan Am crewmen he had helped train in its use when it came out of the Middle River factory five years before.

A few months after Gene Foster went to China, the first B-10s purchased by the Dutch East Indies Air Force, 13 of an eventual 120, were delivered by slow boat to Java, and another Middle River factory pro followed them. Fuzz Furman remembered that it took him thirty days to get to the Dutch East Indies. He took the *Queen Mary* from New York to Cherbourg, crossed France by train to Villefranche, where he caught a Dutch liner. It carried him through the Suez Canal and around the tip of India to Java. For a tall, handsome, twenty-eight-year-old bachelor on his first trip outside the United States, it was quite an adventure.

Furman was the only Martin representative on Java and only one of two Americans at Bandoeng (or Bandung) air base, where the B-10s were stationed. The other American was "a nice guy" named Tarbox who worked for Standard Oil, Furman remembered. Bangoeng, he said, was "real pretty, a cool place on a lake in the mountains, sort of a resort. People would come there from where it was hot."[2]

About four months after arriving in Bandoeng, he met Amelia Earhart and her navigator Fred Noonan. "We had heard about her round-the-world trip on the radio," Furman said, "so when she landed at Bandoeng, I went along with everybody else to see her. Esso was supplying all of her one hundred-octane gasoline, so Tarbox met her, and he introduced me. She had some problems with the exhaust analyzer and the fuel flow meter on her Lockheed Electra. The people of KLM, which was a Dutch airline that flew from Bandoeng to Australia with Lockheed 14s, didn't know too much about this equipment, so I told her if she needed any help, I'd be glad to help her. We used the same exhaust analyzer on the B-10, and she asked me to take a look at it. I found out what was wrong with hers and fixed it. The Bendix flow meter I had never seen before, and I didn't know much about it. It had a cable that ran back to a little alternator, or generator, which created 110-volt current to operate the flow meter. And the shaft that drove that on the engine up front was all worn off. They didn't have one, so I got one from the Army and put it in, and that fixed that."

Noonan, Earhart, and Furman

Earhart and Noonan took off and flew to Surabaja, slightly more than five hundred miles to the east, where the analyzer went out again. "She called me and asked what she should do." Furman said. "She didn't want to continue with it not working, but she didn't want to turn back, either. She wanted to know if she could get it fixed in Surabaja. I told her, 'You'd better come back here.' We had overhaul shops and everything. So she came back the next morning.

"I went over and found that the exhaust analyzer tube, when it broke previously, had put too much heat on that little alternator, and it had melted some of the wiring in there. So we gave it to the Chinese and the Javanese in the engine shop. Using the one on the other side as a guide, they were able to fix it right up. We put it back in, and I think she left the next day. I got a telegram from Surabaja saying it was working okay and thanking me for fixing it."

Amelia Earhart and Noonan were at Bandoeng a total of about four or five days, counting their return from Surabaja. During that time "she was constantly at the airport or in some function with the people in the area," Furman recalled. "In the evening she stayed in her room. She'd even eat in her room. But Fred and I were together all the time. We'd chat in our room and down in the lobby, or we'd talk as we walked around the streets. He was worried about finding tiny Howland Island."

Their plan was to fly from Bandoeng to Lae, New Guinea, then make a long overwater jump, some 2,480 miles, to Howland Island, a pinpoint equatorial atoll in the middle of the Pacific, just about midway between New Guinea and Hawaii. "Fred said, 'If we make that, the rest will be easy.' It was a big deal. I mean when you think about the navigation system they had . . . celestial navigation or dead reckoning . . . you've got to be good to hit that little island. There's a lot of water out there, and Howland Island was only nine miles long by two miles wide and a couple of feet above sea level. Heck, if a cloud got in the way, you might miss it, and they didn't have enough fuel reserve to fly around very long."

Furman said Noonan worried the entire time he was at Bandoeng about time. "He kept four watches, and he would walk around constantly checking those watches with chronometers to ensure accuracy. He knew if he was off a half-second or so, he was going to miss the island. Instruments weren't very good in those days, and Noonan had to do most of his navigating by the stars," Furman said. Amelia Earhart's radio had a voice range of only seventy-five miles, so when Howland Island heard from her that she was low on fuel, Furman figured she had to be within seventy-five miles of her target. It was about a week after they took off from Bandoeng the second time before Furman learned Amelia Earhart and Fred Noonan were lost at sea. "I was at a party the ambassador was giving when we heard about it."

Furman doesn't buy the theories about what happened to Earhart and Noonan: that they were shot down by the Japanese, that they were captured and executed as spies, or that they landed on a reef and starved to death. "I couldn't understand why anybody thought she was a spy. Everybody that was out there in that area knew what the Japanese were doing. I mean there was no secret. Hell, she just ran out of gasoline. Period!" Over the years, Fuzz Furman repeated his story countless times to inquiring newspaper and magazine writers, radio and television reporters, book writers, and anyone else with a theory on what happened to America's best-known aviatrix. As late as 1991, he said, "A guy and his wife from New Jersey— can't remember his name—came to see me. They're writing a book, too, and wanted to know all kinds of things about her airplane: Did it have a life raft? What about one of those hand-cranking signal things? I couldn't tell them. I never went in the airplane. I didn't have to."[3]

Furman returned to the States later in 1937, in time to witness two postscripts to the romantic chapter of the Martin Clippers. Glenn took the occasion of the twenty-fifth anniversary of his historic world record overwater flight from Newport, California, to Catalina Island to return there. But this time he went in style. Instead of the canvas and wire biplane he flew in 1912, he made the trip in a luxuriously appointed China Clipper, and he took his mother along. It was a celebratory occasion with festival crowds, testimonial banquets, glowing newspaper recounts of his accomplishments, and general applause creating a glow in which he and Minta Martin deservedly basked.

The second postscript came in an order for a fourth Clipper to be built for the Soviet Union under rather cloak-and-dagger conditions at Middle River, reportedly for a million dollars. Designated Model 156 but generally referred to as the "Soviet Clipper," it was the largest flying boat in the world, weighing sixty-three thousand pounds, eleven thousand more than its predecessor Pan Am triplets. Its wingspan was 157 feet, compared to 130 feet on the earlier planes. Its first test flight, with Ken Ebel at the controls, was on November 27, and on a cold January 20, 1938, it was flown to Floyd Bennett Field on Long Island.

Furman remembered the Soviet Clipper well: "In New York they took her engines off, her wings, lots of parts, and packed them in crates. Then they shipped that whole disassembled boat to the Soviet Union on the deck of a Russian freighter. We never heard about it again." "Never" was almost eight years. It was known that Amtorg Trading Company, which took possession of the Martin 156 on Long Island, also received a second Clipper in fabricated subassemblies, a third flying boat in detail parts, plus all the tools and fixtures necessary to assemble the two additional boats, as well as blueprints and a license from Glenn Martin to mass-produce the giant flying boats in Russian factories. During World War II there were unconfirmed reports of Martin-like Clippers in the European theater of operations. Did the Soviets ever reassemble and fly their Martin-built 156? Were copies built by the Russians? It remained a mystery until after the war.

Fuzz Furman did a second tour on Java at the request of the Dutch East Indies Air Force. When he returned to Middle River, it was to a promotion as subforeman in final assembly. Once again the Dutch asked for him, this time to be their representative at Brewster Aircraft on Long Island. Brewster was then headed by C. A. Van Dusen, Glenn Martin's longtime colleague from the early days in Los Angeles and later as business manager in Cleveland and Baltimore. The Dutch request spoke eloquently to Martin's reputation as well as to the quality of its planes and people, and Glenn lent Furman to Brewster.

"The Dutch were buying Brewster's Buffalo fighters, and they wanted me to be their man on the spot in the factory to check whether the planes met specifications," Furman said. "I was licensed to pass them. When they first started flying that airplane, the pilot came back and told me the propeller was humming. It was a Curtiss Electric propeller like the ones that were on the B-10. It was driven by a tachometer, which was driven mechanically by a shaft. I couldn't find anything wrong with it, but the pilot kept coming back, complaining about the humming. Nobody knew what to do, and I was getting disgusted because they were just fooling around, and the Dutch needed the airplanes."

Furman contacted a friend at Curtiss in New Jersey. "It was their propeller, and I said, 'I want to borrow an electric tachometer from you people.' They lent me one, and I put it on the airplane and hooked it up. And I told the pilot, 'Go fly it now.' And he did and came back and said it was okay. 'It doesn't hum anymore?' I asked. 'No,' he said. 'Do you know what was wrong?' I asked. 'No,' he said. So I told him: 'That shaft that went from the drive to the tachometer was turning inside its casing, and the casing had so many bends in it that it would get to the point that it would stick, and then it would rip. The propeller was not humming. The propeller is okay. It's the tachometer that you have to do something about.' So that took care of that."

Furman also helped Brewster write a maintenance manual on the Buffalo fighter. "But when they asked me to go to Java for them, I told them, 'No, I've already been there. Twice.' I didn't think much of Brewster, so I went back to Martin's."

With an extraordinary team of engineers and businesspeople in place by 1938 and the company not only stable financially but growing, Glenn decided to go to Europe and see for himself what was happening. He took his mother, of course, and they toured England, France, Germany, Holland, Italy, and Switzerland. His alarming observations of war preparation after visits to German aircraft factories were passed on to the American ambassador in Berlin. They were immediately dispatched to President Roosevelt. On his return to America, Glenn personally submitted reports of his trip to the Army and the Navy, and even recommended in a voluntary appearance before a congressional committee that the United States build a force of long-range bombers.

The committee rejected his advice, although one member conceded the need for short-range planes to defend America's coasts. "We are concerned only with defense," the congressman said. "We want nothing to do with the troubles of Europe. All we want are planes that will defend our shores, that's all." To which the persistent Martin responded, "But what if a foreign power has a bomber that can fly from Europe to drop bombs on Washington?"

"Do you know of any such bomber?" he was asked. "No, but such a plane is conceivable. Oceans and shore lines mean nothing to an airplane. Aviation has advanced so rapidly that few people are aware of what is possible in terms of distance that may be covered and cargo capacity, which may be passengers or bombs," Glenn told the committee.

"Then you believe, Mr. Martin," another member of the committee joined in, "that we should build such offensive airplanes merely because you saw a few thousand planes in Germany . . . that we should turn our efforts to the building of long-range, heavy bombers?" To Glenn's emphatic "Yes," the congressman virtually shouted: "Then you, sir, are a merchant of death."

It was a stinging rebuke, a slap in the face with an epithet he had not heard since the armament debates of World War I. Glenn never would have dreamed that such a charge would be leveled at him. In a low but bitter voice, and trying to control his humiliation and anger, he replied, "I have been at war, sir, since 1913, and now I am ready to be demobilized." He excused himself, stood, and walked out of the hearing room.[4]

At Middle River in 1939, designs were coming off the drawing boards and airplanes were rolling out of the plant at a near-feverish clip. The exception was a small, walled-off space in Experimental, where security guards maintained a close watch. Then one day, to the surprise of the majority of those who had been watching and waiting, a runt of a flying boat appeared on the ramp. Not much bigger than a Piper Cub, the small seaplane had all the lines of the big flying boats, including two engines and twin rudders. But its gull-shaped wing had floats on the tips. It was Model 162-A, a baby seaplane. It was a quarter-scale, two-man flying model of what would become the U.S. Navy's greatest patrol bomber: the workhorse PBM Martin Mariner. From 1940 through 1945, a total of 1,365 Mariners would be produced in ten different modifications, including 32 PBM-3Bs purchased for the Australian Navy.

The piloted miniature was an aviation first. It had only a single motor linked by a belt drive to propellers in twin nacelles. The concept was to proof-test in water and in flight all of the hydrodynamic and aerodynamic characteristics of a radically new type of flying boat before taking the time or expending the cost of building a full-scale prototype. The Navy was so impressed with its performance, it okayed the building of twenty full-size Mariners, the PBM-1, before a full-scale prototype, the XPBM-1, even flew.[5]

The Mariner was the Navy's largest, heaviest, longest-range patrol bomber yet conceived. It could fly 3,450 miles with four thousand pounds of bombs. Living and dining accommodations for crews on long-range missions enabled it to sweep the oceans for enemy submarines and surface ships. First deliveries to the Navy were greatly advanced by performance of the "little Mariner" flying model. Development of the full-sized Mariner was kept a virtual secret until the floor of Middle River's B-Building was nearly covered with full-grown hulls almost 80 feet in length and gull-shaped wings 118 feet in length.

From the base of the hull to the tip of its twin vertical rudders, the Mariner almost equaled the height of a three-story building. At the time, B-Building's 135,000 square feet, although only one-third the size of A-Building, was the largest unobstructed aircraft assembly floor in the world. A 300-by-450-foot rectangle, one end was entirely a door that could be opened to a height of forty-five feet. Erected two years earlier in 1937 contiguous to A-Building, it was part of the original plan of noted Detroit architect Albert Kahn. And of course it met the specifications that Glenn Martin had envisioned would one day be needed to house such leviathans as the Mariner flying boats. Yet for all its immensity, the building's cavernous high-bay interior was made almost Lilliputian by the effect of multiple giant Mariners undergoing simultaneous assembly.[6]

The first production PBM-1 Mariners were delivered in September 1940, and the last in May 1941. A single XPBM-2, designed for catapult launch, successfully demonstrated that capability with a JATO (jet-assisted takeoff) bottle, but additional copies were not produced. The Navy awarded the company a contract for 379 PBM-3s in November 1940, and these planes plus a subsequent order for 360 more were delivered between April 1942 and June 1944 as PBM-3C and 3D patrol bombers, PBM-3R transports, and PBM-3S antisubmarine aircraft. The latter established an impressive record in the Atlantic against the German submarine threat. Nearly all the Mariners would see duty in World War II or Korea.

The Mariner was not the only new plane coming out of the Baltimore plant as the 1930s turned into the 1940s. A new attack bomber, Martin Model 167, had competed for an Army Air Corps

Squadron of Marylands over Libya, 1942

contract but lost to a Douglas prototype that crashed even before competitive flight tests began. In a strongly worded letter to Secretary of War Harry H. Woodring, Glenn protested to no avail. His disappointment soon would be assuaged by heightened interest from the French and British who opened long-distance negotiations for the plane, which became the famous A-22. It would eventually become better known as the Martin Maryland.

Transatlantic telephone traffic increased to the point that Glenn had the metalworking shop build a special bed for his office. It turned out to be as rugged as the airplanes rolling out of the factory. Large enough to accommodate Glenn's six-foot frame, its one-piece, welded steel frame was still light enough so that it could be tipped on one end and rolled on casters into a specially built closet during the day. Aircraft seat belts, specially modified, held the bedding in place.[7]

Shortly after the Nazi panzer push across Poland and Neville Chamberlain's Munich agreement of "peace in our time" with Adolf Hitler—both in September of that year—the first night shift went to work at Middle River, and the number of employees climbed to thirty-nine hundred. Work also began on a new five-hundred-acre airfield to replace the original, which had been outgrown. A ten-thousand-foot runway, capable of handling the biggest airplanes, made the Martin airport the largest private field in the country, a distinction it would hold until it was purchased by the State of Maryland in 1975. Strict security, with identification badges and gate passes, became a necessary part of plant routine. Guards appeared in new blue uniforms with the red, white, and blue Martin "Star" emblem on their shoulders.

Isolationists and others who earlier had hurled the "merchant of death" invective at Glenn now wanted to know how quickly he could tool up to build more planes. Underscoring the urgency of their negotiations for the A-22, a delegation of Frenchmen flew into Middle River and agreed to purchase 115 of the three-man bombers for $11 million. That French buy alone almost equaled the total sales of the previous year.

In February 1939, in an urgent telephone call personally placed to Albert Kahn in Detroit, Glenn Martin ordered a second plant expansion that would more than triple manufacturing floor space. Martin biographer Henry Still reported that phone call in *To Ride the Wind:*

> "Mr. Kahn, I've got to add 440,000 square feet to my plant in a hurry."
>
> "How much of a hurry, Mr. Martin?"
>
> "Eleven weeks," Glenn replied.
>
> There was silence from the Detroit end of the line. Then Kahn spoke, "It's impossible, of course, but we'll do it."
>
> The next day Kahn arrived with his staff of experts and work got feverishly under way.[8]

Kahn himself later noted: "The morning after Mr. Martin's telephone call, I was in Baltimore with an architectural assistant, a structural designer, and an estimator. That day we prepared a number of schemes of plan and construction, showing the comparative steel tonnage. The next day we called in steel contractors. The next day we placed the contracts." Seventy-five days later production had begun on the French A-22 bombers at one end of the new building while workmen completed the other end.

That was C-Building, often referred to by employees as the French Building. It was without precedent architecturally in that it enclosed an area 300 by 450 feet without interior columns, beneath the longest flat-span trusses used up to that time.[9] It brought the total area of the Middle River plant to more than one million square feet, making it the largest aircraft manufacturing plant in the country, if not the world. The addition enabled the French to take possession of attack bombers in just three months and three days, an unheard-of production record, but it was only a hint of things to come.[10]

Two years later Kahn was designing at Middle River Martin Plant No. 2, a government-owned facility about a mile farther east along the Pennsylvania Railroad mainline tracks, across Strawberry Point Road, on the other side of the airport. He virtually duplicated the various portions of the original plant, and in that same year he used the basic scheme a third time for another Martin-operated government plant, at Omaha, Nebraska.

For 1939, the year C-Building was constructed, revenues climbed to $24,169,468, and the backlog of firm orders topped $30 million. Employment in the newly enlarged factory reached ten thousand, prompting Glenn's efficient secretary to pull from the safe the letter he had dictated ten years earlier after his employment prediction had brought laughter at the Baltimore Association of Commerce luncheon. "What shall I do with it, Mr. Martin?" the secretary asked. "Burn it" was the reply. Every day that went by was confirmation of his 1929 forecast. He saw no need to flaunt the success.

Time magazine featured Glenn L. Martin on a cover that year, and *Fortune* wrote glowingly of the manufacturing miracle and the men and women who were masterminding it:

> Push through the door of Building C, the latest addition to The Glenn L. Martin Company's plant at Middle River, Maryland, and the hum of power-driven machinery is drowned in a bedlam of riveting, now low and deadly like the spray of machine-gun bullets, now rising to a high-pitched scream.
>
> Across some 240,000 square feet [actually it was 440,000] of floor space, which by night is flooded in the blue-white light of mercury-vapor overheads, there stretches an array of workbenches, of great and small du-

1939 *Time* cover

ralumin parts, of human hands and faces. Most of the faces are young; and many who work here still wear sweaters bearing their high school numerals or insignia.

Down one side of the building boys swarm about a line of enormous dural wings; at another point they are bucking up rivets in fuselage and tail assemblies; at a third point they fit controls and instruments (the throttles one observes are marked "ouvert" and "ferme" instead of "open" and "shut") into bulbous dural noses. Only at the end of the building does the work integrate into finished product.

There, standing in a far bay, is a line of sleek planes, landing gears in place, twin motors sheathed into wings, each unit representing 30,000 parts brought together into 16,500 pounds of fighting ship.[11]

The Martin A-22, so described by *Fortune*, would be one of the first American "fighting ships" to face the German sweep across Europe and the Mediterranean, even displaying as it did the insignia of French and British allies. It would become a particularly effective deterrent to Rommel's tanks in the Egyptian desert and would contribute to their ultimate rout by the British at El Alamein in 1942.

CHAPTER 16

War Production

■

Even as the production, plant, and population grew, Martin
company employees remained a close-knit family. Increasing numbers of husbands, wives, brothers, and sisters were
hired and became caught up in the spirit that their work engen-
dered. The work force had more than doubled in just a few years. Yet
"Mr. Martin" was a familiar figure on frequent walks through the
manufacturing areas of the plant. Always impeccably garbed in his
special braid-trimmed suits and rather reserved in demeanor—some
thought him aloof, even abrupt—he had the remarkable ability of
not only calling employees by their first names but of knowing the
job each was performing.

As the need for more workers grew, recruiting spread from the
nearby metropolitan areas of Baltimore, Washington, Wilmington,
and Philadelphia to the mountains of the Virginias and the pied-
mont of the Carolinas. The influx of untrained and sometimes min-
imally educated employees (less than a high school diploma)
spurred a need for special educational programs. In conjunction
with Baltimore Polytechnic Institute, one of the city's two major
public high schools for boys, the company set up courses in blueprint
reading. Additional courses were organized at the plant in virtually
every craft required for airplane manufacture, including wiring,
welding, sheet-metal forming, and riveting.

During these late years of the 1930s, new employee benefits were put in place under the direction of Dan Siemon. He had personally interviewed many prospective employees in the early Baltimore days and had become the company's first vice president of industrial relations, the executive in charge of hiring and firing and virtually every other activity directly impacting employees. Siemon was not only generally respected, he was liked.

The industry's first pension and retirement plan was instituted during this period, and two housing developments were begun near the plant. Construction of affordable homes was begun late in 1941, less than a mile from the plant in a community called Aero Acres. An earlier 1940 development called Stansbury Manor offered apartments at reasonable rates in attractive brick buildings. In Aero Acres, Martin people could purchase new two- and three-bedroom frame houses for as little as $1,200 on clean, neat streets with names like Rudder, Aileron, and Fuselage. A half-century later, a local weekly newspaper observed the fiftieth birthday of what it called "America's first planned community" in a front-page series recalling Aero Acres'

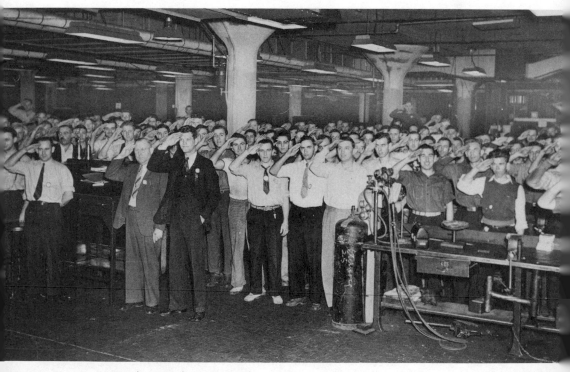

Employee salute, December 1941

"Martin roots" and biographing the aviation pioneer who established it.[1]

Glenn Martin's personal largesse to employees in need, always generously but quietly extended when the work force numbered only twelve hundred in Cleveland, had multiplied considerably as the "family" grew in Baltimore. Medical insurance did not exist in industrial America at the time, but if a Martin family faced major medical expenses, Glenn helped out. If an employee had a problem that Mr. Martin learned about, he tried to solve it. One young woman suffering from curvature of the spine underwent several operations, paid for by Mr. Martin, and her living expenses were taken care of until she was able to return to work. Another employee with a kidney infection was sent to the hospital at Glenn's expense. The company president's personal interest in the welfare of his employees eventually became company policy with establishment of the Martin Foundation. It provided interest-free loans to workers in need, thereby removing such assistance from the charity category. It was a happy, dedicated work force that produced airplanes in many configurations and in record numbers throughout the war, and airplanes were not the only product.[2]

The first electric-powered revolving gun turret for aircraft was developed at Middle River in 1937. It was a hydraulic model designed for the nose of the Navy's PM-1M patrol bomber. It also became standard equipment in the bows and on the decks of Martin Mariners, PB2Y4 Coronados, and PB2Y3s. But the most famous Martin turret—it was infamous to enemy pilots who experienced its withering firepower—was the electric-powered Model 250CE. Developed in 1940, it was Martin's response to Air Corps Commanding General Hap Arnold's edict that power-operated turrets were a "must" for Army bombers. The 250CE was mounted as the dorsal, or top, turret in the fuselage of more than a dozen different U.S. and Allied planes. It provided gunners two .50-caliber machine guns in 360 degrees of horizontal movement and with a vertical firing field of 90 degrees.

When a gunner climbed into the Martin turret, he felt that he had become part of the mechanism. The clear plastic bubble that covered the turret protruded only inches above the surface of the airplane, yet it afforded the gunner maximum visibility. Its swift, smooth rotation enabled him to track attacking enemy fighters with deadly accuracy. More than forty thousand of these turrets were produced by a special Martin division established for that purpose on Sinclair Lane, midway between the Middle River plant and downtown Baltimore. In addition to the Navy patrol bombers and Martin

Martin gun turrets

A-22 Maryland, A-30 Baltimore, and B-26 Marauder, the 250CE turrets were on the Douglas A-20 Havoc, Lockheed's Vega and Ventura, North America's B-25 Billy Mitchell medium bomber, the Boeing B-17 Flying Fortress, Consolidated's B-24 Liberator and B-32 Dominator bomber, as well as the British Lancaster bomber.[3]

Another Martin development widely used throughout the U.S. aircraft industry during World War II was the self-sealing fuel tank, a trademarked product known as Mareng, a contraction of "Martin" and "engineering." Developed by Martin in 1936 and manufactured by the United States Rubber Company, the rubber compound was pumped into the wing or other cavity of an airplane to form a permanent seal for the fuel it held. An uncontained "Mareng cell" was also developed in 1942 for the transportation or storage of fuel independent of a conventional tank. Such cells could transform railroad boxcars into fuel-carrying vehicles. A standard boxcar containing six Mareng cells carried 13,500 gallons of fuel, almost a third more than in a standard railroad tank car.

But airplanes were Martin's major product. In Europe the A-22 was being flown with distinction by French crews who called it the Glenn and highly favored its speed, handling, and availability. The plane was seldom down for maintenance, and the French Armée de l'Air had ordered an additional one hundred of the A-22s shortly before the June 22 surrender of the Vichy government. Only twenty-five of the newly ordered planes reached France, and they, plus those that had survived the Luftwaffe's overwhelming numerical superiority, were diverted either to England or to North Africa. Those sent to North Africa became part of the Air Force of Vichy France, where unfortunately they would be turned on former friends and allies. In some cases, Martin A-22 Glenns, flown by the Vichy French, would meet British A-22s flown by Free French pilots. The English had quickly snapped up the remaining seventy-five undelivered French planes from Martin and further enhanced the A-22's reputation as the "Maryland," the Brits' name for the plane.

Three weeks before Pearl Harbor, Baltimore's *Sunday Sun* carried this account under the headline MARYLAND BOMBERS, A PERFORMANCE REPORT ON MARTIN-BUILT SHIPS IN MIDDLE EAST:

> A notable record of performance by American-made bombers—The Glenn Martin Marylands—was the feature of Royal Air Force activity in the Middle East front during the past week. These bombers made a number of sorties, all marked by outstanding success . . . on the Derna (Cirenaica) harbor and on Bengasi and other North African airdromes.
>
> One afternoon, while R.A.F. flyers piloting Marylands, were bombing Bengasi, two Italian CA-42s decided to join the party. The Italians dived down, confident of at least one victim. They received a warm greeting from the Marylands, and the enemy planes were brought down in a few seconds. Having completed their bombing, the Marylands returned safely to their base.
>
> Another afternoon, a Messerschmitt 109 decided to have a crack at a Maryland, flying 1,000 feet below. A

continuous roar of guns filled the sky, and a few seconds later the Messerschmitt spun to the ground, out of control.

Similar reports of excellent performance by these bombers came from the Libyan coast. At Derna, Marylands destroyed four enemy planes on the ground and later two Messerschmitt 109s. They shot down an enemy fighter at Barca, Eritrea; another Messerschmitt 109 at Bengasi, and dropped many tons of bombs on airdromes, munition dumps, and workshops, and also on a motor transport. . . . It was a Maryland on reconnaissance which spotted the Italian convoy of eleven ships and advised the Royal Navy, which, with no loss to itself, delivered the coup de grace.[4]

The British ordered 185 more A-22s before giving Martin specifications for a successor aircraft. It would become the Maryland's slightly chubby sister, Model 187 in Martin's lexicon, or the A-30 Baltimore bomber, as the world came to know it.

The Baltimore shared the Maryland's good looks, both having so-called frying pan handle fuselages. The tadpolelike taper two-thirds of the way back on the underside of both planes provided an improved cone of fire for the ventral gunner and at the same time increased the planes' speed by reducing drag. The Maryland's extremely narrow nose profile was due to its very slender fuselage, reportedly the result of a collaborative effort of Martin designers Jim McDonnell and Peyton M. Magruder, father of the B-26 Marauder. The story has it that McDonnell placed Magruder in a chair, measured the width of his colleague's shoulders, then added two inches on either side to establish the width of the Maryland's cockpit and its fuselage.[5]

That slenderness gave way to the slightly pudgy look in the 187 because the British wanted Martin to make room for a fourth crewman, more armament, and a heavier bombload. By adding larger, more powerful engines, the British traded range and service ceiling for greater speed and a third more bomb capacity. The Baltimore also carried self-sealing fuel tanks, 211 additional pounds of armor plate, and eleven .30-caliber machine guns, a number later reduced in favor of upgraded .50-caliber guns. Less svelte in appearance because of the resultant fatter fuselage, the Baltimore looked more like a pregnant tadpole, but it remained a very hot airplane.

The Baltimore went into production straight from the drawing

A-30 Baltimore built for RAF

board, without a prototype being built. The Royal Air Force, with its usual thoroughness, put it through 150 hours of exhaustive flight tests that lasted nearly three months. British pilots quickly shortened the Baltimore's name to the "Balt," a moniker of affection they seldom displayed for anything not British, particularly if it came from the "colonies." By all accounts they truly admired the Martin airplane.

Airpower magazine, many years later in an article entitled "Martin's Mercenaries," described the Baltimore and the Maryland as "Martin's Dynamic Desert Duo . . . excellent warplanes, versatile, tough, fast, well liked by their crews, and at least equal in all-around performance to foreign contemporaries," namely the German Heinkel, the Japanese Mitsubishi, and the Italian Savoia Marchetti. Comparing it with other American planes of the day, *Airpower's* associate editor Walt Boyne wrote:

> The British were extremely jingoistic about aircraft, curling an imperial upper lip in evaluations of American planes. . . . Derogatory comments were filed on Seversky products, the early P-40, Bell's P-39, and even our pride and joy, the Boeing B-17. The size of American planes was ridiculed, as were the incredible (to them) creature comforts provided. The most strenuous, and perhaps most

justified, criticisms were directed against speed, maneuverability, and combat survivability.[6]

By contrast, Boyne reported the British, after the flight qualification tests, "very highly regarded" the flying qualities of the Martin Baltimore, calling it "nice to handle" in all conditions of flight. "Maneuverability was excellent, and the normally reserved test pilots were effusive about single-engine performance, stating 'that the Baltimore maintained height [altitude] with greatest of ease on one engine even with the propeller of the dead engine unfeathered.'" The most impressive result to the British, Boyne wrote, "was the fact that no engine or mechanical accessory had to be changed during the entire trial period despite the fact that the plane was maintained in the open during the tough English winter and had been flown to (but not in excess of) all operational limitations."

So pleased were the English that they ordered a total of 1,575 Martin A-30s from 1940 to 1942. The first two orders, for 400 and 575 aircraft, respectively, were prior to the entry of the United States into the war and therefore were made by the U.S. Army Air Corps and reached the British through the Lend-Lease Act. In addition to the British, who flew the Baltimore almost exclusively in the Mediterranean, the plane was flown, and equally admired, by the Free French and the Free Greek air forces, by the Italian Co-Belligerent Air Force, and by the air forces of South Africa and Turkey.

The A-30 Baltimores also saw war service in the Pacific with the Royal Australian Air Force, but the plane's most effective blows were struck in North Africa, from El Alamein to Tunis, mostly in pursuit of Rommel's legions. According to Sir Vivian Gabriel, the head of Britain's Air Mission in Washington during World War II, nine squadrons of Baltimores, operating under the peculiarly unfriendly difficulties of desert maintenance, were in action continuously with the British Eighth Army. Sir Vivian said the Baltimores had a large share in breaking Rommel's lines, continuously dogging the heels of his retreating panzer units. In one week of action over the Libyan battlefield, the air minister said, the A-30s destroyed more than one thousand enemy tanks and wagons, brought down forty-seven German aircraft, and wiped out hundreds of troops. It was during the Tunisian campaign that the Martin Baltimores dropped their 11,111th bomb of the war. As to maintainability in the harsh desert environment, Sir Vivian said, "One squadron of Baltimores had a serviceability mark in 1943 of 81.8 percent, when 60 to 70 percent was considered very good indeed."

30,000 Middle River employees at wartime awards ceremony

When the fight ended in Africa, the Baltimores accompanied the British Eighth Army to Italy, taking part in crushing aerial attacks on Pantelleria, Crete, and Sicily. They later appeared in force over the Adriatic and Aegean seas, where they were flown, as of 1944, by the newly constituted Greek Air Force.[7]

Five Martin bombers, Boyne noted—the G.M.B., MB-1, NBS-1 (another designation for the MB-2), B-10, and the B-26—were "all symbols of American airpower." He concluded the *Airpower* article by saying:

Two other planes belong in that illustrious lineup, two that engaged in far more combat than any except the B-26, but are somehow sadly overlooked because they were "built for hire." These, the Martin Maryland and its portly younger sister, the Baltimore, were used very effectively by our allies serving as flying mercenaries in nine separate air forces. . . .

The British concentrated the majority of their Marylands in the Middle East, where they were used for reconnaissance, bombing, and, with an agressive pilot, as a fighter. (Flight Lieutenant Adrian Warburton . . . scored ten in his Maryland in a very short period of time.)

Despite their Mediterranean influence, it wouldn't be an exaggeration to say that the entire 167 program was more than paid for in another theater of war, when a Fleet Air Arm Maryland threaded its way on the deck through twisting Norwegian fjords to establish that the dreaded super battleship *Bismarck* had departed its anchorage. The news set off a sea chase whose climax was perhaps the only bright British news of 1941.[8]

No less than seven different Martin planes were flying combat missions around the world in the years immediately preceding Pearl Harbor and in the early years of the United States' declared combatancy. Martin PBM Mariners in nearly a dozen configurations and the giant JRM Mars flying boats patrolled the seas for the Navy. Even the two surviving Pan Am Clippers were pressed into military service for transport and medical evacuation missions. The Army's B-10s, which had been produced for six different nations and had gone to China and the Dutch East Indies primarily for service against the Japanese, were joined by the A-22 and the A-30, both of which were committed to combat in Europe and the Mediterranean by America's allies.

The Mariner would become the Navy's multipurpose workhorse seaplane. The first PBM was flown in 1939, and by 1940 the twin-engine patrol bomber was in full production. Early in the war it won its spurs patrolling the Atlantic, where Nazi U-boat skippers came to dread its ability to locate and sink them. In a series of modifications from PBM-1 through PBM-5 and a half-dozen model variations, Mariners were also used for cargo transport, heavy machinery lifting, troop carrying, air-sea rescue, as well as patrol and bombing missions for which they were designed. In a period of not quite fifteen months, beginning June 30, 1942, Mariners operating in the Caribbean and in the South Atlantic off Brazil sank ten U-boats, five of them in sixteen days—from July 15 through July 31, 1943.[9]

One of the most celebrated Mariner actions was by a PBM named Nickel Boat, credited with two German submarine sinkings.

Cleaning paint on PBM

The second also resulted in the capture of the U-boat's skipper, Kapitanleutenant Friedrich Guggenberger, who had been personally decorated by Adolf Hitler for sinking the British carrier *Ark Royal*. The pilot of another Mariner, Navy Lieutenant Joseph A. Japp, received the Distinguished Flying Cross for landing his Mariner in twelve-foot midocean waves, one hundred miles off Bermuda, to effect the rescue of survivors from a torpedoed British tanker.

Primarily as patrol bombers, Mariners took part in Pacific invasions from Kwajalein to Iwo Jima, the Philippines, and Okinawa. Artemus L. Gates, assistant secretary of the Navy for air, paid the airplane the ultimate compliment, one that pleased Glenn Martin particularly because it echoed his early-stated argument in favor of seaplanes. Gates stated after a wartime tour of the Pacific: "The Mariners are more in contact with the enemy than any other type of naval aircraft. You can't move the land planes in until your fields are ready, but I found the seaplanes were moving up practically with the landing operations."

Painted an ominous black, Mariners also earned the nickname "Nightmares" for their dusk-to-dawn search for shipping in enemy harbors. Toward the close of the war, when B-29s were pummeling Japan, the Mariners were deployed in rescue operations, frequently reaching downed American and Allied fliers within minutes after they had ditched planes in the sea.

A report by the U.S. Navy's Bureau of Aeronautics gave eloquent testimony to the open sea rescues the Mariner made commonplace:

The greatest World War II successes in air-sea rescue operations were achieved during the months following the initiation of the campaign for Okinawa. From April to August of 1945, the percentage of survivors rescued was higher than at any previous time during the war. The PBM Mariner was brought into full use during this period: it was able to complete rescues which its predecessors would have shied away from or found altogether impossible.

From April 1 to May 17, there were 132 men rescued out of 186 possible survivors. Of these, 63 were picked up by PBM "dumbos" (Search and Rescue Squadrons), 44 by ships, 18 by PBM squadron aircraft, 5 by VOS aircraft, and 1 by land forces; another made shore unassisted. Thus they rescued almost twice as many downed aviators as any other agency. The most successful group was the six twin-engined flying boats of VH-3 (Mariners). Flying missions from Kyushu to Formosa, VH-3 made 33 rough open-sea landings, of which 21 were made within 10 miles of enemy-held land, and seven while under fire from shore batteries.[10]

Like all Martin-built airplanes, the Mariner was rugged. During a night landing in the water near New York's Floyd Bennett Field, a Mariner struck a sandbar hidden beneath the surface. Twenty-four hours and twenty-six rivets later, the strong ship was flying again. Navy crews and Martin people told a favorite wartime story about the squadron of PBMs caught in a sudden Pacific typhoon. For a day and a half the planes and their crews rode out the savage blow and twenty-foot waves by running the engines at a thrust equal to the one hundred-miles-per-hour winds.[11]

The British procured thirty-two Mariner PBM-3s, the majority of which saw duty in the Pacific; the last one was operational there in mid-1958. Of all its remarkable service, the Mariner embarrassed itself only once, and then distinguished itself. On a cross-country flight over southeastern Arizona in the summer of 1944, a PBM-3 broke an oil line, shutting off one engine. Unable to stay airborne and lacking any water on which to land, the pilot gentled the great seaplane onto Willcox Dry Lake, a sandy lake bed about sixty miles east of Tucson, with only superficial damage. Beaching gear was flown in, attached to the Mariner's belly, and the great seaplane was flown out of the waterless ocean of sand without further incident, recording two firsts in flying boat history. That Mariner henceforth carried the name "Mirage of Willcox Dry Lake" painted on its nose.

Mariners operating from the seaplane tender *Norton Sound* explored the Arctic ice cap in 1946, and later the same year photographed and explored Antarctica. Other PBMs that same year provided logistic support for Operation Crossroads, the first postwar testing of the atomic bomb. When the Korean War broke out, Mariners were the first patrol planes there. Still others patrolled the Strait of Formosa from bases in Okinawa, Japan, and the Pescadores Islands.

The PBM-5 was ordered into production in January 1944, and 590 were purchased by the U.S. Navy and the U.S. Coast Guard in seven modifications, including thirty-six amphibians with retractable landing gear.

The Mariner was big, with its wingspan of 118 feet, and the China Clipper was even bigger, with a span of 130 feet, but Glenn Martin had a still larger flying boat on the drawing boards. Designated Martin Model 170, the Mars was conceived more than three years before America's entry into World War II, and it carried Glenn's last dream of a commercial future for the seaplane. The wingspan of the Mars was two times the one-hundred-foot distance covered by Glenn Martin's first flight at Santa Ana. So big was the seaplane's cargo hold that it could accommodate ninety-one planes the size of Glenn's original craft. Compared to the two largest land-based planes of the day, the Mars could carry nearly twice the cargo of the Douglas DC6 and nearly 26 percent more than the Boeing Stratofreighter, the C-97.

With its two hundred-foot wingspan and a fuselage 117 feet in length, the Mars was truly huge. It was half again longer than the Mariner, its gross weight of eighty-two tons was well over twice as heavy, and it was capable of flying the Atlantic round-trip nonstop. The wing was so long, its span surpassed the 124-foot distance of the Wright brothers' first flight at Kitty Hawk. You could tuck a Mariner

Gigantic Martin Mars

seaplane almost completely under one side and a China Clipper under the other.

Everything about the plane was gargantuan, and it proceeded to set one record after another on nearly every flight it made. The Navy originally ordered a prototype, designated the XPB2M-1, as an extra-long-range bomber, heavily armed. Its launching at Middle River on November 8, 1941, was unique in that it duplicated the launching of a great surface ship rather than an airplane. Mrs. Artemus L. Gates, wife of the then undersecretary of the Navy, broke the traditional bottle of champagne over the flying boat's bow as it slid wingless into Frog Mortar Creek before dignitaries of the Navy, the State of Maryland, and the City and County of Baltimore. When the Mars made its maiden flight the following summer, it was the world's largest aircraft, giving Martin another first.

Martin's chief tester, Ken Ebel, put the great seaplane through its paces, quickly dubbing her the "Old Lady." That nickname stuck, even in the Navy, which decided its newest acquisition should be completed as a transport rather than as a bomber. The progress of the war and the ever-increasing speed of the aerial phase made it obvious that the relatively slow speed of the Mars would make it too vulnerable a target. The planes would make excellent transports, however, capable of moving troops and vital materiel swiftly and in large quantities to almost any place in the world. And that it did in workhorse fashion.

By the fall of 1943, when the remodeled Mars was turned over to the Navy at the Patuxent River Naval Air Station in southern Maryland, she had been stripped of armor, and her huge bomb bays had been sealed. Redesignated the PB2M-1"R" for cargo, the Mars made its first Navy flight on·November 30, to Natal, Brazil, at a gross weight of 148,500 pounds. The Old Lady broke every existing record, carrying 13,000 pounds of cargo a distance of 4,375 miles in 28.3 hours, nonstop. In early 1944 she made a 4,700-mile round-trip from California to Hawaii in 27 hours 26 minutes, with 20,500 pounds of cargo, another world record.

The Navy put the lone Mars into regular service between Alameda and Honolulu and was so impressed with its performance that it ordered twenty of the giant seaplanes built as cargo transports with the designation JRM-1. That was 1944, but when the war ended the next year, the order was cut back to just five aircraft in addition to the original PB2M-1. The five ships were named, as the China Clippers before them had been, for Pacific islands: the Hawaii Mars, Philippine Mars, Marshall Mars, and Marianas Mars. The fifth, the Caroline Mars, even bigger and more powerful than its sisters, was designated JRM-2.

The first JRM-1, the Hawaii Mars, was lost in an early test flight crash in Chesapeake Bay. A fuel leak and resultant fire destroyed the Marshall Mars on a flight from Honolulu. The other four distinguished themselves as troop carriers and cargo ships in the Korean War, averaging five round-trips per week on the Pacific service until late 1955. At that time all four ships plus enough engines and spare parts to keep them flying for years were sold to a Canadian forest fire-fighting company, Forest Industries Flying Tankers, a unit of MacMillan Bloedel Limited, for use as "water bombers."[12] Outfitted with fiberglass-lined plywood tanks, the Mars fire fighters were also equipped with specially designed scoops able to withstand the tremendous strain of taking on six thousand gallons of water, weighing thirty tons, in a single twenty-two-second skimming of a lake. The water mixed with foam could deluge three to four acres of raging forest fires in a single dump. Such fire-fighting sorties by the Mars could be repeated every fifteen minutes, giving the great seaplanes a capacity and frequency unmatched by any other fire-fighting aircraft and equipment. Operators of the Mars estimated that, on average, the water-dropping capability of the Mars saved one hundred fire fighters at least five additional days in extinguishing a forest fire, thereby preserving 275,000 cubic feet of timber that would have been destroyed had the fire continued to burn.

Two of the rugged flying boats died in fire fighting service— the Marianas Mars when it struck the top of a tree in 1960, and the Carolina Mars, which was destroyed in typhoon Freida in 1962. The surviving grand Old Ladies, the Philippine Mars and the second Hawaii Mars, were still putting out forest fires in 1993, nearly fifty years after their birth. Painted fire-engine red and white, they were based on Sproat Lake, Vancouver Island, British Columbia.[13]

Martin's seventh and perhaps most famous contribution to World War II was the B-26 Martin Marauder. Often maligned but more often heralded, this "bring-'em-home-alive" medium bomber became one of the most celebrated American combat aircraft in both Europe and the Pacific from 1941 to 1945. But that's a chapter of its own.

CHAPTER 17

B-26 Marauder, The Stuff of Legends

■

Much has been written, including a half-dozen full-length books, on the B-26 Martin Marauder, the men who flew the B-26, and their heroics. It was truly the stuff of legends, one of the greatest bombers of the war from the standpoint of durability, versatility, speed, defensive firepower, bomb capacity, and precision in bombing.[1] Those who flew in it and loved it far outnumbered those less well trained in its operation, who feared it and came to hate it. A Marauder association is very active even today, with 3,000 members who either flew or worked on the Martin plane. The distinguished record of the B-26 Marauder as a rugged fighting machine is filled with exploits that crowd the pages of World War II history books, exploits that touched the careers of not only an incumbent president but four future presidents of the United States.[2]

The history of the B-26 actually began on January 23, 1939, when the Army Air Corps requested proposals for a new medium bomber with the speed of a pursuit plane. It asked specifically for a twin-engine, five-man bomber with a speed of 250 to 300 miles per hour, a range of three thousand miles, a service ceiling of between twenty thousand and thirty thousand feet, a bomb load of four thousand pounds, and armament of four .30-caliber machine guns. What was wanted was a medium bomber that could fly as fast as a fighter

B-26 assembly

and carry a bombload equal to a heavy bomber. A bomber like that had never been produced before, but if one could be, it might offer the United States a marked tactical advantage.[3]

Martin's response was the design child of aeronautical engineer Peyton Magruder, who had contributed to designs of both the 167-Maryland and the 187-Baltimore bombers. When the new design came off his drawing board in June 1939, only a few weeks before the close of the Army competition, Glenn Martin took one look at the rough drawings and immediately declared it a winner. Seeking out Magruder, he on the spot appointed the lanky twenty-six-year-old project manager for the development of Model No. 179, later designated the B-26 by the Army.

Magruder was assigned the finest engineering and manufacturing talents in the company, and his team prepared a detail specification that guaranteed the airplane would meet the Army's written requirements along with a formal proposal for the assigned number of aircraft at a bid price. Only three other firms entered designs, which were to be evaluated by certain critical characteristics on a prescribed numerical basis. Speed was the Army's most weighted value, with a total of one thousand points possible on all characteristics. When the bids were opened the day after the Fourth of July, Martin was judged the winner; its design was rated at 813.6 points, 140 points better than its nearest competitor. Martin was awarded a contract one month and five days later for 201 aircraft to cost $15,815,000.

One month after the contract signing, construction was begun on Middle River Plant No. 2, a facility having more than 1.1 million square feet. It was situated on the other side of the Middle River airport, about a mile to the east of the original plant buildings. Despite recently added floor space, more than 2.3 million square feet enclosed by Plant 1's A, B, and C buildings, they were filled with A-22s, A-30s, and PBMs. There was no room for another new airplane.

With no time to wait for special authorization and paperwork, the company began construction with its own money even though the addition would be a government-owned facility. Plant 2 would be almost a duplicate of Albert Kahn's architectural design of the original Martin manufacturing complex. Materials were purchased by tons and by tens of thousands of pieces. Tooling for mass production was under way before the new building was completed.

Manufacturing techniques developed for the PBM were honed for the B-26. In what was described as a "new quantity-production system," thirty thousand parts (exclusive of nuts, bolts, rivets, etc.) were assembled into 650 minor subassemblies, which in turn became 32 major subassemblies before final assembly into complete airplanes.

Harry George, who was a supervisor in "manufacturing methods" at the time, recalled the tremendous push to get Plant 2 online and staffed with experienced people. "They really diluted the skills in Plant 1 to staff Plant 2," he remembered. "Everybody was working like hell already, but the production requirements the Army had set for the B-26 meant we were going to work even harder. We had to get the man-hours down by simplifying the work so that fewer people were needed for each function."[4] One of the manufacturing methods they came up with, George said, involved predrilling holes in the flanges of frames that held the material being formed into wings and fuselages. "So instead of laying out rivet holes by hand in each airplane skin, the holes were in the frames holding the skins. All you had to do was drill through the pilot holes directly into the skin. It not only knocked hell out of the time it took to do the job," George said, it maintained "edge distance" for each and every hole, an important margin in preventing rivet pullout under stress.

George had joined the company three years earlier, in 1936, as a seventeen-year-old right out of high school. It was just before the B-26 work began that Tom Soden, "an old Scot who was factory manager, called me into his office and shut the door," Harry said. "This wasn't an everyday occurrence, and I was wondering what I was in for when he told me my hard work had been noticed. He said it was easy to see my heart was in the Martin company, and it was appreciated. 'Effective next month, you're going on salary,' he told me, and then he asked, 'Do you know what that means? It means your heart *and* your soul will be in the Martin company.' Then he handed me the silver-rimmed badge which signified supervisory people. I walked out of there on a six-foot cloud."

George said the promotion effectively meant a cut in pay because as a supervisor he no longer was eligible for overtime pay at time plus a third. He would have numerous management positions in Baltimore and, for the last sixteen years of his career, at Orlando before retiring in 1986 after a half-century of Martin service.

Another bit of Martin production ingenuity born on the B-26 program was a photographic reproduction system. By eliminating much of what had previously been hand layouts by toolmakers, the new process greatly accelerated the manufacturing cycle. Ned I. Stephenson joined the photographic department in 1941, right out of high school and just after the so-called robot draftsman took hold. Ned credits the photo process with speeding up the transfer of hundreds of pounds of original shop blueprints by duplicating them identically on other materials. It could transfer engineering drawings onto coated metal, wood, cloth, paper, Masonite, plastic, or whatever material was required.

"Commercial cameras of the size needed were not available, so special cameras had to be built in the plant," Stephenson remembered. "Copy boards were as large as five by twelve feet, and we photographed the drawings on glass negatives that held tolerances to plus or minus ten-thousandths of an inch."[5] The system was the brainchild of Sid Polk, an engineer in lofting, and Harry Ricker, head of the photographic section at Middle River, according to Stephenson.

The system was also sold commercially as Martin Multi-Mulsion and was a big hit with artists and others who wanted to transfer original drawings and photographs to a variety of materials, including china and silver. Ned Stephenson spent forty-eight years with the company before retiring in 1989 in Denver, where he headed the photographic department.

B-26 production called for many revolutionary innovations in manufacturing, including spot welding for secondary structures, stretch press for making large, curved pieces of skin for the fuselage, more castings and forgings than in any comparable aircraft, fewer detail parts, and fewer rivets. In a move to accelerate production, the Army concurred in the company's recommendation to skip a prototype. The Marauder went straight from the drawing board to the flight of the first production airplane, lopping three years off the normal development cycle.

What a beauty that first plane was. The fuselage was cigar-shaped, sleek and cylindrical, 58½ feet in length and tapered on both ends, the tail more so than the nose. In fact, its aerodynamically perfect fuselage earned it the nickname of "Flying Torpedo." The high wing was a clipped 65 feet (lengthened to 71 in later models), and the nearly 10-foot vertical tail was accentuated by an eight-degree dihedral of the horizontal stabilizer. It could carry four thousand pounds of bombs on a five-hundred-mile mission at speeds in excess of three hundred miles per hour, and still make the return trip home.

Adding to the B-26's great look was the fact that it sat upright on tricycle landing gear, its sleek fuselage parallel with the ground. There was one exception. As part of the development in the late forties of the B-48 and the B-51, two jet bombers that didn't get beyond prototypes, a B-26 was modified to test a "bicycle" landing gear. It consisted of a single wheel under the nose of the plane, a double-wheeled but single landing gear under the fuselage in a straight line with the nose wheel, and then smaller outrigger wheels under each wing tip, like training wheels on a child's bicycle. This Martin innovation earned the modified Marauder the additional sobriquet of "Middle River Stump Jumper."

Bill Compton, who went to work for the company in 1947 as a test pilot and put in more than forty years before retiring in 1988 as head of the corporate aircraft department, remembered how the "Stump Jumper" got its name. "We affixed two-by-fours to the runway about every two feet, then ran that B-26 with the bicycle gear back and forth across those strips of wood to test the ruggedness of the wing-tip landing wheels."[6] Although the B-48 and B-51 would never become production aircraft, the Martin-developed bicycle landing gear was the model for what later became standard gear on Air Force B-47 and B-52 bombers.

On November 25, 1940, the first B-26 rolled out of Plant 2 and onto the flight line with chief test pilot Ken Ebel, by then also chief engineer, in the left seat and Alexander Melewski in the right. Melewski was not a test pilot, but he worked in engineering flight test, and Ebel had recruited him for the first B-26 flight because there were no volunteers for copilot.

They taxied the length of the field a few times, then took off into a cold northwest wind. A throng of people who had built the plane, plus Peyton Magruder, Glenn Martin, Army officers, and covering press, cheered until hoarse as the sleek cigar-shaped B-26 cleared the power lines paralleling Eastern Avenue and the railroad tracks and climbed gracefully into the sky. The entire process from design through production and successful first flight test had taken little more than a year from the contract award—fifteen months, to be exact, without a prototype. It was an industry eye-opener.

Exactly three months after that first flight, Marauders began flowing to Army airfields. Even the second plant at Middle River was not sufficient to maintain the delivery of 5,266 Martin Marauders, the number eventually produced. On March 3, 1941, ground was broken at Fork Crook, Omaha, Nebraska (later renamed Offutt Air Force Base) for an aircraft assembly plant dedicated to the production of B-26 bombers. The Glenn L. Martin–Nebraska Company built and operated the plant for the government, and the Martin Omaha plant, as it came to be known, made history of its own.

On December 8, only eighteen hours after the attack on Pearl Harbor that would make that a "day that will live in infamy," fifty-three of the first fifty-six Marauders to be built took off from Virginia's Langley Field headed for the Pacific. After a brief interlude on coastal defense duty from a base at Muroc Dry Lake in California, the Marauders proceeded to Australia. The B-26 not only defended that island nation from the Japanese but fought the enemy at Guadacanal, in the Coral Sea, and all over the Pacific. Not a single B-26 was lost nor a single crewman wounded in the first six months of the

United States' formal entry in the war, so effectively did the plane perform in scores of Pacific combat missions.

"I was inspecting the coordinating fixture for a B-26 fuselage section when the plant superintendent got on the loudspeaker to tell us the Japanese had attacked," Adolph Vlcek recalled thirty-seven years later. Vlcek, who was hired as Employee No. 577 in 1930, spent forty-nine years with the company before retiring in 1979. It was in 1978 as technical director for manufacturing programs in the Baltimore division that he recalled some of those early days as well as the war years. In an interview for an article in *Martin Marietta Today* magazine, Vlcek said he was in Plant 2 working as superintendent of detailed manufacturing on the Marauder on the Sunday that Pearl Harbor was bombed. "When President Roosevelt said the aircraft industry was going to build fifty thousand planes a year, the politicians said it was wishful. Our industry did it in ten months. We didn't do much flag waving around our plant," Vlcek added, "but when FDR came over and drove through the plant, you could sort of feel a sense of urgency rising."[7]

He remembered "the heroines of the day." "We had women

Marauders poised for delivery at Middle River, Maryland

who could drive fourteen thousand rivets in eight hours; you could say Americans are hell for an objective. Listen, we never thought of failing. We opened with thirty-five a month as our B-26 goal, and at the end of the month we had delivered thirty-five. But one day you could walk into the assembly area and not a plane was in sight. So we set up a continuous line. I can hear Wimp Sattler—he was the general foreman—calling, 'Clear all stations, move that plane,' " Vlcek said. "If the guys on a station weren't through with their job, they had to go with the plane to the next station, finish their jobs there, and then hurry back to a new plane that moved in."

Big for his age, Vlcek was only fifteen that spring day in 1929 when he took a trolley ride from downtown Baltimore to Middle River. He struck up a conversation with a stranger who turned out to be the plumbing contractor on a new plant being built there. "He offered me forty cents an hour to help unload the freight cars that brought in pipes, valves, and all the fittings," Vlcek said. "It was depression time. That was big money." The plant was finished two days before Christmas, and the plumbing contractor laid off Vlcek. He returned on January 29, 1930, and was employed by the Glenn L. Martin Company as a metal bench helper.

Among others who attested to the B-26 as a rugged fighting machine was a future president of the United States, at that time a junior congressman from Texas and a lieutenant commander in the Naval Reserve. Lyndon Baines Johnson was sent to the South Pacific in the spring of 1942 on a fact-finding mission by President Roosevelt. His assignment was to be the president's eyes and ears on how the war was progressing and what "our men in the field needed." Despite instructions to the contrary and a military escort with orders to keep the commander/congressman out of harm's way, Johnson talked his way aboard the "Heckling Hare," an original short-wing B-26 of the Twenty-second Bomb Group, and flew as an observer over enemy-held New Guinea.

On a harrowing bomb run over a "suicide" target, the heavily fortified Japanese air base at Lae, his Marauder was jumped by seven enemy Zeros when it had to drop out of formation after losing a generator. Riddled by Japanese gunfire, the Heckling Hare was credited with shooting down one attacker while fighting off the others. It returned safely to its base full of holes, both literally and figuratively, but with crew and distinguished observer safely aboard. For that particular mission, each crew member of the Heckling Hare, including presidential special observer Lyndon Johnson, was awarded the Distinguished Service Medal by General Douglas MacArthur.[8]

Back home, the pace of the war had increased demand for the B-26, while at the same time it reduced the training cycle for its crews. Three takeoffs and three landings, and you were a B-26 pilot; that's all the transition training they were getting. The Marauder's landing speed of 115 miles per hour, unusually "hot" for a medium bomber, was actually faster than the cruising speed of the training planes the rookie pilots flew. Its high load factor on a relatively short sixty-five-foot wing made the airplane unforgiving of pilot error, particularly as less experienced, inadequately trained crews began flying it. These flight characteristics earned it a number of sobriquets, in addition to "Flying Torpedo." Early in the plane's wartime career that ultimately spanned six years, its nicer nicknames included "Flying Prostitute" and "Baltimore Whore" (no visible means of support). The B-26 was a pilot's airplane to the experienced regulars who first learned to fly it and took it to the Pacific. They told fantastic tales of its rugged durability, including stories such as the Heckling Hare's mission with Lyndon Johnson.

But early modifications directed by the Army Air Corps added weight to the B-26 and increased the potential for error in the hands of inexperienced pilots. By the beginning of 1942, the normal gross weight of the Marauder had increased to 31,527 pounds, nearly two and a half tons above its designed 26,625-pound gross weight. The frequency of training accidents also increased, particularly on single-engine drills. "One a day in Tampa Bay" and the "Widow Maker" became perjoratives for the B-26 at MacDill Field, a training base on Florida's west coast.

Finally an official inquiry was held by Congress under the direction of Senator Harry S. Truman, whose subcommittee became known as the Truman Committee. Fuzz Furman, as a foreman in final assembly, had set up the first production line for the B-26, the first cost controls, and an open-stock binning system; he was senior general foreman at the airport when the Truman Committee visited the plant.

"I can't remember Truman being there," Fuzz said. "People tell me he was there, but I didn't see him. His committe people were everywhere, including the airport where a guy named Colby, who wore glasses, put on a show which he wasn't supposed to do with a B-26. He just happened to be up there flying. He exceeded every limitation on the airplane—speed, manifold pressure, RPM, everything—but he really flew that airplane around. He hadn't been scheduled to peform for these folks, and if something bad [had] happened to that airplane with that committee watching . . . but it didn't, and I guess they were impressed. The pilot was fired on the spot when he landed the airplane," Fuzz said. "We couldn't find anything wrong with the engines, but we changed them anyway because we knew all their limitations had been exceeded."[9]

The Truman Committee may not have been as impressed as Furman was with that demonstration. It recommended that B-26 production be halted. When word reached the South Pacific, veteran Marauder pilots and combat leaders went to bat for the airplane, and only a concerted campaign by the Air Corps kept the program alive. A military review board created by Army Air Corps Chief Hap Arnold recommended four things: improve the training of pilots, improve the maintenance of the aircraft, halt overloading, and lengthen the wing of subsequent models to increase single-engine performance so that it would be easier for average pilots to fly.

General Arnold appointed one of his top commanders, Brigadier General James H. "Jimmy" Doolittle, to implement the recommendations. Doolittle, who earlier that year had distinguished himself as the leader of the Tokyo raiders in another twin-engine medium bomber, quickly became a fan of the B-26. In fact, he later chose a B-26 for his personal aircraft. Doolittle recruited the Air Corps's top test pilot, Vincent W. "Squeek" Burnett, as his technical adviser on the B-26 "rescue" operation. At the time, Burnett was assigned to the ferry command at Baltimore's Logan Field, where he flight-tested and checked out pilots who would be ferrying all manner of aircraft from the States to combat theaters, including B-26s flown directly from Martin's Middle River airport.

Burnett's introduction to the B-26 had been somewhat of a miracle in itself and further underscored his unusual abilities as a pilot, according to J. K. Havener in his history, *The Martin B-26 Marauder*. "All his thousands of hours of flying time had been single-engine . . . but checking out the 'Widow-Maker,' which would have been a terrifying experience to anyone else, proved to be a 'piece of cake' for Squeek."[10] After less than a day familiarizing himself with the B-26 on the ground, a pilot took him up for a spin around the field, then told Burnett to land it. Of course he did, and there was no need to give him additional instruction. For Burnett, the B-26 was love at first sight. He considered it a pilot's airplane, and when Jimmy Doolittle asked him to take on the special assignment, he jumped at the opportunity.

A large part of the training problem, Doolittle reasoned, was that young pilots went from primary training to basic trainers to advanced trainers before receiving their wings. After graduation

General Jimmy Doolittle with B-26

from flight school, they were sent directly to B-26 transition schools, a very difficult step without having flown multiengine aircraft. Even those with twin-engine training had never flown a plane with tricycle landing gear, so the Marauder, with its nose wheel, was a "step up in difficulty for all new pilots," General Doolittle concluded in his autobiography, adding:

Hap [General Arnold] asked me to check into the problem and recommend whether or not the B-26 should continue to be built. I checked out in it at the Martin factory near Baltimore and liked it. There wasn't anything about its flying characteristics that good piloting skill couldn't overcome. I traveled to several flying training schools and B-26 transition units, gathered the student pilots together, and asked them what they had heard about the B-26 airplane. Almost all said they had heard it wouldn't fly on one engine, you couldn't make a turn into a dead engine, and landing it safely on one engine was just about impossible.

To prove them wrong, I lined up on the runway, feathered the left engine during the takeoff roll, and made a steep turn into the dead engine, flew around the pattern, and landed with the engine still inoperative. I did it again in the other direction with the right engine feathered. And I did this without a copilot, which made a further impression. This convinced the doubters that all of these "impossible" maneuvers were not only possible but easy if you paid close attention to what you were doing. I had no trouble getting volunteers after each demonstration.[11]

Jimmy Doolittle told of another time when he took Major Paul W. Tibbets, Jr., up for a ride. Tibbets later became known to the American public as the pilot of the Martin-built B-29 the *Enola Gay*, which dropped the first atomic bomb on Japan. "Paul was one of the pilots who had flown General Eisenhower down to Gibralter and was partial to the B-17 because he felt the role of the B-26 as a medium bomber would be limited," Doolittle said. "He [Tibbets] wanted to fly the big ones, but I wanted him to see what the Marauder could do." Doolittle, in his autobiography, quoted Tibbets's memoirs:

> Doolittle then shut down one of the engines and feathered the propeller. He got the plane trimmed and we did some flying on one engine, turning in both directions, climbing, making steep banks. The Marauder was a tame bird with Doolittle at the controls. Suddenly he put the plane into a dive, built up excess speed, and put it into a perfect loop—all with one engine dead. As we came to the bottom of the loop, he took the dead propeller out of feather and it started windmilling. When it was turning fast enough, he flipped on the magnetos and restarted the engine as we made a low pass over the airfield. We came around in a normal manner, dropped the gear and the flaps, and set the B-26 down smoothly on the runway. The pilots and operations people who had been watching us were impressed. The flight was an important start toward convincing them that the B-26 was just another airplane.[12]

General Doolittle called the Martin B-26 "an airplane to be respected but not feared." He recommended that the B-26 continue to be built, that transition training be improved and lengthened, and that subsequent models have longer wings to increase the safety

Airmen learn B-26 maintenance

margin. All of these things were done. When Doolittle returned to England to direct Air Corps operations over Europe, Squeek Barnett, who by then was a uniformed colonel, took over the B-26 training task. He demonstrated by example, as had Doolittle, the flyability and maintainability of this remarkable airplane, thereby assuring its continuance and the excellent combat record it achieved in World War II.

As one solution to the B-26 problem, Martin test pilots, led by test chief Orville E. "Pat" Tibbs and engineers William B. Bergen and George Trimble, among others, went into the field to demonstrate and teach pilots who were new to the aircraft. Air Corps pilots and mechanics, five hundred at a time, were assigned to the Martin plant, where they were schooled on proper maintenance procedures in what came to be known as the "College of B-26 Knowledge." Through these combined efforts the training accidents soon dwindled in number, and aside from the lengthening of the wings, unnecessary modifications to the airplane were avoided.

Glenn Martin, whose pride in the quality of his products was shared by his employees, had taken each accident as a personal affront and responsibility; he grieved for each pilot lost or injured. But his faith in the airplane never flagged, and he actively prodded his employees and the customer until conditions improved. He had closely followed the success of the first airplanes, which had gone to the Pacific with the 22nd Bombardment Group soon after the attack on Pearl Harbor.

Marauder exploits began to multiply after nine of the aircraft attacked the Japanese base at Rabaul in April 1942 with only one plane lost. In the Battle of Midway, four Marauders with torpedoes slung under their bellies (a Martin innovation) penetrated fierce antiaircraft fire and swarming Zero fighters to attack the Japanese fleet. All planes returned safely, one of them with more than five hundred holes from bullets and shrapnel. It had to make a crash landing because one of those holes had flattened a tire.

November of the same year saw Marauders in their first action in North Africa, a campaign in which the airplane performed outstandingly as part of the Twelfth Air Force.[13] At El Alamein in Egypt, the B-26 joined Martin A-20s flown by both Vichy French and Free French fliers, fighting each other, as well as the British-flown Martin A-30s. It is the only time recorded in the history of aerial warfare that one manufacturer had three aircraft in a single battle.

As the man whose name and reputation rode with every plane, Glenn Martin cherished the telegram he received from Army Air Corps Commanding General Arnold:

> Martin B-26s, attacking without fighter escort, drove off intercepting German fighters in a convincing demonstration of the bomber's defensive firepower just reported to me from the North African campaign. Five Messerschmitt 109s intercepted 11 B-26s at 4,000 feet.... When the scramble cleared up, two 109s were shot down and a third claimed as probably destroyed. There was only minor damage to one B-26. I extend to you my congratulations and thanks for a tough and durable airplane that will help us win the war.

In addition to the Twelfth Air Force in North Africa, the Martin B-26 was used extensively to "soften up" the enemy in the Mediterranean, Italy, France, Holland, Belgium, and Germany prior to the invasion of the continent. Marauders flew thousands of missions as part of the Eighth and later the Ninth Air Force based in England. At least seven B-26s completed one hundred missions each before D-Day, and one nicknamed "Mild and Bitter" completed one hundred missions a full month before the invasion. By the time the war

General Hap Arnold and Martin

ended, more than 250 different Marauders had each completed one hundred combat missions.

Perhaps the most celebrated Marauder of all was aptly named "Flak Bait." It completed 202 missions and had the additional distinction of having been shot up more than any other combat aircraft. Flak Bait was struck by enemy fire a thousand times and continued flying with a patch on every replaceable surface area. Flak Bait was

D-Day Marauders over channel

the hero of a book by the same name written by Devon Francis. The nose section of this famous airplane was preserved and is one of the permanent exhibits in the Smithsonian Institution's Air and Space Museum in Washington.

Undoubtedly the proudest accomplishment of the Martin Marauder came on D-Day, 1944, when it was chosen by General Eisenhower and his air commanders to spearhead Operation Overlord, the invasion of the continent of Europe. On that rainy, windy sixth of June dawn, Martin B-26 Marauders of the Ninth Air Force's 344th Bomb Group were an integral part of the greatest air, sea, and land armada in the history of mankind. They drew the lead position to fly into coastal Normandy and pulverize German gun emplacements minutes before American troops crossed the beaches. Behind the Marauders came waves of other American and British bombers and fighters, more than five thousand surface ships, and an initial landing force of more than one hundred thousand troops.

Normally assigned to mission altitudes of ten thousand feet and above, the B-26 pilots had been warned of low scuddy weather and had been ordered to "come in at treetop level" if necessary in order to see their targets. They actually crossed the channel only a thousand feet above the invasion flotilla and were able to climb to only three thousand feet for their bomb runs on the coastal fortifications above Utah Beach.

Spearheading the Ninth Air Force's 269 Marauders were six B-26s known as "The Six Hundred" for the total missions they had flown, each having completed one hundred or more. They were Littjo with 117 missions, Rat Poison, Bar Fly, Ye Olde Crocke, Blazing Heat, and Slightly Dangerous.[14] The B-26s dropped their bombs at exactly 6:20 A.M., nearly daylight, just ten minutes before the American invasion troops hit the beach. The Martin Marauders altogether dropped 4,404 bombs, each weighing 250 pounds. The size of the bombs had been chosen deliberately to wreak sufficient havoc on German underground gun emplacements without leaving craters so large they would impede following waves of Allied tanks.

At their low bombing altitude, the Marauders caught plenty of flak, as Lieutenant Emmett Lancaster, the copilot in Marauder 71★D, could attest. His B-26, piloted by Lieutenant R. J. "Whitey" Schwaergerl, was leading a flight in the third box of eighteen aircraft of the 497th Squadron of the 344th Bomb Group. According to Lancaster:

> We were leading the next-to-last flight, stacked down from the cloud base to around 3,000 feet. As we started our run on the beach, we came under heavy ground fire. The aircraft immediately in front of us blew up, and another skidded beneath us trailing flame and smoke; pilot and copilot both slumped forward over the controls. A shell slammed into the left side of [our] radio compartment with an explosive force that stung my feet through the floor panels, and the ship lurched momentarily out of control, instruments gyrating wildly. We dumped our bomb load, feathered the left engine, and began to lose altitude.[15]

Lancaster and the crew of Marauder 71★D limped back across the channel "low and slow," as he put it many years later from his home in Tempe, Arizona. As an aviation artist he painted a graphic depiction of that mission, which became the cover design for J. K. Havener's book, *The Martin B-26 Marauder.*

Lancaster's painting of B-26s

Martin Marietta, the corporation, would return to Normandy nearly a half-century later, not far from those grassy B-26–made craters and broken concrete gun emplacements that are a memorial to the American Rangers of the Second Batallion. The Rangers scaled the vertical one-hundred-foot cliffs of Marauder-softened Pointe-du-Hoc to eliminate what would have been withering German fire on the landing beaches of Omaha and Utah.

The location is less than an hour from the Battle of Normandy

Memorial at Caen, a teaching museum dedicated to peace; its construction was partially funded by Martin Marietta. It is part of a 1994 multinational fiftieth-anniversary commemoration of that D-Day invasion, which literally rose as a high tide out of the English Channel, engulfed the Norman countryside, and eventually inundated all of France and much of Europe in a liberating flood of freedom. The process begun that day would be crowned in the early 1990s with the fall of communist governments throughout eastern Europe and the subsequent democratization of the Soviet Union and its fifteen republics.

As part of the Caen memorial, the twelfth-century Abbaye d'Ardennes, just outside Caen, has been given by the French to the U.S. Battle of Normandy Foundation, which will turn it into an American study center. College students from each of the fifty states will be able to spend a semester in France examining the political and social causes of war as well as the evolution of the peace that ensued.

There was considerable postwar speculation, although no definite proof, that a group of B-26 Marauders had been sent to the Soviets during World War II and that they had seen action in the hands of Soviet pilots, who trained in B-26s either at Wright or at Patterson fields in Dayton, Ohio. But as to an actual transfer of Army Air Corps aircraft to the Soviets, either as part of the Lend-Lease program established by President Roosevelt prior to America's entry in the war or by other means, no record is known to exist.[16]

Fuzz Furman, who was flight line foreman at Middle River during production and delivery of many of the B-26 aircraft, said no Marauders were sent to Russia from the Baltimore plant and he did not know of any Russian women pilots training in the aircraft at Middle River, as reported by another source. "The only women pilots at Middle River in those days," Furman said, "were both Brits and American women flying planes for the Ferry Command."

A total of 5,266 B-26s were built by Martin during World War II—3,681 in Baltimore and 1,585 at the Omaha plant. They flew more than 110,000 sorties and dropped 150,000 tons of bombs, most notably in raids on Normandy, Florence, Naples, the Abbey Monte Cassino, Rome, Chartres, and the Seine River bridges. The B-26 loss-in-combat ratio was one-half of 1 percent, the lowest of any Allied bomber. The airplane claimed these other distinctions:[17]

- First Allied bomber in European Theater to complete one hundred missions, Mild and Bitter, on an afternoon raid on a Nazi airfield at Evreux/Fauville, France, May 9, 1944.

- First Allied bomber in European Theater to complete two hundred missions, Flak Bait, actually completed its 202nd mission from Airfield Y-89 at Le Culot in May 1945.
- First Army bomber to use torpedoes in World War II—standard two thousand-pound naval aerial torpedo slung from external keel rack.
- First twin-engine medium bomber to carry greater payload of bombs than B-17, the heavyweight bomber of the day.
- First U.S. Army plane to carry power turret, Martin 250CE.
- First World War II U.S. aircraft to use weapon pods—two .50-caliber machine guns on either side of the forward fuselage.
- First all-Plexiglas bombardier's nose, another Martin innovation.
- First combat aircraft to use butted seams for skin covering, enhancing the flow of air and increasing speed.
- First combat bomber to employ all-electric bomb-release mechanism.
- First combat U.S. aircraft with self-sealing fuel tanks, a Martin invention, Mareng Cells.
- First flexible tracks for transferring ammunition from bomb bay storage racks to tail gun, a Lionel development for Martin.
- First combat aircraft to substitute plastic for metal in more than four hundred parts.
- First aircraft (Middle River Stump Jumper) to test bicycle landing gear that was later adopted for B-47 and B-52 air force jet bombers.
- First medium bomber modified for tow target use in aerial gunnery training because of its pursuit-plane speed; designated the AT-23 and later changed to TB-26.

Perhaps the most fitting epitaph for a magnificent fighting machine is contained in the epilogue of the book *Marauder Men* by Major General John O. Moench, U.S. Air Force (Ret.):

> Maligned in the beginning, the final record of the Marauder was outstanding. The Glenn L. Martin Company had designed a truly superior aircraft although, admittedly, it was well ahead of its time.... Around the Marauder there developed a group of strong, dedicated men.... These were the Marauder Men—heroes who became special persons not just because they were special but because they had fallen in love with and married the Martin Marauder.[18]

CHAPTER 18

"Rosie the Riveter" and Other Wartime Phenoms

■

I n the peak production years of World War II, the saying around Baltimore was "Everybody and his brother or sister works at Martin's." Not literally true, of course, but employment did swell to more than fifty-three thousand men and women in the four Baltimore locations, including the two plants at Middle River, the turret production facility on Sinclair Lane, and the Canton warehouses. In addition, fourteen thousand were employed by the Glenn L. Martin–Nebraska Company at Omaha.[1] Built originally as a second source of B-26 production, Omaha developed an even greater fame little known until after the war.

There were many wartime manufacturing "firsts" established by the Glenn L. Martin Company, but a first of another kind occurred on October 20, 1941, when nineteen women were hired to work on the factory floor. On that day "Rosie the Riveter"[2] was born. Of course, women had been major players in the early aeroplane days, stitching fabric wings and other cloth surfaces, but the metal manufacturing areas of the aircraft industry, including hot forges, metal cutting and bending, and the noise and physical exertion associated with those processes in those days generally had been perceived as a man's world.

There was considerable opposition to the idea of women in

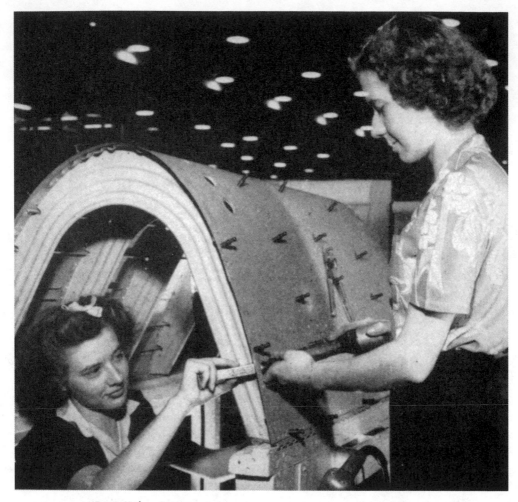

"Rosie" the riveters

"this harsh male environment," but Glenn Martin was willing to give it a try. A man years ahead of his time and a trendsetter in many areas besides design and engineering, he was, in reality, an early advocate of equal rights for women. He had long encouraged and even featured the distaff side in his flying. Aircraft metals were light and easily handled, he reasoned. Much of the work required skills women had honed to perfection in the household, skills requiring great patience, perseverance, and concentration—all attributes Glenn believed women possessed in greater abundance than most men. A single B-26, for example, consisted of twenty-five thousand parts and required three hundred thousand rivets and the drilling of hundreds of thousands of holes. Miles and miles of wiring that had to be gathered into harnesses required deft manual skills, he reasoned. The aircraft industry was an excellent environment in which to try this "employment experiment," he judged correctly. By March 1942, there were two thousand women working as Martin riveters, welders, and operators of drill presses, punch presses, sanders, electrical assemblers, and a variety of other jobs. Within a year of Martin's initiating the idea, there were thirteen thousand women holding down assembly line jobs in the aircraft industry.[3]

At the Omaha plant, where women eventually made up 40 percent of the work force, the company issued a handbook on the proper attitude to be displayed toward female employees. Although such a document would stir a hornet's nest of protest in the 1990s, it was a model of well-intended advice on the male-dominated factory floor of 1941.

A half century later, Delores "Dee" Parker was one of hundreds of women who worked in Orlando on the target identification and pilot night vision system, known as TADS/PNVS, for the Apache helicopter. She is a second-generation Martin Marietta woman, who vividly remembers her childhood fifty years ago in Omaha, when her mother was in the original contingent of Martin-Nebraska women and a riveter as well. In addition to working final assembly on B-29s, Parker said her mom, Marie Calk, was one of the first to be designated a "woman's counselor." She was given a handbook entitled *Why Were You Hired as a Counselor?* It answered that question with statements about women that would be totally unacceptable today, such as:

> We had to hire women; we don't know how to handle them. They weep; they're absent, they quit; the men don't know what to do about them, so we hired a woman's counselor. And there you are—the new counselor—bewildered and uncertain. "What do I do, and how do I do it? Who is my boss? Where do I start?"[4]

"That was the company's guide in those days to the 'woman's counselor,' my mom, Mrs. Marie Calk, and she really worked hard at it," Delores Parker said. "She even brought some of the women home to stay with us for a time until they could find places of their own. Our house only had two bedrooms; but Daddy had made the back porch as long as the house, and he put two double beds out there so we could have extra room. I have a sister, who is two years younger, and Mom would say, 'Dee and Marilyn, we're going to have to put you out on the porch so that we can give so-and-so your bedroom. Her husband was killed in action and she doesn't have anybody else. Just pretend she's your sister.' And Mom would bring the gal home, and she'd stay maybe six months. Then pretty soon she'd leave and here would come another one, maybe this time with two little kids. So we'd be babysitting and helping them out."[5]

■

EVEN BEFORE B-26 PRODUCTION WAS completed in 1944 with the rollout of Tail-End Charlie—the 5,266th Marauder and the 1,585th built in Omaha—the Nebraska plant was being expanded and tooled for production of another airplane. It would be the B-29 Superfortress, a Boeing airplane for which Martin Omaha would become an important second-source producer, one of four plants set up to supplement B-29 production at Boeing's Seattle facility. Included among the 531 B-29s that would be built in Omaha were the two that dropped the atomic bombs on Japan. Their mission not only brought the Japanese to the surrender table and World War II to a close but obviated any further need for the Martin-Nebraska plant or, for that matter, any further war production.

But in the midst of the war, Omaha was a pressing new entity. When the government decided to build it, a contract was given to the Martin company for the construction as well as the operating management of the finished plant. In addition, there were three government-prescribed automotive subcontractors chosen for their presumed knowledge of mass production.

Although the aircraft industry was by that time setting mass production records undreamed of by automobile or any other prewar manufacturing effort, the government decided that Goodyear Aircraft Corporation, Hudson Motor Car Co., and Chrysler Corporation would be teamed with Martin for the manufacture and assembly of the B-26s in Omaha. The decision was not unreminiscent of the thinking that gave the automotive industry dominance over the fledgling aeroplane makers prior to World War I. This time the outcome would be spectacular, an indication of the superb results of mass production—to the credit of Glenn Martin's team and like companies in the aircraft industry.

In the spirit of the government's pact, Glenn Martin hired an automotive man, Lincoln R. Schafe, to be the first general manager of Martin-Nebraska. Schafe had been general manager of the Fischer

B-29s at Omaha plant

Division of General Motors in Cleveland and was therefore well suited to managing the diverse procurement that produced the B-26. Forty percent of the plane was to be made in the Omaha plant, and 60 percent would come from factories of the three subcontractors. All four groups of employees made a pledge, inscribed in bronze:

TO THE MEN WHO FLY THIS SHIP

We, the men and women who helped build this airplane, were ever mindful that your lives and possibly our futures might depend on how well we did our jobs. We, therefore, pledge that every detail of construction of the airplane was completed as carefully and thoroughly as though we were to fly it ourselves.[6]

217

The pledge was vintage Glenn Martin. He believed it, and it was inculcated in those who worked for him, whether in Nebraska, Maryland, or wherever the company's fortunes would take them. Although not so named at the time, the pledge was the embodiment of a corporate culture that two decades later would take the name of and become widely known as mission success.[7]

When G. T. "Tom" Willey succeeded Schafe as vice president and general manager at Omaha in February 1943, the plant had been rolling out B-26s on schedule for two and a half months. It then went thirty-three months from that date until the war's end without missing a production schedule. Tom Willey was an Englishman of some reputation. One of the legendary production giants of the Martin company, he had already been with the company fourteen years before being named to the Nebraska position, but more important, he had been working in aviation for twenty-five years. A native of Bristol, he had started with the Bristol Airplane Company right after World War I and had worked his way across the Atlantic and into the States by way of Vickers in Montreal.

Earl R. Willhite, who spent forty-six years with the company and knew G. T. Willey well, remembered the man's humorous foibles as well as his marvelous skills as a factory production boss. "The man did not know the word 'can't' nor was he very tolerant of anyone who spoke it," Willhite recalled.[8] A very religious man in his private life, Tom Willey was an eloquent and forceful speaker, a lay preacher who was never heard to utter a swear word. "But when riled, he really blustered, and his 'goldurn' was guaranteed to wither whomever he had targeted," Willhite said. He had a well-earned reputation for verbally bracing victims against the wall if he suspected them of carelessness or, worse, not trying. Willhite laughed about the time Willey changed the wrong tire on his own car during a rainstorm. But he remembered him equally for his disciplined approach to factory production and as "one of the kindest of men," considerate, and caring of those who worked with or for him.

Willhite, a twenty-three-year-old spot welder in the sheet metal department who had won three simultaneous awards for production improvement suggestions, did not know Willey when he first ran into him at Middle River before Willey was assigned to Omaha. The company was building a sheet metal engine mount, the first ever built, and it had a lot of complications and engineering problems. Willhite was the liaison between the job and tool planning.

"I had just come into D-building when I saw this crowd of

people and this guy in a suit, bronze badge and all, telling them: 'Do this. Do that. Do this. Do that.' I didn't know who he was, but people were scurrying around, and I knew what he was telling them wasn't going to work. So I waded through the crowd and said, 'I beg your pardon. I don't think we can really do what you want.' The man turned to me and asked, 'Who are you?' and I told him, 'I'm Earl Willhite. I'm the liaison assigned to this job.' 'Well, young man. Do you know how to do it?' he demanded. 'Yes sir, I do know.' And he said, 'Well then, go ahead and do it!' "

Willhite said Tom Willey walked off and the crowd dispersed, all except one fellow who asked him if he knew the person he had been talking to. "I said, 'I haven't the slightest notion.' 'That was Tom Willey, and he is in charge of the whole works,' he told me. Then he told a story about how Willey, only a couple of weeks earlier, invited one of the supervisors to take a walk with him. They walked to the front gate, where Willey put the supervisor out and told him, 'Don't ever come back.' "

Just a few days after Willhite's initial encounter, he was called to the office, where Willey suggested, "Let's take a walk." As they walked outside, Willhite said, "I'm thinking: 'Oh, boy, we're going towards the gate. Am I going to be the second one?' Only we get to his parked Cadillac, and he says, 'Get in. Take a ride with me.' So we rode around awhile, and he wanted to know how long I had been there and what experience I had. I still thought we were going to drive out the gate, and that would be it. But he apparently appreciated me speaking up, sorta getting him out of a pinch. We became good friends, and I really respected and liked him."

Two months after taking charge of the Omaha plant, Tom Willey hosted the President of the United States. On April 26, 1943, accompanied by Nebraska governor Dwight Griswald and Glenn Martin, President Roosevelt rode in an open car on an hour-long tour of the B-26 assembly line. It was on this visit, Willey would tell associates many years later, that the president and commander-in-chief took him aside, without any aides or secret servicemen, and confided that the Martin Omaha plant had been chosen to build a second plane, the Boeing B-29 Superfortress.[9]

Within the month it was announced that the Martin-Nebraska plant would become a second-source producer of the Boeing plane. Tom Willey always attributed that contract to the exceptional record of on-time, top-quality production of the B-26 by the Omaha employees, an achievement that continued through production of 536

FDR, governor, and Martin tour Omaha plant

B-29s. The plant and its employees won the Army-Navy "E" flag for production excellence, then subsequently added three white stars to it for the equivalent of four successive awards.[10]

In the summer of 1944, the government asked the four second-source producers of the B-29 how long it would take to modify a select few of the planes to carry an inordinately large bomb. Time rather than cost was the critical item, they were told, and there should be no negative impact on regular production. Three of the four respondents estimated it would take three to four months and that it would have a negative impact on the production line. Omaha said it could do the modification in six weeks.

Willey's plant got the job, and work on the secret modification began in the fall of 1944 when the Army Air Corps asked the plant to design a carrier capable of hauling a special bomb. Working seven days a week, Martin engineers completed the work in six weeks. An inert bomb, a reasonable copy of the real thing, was brought to the plant for trial installation by Colonel Paul W. Tibbets, Jr. (the same pilot who earlier had been introduced to the B-26 by General Jimmy Doolittle). Tibbets named the Martin-built B-29 *Enola Gay* after his mother. The Omaha plant subsequently manufactured some twenty of the specially designed B-29s. Only one other would see that special use, however.[11]

At 8:15 in the morning (Japanese time) on August 6, 1945, the *Enola Gay,* piloted by Colonel Tibbets, dropped a single atomic bomb weighing nine thousand pounds on Hiroshima. That bomb, called "Little Boy," exploded over the city with the force of twenty thousand tons of TNT, the equivalent in power of what two thousand B-29s could carry in conventional explosives. When the Japanese still refused to surrender, another Martin Omaha–built B-29, this one named "Bockscar," dropped a second A-bomb three days later on Nagasaki. Japanese surrender followed within a week. Thus painfully ended World War II, yet saving the lives, it was estimated, of hundreds of thousands of American and Allied servicemen, as well as Japanese who would have been killed had the war continued with an invasion of Japan's main islands.

At the time of the Nagasaki bombing, and for some time after, there was considerable confusion as to the identification of the second atom bomb–carrying B-29. In what has been described as "the greatest identification snafu of World War II, Bockscar was not identified with the historic Nagasaki mission for more than a year after the war ended. A third Omaha-built B-29, "The Great Artiste," was flown on the Nagasaki mission as an instrumentation plane. Its pilot that day was Captain Frederick C. Bock, whose regular plane was Bockscar. But the official Air Force communiqué as well as published accounts, including those given by eyewitnesses, listed The Great Artiste as the Nagasaki bomber.

The confusion came about this way: Prior to the mission, with nicknames removed from both aircraft, Major Sweeney and Captain Bock exchanged aircraft in order to avoid transferring some sensitive scientific instruments. Because Sweeney had been assigned to the bomb-dropping mission, and in fact did fly it, it was assumed he was piloting his regular aircraft, The Great Artiste, and so it was reported officially. Further complicating the "official" snafu, Bockscar's fuselage identification number, 77, was later changed to 89, the number of The Great Artiste, and to this day still displays that number as it stands on permanent exhibit in the Air Force Museum at Wright-Patterson Air Force Base, Dayton, Ohio.[12]

The war's end also meant the closing of the Omaha plant, which had compiled the longest on-schedule production record of any aircraft manufacturing plant in the country—thirty-three months without a missed delivery. The nation's wartime production chief,

William Knudsen, called Tom Willey "the hardest-hitting production man I ever knew,"[13] a fitting tribute to a man who would go on to become, before his retirement in 1967, vice president of manufacturing for the Glenn L. Martin Company, the first general manager of Martin's test and launch operations at Cape Canaveral during the early days of the rocket business, and finally vice president and general manager of the Orlando division.

■

EVEN THOUGH MARTIN PLANES were reaching the war before America's involvement as a combatant, the pre–Pearl Harbor atmosphere around Middle River was somewhat less charged. It was in 1940 that a twenty-two-year-old from Pitman, New Jersey, the ink still wet on his engineering diploma from Drexel University, joined "Martin's" and was assigned to the engineering laboratories. His name was John Donald Rauth, and his first assignment was "a very special secret project for Mr. Martin," he was told. Taken to a small room in the instrument lab, young Rauth was equipped with a jeweler's drill press, a bushel of freshly shelled kernels of corn, and a mortar and pestle. Gordon Bell, who ran the lab, told the newcomer his task was to drill a small hole in each kernel of corn, being careful not to punch the hole all the way through the kernel.

When he had drilled each and every one of the tens of thousands of corn kernels, he was to use the mortar and pestel to prepare a pasty mixture that he was to carefully stuff into each kernel. Working the majority of three days, including Saturday and Sunday, Rauth completed the task and reported back to Bell. "Could I know what this is for?" he asked, at a loss to see what relevance his task had to the airplane business. Bell explained that the pasty substance Rauth had painstakingly prepared and stuffed into each carefully drilled kernel contained a harmless drug. The doped corn was to be mixed with hundreds of pounds of regular corn and spread across Mr. Martin's Eastern Shore farm. The migrant ducks and geese hopefully would eat it and fall unconscious just long enough to be banded. It was all part of a study Glenn was making of wildfowl migratory habits.

"What the 'old man' hadn't figured on," Rauth said with a laugh many years later in recalling the incident, "was that the ducks and geese were too smart." They ate all the good corn and left the doped stuff for the less discriminating chickens, which were found by the hundreds, unconscious on their backs, much to the chagrin of neighboring farmers.

Whether Don Rauth was the only engineer so assigned or one of many—some recall a whole roomful of fledgling engineers, multiple drill presses, bushels of corn, and pots of dope—is not important. The incident became a favorite story told about Mr. Martin around the factory. It did nothing to deter young Rauth, who went on to become successively and successfully chief project engineer for all systems development, general sales manager, director of materiel, vice president and general manager of, first, the nuclear division and then all strategic missile and space activities, president of the aerospace company, president of the aluminum subsidiary, and president and a director of the corporation.

Ultimately, J. Donald Rauth became the corporation's third chief executive and chairman of the board for nearly five years prior to his retirement in 1983. His entire professional career of forty-three years was spent with one enterprise, the Glenn L. Martin Company and its successor, Martin Marietta Corporation. Not a bad mark for a young engineer whose first assignment involved a lot of corn and the precision use of a jeweler's drill press.[14]

■

PATRIOTIC FERVOR RAN HIGH throughout American industry during World War II, and workers in the aircraft industry, and the Martin company in particular, took no backseat. Reports from the war front repeatedly extolled the virtues of Martin aircraft in the fight. Fliers on leave, military brass, and government officials were frequent visitors to the Baltimore and Omaha plants. Glenn Martin's legion of Hollywood friends from his early days in California, many of them stars, plus others in the entertainment world toured the plants. VIPs visiting the Martin plant at Middle River in a virtually constant stream included not only members of Congress and Army, Navy, and War Department officials but also heroes from the war front and foreign dignitaries. The fliers and the heads of governments always brought high praise for the performance of Martin planes they had operated or planes that had been flown by their armed forces.

In February 1942, the company launched *The Martin Star,* a picture-filled, glossy employee magazine with a color cover. Its name was taken from the company's long-used commercial symbol, a five-pointed white star bearing the words "Martin U.S.A." on a field of blue enclosed in a red and white circle. The cover photograph on volume I, number 1, was of three men standing at attention; a helmeted soldier and a sailor flanking a white-coveralled Martin factory

Morale-boosting war news

worker with drill in hand. Inside, in the "Message from the Chief," Glenn extolled his fellow employees as "Soldiers of Industry . . . [who] strike decisive blows for freedom" in forging the weapons that beat down the enemy.

The lead editorial, titled appropriately "Hitch Your Wagon," dedicated the *Star* as the journal of an organization "grown too great for the word of mouth to suffice in our common dealings." "Time was when all Martin folk knew each other; when there was a close personal bond between us. But now we are one of the great industrial concerns of the nation, with the most important job in the world. . . . It is essential that we preserve our personal ties . . . that we know what is going on . . . that we understand the common aims so that our individual contributions, large or small, may be given full effect. It is to this end that *The Martin Star* is dedicated."[15]

Another issue[16] that same year announced the creation of the "Order of the Purple Martin," a badge of honor to be awarded Martin employees, principally inventors, when their work became the subject of a patent. Its symbol, a patented design by Glenn himself, consisted of a purple martin in full flight silhouetted against the Martin Star. It was awarded as a lapel pin with scroll and was personally presented by Mr. Martin as soon as a patent was issued.

The bird was chosen by Glenn not only because of the name but also because of its hemispheric range from Alaska to Brazil, its 106-miles-per-hour speed of flight (about the landing speed of the B-26), and its tenacity as a fighter against larger bullying birds. Although still in existence as an award for patent holders, the pin is no longer given.

The same issue of the magazine that announced the Purple Martin award also carried a red, white, and blue card that employees were urged to tear out and "paste up for all to see."[17] Typifying the pride and patriotism rampant throughout the company in the 1940s, it pledged:

> I AM GOING TO WIN THIS WAR!
> I AM GOING TO WIN IT PERSONALLY!
> I AM GOING TO WIN IT QUICKLY!
> My reasons for doing this are entirely my business.
> I AM not asking for any help in this matter,
> FOR I SHALL GO AND GET ANY HELP THAT I MAY NEED.
> Those who feel as I do shall receive my utmost cooperation.
> OTHERS HAD BEST KEEP OUT OF MY WAY.
> I thank God for my good health and the opportunity before me.
> (Signed)   (Dated)

During the war years, the entire Middle River facility had been camouflaged against the eventuality of an air raid. It was an elaborate subterfuge that included painting the roofs of the factory buildings, hangars, and airport runway and erecting huge, tentlike canvas coverings over the acres of automobile parking lots. Seen from the air, the deception changed the course of the river and the coastline, making it appear there was a community there instead of the mammoth plant and airfield.

On Palm Sunday, 1942, Baltimore and its surroundings awoke to one of the area's heaviest spring snowstorms. More than twenty-two inches of wet snow fell that morning, and the weight on the canvas camouflage coverings at the Martin plant snapped supporting poles as if they were matchsticks, dumping canvas and tons of snow on the cars beneath. It was weeks before the mess was cleared and the cars that weren't damaged could be liberated.

The class of '43 at Baltimore City College remembered that snowstorm for more than the extended Easter holiday it provided during their junior year. As part of the war effort, students who took wood shop at City, Poly, and the area's other high schools had been recruited to build the tent poles that supported the camouflage netting, and they got to do it again when the broken poles had to be replaced. One of the Poly students was Phil Rogers, whose dad, Philip Quiggle Rogers, worked at Martin's and lost the family car, a 1941 Chevrolet, to the collapsed netting. Young Phil, a high school freshman at the time, later spent more than forty years working for the company in Baltimore, Orlando, Vandenberg, and Denver. His father was an employee for twenty-eight years; Phil's first wife, Shirley, for a year; his second wife, Sandra, more than twelve years; his mother-in-law, Helen Milligan, thirty years; his son, Jeffrey, and Jeffrey's wife, Leslie, more than a dozen years each; his youngest son, Paul, briefly with the company at Vandenberg while a college student; Phil's sister, Diana, six years; his brother, Harry, more than thirty-five years; and Harry's wife, Eva, more than twenty years. In all, eleven Rogers kinsmen worked almost two hundred years, cumulatively, with the company, and some were still counting their service in 1993.

Wartime spirit received an added boost when President Roosevelt, who had toured the Omaha plant in the spring of 1943, made a similar tour of the Middle River plant. "It was one of the biggest memories I have of those days," Earl Willhite said. The other was seeing the B-26s take off from the Martin airport directly for combat. "That was the greatest feeling of pride and accomplishment because you felt we were in it and the planes we were building were going right to the front where they were needed," Willhite said.[18]

"But when the president came to the plant, that was very special. They drove his open car right down the aisles of the factory. The president waved to us, and Glenn L. and Governor Herbert J. O'Conor were sitting in the car with him. Of course, we were all Roosevelt people in those days. As far as we were concerned, he had stopped the depression. It was kind of a thrill to see him close up. Then later, when he died, we were all out on the tracks in front of the plant when his funeral train went by." Earl Willhite remembered "both times very vividly."

■

THE END OF THE WAR wrote epitaphs for both the China and Philippine Clippers. For the Philippine Clipper, it was a rather dramatic ending. As *Air & Space* magazine reported thirty-eight years later: At 6:30 in the morning of December 8, 1941, the Philippine Clipper took off for a routine ten-hour flight from Wake to Guam, fifteen hundred miles to the west. Across the international dateline to the east in Midway and Hawaii, it was still December 7. As the Philippine Clipper disappeared in the distance, the senior military man on Wake, a Navy lieutenant, received a terse message from naval command in Honolulu: "Oahu under attack." Confused momentarily, he thought it might be the Navy gunboat *Oahu*, then on the Yangtze River in China, until a second message identified the attack as being at Pearl Harbor on Hawaii's Oahu Island.

The Philippine Clipper was radioed to turn back, aborting its last peacetime flight. Immediately unloaded, it was refueled and was being stripped of all unnecessary furnishings with the intention of sending it out to search for the Japanese fleet when bombs began falling on Wake. Riddled with bullets, but none below the water line and otherwise undamaged, the Philippine Clipper escaped the Japanese and spent the entire war in Navy service, as did the China Clipper. Both Martin planes were used to ferry soldiers, sailors, and medical supplies between San Francisco and Pearl Harbor almost daily.[19]

Neither plane lived to see old age, however. On January 21, 1943, during a severe storm, the Philippine Clipper flew into the side of a mountain north of San Francisco and was destroyed, killing all on board. The China Clipper did survive its military service and was returned to Pan American. It took up a scheduled passenger run, this time across the Atlantic, from Miami to Leopoldville in the Belgian Congo, with intermediate stops in the Caribbean.

On January 8, 1945, after leaving Miami at 6:08 A.M. as Pan Am Flight 161, the China Clipper banked for its landing approach over the bay at Port of Spain, Trinidad. Apparently the captain was confused by the glassy surface of the water and misjudged his altitude and his angle of descent. The big ship struck the water sooner than anticipated and broke in half. Nine crew members and fourteen passengers were killed instantly. Seven survived the crash.[20]

PART V

New Directions
1945–55

■

CHAPTER 19

Peace but Not Prosperity

■

T he August end of hostilities in the Pacific, following by
three months the German surrender in Europe, had an
almost immediate impact on the aircraft industry back
home in America. Specifically for the Glenn L. Martin Company,
peak employment levels dropped dramatically. All operations at the
Glenn L. Martin–Nebraska subsidiary ended almost overnight, and
the jobs of its ten thousand workers ceased to exist. The government-
owned facility was mothballed and quickly turned over to the government. Many years later the buildings became part of the
headquarters of the Strategic Air Command.

There would be life after war for the Middle River complex, but
on a drastically reduced basis. Plant 2, entirely government owned,
would see production of aircraft for a time and, later, nonproduction
life as a government warehouse and documents storage depot. The
wartime work force, which had peaked at more than 53,000 for all
the Baltimore facilities, stood at approximately 34,000 the day the
war ended. Within one month there were 10,000 fewer Martin jobs
at the Middle River plant and only 14,250 in the entire Baltimore
area. The sales dive was even more precipitous, from $356,162,188 at
the end of 1945 to $37,640,958 a year later, an almost tenfold drop
in twelve months.

Several military projects would continue, but the all-out war
effort had allowed no time or resources to plan for a peacetime

Postwar Middle River

future of plowshares instead of swords. In fact, the government had all but prohibited such planning by fiat with its contractors. A month after victory in Japan, "V-J Day," Glenn wrote to his old friend and early patron, Frank Garbutt, in Los Angeles:

> V-J Day came with such suddenness that the government was far off-base as far as reconversion is concerned. We have found ourselves in the midst of a very exciting struggle to save some of the industrial debris floating around on the sea of uncertainty.... We were not permitted [while the war was on] to do any engineering or research work of any kind on postwar business or designs of any description, except war designs, as ordered from time to time by the government. . . . We are in for rather intensive planning to hold our productive strength until orderly business can be established.[1]

Those few new designs allowed by Martin's customer that might have commercial application included the JRM-1, the giant Mars seaplane, which had its first flight slightly more than one month before the war ended. Three of them were completed and delivered to the Navy in 1945.

On October 16, 1945, the veil was lifted from the ten-year-old mystery of another Martin flying boat, the Soviet Clipper. An official press release issued by the Martin company and quoting "Russians in a position to speak authoritatively" disclosed that the Soviets did indeed reassemble and fly the Martin-built 156. What's more, they built a big plant to manufacture the flying boats on the Sea of Azov in the Crimea. The plant had been completely tooled and production begun, with the first Russian-built Clipper being readied for flight, when the Nazis overran Kiev, Kharkov, and Odessa. Rather than have the factory and seaplanes fall into enemy hands, the Russians blew up the plant together with the completed and partially completed ships, according to the news release.

The original Martin-built 156—the Soviet Clipper—flew throughout 1941 and 1942 from bases on the Black and Caspian seas, the Russians said. Stripped of her luxurious fittings and all nonessential weight, the Soviet Clipper's twenty-four-hundred-mile range was greatly extended. By operating from Caspian bases eighty-five feet below sea level, the big clipper was able to take off with loads heavier than its sixty-two-thousand-pound gross weight limitation. The release said the Soviet Clipper flew patrol bombing missions, carried paratroops, and was used to evacuate wounded after the Nazis smashed through Crimean defenses and reached the Black Sea. Still quoting Russian sources, the Martin release turned to prose in describing the big plane's repeated "defiance of the Luftwaffe's aerial might":

> The Clipper was flown into Sevastopol night after night to evacuate wounded men during the historic siege of the Crimean city. Flying without fighter escort through moonless skies, she swept low over the Romanian seaport of Constanza, setting great fires in the surrounding oil fields. In dim twilight, she frequently dived through the overcast to drop paratroopers and supplies to the hard-pressed garrison fighting in the rubble that was once Sevastopol.[2]

What the release did not say and what still remains a mystery is what happened to the Soviet Clipper *after* the war.

P5M Marlin in production

Marlin rendezvous with sub

Also in 1945, an experimental modification of the war-veteran PBM series Mariners, the XPBM-5A, was about to be rolled out of the factory. It was identical to its predecessors except that it had been made amphibious by the addition of wheels and was accepted by the Navy after its first flight on December 10 of that year. Thirty-seven of the versatile amphibians, which also carried JATO bottles—the acronym for Jet-Assisted Takeoff—were produced in the next three years.

Also in the design pipeline as the war wound down were two other Navy planes—the AM-1 Mauler, a carrier-based, torpedo dive-bomber of unprecedented speed, armament, and maneuverability, and the P4M Mercator, a land-based patrol bomber. Nicknamed the "Able-Mabel," the Mauler was the heaviest and largest aircraft ever built for operation from a carrier deck. It was built around the same R-4360 Pratt & Whitney engine used on the giant JRM-2, the fifth and largest of the MARS flying boats. It had more range, more payload, more firepower, more of everything. With a gross weight of 29,332 pounds, the Mauler almost doubled its own weight with armament, including three 2,200-pound torpedoes, twelve 250-pound bombs shackled beneath the wings, and four twenty-millimeter cannon mounted in the leading edge of the wings. It could fly at more than 350 miles per hour and had a dive speed in excess of 500 miles per hour. Although it never saw action in World War II, the Navy purchased 152 Maulers between 1946 and 1949.

The Mercator was designed primarily for reconnaissance to replace the Navy's aging fleet of Lockheed PV-2 aircraft. Its two Pratt & Whitney 4360 internal combustion engines gave it a range of three thousand miles, and it was equipped with two Allison jet engines, housed in the same pods with the regular engines, for additional take-off thrust. It was one of the first aircraft to combine the two forms of propulsion, not counting the conventional JATO bottles used on some aircraft such as the Martin Maulers. Only twenty-one Mercators were bought by the Navy, the first in 1946 and the last in 1949.

Although the Mauler and Mercator programs enabled the company to hold its "productive strength," as Glenn phrased it, in the immediate postwar period, he envisioned permanent employment of eighteen to twenty thousand people. If he could reemploy some of those talented, experienced aircraft builders from the thousands who had been furloughed after V-J Day, they could turn out civilian aircraft in addition to whatever limited military planes the government would procure in peacetime, he reasoned.

Within months of the Japanese surrender, Glenn did two things:

He set a group of designers to work on a two-engine commercial airliner, the 2-0-2. The commercial airlines had not had a new plane since before the war, and all of their equipment had been badly overworked in the war effort. He also seized what would be a temporary opportunity to fill the airlines' equipment needs sooner by converting war-developed military cargo and troop-carrying planes, notably the Douglas C54.

When the Army Air Transport Command announced that hundreds of its big four-engine troop carriers would be surplused and sold to commercial operators, the Martin company moved swiftly to capture this reconversion business. Flooding the market with surplus military transports had the effect of delaying development and manufacture of new designs, but Martin made the most of the new business opportunity. Salesmen called on virtually every airline, offering the Martin plant and experienced people for the modification work. It did not hurt that Martin's reputation for producing the Marauder, the Maryland, the Baltimore, the Mariner, and the China Clipper had preceded salesmen making their calls. Nearly every domestic airline and several foreign carriers contracted with the company for conversion of the government surplus C-54 Army transports they had purchased. Martin turned them into gleaming, handsomely appointed and upholstered civilian airliners.

Fuzz Furman said B and C Buildings, which had been crowded with Mariners and Mars flying boats only a few months before, were wall-to-wall in C-54s. "We'd strip them down to the shell and completely replace everything," Furman said. "We could turn a plane around in ninety days, and we were doing it for the major lines, Trans World, Northwest, Capital, Chicago Southern, China National, Braniff, Northeast, American, KLM—you name it."[3]

One of the planes was for Chiang Kai-shek, according to C. E. "Buzz" Showalter, who worked on the C-54 conversions "hooking wire and stuff." The airplane being outfitted for the Chinese Nationalist president "had all gold fittings and gold plating," Showalter recalled. "It was a beautiful airplane." Some others were under conversion for Eastern Air Lines, and Showalter remembered Eddie Rickenbacker, Eastern's president, coming through on an inspection trip. "He was one tough bird. If he saw something he didn't like, he would chew and chew—not on me, of course, but on my boss. He was something, really tough."[4]

During 1946 and 1947, Martin remade a total of 110 C-54 military transports into commercial airlines and modified two hundred Douglas C-47s, the military version of the civilian DC-3, into target-towing aircraft for the Air Force. It was good business and kept the work force in place for the Martin designs that followed. Most notable was the "2-0-2" twin-engine, forty-four-passenger commercial airliner. It was Martin's bid to grab a relatively small but untapped market for a medium-range plane that the company expected would put it solidly in the postwar civilian airplane business. No such plane existed, and if the company could get the jump, it would not have to compete with larger competitor aircraft, notably the Douglas DC-6 and the Lockheed Constellation. Both already existed in military versions and were readily convertible to civilian commercial service.

It was not a bad gambit, and in a relatively short time the company had tentative orders from seventeen airlines for 327 of the new planes, mostly the "2-0-2," but also for the "4-0-4," a pressurized version. It was a good-looking airplane, thanks in part to Glenn's personal design stamp; it was his pet, but it wasn't without problems. George Trimble, a thirty-year-old aerodynamics engineer for the company, was asked to get involved with the 2-0-2. Pat Tibbs was having trouble getting the new plane flight-certified by the Civil Aeronautics Authority. Trimble said, "Pat and I had worked closely on the first B-26s built in Omaha and had gotten to know each other pretty well, so he asked if I'd take a look and see if I could fix the problem. That's when I first met the old man—Mr. Martin. I was called up to his great big office. I'd never seen one that big. And he had drawings of the airplane—side views and everything—and he told me 'I don't like it.' Dihedral was his pet project, and he wasn't too interested in some punk kid telling him something was wrong with his plane. But there wasn't enough angle in the wing, and Mr. Martin didn't like the way I had bent them.

" 'I'm sorry,' I told him. 'I don't either like it or dislike it, but I don't think it will fly unless we put that much angle in.' And he said, 'Well, would you care if we reduced the dihedral two degrees? I think it will work all right at two degrees.'

"If you can imagine, I was plenty scared," Trimble added, "but I believed in what I was doing and I had a lot of good reasons for doing it that way. So I told him I didn't think it would certify his way, but we went back to the wind tunnel and tried it both ways.

"Glenn L. was awfully smart, from what I could see, and he had lots and lots of experience, only not with the CAA; those guys wanted an airplane to fly 'hands off' before they'd certify it."[5]

George Rodney is fond of another memory of Glenn L. and the 2-0-2 design. Rodney, a Carnegie Institute of Technology mechanical engineer "with an aero option" won his Army Air Corps wings at

Liberal, Kansas, which is steeped in early Glenn L. Martin folklore and fact. He started with the Martin company in 1945 as an aerodynamicist and was working for Trimble, who had talked him into being a test pilot. The first aircraft he flight tested for the company was the 2-0-2, which is when he first encountered Mr. Martin.

"We had a directional stability problem on the early 2-0-2," Rodney said, "and had to put some more dorsal [top] fin on it. We ran some wind tunnel tests at MIT on about three different dorsal fin shapes. We had arrived at them more or less just by drawing lines on paper. We wanted to have as small a tail as possible because of weight, but we decided to build all three, then start with the smallest and work up to the point where we didn't need any more.[6]

"Well, Glenn L. wandered in one day and saw those three dorsal fins sitting there. 'That's ugly,' he said, looking at the smallest, which we had hoped to use. 'Use this one,' and he pointed to the biggest. So that's the one that ended up on the airplane. Mr. Martin liked it because it had the best lines. He was a stickler for good design. We never did find out whether that fin was optimum or not."

George Rodney later became one of Martin Marietta's most famous test pilots, and in more than forty-one years with the company he figured prominently in engineering, test, and quality control on such major programs as the P6M SeaMaster, the world's first jet seaplane; the 2-0-2 and 4-0-4 commercial airliners; the Titan intercontinental ballistic missile; and Skylab, the world's first space station. He left the company in 1986 when the National Aeronautics and Space Administration drafted him to be its "safety czar" and chief of quality in the wake of the Challenger Space Shuttle accident. His formal title at NASA was "Associate Administrator, Office of Safety and Mission Quality," a position he filled with distinction until he retired in 1992.

Unfortunately, initial enthusiasm that had created tentative orders for more than three hundred of the new 2-0-2 planes was not sustained. By the time it went into service with Northwest Airlines, which bought twenty-five in 1946 and 1947, and Trans World, which purchased a dozen in 1950, plus a half-dozen more sold to airlines in Chile and Venezuela, competitor planes had taken over the medium-range market.

One of the major disappointments of the dwindling airline interest in the 2-0-2 involved Eddie Rickenbacker, the colorful and celebrated aviator and World War I ace, who was president of Eastern Airlines. He had visited the plant and had personally taken an option on a quantity of 2-0-2s with Glenn. But he later changed his mind.

Many in the company felt he should have left some money on the table, but he didn't. Glenn Martin graciously honored Rickenbacker's change of mind and let him walk away with a handshake. When Martin later came out with a pressurized version, the "4-0-4," Rickenbacker purchased sixty of them, and forty-one went to Trans World. Combined sales were well below projections, however.

One of the dozens of stories about "Captain Eddie" was told by Don Rauth, who was working in sales and service. Rauth was assigned to be Rickenbacker's host on one of the airline executive's whirlwind visits to the plant to check on progress of the new planes. Rauth took him to final assembly to see the first 2-0-2, which was then close to delivery.

"The workers, all women, were doing the interior fabric lining, stitching and sewing and so forth. Captain Eddie, wearing his famous wide-brim hat, walked all the way through to the rear of the airplane

Rickenbacker, Martin, and 2-0-2

where the lavatories are. He didn't say boo to anybody," Rauth said, "just took down his trousers and sat on the john. Then he cussed a bit, and with all those women listening, bellowed, 'Who in hell ever designed this seat? You can't even get your "blank and blanks" in it.' He was a different personality, not the normal VIP we were used to."[7]

On another visit to see the 4-0-4, Rauth said Rickenbacker "raised cain about the physical attributes of the Eastern falcon," the bird in the airline insignia that was being painted on the tail of the plane. It depicted a falcon about to land, its feet and claws extended, its wings up.

" 'Where in hell did you get that falcon?' " Rauth said Rickenbacker demanded. When told it was from Eastern's own art department, the airline executive insisted it was not, and "nothing would satisfy him until we got one of his own art people to come to the plant and confirm that the Eastern falcon was so endowed and really did look like that."

Without question, Martin had been the first to offer a medium-range commercial transport, and at the time of peak airline interest was the only manufacturer in the field. More than one prospective buyer asked for complete drawings and specifications and more time to look at them in detail, Rauth said. Always the complete gentleman, although perhaps a bit naive in such matters, Glenn obliged them.

Although Martin had been the first, competitor aircraft that were similar in appearance and performance eventually captured the market. George Rodney believed the problem was the company's misreading of the customer's real need. "Usually those commercial airplanes have a lead airline. Although United, Northwest, and practically everybody else had peripheral interest, the lead airline was American. They were the ones forcing development of a 2-0-2-type airplane," Rodney said.

"The gimmick was that they really wanted a pressurized airplane, and Convair recognized this. We weren't quite smart enough. At that time the industry really didn't have pressurized airplanes, and there was a significant amount of risk in building one. American Airlines wasn't sure one could be built. They talked to us about it, but we built a nonpressurized airplane, the 2-0-2." Convair built the pressurized 240, which worked, and it stole the market. The two planes looked very much alike. In Rodney's opinion, "the 240 wasn't quite as good a flying machine as the 2-0-2, but it was pressurized, and it was what the customer really wanted."[8]

Rodney said Martin tried to play catch-up with the 4-0-4 and at

Airliners in production for TWA

the same time followed the lead of another customer, United Air Lines. UAL also wanted a pressurized plane but one smaller and faster than the 2-0-2. As the lead airline pushing it, Rodney said, UAL "encouraged us into building the 3-0-3. It was all of those things they wanted, really a neat airplane. Pilots loved it. But we had not done any total market research ourselves. Plus by that time we couldn't afford to produce a third transport."

Meanwhile, the 2-0-2 was flying with Northwest and TWA, and a half-dozen had been sold to two airlines in South America, LAN of Chile and LAV of Venezuela. The legendary Howard Hughes, then head of TWA, was active in his company's purchase of the 2-0-2 and later the 4-0-4, and George Rodney got to know and fly with him on more than one occasion. Rodney spent about six weeks at the Hughes factory in Culver City, California, first with the 2-0-2 and later with the prototype of the 4-0-4, demonstrating single-engine takeoffs, loss of an engine at various speeds and altitudes, and in other competition with Convair planes. Rodney said, "We did real well, and the

Convair almost crashed, which was one of the things that helped sell the Martin planes to TWA.

"Howard Hughes would come out and fly, always at night," Rodney said, "and always he'd have somebody with him, usually [Hollywood starlet] Terry Moore at that time," which was the late forties before Hughes became a total recluse. "We'd fly over to Las Vegas and to Palm Springs and places like that. Sometimes, if Hughes didn't want to pilot the plane himself, he'd call me . . . always in the middle of the night . . . and say, 'Hey, want to join me?' and I'd say, 'Sure.' He wouldn't think anything about calling at three o'clock in the morning and say, 'Meet me in ten minutes.' Then we'd go off to the Beverly Hills Hotel or some other posh place and have breakfast or dinner, or whatever meal he was having, before we flew. He never carried any money," Rodney said. "He usually had this real sneaky character around who took care of the money. I can't remember his name, but later on he got into a lot of trouble . . . and went to jail."

Rodney said Hughes was very shy, "but he was very thoughtful, very polite when he was with you. He was a good pilot, but he didn't pay attention to any of the rules. When we'd fly instruments, I'd file the instrument plan. It always would be in my name. And ol' Howard would sit in the left seat and just fly straight ahead for wherever we were going. It didn't matter what the flight plan called for. I would radio in that we were over such-and-such a checkpoint when sometimes we were a hundred miles away. Luckily it was before radar," Rodney added. "I was trying to keep my license."[9]

Rodney remembered that the employees at Culver City took Hughes's original Constellation out of the hangar every day and had it warmed up in case the eccentric billionaire wanted to fly it. Rodney also had a private tour of the Spruce Goose, the mammoth plywood seaplane that Hughes built but flew only once and then only a few feet off the water. "He knew I had a lot of time in seaplanes, and we talked about my maybe flying the Goose one day," Rodney said, "but nothing came of it. I had not decided I really wanted to fly the thing even if he had offered, but I did go through it." All in all, George Rodney found Howard Hughes to be a "very interesting man."

Hughes and TWA turned out to be Martin's biggest customer for commercial airlines. The airline purchased twelve of the 2-0-2s and forty-one of the 4-0-4s. What eventually complicated the sale of additional planes to other lines was the crash of one 2-0-2 and the severe damage of another late in the summer of 1948 during a violent storm over Wisconsin. Northwest Airlines blamed both accidents on metal fatigue and the design of the wing. Martin blamed

Northwest for allowing the planes to fly in such severe weather. All 2-0-2s were grounded for a time, further weakening an already moribund sales effort.

Subsequent success for the pressurized 4-0-4 appeared more likely until the invasion of South Korea put the nation on a wartime footing again. Prioritization of airplane materials and parts all but closed down 4-0-4 production. It was the final straw. When all was said and done, the company had lost its corporate shirt betting on commercial aircraft.

A series of ads in 1946 on the Martin 2-0-2, "New Queen of the Airways," had trumpeted what the plane would mean to airline operators, to airline pilots, to airline executives, to traffic and operations personnel, and to airline hostesses. But the queen became a wallflower, as did the 4-0-4.

Once the bugs had been worked out of the 2-0-2, the airlines that had purchased and operated the two Martin planes found them dependable and economically profitable to fly and maintain. Both aircraft went on to serve well mid-America's "short-haul" flying public. The only problem for their manufacturer was limited production. As with the 2-0-2, pricing on the 4-0-4 had been unrealistic, far below the cost of building the planes. The break-even point at which development costs are recovered and subsequent sales become profit was never reached. Both planes had missed the volume market. There simply were not enough buyers. As a result, there was a net 1947 loss of $19 million, and that red ink, combined with renegotiated wartime profits and other write-offs, plunged the company heavily into debt. Glenn had seen it coming. In May 1947 he asked the Reconstruction Finance Corporation for a $25 million loan. He was granted $16.6 million with the proviso that dividends be restricted and no new experimental programs be started without the agency's prior approval.

There was other, more promising activity at the company, but little of it was immediately profitable. Along with the commercial aircraft, Martin had developed a family of aircraft ground-support equipment—movable passenger boarding ramps, freight-handling trucks, luggage conveyors, and other paraphernalia that it sold successfully. Unfortunately, these products were never pursued as an independent business line, even though such basic equipment, successively modernized through many generations, remains in widespread use throughout the industry close to a half-century later.

There were also new "pilotless systems"—as missiles were called in those days—coming out of government research laboratories.

Even while the company was pursuing the commercial market, Uncle Sam was encouraging Martin and like firms to bid on the new programs. One was the TM-61 Matador tactical missile for the U.S. Air Force. Another was Lacrosse, a truck-mounted surface-to-surface missile, for which the company won a contract from the Army. For the Navy there was the Gorgon IV, an experimental subsonic ramjet and one of the earliest proof-of-principle missile programs, and Oriole, a Navy air-to-air test missile. Oriole had an active X-band radar, which meant it emitted its own beam to the target. When it received an echo in return, it would home on that bounce-back of its own energy source, much like a bat does with sound waves. Only sixteen Orioles were built, but the Martin test missile was the progenitor of the Sparrow missile, still in use by the Navy in the nineties.

Don Rauth, who was project manager for both Gorgon and Oriole, recalled the test program on Oriole: "The BAR [Bureau of Aeronautics Representative] flew an airplane as target for the Oriole radar, which we had installed in the nose of an Oriole missile mounted on the roof of the Middle River engineering building. We'd be on the target, then we'd lose it, track it, then lose it. Up in the airplane, the BAR could tell us without error when we were on him and when we had lost him. He didn't have any instrumentation to indicate it, but he said when that radar was on him, he got a peculiar taste in his mouth. It was amazing," Rauth said, "like tooth fillings that vibrate."[10]

There were also two new Martin-developed prototype airplanes built for the Air Force during the late forties. One was the XB-48, a six-jet medium bomber designed to Air Force specifications as a conservative backup in the event the more innovative Boeing B-47 didn't work out. Only a prototype and one copy were built. The other new design was the country's first tri-jet, an experimental support bomber designated the XB-51. It was one of the first airplanes to have a rotating, or variable-incidence, wing. It had tricycle landing gear and a tall flying tail, plus other innovations. But it was a complex airplane, and the tactical Air Force wanted something very simple, not only to fly but to maintain. Several of the XB-51's best features would be built into the B-57 at a later date.

The only production programs keeping the company afloat were the AM-1 Mauler, the PBM-5A amphibian Mariner, and the P4M Mercator. And under a contract from the Naval Research Laboratory, Martin began work on a high-altitude sounding rocket called Viking. It was an outgrowth of captured German V-2 missiles that rained destruction and death on England during the war.

Although sales climbed from $23 million at the end of 1947 to more than $72 million twelve months later, there was another net loss for 1948 of $16 million. Compounding the slower-than-anticipated growth of the civilian airplane market was the onset of the Berlin crisis in the spring of 1948. Although a spur to military procurements, it put in abeyance commercial airline spending for new planes.

In the fall of 1948, just twoscore years from his earliest attempt at airplane building in Santa Ana, Glenn and his mother decided to mount a sentimental return to his airplane beginnings. He was sixty-two, she a frail eighty-four. George Rodney was given what he described as "the magnificent sum" of $45,000 to convert the original 2-0-2A to a lush executive airplane. "The number one airplane never had an interior," Rodney said. "So I went around to all the supply houses, buying the biggest bargains I could find . . . upholstery, swivel chairs, couches, carpeting. And we cobbled up a pretty nice interior, sort of an executive suite."[11]

With Rodney and Carl Storey, a retired Army colonel who was in marketing on the commercial side of the house, as pilots, Mr. Martin and Minta took off across the country—to Cleveland, then to his Kansas boyhood towns of Salina and Liberal, and finally to California, to San Francisco and Santa Ana.

"One of the things that was notable about the trip," Rodney remembered, "was keeping a supply of the ol' man's favorite drink on board. Of course, he didn't drink anything alcoholic, but he always served and liked to drink what everybody thought was a sparkling white wine. It wasn't. It was just unfermented Catawba grape juice. You can still buy it, but in those days it was hard to find just anyplace, especially in quantity. Carl and I would chase all over the place in every town we landed so that we'd always have a supply on board."

Rodney had one other outstanding memory of that fortieth-anniversary flight back into the Martins' history. "It was when we landed in San Francisco and opened the door. This beautiful girl comes charging up the ramp. She shouts, 'Glenn!' . . . grabs him, and literally smothers him in hugs and kisses." It was Catherine Irvine, Glenn's first close female friend from Santa Ana—the one to whom he threw floral bouquets from his airplane—and one of only two girls with whom he was ever linked romantically.

"She really gave him and his mother a chase while we were in San Francisco, and she fixed Carl and me up at the Olympic Club, the most exclusive club in the Bay area. Rooms, meals, golf . . .

everything. We couldn't pay a dime, even a tip. We were Miss Irvine's guests the whole time we were there.''

In Santa Ana, former neighbors, friends, and the city's leaders rolled out the red carpet and feted the man who had "begun it all" in their midst. And by his side, as she had always been, was his mother Minta.

■

WHILE THE MARTIN COMPANY'S postwar landscape was hazy with disarray and red ink, just the opposite was true of American-Marietta. The company emerged from the war years more robust than ever; with sales of $13 million, compared with $3 million in 1940, it was poised for the greatest period of growth in its history. Correctly sensing that the end of hostilities would mark the beginning of a civilian boom in home building and construction of all kinds as millions of servicemen returned home, Grover Hermann set his sights on acquiring companies in these markets as well.

He hoped such a dream would be realized for his oldest son, Grover, Jr., who prior to the war was already being readied to follow his father into the business. But four months before the war's end in Europe, young Grover, a captain in the Eighth Armored Division, was killed in Germany. He was not yet thirty when a sniper's bullet found him on a road outside the Moselle River town of Trier, not far from the Luxembourg border, on his first day of combat, January 26, 1945.

This tragedy in the fifty-fifth year of Grover's life was followed closely by a second personal trauma. Later that same year, Hermann's marriage of thirty-one years to Hazel Hessinger, his high school sweetheart, ended in divorce. On October 27, Hermann's longtime secretary and confidante, Sarah Robertson Thurmond, became his second wife. From that time on, Grover Hermann appeared to breathe even more dramatic growth into the company he had created. There is no question that the year 1945 was a turning point in his personal life, and it clearly marked a watershed in the history of American-Marietta.[12]

During the years 1940 to 1948 that American-Marietta was picking up fifteen new companies, most of them in paint, total United States sales for that industry doubled. But for the same period, American-Marietta revenues skyrocketed to more than $37 million. Sales by the close of 1948 were twelve times the 1940 level of nearly

$3 million. Better than half of that remarkable increase had taken place in the three years following the war's end.

In 1947 the company offered its securities on the public market for the first time in its thirty-four-year existence, its common stock to be sold over the counter. By 1950, through aggressive growth in existing businesses and increased numbers of acquisitions, American-Marietta's net profit reached almost $3 million. That was the equivalent of 1940's total revenues and a handsome earnings return of nearly 7 percent on sales of $44 million. The company employed three thousand people in fourteen different businesses, including two dozen plants manufacturing paints and varnishes distributed through forty-six branches nationwide.[13]

Sales increased by nearly 50 percent to $65 million in 1951, and took another 15 percent hike to $75 million in 1952. That's the year Grover went into household cleaners and the home trade with the acquisition of 88 percent of the stock of O'Cedar Corp., maker of furniture polish, waxes, and Jonny Mops, a real household name.[14]

The "A-M" brand of paints ranked right alongside the country's leading paint producers, names such as Sherwin-Williams, duPont, Glidden, and National Lead. If its name was not as well known to consumers, it was because American-Marietta sold directly to other manufacturers. After all, the industrial market is "where demand is pretty constant and where quality is important," one of the company's production chiefs told *The Wall Street Journal* in a flattering front-page writeup headlined AMERICAN-MARIETTA'S RULE FOR RAPID RISE: EXPAND BY PURCHASING GOOD SMALL FIRMS.[15]

CHAPTER 20

Missiles and Rockets and Airplanes, Too

■

When Glenn and his mother returned home, none of the company's problems had gone away. Glenn once again had to confront the discouraging realities of trying to redirect an essentially government-driven armaments enterprise into a peacetime, civilian economy no longer in need of, or interested in, the "swords" of war. The 2-0-2 and the 4-0-4 were to have been the company's "plowshares," but the goal of Isaiah's prophetic vision was not easily attainable for much of the wartime aircraft industry. It certainly was not for the Martin company.

The return to his Midwest and West Coast beginnings had been, in a way, Glenn's last hurrah, a fitting climax to the decade of the forties, easily the most important and satisfying period of a long and lustrous career. He had clearly and early seen and publicly forecast Tennyson's "vision of the world, and all the wonder that would be."[1] He had not only predicted but helped realize "nations' airy navies grappling in the central blue," and he had also been the first to predict "the heavens fill with commerce." But that specific Tennysonian vision would elude his personal satisfaction of building very many such aerial vehicles of commerce.

None of the company's war-developed aircraft was readily adaptable for commercial transport. The only plane that might have been even remotely suited to civilian use was the giant troop-carrying Mars. Company postwar advertisements did their best to tout its commercial potential. Dramatic pictures and prose depicted multideck cruise ships with wings, a "125-ton airliner" able to "circle the globe on a two weeks' vacation with ample stopovers for sightseeing." Even earlier ads in 1939 and the 1940s had hinted at "stratosphere liners" that would span peacetime oceans of the future.[2]

A decade later, Glenn reveled in a Naval Transport Command statistic that credited the five Martin Mars seaplanes with carrying 250,000 passengers without a single fatality. But they would never transport commercial passengers as he had hoped. Multistoried stratospheric planes envisioned by Martin advertisements would indeed be developed—the most notable Boeing's 747—but they would be land-based, not the seaplanes of Glenn Martin's dreams.

While the thirties had produced two technological marvels in the Collier Trophy–winning B-10 and the China Clipper, the decade for the most part had not been a rouser from a business standpoint. All that changed in the first half of the forties. Along with business success came well-deserved recognition. The aerial armadas of war had been grim proof of Glenn's prophecies, and the magnificent machines produced in Martin factories were superb instruments of the victory over his country's enemies.

In addition to his company's technological powers, Glenn had become a champion of employee morale and well-being. Having hired the first women factory workers in the industry, he was also a leading proponent of the five-day workweek. Glenn had testified before a congressional committee that even during wartime the five-day workweek was the most efficient in terms of production. "Every man [and woman] should have a day a week to develop a hobby and a day for church," he said, unmindful of the fact that he seldom limited his own workweek to five days.[3]

In 1941 he had been awarded the Daniel Guggenheim medal by the Institute of the Aeronautical Sciences for his "contribution to aeronautical development." The next year, with a gift of $500,000 in company stock, he established in the IAS the Minta Martin Aeronautical Endowment Fund. Also in 1942, he received the Lord and Taylor Design Award. He also gave gifts of $1.7 million in 1944 and $800,000 in 1945 to the University of Maryland for the establishment of a school of engineering, and it became a reality in 1947 as the Glenn L. Martin Institute of Technology.

In addition to a seat on the University of Maryland's Board of Regents, Glenn was a trustee of the Baltimore Association of Commerce (the very group that had scoffed at his 1929 employment predictions), a member of the Maryland Commission on Postwar Planning and Development, and a member, as well as president in 1943, of the National Aircraft War Production Council. For some years he had been president of the League of Maryland Sportsmen and a trustee of the American Wildlife Foundation; and in 1943 he was recognized as America's outstanding conservationist with the *Sports Afield* trophy.

While serving on the mayor's committee to build a new Baltimore stadium as a memorial to the city's war dead, Glenn submitted a proposal in the spring of 1945 for an enclosed stadium with an innovative "floating roof." The idea of huge expanses unencumbered by support structures was not new to airplane manufacturing, but it would have been the first use of such a concept in a public building, and would have made the facility the nation's first all-weather stadium. Held in place by air pressure, the roof would have been anchored by rings to an independent perimeter wall built around the playing field and seating galleries, according to a May 2, 1945, newspaper account in *The Sun*. In what was called "the final report of the stadium committee," Jan Porel, an assistant to Glenn Martin and technical adviser to the committee, was quoted in the newspaper as telling Mayor Theodore Roosevelt McKeldin that an air-locked building "could be 'pumped up' and the roof raised to its suspended position in an hour and a half. Yet with all doors and windows open and the pumping machinery shut off, it would take a month for the roof to descend to the position in which it was built, and even then it would be twenty feet above the heads of spectators in the stadium."[4]

Three years later city fathers still were debating the merits and costs of a proposed memorial stadium. Glenn, who by then was chairman of the stadium commission, resigned in protest when the then mayor, Thomas D'Alessandro, was said to be wedded to building the new stadium on the site of the old one, thereby prejudicing the commission's consideration of three sites from an original list of twenty-two. Glenn's idea for an enclosed arena with a floating roof had been dismissed months before when W. W. Emmart, architect and onetime member of the Commission on City Planning, issued a statement quoted in *The Sun* of June 6, 1948, that said "a roof over a stadium is anathema, contrary to all traditions and expensive."[5]

With all of his laurels, activities, and the fantastic forties fading rapidly behind him, he had to face up to the devastating prospect of seeing his company destitute. It was not an acceptable course. When the banks rebuffed him on additional borrowing, he turned once more to the government to avoid bankruptcy. In doing so, he reluctantly had to agree in September 1949 to give up day-to-day control of the company, a Reconstruction Finance Corporation condition for additional financing. The presidency of the Martin company passed to Chester Pearson, a forty-two-year-old outsider brought in from Curtiss-Wright. Glenn was elected chairman of the board, a newly created position, at the same $60,260 salary Pearson received. It was the fall of 1949, Glenn's sixty-third year, but the winter of his life. He would remain intimately active in the affairs of the company, of course, but someone else would be directing the company on a daily basis. In the role of chairman, Glenn spent nearly two and a half more years—years that inexorably fixed the company's future course even if no one, including the founder, knew at the time what that course was to be.

On January 20, 1949, the nation's first tactical missile intended for operational duty was fired from a sandy projection of Florida's Atlantic coast, then an annex of the Banana River Naval Air Station at Cocoa Beach, Florida, and later Patrick Air Force Base. The missile was the Air Force Matador, a Martin-developed radio-guided, jet-speed, pilotless bomber, and the launch site would become Cape Canaveral, or more formally Station No. 1 of the Air Force's Atlantic Missile Range. Although called a bomber because aircraft nomenclature was hard to shake in those first days of the nation's missile program, the entire Matador vehicle was a flying bomb. Nine hundred seventy-one Matador missiles would be produced by the company between 1949 and 1957, and it would be followed by the TM-76 Mace, a longer-range much-improved guidance. A total of 295 Mace missiles were built.

Martin's factory representative at the Cape for the first Matador firing was Kenneth W. Traut, a lanky thirty-year-old who had already spent ten years in the Baltimore plant. Traut had first gone to Florida for the company in 1943 to modify PBM-ls based at Banana River Air station. He made many visits before moving there permanently in 1956. But he remembered particularly that first trip by overnight train with Carl Hansen. The two of them had been sent to Florida from Middle River to install "interrupters" on the gun turrets of the PBM to prevent overzealous Navy crewmen from shooting off the plane's vertical stabilizer.[6]

The first and only government contractor employee at the Cape for a time, Ken recalled the snakes, alligators, and mosquitoes that had infested the marshes which made up most of Canaveral behind

Matador "pilotless bomber" launch

its beautiful sand beaches. He spent forty-one years with the corporation, the last twenty-four at the Cape, where he took part in more than 250 Martin missile launches and was witness to virtually every missile and rocket launch of America's first quarter-century in space.

Before taking medical retirement in 1980, Traut directed Martin's customer requirements at the Cape for nearly two decades, working first for the legendary Tom Willey of Omaha fame, who was vice president and general manager when the launch operation there became a full-fledged test division of the corporation. Then, successively, Traut worked under George E. Smith, O. E. "Pat" Tibbs, Joseph M. Verlander, John A. Coryell, Felix J. Scheffler, Robert D. Rhodus, and Wendell E. Fields as each of them directed Martin's Cape operations. Traut also had a green thumb and became a cultivator of hibiscus, wild orchids, and almost anything else that grew and flourished in Florida's sunny climate.

That same year, 1949, that Martin people were firing Matadors off the East Coast, others were launching a research rocket vertically from the Southwest's desert. It was the Viking high-altitude research rocket, probably the most significant change-of-direction program for the Martin Company in those days. The chief engineer of the program was a thirty-year-old with a crew cut and bifocals who later took up the bagpipes. William G. Purdy had joined the company in 1941, fresh out of college, and like every new engineer was assigned to "menial drafting chores" at the Rouse Building on Redwood Street in downtown Baltimore. "We called it the 'Rouse College of Wasted Knowledge,' " Bill Purdy remembered. "We were trained by a strict old German named Reimann. We had to heavy up drawings and generally just mess around ... menial drafting work ... until someone picked us for a real job at the plant."[7]

Purdy was eventually picked by Bill Bergen to join the Vibrations Group, which Bergen headed and which included three other young engineers: Welcome W. Bender, George S. Trimble, Jr., and Edward G. Uhl, all of whom would one day rise to prominence in the corporation. The Vibrations Group, part of a new technology, placed instruments in various areas of an airplane in an attempt to predict flutter, a bugaboo of high-performance aircraft.

Bergen later took over flight testing, and then the "pilotless aircraft group." He asked Purdy to join the group, assigning him as project engineer on Viking, a single-stage upper-air research rocket for the Naval Research Laboratory. Viking was patterned very much after captured German V-2 rockets except for a couple of notable Martin innovations that Purdy said "really stuck and became basic in all rocket design after that." One was the use of fuel tanks as integral to the structure of the rocket; tank walls doubled as the rocket's exterior casing, thereby saving considerable weight. The other innovation was gimbaled engines that could be tilted in any direction to counteract and control side forces, thus stabilizing a rocket vehicle during ascent. They would not be demonstrated until later, however.

"One other innovation that we nearly accomplished but didn't have the money to do was to take off the fins," Purdy said. All rockets had fins at the time, and the Viking had huge fins, which Purdy said were a source of destabilizing forces because they could not be lined up exactly. "Some of the control force had to be used to compensate for the fins' misalignment," he added. "If we had been able to build the gimbaling system with enough sensitivity so that we didn't need fins at all, that would have fixed it. We did that design and demonstrated it later on Vanguard. But basically the Navy lab didn't have the money to take the fins off of Viking."

Three other charter members of that rocket design team were Jim Burridge, Dick Lea, and Irwin "Win" Barr, who collaborated on a number of other innovations, Purdy said. "One was the 'Barr Cart,' an arrangement for transporting the Viking rocket. It consisted of a framework with two wheels that attached to the base fins. Using the rocket as its own limber pole, the Viking could be towed and guided by a castered wheel attached to the nose of the rocket," Purdy said. Sort of a tricycle bolted to the rocket, it gave the forty-five-foot-long Viking the appearance of a "fantastic dachshund," in the view of Milton Rosen, the Navy project chief. Barr tested his contrivance by driving it around the Middle River plant at forty miles per hour with the rocket in tow. Barr later left Martin, along with Joel Jacobson and several other engineers, to form Aircraft Armaments Inc. Burridge and Lea ended up in Denver, as did Purdy when that plant was built.

The original contract called for ten Vikings, although ultimately fourteen were built and flown, all but three from White Sands Proving Ground in New Mexico. The last two were launched from Cape Canaveral as test beds for a subsequent rocket, the Vanguard. Purdy and his Viking team spent a good deal of time traveling between Baltimore and El Paso, Texas, gateway to the Army's Fort Bliss, which was the across-the-stateline support base for White Sands. Bliss at the time was also the housing base for Wernher Von Braun and his group of German rocket scientists who had surrendered to the United States rather than be captured by the Russians at the close of World War II.

"The Germans had not yet been moved to Redstone Arsenal,"

Viking high-altitude rocket

Purdy recalled, "so they were kind of incarcerated in a sense at Bliss—I'm not sure whether for our protection or theirs. But they were the source of all rocket knowledge at that point in time . . . a very respectable group of people. The connection we made with Von Braun and his Germans continued on into the Titan era. So, basically, that's when the rocket business started for Martin, in 1946 and 1947."

Martin's field chief on Viking was J. Preston "Pres" Layton. John Youngquist, who would later play prominent engineering roles on both Vanguard and Titan, was in charge of propulsion, and the operations manager was Paul Smith, a product of Martin's Middle River shops. Smith had the reputation of being able to do anything and everything on Viking, which earned him Navy project chief Milt Rosen's approbation of "mechanic *par excellence.*"

Although Viking racked up sophisticated accomplishments in basic rocketry as well as high-altitude research up to the fringes of space, all was not sophistication, Purdy remembered. Practicality and resourcefulness played their parts, and trial and error was the rule of the day. An example of practicality occurred right at the beginning of the program in the matter of determining the size of the rocket. Purdy said the diameter was fixed at thirty-two inches, not for any engineering consideration but because that was "the widest piece of standard rolled aluminum sheet we could find."

The first Martin Viking was launched May 3, 1949, from White Sands Proving Ground in New Mexico. It reached a speed of 3,450 feet per second and climbed fifty miles, neither figure a record, but it carried 464 pounds of special instruments to measure upper-air pressure and temperature, and that was significant. The next one attained only thirty-two miles in altitude due to premature cutoff of the engine. "Number 3 went west," Purdy said, "because I set the trim tabs wrong—pure and simple," although it did reach a height of fifty miles and a speed of 3,440 feet per second before range safety sent a radio command to cut off the engine.

But in a 1950 firing from the deck of the USS *Norton Sound* in the South Pacific, Viking No. 4 soared to 105 miles, a single-stage rocket high-altitude record soon toppled by Viking No. 5, which made history with an altitude record of 108 miles. "Then we changed the fins from stainless steel to aluminum," Purdy said, "and No. 6 did a cartwheel in the night sky when those aluminum fins buckled." Having learned something about fin design, it was back to the old fins for No. 7, which established another record at an altitude of 136 miles.

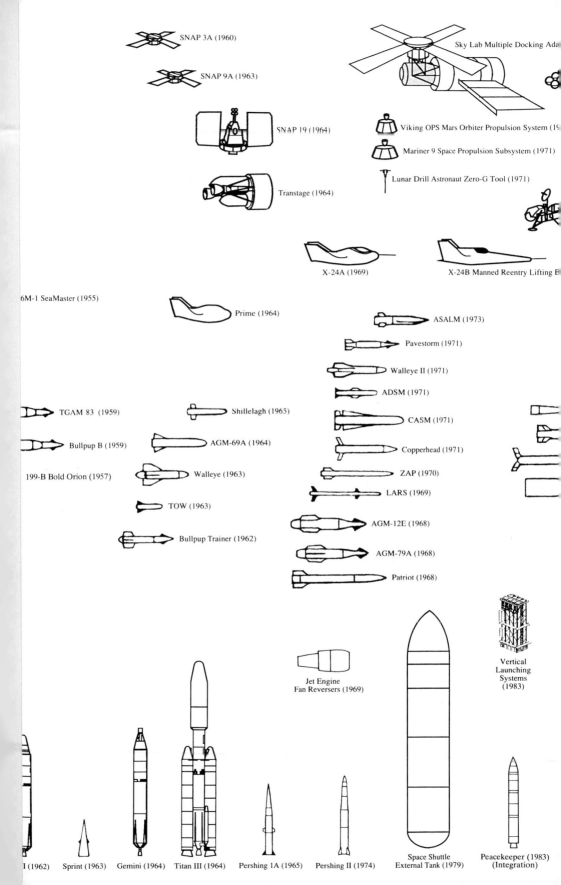

SNAP 3A (1960)

SNAP 9A (1963)

SNAP 19 (1964)

Sky Lab Multiple Docking Ada

Viking OPS Mars Orbiter Propulsion System (19

Mariner 9 Space Propulsion Subsystem (1971)

Lunar Drill Astronaut Zero-G Tool (1971)

Transtage (1964)

X-24A (1969)

X-24B Manned Reentry Lifting B

6M-1 SeaMaster (1955)

Prime (1964)

ASALM (1973)

Pavestorm (1971)

Walleye II (1971)

ADSM (1971)

TGAM 83 (1959)

Shillelagh (1965)

CASM (1971)

Bullpup B (1959)

AGM-69A (1964)

Copperhead (1971)

199-B Bold Orion (1957)

Walleye (1963)

ZAP (1970)

TOW (1963)

LARS (1969)

AGM-12E (1968)

Bullpup Trainer (1962)

AGM-79A (1968)

Patriot (1968)

Vertical
Launching
Systems
(1983)

Jet Engine
Fan Reversers (1969)

I (1962)   Sprint (1963)   Gemini (1964)   Titan III (1964)   Pershing 1A (1965)   Pershing II (1974)   Space Shuttle
External Tank (1979)   Peacekeeper (1983)
(Integration)

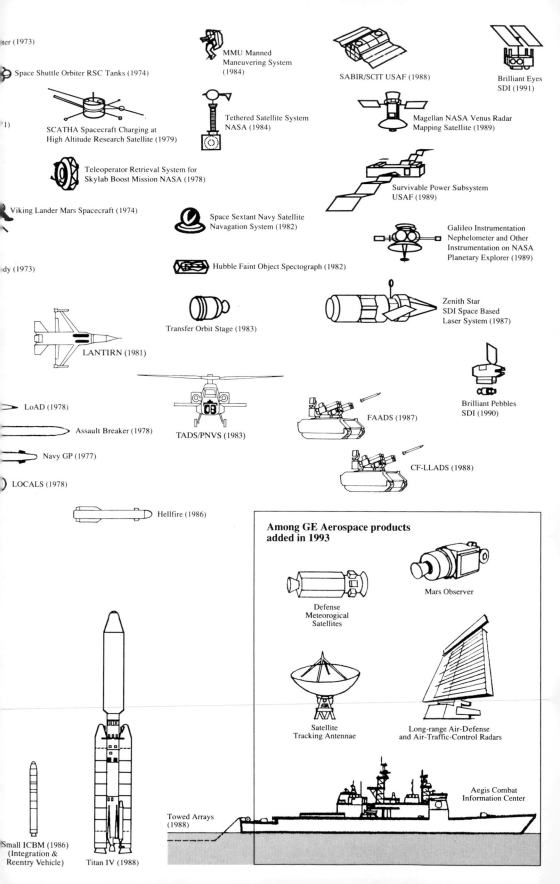

iter (1973)

Space Shuttle Orbiter RSC Tanks (1974)

'1)

SCATHA Spacecraft Charging at
High Altitude Research Satellite (1979)

Teleoperator Retrieval System for
Skylab Boost Mission NASA (1978)

Viking Lander Mars Spacecraft (1974)

dy (1973)

LANTIRN (1981)

LoAD (1978)

Assault Breaker (1978)

Navy GP (1977)

LOCALS (1978)

Hellfire (1986)

MMU Manned
Maneuvering System
(1984)

Tethered Satellite System
NASA (1984)

Space Sextant Navy Satellite
Navagation System (1982)

Hubble Faint Object Spectograph (1982)

Transfer Orbit Stage (1983)

TADS/PNVS (1983)

FAADS (1987)

CF-LLADS (1988)

SABIR/SCIT USAF (1988)

Magellan NASA Venus Radar
Mapping Satellite (1989)

Survivable Power Subsystem
USAF (1989)

Galileo Instrumentation
Nephelometer and Other
Instrumentation on NASA
Planetary Explorer (1989)

Zenith Star
SDI Space Based
Laser System (1987)

Brilliant Pebbles
SDI (1990)

Brilliant Eyes
SDI (1991)

**Among GE Aerospace products
added in 1993**

Defense
Meteorogical
Satellites

Mars Observer

Satellite
Tracking Antennae

Long-range Air-Defense
and Air-Traffic-Control Radars

Aegis Combat
Information Center

Towed Arrays
(1988)

Small ICBM (1986)
(Integration &
Reentry Vehicle)

Titan IV (1988)

During a captive firing, an engine-only test in which the rocket remains bolted to the launch stand, Viking No. 8 "inexplicably got away," Purdy said, setting an altitude record of sorts for a captive firing, about four miles straight up before burying itself in the sand about as many miles across the range. No. 9, the first Viking with a larger airframe, was successful at an altitude of 135 miles. With only two out-and-out failures in nine launches, the research program was progressing rather well, especially for those days.

Viking No. 10 was in countdown for a launch attempt when a misfire caused an explosion and fire in the engine compartment. "The fire played hell with the engine without demolishing it," Purdy said, but the electrical system was knocked out, "and the rocket just sat on the launch stand and burned." The water deluge system failed to extinguish the fire totally, and there was no way to open vent valves that would have permitted dumping fuel and oxidizer from the tanks. Only a thin aluminum wall separated the fire from a tank full of highly combustible peroxide, and without venting and unloading, Purdy said, the inevitable change in pressure would have collapsed the tanks and destroyed the entire rocket.

Resourcefulness by Martin's Paul Smith, Range Fire Chief Ernest Boyd, and the Navy program officer Lieutenant Joe Pitts saved the day. Smith volunteered to leave the safety of the sealed blockhouse to redirect a fire hose and extinguish the remaining fire. Chief Boyd gave his permission and went along to help. With the fire finally out, the problem of the unvented tanks and mounting pressure still threatened destruction. Borrowing a carbine rifle from the guard on the blockhouse door, Lieutenant Pitts carefully fired a bullet into the Viking's alcohol tank, thereby venting it and saving the rocket.[8]

Somewhat charred and misshapen, Viking No. 10 was shipped back to the factory, repaired, and returned to White Sands, where on March 7, 1954, it equaled the previous high-altitude mark of 136 miles. The bullet, incidentally, was recovered from inside the tank during the rocket's refurbishment at Middle River and was given to Lieutenant Pitts as a souvenir.

Viking No. 11 was the world-beater at 158 miles of altitude, returning the first pictures of Earth taken from space. The twelfth and last Viking in that program was also successful, reaching 144 miles. Within the year Martin and the Naval Research Laboratory were selected for Project Vanguard.[9]

While pilotless Matadors and high-altitude Vikings were inexorably pointing the company's future path, three new airplane programs were born in the eight years (1948 through 1955) that brought the Glenn L. Martin Company from primarily an aircraft producer to the design, development, and manufacture of missiles and rockets. Two were Navy seaplanes, the P5M Marlin and the P6M SeaMaster, and the third was the Air Force B-57 tactical bomber. The P5M and the B-57 would become major production and modification programs for the Middle River plant prior to the eventual phaseout of aircraft production in 1960.

The P5M birth actually occurred early in 1946 as Model 237 when the company set about designing a replacement for the Navy's aging fleet of Catalina, Colorado, and early Mariner flying boats. On June 26 of that year, the Navy formally contracted for the prototype, to be designated P5M-1 and later dubbed the Martin Marlin. It would have a pair of standard Mariner gull wings and a heavily modified Mariner hull with a longer afterbody that operated more smoothly in rough water. Below the waterline at the stern were Martin-designed "hydroflaps" that acted as water brakes to slow the Marlin on landing. Operated individually in combination with reversible propellers, the hydroflaps also gave the new flying boat significant maneuverability on the surface. Instead of the Mariner's twin vertical stabilizers, the P5M-1 had a tall single tail fin. Weighing nearly thirty-seven tons, the Marlin had a maximum speed of 234 miles per hour and a cruising speed of 150 miles per hour, with a range of three thousand miles. The prototype flew in 1948, and the Navy purchased 121 of the dash-1 Marlins, primarily for ASW (antisubmarine warfare) duty between 1951 and 1954. A conventional low horizontal stabilizer would become a T-tail on the P5M-2, a modification with a longer range and greater capacity. The Navy ordered 117, extending production into 1960.

Before the company was a year into production of the Marlin, the Air Force expressed interest in a new tactical bomber, its first postwar ground support aircraft. Martin's answer was the XB-51, the swept-wing trijet with rotating bomb bay door that had made its first flight on October 28, 1949. Ultimately, in the interest of economy and time, the Air Force decided against risking a new design, opting instead to adapt an already flying British bomber, the Canberra. Martin was awarded the task, and the American version of the Canberra became the twin-engine B-57, a sleek Air Force mainstay with missions ranging from high-altitude bombing and reconnaissance to low-level night interdiction.

Pratt & Whitney J75 engines were chosen to replace the Canberra's Rolls-Royce power plants, 20-millimeter cannon were placed in the leading edge of the wings, and the rotary bomb bay developed

Experimental XB-51s

for the XB-51 was adapted to the B-57 redesign. A Martin invention, the rotary bomb bay when open permitted speedy external attachment of bombs to racks attached to the door. When loaded, racks and bombs—the entire mechanism—rotated into a closed position.

In 1953, when flight testing began on the B-57, Martin test pilots Pat Tibbs and George Rodney were known around the Middle River flight line as "Captain All-ass" and "Captain No-ass." Tibbs drew the former appellation because of the 265-or-better pounds he carried on a six-foot frame, and Rodney the latter designation because at six-foot-five, his 170 pounds scarcely cast a shadow. The two men were great friends and members of the same mutual admiration society.

Test pilot was about the last thing you'd think of when looking

Rodney, Tibbs, and B-57

at Pat Tibbs. Both his height and his girth made him an unlikely candidate for a test pilot, as a national television audience found out. Tibbs was a guest on the popular quiz show of the 1950s, "What's My Line?" and, of course, he stumped the panelists. They guessed a variety of vocations from priest to banker, but none came close to guessing he was a test pilot.

Pat Tibbs was living proof, however, that looks can be deceiving. Rodney called him "one of the great natural fliers of all time. He would get in an airplane, and it just became part of him. Most of us test pilots worked to fly, and we had to. We tried to understand the airplane and all of its aerodynamics, how it was built, and all that. We would approach the flying, regardless of our skill, in a very controlled fashion. But Pat, we used to say, didn't get into an airplane; he put it on, and it became part of him. He was something to fly with—just an outstanding guy."[10]

One model of the B-57, the "D," was built ostensibly as a high-altitude test bed. Its 110-foot wingspan (the regular B-57 wing was 64 feet) enabled the B-57D to loiter at relatively slow speed above eighty thousand feet. That was higher than altitudes later flown by the infamous U-2 spy plane of Francis Gary Powers, shot down by the Soviets in 1960 to the considerable international embarrassment of President Eisenhower and his disarmament negotiators.

Twenty of the high-flying D model were built. George Rodney remembered its remarkably short development time. "We had done a little bit of preliminary study, of course, but from the time we got the go-ahead to build it until it literally was flying over the U.S.S.R. was something like eighteen months." Recalling the compressed schedule, Rodney said the structural test involved setting the plane up on blocks because its overly long wings drooped so much. "Then we tied down the airplane, put ropes on the wing tips, and a bunch of us got out there and pulled down on the ropes, then let them up, then pulled down, and let up. That got the wings going in natural

B-57 production

frequency until we made the maximum excursion the engineers said would give us the structural demonstration. That was the only proof test we did on the whole damned plane. Then we flew it."[11]

Rodney flew the B-57D on its first flight and for a total of about sixteen hours. "I had about five or six things that I thought ought to be fixed. The Air Force came in and flew it for twenty hours, and they wanted to fix three of the things on my list, plus one other. We fixed them all. I flew it another twenty hours or so. Meanwhile, we were packaging and installing all the electronics, after which I flew a few more hours, the Air Force flew a few more hours, and the combat crews came in for a few additional hours. Then off they went to keep watch over the Soviet Union." And that pretty well told the expediency of the B-57D program, in Rodney's view. "It was doing the same things the U-2 did, only no one ever heard about it."

In all, Martin built 403 of the B-57s over the next four years in six different models, more effective configurations than any other

High-altitude RB-57D with normal-wing version

USAF aircraft. Then in the mid-1960s, close to four hundred B-57s originally produced by the company returned to Middle River under new Air Force modification contracts. Most of this work involved new electronics, and these airplanes saw extensive duty in Vietnam. B-57s continued flying in U.S. Air Force and Air National Guard service into the early 1980s, the last squadron being retired in Vermont in 1982.

Flight testing in the 1950s was headed by Tibbs as chief test pilot, and Rodney, as number two, was chief of experimental flight testing. Ken Ebel, who had test-flown more Martin airplanes than any other pilot, was by then chief of engineering and had given up test-piloting. Others in that unique cadre of Martin test pilots, according to George Rodney's recollection, included Ray Nestle, Dutch Gelvin, Chris Kristoferson, Tommy Taylor, Bob Turner, Tom Lloyd, Don McCusker, Eddie Ball, Jim Frost, Shelly Yates, Clay Ingraham, Victor Tomich, and Tom Cobb. Another test pilot who rivaled Tibbs in size and weight, and was by Rodney's description "a pretty good flier to boot," was William B. "Big Bill" Johnson. He quickly became known affectionately as "All-ass No. 2" and just as quickly became a great admirer of the incomparable Pat Tibbs, about whom he told the following story:[12]

The Martin airport at Middle River was on the edge of the water and was frequently under siege by sea gulls who were a hazard to jet planes taking off and landing. According to Bill Johnson, Pat Tibbs as chief of flight testing kept a twelve-gauge shotgun in his office and fired it in the air to clear the runway when the sea gulls became too thick.

There also was a red fox, probably attracted by the sea gulls. Frequently sighted, it caused no particular problem until one afternoon it ran across the runway, causing a landing plane to swerve and blow a tire. That was all Pat Tibbs needed, according to Johnson, who was in the radio room when he heard his code name called in Pat's most urgent tone: "Redbird Twelve, Redbird Twelve, come to my office." "Whenever Pat called one of us," Johnson said, "you knew you were going to get a lecture, maybe a pat on the back, or an invitation to Wilhelm's, which we called 'Hangar 7,' to have lunch. Only this time he wanted to get the fox. He took his shotgun, and we went out to the station wagon we always kept next to the door. It had fire extinguishers, first-aid kits, and other things we might need in a hurry sometime. Pat lowered the tailgate and sat back there, and told me to drive the wagon along the runway and get him close enough to the fox so he could shoot it.

"We were going along about thirty miles an hour, and I was so intent on following that fox that I didn't see a drainage ditch. When we hit it, as you might guess at that speed, Pat was bounced pretty high, and I drove that wagon clear out from under him. He landed on his butt, and both barrels of that shotgun went off, 'blam! blam!' The fox kept right on running, only faster, and I was still chasing it, figuring Pat had missed. I didn't know I had lost Pat until I looked around some distance down the runway, and he wasn't there. He had a few choice expletives for me when I got back to where he was dusting off his pants and his pride," Johnson said. "It was all I could do to keep from laughing, but we never did see that fox again."

The fox hunt wasn't the only time Tibbs took to the Middle River runway in something other than an airplane. Rodney recalled another time that he, Tibbs, and Fuzz Furman, who ran the airport, drag-raced their automobiles on the landing strip after hours. Rodney drove a Studebaker Golden Hawk, Tibbs an Oldsmobile, and Furman a Buick, which Rodney said "he mothered to death."

"Both Fuzz and I were constantly beating Pat's car," Rodney said, "and he got fed up." So he went out and had a turbo put on his Olds. Tibbs clued Rodney in on his secret, but when the Olds outran both the Studebaker and the Buick, Fuzz couldn't wait to see the winning car. "Okay, let me see what you've done to the car," he demanded of Tibbs. Rodney said it was the infancy of auto turbos, and that was the last thing Fuzz would have guessed. So Tibbs fibbed a bit and told him it was the same old car, "just tuned up a bit." Of course when Fuzz raised the hood, he discovered the turbo hook-up—to his chagrin and the loud laughter of his two pilot friends.

CHAPTER 21

Receivership: New Pilot
at the Controls

■

I n spite of the successful aircraft programs and new beginnings in missiles and rockets, the financial drain of the commercial airplane venture proved too much, and the
government customers and the banks began pressing the company
to strengthen its books or face closing. Additional loans, basically
guaranteed by Martin's Navy customer, were necessary from the Reconstruction Finance Corporation and the Mellon Bank.

By the end of 1951, the company was once again on the brink
of financial collapse. Only the fact that it was producing planes for
the Korean War, deemed essential to the national welfare, prevented
formal bankruptcy proceedings. Although the RFC held the first
mortgage on the company, the Air Force and Navy could not agree
on a course of action, so the matter fell to Charles E. Wilson, director
of the Office of Defense Mobilization. He ruled against bankruptcy
and approved a complex refinancing. The Navy would advance the
company enough money to keep it going until a permanent solution
was found.

The major condition of the arrangement was another change
in management. Chester Pearson, who had taken the presidency
little more than two years before, stepped down to vice president,
and a young man brought in by the Mellon interests became presi-

dent and chief executive. George Maverick Bunker, then forty-four, had been chairman of Trailmobile Corporation at Cincinnati, where he had earned an excellent reputation for his executive abilities and reorganization skills. It was apparent that he had been brought to The Martin Company to take complete charge. Henry Still described the change in his biography of Glenn Martin:

> No one could bring himself to tell Glenn of this decision, though all was done to prepare him for the blow. When Bunker arrived in Baltimore by train February 21, 1952, he was met at Union Station by Howard Bruce, a longtime board member and friend of Glenn's, who had been instrumental in the behind-the-scenes actions to save the company.
>
> At the board meeting, Bunker was elected president and chief executive and Glenn was made honorary chairman of the board. Glenn was stunned into speechlessness. He sat ashen-faced at his desk after the meeting, absent-mindedly toying with a model of the Viking, when Bruce came in.
>
> "I know you'll understand, Glenn. What we're doing is for the good of the company," Bruce told him gently. Then realizing and respecting Glenn's silence, Bruce quietly withdrew.[1]

When Glenn returned to his office the next day, he found that a large table had been placed squarely against the front of his massive desk, and across from him sat George Bunker. They shared the space for less than a day. Glenn gathered up his personal belongings and moved into an office provided for him twelve miles away in a downtown Baltimore bank building. As the largest single stockholder, he remained on the board of directors and was honorary chairman.

At the first session of the board of directors under the new management, Glenn sat silent and expressionless while Bunker conducted the meeting. When finally asked if he wished to say anything, Glenn reportedly spoke slowly and with quiet dignity. "Gentlemen," he said, "to show my good faith and my concern for the welfare of the company, I am willing to place voting control of my stock [26 percent of outstanding shares] in the hands of trustees." George Bunker extended his hand, Glenn shook it, then nodded to others around the table as he left the room.

The date was six months shy of the fortieth anniversary of the 1912 founding of the first company to bear Glenn Martin's name in California. No one had noticed that the new president's initials, G.M.B., stood for Glenn Martin Bomber, the actual designation of one of the company's early planes.

Bunker and Martin remained cordial, if not friendly, even appearing together the following summer at the annual employee picnic and open house at the Middle River plant. The Korean conflict had almost doubled employment, from 7,400 in 1949 to 14,500 in 1951, and it passed 22,000 by the summer of 1952, when Harry George, his wife Hazel, and three young sons, Bill, Dick, and Tom were among thousands of families attending family day. The Georges were among many who stood in line to shake the hands of the founder and the new president.

It was the first Martin Family Day that Minta Martin missed. At eighty-eight, she was virtually bedridden in their Baltimore home, under the constant care of doctors and nurses and the close atten-

Martin and Bunker and the George family, 1952

tion of a devoted son. From the picnic he brought her a carnival hat with the inscription OH YOU KID! which drew a laugh from the frail "Grand Old Lady of Aviation" when he perched it on her head.

She lingered for less than a year, and when she died on March 14, 1953, at eighty-nine, Glenn lost not only his mother but his best friend and closest confidante. He had her entombed with his father Clarence in the mausoleum at Santa Ana's Fairhaven Memorial Park. In her memory, Glenn gave the First Presbyterian Church of Santa Ana a splendid new organ and carillon bells. He arranged with the Reverend O. Scott McFarland, pastor of the church and a longtime Martin family friend, to have the bells peal every hour on the hour each weekday between 9 A.M. and 7 P.M. and to play a hymn at 5 P.M. It remains a tradition of downtown life in Santa Ana.

After his mother's death, Glenn spent less and less time in Baltimore. Both his downtown office and his home were lonely places. He began spending most of his time at Glenarm, his beloved Eastern Shore farm, where he had had a glass observation tower built on the roof. For hours and sometimes days, binoculars in hand, he delighted in the large number of wild geese and ducks that were attracted to his sanctuary.

He did maintain contacts at the plant, who kept him apprised of developments, the latest contracts won, first flights, and new sales. He took satisfaction in news accounts of P5M exploits in the China Sea off Korea, of 4–0–4s in regular airline service, of the new B-57 tactical bomber beginning service with the Air Force. And even though he would remain foremost an aviator, he closely followed the progress of the new programs such as Matador and Viking. His pride was enormous when his Martin team was selected to develop first Vanguard, a three-stage rocket that would launch a U.S. satellite, and then a new intercontinental ballistic missile, which the Air Force would call Titan. He had employed many of the bright young engineers who were now winning and managing these programs, and he had encouraged them to go after the new "pilotless aircraft" business.

In the fall of 1953, Glenn was accorded a singular honor: selection for the second time in his life to deliver the Wright Brothers Lecture, this time by the Institute of the Aeronautical Sciences. It was recognition by his peers for a career rich in achievement. In 1931 he had presented the Wilbur Wright Memorial Lecture before the Royal Aeronautical Society in London. The repeat of that honor came on December 17, 1953, when he delivered the seventeenth lecture to the American counterpart organization on the occasion of the fiftieth anniversary of flight. It was the valedictory of a pioneer who had not only seen the entire remarkable age of flight but had himself frequently pointed the way.

Speaking before a packed audience in the U.S. Chamber of Commerce auditorium in Washington, D.C., Glenn Martin called it a "humbling experience to review the first half-century of flight in America":

> I am happy to assay this task because of the deep sense of obligation I feel toward aviation. It has been the central theme of my life, and it has been the most demanding yet the most rewarding of any field of work I could possibly have chosen. I hope that I have made some contribution to it, no matter how small. If I have, however, it has been only as a member of a continuing team of enthusiastic and loyal coworkers who have shared with me the triumphs and the failures of these interesting years.
>
> The Wrights brought to aviation the scientific approach to invention in which intuition and logic are used as a leavening for the diverse technical facts at hand.
>
> I was closely acquainted with Orville Wright for many years, first as friend and later as business associate, and I can say that he was the most honest man I ever met. I am convinced that it was this devotion to truth—in all things— that lay at the root of the Wright brothers' success in creating the airplane. It has been honest men who have built our great industry and who will guide its sound growth in the future.
>
> The quality of honesty in daily dealings is an infallible guide to a man's capabilities in the engineering and scientific fields. Structures and machines are unforgiving of the cheater and inevitably indict those who toy with the facts.
>
> The real legacy of the Wright brothers to their contemporaries was the single truth that flight had been achieved. With this fact in hand, the rest of us were able to sweep all difficulties before us and rush to our individual successes. It is the haunting fear that what he is trying to do is impossible that corrodes the will of the inventor Once this fear is removed, the spirit overrides all problems and moves quickly to the fruition of the dream. All of us who followed the Wrights lived beyond such fears.

I have had many years in which to recall my first flight and to attempt to express the experience in words, but I have always failed. Leaving the ground for the first time in a machine of your own design, which you have built with your own hands, is simply an indescribable experience.[2]

His lecture went on to review the materials and technologies, the problems and accomplishments of fifty years of flight, and he noted that "in a free independent society there can be no grand guiding hand controlling the destiny of an industry or a people." He added:

The modern airplane constitutes an integration of thoughts and lifetime work of more individuals than any other industry on earth. This integration was accomplished not by fiat but by understanding cooperation between its many and diverse elements. This interplay of really diverse avenues of human effort is a monument to man's dependence upon other men.

It has been only the unfettered freedom of America which has created this giant team of cooperating individuals which is our modern aircraft industry. We have the aerodynamic knowledge, the structural materials, the power plants, and the manufacturing capacities to perform any miracle in aviation.[3]

Turning to manufacturing costs, he addressed the "pronounced apathy of the American people for the flying machine they invented." Throughout his lifelong participation in aviation, Glenn said he had witnessed public criticism of the high cost of aircraft.

I do not know why our citizens heartily approve substantial profits in the manufacture of automobiles and household appliances but become incensed when the word "profit" is even associated with the design and production of vital weapons of national defense.

Without profits there can be no research, no advanced machinery and equipment, no progress of any sort. Without profits available for expansion of potential, that expansion becomes the responsibility of the government.

And that responsibility, unchecked, leads inevitably to the political and economic system we are attempting to defeat throughout the world.

There is a proper role for the government in aviation progress. As a customer, it must establish clearly and precisely the goals that we will be required to meet. It must assume the financial cost of the research and development work required in the perfection of that goal. It must make certain that this nation has at all times a strong aircraft industry, a healthy and progressive accessory and equipment industry, an experienced and capable airline industry, and a reservoir of educated and skillful young men coming forward to man these industries.[4]

Costly as it may seem, Glenn predicted, the burden of this government role "will be borne cheerfully by an enlightened American citizen once he understands its full significance to him and his progeny." In closing what had been, without doubt, the most eloquent and deftly delivered public presentation of his life, Glenn confidently predicted:

- interstellar spaceships with speeds of twenty-five thousand miles per hour
- giant two-hundred-passenger jet airliners that would cross the continents and the oceans in literally zero time in the westerly direction
- fully automatic airline flight operations through electronic guidance and control equipment
- reductions in the cost of air travel to amounts well below any other form of transportation

All of the predictions did not come true, of course, but most were greatly exceeded. Two others—"helicopters carrying all airline traffic of less than 150 miles" and "nuclear-powered aircraft"—did not materialize, although The Martin Company, under government contract, studied the feasibility of powering aircraft with nuclear power. It was determined that the cost would preclude the feasibility.

He also predicted flying boats with speeds matching their land-based equivalents, and six months after his Wright brothers lecture he saw that vision not only realized but surpassed. It happened on July 14, 1955, with the maiden flight of the world's first jet-powered seaplane, the Martin-built supersonic XP6M SeaMaster. It would be for Glenn the last of many Martin historic firsts. Six months later, on December 4, 1955, Glenn Luther Martin died.

He had been hospitalized in Baltimore just a month before his death with a severe cold and a virus infection. He had recovered sufficiently that his physician, Dr. W. Kennedy Waller, allowed him to return to his Georgian farmhouse on the Eastern Shore for Thanksgiving. Dr. Waller went along to make certain his famous patient and close friend continued his recovery and did not overexert.

Early on Sunday, December 4, as was his daily bent, Glenn climbed to the rooftop crow's nest to watch the dawn arrival of wild fowl. Dr. Waller was with him, and as the two men watched the sun come up, a long V-formation of geese swooped down to feed on the cornfield. "You know, Doc, I'd like to spend the rest of my life right here," Glenn confided.

Dr. Waller went downstairs to have his breakfast. When Glenn had not joined him by the time he finished eating, Dr. Waller returned to the roof. Glenn was unconscious on the deck, the binoculars still clutched in his hand. He had suffered a cerebral hemorrhage but was still alive. Rushed to Baltimore's University Hospital, he died that night without regaining consciousness.[5]

■

THE MARTIN 2-0-4 BEARING the Flying Dude's body on his final flight to Santa Ana passed just south and a little west of Denver, Colorado. Coincidentally but appropriately, the plane flew almost directly over the Rocky Mountain foothill site newly selected for the company's Denver plant, where much of his company's future would take place. It was appropriate that the plane carrying Glenn's body was a combination of the two commercial aircraft he had loved so well and in which he had put so much faith. Basically a 2-0-2, the plane had been modified as a demonstrator for the 4-0-4 program and later served for a number of years as the flagship of the company's corporate fleet, where it was known affectionately as the "Two-by-Four," until replaced by a pure jet.[6]

Glenn's funeral on December 9 was from Santa Ana's First Presbyterian Church, the same one he had attended as a youth, with Dr. McFarland officiating as he had at the funerals of Glenn's father and mother. The Minta Martin organ and carillon played, and aviation's great were honorary pallbearers for the man who had given them their start. Among them were Lawrence D. Bell, president of Bell Aviation; James McDonnell, president of McDonnell Aviation;

William E. Boeing, founder of Boeing Aircraft Company; J. H. Kindelberger, chairman of North American Aviation; Donald W. Douglas, president of Douglas Aircraft; and Robert E. Gross, president of Lockheed Aircraft. Other honorary pallbearers included Admiral Dewitt Ramsey, president of the Aircraft Industries Association; Grover C. Loening, aviation pioneer and consultant to the National Advisory Committee for Aviation; Vice Admiral Emory S. Lamb, former president of the Air Transport Association; Major Lester Gardner, former managing director of the Institute of Aeronautical Sciences; U.S. Senator Frank Carlson of Kansas; Thomas Herbert, former governor of Ohio; and Dr. Wilson H. Elkins, president of the University of Maryland, plus Eric Springer, a vice president of Douglas Aircraft, who had flown with Glenn in the early days and was a test pilot for him in Cleveland. Interment was with his mother and father at Fairhaven Memorial Park. Roy Beall, his mechanic and early friend who had helped build Glenn's first airplane and had often pushed it onto the field, helped guide his casket into its niche in the mausoleum wall. Among the mourners were Hollywood stars Claire Windsor and Mary Pickford, along with Joe E. Brown, the Creston, Iowa, tumbler who went on to become one of the greatest entertainers of stage and screen.[7]

Glenn died a very wealthy man. His sizable block of Martin company stock, although reduced to 13 percent by the time of his death, was still the largest individual holding. It had significantly increased in value under the company's new management and swelled the value of his total estate to an estimated $20 million. What had always seemed a very small family increased fivefold almost overnight as a profusion of cousins came out of the woodwork to claim the estate. Four remote first cousins, twelve second cousins, and four even more distant cousins claimed the inheritance. Glenn had made specific provisions in a will that was never completed. A token trust fund of $50,000 was established for his sister Della, who had been in a mental institution for fifty-one years, since she was twenty-two. Glenn had assumed responsibility and paid for Della's care after Minta Martin's death, visiting her on his occasional visits to California.

The will bequeathed $2 million to the University of Maryland, to be added to the Minta Martin Aeronautical Research Foundation. There were bequests of $100,000 each to the First Presbyterian Church and Hoag Hospital, both in Santa Ana. Fifteen other charities were to share $1,625,000, leaving $16 million that the cousins hoped to split. But Maryland law provided that the residue beyond specific bequests went to the next of kin. Without question, that was

Santa Ana family crypt

Della. She had learned of her famous brother's death while watching television in a San Gabriel Valley sanitarium. Friends of the Martin family who knew about Della had her released in their care, took her to their home, and hired an attorney to serve as her guardian.

After a year of protracted court fights, Della's guardian, James C. Sheppard, was authorized to divide the estate according to a complicated court-dictated formula. Della was to receive 70 percent of the total estate outright and income for life from another 15 percent. The remaining 15 percent and a "share alike" upon her death was to go to the four first cousins, Ross N. Enlow, Florence E. Lundstrom, Reba W. Schoeggl, and Bessie H. Baker. The sixteen other assorted cousins received $10,000 each.[8]

Even after federal and state taxes took $8 million from the gross estate, Della Martin was left a very wealthy woman. She also was free, having been declared medically sane. Although suffering from cultural underexposure, she moved into her own home in Pasadena, where she lived nineteen more years in the care of a companion-housekeeper and a nurse. When Della died in 1974, her body, too, was placed in the family crypt behind a marble plaque bearing her name in her own handwriting. Glenn had had it prepared many years before to match signature plaques for his parents and himself.[9]

■

AND WHAT WOULD BE the legacy of Della Martin, whose lifetime of cultural "underexposure" had deprived her of even the smallest share of her brother's fame? In the Library of Congress on Capitol Hill in Washington, D.C., there are fifty-five thousand pieces of Glenn L. Martin memorabilia—correspondence, scrapbooks, pictures, and clippings collected by Glenn and his mother over the course of his career. As part of his estate, these materials went to Della. This rich trove of aerospace history can be found today in the Manuscript Room of the Library of Congress's James Madison Building, where it resides as a permanent collection, donated to the library in the name of Della Martin after her death.[10]

CHAPTER 22

Onward and Upward and One Last Airplane

■

The company's net sales, which had dipped to $68,480,519 the month before Glenn stepped aside, had increased to a robust $271 million by the close of 1955, the year he died. Much had been done by the new management to accomplish the turnaround, which benefited more than a little by luck and timing. The huge losses incurred on the commercial airplane ventures had generated huge tax credits. The company had been selected to build the Vanguard satellite launcher for the International Geophysical Year, and almost at the same time it competed for and won a contract to design and manufacture the nation's largest and most powerful intercontinental ballistic missile. Meanwhile, two aircraft, the P5M seaplane and the B-57 tactical bomber, were being produced in numbers for the Navy and Air Force, respectively, and there would be one last new airplane.

In that same pivotal year of 1955, Martin engineers were firing the twelfth and last Viking rocket at White Sands, where only a few months before they had established a high-altitude record by firing one 158 miles straight up into the fringes of space. That Viking, No. 11, also sent back the first pictures of Earth ever taken from space.

Bill Bergen, who only the year before had introduced a new management technique called "systems engineering," was elected

"Half bird, half fish"

Rodney at controls

executive vice president of the company. His concept, one of several put in place by the Bunker management, may have been as significant as any single technical accomplishment in the company's long history. Bergen's management system set up a single multidisciplined engineering function for each program or project in the factory. The concept was quickly expanded to cover all functions from design through manufacturing and distribution under the broader designation of "systems management." In effect it made each hardware program or project in the company a separate autonomous unit headed by a project manager with a chief engineer and directly supported by all the traditional disciplines—aerodynamics, structures, electromechanical, electronics, production design, and flight test. To this organization was added the other functional areas—manufacturing, sales and service, procurement, and quality—each assigned directly to the project manager. As Bergen described it at the time in a paper published by *Aviation Age* magazine:

> Within the company we have created a number of miniature companies, each concerned with but a single project. The project manager exercises overall product control—in terms of an organization of all skills.[1]

Bergen, who had been hired by Glenn Martin, later became president of the company under George Bunker. His systems management brainchild was a widely used model within the Martin company and was broadly copied throughout the industry. Although subsequently a well-accepted and routine method of managing, the concept was extremely innovative at the time.

One of the early programs to be "systems managed" in the mid-fifties was the Navy's P6M seaplane. "Half bird, half fish," as one reporter described it,[2] the SeaMaster was the last complete airplane designed and built by The Martin Company. Painted midnight blue with a white underbelly, its graceful beauty conjured up the image of a killer whale. The P6M quickened the pulse of flying men and captured the hearts of practically everyone who saw it.

Perhaps George Rodney loved it more than most. He was in the left seat on the first flight of each of the sixteen SeaMasters built. Thirty-seven years after he first flew the "P-Six," he could still rhapsodize about the plane, both as a thing of beauty to behold and as a machine of incredible mechanical grace and performance.

The SeaMaster was designed to be the linchpin of the Navy's new global mobility concept. The world's first jet seaplane was to

SeaMasters aloft

have been based in floating seadromes, refueled by submarines in all parts of the world. But changing budget priorities, especially an admiral's dream of a nuclear Navy, sank the SeaMaster as a program before completion of flight testing. Of the sixteen seaplanes built and flown hundreds of hours, the first two YP6M evaluation models were lost in test accidents that were eventually attributed to design error in the flying T-tail.

The Martin test pilot, Maurice B. Bernhard, and two others flying as company engineers, Herbert D. Scudder and James Hentschel, died December 7, 1955, in a crash of XP6M-1, along with a Navy pilot, Lieutenant Commander Victor Utgolf, who was making his orientation flight in the jet seaplane. Almost a year later, a Martin test crew of four was more fortunate when they ejected from the second experimental SeaMaster after it, too, went into an inside loop. Surviving that accident were pilots Guy Cunningham and Bob Turner, along with Bill Compton, who was flying as the flight engineer, and Tom Kenny, a test engineer on his first airplane ride.

Compton was able to laugh about his narrow escape many years later. Before takeoff he had personally strapped Kenny into a seat in the rear of the plane, admonishing the nervous first-timer: "Now remember! If you feel a draft, you want to punch out of this thing." Compton said the four of them parachuted into a swamp near Odessa, Delaware, east of Dover. "We were soaked and colder than hell but otherwise unhurt when they picked us up and flew us back to Middle River," Bill recalled. "First thing we had to do was be debriefed by Pat Tibbs on everything we could remember about the flight; first the pilots, then me. When Kenny's turn came"—Compton laughed as he remembered Kenny's report—"Bill told me if I felt a draft, I was to get out of there. Well, I heard a noise and felt a draft, too, so I got out of there. And that's all I know."[3]

Compton flew three more years as a Martin test pilot, and then for twenty-eight years he piloted corporate aircraft, the last five as director of that department before retiring in 1987 after more than forty-two years with the corporation.

Discovering the cause of the second SeaMaster crash taught George Rodney a significant lesson he would never forget in a long career in quality control and troubleshooting. The first accident, which claimed the lives of three of Rodney's friends and fellow test pilots, was never fully reconstructed, he said. "We thought it was an aerodynamic problem," George said. "Hell, I spent almost a year working on it, but it wasn't until the second accident that we discovered the original wind tunnel data on the flying tail was bad. Instead of arithmetically adding the sine convention of some of the data, it had been algebraically added, or vice versa, I can't remember which. A lot of us were embarrassed because none of us was quite smart enough to go back to the absolute raw wind tunnel data. That's a lesson I never forgot."[4]

Rodney called the P6M "a pilot's dream, one beautiful airplane. It took all the seamanship out of seaplane flying. I could take any B-52 pilot and transition him into that airplane in an hour or two, even though he had never flown a seaplane in his life."

Rodney was not alone in his admiration for the seaplane. Only

Martin engineers briefed by NACA, 1957[5]

three months before the first crash, Navy officials called the P6M "unusually promising,"[6] and in November it had been demonstrated to the highest-ranking officers of both the United States and Great Britain. Admiral Arleigh Burke, chief of naval operations, called it a "wonderful airplane" and said the Navy wanted to "get as many as we can get approval for each year." Equally enthusiastic about the SeaMaster was Burke's British counterpart, Admiral Louis Mountbatten, first lord of the admiralty. Even the U.S. Air Force was interested. General Thomas D. White, then vice chief of staff, hinted that the Air Force was looking at the P6M, possibly for adoption as an atomic bomber.

Even without the accidents, which slowed the evaluation phase, Rodney believes the program was "doomed to politics and the budget and the Navy's changing concept." The problem with the P6M fundamentally, he said, was that it was a strategic bomber, "and no way could the Navy ever admit to the thought that it was going to do strategic bombing." Adding to that political complexity, the Navy's budget about that time became heavily skewed toward a nuclear Navy.

When it became apparent that the program was to be terminated, Rodney said he personally tried very hard to get General Curtis LeMay, Air Force deputy chief of staff (later chief of the

Strategic Air Command) to fly the SeaMaster. "Twice we had him scheduled to come over to Baltimore to fly it, but both times something interfered, and we never got him in the airplane. Curt LeMay would have fallen in love with it," Rodney believed. When the cancellation order finally came through in August 1959, the Navy directed that the remaining fourteen SeaMasters be cut up for scrap metal. "Not even one for the museums," Rodney lamented.

Little more than a year later, after delivery of the 239th and last P5M Marlin seaplane, The Martin Company formally announced it was exiting the manufacture of aircraft to concentrate on missiles, rockets, spacecraft, and electronic systems. By best count, the company in its first half-century produced 11,155 airplanes, more than 9,000 of them during World War II and the aircraft buildup leading to the war, 1935 to 1945.

P6Ms on Strawberry Point ramp

Well before the airplane's demise in Martin's inventory of production programs, the company's new leader, George Bunker, had begun firmly steering the corporate ship in the direction of the products he believed would make the company's future. The formal announcement a few years later that the country's oldest and most prominent aircraft manufacturer was "leaving" the airplane business did not say that, in truth, it was more a case of the airplane business leaving Martin—at least the types of airplanes that Martin had made famous, tactical bombers and giant seaplanes.

So in addition to the financial and managerial acumen that George Bunker brought to the enterprise, his market strategy was remarkably sound. He was not an "airplane man," to be sure, and perhaps that lack of focus was the company's salvation. Long before the merger that would truly diversify the company's product mix, Bunker had begun a diversification that mixed missiles and rockets with airplanes—for a time—but also with nuclear systems, electronics, communications and information systems, and a dozen other disciplines that eventually made up the world of aerospace.

In fact, in the councils of the Aircraft Industries Association, in which Bunker became a quiet but driving force, he was a primary voice in expanding the industry's public identification from aviation and aircraft to air and space, including the artful (some would have said awkward) coining of the term "aerospace."[7]

■

BUNKER HAD A STRONG BELIEF, confided on occasion to close associates, that a company like Martin that lived primarily on government contracts had a dual obligation to support and foster basic industry and research. In that spirit, he established in 1955 the Research Institute for Advanced Studies in Baltimore "to observe the phenomena of nature and to encourage, promote, and support investigations in search of underlying knowledge of these phenomena . . . to discover fundamental laws . . . and to evolve new technical concepts for the improvement and welfare of mankind." Sharing that conviction were George Trimble, then head of advanced programs for the company, and Welcome W. Bender, who was named the first director of RIAS and served in that position until 1963, when he was succeeded by Kenneth Jarmolow.

RIAS attracted some world-class contributors in mathematics, physics, biology and materials science. Chief among them was Dr. Solomon Lefschetz, senior professor emeritus at Princeton Univer-

RIAS scientists, 1960, in Baltimore.[8]

sity and renowned in the fields of topology and nonlinear differential equations, which won him the National Science Medal from President Lyndon B. Johnson in 1964. His presence attracted many young, innovative basic mathematicians, including Dr. Rudolph Kalman, whose Kalman Filter Theory was later widely applied in robotics, automation, and aerospace.

Another of the Laboratories' principals was Dr. Bessel Kok, from the Netherlands, one of the world's leading figures in the area of photosynthesis. While conducting research on spinach leaves, he discovered P-700, a constituent of chlorophyll that plays a key role in the process by which plants employ light, water, carbon, and oxygen in their growth and productive processes. Others included British-born metallurgist Dr. Albert R. C. Westwood. His theories on the behavior of materials from an atomic and subatomic perspective suggested ways of preventing catastrophic failures in various metals and ceramics and of "customizing" materials to improve their performance and fabrication. Bert Westwood became the third and longest-serving director of the research center, from 1974 to 1990, after its name was changed, in 1973, to Martin Marietta Laboratories and its mission became less basic and more directly applied to corporate programs. In 1993, when Martin Marietta became the managing contractor for Sandia National Laboratories, Dr. Westwood became vice president for research and exploratory technology.

CHAPTER 23

Vanguard: In More Than Name

■

W hile Bunker is generally conceded to have set new directions for the modern-day Martin company, he would have been the first to credit much of the company's "marketing smarts" in those transitional days of the fifties to his close associate and good friend Jess Sweetser. A big, handsome man with thick, bushy eyebrows and a resonant voice, Sweetser was something of a legend in the world of sports. At the age of twenty he had won the United States Amateur Golf Championship, and four years later, in 1926, he became the first American to win the British Amateur title, beating among others golfing great Bobby Jones.

Glenn Martin had hired Sweetser in February 1950. Three months later he was promoted to vice president for sales and requirements, a position he retained when Bunker took the reins two years later. He worked for the company a dozen years until retirement, and on the golf course he continued to shoot his age or better from the time he was sixty-seven until he died in his eighties. When he retired in 1962, Sweetser was succeeded in the sales and requirements position by another who was as personable and forceful and whose share of fame was earned on a competitive playing field not as gentlemanly as golf. His name was Thomas G. Pownall.

Sweetser's athletic reputation preceded him wherever he went in business, particularly in the "customer's shop." Friends and business associates alike vied for his company on the golf course. In addition, Sweetser was the consummate company representative. "Sartorially impeccable, unfailingly courteous," as one chronicler described him many years later, he also was an excellent salesman. He knew how to listen to a potential customer and find out his needs and wants when it came to new systems.[1]

Bill Purdy said it was Sweetser who doggedly tracked the Air Force requirement for a second intercontinental ballistic missile and who focused management's attention on going after the contract. It was at the same time, 1955, that the company was chosen by the Naval Research Laboratory for the prime contract on Project Vanguard. The contract, announced on October 7, came just forty days after President Eisenhower officially proclaimed that the United States would launch instrumented, man-made satellites as its scientific contribution to the International Geophysical Year (IGY), an eighteen-month period of scientific study and exploration by sixty-seven nations that was to begin July 1, 1957.

Vanguard was to have been this country's and, Americans thought, the world's first Earth-orbiting satellite. The competition to build and launch a satellite had been among the three armed services: Army, Navy, and Air Force. The Army's entry was the design of the German team headed by Wernher Von Braun and was patterned pretty much after V2 technology from the war. The Air Force entry, based on the Atlas missile just then emerging as the nation's first intercontinental ballistic missile, was the largest of the three. It was a giant compared to the pencil-thin, very much more sophisticated Vanguard rocket, which was inspired by the successful Viking Program and proposed by the winning team of Martin and the NRL.

In the government at the time, and particularly among the decision makers who would actually influence the Vanguard decision, there was concern that nothing should interfere with the nation's development of a military missile capability as a counter to similar efforts in the Soviet Union. That concern weighed heavily against the Air Force approach with the then-fledgling Atlas ICBM, and all but ruled out the Army's proposal; there were also unspoken misgivings, if not outright distrust, of the "German crowd" of Von Braun rocket scientists.

"I remember some of us felt," Bill Purdy said, "that because the program was a scientific one . . . a noble undertaking with a peaceful purpose . . . that somehow the services ought to have found a way to collaborate on the approach. But it didn't happen. We

[Martin] were pressed very hard by NRL to actually commit ourselves to a program of adapting the Viking design to something that would carry a satellite "[2] Actually, from the standpoint of technical grasp, Purdy said, the Germans were further along, but as far as the hardware, Viking was probably more advanced.

"About the same time, within the company, Jess Sweetser was really bending our ears talking about a backup ICBM that the Air Force was going to develop," Purdy added. "It was huge. Even in those days it obviously was a gigantic project. It didn't have a name at that point in time. We weren't really sure that it was a serious program. And again some of us felt—I know I felt—that we weren't ready for something that large, that we really should concentrate on Vanguard and give the Atlas backup the go-by."

Sweetser's bulldog persistence in pressing management to bid on the work, plus the technical assessment of engineering talents such as Purdy, Bergen, and Trimble, convinced George Bunker to go after the new ICBM program at the same time the company was developing the Vanguard rocket. It was a fairly gutsy decision to make. Not only had the company just won the Vanguard competition, but its competitors for the new ICBM were Lockheed and Douglas, both of which were doing important work for the Air Force. Both companies were much better known than Martin in the particular type of shop that would be handling the proposal.

Once the decision was made to do both, Purdy said, "we were in the position of having to split the Viking group two ways, half going to Vanguard and half to the new Air Force proposal." But before the team was divided, Purdy, as head of the recently completed and highly successful Viking rocket program, drew the assignment in the late summer of 1955 of representing Martin in negotiations with the Navy that set the time schedule and scope of the Vanguard contract. The commitment was to build a workable launch vehicle that would place one satellite in orbit around the Earth within the eighteen-month International Geophysical Year, or before the close of 1958. The cost was estimated at approximately $13 million.

The Martin program manager for Project Vanguard was Elliott N. Felt, Jr. Donald J. Markarian was named chief engineer, and the chief of flight testing at Cape Canaveral was Robert Schlecter. His sidekick as operations manager of the launch team was a young crew-cut West Point–trained engineer named Stanley Welch. All but Welch were engineering veterans of the Viking program. Purdy's efforts were redirected to the other company team going after the

Air Force contract for a new ICBM. Less than four months later, in the closing days of 1955, The Martin Company won that job, too. It was chosen to be the prime contractor for the Air Force's newest, most powerful ICBM, the Titan. It was a heady time. The country's oldest and most prominent maker of airplanes had become virtually overnight a premier producer of missiles and rockets for the new aerospace age.

VANGUARD

To many who were there at the time and to others in a position to know, including many of the gatherers and writers of history, the Vanguard Program was an outstanding success. It did not put the world's first satellite into orbit, or even the first American satellite so to that end it failed. But it was, as the dictionary defines the word *vanguard*, the advance guard, the leader, the forefront in any movement, field, or activity. The program contributed a long and impressive list of technological firsts to the generations of rocket, missile, and spacecraft systems that followed.[3]

To millions of others—both lay and professional—who were whipped into a frenzy of self-doubt by technology-innocent reporters and headline writers intolerant of the research process of trial and error, Vanguard was a dismal failure. It had not beaten the Soviet satellite, Sputnik, into orbit. America's prestige, educational veracity, and technological virility had been called into question, or so it seemed at the time. The result was a massive shudder of the national corpus, resulting in a restructuring of teaching techniques in schools and a new emphasis on science, among other things.

In hindsight, it is difficult to know what might have been had priorities been different, had the United States' scientific program not taken a lower priority than considerations of national defense, including the development of a nuclear deterrent and the ICBM as a means of delivering it. In any case, Martin men and women were at the heart of both efforts. The roles they played contributed significantly to the course of history not just in the United States but throughout the free world, and what would become an even larger world community of free nations and peoples.

When the first slender Vanguard rocket reached Cape Canaveral, it was several months and many millions of dollars off original schedules. The reasons were many. Never before had anyone tried to compress so much instrumentation and electronics into such a small package. Not only was the rocket itself small, only forty-five inches in

Vanguard failure, 1957 . . .

. . . and success, 1958

diameter and seventy-two feet in length, but its fuels, electrical and hydraulic systems, staging mechanisms, controls, handling structures, and tracking network were virtually all new. There were to be a dozen launch vehicles in all. The first six would be test vehicles designated TV-0 through TV-5, the initial pair being modified Vikings left over from that program. TV-4 and TV-5 were to carry experimental satellites in the "unlikely event" they reached orbital velocity and altitude. But only after analysis of the six test vehicles would the six satellite vehicles, or SLVs, be launched. The program, by formal mission definition, called for only a single Earth-orbiting satellite by the end of 1958, the close of the IGY. Much would occur to alter those objectives.

The first two test vehicles—the modified Vikings—were completely successful, in December 1956 and May 1957. But when the Soviets launched the world's first Earth-orbiting satellite, Sputnik I, on October 4, 1957, the din in the American press and the American political community could be heard around the world. America had been beaten. We had lost the "race" to be first. Another Vanguard test vehicle was successful three weeks later. It consisted of the new first stage topped with inert second and third stages, but without a satellite, its success was not good enough. The pressure was on, from the White House down, to match the Soviet feat. "Get something up there! Anything!" was the cry.

Kurt Stehling, Vanguard propulsion group head for the Naval Research Laboratory, put it in focus years later, rationalizing in his book, *Project Vanguard:*

> After Sputnik I a great geyser of asininities erupted in the United States. One of the more foolish manifestations of our post-Sputnik era was the cry that education (or the lack of it) was responsible for our missile and space "setback." But surely the most foolish notion of them all was the common belief that Vanguard was ready and able to rake the chestnuts out of the space fire. The country now had the satellite fever . . . and the spotlight focused on Vanguard.
>
> All at once the early altruistic IGY considerations went out of the window and a satellite was demanded— any satellite, it seemed, would assuage the national pride. . . . The decision, well meant but silly, to place a "baby" satellite in our untried test launch vehicles and then *publicize* this was going to unleash a whirlwind.[4]

At a White House meeting with President Eisenhower, Vanguard project director Dr. John Hagen emphasized that the next Vanguard rocket, TV-3, the fourth test vehicle and the first Vanguard with all three stages live, would be strictly experimental. Any announcement of its planned orbital attempt would be premature, he said. To Hagen's chagrin, press secretary Jim Hagerty, in a White House news release the next day, proclaimed that the upcoming shot would launch the first United States satellite.[5]

TV-3 was set to be launched in December. It was to have been the first flight test of the second-stage propulsion system and the first test vehicle with the complete guidance and control system. Because of the pressure to match the Russians, it also carried a four-pound, grapefruit-sized satellite. One second after ignition, with much of the world watching expectantly, the pencil-thin Vanguard rocket lifted ever so slightly, then settled back on the launch stand and exploded. The tiny satellite, sprung from the rocket's nose, rolled across the concrete launch pad, beep-beeping its tracking signal as if it had been released in space. Faulty ignition had caused the first-stage engine to lose thrust, and the smoke and fire of the failure consumed what was left of the nation's already tarnished pride.

To the NRL-Martin launch crew, it was the ignominy of ignominies. No one outside the program seemed to realize it was a brand-new rocket. Failure had not been unexpected. It was only the fourth of six tests planned before even the first attempt to launch a satellite. Only three days before that heartbreaking explosion on the pad, Martin Company vice president George Trimble had flatly predicted at a business meeting in Melbourne, Florida, that the first complete Vanguard launch vehicle would not succeed in placing a satellite in orbit. He based his statement on "the prevailing mathematics of trial and error"—normally three failures in every seven tries—"in this kind of testing experiment." Public chagrin and hurt pride needed a whipping boy, and Vanguard was it.

Back in Baltimore a few weeks later, project engineer Don Markarian learned just how strong the feeling was. He had trouble getting a painter to work on his house. "Finally," he recalled later, "one of the men I approached had the courtesy to level with me. 'To tell the truth, Mr. Markarian, I don't feel much like working for anyone connected with Project Vanguard.' "[6]

Not everyone was so critical. Many in high places, including the president and vice president, tried to rationalize the failure, even sending encouraging messages to the Vanguard team. President Eisenhower, in a conversation with Dr. Detlev Bronk, president of the

National Academy of Sciences, asked, "Were we Americans the first to discover penicillin?" Bronk replied, "You know the answer to that, Mr. President." "And did we kill ourselves because we didn't?" the president asked, again being assured he knew the answer to that as well. And Murray Snyder, assistant secretary of public affairs for Defense, chastised reporters for "exaggerated optimism" in covering events leading up to the TV-3 failure, particularly in view of the "great restraint exercised" by the Department of Defense in stressing the preliminary test nature of the launch attempt.

Ten years later, Charles A. Lindbergh, a man who had felt the intensity of press coverage from differing perspectives, noted that "the effect of a superficial and sensational press . . . has retarded the development of many important projects, Vanguard among them. It places such an unrealistic penalty on development errors that increased costs and delays result through excessive attempts to avoid them."[7]

And so it went that bleak winter of 1957, until Wernher Von Braun's Army team, headed by Major General Bruce Medaris at Redstone Arsenal, Huntsville, Alabama, was officially turned loose to attempt a satellite launch. They did so successfully on January 31, 1958, with a modified military missile, the Jupiter-C, which boosted Explorer I into orbit as the first United States satellite.

The U.S. Navy–Martin team would have to wait another month and a half, until March 17, 1958, when TV-4, the fifth test vehicle—complete with a shamrock taped to its side—placed fifty-seven pounds into an elliptical orbit that is expected to last one thousand years. The initial perigee, or closest distance to earth, of the four-pound satellite was 406 miles. Its apogee was 2,465 miles.

A second Vanguard satellite, weighing 23.7 pounds, plus its 47.08-pound third stage, was boosted into space on February 17, 1959, by SLV-4, achieving an orbit expected to last at least two hundred years. The program's third satellite, SLV-7, orbited on September 18, 1959, was the last Vanguard. Actually a backup to an earlier test vehicle, it placed 94.6 pounds in orbit, including a 52.25-pound satellite expected to circle the Earth for at least fifty years. (A fourth Vanguard satellite, SLV-1, achieved orbit, but only briefly, on May 27, 1958.) Vanguard's bottom line? Four satellites placed in orbit, three of them for extended lifetimes, out of seven attempts (actually, only six were planned).

George Trimble's statistically based forecast of three failures in seven attempts, or four successes, was the Vanguard program's final box score—not too shabby for a program objective of one satellite

(TV-4) in Earth orbit during the IGY. Vanguard's record was actually double the success rate of U.S. launch vehicles during those early years of the space age. John Goodlette, who played major engineering roles on Titan, Pershing, the Viking Mars Lander, and many other programs, observed thirty years after that "Vanguard was not a resounding example of mission sucess" in what would become the company's predilection for that term. But he agreed that the Vanguard program had these notable achievements:

- First multistage launch vehicle.
- First use of gimbaled engines.
- First rocket use of hypergolic fuels, white fuming nitric acid, and unsymmetrical dimethylhydrazine (UDMH), which ignite spontaneously on contact, and the first use of UDMH, the second-stage fuel.
- First high-altitude ignition of liquid rocket motor.
- First fiberglass-encased third-stage solid rocket motor.
- First launch vehicle to navigate with self-contained airborne guidance.
- First use of a "strapped-down" gyro platform.
- First efficient roll control of a rocket using rotatable exhaust jets of the first-stage turbopump.
- First use of miniaturized circuits and batteries and first space use of solar cells.
- First complete reliability analysis, through telemetry, of the performance of every part of every vehicle fired, whether successful or not.[8]

Scientists at the National Academy and many in the National Aeronautics and Space Administration acknowledged Vanguard "as a progenitor to all American space exploration," wrote authors Constance McLaughlin Green and Milton Lomax in their book, *Vanguard: A History*. In a preface to that history, Charles Lindbergh wrote:

> That the spectacular and psychological exert tremendous influence on life is obvious. That we underestimated this influence in planning our early satellite program is just as clear. That, in hindsight, we should have changed the relative priority between missiles and satellites can still be argued. . . . In rational analysis, two facts emerge to silhouette against a turbulent background.

The Project Vanguard objective was accomplished during the International Geophysical Year, as planned, and our military forces achieved a retaliatory power before the Soviet Union could have destroyed our civilization by a ballistic missile attack. Both programs were successful despite the many obstacles encountered.

. . . To this decade-later evaluation, I believe it is pertinent to add that Project Vanguard contributed in major ways to the manned lunar orbitings and landings in which principles of scientific perfection were maintained and America was first.[9]

Green and Lomax concluded: "The engineering feat of designing, constructing, and testing within thirty months a vehicle that could and did launch an Earth satellite was in itself extraordinary, especially at a time when the art of rocketry was still in adolescence." Von Braun himself called Vanguard's accomplishments a "miracle."

PART VI

Diversification

1955–65

■

CHAPTER 24

Time of the Titan

■

I t had no grand name when first conceived. The Air Force called its secret alternative concept for an intercontinental ballistic missile XSM-68, for "Experimental Strategic Missile." The as-yet-to-be-designed missile would also be designated WS107A-2, the first two letters standing for "weapon system." Atlas had been designated WS-107A, and this was to be the second ICBM, thus the 2. Its design would draw heavily on innovations and technologies developed successfully on Vanguard. Even though much stouter in diameter, its ultimate bullet shape would also reflect Vanguard's trimness. That it would be the first of a long and distinguished line of missiles and space boosters—an entire family of Titans—no one could have guessed in 1955.

It was apparent at the time that the Air Force wanted its new ICBM developed away from either coast, outside the range of a missile-firing submarine. Bill Purdy said this caused quite a bit of controversy among the other contractors hoping to build the new system. Douglas and Lockheed were both competitors; both had missile operations in California and were not too keen on moving elsewhere. Boeing in Seattle was also posturing competitively, based on its missile experience with the Matador-like Bomarc, but only briefly.

For The Martin Company, "it turned out that George Bunker was looking for an excuse to open a new division," Purdy said, "so there wasn't any feeling of opposition about moving to a new spot."[1] With that decision made, the rocket-experienced group that had been broken off from the Viking-Vanguarders was further subdivided. "Bunker thought half of us should work the proposal effort from Baltimore," Purdy said, "with the other half moving to California where the customer lived," specifically the Western Development Division of the U.S. Air Force's Air Research and Development Command.

The Western Development Division, formed less than a year before, with offices in the Los Angeles subdivision of Inglewood, was commanded by newly starred Brigadier General Bernard Schriever. Earlier, when Schriever was stationed in Washington, D.C., as director of the Air Force Office of Development Planning, Jess Sweetser first began tracking Air Force interest in a second ICBM. He and Schriever became friends and occasional golfing companions.

"Benny" Schriever, to those who knew him best, was generally conceded to be the father of America's strategic missile program. In his new, high-priority assignment developing the land-based missile element of the nation's strategic defense, General Schriever had the strong assistance of the Ramo-Wooldridge Corporation, which provided his command with technical direction. Its principals were Drs. Simon Ramo and Dean Wooldridge, two bright scientists who had been performing long-range analytical studies for the Air Force.[2]

Purdy remembers that when he visited Si Ramo to inform him that Martin intended to set up a group in California, "he was very nice about it, but he told me the kind of skills we needed 'are really in scarce supply, and I doubt that you're going to help yourself by putting half your scarce skills out here and half back in Baltimore.' We went ahead and did it anyway," Purdy said. Whether it was a significant factor in winning the contract, he could only guess. Moving the team to California definitely increased The Martin's Company's knowledge of the customer, and it undoubtedly raised awareness and familiarity with the Martin proposal team among people in that particular Air Force division.[3]

Purdy remained in Baltimore with the base group, and Jim Burridge was sent to California to head up the other half of the proposal group in Santa Monica offices. John Youngquist of Viking fame went with Burridge. At about the same time, the company conducted an extensive survey to determine the site of the new organization. Purdy said the survey started with George Bunker,

Purdy and Burridge in Titan control room

whose first reaction was that the company needed to go to Denver. " 'There's no better place to live than Denver' was Bunker's rationale," Purdy said. After surveying about ninety-eight different locations throughout the country, Denver was the odds-on choice, and the proposal to the Air Force was based on setting up a new division to build the missile in Colorado.

As the deadline for submitting the proposal neared and details were finalized, the effort was concentrated on the West Coast, where Purdy had moved to lead the final push. By that time it was clear the Air Force wanted a true alternative ICBM—a more advanced design, not merely a backup. The Atlas was basically a thin-skinned—thinner than a dime—inflated aluminum balloon. It could stand upright only when pressurized and filled with propellants. Its propulsion consisted of three side-by-side engines burning from the ground up, essentially a single-stage rocket, although it was referred to as a stage and a half because the outer two engines, attached by a skirt, dropped off at burnout, leaving only the center, or sustainer, engine burning to orbit.

The Air Force specification for the new design spelled out the range, speed, time to target, guidance, and throw weight, or size of the warhead. Left to the bidding contractors was the type of missile, its configuration, whether solid or liquid propellants, number of engines, and staging techniques. In other words, Purdy said, it was virtually wide open as long as it was better than the Atlas. Lockheed's approach involved multiple rockets clustered or strapped together. Douglas had another concept.

Martin's proposal called for two liquid-propellant stages with rigid framework of a copper-aluminum alloy the thickness of a half dollar. Tankage walls would be integral to the rocket's walls, à la Viking and Vanguard, for weight saving. The first stage would be powered by twin 150,000-pound-thrust engines, and the 80,000-pound-thrust second stage would be separated and ignited at high altitude, well above most of the Earth's restraining atmosphere. A bold approach, it would be the first application of high-altitude ignition under virtually gravity-free conditions, or zero-g, to a *large* liquid rocket engine. Vanguard's second stage had proven the principle, but Titan would be the first large-scale application of ignition at high altitude.

Titan would stand ninety-eight feet in height, its first stage ten feet in diameter tapering down to an eight-foot-diameter second stage. It had to be able to hurl approximately 3,800 pounds, made up of its warhead and the reentry vehicle, a distance of 5,500 nautical miles. Perhaps most significant, from the standpoint of growth and future missions, the design would be modular, or building-block, in approach, meaning that the basic configuration could be grown in size or modified by add-on units. The true significance of that approach to future business was incalculable at the time. Another distinguishing feature of the Martin proposal was that a new Rocky Mountain facility would be dedicated to the development, manufacture, and testing of this one missile system, a place "where an engineer's drawing line can be transformed into a complete weapon system, including design, fabrication, and captive testing."

The Air Force had backed off on security considerations that originally dictated a midcontinent manufacturing location. That had become a moot point by the time final proposals were submitted. By then, however, Martin's management was dedicated to moving to Denver, "so we actually had to sell the Air Force on their own original idea," Purdy said, while the competitors proposed building the missile on the West Coast, literally in the customer's backyard.[4]

When it came time for the formal oral presentation that accompanied the printed volumes of the written proposal, Purdy and Jim Burridge were the presenters. Somewhere near the end of

Denver plant, Rocky Mountain home of the Titan

Purdy's part, he said, Dr. Ramo came into the room and asked, "What do you think is your most critical problem?"

"I sweat like a pig when under stress," Purdy said, "and I was sweating and mopping my brow with my handkerchief when I told him, 'There are two, I think. One would be the staging issue, and the other would be attaining the reliability that is necessary for the operational hardware.' Ramo nodded his head and walked out of the room. I didn't know whether that was the answer he wanted . . . whether I had failed or not."

They definitely did not fail. Purdy said the decision on the winner was made quite rapidly. "I remember when we learned we had won, there was definitely a feeling of accomplishment. As we were leaving the Air Force office, I can remember the glum look on the faces of the losing team. They had had the inside track, we thought, so we felt good about beating them. But we could empathize with their disappointment, knowing the amount of work they must have put into their proposal."

Even before the award of the contract, which came in December 1955, Chairman Bunker and Bill Bergen, along with Ross B. Hooker, Jr., the company's director of facilities, headed west in hopes of quietly putting together the remote acreage required for the new plant. Although welcomed warmly by Chamber of Commerce officials and other city leaders, the venture almost came unglued when the Martin people were placed in the hands of a real estate broker who did not take their interest too seriously. He apparently was working his own agenda, convinced that he was on the ground floor of rumors that had Boeing, the big airplane maker, coming to town. No one knew where that rumor originated. As a result, the Martin people were shown nothing that came close to their needs. They were preparing to leave town when word got back to Calvin Snyder, director of the Chamber of Commerce, who prevailed upon them to stay a few more days.

Taking the matter into his own hands, Cal Snyder, with the help of his associate Bill Gibbons, in the space of a weekend put together seven thousand acres of property in the foothills of the Rockies, near Littleton, a community of five thousand a dozen miles southwest of downtown Denver. Although the property involved many parcels held by a variety of nonresidents—some of them second and third generations from original owners—all were contacted and sale commitments obtained before Bunker and his associates left town.[5]

Options were taken on the property before Thanksgiving, the Titan contract was won in December, and siting surveys began before

Christmas. Beal Teague was one of three engineers who surveyed the high ground behind the hogback—the outcropping of Colorado red rock—where the plant would be built. "I was standing on a hill near what is now the entrance," he recalled years later. "Right then and there we picked out the site for the first test stand."[6]

Those who selected the overall property had done well. Sound propagation studies involved placing scores of listening devices scattered in a 360-degree circle as far away as Boulder to detect simulated sound waves at decibel levels expected from engine tests. Natural folds of the rugged landscape effectively contained the sound except when there was a temperature inversion. Then the sound would sometimes be bounced across the county. But even under such conditions, the disturbance was momentary, and the sound, remarkably, was no greater than that made by a loud truck.

Ground was broken for the plant on February 6, 1956. The first cadre of employees had moved from Baltimore to Denver shortly after the New Year, establishing offices in the old Shell Building, just behind the State House in downtown Denver. The overflow moved into the Keith Building a few blocks away. Two hundred engineers and facilitators from Middle River were in place by the spring, and local hiring began. Just 299 days after ground breaking, the engineering building was completed. The sprawling manufacturing building was completed soon after, and employees occupied their new Denver division that fall. Static test stands, propellant-loading facilities, machine shop, and other ancillary buildings soon followed. Al Varrieur, veteran Baltimore engineer, was the first general manager, and Bill Purdy was named chief engineer.

From that moment on, Purdy said, "it was Katie, bar the door. Basically, the problem was we were putting together a weapon system and an organization and a facility—all of them brand new—at the same time. And all of them were unprecedented in size." An early Martin estimate in the proposal process put the cost of the new ICBM at something like $90 million, Purdy said. "We were far off the mark, and the customer knew that. They were smarter than we were in that regard. Even in those early days it was a several-hundred-million-dollar program."

The new system would be called Titan, after the sons of Uranus and Gaea in Greek mythology, and so would be their sons—creatures of enormous size, power, and influence. This Titan would be all those things. Practically everything about the new program was unprecedented. No one had ever put such a system together. Relationships with the new customer and even among Martin people were

President Eisenhower views Colorado test stand

tentative. "We were a bunch of strangers who didn't understand each other and sometimes didn't want to understand each other," Purdy said. "To make things more complex, the Air Force had developed a philosophy, through bitter experience, of testing everything on the ground before it flew. And they meant literally everything . . . simulating flight to the greatest degree possible."

With a multistage rocket, one of the big unknowns is staging at altitude. Although it had been done before in much smaller vehicles, one of them the Vanguard, experience with big rocket motors and large amounts of propellants was "essentially zilch," Purdy said. So one of the test programs the new Denver division had to establish was a captive staging process involving a three-hundred-foot tower. It had to be rugged enough to handle the firing of a partially loaded first stage, followed by separation and firing of the second stage, both of them restrained during the static firing. Unlike the Viking that got away in the early days at White Sands, such an incident would be unthinkable in the metropolitan Denver area. If it sounded like something that couldn't be done on the ground, that was exactly what the Air Force and Martin finally concluded. It would not be worth the cost of building a structure so strong that it could destroy the second stage before it broke loose.

Another of the young Titan engineers—they were all in their late twenties and early thirties—who agreed with Purdy's assessment that the state of missile knowledge in those days was at best limited was Laurence J. "Larry" Adams. Jim Burridge recruited him to make the move from Baltimore as head of the stress group. "In about ten milliseconds I said yes," Adams recalled. "I never even talked to Peggy [his wife]" or to Jerry LaFrance, his boss at the time. Adams had been with the company about seven years and had worked on most of the missile and rocket programs, including Oriole, Matador, Mace, and Viking. "When we got to Denver, we were on a crash schedule, working ten hours a day, six days a week," Adams said. "That was our standard schedule. Cryogenics was one of the critical areas we were working particularly hard because we didn't know much about the supercold liquids that were going to be our propellants. I didn't know anything about them, especially how they would affect the metals we were using.

"We were welding 2014 aluminum . . . an alloy then called ST14 . . . which up until that time had been considered a nonweldable metal. It's a high-strength alloy, and we needed as much strength as we could get." The University of Denver, where a comprehensive

Titan production

research program had been established, ran a whole series of tests at cold temperatures and warm temperatures to characterize the welds. Adams said the concern was that the whole tank structure might shrink or contract when filled with propellants that were minus 297 degrees Fahrenheit. "If the metal became wavy and distorted, the stage could lose its load-carrying ability."[7]

Among the tests was a full-size simulation using a tank ten feet in diameter and fifteen feet long. In order to save on liquid nitrogen, which was used in place of liquid oxygen, they filled the majority of the tank's volume with big steel plugs. "So there we were, pumping liquid nitrogen," Adams said, "and we pumped away and pumped away and pumped away until we were far beyond the quantity planned. And we kept hearing these big CRACK! BANG! BOOM! sounds. My God, that stuff makes noise when it contracts. Well, it turned out that all that steel became very brittle in the intense cold and busted all to pieces, so instead of large chunks filling the space, we had steel pebbles and dust, practically, and the space was filling up with liquid nitrogen."

Another time, Adams recalled, they were testing fifteen-foot-long salami-shaped bottles designed to store liquid hydrogen that was needed for pressurization within the larger liquid oxygen tank. The idea was that the colder you could store liquid hydrogen, the more you could hold in a small container—another volume and structural-weight-reduction consideration. As with practically every-thing in the design of such rockets and missiles, the more weight you saved in the vehicle itself, the more payload you could lift.

"So we built a small, concrete-lined pit up above the plant, behind one of the hills, and we laid the salami tank in the pit," Adams said. "We had the salami tank rigged so that as we filled it with liquid nitrogen, we could pressurize it to the point of breaking it, in order to determine its strength. We were also going to fill the pit with liquid nitrogen to keep the salami tank as cold as possible. So the service department delivered the liquid nitrogen, and the guy in charge of that was a young fellow by the name of Charles E. Carna-han. He had a line running from his truck up over the revetment we had built to hide behind during the test and on into the pit. Once again we pumped away and pumped away and pumped away and never got anything out the other end. Turns out—of course it's obvious when you stop and think about it—the damned liquid ni-trogen was turning to gas by the time it got to the end of the line, and all we were doing was spraying gaseous nitrogen around. It was an-other one of those dumbnesses with cryogenics we learned about the hard way."[8]

There were even more "stressful" moments, Adams recalled, on the way to producing the free world's most powerful ICBM and what would become, without question, the most successful space launch vehicle. One involved simulation of the gravity force (g-force) the propellants and tankage could expect to receive at Max-q, the point at which the missile climbing through the dense atmosphere is subject to maximum dynamic pressure, or that point where the aero-dynamic load on the missile is most severe. Attached at each quad-rant of the ten-foot-diameter-base of the Titan's first stage were four large longitudinal braces, called longerons, which not only took thrust loads from the engines but provided mounting points for the giant missile to sit on its launch stand. In a design dedicated to maintaining the integrity of the tanks, specifically by not drilling holes that could possibly leak, these longerons were spot-welded to the missile.

"We had set up what we considered a very esoteric spot-weld test in the Vertical Test Facility," Adams said. "Anticipating gravity forces of six-g's, we loaded the tanks with lead shot six times as heavy as the propellants would weigh. There this beauty was, sitting there in all its glory, the tank full of lead shot, when the damned spot weld let loose, and the whole shebang fell through the bottom. We totally destroyed the structural test area; I mean absolutely, totally destroyed it. That was one of the lowest days of my life. I was head of the stress group."

Others who played key roles on the engineering ground floor of that ambitious program included Caleb B. Hurtt, John D. Goodlette, David S. LeVine, John Hedgepath, Hatch Wroton, and Walter O. Lowrie, in addition to Jim Burridge and John Youngquist. Larry Adams, like others, would move on to bigger and more stressfully responsible positions, including general manager of the entire Denver complex. Adams followed Bill Purdy in that job. He became best known three decades after the early Titan Days as Martin Marietta's president, chief operating officer, and a member of the board of directors, until his retirement in 1991 after forty-three years with the corporation. Caleb Hurtt, better known simply as "K" (the letter, with no period, like the "cay" sound in his first name), also scaled the corporate heights in his thirty-seven-plus years with Martin Marietta. After working on Titan I and III, he became program manager on Skylab, then followed in the footsteps of Larry Adams as general manager at Denver, president of the aerospace company, and eventually president and chief operating officer of the corporation and a member of the board of directors.

Dave LeVine was something of an anomaly, to use a pet word of the engineers. He was an industrial engineer, not an aerodynamicist or degreed in electronics or flight controls or fluid dynamics or any of the other aerospace engineering specialties. He had been in plant engineering at Baltimore, and when Bob Blakey was moving to Denver in 1955 to head up manufacturing in the new plant, he asked Les Lippy to be factory manager and LeVine to be chief of industrial engineering. When the technicians for the Titan test stands "up on the hill" were assigned to LeVine by a quirk of personnel administration, he was into test engineering as well as plant engineering. It would be but the first of many anomalies in Dave LeVine's remarkable thirty two year career with Martin Marietta.

The first Titan reached its Cape Canaveral launch complex late in 1958, a remarkably swift two years and two months from completion of the plant and almost exactly three years after Martin's selection as the prime associate contractor for the system. Awaiting the missile at Canaveral was the most experienced test flight operations crew any missile and rocket contractor had ever assembled. Recognizing the inherent intellectual arrogance of most engineers, particularly when dealing with hardware they design, the company had established an autonomous test division at Canaveral. It was a corporate organization with its own general manager, independent of

Titan I test flight

any engineering or manufacturing arm of the company. The theory was that a test division, in order to properly "wring out" a new system, needed to be free from influence by management or control by the manufacturing organization. The concept was enthusiastically embraced by Martin's various customer organizations. They were the ones, after all, who eventually had to take over a system and operate it reliably without benefit of the design engineers and their penchant for perpetual tinkering. The Canaveral approach was "If it doesn't work, don't fix it—send it back."

Heading the Martin Canaveral division when Titan arrived was none other than that redoubtable Brit Tom Willey, of Baltimore and Omaha production fame. Flight test programs already in the division's capable hands when the first Titan arrived were Matador, Mace, and Vanguard. They would be followed by Pershing, Titan II, the 199-B Bold Orion, the first space-bound nuclear power supply for the Navy's Transit satellite, the Gemini-Titan Launch Vehicle, Titan III and IV, and the Commercial Titan. In fact, at one time in the late fifties, there were so many different test programs on the Canaveral division's plate that Martin was responsible for at least a launch a week from Cape Canaveral. Some weeks there were three or four Martin launches, occasionally two on the same day. In the first thirteen years of Canaveral's existence as the launch site for the Atlantic Missile Range, one-third of all U.S. missiles launched had been built by the corporation.

Reporting to Willey were all the regular staff functions—personnel, finance, procurement, engineering, quality, even public relations. Each supported flight test programs assigned to the Cape by the manufacturing divisions of the corporation. And managing those test programs were some of the most senior in experience—if only "kids" by age—missile and rocket veterans in the industry.

Titan had been at the Cape less than a month when Willey requested that Dave LeVine be transferred from Denver to the Cape to take over Titan launch operations. Willey and LeVine were kindred spirits in many ways. Both ardently pursued outside avocations—Tom as a lay preacher, Dave as a golfer, skier, and fisherman—with the same passion they applied to their work. Both were very direct, no-nonsense, hands-on managers, and each was a bug on cleanliness. LeVine reflected many years later that his cleanliness fetish "undoubtedly came from Tom" in the early fifties when they had worked together on the factory floor in Baltimore. Both believed a clean work area inspired clean work habits and, therefore, a cleaner product.[9]

Another pro transferring to the Canaveral division with the initial Titan was Richard C. Lea, who, as manager of the first test stand at Denver, had shepherded the missile through static testing. Lea became chief engineer for Titan testing at the Cape, and Dave LeVine credited him with being "a tremendous force," both at Denver and at Canaveral, in preparing Titan for launch. "Dick was energy-oriented, a ball of fire, yet calm and thoughtful," LeVine said. "He brought unquestioned integrity and authority to the launch program." When Lea later rotated back to Denver, his replacement at the Cape as chief test engineer on Titan was "K" Hurtt.[10]

Jim Burridge was another to whom Dave LeVine gave the highest marks as a person and as an engineer. "Jim was A-Number-One, my absolute salvation after I arrived at the Cape. I could call Denver with a problem at any hour of the day or night, and Burridge would immediately work on it," Dave said. "It wasn't unusual for me to wake him at one or two in the morning. He would go into the plant and call back in a couple of hours with either the solution or a suggested fix that generally worked."

Others in the Canaveral division in those early days of missile flight testing included, in addition to Schlecter and Welch, Leonard Arnowitz on Vanguard; Eugene Mommer on Mace; and on Titan, in addition to LeVine and Lea, Stanley Albrecht, Bob Neff, Neil Jones, Jim Stoms, and Warren Opitz, to name only a few. Riding herd on quality control were pros Joe Kraczyk (who would later change his surname to Taylor) and Haggai "Guy" Cohen. Another launch team regular was Romeo Thibedeau, better known as "Whitey." Like Joe Kraczyk, Whitey had problems with people mispronouncing his last name. He went to court and had his name changed to Robert Tibbs. Throughout a long career that included representing Martin Marietta for many years in Huntsville, Bob Tibbs was still called Whitey.

The public relations slot was the first full-time position of its kind for any contractor at Canaveral. Therein rested a vignette on the general atmosphere pervading those early days in the development of the nation's missiles and space rockets. The company was smarting under the blistering floodlight of negative headlines and the general lack of public understanding experienced with Vanguard. So it hired and sent to Canaveral in December 1958 a young news wire writer and editor who had been covering the budding space program from the Baltimore bureau of the Associated Press. His principal assignment was to interpret in lay language for generally nontechnical reporters the highly technical jargon of engineers and technicians, and the raison d'être of their hardware. He had

President Kennedy receives Titan II briefing at Canaveral

been aboard less than twenty-four hours when he was summoned before Major General Donald N. Yates, commanding general of Patrick Air Force Base and the Air Force's Atlantic Missile Range, of which Canaveral was Station No. 1. General Yates, a diminutive man physically, had a truly commanding presence and could bellow like a lion. One of his chief concerns was maintaining security for many of the classified programs assigned to his charge. And although not every program was classified, one of the general's proclivities was control of all launch schedules, regardless of national defense considerations.

Members of the press corps, who by and large were denied physical presence on the Cape—with rare exceptions in the early days—devoted much of their waking hours to circumventing the schedule blackout. The newspeople reported what was going on by using every means available to them, including long-range telescopes, traffic patterns, aerial surveillance, and an extensive network of Cocoa Beach bartenders and waitresses who seemed to know whenever a launch was scheduled, due mostly to the patronage, or lack thereof, of their regular customers.

Into that highly charged atmosphere of intrigue and exposure strode the newly hired Martin PR man, reporting specifically as directed to the commanding general's second-floor office at the Patrick Headquarters Building. After exchanging pleasantries with the receptionist, he opened the door and stepped hesitantly into General Yates's private office. No sooner had he entered than the general sprang from his chair behind a massive mahogany desk, which was mounted on a platform in the far corner of the enormous room. It gave General Yates a towering presence, despite his five-feet six-inches, as he jabbed a finger in the direction of the startled newcomer and shouted: "I need you here like a [expletive] hole in the head. You'll be just another damn leak to the press."

As time passed, launch schedules became public and press access to the Cape gradually improved. So did newspaper and radio coverage, and with it public understanding of the fledgling industry, which in those days seemed to blow up more things than it put up. At a time when the words *hold* and *scrub* and *random failure* were the rule rather than the exception, press and missile engineers alike looked forward to "random success." Much of the improvement in press relations was credited to the good offices and sound advice of Colonel Sidney Spear, General Yates's chief of public information. In time the general himself mellowed somewhat, and he and the Martin PR man actually became nodding acquaintances, both enjoying the mutual friendship of innkeeper Tommy "Wild Man" Dougherty and his late-night sing-alongs in the bar of the old Trade Winds Hotel, eighteen miles south of the Cape at Indialantic, Florida.[11]

The first Titan, its second stage inert, flew successfully from Canaveral Launch Complex 18 on February 6, 1959. Numbers 2, 3, and 4 were also good, forming an unprecedented string of successes for a brand-new program. Success would be short-lived. The fifth Titan blew up on the pad, and there followed two more failures that tested the mettle of test crews and design engineers before Titan got back on track.

Among those witnessing the spectacular though devastating first blowup of a Titan were George Bunker and General Bernard Schriever. As head of Titan launch operations, David LeVine, who rated the launch of the first Titan as the greatest personal moment of his career, would always remember the day Titan No. 5 exploded like it was yesterday.

"Even before we knew the cause, Bunker and Schriever wanted to know how long it would take to fix the launch stand," LeVine said. "I told them we could have another missile on that stand in four weeks, and they both responded with an incredulous 'bullshit.' We actually had it repaired and another missile up in twenty-three days, and Bunker was impressed."[12] That may have been the beginning of what developed into a close relationship—both professionally and personally—between Bunker and LeVine. But more important, the recovery from the Titan failure demonstrated a fundamental trait that would forever characterize the company and set it apart from others in the eyes of its own people and, it was hoped, in the eyes of their customers.

"When the Titan blew up, we knew we had a problem," LeVine said. "But there was no finger-pointing, even after we discovered the cause. We simply turned to getting it fixed and took corrective action to ensure its not happening again. I think the Air Force and other customers have always thought of Martin Marietta that way. We never alibied or pointed fingers. We just said, 'Here's the problem, let's fix it,' and then moved on."

When the failures set in and before the program "got well," George Bunker moved to Denver and personally took charge of the program. It was, of course, a dramatic move for the chief executive of a large corporation to make. But he knew that his presence in Denver would automatically accomplish two things immediately. It reassured the customer that something was being done to fix the problem and that it had the top man's attention, and it alerted every man and woman in the Denver organization, particularly those on the Titan program, that the problem had the boss's close attention and, therefore, it had better have theirs as well.

About the time Bunker moved to Denver, two Baltimore veterans were drafted to make the move as well. George Rodney, who in 1969 had seen his beloved P6M SeaMaster scrapped by the Navy, was tapped to move to Denver as head of Titan testing, and Vernon Keene was transferred to run manufacturing. It would be Rodney's transformation from airplanes to missiles and spacecraft. A short time later George Smith was transferred from Canaveral to be general manager of Denver. These three would be among the nucleus of a team to help transform Denver from a Titan-only missile manufacturer into a full-fledged player in the broader field of astronautics.

One incident during Bunker's time of running the Denver operation is printed indelibly on "K" Hurtt's memory. Hurtt said he was in his office in the Little Cambridge Dairy location wrestling with the solution to a Titan problem when Bunker wandered in.

"I was struggling with whether to go with a solution that would have been very good for the program but not so good for Martin Marietta in terms of additional sales and profits. When I told George, he threw up his hands and said, 'Oh my God, is that all that's bothering you? You shouldn't waste your time on that one. It's a no-brainer.' " And Hurtt said he remembers Bunker "so clearly telling me to absolutely always vote for your program. Never vote for your perception of anything other than what is best for your program because in the long run it also will be the best thing for the company."[13]

In just about a year, success returned to Titan R&D testing with the seventh flight, and eleven more completely successful flights, with only two out-and-out failures in eighteen R&D flights, followed during 1960. The ultimate record for Titan I research and development flights was forty-four complete successes out of sixty-seven tests, a remarkable 66 percent rate of success for those early days of ICBM development. Titan I became operational with the Air Force on schedule in August, 1962.[14]

There was an almost poetic postscript to the development story of Titan earlier that year. It occurred on January 29, 1962, one of Florida's clearest winter evenings, with the forty-seventh and final Titan I R&D flight from the Cape. Launch had been scheduled for afternoon, but repeated holds in the countdown delayed it just beyond sundown. Martin Caidin, a colorful writer and prolific author and one of the covering horde of newsmen, described the launch in his 1962 book *Rendezvous in Space:*

> Thirty-one minutes past six o'clock the launching pad exploded in a glorious burst of golden fire. Light flashed in all directions as the Titan broke free of gravity and began her ride away from earth. It was impossible to see anything but light—savage, intolerable golden light . . . so intense that it bleached the blackness out of the night.
>
> The golden fireball lifted above the earth to announce the sound . . . a great knife of sound [that] split the sky asunder. . . . It punched at you and embraced the body and everything seemed to vibrate just a bit in resonance with the cry of the *thing.* . . . She rose, faster and faster, accelerating rapidly. The flame revealed thin hollow tubes of fire within which shock diamonds paraded in an endless stream. . . . The yellow became deep red and— suddenly—Titan was free of darkness. It was still early night . . . but Titan, rushing from night back into daylight, was struck by the sun already well disappeared beyond the horizon. First the flame became a blood color, then a rich orange with increasing height. Where Titan was, a man could no longer breathe; the giant plunged into the lower edges of space itself.[15]

As Titan's twin first-stage engines shut down, there was a moment without fire before the second-stage engine burst into life, and the heavenly panoply intensified. Alvin B. Webb of United Press International News, watching the launch with Caidin, called it "one of the most awesome and beautiful sights of the space age." And Caidin's rhapsody continued for what he described as "600 seconds of sorcery":

> . . . a glistening halo appeared around the burning upper stage. Ionized gases from the accelerating rocket rushed about in all directions, causing the halo to spread with tremendous speed . . . wider and wider, a huge pulsating teardrop that became a pale green . . . then glittering spots of pink and purple. . . . Soon we watched the light coming back at us in whorls and eddies, great glittering spirals, one after the other, a plasma whirlpool in the heavens far

above the upper edges of the planet's atmosphere. . . . It
was the most fantastic, beautiful sight I have ever seen.

So thought Marty Caidin in describing the incredible display witnessed by tens of thousands on the East Coast, from Florida to the
Carolinas. Police switchboards were flooded by callers wanting to
know its source. A meteorologist in the Miami Weather Bureau
dubbed it "Aurora Titanalis," and as such it would go into the
record books, a fitting climax to the Titan I test program and a
herald of Titans to come—Titan II, the Gemini-Titan Launch Vehicle, Titan III, and Titan IV.

Well before the original Titan completed its R&D launches and
took its place in the front line of the nation's strategic defense, a
vastly improved, more powerful successor was on the drawing boards
in Denver. Titan II was conceived to meet the growing fear in the late
fifties that the Soviets were developing superior nuclear warheads
and the missile capability to hurl them accurately at U.S. targets.

While the Air Force developed the need, Martin, as the inte-
grating contractor, and its associate contractors—Aerojet-General
Corporation for the engines and General Electric, replacing Avco
Corporation, for the reentry vehicle—came up with a system that
would be not only a logical modification and expansion of the Titan
design but a next generation dramatically improved in operational
simplicity and efficiency as well as maintainability and readiness. The
A.C. Sparkplug Division of General Motors was the associate contractor for the inertial guidance system, which had been developed by
the Charles Stark Draper Laboratories of Massachusetts Institute of
Technology. It would replace a radio guidance system that Bell Telephone Laboratories had furnished on Titan I.

The modularity of the original Titan design simplified its
growth. By fattening the second stage to the same ten-foot diameter
as the first and by lengthening both stages, the quantity of propellants could be increased significantly. In addition to the far more
accurate and pre-programmable inertial guidance, it was decided
that the new missile would use propellants that were storable at room
temperature and ablative materials for protection against aerodynamic heating and to protect missile surfaces from the heat of rocket
exhaust. The foremost and potentially most difficult requirement
called for the launch of the missiles from the depths of their silos
rather than lifting them to the surface, thereby dramatically short-
ening response time.

Improvements in the Titan II were startling. The number of

airborne electrical relays was reduced from forty-nine to seven, umbilicals from thirty-two to four, and valves and regulators from ninety-one to sixteen. On the ground, the simplification was even greater. Major underground structures were more than halved, dropping from forty-two to eighteen. Six thousand feet of underground tunnels required to support Titan I were reduced to 945 feet. Electrical power requirements per squadron dropped from 12,000 kilowatts to 2,700 kilowatts. Per missile, the interconnecting cables, wires, and terminations were cut in half, dropping from 11,794 to 5,820. As a result of this vast reduction in complexity, there was only one-tenth the number of periodic checkout functions (35 compared to 322) and one-tenth the number of launch functions (23 compared to 230).[16]

Titan II development began in June 1960, and the test program was significantly shortened, thanks to the simplified design and the increased level of confidence from the outset that the system would be more reliable. Titan II did not disappoint. Only thirty-three R&D missiles were launched, and twenty-five were completely successful, including the final thirteen. The R&D program was so successful and the Titan II so reliable that it was selected by the National Aeronautics and Space Administration as the launch vehicle for the two-man Gemini spacecraft, the middle phase between Mercury and Apollo of America's quest to place men on the moon.

Along with developing a reliable intercontinental ballistic missile, the Air Force was equally concerned with basing it. Some sort of hardened site that offered protection against possible Soviet ICBM attack was definitely required. Some in the company suggested drilling holes in Goat Mountain right above the plant and launching the Titans angularly from inside the mountain. As far-fetched as it sounded, word got back to the Air Force, and the result was underground silos buried beneath huge steel and concrete doors.

Don P. Herron, who was Martin-Denver's director of public relations at the time, credits a chance meeting with the Strategic Air Command's Major General David Wade with facilitating the basing decision. It was at an Air Force Association annual meeting in Dallas, Herron recalled. He was having an early breakfast in the hotel coffee shop and was deep in the morning newspaper when "a gentlemanly voice asked, 'Do you mind if I join you?' I looked up at a shoulder full of stars and it was General Wade. Although I didn't know him, I recognized him as one of the SAC officialdom attending the conference, so I invited him to join me and introduced myself as working for Martin at Denver.

" 'Oh, the Titan,' the general responded. 'You're the very person I'm looking for. I understand you fellows have a concept for basing the Titans in holes in the mountain rather than hardening them on the surface.' " Herron confirmed that fact and described the concept as well as others that were being considered by his colleagues back in Denver. "General Wade was getting more excited by the minute. 'This is going to change the whole picture,' he told me. 'I need to get in touch with your people and come out because we're interested.' " General Wade was as good as his word, Herron said, and visited the plant within the week.[17]

That was the beginning of silo basing, for which Martin was awarded a contract even larger than the original Titan order. Even before Titan I became operational in 1962, the underground basing concept would offer a whole set of new challenges in developing the missile's operational test facilities at Vandenberg Air Force Base in California. As the prime associate, or the industrial systems manager, The Martin Company oversaw that activity as well.

The first Vandenberg installation was the Operational Systems Test Facility, better known in typical Air Force alphabet soup lingo as OSTF. During the final checkout as the prototype for the operational sites, a Titan had just been raised by elevator 125 feet to the surface of its silo. There it stood in all its 110-ton glory fully loaded with liquid oxygen and RP1 fuel, when the elevator brake mechanism failed. The entire assembly plunged to the bottom of the silo in a devastating explosion of such force that the OSTF was destroyed beyond repair. As a result, the first training facility had to be rushed to completion and assigned double duty in checking out the operational procedure. Needless to say, the brake system for its elevator was redesigned by its subcontractor.[18]

In addition to developing and testing first Titan I and then Titan II in their R&D programs, then developing the operational test programs at Vandenberg, the company had the added responsibility for activation of the underground sites, aptly called "complexes." And complex they were, with massive concrete silos, bunkers, fuel storage cells, electronic control systems, and a command center—a virtual city buried deep within the earth. The activation task may have been the most awesome. Al Kullas, Denver's chief engineer at the time and one of the original transferees from Baltimore, best described the pressure-kettle atmosphere that existed:

It was a program best represented by a spectrum of feelings that ranged from the cryogenic temperatures of liquid oxygen to the most heated of human passions on a hot day in July. People worked all hours of the day and night for many months. Tempers flared, and I recall refereeing disputes between key Martin and subcontract people that approached fisticuffs. But it was because there was such tremendous commitment to the task and to successfully getting the job done.[19]

The initial nine operational silos making up the first Titan squadron were constructed on the bombing range at Lowry Air Force Base, east of Denver. That would be about as close to home as Vernon R. Rawlings would get for much of the four years he headed up the operational siting of the two Titan systems. Rawlings was a Baltimore boy. He had joined Martin in 1939 and earned his company spurs during the war as a manufacturing prodigy of Tom Willey.

As an assistant to Willey in the war years, Vern remembers attending staff luncheons with Mr. Martin in the Middle River executive dining room. "We would all get there at least five minutes early, and we'd stand stiffly behind our chairs until Mr. Martin came in precisely at the time set for lunch. It was very formal—tablecloth, silver, and wineglasses filled with Mr. Martin's favorite, nonalcoholic white grape juice. No one spoke unless spoken to, but Mr. Martin always managed to go around the table and engage each of us in some dialogue," Rawlings said.[20]

That was years before Rawlings was tapped for the activations task, and little did he know that he would also be the head man at Middle River, as vice president and general manager, from 1962 to 1970. When ICBM "site activation" began in 1959, Martin created an activation division with Rawlings as general manager. In that job he was virtually the industry czar, reporting to his Air Force counterpart and essentially his only boss, Major General Thomas Patrick Gerrity. "He was, without doubt, one of the finest officers and gentlemen you'll ever find," Rawlings said. "He supported us totally in everything."

Everything was just that—site preparation, construction, installation of the missiles, and initial flight readiness. It has been described as the largest, most complicated engineering-construction project ever attempted. It was a turnkey operation with Vern Rawlings and his activation division directing the activities of seven major associate contractors and about two hundred other subcontractor and supplier firms. "One absolutely superior team" Rawlings called it. "The managements of each of those companies and their twenty-three thousand

Rawlings, General Curtis LeMay, George Smith in Titan silo

employees assigned to Titan site activation were hell-bent on getting the job done right and on schedule, which meant as quickly as humanly possible."

Bill Purdy said he doubts "whether anybody could have done the job Vern did" on activation. "He was incredible. He understood the politics of admitting a mistake and making mileage out of it. Where the ordinary person would defend against criticism, Vern would say, 'Yes, I did it. I'm sorry. I'm going to work like hell to fix it.' And the Air Force loved him because he did work like hell to fix it."[21]

In describing Vern Rawlings's philosophy of identifying problems and owning up to mistakes, then fixing them, Purdy put his finger on what may be the most important ingredient of Martin Marietta's long-running success as a government contractor. It began in Cleveland under Glenn Martin, and to the present day it is one of the distinguishing features of the company's corporate culture. Certainly it is the most frequently cited by employees, retirees, and customers and is essential to the corporation's overall dedication to mission success.

In addition to the Lowry installation, Titan squadrons went into Marysville, California; Mountain Home, Idaho; and Rapid City, South Dakota. There would be a total of fifty-four operational Titan I missiles, each fueled and poised vertically in its underground silo in strategic defense of the United States. With specific targets programmed into the guidance computers of each missile, the Titans represented a deadly deterrent that served its purpose well in those head-to-head confrontational days of a very cold war with the Soviets.

When it came to Titan II, storable propellants made possible almost instant launch, and that called for firing the missiles from underground. On the scale of a 110-foot-tall missile belching 430,000 pounds of flaming thrust, it had never been done before. The very idea raised serious engineering disagreements between "the airborne guys and the ground guys," Robert Molloy remembers. At the time Molloy was in charge of ground system integration for the new Titan. A drastically simplified flight system would mean equally less complex ground-related facilities. The only real problem appeared to be the concept of firing from underground.[22]

"Our own missile guys said you couldn't do it," Molloy said, "and so there was a shootout in Al Hall's office." The chief engineer at Denver was Dr. Albert C. Hall, a tall, lean, serious man not generally given to mirth or light talk. Molloy said "the airborne guys were determined: 'We're not going to launch that missile out of the hole.' And the ground team was saying, 'By God, we've got to launch out of the hole, and you can do it.' "

Molloy said the reason his team was so sure was that "the British had run scale tests on a thing called the Blue Streak, an intermediate-range missile that, like the Atlas, had to be pressurized all the time. They had run one-sixtieth- and one-sixth-scale tests and had done all the work we needed to determine the barometric relationship between the missile diameter and the diameter of the hole so that you had the right aspiration rate and could control the bird as it came out." That was Friday afternoon, Molloy said, and Al Hall gave him the weekend to prove that structurally and control-wise the bird could be flown out of the hole. He did prove it, and that became the approach Al Hall accepted, and eventually so did the Air Force.

Final proof of the fire-from-the-hole pudding came on February 16, 1963, when a Titan I rose majestically from a Titan II operational test silo at Vandenberg between twin exhaust plumes of black smoke spewing from openings on either side. All that remained was for Vern Rawlings's activation team to construct, check out, and plant the missiles in underground sites at Little Rock, Arkansas; Wichita, Kansas; and Tucson, Arizona. That herculean task was completed on schedule in 1964. A total of 141 Titan II missiles were built, and 54 of them were placed on operational status. There they stood sentinel

Titan I test of Titan II silo launch

for twenty-three years, a symbol of force against Soviet aggression and the most powerful keeper of the peace until deactivated as part of the START treaty on July 23, 1987.

Titan was not the only program in the Denver plant, but it was the reason for the Denver plant's establishment. In its many forms, Titans have been the bread-and-butter programs there for nearly four decades.

A PHILOSOPHY CALLED "MISSION SUCCESS"

Perhaps one of the most beneficial fallouts of the Titan development story was the birth in 1966 of a formal program called "mission success." It would spread throughout Martin Marietta and over the years stamp itself in the minds of employees and customers alike as a significant ingredient of the corporation's culture. Twenty years later Robert W. Morra, a young engineer at the time, would describe "a single-mindedness toward mission success as perhaps the most significant attribute of Martin Marietta employees."[23]

This attitude did not just happen, Morra said. The concept was born out of an analysis of early 1960 missile failures throughout the industry and the shared conviction of the Air Force and Martin Marietta that "we can no longer tolerate failure." The objective of the first formal organization, known as the Launch Vehicles Mission Success Organization, was to ensure that no physical or technical deficiencies would exist—in the launch vehicle or associated equipment at the time of launch and throughout the flight phase—that would compromise the accomplishment of any mission objectives. The man who drew the initial assignment in 1966 of directing mission success was Walter O. Lowrie, who later would become prominent in management not only of the Titan program but of the Viking mission to Mars, as well as head of the Orlando operation.[24]

Although that was the beginning of the formal program known as mission success, the name may have originated a year before. According to Arthur L. Welch, the Denver operation was about to receive a visit from an Air Force general who was desirous of motivating the Martin people, and Denver general manager Bill Purdy was anxious to give the Titan quality program a name that would satisfy the general. "Mission success" was suggested, and it stuck.[25]

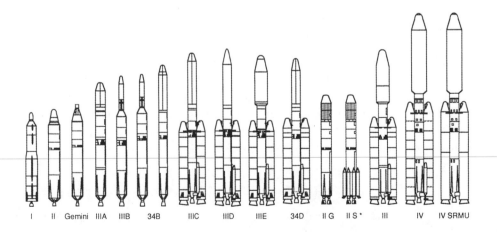

I   II   Gemini IIIA   IIIB   34B   IIIC   IIID   IIIE   34D   II G   II S *   III   IV   IV SRMU

Evolution of Titans

CHAPTER 25

Pershing: A Gamble That Paid Off

■

George Maverick Bunker was an excellent poker player and at times was known to live up to his middle name. Although he could not be called a nonconformist, the head man of the Martin company could be found on occasion somewhat apart from the herd. So it was in 1956, a year in which the odds were stacked heavily against the company's winning another major contract. But Bunker, betting strictly "on the come," placed a wager even before the cards had been dealt or the game identified by building a brand-new plant without a major new program to put in it.

In one sense he may have figured he was on a roll. Only the year before, Martin had won the Air Force's new Titan program and was in the process of building the Denver plant in which to manufacture it. That contract had followed closely on the heels of Martin's selection to build the Navy's Vanguard satellite launcher, a program already behind schedule and under enormous pressure to perform, including a push by Wernher Von Braun's Army team of German rocket scientists to put the first American satellite in space. The odds were long against the company's winning a third major program.

Such was the atmosphere early in the year when the Martin chief executive paid a courtesy call on Major General John Bruce

Medaris, commanding general of the newly created Army Ballistic Missile Agency at Huntsville, Alabama. General Medaris, slim and ramrod-straight, with iron-gray hair and crisp mustache, was not a West Pointer. He had been a Marine in World War I, spent ten years in the Army of the 1920s, and had returned to civilian life for a decade. Reenlisting at the outbreak of World War II, he had risen through the ranks to deserve the accolade of being a soldier's soldier. Politically astute and well aware of the merits of good press, Medaris was Von Braun's boss and knew what a responsibility and a treasure he had in the former Peenemünde team.

As Medaris himself described it many years later, the purpose of Bunker's visit was not a direct solicitation for Army business. Bunker simply was calling on the commanding general of a new organization to "inquire how Martin company could best be of service to the objectives of the Army's missile programs."[1] It would be "extremely advantageous" to the Army, Medaris frankly told Bunker, if some aerospace company saw fit to build a plant somewhere between Huntsville and Cape Canaveral, the primary launch site for long-range missiles. George Bunker thanked the general and left. Before the summer of 1956 turned into fall, the Martin company had quietly acquired ten and a half square miles—a total of 6,777 acres—of central Florida pasture and orange grove, ten miles southwest of the Orange County town of Orlando. A somewhat sleepy market town for the surrounding citrus groves and cattle ranches, Orlando was also something of a banking center. It had very little industry and was perhaps best known outside Florida for its Herndon Airport, a two-way funnel for the hordes of missile and rocket scientists and engineers and the swarm of covering reporters, photographers, and television personalities streaming to and from Cape Canaveral, fifty miles to the east.

It was to Orlando that George Bunker and Edward Uhl, his vice president of operations, flew on August 23 to pay a call on Linton Allen,[2] chairman of First National Bank (later SunBank). They told him they were looking for land, maybe five hundred acres or so, on which to build a manufacturing plant. Unlike Baltimore when Glenn Martin first attempted to relocate his company in 1928, or even Denver, which almost missed attracting the company when first approached in 1955, the Orlando civic leaders could not have been more accommodating. Allen took them to lunch with Mayor J. Rolfe Davis and within the day introduced them to Billy Dial, a director of the bank and its attorney, and Milton Blanck, manager of the Orlando Industrial Board. Blanck, in turn, involved Dean Downs, a real estate broker. A few days later the Orlando leaders flew to Baltimore to brief the Martin company's board of directors on available sites, two of them the size specified at a cost of between $500 and $600 an acre, and a third, sixty-four-hundred-acre tract costing $200 an acre. The company chose the larger parcel plus several hundred additional acres, and Allen hurried back to Orlando to take an option on the land with $1,500 from his own pocket.

Billy Dial recalled forty years later how a handful of people, including the governor, met all of Martin's needs—guaranteeing new roads, utilities, and sewage—within a matter of days. "We knew it would be a big payroll," Dial recalled in an *Orlando Sentinel* interview thirty-six years later. "The employees all would need homes and shopping centers." The Martin people said they would need water and power, Dial said, "and Curtis Stanton, general manager of the Orlando Utilities Commission, said he could supply those." The county did not have sewer service, so it created a sewer district with Martin as the sole customer. "They said they needed roads, and I told them we could get a road out there," Dial added. "George Bunker asked what authority I had to make such a promise. I told him I was on the State Roads Board and had already talked to the governor about it. He asked if we could see the governor, [and] we flew up that afternoon [to Tallahassee]."[3]

Ground was broken five months later, and on December 4, 1957, Florida governor LeRoy Collins cut the ribbon as the company

Allen, Gov. Collins, Bunker, Uhl open Orlando plant

opened on its Sand Lake Road property, a sprawling two-story manufacturing building marked by a soaring water tower, forever after
known as the Green Onion. The land had cost only $1.95 million,
but the Martin company put $18.5 million into the five-hundred-
thousand-square-foot, ultramodern plant, at that time the largest
building in Florida. It was quickly occupied by twenty-three hundred
employees who had been working since January out of leased quarters in East Orlando. The core of this group included key people
transferred from Middle River along with three existing Baltimore
programs, the Army's Lacrosse surface-to-surface guided artillery missile, an Army electronic air defense command center known as Missile Master, and the Bullpup air-to-surface missile, a joint Navy and
Air Force program.

Phil Goebel, one of the first new hires when Glenn Martin
moved his company to Baltimore, was the first Martin employee
transferred to Orlando. "I used to meet the airplanes coming down
and show the fellows—engineers and others the company was trying
to influence—all around Orlando, trying to interest them in making
the move. They'd ask me, 'What the hell are you doing down here?
Are you coming down here to die?' That's because there was nothing
to do in Orlando at night. All the blinds were down and the lights
turned out. They'd roll up the sidewalks at sunset."[4]

Laid-back Florida town that it was in the fifties, Orlando did
work its magic on visitors from the cold North. Many succumbed to
its myriad lakes and semitropical climate, the sight of Spanish moss
hanging from scrub oak trees. Warm breezes sweet with the perfume
of orange blossoms rustled the palm trees. These were among the
attractions Dan Siemon used as Martin's vice president of industrial
relations in his efforts to staff the new division. Siemon visited Orlando about every three weeks to review the process, Phil said. "I
lived at the Cherry Plaza Hotel on Lake Eola, and Dan Siemon would
stay at the Langford in Winter Park. I'd go over and have dinner with
him and tell him about certain people and whether they were interested in transferring. Then he would go back and make the deals
with them. It was quite exciting."

Missiles and jobs were not the only things the Martin company
brought to Orlando. The Baltimoreans who transferred to Florida to
form the nucleus of the work force brought with them some of the
traditions of the "Land of Pleasant Living," as the beer commercials
described Maryland's Chesapeake Bay. One tradition was a love of
fresh oysters and steamed crabs. The Martin Baltimoreans were surprised and pleased to find Florida oysters succulent and sweet even

if smaller than bay country bivalves. To their amazement—and it wasn't something they'd admit to folks back home, but it was true—Florida blue crabs were every bit as big and meaty as they had been in Baltimore. But the Floridians served only the crab claws—"fingers," they called them—as cocktail fare. Nobody steamed and ate the whole hardshell crab. At least nobody did until Tony Bressi arrived in Orlando.

Bressi, who had moved to Orlando with the Lacrosse program and later went to Huntsville on the Pershing program, decided central Floridians didn't know what they were missing, so he staged a small crab feast on Lake Fairview—then another and another, each one getting larger. He sent to Baltimore for the crabs until he discovered that the local crab crop was pretty good. Bressi's steamed crab feasts soon became so popular that he formed the first Italian-American Club in Orlando primarily for the purpose of eating crabs. To this day, they still have crab feasts regularly at the Italian-American Clubhouse built in 1972 in Orlando's Azalea Park, but you now can buy steamed crabs to take out from a number of emporiums throughout central Florida thanks to a Baltimore tradition that moved south with the Martin folks.

Frank Vitek was another old-timer from earliest Baltimore days who was one of the first transfers to Orlando. An electrician and pipefitter by trade, Frank had originally been hired out of the Baltimore shipyards. He claimed the distinction of opening the first railroad boxcar of equipment arriving from Cleveland at the Canton warehouse in 1929, before the Baltimore plant was even built. He had twenty-eight years of service, most of it in materiel control, by the time he moved to Orlando.

"Before I came down with the Bullpup," Vitek said, "Buzz Showalter and some of the other guys who were already in Orlando were having trouble getting parts and things from Baltimore. They were calling all the time, complaining, 'We can't get this, we can't get that,' nuts, bolts, standards, all kinds of things. We had an airplane making the round-trip every day with people and parts. So I flew down one day to get the layout of things, and I told Buzz, 'Give me your list, and I'll call Baltimore right now and tell them to put them on tomorrow's airplane.'" Vitek was chief of stores at the time, and the materiel people in Baltimore still worked for him. "So I made the call, and the items were on the plane the next day.

"Well, Buzz sorta liked that super-duper kind of service, and by the end of a week I had spoiled him to the point that he called up my boss in Baltimore, Ed McDonald, and asked for me. I was only supposed to be in Orlando for a couple of weeks," Vitek recalled, "but Buzz didn't want me to go back. I told him I had another man, just as good, who was all ready to transfer, but nothing would do until I came. So eventually I went home, packed up our things, and we moved to Orlando." That was 1957, and Frank Vitek put in fifteen more years with the company before retiring in 1972 after forty-three years of service.[5]

C. E. "Buzz" Showalter was manufacturing manager on the Lacrosse program in Baltimore at the time the Orlando plant was established. Jack Libby was the operations director, and Gene Foster, who had moved with Glenn from Cleveland in 1929 and who took the B-10 to China in the thirties, had sales and service for Lacrosse. It wasn't long after the company decided to purchase the land in Florida, Buzz said, that "a bunch of us, about twenty, were on the company plane, headed for Orlando." Included in the group were Jim Halpin, who was directing the Bullpup program; Dave Smith, manufacturing manager for SysNet, which became Missile Master; Jack Libby, Jim Dunlap, and Ed Uhl, a vice president of the company who became the first general manager of the Orlando plant.[6]

The plane was met by Utilities Commission chairman Curt Stanton and realtor Dean Downs. "They put us up at the Langford Hotel in Winter Park and treated us royally," Showalter remembered. "Dean showed us all over town—both property we could lease temporarily until the factory was built as well as residential areas. As far as Lacrosse was concerned, I picked a building on Ewell Street because it had plenty of parking and adjoined Herndon Airport. If I needed something from Baltimore, I could get it right off the airplane. The building was hotter 'n hell because it wasn't airconditioned, except for my office, but it had lots of advantages." The buildings on Ewell Street became temporary home for the division until the Sand Lake plant was built.

When it became time for Showalter to make the permanent move to Orlando, he said he was one of the first to buy a house. He had been named superintendent of final assembly and acting director of manufacturing until his boss, John Mason, could make the move from Baltimore. "John suggested that I might want to look around longer before deciding on a home, but I told him, 'Nope. I've found what I want. Etta [Buzz's wife] likes it. It's near the schools, and I've got work to do. I can't be playing around, building houses and so forth.' We had no trained people, nothing but orange pickers," Showalter said, "and I was trying to put a crew together."

Such was the gung ho spirit of the Martin veterans who moved south from Baltimore in 1956 and 1957 to people the new Orlando division of "The Martin Company," the corporation's name having been formally shortened on April 22, 1957. Before the year ended, the Orlando plant was completed, making, with Baltimore and Denver, the company's third manufacturing facility.[7]

On January 7, 1958, the Department of Defense authorized General Medaris's Army Ballistic Missile Agency to develop a new solid-propellant ballistic missile system to replace the Redstone. With "selective range," it would be designated an SRBM. Medaris's entire military career had marked him as a man of action, and he quickly made certain that his superiors in the Defense Department would not have a change of heart. Within eleven weeks of the authorization to proceed with development, the Army Ballistic Missile Agency had drawn up specifications for a Redstone-S (the S stood for solid propellant), invited proposals from industry, evaluated them, and awarded the contract. By any standard it had to rank as the all-time speed record for a major military weapons procurement.[8]

To be sure, General Medaris had a few things working for him. One was the extraordinary authority given him by Secretary of the Army Wilber M. Brucker when the Army Ballistic Missile Agency was created. Another was the unparalleled experience and technical expertise built into the organization, namely the disciplined methodology of Wernher von Braun and his team of Germans. Added to these pluses was the decision, less than ten days after the authorization, to name the missile after the Army's most illustrious hero, General of the Armies John J. "Black Jack" Pershing, who had commanded American expeditionary forces during World War I. That public relations move, added to the near-universal approval rating already earned by the Huntsville team when its Jupiter-C rocket successfully orbited the first United States satellite on January 31, gave the Medaris team all the clout needed to advance its new program.

Within a week after the Explorer I launch, the Army's Huntsville command issued a "request for proposal." It went to seven companies carefully winnowed from a list of 121. Two criteria were paramount for firms on the final list: ballistic missile experience and plant location in relation to Huntsville and Canaveral. The RFP asked for engineering design, development cost, manufacturing time, and testing schedule for a mobile system. The missile had to be capable of carrying a nuclear warhead, be easily transported anywhere in the world by helicopter or other aircraft, and be quickly emplaced and fired by combat troops under the worst extremes of tropical heat and arctic cold. The seven firms asked to submit proposals within only thirty days were Chrysler Corporation, which had taken on production of the Redstone missile after Von Braun's people had developed it; Lockheed Aircraft Corporation, already developing the Navy's Polaris submarine missile; Douglas Aircraft, then building the Thor intermediate-range ballistic missile for the Air Force as well as the Army's Nike-Zeus anti-ICBM missile; the Convair division of General Dynamics Corporation, builder of the Air Force Atlas ICBM; Firestone Rubber Company; and Sperry-Rand Corporation.

The seventh company was, of course, The Martin Company, which had produced the air-breathing cruise missiles, Matador and Mace, for the Air Force and was currently manufacturing the much smaller Bullpup air-to-ground missile for the Navy and Air Force and the Army's Lacrosse artillery missile, none of them ballistic. But Martin was well qualified: It had developed the Viking high-altitude sounding rockets for the Navy and was continuing development of the Vanguard and Titan programs, all of them ballistic.

Ed Uhl, vice president and general manager of the new Orlando facility, was a former Army ordnance officer and co-inventor of the famed World War II bazooka, a hand-held antitank rocket launcher. An innovative engineering conceptualist with a reputation for being a hard-nosed manager as well, Uhl drew the assignment of pulling together a team of the best talent in the company that could produce a winning proposal in the one month allowed for response. He picked as proposal manager his chief engineer, Sidney Stark, an eleven-year veteran with the company who had a proven track record. It included the leadership of efforts that had won prime contracts for both the Bullpup and Lacrosse missiles. Stark chose Ralph Draut for design of the missile, Jack Libby for design of the sizable complex of ground support equipment that would be needed to transport, erect, power, aim, and fire the missile in combat; Nicholas De Pasquale to plan the engineering and field test programs; Buzz Showalter for manufacturing; Dick Bonnel for procurement planning; Arthur Ahlin for contracts; and Gene Ahearn as finance manager, who would have to come up with a winning cost figure. All had reputations for getting things done, for doing them well, and for doing them on schedule.

Gene Foster—a real utility infielder, everybody's "Mr. Everything," no matter what the program—drew the job of logistics planning. It was perhaps the most critical and certainly the largest aspect of the entire Pershing program. The term *logistics* on the Pershing program included everything in the broadest military definition of the term—shipment or transportation of all components, spares, personnel, and documentation throughout the development, testing, and deployment of the system; preparation and dissemination of all instruction, repair, and training manuals; development of training programs as well as supervision of the actual training; and development of operational schedules for resupplying both equipment and personnel. It was a huge task.

An isolated hangar at Orlando's Herndon Airport, ten miles from the main plant, became the spartan quarters of the proposal effort. "Building 3" was its only designation, but it was home to the proposal team for thirty days and nights. On March 4 the proposal was completed and hand carried to Huntsville. Its four volumes, totaling about six hundred pages and measuring only six inches thick when stacked one on top of the other, would have been something of a mini-wonder alongside proposals that were ten times that size only a decade later.

Sid Stark, on Uhl's last-minute instruction, had designed an "eye-catching" cover meant to distinguish the Martin proposal from all others. It was plain except for two playing cards, the ace of diamonds and the jack of clubs, plus the single word "Pershing." Uhl was wildly enthusiastic about the "Black Jack" symbolism until a visitor from headquarters told him it could be interpreted as "Don't gamble on Martin." The cover art was quickly and quietly dropped.

A few days after submittal of the written proposal, Martin and each of the other six competitors was invited to Redstone Arsenal for oral presentations. Three Martin people went: Sid Stark was there to present the engineering aspects. Ed Uhl fleshed out administrative, financial, and logistical details of the proposal. The third man was George Bunker, Martin's president, who flew down from Baltimore to play out the hand he had picked up nearly a year before when he gambled six thousand acres of Florida scrub land and a brand-new plant without knowing either the name of the game or the color of the first card. He was in Huntsville to lend the company's full weight to the Martin proposal. Presentations were tightly scheduled: four hours in the morning for one company, four hours in the afternoon for the next. No company was allowed to hear another's presentation.[9]

Presiding over the selection board was Dr. Arthur Rudolph of Germany's underground Mittelwerk V-2 plant fame. He was flanked by six colonels, three each from the Ordnance Corps, which would oversee development of the Pershing missile, and the Corps of Artillery, which would have to fire it.[10]

Russ Brinley, freelance writer and onetime Martin public relations representative, interviewed some of the participants many years later. He described Stark's presentation: "as spare as the man's name." He had no slides, no film, no fancy charts or graphs, no handouts or visual aids of any kind. Stark's plain and serious demeanor, evenly pitched voice, a piece of chalk, and a blackboard were his only tools. He drew a missile that would be thirty-four feet in length and have two identical stages and a sharply pointed warhead. The savings of developing only a single solid-propellant motor were obvious, he told the selection panel. Moreover, the economies would multiply throughout the life of the program by eliminating the need for separate static tests, separate handling apparatus, separate maintenance and inspection procedures, crating and shipping, field handling, training, instruction manuals, and documentation. This cost-saving approach appeared to impress the board, Stark noted.[11]

Uhl stressed the fortuitous location of the Orlando plant and its cost significance to the program. Its proximity to the Cape, he said, would permit field demonstration of the Pershing's mobility by assembling an entire unit at the plant, then moving it the fifty miles to the Canaveral launch site where it could be fired down the Atlantic Missile Range in full simulation of tactical conditions. The Martin presenters believed this also impressed the board.

Bunker wrapped up the Martin presentation with a pledge of full corporate support in both funds and facilities, including an offer to construct an additional building at the Orlando plant to house engineering and administrative personnel assigned to the project. Overall, the Martin proposal called for seventy-seven test missiles at a cost of between $105 million and $110 million, a modest program compared to what the developmentally experienced Army panel and their Peenemünde-trained backup considered adequate.

The Martin presenters returned home for a two-week nail-biting wait, unaware that they were the early odds-on choice of Dr. Rudolph and the selection panel. Nor were they aware of the high-level machinations that followed the Huntsville choice of Martin. According to reports at the time, later confirmed in interviews, the Army from the outset of the Pershing procurement process harbored a bias against contractors who, in the Army's eyes, were too closely allied with the Air Force. If that prejudice applied, only Chrysler and Firestone of the seven bidding firms could be classed as nonaerospace.

In addition to the alleged bias against the Air Force and its "captive" contractors was an ongoing interservice rivalry over roles and missions. The Air Force considered itself sole proprietor of strategic defense and therefore ballistic missiles in general. It was already building Thor, Atlas, and Titan. The Navy had broken the mold with its submarine-launched Polaris, a ballistic missile then in development, and the Army was attempting to do the same with Pershing.

Almost from the beginning of the procurement, General Medaris in Huntsville had been receiving signals from Washington that Army Secretary Brucker was under severe political pressure to steer the Pershing contract to the State of Michigan, where the automobile industry was suffering through the low point of the late fifties recession. Since Chrysler was the only firm on the bidder list from Michigan, such a move would have made a sham of the entire proposal-soliciting process. General Medaris did not buy it, and when he and Secretary Brucker met on the subject, the general gave the former Michigan governor an out.

"Just tell them, Governor, whoever they are, that the matter is out of your hands," he advised Brucker. "By the authority you delegated to me in setting up the Army Ballistic Missile Agency, selection of a contractor is solely the responsibility of ABMA." Brucker apparently agreed with that reasoning, and the matter was thought to be closed.[12]

The selection board took only a few days before deciding on Martin as the best company to build the Pershing, a decision based not only on technical merits but on anticipated cost savings that could be realized as a result of the convenient Florida plant location. General Medaris concurred in the selection, but when it was forwarded to Washington, all hell literally broke loose. The date was March 13. Russ Brinley described the scene:

> Secretary of the Army Brucker was in a desk-thumping mood when he summoned Medaris and Rudolph to Washington for a personal briefing on their decision. Brucker was incensed that a company that had abandoned the aircraft business and run into serious difficulties in the highly publicized Vanguard satellite program had been selected to develop the Army's only remaining long-range weapon.
>
> His short legs dangling from his swivel chair, Brucker waved in the faces of Medaris and Rudolph a handful of "bad" press clippings about the technical difficulties and spectacular disasters that had plagued Vanguard. How could they justify putting "his" missile in such untrustworthy hands? Medaris, however, remained obdurate. He

would stick by the selection. Brucker remained equally obdurate. He would stick by his objection.[13]

It was impossible to distinguish from a distance of three decades whether Brucker's objection was a genuine concern about the capabilities of The Martin Company or a last-ditch attempt to salvage the contract for the State of Michigan. The only demonstrable historic fact is that he *did* object, and the award of the Pershing contract *was* delayed. Edward J. Cottrell, who at the time was the Department of the Army's civilian chief of public information and therefore Wilber Brucker's principal spokesman, confirmed that the air was charged and that Martin representatives were circling his Pentagon desk.[14]

"Whenever I turned around, there was C. B. Allen or Joseph M. Rowland at my elbow wondering whether a decision had been made," Cottrell recalled. Allen was a special assistant to the Martin president, and Rowland was director of public relations. Four days later, on St. Patrick's Day, Martin's Vanguard rocket placed a twenty-one-pound "grapefruit" satellite into orbit around the Earth. It was the second U.S. satellite. The first had been Explorer I, launched only seventeen days before by Medaris's Army Missile Command.

Within the week Secretary Brucker telephoned General Medaris to give his approval of Martin's selection as the Pershing prime contractor on two conditions: (1) that the Martin Orlando plant be placed under the cognizance of the Army rather than the Navy, whose Bullpup missile was until that time the plant's most lucrative contract, and (2) that George Bunker write a personal letter to the secretary detailing the technical problems encountered in the Vanguard program and the corrective actions taken to remedy them. Both conditions were met almost immediately; Sid Stark and Ed Uhl personally delivered to Medaris on March 21 the written assurances Brucker had demanded. Back in Orlando the next day, Ed Uhl took a telephone call from Huntsville and immediately called Stark at home. "We got it!" was all he said. It was Saturday, March 22, 1958.

The Pershing program ran for thirty-four years, through two major growth modifications. It was one of the most successful in terms of performance, schedule, and cost in the annals of military history. It also produced more than $4 billion in sales for the company. The most important accomplishment, however, was Pershing's use as a strategic and political instrument of world peace and disarmament and, therefore, as a major contributor to the collapse of communism and to the end of the Cold War.

The ultimate testimonial to the reliability that Martin built into

Stark, Goodlette, Willey with Pershing

the Pershing system and its effectiveness as an instrument of peace was given on September 8, 1988, by Vice President George Bush. Speaking at the Longhorn Army Ammunition Plant in Longhorn, Texas, on the occasion of the Army's destruction of Pershing motors under terms of the International Nuclear Forces Treaty, the vice president said: "The Pershing missile system strengthened deterrence and was concrete evidence of United States resolve. If we had not deployed . . . [Pershing] there would not be an INF Treaty today." Secretary of State George P. Shultz further elaborated three months later when he told the annual meeting of Private Sector Committees of the United States Information Agency that the Soviets would not have even come to the START Treaty negotiations had not the U.S. deployed the Pershing missile in then-West Germany.[15]

CHAPTER 26

Making Good
on the Promise

■

Army Secretary Brucker and General Medaris would both live to see their judgment in selection of the Pershing contractor rewarded. Uhl and Stark, along with Art Ahlin, who had been designated Pershing contract manager, and Jack Libby, who was assistant program director to Stark, returned to Huntsville the following week for two days of protracted "contract negotiations," including some very frank discussion with General Medaris, who left no doubt as to who was in charge of the program.

On the day of their arrival in Huntsville, the afternoon newspaper carried the Army announcement of Martin's selection to build the Pershing. Stark said the sessions were more a case of listening and taking careful notes than negotiating. The lecturer was Dr. Rudolph, who in painstaking detail spelled out exactly what he expected from Martin. Prior to Pershing, the Army had been accustomed to having complete design responsibility for a weapon system. This "arsenal concept" had been in effect for both Redstone and Jupiter missiles, both of which had been essentially designed and developed at Huntsville and then given to Chrysler to manufacture. General Medaris had hoped to have the Pershing developed the same way, but Pentagon superiors decided even before bids were solicited that the design should be performed by the prime contractor. Still, Medaris and Rudolph made it abundantly clear that they would continue to be involved in every detail of the program, including design.

After two days of discussions, General Medaris summoned Stark to a meeting with Wernher Von Braun and Colonel C. A. Heath, the ABMA chief of staff. In front of his top aides, General Medaris told Stark he wanted to make one thing perfectly clear: "You are now working for me. If anyone outside of this organization attempts to contact you or influence you in any way on matters concerning the Pershing program, you are to report that contact immediately to Colonel Heath here. Is that understood?" Stark acknowledged that he understood—and he would not wait long before his new understanding was put to the test.[1]

Meanwhile, Ahlin and Libby had been cooling their heels, frustrated that no one had even mentioned a formal contract. So they hopped in their rental car and drove one hundred miles south to the headquarters of the Army's Birmingham Ordnance District. There, within a matter of hours, Ahlin had signed a preliminary letter of contract committing The Martin Company to the Army's terms. On Friday, March 28, the Army publicly acknowledged that it had entered into a contract with Martin for the design and development of its new medium-range ballistic missile as well as for production, testing, maintenance, training, and field services.

Less than a week later Sid Stark, back in Orlando, received an unexpected visitor. Neatly dressed in sports coat and tie, the gentleman explained that he was vacationing nearby and had simply taken the opportunity to drop in and offer his views on the new Army system that Martin was developing. Stark listened attentively, taking occasional careful notes. At the conclusion of their conversation, he thanked his distinguished-looking visitor for coming and walked him to the lobby. After returning to his office, Stark immediately telephoned Colonel Heath in Huntsville.

"I have just had a contact from outside your organization," Stark reported. Who was it? Heath wanted to know. "He told me he would be satisfied with a five-hundred-mile range if the system was reliable and could be delivered early," Stark continued. Again, Colonel Heath persisted in wanting to know who had told Stark this. "He also told me that he didn't want the combat capability of the system in any way compromised by a requirement for helicopter transportability," Stark said." "Well, who are you talking about? Who contacted you?" Colonel Heath insisted. "His name is Maxwell Taylor," Stark calmly replied. "I believe he's the Army Chief of Staff."[2]

Thus was established, on April 1, 1958, the initial range of the Pershing. Although the Army's role and mission were limited on paper to two hundred miles, a range of four hundred miles was eventually approved for Pershing I. That range would later be expanded to fifteen hundred miles to satisfy a NATO requirement that put the most heavily developed areas of the Soviet Union within the deterrent reach of a more powerful Pershing II stationed in West Germany.

Much later Rudolph confided to Stark that the marathon nature of the contractor orals tended to blur the separate company presentations, but he had been impressed by two details of the Martin presentation. He thought Stark's detailed list of the economies of having two stages identical was "interesting and innovative." The other was Ed Uhl's description of the cost significance of plant location and the benefit it would be to tactical mobility demonstration. The Army later abandoned the identical stage idea, opting instead for two distinctly different stages powered by motors from different propellant manufacturers. And the idea of moving a Pershing fire unit over the road from the Orlando plant to Canaveral had to be abandoned because of safety and scheduling requirements on the Atlantic Missile Range. At the time of the orals, however, Dr. Rudolph credited both ideas with helping Martin win the contract.

So began the extraordinarily successful development of the Pershing mobile missile system. It progressed through three growth modifications over more than three decades. The program became a model of American military-industrial managerial partnership. It produced an effective weapon system that was adaptable to military requirements and tactical concepts without crippling technical problems, schedule delays, or cost overruns. In fact, Pershing frequently produced annual cost underruns, which in most cases the Army chose to plow back into product refinements.

The first version, mounted on tracked vehicles, went to the troops in October 1962 with activation of the first Pershing missile battalion at Fort Sill, Oklahoma. Following extensive testing in the extremes of arctic Alaska and tropical Panama, Pershing units became operational in 1964 in West Germany, both with the U.S. forces stationed there and with Federal Republic of Germany troops. A firing unit consisted of the missile mounted on its tracked erector-launcher plus three other tracked vehicles carrying radar and command and control equipment.

When it became apparent that the system would be required to travel more on paved roads than on rough terrain, Pershing Ia mod-

Pershing elevated for launch

ifications involved the conversion of the carriers from tracks to wheels. Because the system was already in the hands of field forces in the United States and Europe, a unique exchange program did just that in the fall and winter of 1969 and 1970. Without lessening the operational readiness of any missile units already deployed, "Operation Swap" delivered approximately four thousand pieces of Pershing Ia equipment directly to field forces who exchanged them, one new for one old piece, on a battalion-size scale.

Operation Swap was accomplished entirely outside of normal Army supply depot channels and marked the first time that the Army utilized the technology, manpower, and services of an industrial contractor—in this case The Martin Company—to not only manufacture and package a system but to test it, marshal it, and deliver it directly to the troops, ready to use and complete with spare parts and tools.

Just as it had been a factor in awarding the contract, the location of the Martin-Orlando plant was key to the Army's decision to augment its own supply system with Operation Swap. All the replacement Pershing equipment was marshaled and tested dockside at Port Canaveral. There it was loaded on special Navy cargo vessels, a complete battalion's worth of equipment per ship, for the voyage to Bremerhaven, Germany. Once in Germany, the equipment was driven to a staging area, where Pershing-firing batteries took turns coming in to exchange their old gear for the new models.

From start to finish, approximately one hundred Martin technicians, working at Port Canaveral under the direction of Martin's Operation Swap manager Marvin J. Colvert, completed the process in just three months. To have accomplished the same task under normal depot procedures, the Army estimated that twenty thousand individual requisitions would have been required from supply officers. As it was, only a handful of paperwork provided operational field units with improved, faster firing and more reliable ground support elements of the U.S. Army's and NATO's mightiest and most dependable deterrent.

In all, 754 Pershing I and Ia missiles were built, and there were 276 Pershing IIs, for a total of 1,030 missiles.

Pershing II was a dramatic advancement in the system. Accuracy was honed to near perfection, and more powerful stages tripled its range to meet NATO requirements. Even though essentially a new missile, its reliability was so predictable as to allow for development and testing concurrent with deployment on a schedule intended to counter a 1980s Soviet threat of SS20 and other medium-range missiles pointed at western Europe.

Silent sentinel in Germany

During its operational lifetime, the accuracy of Pershing II was classified, although it was no secret that it was deadly accurate. Even the Soviets knew it was accurate enough, as Secretary of State Shultz made clear in crediting Pershing's deployment in West Germany as a key factor in driving them to the treaty table. Exactly how accurate was it? After the missile's destruction began in 1987 as part of the START II Treaty accords, the classification was relaxed. The Army now confirms that if a Pershing II had been fired from the backyard of the Martin Marietta plant at Orlando, its guidance system could have placed it precisely in the interior courtyard of the Pentagon, seven hundred miles to the north. What's more, it could have hit the luncheon kiosk in the center of that courtyard. And it could have done it five times in five firings.[3]

With the exception of Uhl and Stark, both of whom later left the company, most Pershing principals, both in the company and at Huntsville, remained with the program throughout most of its long life. Tom Willey, who moved from the Canaveral division to succeed Uhl as Orlando's head man, and Jack Libby, who replaced Stark as Pershing program director, left indelible management imprints on Pershing, as would John Goodlette, Nick DePasquale, Don Hickman, and many others who played prominent roles in its development and deployment.

Willey's arrival in Orlando was fortuitous for all the programs in the plant—Bullpup, Lacrosse, and Missile Master, as well as Pershing. But it was on the latter program that a meshing of Medaris's and Willey's personalities had a particularly salubrious effect. Those who worked with them noted an affinity of personal and management philosophies "that virtually precluded argument and substituted action for extended discussion whenever technical or management problems arose. The two men came to know each other so well that when a problem did arise, they merely had to acknowledge that it existed. They did not have to tell each other how to solve it."[4]

That same practice of quickly stepping up to problems and fixing them before they became insurmountable hurdles had become a trademark of the company. As simple and direct as calling a spade a spade, it had been practiced by Glenn Martin throughout his lifetime and was emulated by many of his hard-driving students and their successors at all levels of the enterprise. The same management attitude had been notable in the mammoth and complex Titan activation program directed by Vernon Rawlings, who not surprisingly was a Willey disciple from wartime manufacturing in Baltimore.

Probably the single trait that allied Willey so closely with Medaris, in the view of those who knew both well, was that each understood and practiced a primary tenet of good command or good management: "Hit the top, then check to see what comes out at the bottom." After giving the command, if you aren't satisfied with what is happening at the lower levels of the organization, you must hit the top again, even harder. Scarcely a day went by that Tom Willey did not visit some portion of the vast array of machine shops, assembly lines, fabrication centers, and laboratories under his responsibility.

When he retired in 1974, Gene Foster had been on the Pershing program for seventeen years and was known both inside the company and within the customer's shop as "Mr. Pershing." For the first three years, as director of logistics, Gene was responsible for training the Army's artillery board at Fort Sill, Oklahoma, as well as the guided missile instructors and the instructors at the Missile Command in Huntsville. In 1961 he went to Germany to represent Martin on the Department of the Army's international sales team, which was responsible for the sale of Pershing to the Federal Republic of Germany's Air Force. On his return to Orlando in 1962, and for the next twelve years until his retirement, Gene Foster represented the company during the training and commissioning of four field artillery battalions in New Mexico and Utah. He also took part in the firings of 280 missiles, including those by West German squadrons at Cape Canaveral.

Stanford Welch, the boy test conductor from Vanguard days, was still only in his thirties when he transferred his droll sense of humor and West Point fetish for countdown discipline to the Pershing flight test program, which he directed through all its success from 1969 to 1974, when he became director of engineering at Orlando.

CHAPTER 27

"Zero Defects" Was Invented Here

■

It was during Tom Willey's tenure as general manager of the Orlando division in the early 1960s that the quality control program "Zero Defects" was conceived and established plantwide. Aimed at perfection and at doing it right the first time in manufacturing and all industrial endeavors, the program swept through the Orlando plant, the entire corporation, most of the aerospace industry, and through many commercial organizations as well. Many customer organizations also adopted the approach, although sometimes its principles were practiced under other names. Although sometimes degraded to sloganism alone, Zero Defects was the granddaddy of all the quality control programs that followed, including quality circles, total quality management, and a host of others.

A revolutionary approach to quality assurance, Zero Defects was generously offered by the company to all other aerospace companies and other industries. Hundreds of firms, notably General Electric, ITT, and Montgomery Ward, applied Zero Defects to their operations, and word of its success attracted international attention, including Great Britain's Rolls-Royce and a number of Japanese companies. It was adopted totally by the U.S. Army and under other names by the other armed services. The Orlando division credited the Zero Defects program for a 25 percent reduction in the overall plant rejection rate, including defective hardware and documentation, and for a 30 percent reduction in scrap costs.

Zero Defects was the brainchild of a gifted and articulate young engineer named Philip Crosby, who conceived it while working as quality control manager on Pershing. The program was as simple as its name: If you strive for perfection, which is zero defects, you unquestionably will have control of product quality. Jim Halpin, another Baltimore original who came out of the shops and contract administration before transferring to Orlando, was Crosby's boss as director of quality control. Halpin not only encouraged Crosby but actively promoted "ZD," as did Tom Willey, who insisted that all departments—not just manufacturing—practice ZD. Secretaries, public relations writers—indeed, everyone—were encouraged to perform error-free work.

Joseph S. Taylor, a longtime Martin quality control professional who took the program to Baltimore and applied it to the Gemini Launch Vehicle in 1962, recalled that Willey convened an industry-wide conference on the subject in Washington and helped promote the program in the Missile Command and other Army organizations. Taylor gave Halpin and Willey much of the credit for promoting and popularizing the program.[1]

Halpin wrote a book in 1966 in which he called Zero Defects "a commonsense method of quality assurance through prevention rather than detection." He later said about the book:

> I would like to think [it] is about people because people are the essence of the Zero Defects concept. Zero Defects is simply a method of assuring that each individual within an organization realizes his importance to that organization's product or service and, conversely, that each member of management realizes and recognizes the important contribution of each person reporting to him.
>
> I define Zero Defects as a management tool aimed at the reduction of defects through prevention. It is directed at motivating people to prevent mistakes by developing a constant, conscious desire to do their job right the first time.[2]

Robert E. Brooker, president of Montgomery Ward, one of the adopters of the program, wrote in the foreword of Halpin's book: "Zero Defects is, in my opinion, the outstanding quality program of the decade, if not the century."

Zero Defects kickoff with Gemini astronauts and Rawlings (center)

Phil Crosby was later wooed to ITT, where Zero Defects became an important program. Ultimately he established his own company and became a very successful, widely traveled author and lecturer on the subject of quality control in general. The Japanese applied Zero Defects most effectively to the manufacture of automobiles in the late 1960s and 1970s, and by the 1980s it had come full circle (no pun intended), with Americans envying and copying Japanese quality production techniques, one of them called "Quality Circles."[3]

Stories by and about Tom Willey are legion and legend among those who worked with him and for him. Relatively short in stature, he was solidly built with a bit of a barrel chest. Nattily attired, he moved with a purposeful gait that left little doubt about his direction or purpose. He had a firm, well-modulated speaking voice, crisply English-accented and commanding of attention. Although a man of considerable charm, he brooked absolutely no nonsense on the job. He did not like excuses, and he would not abide the word *can't.*

Zero Defects fit neatly with Willey's penchant for orderliness. He was a stickler not just for order but for cleanliness and openness. He disliked dust, debris, and clutter, and unnecessary partitions, walls, and enclosures of any kind. And he was particularly intolerant of closed doors, which he felt hid or obstructed. The Orlando plant had been designed with flexibility paramount. Anything that was not load-bearing, including doors, partitions, walls, and even stairwells and elevators, could be unbolted and moved. Such "facility mobility" allowed optimum adaptability to changing production or contract requirements. On his frequent tours of the plant, Willey was quick to note a new closed door. If there was no compelling reason for a door's being there, he would order its removal or direct that it be glass-paneled so that you could see through it.

Ed Cottrell, a member of Willey's senior staff, was in the habit of closing his office door every Monday afternoon while conducting his department staff meeting. The office was just across the hall from Willey's on "checkerboard square," the executive office area so called because of the prominent black-and-white tiles that covered the floor. Invariably, once or twice a month in the middle of the staff meeting, the closed door would be flung open and the head man— right hand on the knob and left hand braced against the door frame—would lean in with the question: "Everything all right in here?" Assured that everything was fine, Willey would close the door and go about other matters.

He ran a taut ship, but unlike the Navy tradition of that term, Willey provided no "ration of rum," either literally or figuratively. Like Glenn Martin, Willey did not drink, swear, or smoke. And under his management of Martin Orlando there were no coffee breaks or coffee or cigarette vending machines in the factory—in fact, no vending machines of any kind. The only machines Willey permitted in the manufacturing area were machines that performed work.

"The trouble with coffee breaks," he was frequently heard to say, "is that they start out at fifteen minutes, then stretch to twenty minutes, and pretty soon everybody is away from his machine or workplace for half an hour. Twice a day, this amounts to an hour lost from an eight-hour day. That's five hours a week per person, multiplied by the number of our employees. We have eliminated that problem by just eliminating the coffee break."[4]

The prohibition against coffee in the workplace actually went back to Glenn L. Martin and early Baltimore days. Story has it that before the time of photocopying, an upset cup of coffee once ruined an expensive set of engineering drawings of a new airplane, and Glenn Martin himself forbade coffee drinking on the job thereafter. Coffee breaks were allowed in the company other than in the Orlando plant, but the ban on consumption at the point of work was not lifted until well into the decade of the sixties—coincidentally, after Tom Willey's retirement.

Another of Willey's firm convictions, frequently expressed, was that desk tops were intended as work surfaces. He could not abide people sitting or even leaning on desks. In administrative and engineering areas of the plant, desks were lined up end on end with no room for chairs other than one for the user of each desk. New employees were well briefed on the boss's feeling about desk sitting, and with no place to sit or even lean, visits between desks were generally brief. Visitors unfamiliar with the "never sit on the desk" rule were occasionally embarrassed.

Russ Gambill, a guidance and control engineer visiting the Orlando plant from Redstone Arsenal, vividly recalled one instance where he and three other Army civilian engineers sat perched on the edges of desks conferring with their Martin counterparts. Tom Willey happened by, and without inquiring who they were, brusquely ordered them off the desks. They meekly complied without a moment's hesitation or thought about who worked for whom. Willey, who would never have considered addressing a customer representative in that manner, presumably never knew their identity, and the incident added to the mystique of the man.

Even with so many idiosyncrasies of style, Tom Willey was a man without guile, affectation, or egotism. He simply was 100 percent uncomplicated Tom Willey. And he preferred being addressed as "Tom" by anyone and everyone. Russ Brinley recounted an occasion when Willey had scheduled an award presentation in his office for a female employee who had established a record for consecutive defect-free soldering connections on Pershing wire harnesses. Photographers Bernie Markel and Tom Hammer had the assignment, Markel taking the picture while Hammer held the floodlight at the proper angle. As Willey and the awardee froze in the handshake position, Markel shot a glance at Tom Hammer and said, "Tom! Close those window blinds. I'm getting a glare in my lens."

"Oh, sure," answered Tom Willey, dropping his pose and striding quickly to the window, where he obligingly lowered the blind before Tom Hammer could put down the light he was holding. It was vintage no-pretense Tom Willey, promptly complying without question when he heard "Tom."[5]

One of the better Tom Willey stories, one that spoke eloquently to his audacious confidence in everything he did, was told by Joe Taylor. It was when Taylor headed quality control in the Canaveral division and Willey was general manager there. Taylor was a knowledgeable sailor and did a good bit of fishing in his sixteen-foot motorboat. Willey, on the other hand, was not a real sailor in the true sense of the word; he owned a twenty-one-foot cabin cruiser that he was in the habit of running aground in the shallow waters of the Indian River. One evening Willey and his wife Elizabeth invited Taylor and Ken Traut and their wives to cruise to Palm Beach for dinner and the night. It was suggested that the three wives accompany Willey on his boat and that Taylor and Traut follow in Taylor's smaller boat.

As tactfully as he could, Taylor suggested they go slowly through the narrow twisting channel that navigated Stuart shoal, about midway between their departing point of Indialantic and Palm Beach. "Tom liked to go fast," Taylor said, "and the next thing we saw was this rooster tail of sand and water as Tom sliced right through a sandbar."

Without further incident, however, they reached their destination and tied up at the city marina. "Some old guy on the dock was giving Tom a hard time," Taylor said, "and Tom apparently didn't pay close attention to what he was doing." The group checked into a motel, cleaned up, and went to dinner. Afterward, when they checked on the boats before going to bed, Willey's was under water, stern first, with only the top of its cabin protruding. "Tom was convinced there must have been a leak, and although it was midnight, nothing would do but that we bail out that boat right then. There weren't any leaks," Taylor said, "and Tom didn't take too kindly to my suggestion that he had tied the bowline too tight and his stern lines too loose. 'Goldurn, why didn't you tell me?' he wanted to know."[6]

It was another Willey story frequently retold with laughter, even in Tom's presence.

CHAPTER 28

Martin Meets Marietta

■

By 1961, Grover Hermann's American-Marietta Company had blossomed into one of America's largest corporations. The modest business that began in 1913 with Charles Phelan's magic asphalt paint formula and $5,000 that Grover's dad put up had grown into one of the major players on the Fortune 200 list. Sales totaled nearly $400 million.

Still, Grover Hermann was restless and perhaps ready to slow down at seventy-one, although he would never have admitted it. He had lived for his company and had few other interests, aside from a growing penchant for philanthropy and the companionship of his wife Sally. Comfortably settled, when he wasn't traveling, in the beautiful home he had built for Sally amid the Monterey pines of a Pebble Beach bluff overlooking the Pacific, Hermann pretty much limited his leisure activities to reading and walking. He still owned four horses, although he had long ago given up riding.

His life's focus, American-Marietta Company, had become a money-making machine, but it was also becoming increasingly difficult for him to manage it effectively. In spite of its size and wide diversification, many of its products were closely linked to construction markets and therefore somewhat at the mercy of cyclical swings that periodically depressed those markets. Perhaps it needed better balance, he reasoned—ideally, some government business, which typically boomed when the civilian economy slowed.

With this in mind, Grover Hermann spoke with a stockbroker acquaintance in Trenton, New Jersey. He suggested to the broker, John F. Donoho, that he keep his eyes and ears open for any "promising opportunities" that had "strong management." Donoho was married to a Maryland Eastern Shore girl, and the couple frequently spent weekends at her family home in Queen Anne's County. Their property bordered Blakesford, a nineteenth-century mansion set amid the oaks of a twelve-hundred-acre estate on Queenstown Creek and the Chester River. It was the country home of Clarence and Eleanor Miles, with whom the Donohos were acquainted. Clarence Miles was a prominent Baltimore attorney and a founding partner of the law firm of Miles and Stockbridge, and at the time he was serving full-time as general counsel of The Martin Company.[1]

Thus it was an easy thing and not too coincidental that John Donoho happened to mention Grover Hermann's interest to country neighbor Clarence Miles. Miles knew that his friend and employer, George Bunker, might be more than casually interested in diversifying. At that time, Bunker had already concluded that a company devoted exclusively to military hardware was going to have a tough time. He wanted to join Martin with something that had a commercial flair and opportunity. So a meeting was arranged. When Grover Hermann called on Bunker, the two men quickly saw the merits in putting the two firms together. A merger, they concluded, could supply the balance that both firms lacked. It would bring to Martin the commercial business that Bunker sought to offset the periodic lows in government buying, and Hermann found in Martin the countercyclical government business that he felt American-Marietta needed.[2]

The resulting marriage of American-Marietta Company and The Martin Company created Martin-Marietta Corporation, incorporated in Maryland on October 10, 1961. The hyphen, inadvertently used by attorneys formalizing the merger, was quickly and legally dropped. One of the biggest mergers of the day, Martin Marietta Corporation had combined sales of $1.2 billion and earnings of close to $45 million. It employed more than fifty-six thousand people at 350 plants in all the forty-eight states, in Canada, Mexico, and thirteen countries overseas. Stockholders numbered seventy-five thousand. Those who had owned Martin stock received 1.3 shares of common stock in the new company for every share they held in Martin. The holders of American-Marietta common exchanged their

Bunker and Hermann at New York World's Fair, 1964

stock share for share. George Bunker became president and chief executive officer, and Grover Hermann was chairman of the new board of directors.[3]

In addition to a greatly expanded line of the original paint and varnish products, American-Marietta brought to the merger its prominence as a leading manufacturer and distributor of adhesives, resins, and chemicals. There were textile dyestuff, printing inks of every color and description, sealants, refractories, and metallurgical products, including metal powders, pigments, abrasives, and alloys. The company produced machinery, equipment, and construction materials, included brick and tile, cement admixtures, and electrical products. It was the nation's largest producer of chemical-grade lime and concrete products, and the seventh largest producer of cement. American-Marietta had become one of the country's first true conglomerates, even before that term became popular on Wall Street. It even made household cleansing products, among them furniture polishes, waxes, and the well-known O'Cedar Jonny Mop.[4]

Combined with Martin's aerospace products, the new company almost defied easy description except for Wall Street reporters and headline writers who delighted in saying its products "ranged from sewer pipe to satellites" and from "missiles to mops." Analysts had difficulty comprehending exactly what it was. It fit no clear-cut market categories. Even Martin Marietta people had difficulty describing it, as evidenced by one of the earliest public promotional attempts. In May 1962 the corporation purchased the expensive sponsorship of a prime-time television show, an hour-long debate of sorts between astronaut John Glenn and Soviet cosmonaut Gherman S. Titov. As the commercial opened, the camera drew back to reveal a stage heaped with neat clusters: missile models, paint cans, bolts of colored cloth, piles of stone, electronic devices, machinery, concrete forms; and in the center of the stage was a huge circular piece of sewer pipe.

Through the center of the sewer pipe circle brightly stepped the commentator with a wave of the hand and a hearty "Hi there. I'm from Martin Marietta. You say you've never heard of Martin Marietta? Well . . ." and he proceeded to enumerate the products surrounding him. The commercial went downhill from there, communicating only bigness and confusion, not focus or investment value.

It took almost seven years to sift through and sort out all the companies and plants in the American-Marietta conglomeration and dispose of, either by sale or liquidation, those companies that did not align with the corporation's major business thrusts—aerospace, construction materials, and chemical specialties. The firms dealt off either did not conform to logical product or market groupings or simply were incompatible with corporate goals or efficiencies of good management. Aside from several broad categories, Grover Hermann had collected American-Marietta elements based on two simple criteria: They had to be well managed, and they had to be profitable and have good potential for growth. Most of the companies met those goals.

Among the first to go were O'Cedar with its household cleaning products, Steel City Electric with its electrical junction boxes, Pulverizing Machinery, Metals Disintegrating, and United Brick & Tile. The entire paint and finish business—some forty companies—was sold in 1963. The concrete pipe and products companies—ninety operations in all, plus nine stone quarries and two lime operations—were disposed of between 1963 and 1965 under terms of a federal antitrust divestiture agreement negotiated earlier. It precluded American-Marietta, and therefore its successor, Martin Marietta, from owning finished concrete product businesses as well as companies that furnished raw materials for concrete, such as cement, lime, and the specific aggregate operations that were divested under the same order. Such vertical integration of an industry, the Federal Trade Commission ruled, was in restraint of fair trade.

With all those businesses gone by the close of 1968, Martin Marietta had been streamlined dramatically. It was still widely diverse in product lines, but it now had "purposefully diversified," management told the financial community, and was a "corporation capable of growth and of sustained capacity for profit." There were four distinct businesses—cement, chemical products (printing inks, textile dyestuff, industrial sand, and chemical admixtures for concrete), construction aggregates (then called Rock Products and consisting of crushed stone, sand, and gravel), and aerospace (systems for space and defense).[5]

Aerospace contributed about two-thirds of total sales, which the divestiture had reduced to $682 million, approximately half the merger-year total. Earnings of close to $40 million had held approximately equal to 1961, and the commercial companies were responsible for two-thirds of that profit. In addition, the corporation had accumulated a cash nest egg of several hundred million. *Fortune* magazine headlined the cache THE MILLIONS UNDER MARTIN MARIETTA'S MATTRESS in an article speculating on possible investment and acquisition opportunities.[6]

Readers of the magazine, including Martin Marietta employees and stockholders, did not have long to wait to find out where the millions would be invested. George Bunker added a fifth leg to the corporate stool in 1968 with the purchase for $107 million of 41 percent of the stock of Harvey Aluminum, a Los Angeles–based, fully integrated "mine-to-market" aluminum company. Martin Marietta ownership was increased to 83 percent in 1969, and the aluminum company became a wholly owned subsidiary several years later.

The acquisition of Harvey Aluminum boosted the corporation's sales total once again to near the billion-dollar mark and increased earnings by almost 20 percent, to nearly $50 million. The addition of the fifth business also established the look and scope of Martin Marietta Corporation for the next dozen years.

A "SUPERIOR" MOVE: PEBBLES TO PERIGEES

At the time of the merger, size and scope were among the concerns of some members of the board of directors. Those who had come aboard with American-Marietta were less than sanguine about what they were getting into. W. Trent Ragland of Raleigh, North Carolina, was a good example. His Superior Stone Company had been in the American-Marietta family for only two years prior to the merger with Martin, and he was still getting used to being "acquired." The Superior acquisition was Hermann's first venture in stone. Engineered personally by Grover, it was almost a fluke, according to Ragland.

The scion of a prominent Raleigh family, Ragland had grown up in the aggregates business. His father, William Trent, Sr., and his uncle, Edward Ragland, had preceded him in the aggregates business, as had Trent's grandfather, William Ragland. The senior Raglands had been in the stone business from before World War I, the earliest days of the crushed stone industry. Trent said he "came pretty close to being born" in the old Bald Mountain Quarry near Albemarle, where his father and uncle were producing giant jetty stone for a breakwater and new harbor at Cape Lookout, near Morehead.

"My parents lived in a tin shack on the edge of the quarry, and every time they blasted, my uncle Edward would toss stones onto the tin roof to tease and frighten my mother," Trent said.[7] She eventually went back to her home in Salisbury, where Trent was born. When the war broke out, the Raglands shut down the quarry and joined up. The Cape Lookout harbor project was never resumed, and the Ragland brothers returned from the war to work in the old Neverson quarry, producing stone ballast for railroad right-of-ways throughout the Southeast. Trent grew up around the quarries, helping his father and uncle. "The only thing I ever wanted to do was be in the stone business, too," he recalled many years later. But he had no idea that one day he would take his company into a huge conglomerate like American-Marietta or an even larger enterprise like Martin Marietta.

The senior Ragland brothers and a fellow employee of the Southern Aggregates Company, Henry Shaw, decided in 1939 to go into business for themselves. "They borrowed two hundred thousand dollars from my granddaddy and his sister, and started Superior

Mountains of aggregates to build the nation's infrastructure

Stone Company," Ragland said, "and that was the last dollar ever put into the business. All the growth since that time has been generated internally."

At the time they formed Superior Stone, the Raglands had people on the payroll but "no plants, no equipment, no nothing coming in," Trent added, so they decided to put Mr. Shaw into the concrete pipe business. "The state was making its own concrete pipe down at the prison. They had a one-man pipe machine and this guy running it. My daddy bought the pipe machine from the prison, got the prisoner who was running it paroled, and started North Carolina Products Company, with Mr. Shaw in charge. Since the state no longer had a machine, they had to buy pipe, and the company grew into a pretty large, multiplant business. By 1939 it had four or five plants around the state and was very successful, as large as any pipe company anywhere else," Trent said. His father and uncle owned some of the pipe company stock, and Henry Shaw was a stockholder in Superior Stone and on its board of directors.

At about that time Ragland met Grover Hermann, a roundabout introduction that, according to Ragland, happened this way: American-Marietta owned a number of concrete pipe plants all over the country, and Hermann went to Carolina to look at North Carolina Products Company and also Carolina Concrete Pipe Company in Charlotte. He purchased Carolina Pipe, but he told Henry Shaw he couldn't make a deal with him because antitrust laws would not permit him to buy a second pipe plant in North Carolina. Then, according to Ragland, "Mr. Shaw, who was anxious to liquefy his holdings, asked, 'Well, have you ever thought about going into the aggregates business?' And Mr. Hermann said, 'No! What's that?' So Shaw told him there was a fine company over in Raleigh named Superior Stone that he should look at, and he explained to Mr. Hermann "what an aggregate was—how they 'made little ones out of big ones.' "[8]

Hermann returned to Chicago but later made another visit to North Carolina, this time with his vice chairman, Ray Oughton. They discussed with Trent and his father the possibility of buying Superior Stone Company. When the Raglands suggested a price, Trent recalled, "Mr. Hermann would say, 'Oh, let's see. No, I don't think we could possibly do that. Could we, Ray?' And Ray Oughton would say, 'No, sir.' Anyway, we gave them all the information they requested about the business, and they took it back to Chicago. Their proposal was not very interesting to us, so we asked them to return our information, which they did."

That was October 1958. Four months later, on February 8, 1959, Ragland said, "Mr. Hermann telephoned me and said, 'I've got to make a trip down your way anyway. How about stopping by and visiting again?' I think he had waited long enough to see if we were going to do anything. And so he came on down. I met him at the airport one evening about six o'clock. I had told Anna, my wife, I was going to meet him, and she asked if I wanted to feed him supper at the house. I told her no, we'd go straight to his hotel. But on the way into town I asked if he'd like to stop by the house to meet my wife, and he said, 'Certainly.' So we drove home, much to Anna's surprise because she wasn't expecting him at all.

"I offered him a little drink, which he accepted, and we sat there and talked and talked. 'Would you like another drink?' I asked, and he said 'Yes, fine.' Well, I reckon we had three or four drinks, just the two of us, and talked and talked. I don't know what about. It wasn't until much later, after I got to know him, that I learned he didn't drink at all. I was so embarrassed. But he drank that night, just to be sociable, I reckon. Finally, Anna came into the room and asked, 'Mr. Hermann, would you like something to eat?' And he replied, 'Well, that would be very nice.' So she fixed a roast beef sandwich about ten o'clock. We got along just grand . . . had a good time. I don't remember what the hell we talked about, but it wasn't the business. I finally drove him to his hotel, and we said good night."[9]

The next day, Ragland said, Hermann met with him and his father for much of the day at the stone company offices, "and we agreed on a deal." Then Hermann sent for American-Marietta's general counsel, who arrived the next morning and dictated a legal agreement. The acquisition of Superior Stone Company, with its thirty-three quarries in North Carolina, Georgia, and Virginia, was completed two months later, on April 22, for five hundred thousand shares of American-Marietta stock valued at $26 million. With Superior Stone, American-Marietta had entered a new and different business; its product, construction aggregates—crushed stone, sand, and gravel. Hermann would rapidly expand his aggregates holdings, acquiring a dozen more stone companies in the next fifteen months. It was a capital-intensive business, requiring considerable investment for plant and equipment, but aggregates would also be one of the most profitable of Grover Hermann's many enterprises.

Ragland was elected to the board of American-Marietta, and over the next two years, before the merger with Martin Marietta, he came to know Grover Hermann quite well. "Although Mr. Hermann was pretty relaxed that night in my home," Ragland said, "he was not a relaxed man by nature. He was really very nervous, almost jumpy. He had very definite ideas about everything. I don't mean he wasn't congenial. He was very congenial, very cordial. But he was always working. I think his mind was constantly working the business."[10]

Ragland called Hermann basically a salesman. "He would sell you on his company's stock. He was just as quick as he could be. Anything you brought up about any aspect, he'd have a ready answer."

Trent Ragland's position as a director of American-Marietta and as somewhat of an arm's-length friend and occasional confidant of Grover Hermann gave him a unique perspective on the merger with The Martin Company: "I was with Mr. Hermann in Atlanta or somewhere before the Martin thing was raising its head, and he said, 'Trent, you remember when we were talking about getting together as a company, you raised the question of why our stock was not listed on the New York Exchange? That was a concern of yours, I recall. Well, I've given it considerable thought, and I think I've found a way to solve your problem.' He said, 'The Martin Company is listed on the New York Stock Exchange. Think of that. If we merge with them, your stock will then be on the New York Stock Exchange. Isn't that wonderful?'"

Ragland said he had heard of Martin bombers, but that was all he knew about the company. And the next thing he knew, he was summoned to Chicago for a board meeting to vote on the merger. He checked into a Chicago hotel the night before and almost immediately was contacted by Robert E. Pflaumer, American-Marietta's president. "Bob Pflaumer told me what a terrible deal a merger would be and how, 'they' were not going to get away with this one; we couldn't let this thing go through."

Ragland said Pflaumer and Hermann had been extremely close. "Bob was the executor for Mr. Hermann in his will and trustee for his children . . . everything. And when Mr. Hermann died, Bob was going to vote his shares . . . I mean all that kind of thing. But when the merger came up, I think Pflaumer saw little place for Pflaumer, so he fought it. There were several other directors who were opposed, who wanted to know, 'Why are we doing this? We're doing great like it is.' So we had a lot of conversation with different ones. Bill Cabaniss [William J.], head of Southern Cement, was one I particularly remember.

"When we sat down at the board meeting the next morning, Mr. Hermann was at the head of the table, Bill Cabaniss sat next, then me, and I can't remember who was on the other side of me, except he also was dead-set against it. So I really didn't know which way to go," Ragland said. "I was just a country boy out there in Chicago voting on something of this size, and I really didn't know how to vote. You'd listen to one and be sure that was the way to go, and then you'd listen to another and you knew damned well *that* was the way to go.[11]

"Right off the bat, Bob Pflaumer moved to have a secret ballot, but Mr. Hermann said, 'No! We're not going to have a secret ballot. We're going to poll the directors, one by one.' And he and Cabaniss went back and forth on that issue for a while, with some of the others joining in. I just sat there thinking to myself; 'Well, hell, you know Mr. Hermann's the boss. This is what he wants, and I'm working for him, so I oughta vote for it.' I really didn't know why, exactly, except he was the boss and my relationship was with him.

"We finally got around to polling the directors," Ragland said, "and poor old Cabaniss was sitting there as number one. He said, 'Sorry for this, Mr. Hermann, but I must vote no.' Then it was my turn, and the fellow on the other side of me had told me he also was going to vote no, but I said, 'I vote yes.' That next fellow, the one whose name I just can't remember, apparently changed his mind, and he voted 'yes' also. Well, that gave it momentum, and it was 'yes' all the way around the table until it got to Pflaumer, who said 'no.' " Not long after that, Cabaniss was no longer seen, Ragland said. "He was just gone, and Bob Pflaumer went, too. I don't know what got into him. He went to the first joint meeting of the two boards in Washington and raised about fifteen questions about something we were asked to vote. Why he did, I don't know. He had the questions all written out and just ticked off all the reasons whatever we were voting on was wrong. Of course it didn't endear him to the group, so he, too, was soon gone."

Ragland had another lasting memory of that first meeting of the new corporation. Grover Hermann, as chairman, was running the meeting, and George Bunker, the president and chief executive, sat next to him. After all the formalities and pleasantries, "Mr. Hermann said one item that needed approval was the purchase of another paint plant in Los Angeles. 'It's a very good operation,' he told the directors, 'and we've told the people we would pay seven hundred and fifty thousand dollars for it. We'd like to proceed with that approval if there are no objections.' "

Ragland said, "Mr Bunker offered to go out and look at the property and give his appraisal, and Mr. Hermann replied, 'That would be fine, but we need to go ahead and act on this today.' Mr.

Bunker said no, he wanted to look at it first. Mr. Hermann told him there were other people trying to buy the property, that we were lucky to get such a wonderful deal. We had already told the people we were going to buy it, and it might get away from us if we didn't act on it right away. Mr. Bunker told Mr. Hermann, 'I'll go out there and look at it just as soon as you would like me to and let you know.' " Ragland said it was deathly quiet in the room, "and I said to myself, 'There it went.' That was the moment the power shifted hands. American-Marietta stockholders had two-thirds of the stock and none of the power from that minute on."[12]

George Bunker's style was quite different and very direct. He was unfailingly courteous, never raised his voice with anyone, and dealt only with large issues, leaving the how and the why and the details to others. One story that illustrated his directness occurred early in his tenure as Martin president. While making his first flight on the company airplane, Bunker was served a sandwich and asked the steward for some ketchup. "I'm sorry, sir," the steward replied. "We don't have any ketchup." Well, how is it, Bunker wanted to know, that there is no ketchup. "Well, sir," replied the steward, "we don't have much call for it. Once you open a bottle of ketchup, you know, if you're not very careful, it kind of spoils. That's very wasteful, sir, so we just try not to be wasteful."

"I want you to know, young man," Bunker is said to have told the steward, "that while we have been talking, we probably have spent enough money on fuel for this airplane and on salaries for the pilots, and for you and me and the others on this plane, that we could have bought maybe a thousand cases of ketchup. So from now on, every time we take off I want a new bottle on this table."[13]

Although he would hold the title of Martin Marietta chairman from 1961 to 1965 and be honorary chairman for another year, Grover Hermann never played an active role in the management of the new corporation. At seventy-one he left the task of sorting out the pieces and shaking down the organization for the long term to George Bunker and others. He was a very wealthy man as a result of selling the company he had built, and in his retirement philanthropy became nearly a full-time passion. Many institutions of learning and other worthy causes benefited from his generosity over the remaining seventeen years of his life.

Ragland told of a visit he made to Chicago in 1962, a short time after the Martin Marietta merger. Accompanying him was William G. Ross, a Superior Stone vice president. Bill Ross was a staunch Presbyterian, active in his church and in Peace College, a small, ninety-year-old church-owned Raleigh institution that was experiencing hard times and was about to be consolidated with two other church-supported schools. Ross didn't like the prospect at all, and knowing Grover Hermann was also a Presbyterian, he asked Trent what he thought about asking Hermann to help the college with a contribution.

"Well, if you ain't got a bit of sense," Ragland said he told his associate. "Mr. Hermann hardly knows where Raleigh is, much less anything about Peace College, for crying out loud. So I don't believe you ought to do it." But he didn't tell Ross he absolutely couldn't. Later, when he, Ross, and Hermann were walking down Michigan Avenue after dinner, "the first thing Bill Ross said was, 'Mr. Hermann, would you be interested in helping a little college down in Raleigh that needs some money?' And they chatted about it a minute or two."

Ross returned to Raleigh the next day, and Ragland took a plane for New York with Hermann. "Right out of the blue he turned to me and asked, 'What about this Peace College thing, Trent?' " Ragland had never set foot on the campus. "I had never paid any Peace College bills or had a member of my family go there. I knew absolutely nothing about it. But I told him, 'Well, I think it's a very good thing, Mr. Hermann.' And with that, he told me, 'You can tell Bill Ross I'll send him three hundred thousand dollars, and sometime I'd like to come down and look at the college.' " Back then, Trent said, "that was like three million dollars, and it saved Peace College and gave people the idea that 'Wow, if that guy will do that . . . ' and right at that point it determined the future of the college, which has prospered ever since."[14]

Over a period of years Hermann gave more than a million dollars to Peace College, which named buildings and a scholarship for him. He was equally generous to a number of other schools of higher learning, including Northwestern University, where his oldest son had attended before his death in the war. To Massachusetts Institute of Technology, where George Bunker had received an engineering degree, and to its Alfred P. Sloan School of Management, where promising young Martin Marietta executives have been sent for many years, Hermann gave $1.5 million for a new building, which bears his name. Many other institutions shared in the Hermann largess, including St. Paul's School for Boys in Baltimore and churches, schools, and hospitals in his native town of Callicoon, New York.

HONORS AND MR. JEFFERSON'S SILVER CUPS

Eight months after the consolidation of the Martin Company and American-Marietta to form Martin Marietta Corporation, one of the corporation's proudest traditions, the Honors Night award, was established in 1962. Originated on the aerospace side of the house to acknowledge superior technical accomplishment, Honors Night was expanded in 1967 to include all elements and endeavors of the corporation, both aerospace and commercial, and has become an annual highlight in recognition of exceptional employee achievement. The principal award is a suitably engraved sterling silver Jefferson Cup, a copy of one crafted for the third president of the United States and symbolic of his diverse creative skills and talents. Jefferson Cups are presented each year to a select group of approximately fifty employees who excel by "unusual ability, extraordinary effort, or selfless dedication to accomplishment." Additional awards, also presented at a sumptuous black-tie dinner in the nation's capital, go to the corporation's engineer, inventor, author, and manager of the year.

PART VII

The High Ground

1965–82

■

CHAPTER 29

Gemini:
Two by Two into Space

■

The selection of Titan II as the launch vehicle for the two-man Gemini space capsule was made by the National Aeronautics and Space Administration on December 7, 1961. That the decision came three months before the start of Titan II development tests may not have been a true measure of the high confidence the Air Force, NASA, and the company placed in the reliability of the yet-untested missile. There was no other booster rocket with the lifting capacity. Gemini was to be the middle step in America's path to a Moon landing. Mercury capsules, each containing one astronaut, were already being launched by Atlas missiles in the first step. True to its zodiac sign, Gemini would carry twins, two astronauts at a time. Its mission would include rendezvous and docking with other spacecraft to prepare Apollo astronauts for the tasks they must master in the third step, actual flights to, and landings on, the Moon.

To overcome anticipated reluctance on NASA's part to having its Gemini booster rocket possibly play second fiddle to development of the Air Force Titan II as an ICBM in Martin Marietta's Denver plant, the company proposed building the Gemini-Titan II Launch Vehicle in the Baltimore plant. And the Air Force Systems Command, which had the government responsibility of supplying the

Gemini launch vehicle to NASA, issued a contract to Martin Marietta Baltimore on January 26, 1962. Titan tanks would be manufactured in Denver and shipped to Middle River, which was already the supplier of tank domes, skirts, midsections, and other Titan components. The Baltimore plant would assemble the entire rocket and "man-rate" it for its astronaut-carrying missions.

Two pros at accomplishing tough jobs in an efficient manner drew assignments of putting together the Gemini-Titan team and running it: Bastian B. Hello, better known as "Buz," was named program director, and the veteran factory foreman, feisty Fuzz Furman, was given the manufacturing responsibility. Plant wags affectionately dubbed it the "Buz and Fuzz Show," and it would be one of the most successful programs in Martin's long history.

Both NASA and the Air Force were keen on making the Gemini-Titan program special, and to that end Hello and Furman turned full attention. Portable, air-controlled clean rooms were installed at various points throughout the factory, wherever Gemini-Titan parts were being machined or handled. In order to set apart final assembly of the rocket, Furman had a concrete pad poured in the D Building manufacturing area of the Baltimore plant. Six inches thick and measuring larger than a football field in length and width, the concrete floor was painted a bright green. It became known as the "Green Pad," its glossy finish was kept waxed and sparkling clean. There Fuzz Furman and his team held forth, and access was strictly controlled.

Leonard Mitarotondo, who had worked for Furman in flight testing, was in charge of the Green Pad. "When Fuzz was in charge of the airport, we were scared to death of him," Mitarotondo said. "He was always picking up pieces of paper and raising cain because we didn't keep it clean enough. When I really got to know him on Gemini, I discovered he was a real gentle man, not nearly as fierce as most people thought he was."[1]

But he was fierce enough to command absolute attention, not just from those working with him but from anyone in the plant who might cross his path. He insisted that the Gemini-Titan be special. Fuzz Furman ran the manufacturing program, and particularly the Green Pad, with a benign iron hand. He brooked no interference or delays by other departments, either those supplying his production line or those waiting to test the finished product. There were few challenges to his authority. His many years on the factory floor and in test operations on the flight line gave him remarkable insight into the entire production process, and the Gemini-Titan Launch Vehicle

Gemini-Titan in vertical test

benefited from his close attention to detail, quality, and performance.

"It was woe to anybody who stepped onto that Green Pad without proper credentials," Buz Hello remembered, "or without complying with the Fuzz-dictated cleaning routine," which included vacuuming shoes and clothing.[2] Hello and Furman had worked closely on the military manned space program, Dyna-Soar, which barely got off the drawing boards, and earlier on the P5M seaplane program, which Hello headed. Furman was in charge of the flight line at that time, including the waterfront, where high-speed powerboats, nicknamed "Fuzz Boats," accompanied the big seaplanes until they took off and then on landing nudged them into their moorings.

Always open to suggestion or constructive criticism, Furman sometimes had difficulty containing his frustration with newcomers who thought they knew it all. Both Hello and Mitarotondo remembered one such occasion early in the program that had to do with "man-rating," a many-sided process conceived by the Air Force and Martin Marietta to assure utmost reliability in the modification of the Titan II missile into an astronaut-carrying rocket. A young NASA engineer was lecturing on the importance of quality and the fact that "men will be riding on this rocket" when Furman asked in a loud voice, "Who do you think has been riding in all those airplanes we built over the past fifty years? Monkeys?"

The comment was vintage Furman. It was well taken and did nothing to dampen the philosophy of "man-rating" or Furman's ardor in carrying it out. All changes from missile to space launch vehicle were aimed at maximizing the probability of astronaut survival, and of course the astronauts themselves were enthusiastic supporters of the program. Specifically, the modifications included the addition of the Malfunction Detection System (MDS), redundant flight controls, and redundancy added to the vehicle's electrical systems. The company's own error-prevention program, Zero Defects, was already in full swing at the Orlando plant. Joe Taylor, Baltimore's director of quality control, enlisted astronauts Virgil I. "Gus" Grissom and Gordon Cooper, who would be among the first to fly the rocket, to take part in a Middle River ceremony that established ZD on the Gemini program and throughout the plant.

A special worker certification program was another facet of man-rating. It involved recruiting the most qualified people in the plant to work on Gemini-Titan, then putting them through special orientation courses to certify them for the program. Each was especially badged to the job, and the workers' performance and knowledge were constantly evaluated and documented. Special toolboxes, painted Air Force blue and individualized with each worker's name, were another Furman innovation. They not only distinguished Gemini-Titan people but served as a handy check that tools and meters were correct and properly calibrated. No other tools were allowed on the Green Pad, and visitors had to prove they weren't carrying a screwdriver or anything else that might damage the launch vehicles.

A special Gemini symbol was designed, consisting of a circle containing the Roman numeral II with twin stars representing the astronauts. By means of seminars the Zero Defects program was extended to subcontractors and vendors who were supplying Gemini-Titan with "critical parts"—any item whose performance was deemed critical to the success of the mission and the lives of the astronauts. Parts were designated critical only after careful review of every component in the launch vehicle. Once so designated, a sticker or tag bearing the Gemini symbol and "critical part" in red letters was applied to it at the vendor's plant.

From that moment on, every piece of paper associated with the part—drawings, subcontracts, specifications, shipping papers—identified it as critical, and special procedures controlled its production, handling, and installation. Supplier parts designated critical were stored in special locked cages when received at Middle River and were kept there until needed for assembly on the launch vehicle. Only then could they be checked out by carefully trained Gemini personnel certified to handle them. Special blue flags bearing the Gemini symbol in gold became coveted awards for subcontractors and vendors meeting Gemini-Titan certification and delivery schedules.

The Malfunction Detection System the company designed for the Gemini-Titan was in essence an electronic stethoscope that automatically checked the performance of every system in the giant rocket in the three seconds between ignition of powerful first-stage engines and liftoff. If anything was awry, the MDS would signal the problem on a visual display in time for the astronauts to shut down the engines before liftoff. The MDS also had the ability to switch automatically to the backup system if it detected a malfunction in the primary flight control–hydraulic systems where astronaut reaction time would be too slow.

Each Gemini-Titan II, on completion of its vertical test, was trundled stage by stage on special wheeled carriers, called transtainers, to the Martin Airport where giant Air Force cargo planes loaded them for the flight to Canaveral. Most times the carrier was the C-133B Douglas Cargomaster of the Military Air Transport Service, but occasionally it was the "Pregnant Guppy," a modified Boeing Stratocruiser that broke open in mid-fuselage for loading. A weird, winged contrivance, it looked more whale than aircraft.

Accompanying each launch vehicle on the flight was the "launch vehicle chaperone." There were five of them—Jack Lovell, Paul Hess, Norm Brady, Lloyd St. Ours, and Richard Howell—who were rotated among the ten manned and two unmanned Gemini-Titans. Each followed his assigned vehicle from the time its tanks were fabricated in Denver, through manufacturing and vertical test in Baltimore, to the Cape for launch preparation, and until completion of post-flight analysis. The chaperone was the one person responsible for ensuring that everything humanly possible was done to make each of the ten thousand parts in a Gemini-Titan II launch vehicle operate properly.

The chaperone was a catalyst between all program elements. His job was to ride herd on everyone connected with the booster, from suppliers to even his Martin superiors. He was responsible for keeping close tabs on each step in the production, test, and launch preparation, logging every change made to any system, and documenting that every check and test had been properly performed. "Our job," said Lloyd St. Ours, speaking for all the chaperones, "is

Pregnant Guppy loads Gemini-Titan

to make sure that none of the little problems falls into a crack and is forgotten." St. Ours was well qualified for the job. He represented the company at Canaveral when Complex 19, the Gemini-Titan II launch stand, was under construction. Prior to that he was in Baltimore for three years helping to develop all the ground equipment needed to support the Gemini launches. He had grown up with the Titans in Denver in the late 1950s as a project representative for in-silo development of both Titan I and Titan II ICBMs. He began with the company working on the anti-icing system for the 4-0-4 commercial airliner, then was a senior development engineer on PM-1, the world's first air-transportable nuclear power plant.[3]

Of his role as chaperone for the Gemini-Titan Launch Vehicle, St. Ours said, "We must be certain during production and testing that every problem, big or small, is followed up and that the proper corrective action is taken." All problems were obviously taken care of on the flight test of the first rocket, designated GT-1 for Gemini-Titan Launch Vehicle No. 1. It flew on April 8, 1964, just two years and eleven days after the award of the contract, lifting a production model of the Gemini spacecraft into orbit after a perfect no-holds countdown. With a second successful unmanned flight, GT-2, on January 19, 1965, Major General Ben I. Funk, commander of the Air Force Systems Command, declared the Gemini-Titan II ready for manned flight.

And Martin Marietta's Canaveral test division was ready to launch the astronauts. The company's Cape operation by then was headed by none other than Pat Tibbs, the company's "Mr. Test" himself. As vice president and general manager, Tibbs brought his sizable presence and near-legendary fame as a test pilot to Canaveral, where he was following in the oversized footprints of two predecessors of considerable reputation; Tom Willey and George Smith (the veteran Baltimore engineer and program manager who had moved to Orlando to succeed Willey on his retirement from the company). Directing the Gemini-Titan program for Tibbs was Joseph H. Verlander, former Navy pilot of Martin PBMs, whose launch team had already put the two unmanned vehicles into orbit and was eagerly awaiting the opportunity to safely launch all the Gemini astronauts.

It had been almost five years since the company had rolled out its last airplane, and the contagion of having humans back in the loop again on a Martin Marietta system was apparent throughout the company, but most especially in Baltimore and at Canaveral. The astronauts were frequent visitors at Middle River. Now it was Canaveral's turn, and there was an almost proprietary pride in Verlander's

Gemini astronauts at Middle River

organization that "our astronauts" actually were going to fly on rockets that "our [Martin Marietta] people" built.

Francis Xavier Carey, the company's chief test conductor on Gemini, was typical of the Canaveral breed at that time—short on years but long on experience. Only thirty-two, Frank already had fifteen years of hands-on experience with guided missiles and ballistic rockets. He had started in 1950 as a seventeen-year-old crew chief in the first Air Force pilotless bomber squadron, working on Martin Matador guided missiles. Carey progressed through the Rascal missile program, then the Navajo and X-10 programs for North American Aviation, and on the Snark missile for Northrup before joining Martin in 1958. Beginning as a flight controls technician, Frank took part in twenty-six Titan launches, working his way up to test conductor and then moving in the same capacity to the Titan II for the first five development flights of that ICBM before transferring to Gemini-Titan.[4]

It was Carey who directed the countdown in the blockhouse of Complex 19 on March 23, 1965. At T-minus-100 minutes, or one hour and 40 minutes before scheduled liftoff, astronauts Gus Grissom and John Young climbed into the spacecraft atop GT-3. The countdown and picture of the launch scene had been piped into the Middle River plant for employees to see on television monitors scattered throughout the work areas. Adding to the drama, network television crews were in the plant with name newscasters in place should the TV anchormen at the Cape wish to switch to a factory scene during holds in the count. At Canaveral, Martin engineers had been assigned to CBS, NBC, and ABC to serve as "technical advisers" to Walter Cronkite, David Brinkley, and the late Jules Bergman, respectively. More than 650 reporters and newscasters from all parts of the United States and a dozen foreign countries were at Canaveral to witness the launch.

It was a heady time. The astronauts were like family, and as millions around the world—certainly everyone in Middle River—held their collective breath, the countdown clock touched zero. Flames erupted from the base of the Gemini-Titan Launch Vehicle, and at 9:24 A.M. it rose majestically from the launch stand, crackling and thundering as it lifted Grissom and Young smoothly into space. They circled Mother Earth three times before splashing down in the Pacific as planned just seven minutes shy of five hours after their liftoff from the Cape.

There were four more manned missions that year, including the first space walk, GT-4, June 3–7, when Ed White left the space-

Astronaut Ed White on first space walk

craft on a tether for twenty minutes; the longest manned spaceflight, GT-7, December 4–18; and the first rendezvous in space, GT-6, December 15–16, with GT-7. Five more missions were flown in 1966, including the first docking with another spacecraft, GT-8, March 16, and the tenth and last manned Gemini, GT-12, commanded by James Lovell. On that almost five-day flight, November 11–15, astronauts Lovell and Edwin Aldrin repeatedly docked and redocked their Gemini with the unmanned Agena spacecraft. Aldrin also set a new record for extravehicular activity, spending more than five and a half hours outside the spacecraft, twice standing in the open hatch and once maneuvering around the exterior, tethered to the spacecraft by an umbilical line.

Only once in the entire program was there an engine shutdown before launch, and on that occasion the Malfunction Detection System performed exactly as it had been designed to perform. The only real heart-stopping vehicle in the lot was GT-6. That mission actually had a false start on October 25, 1965. Astronauts Wally Schirra and Tom Stafford were in the Gemini spacecraft, their liftoff scheduled for 10:41 A.M., or exactly 101 minutes after the launch of an Agena, which was to be their rendezvous and docking target. The Agena spacecraft was launched by an Atlas precisely as scheduled at 9:00 A.M., reached orbit, and was separated from its booster. Just after the start of the Agena main engine, ground tracking stations lost all contact with it. Without a target to chase, the launch of GT-6 with Schirra and Stafford was scrubbed.

Without the target spacecraft in orbit, NASA officials decided that rather than lose the rendezvous opportunity—one of the principal objectives of the program—they would attempt to rendezvous two Gemini spacecraft. Since GT-7 was at the Cape, awaiting its own launch day, NASA opted to put it up first as the target, with GT-6 to follow in its original role as the chasing spacecraft. Gemini-Titan 6 was removed from Launch Complex 19 on October 28 and placed in bonded storage. GT-7 was erected in its place and launched just thirty-six days later, on December 4, with astronauts Frank Borman and Jim Lovell slated for a history-making two weeks in space.

Eight days later, on December 12, in what was the fastest turn-around time for a rocket to be removed from its launch stand, re-erected, and readied again for launch, astronauts Schirra and Stafford once more lay on their backs in the cramped Gemini capsule awaiting the kick of GT-6's mighty first-stage engines. At exactly 8:37 A.M., after a perfect countdown, the twin engines roared into life. For a full second and sixteen hundredths of another, the fire belched from the rocket still bolted to its launch stand while engine thrust built and the Malfunction Detection System and the Master Sequencer in the blockhouse completed monitoring all critical systems. With less than two seconds remaining in that process before liftoff, the powerful engines shut down. The MDS had detected an umbilical tail plug prematurely dropping from the vehicle and automatically ordered the cutoff, as it had been designed to do.

Schirra and Stafford admitted later that it was the longest wait of their lives—from shutdown of the engines until all ordnance devices on the launch vehicle could be disarmed and they were allowed to climb out of the space capsule. Their extraordinary fortitude in not taking the astronauts' escape option of pulling a D-ring that would have blasted them free from the Gemini capsule and the launch stand saved the day. Program manager Buz Hello later praised Schirra's and Stafford's "exceptional personal bravery" in sitting out those agonizing minutes after GT-6 shut down while their booster was being disarmed. They obviously knew and had great confidence in their launch vehicle, its malfunction detection capability, and the people supporting them, and acted accordingly. Had they panicked

and ejected, they could have destroyed the spacecraft, perhaps causing the rocket to explode, and possibly losing their lives. Instead,
three days later, after a perfect countdown, Schirra and Stafford were
boosted into orbit by the same GT-6 rocket in time to make man's
first historic rendezvous with another spacecraft. They maneuvered
their Gemini 6 within easy waving distance—one foot, to be exact—of Lovell and Borman waiting for them in the Gemini 7 spacecraft.

With the conclusion of the GT-12 mission, November 11–15,
1966, the program was complete and 100 percent mission successful—ten manned missions flown in just twenty months. Each Gemini-
Titan Launch Vehicle performed perfectly in flight and with launch
regularity unmatched before or since in the U.S. astronaut program.
Martin's Air Force contract for the launch vehicle had been one of
the first incentive-award-fee arrangements in the space program and
one of the most stringently written up to that time. No fee was
collectible by the contractor unless and until all missions had been
flown successfully. Needless to say, the company earned and collected practically the entire incentive fee available, some $14 million,
which was all but $25,000 of the total award provided by the con-
tract.[5]

■

THE TREMENDOUS SUCCESS OF THE Gemini program cemented what
had already been strong camaraderie among Martin people at Canaveral. All were pros, tested by time and fire in many programs of the
company before going to Florida. They worked hard and they worked
long hours, and when they had free time, they liked to play equally
hard. Pat Tibbs was a boss easy to respect and just as easy to like. He
loved to play golf, but he mostly liked to play winning golf. And if he
couldn't do it with his own handicap, which was about a fourteen, he
did it by teaming with John H. Boyd, Jr., his feisty public relations
director who, when he was "on," was capable of shooting in the mid
to low seventies. As a golf twosome, Pat and Jack were the scourge of
central Florida, taking on customers or competitors with equal result. There was no such thing as "customer golf."

Whenever there was a monetary exchange after one of their
matches, particularly with newcomers Tibbs had not met before, he
was fond of demonstrating the finger dexterity that still attested to
the reflexes which had made him such a remarkable test pilot. Pat
would wager that he could catch a crisp bill dropped vertically be-

tween his outstretched thumb and forefinger held about a half-inch apart. He never missed collecting on the bet, which generally was the size of the bill he had caught.

In addition to golf, Pat Tibbs had another passion with which he constantly wrestled: eating. Although he still flew occasionally in a small private plane he kept at Melbourne, Pat's test-piloting weight of around 230 pounds ballooned a bit when he started "flying" a desk, and he made a considerable public show of dieting. He would frequently invite his Martin colleagues to dutch lunches, then make them feel guilty if they ate more than the bare, well-done hamburger that he ordered without bread. Lunch with Tibbs ended always short of dessert, but not infrequently in midafternoon he would steal away from the office, solo, for a quick hot fudge sundae, liberally topped with nuts and whipped cream.

Pat Tibbs had flown more than one hundred different types of airplanes during his long career as a test pilot and admitted to being unable to fly only one, a German Focke-Wulf 2, captured during World War II. "I started to test it," Tibbs once recalled, "but I couldn't fit into the cockpit. I was too tall and couldn't pull the canopy shut over my head. I wonder if the Nazis used midgets to pilot those Focke-Wulf bombers," he said with a laugh.[6]

During his five years in Florida as general manager of Martin Marietta's Canaveral division, Pat Tibbs added to his illustrious career 137 missile and rocket launches, including 14 Maces, 52 Pershings, 31 Titans, 23 Titan IIs, 5 Titan IIIs, 12 Gemini-Titans, plus 10 pairs of astronauts.

The Gemini program was a tremendous catharsis for the new Martin Marietta, which had made a strenuous run for the Apollo spacecraft contract in 1961. In fact, the company was informed that its proposal was the winner, only to have the prize snatched away in a matter of hours and given to another bidder. "Sour grapes!" some might say, but it was fact. On November 28, 1961, at about three o'clock on a Friday afternoon—the usual time for such big contract announcements to be made—George Bunker received a telephone call from Oklahoma's Senator Robert Kerr advising him that the company's proposal had been chosen the winner in the hotly contested competition to build the command module that would carry three astronauts to the vicinity of the Moon in Project Apollo. The official public announcement would be made soon after the stock market closed, Bunker was told.

Bunker shared Kerr's confidence with a few associates in the company's headquarters at Friendship, Maryland, including President Bill Bergen, and Vice President George Trimble, who had actively worked on the proposal. Don Herron joined the elated group in handshakes and backslapping before getting into his car and driving into Baltimore on a previously planned errand. On his way back to the office, about five o'clock, Herron heard on the car radio that the Apollo contract had been awarded to North American Aviation.

"I almost lost control of the car," Herron said. "Honest to goodness, I started talking back to the radio, 'Hey, that's crazy! You must be wrong!' But it wasn't wrong, as I found out when I got back to the office. The place was like a morgue . . . everybody almost in tears . . . either badly dejected or terribly angry."[7] There was no mistaking the fact of Senator Kerr's call or that he had been informed of Martin Marietta's selection for Apollo. Then who changed the decision, and why?

There was no explanation from NASA, and if Bunker ever received an explanation from Kerr, he kept it to himself. To its everlasting credit and in keeping with its reputation, Martin Marietta did not protest the Apollo award to North American despite bitter disappointment at not winning that most sought-after program. Only one official public explanation of the switch ever surfaced, and that was six years after the fact, after three astronauts died in the Apollo fire on the test stand at Canaveral. During Senate hearings into the accident, which killed Virgil I. "Gus" Grissom, Roger Chaffee, and Edward White, Maine's Margaret Chase Smith asked NASA Administrator James E. Webb if it was not true that initially the Source Evaluation Board had chosen Martin Marietta as winner of the Apollo competition? Webb confirmed that Martin Marietta had been the numerical point-winner in all areas judged by the board. Webb said that decision was overturned and the award given to North American after he, Deputy NASA Administrator Dr. Robert C. Seamans, Dr. Hugh Dryden, and Dr. Robert Gilruth "reevaluated" North American's experience and capability in developing high-performance manned flight systems.[8]

Six years later, in 1967, George Trimble took a leave of absence from the company to join NASA as deputy director to Dr. Gilruth at the Manned Space Center, Houston. "One of the first things I did after finding my office," Trimble said, "was go to see the fellow who for a number of years had been involved in all of NASA Houston's proposal evaluations. He told me Martin Marietta had won the Apollo command module technical proposal 'hands down' and that we also had the best management proposal."[9] The confirmation was healing salve to the bruised egos of Trimble and others who had worked on what they "just knew" was a winning Apollo proposal. Trimble said the contract went elsewhere for several reasons. "First of all, the NASA guys had worked with North American for a long, long time and knew and had confidence in their people. But I think the thing that really did it was that Martin had just won Titan II, and NASA figured, 'We'll be standing in line behind that Air Force job, and that's not what we want.' " Trimble said he could not fault that reasoning. "Martin had just won the Titan II, and to win Apollo also would have been too much for one company. I think fairly smart people figured that out."

Trimble said he did not think NASA would have given Apollo to Martin Marietta "unless they could have gotten the Air Force to put the Titan contract someplace else, and the Air Force had nowhere else to go: we were the logical guys who could do Titan II. So they figured this was 'best for the country.' They had a need for Titan. Besides," he added, "I know all those guys at North American who won Apollo, and they were a damned good bunch of people and did a good job."

An ironic footnote to that bitterly disappointing loss of a prestigious contract—particularly for those who had put together a winning proposal—was written eight years later, in 1969, when Neil Armstrong took mankind's first step on the Moon. Back on planet Earth, three former, longtime Martin Marietta aerospace engineers held management positions in the Moon-landing program: Trimble was at NASA Houston; Bill Bergen, who had left Martin in 1961, was head of North American's space division, with primary responsibility for Apollo; and Bastian Hello, who had been recruited by Bergen to help the Apollo program recovery after the 1967 fire, was in charge of management oversight on the program.

CHAPTER 30

The Innovators:
PRIME, SNAP, and 199B

■

B efore the Gemini program ended, the company had begun a new unmanned space program that would have
considerable ramifications for future manned flight. Buz
Hello was tapped to head the new Air Force project and moved from
the Gemini-Titan Launch Vehicle program in 1965, after the third
manned mission, to tackle the new assignment. Called PRIME, an
acronym for Precision Recovery Including Maneuvering Entry, it was
a wingless flight vehicle that derived its aerodynamic lift from its
body shape alone and was therefore called a "lifting body." PRIME
was the precursor of two manned vehicles built by the company, and
it provided valuable research, both in aerodynamics and reentry, for
design of the Space Shuttle, which did not yet exist as a program.

PRIME was a good-looking aerodynamic shape. Flat on the bottom, its bulbous top swept like a wedge from a narrow, rounded nose
to a wide tail flared into twin vertical stabilizers. The configuration
had developed from more than a dozen wind tunnel models and one
remotely controlled scale model that company engineers had been
experimenting with for more than a dozen years. The vehicle the Air
Force finally funded in the PRIME program measured 6½ feet in
length by 4 feet at the widest spread of its wedge shape. It was
covered with a reddish brown ablative material, a rubbery epoxy

PRIME lifting body

X-24B piloted lifting body

resin that Martin had developed, which was squirted into each cell of a honeycomb framework covering the vehicle's external surface. The thick oozy material was applied with a gun much like one used by a pastry chef to ice a cake. The entire vehicle was then baked until the ablative hardened, after which it was carefully sanded to the exact thickness and shape called for by the design.

Four PRIME vehicles were built in the Baltimore plant, and three were launched atop Atlas missiles from Vandenberg Air Force Base between 1965 and 1968. The lifting bodies were boosted into the lower fringes of space, above one hundred thousand feet, then pointed back toward Earth. Skipping like a stone off the dense atmosphere, the PRIME vehicles had a landing footprint that ranged in length nearly across the United States, with a width of two thousand miles. After descending below ten thousand feet, a parachute popped, and the vehicle was snared in midair by an Air Force C-123 plane, which returned it for analysis of its ablative skin and other information. All program objectives were accomplished with three vehicles, allowing the fourth to be used as a benchmark for comparative purposes.

With 100 percent mission success on PRIME, which proved the reentry characteristics of the lifting body, the Air Force contracted with the company to build a manned experimental vehicle, the X-24. It would explore the lower regions of the reentry corridor from the fringes of space, where PRIME ended its flight, through the atmosphere down to landing. Designed with the same lifting body shape—flat bottom with a rounded, bulbous top—the X-24 was 24½ feet in length, approximately 13½ feet at the widest part of its wedge shape and only 10 feet 4 inches from the ground to the top of its fins. It was first carried aloft under the wing of a modified B-52 bomber on April 17, 1969, and released at forty-five thousand feet for an unpowered flight. First powered flight was on March 19, 1970, and on the first supersonic flight six months later, the X-24 reached a speed of Mach 1.18, or 783 miles per hour, at 67,900 feet.

Powered flight, which averaged fifteen minutes on each drop test, was made possible by a small Thiokol XLR-11 rocket that provided eight thousand pounds of thrust, after which the X-24 was maneuvered in a powerless glide averaging three and one-half minutes to a landing at Edwards Air Force Base in California. There were also two five-hundred-pound-thrust Bell rockets for optional use if needed on landing. During twenty-six flights over a period of more than two years, the X-24 lifting body reached a maximum speed of 1,048 miles per hour and achieved a maximum altitude of 71,400 feet. Although the wingless wonder flew pretty much like a brick, it provided the Air Force and NASA, which shared the results, valuable data on the merits of the lifting body concept.

Upon completion of the X-24 research program, the Flight Dynamics Laboratory of the Air Force Systems Command and NASA's Flight Research Center at Edwards jointly funded a more advanced lifting body vehicle, the X-24B, which Martin-Denver built and flew in 1973. Using the cockpit, engine, basic structural framework, and subsystems of the X-24, the "B" modification was thirteen feet longer and almost six feet wider while maintaining the same height, or thickness, of the earlier craft. The larger, flatter delta shape doubled its lifting surface and improved its aerodynamics. Maneuverability, which in the original X-24 permitted a range of one thousand miles to either side of its flight path, increased almost threefold in the X-24B. The flight programs of all three lifting body research vehicles contributed significantly to NASA's Space Shuttle Orbiter, which is a design derivative of the Air Force–Martin shapes flown as PRIME, X-24, and X-24B.

DRILLING FOR MOON ROCKS

Martin's space systems division, which developed the Gemini-Titan II Launch Vehicle and the lifting bodies, was one of three located in the Middle River complex in the early sixties. The others were the nuclear division and the electronic systems and products division. Much of electronic systems was spun off and joined with elements of Thompson Ramo Wooldridge in 1964 when George Bunker and Simon Ramo formed Bunker Ramo Corporation. Martin Marietta owned 91 percent of Bunker Ramo for many years but gradually reduced its stake below 19 percent and finally sold the remainder to Fairchild in 1979.

Within the multidivisional Middle River complex, three other history-making space developments took place before the company's space charter was passed in 1977 to Denver. One was the design and development of a lunar drill and other zero-gravity tools that would help the Apollo astronauts recover meaningful samples from the surface of the Moon. The second was the development of the country's first air-launched ballistic missile, which also became the first missile to intercept a satellite in a deliberate near-miss demonstration. And the third was the development of the first nuclear power source ever to fly in space.

The lunar drill developed by the company was put together at Middle River by a handful of innovators working in the mid-1960s under the direction of Donald Crouch. Although designed primarily for use on the Moon, it was not proper to call it a lunar gravity tool. In actuality the drill and other devices developed at the same time were "reactionless" or "zero-reaction" tools. They imparted no reactive force on the person operating them. If an astronaut were to use a normal power tool in the zero gravity of space or on the Moon, where gravity is less than one-sixth of Earth's, he or she would be spun in the opposite direction of the tool's torque. So the trick was to design tools and instruments that would allow astronauts to do meaningful torquing tasks, such as drilling holes to take core samples from the lunar surface or tightening and loosening bolts on an orbiting spacecraft.

Working with crosstown neighbor Black & Decker Corporation as a subcontractor, a drill and assorted bits and bit extenders were developed. Apollo astronauts used the tool in 1971 to drill holes ten feet deep in the lunar surface and retrieve rock cores, which were returned to Earth for study. The company also developed, under contract to NASA, an entire toolbox of assorted devices for use in space. Included was a glue-gun of sorts that enabled astronauts to affix handholds and other fastening devices on the exterior of spacecraft to facilitate their extravehicular chores.

Zero-reaction drill on moon

FIRST SATELLITE INTERCEPT

Perhaps the most innovative and advanced development for its time was a very modest, dollarwise, Air Force program designated 199-B, also known as Bold Orion. It was a three-stage, air-launched ballistic missile put together in 1959 at Middle River by a handful of engineers and technicians in an innovative "skunk works"–type program headed by George Smith. Joe Verlander, who was in charge of flight testing Bold Orion, has the most comprehensive memories of the 199-B. It was only his second job with the company after working as manager of flight testing on the P6M.

Verlander had been a "blue-and-gold naval aviator" in the closing days of World War II and later in Korea. He had flown about fifteen different airplanes, but the one he had the most time on was the Martin PBM. He was the youngest patrol flight commander in the Pacific when the big war ended and "everybody else went home," so he was among the first Navy airmen to go to Korea when fighting started there. "In fact, we were on the way back from seven months in Hong Kong, the Philippines, and the Marianas . . . being relieved by a regular squadron . . . when the Korean thing started," Verlander said. "We got back as far as Pearl Harbor and they turned us around. Our job was to look for Russian submarines and Chinese landing forces, and it was fascinating for a time."[1]

In 1956, Verlander was transferred back to the States, assigned to the Navy's special weapons wing at Sanford, Florida. He was slated for carrier duty as a shipboard officer, but because he wanted to continue flying, he flew into Washington, D.C., to "see the commander who assigns lieutenant commanders." The commander was going to lunch and didn't want to be bothered, Verlander said, and "it made me so mad that I hopped on a train to Baltimore where Martin was hiring twenty-six thousand people for seven major programs. The Titan had just been won, Matador was coming along, there was the Missile Master air defense control system, Lacrosse, Bullpup, the P6M SeaMaster, and the entire series of B-57 jet aircraft. It was a fascinating place," Verlander said, "so I told them, 'Hey, I've been flying your airplanes, and I'd like a job.' I had four interviews, and when I returned to Sanford, Connie [his wife] said the telephone had been ringing off the hook. I had three offers from Martin as a senior engineer at five hundred and eighty dollars a month. As a lieutenant commander with flight pay, I was making seven hundred and seventy-seven dollars a month. But Connie and I kicked it around and said, 'What the heck. It's better to stay together than go back to sea if I can't fly.' So I turned in my resignation to the Navy and we moved to Baltimore."

The Bold Orion originated from a program Martin lost, Verlander said, called Hound Dog. It was an air-launched cruise missile with a turbojet engine, and North American won that Air Force contract over Martin's ballistic missile approach. Baltimore had very active advanced programs at the time, and Verlander said, "some of our young lads went up to Wright Field after we lost Hound Dog and found a major who had five million dollars. They told him for five million they could put together a program that would demonstrate the feasibility of an air-launched ballistic missile, which nobody had done before."

A ballistic missile normally would be launched vertically, but the Martin team proposed dropping it from a B-52 and having it ignite and pitch up under its own power into a typical ballistic trajectory. What's more, they promised it would fly two hundred miles. Verlander said advanced programs was an "enormously talented group of people. George Smith was the program manager and Jack Bitner the technical director, and there was Howie Schick and Monroe Duke. John Rickey, chief aerodynamicist, was "a remarkable guy," who later did all the initial aerodynamics on the lifting body.

"We came up with a bunch of configurations and went through as many wind tunnel testing hours as were applied to any major airplane program," Verlander said. The Air Force "bailed" a B-47 to the project, which Martin test pilot Bill Johnson flew, and the Martin 199-B crew would load up the missile themselves and fly from Middle River to Cape Canaveral, where they would schedule time over the Atlantic Missile Range. "The first one we launched went totally unstable," Verlander said. Three more also didn't work, each after modifications. Still well within their $5 million budget, it was "just a case of cut and paste. We were having trouble with it going unstable in roll, so on number five we put in a rate gyro, and it went two hundred fifty-six miles.

"So then the guys said if we could find a Vanguard third stage, we could add it to the Sergeant as a tapered-down second stage." That's what they did, inserting the Vanguard stage between the first stage and the control section, and moving the canards up front. "We fired one of those son-of-a-guns and got eleven hundred miles, which impressed everybody."[2] By that time the Air Force's cruise missile experimentation had become a three-legged race, he said, with one contractor using a B-58 to demonstrate a subsonic rocket and the other demonstrating a ground-launched rocket with a boost glide, similar to what the Germans had planned to use against New York City in World War II.

Verlander said the Bold Orion was the only one of the three programs that accomplished its mission. It actually demonstrated the feasibility of air-launching a ballistic missile and at the same time produced "some excellent reentry data and some good basic science." Ultimately, the program fired sixteen missiles, and there was one left over when the money ran out.

The team was kept together working on other proposals, including a satellite interceptor called SAINT, which Martin lost to RCA. That program was eventually canceled, and then Martin was given Air Force approval to launch its last Bold Orion on a satellite intercept demonstration mission. It took place in 1958. With "Big Bill" Johnson flying the B-47, the Bold Orion was released over the Atlantic Missile Range at an altitude of thirty-five thousand feet and flew ballistically one thousand miles into the vicinity of Wallops Island, Virginia, and the orbiting Explorer 6 satellite, thereby demonstrating the feasibility of satellite intercept. The date was almost thirty-five years before a ballistic rocket named Pegasus would be used in virtually the same fashion to launch small satellites from an aircraft in the last decade of the century.

First Nuclear Power in Space

Martin's Nuclear Division actually pioneered an entire family of Systems for Nuclear Auxiliary Power, better known as SNAP nuclear generators, but more properly as radioisotopic thermoelectric generators, or RTGs for short. These "nuclear batteries" were based on a physical principle, discovered in the nineteenth century by Thomas Johann Seebeck, that an electromotive force is generated when a circuit containing dissimilar metals is heated at one end and cooled at the other (the basis for thermocouples used to regulate furnaces and other devices). In the case of the SNAP systems, heat resulting from the decay of radioactive isotopes fueled generators that could operate virtually unattended for many years and therefore were ideal for space, undersea, and remote operations in other extremely inhospitable environments.

Don Rauth, who in 1957 was general manager of the Nuclear division, selected a young nuclear physicist and World War II veteran, Dr. Jerome G. Morse to head the SNAP program, a pioneering effort not only in nuclear energy conversion for peaceful applications but also one confronting major challenges in materials development, manufacturing, and safety testing. The first, SNAP 1, was a grapefruit-sized device developed as a research model. It was presented to the public in a White House demonstration for President Eisenhower on January 16, 1959, and the next day made the front page of *The New York Times* under the banner headline: U.S. UNVEILS AN ATOMIC BATTERY.

"As a consequence, Martin stock soared," Morse recalls, "and we were elated, thinking this public attention would hasten the funding we needed to develop operational SNAP generators." Instead, the reaction in government circles was one of concern and caution: What if an accident occurred? What would be the reaction of the Soviet Union if a SNAP generator from a failed satellite launching fell on its territory? To allay such fears, the company embarked on a series of exhaustive safety tests for some years to make certain the SNAP 3A, developed for space applications, would not leak radioactive material in the event of a launch accident. Not only did Morse's teammates prove the safety of their cantaloupe-sized generators, in the process they developed the world's standard for safe use of strontium-90, the RTG's radioisotopic fuel.[3]

Technology was easier to overcome than politics, however, and it wasn't until the John F. Kennedy administration that the White House gave the green light to the launch of a SNAP-powered satellite. On June 29, 1961, the SNAP 3A soared into space as part of the Navy's Transit 4A navigation satellite, marking the first use of nuclear power in space. The 2.7-watt generator, supplying electricity for two of the satellite's four transmitters, continued to operate for many years and on its sixth anniversary in space had traveled more than 868 million miles. A second SNAP 3A was launched November 15, 1961, as part of the Transit 4B satellite.

The nuclear division continued to make history throughout the sixties with a series of one-of-a-kind SNAP generators, each of them firsts. One powered a Coast Guard sea buoy, a second the Baltimore Lighthouse in Chesapeake Bay, and a third a Navy weather buoy in Antarctica. Others powered a floating Navy weather platform in the Gulf of Mexico, a Navy underwater navigation beacon, and an offshore oil platform. Others included SNAP 9A, two of which were produced for Navy Transit 5 satellites, and SNAP 11, a 25-watt demonstration RTG for NASA's Surveyor moon probe. Fueled with the largest amount of curium-242 ever assembled, SNAP 11 successfully completed a ninety-day simulated Moon mission in October 1966. A 30-watt generator, SNAP 19, was the first to wholly power a satellite.

That same year Martin Marietta assumed management at Que-

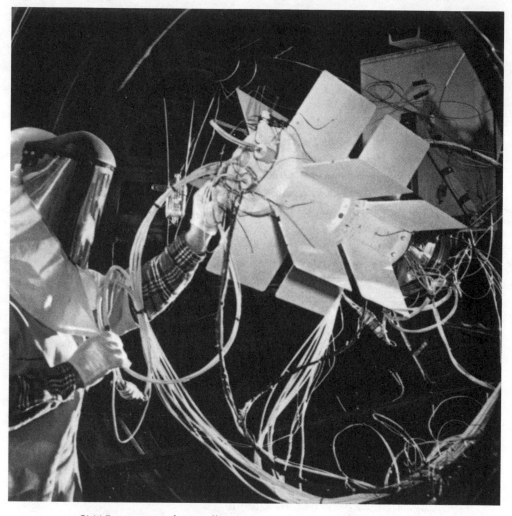

SNAP generator for satellite

hanna, Pennsylvania, of the first industrial processing on a large scale of strontium 90 as fuel for the nuclear Lightweight Commercial Generator (LCG-25). The Navy purchased three LCGs, installing the first as the power source for an oceanographic measuring station in the Bering Strait off the coast of Alaska.

Martin-Nuclear, in the same time frame, produced a number of portable medium-power nuclear plants (PM) for special applications. PM-1 was the world's first air-transportable, 1,000-kilowatt power plant, the prime power source for an air defense system radar installation on a mountaintop at Sundance, Wyoming. It also delivered 7 million Btu per hour of steam, heated by its highly enriched uranium dioxide fuel, to warm Air Force buildings at the site.

PM-3A was a fifteen-hundred-kilowatt portable nuclear plant built under AEC contract for the Navy as the prime power supply for the U.S. scientific exploration base at McMurdo Sound, Antarctica. It also produced 650,000 Btu per hour of steam to operate a seawater distillation plant at the site. The nuclear plant was shipped by air from the Baltimore plant in November 1961, just fifteen months after the award of the contract, and began supplying power to the McMurdo base on July 9 of the following year.

The last nuclear power plant produced by the company was a mobile, high-powered nuclear plant designated MH-1A for the U.S. Army Corps of Engineers. With an output of 10,000 kilowatts, the reactor was mounted in the hold of a jumbo-sized Liberty ship rechristened the *Sturgis*. It could be towed to port sites cut off from

Rauth in Antarctic gear

normal sources of electricity because of military action or peacetime disasters. As the world's first floating nuclear power plant, it achieved criticality—a self-sustaining nuclear chain reaction—at Fort Belvoir, Virginia, on January 25, 1967. Operating totally independent of shore fuel logistics, the MH-1A could supply the electrical needs of a population of ten thousand for as long as two years.

Much of the nuclear division was sold to Teledyne in 1965. The remaining elements, including the RTG technology, became Offshore Systems, Inc., which was formed in 1968 to apply the radioisotopic generator technology to the operation of wellhead control systems for sea-bottom oil wells.

CHAPTER 31

A Balancing Act and Adventures in Aluminum

■

L
ess than ten years after the marriage of Martin and American-Marietta, the balance that George Bunker and Grover Hermann had sought in forming Martin Marietta was beginning to be evident. The Martin contribution of government defense and space contracts, which represented nearly 70 percent of the corporation's $1.2 million in total sales the first full year of the merger, ceased to dominate the diversified corporation, dropping to about half of the 1969 total. Aerospace would account for only 44 percent of total revenues in 1974.

Bunker had brought in Joseph E. Muckley, a Seattle timberman, as executive vice president. Although he was the second in command, Muckley particularly oversaw the commercial operations and paid close attention to the corporation's finances as chief financial officer. Mary Jane LaBarge, who was executive secretary to both Bunker and Muckley for a time at the merged company's Manhattan headquarters on the fiftieth floor of 277 Park Avenue, later became Martin Marietta's first female senior executive and corporate officer, serving from 1977 to 1984 as the corporation's secretary.

The commercial side of the house, with less than one-third of the sales, produced 58 percent of earnings the year of the merger and would increase that contribution to nearly 70 percent of 1969 profits. That was the year Martin Marietta really became a full-fledged player in the aluminum business, increasing its previous minority interest in Harvey Aluminum to nearly 83 percent. Although it would not become a wholly owned subsidiary for five more years, Martin Marietta control brought full consolidation of Harvey's financials, and Wall Street referred to it as the "fifth leg on Martin Marietta's stool," alongside aerospace, cement, construction aggregates, and specialty chemicals.

The aluminum subsidiary was an interesting company—a fully integrated aluminum enterprise from mine to market. It held a major position in a consortium that controlled the richest supply of bauxite in the world, in West Africa. The bauxite ore was shipped from Guinea to the U.S. Virgin Islands for processing into alumina to feed smelters in the U.S. Northwest. Raw metal from the smelters supplied a sheet plant and rolling mill in Kentucky and a forge and extrusion plant in southern California. The company also processed its own carbon coke for the smelting process, and held an exceptionally favorable contract for hydroelectric power—electricity being a major ingredient for making aluminum.

Yet as big—close to $200 million in sales—and self-sufficient as it was, the aluminum company was relatively very small in an industry of giants. Fifth largest, it could claim only a tiny piece of the action compared with the big four—Alcoa, Alcan, Reynolds, and Kaiser. Before Martin Marietta acquired it, Harvey Aluminum was essentially a close-knit family-owned operation, which was the way the Harvey family ran it and seemed to like it. Leo Harvey, a Russian immigrant who had made a small fortune in machine tools and the scrap business, put the aluminum company together after World War II with his sons Homer and Lawrence. In some cases the plants themselves had been pieced together without much regard for appearance, worker safety, or what would become the environmental standards of the eighties.

Martin Marietta's management jumped on the challenges with vigor. George Bunker named Don Rauth, president of the aerospace division, to head the aluminum subsidiary, and he appointed Tom Pownall to succeed Rauth in aerospace. The two appointments, coincidentally, set in place what eventually became the corporate line of succession to the office of chairman and chief executive for both.

Bunker began the supervision of the millions of dollars that would be invested in the aluminum properties over the next decade. Bunker also brought Frank X. Bradley over to the aluminum company from aerospace, thereby setting up Bradley's eventual succes-

Coils of aluminum

sion to president of the aluminum subsidiary. The correction of
conditions at an aluminum refinery on St. Croix, U.S. Virgin Islands,
and the smelter at The Dalles, Oregon, where fumes were cleaned
with massive rooftop collectors, began under Don Rauth's tenure as
first president of the aluminum subsidiary. A gun-toting general manager at St. Croix was replaced by Jose Bou, a Cuban-born longtime
employee fluent in the Cruzan tongue. Between Bou and John de
Visser, whom Bunker brought back from a sales post in Germany to
be the aluminum company's director of public relations, a dramatic
transformation took place within the plant as well as in the company's participation in the life of the island community. The St.
Croix turnaround was a dramatic red-to-green transformation; the
red mud fields surrounding the plant were turned green with grass
and other plantings. Runoff was halted, and mangrove seedlings
were planted in the tidal marsh. Historic ruins on the property were
restored, and the plant recreation field became the site of an annual
Christmas circus and party for the island's native children.[1]

■

ALTHOUGH LACKING MUCH OF the technological sophistication and
gee-whiz appeal of aerospace, there was considerable pizazz and a
certain romance to many of the end-products and markets for Martin Marietta's commercial wares. Many of the world's most striking
architectural structures owed their beauty or strength—or both—to
the company's chemical admixtures for concrete. A high percentage
of the nation's green-glass wine bottles, as well as many TV tubes and
auto windshields were made with Martin Marietta silica sand, and
color abounded on the printed page, in plastics, and on fabric,
thanks to the corporation's printing inks and dyestuff.

Another segment of Martin Marietta commercial business during the two decades, 1961–82, was cement. Depending on varying
annual capacity of the industry, the corporation fluctuated between
fourth and fifth largest in the United States. Its nine plants were
situated up and down the East Coast from Maine to Georgia, and
from Alabama to Oklahoma and back up through Iowa and Michigan. Like aluminum, cement was a large sponge for the corporation's capital investment over two decades, but it was an investment
well advised in view of large federal expenditures—$40 billion on a
new interstate highway system—and a general boom anticipated in
construction.

Of the original nine cement plants that were part of American-

Maine cement plant

Marietta, two were disposed of, five were expanded or substantially rebuilt, and two new plants were added in Colorado and Utah. Martin Marietta was a major force in cement nationally, with company names and plants grounded in the very origins of the industry in America. In fact, when it came time to unite six separate regional companies under a single Martin Marietta Cement banner, great care was taken to retain some of the oldest brand names in the business: Dragon, Dewey, Magnolia, and Capitol. Surprisingly, none of the individual company presidents was wedded to the individual company names. They welcomed the market strength that unification under the Martin Marietta name would bring. They insisted, however, on retention of the colorful symbols marking their products—a red dragon, a magnolia leaf, Dewey's iron cross, the Capitol's dome. Many of the end users—the laborers who mixed the cement, aggregates, and water to make concrete—could not read, and the

symbols on the bag gave the product instant recognition and therefore brand-name identity, they said.

As pedestrian as cement manufacturing is to the man in the
street, Martin Marietta's cement operations were peopled with personalities, particularly some of the unit presidents. Much of the product was sold in bulk quantities measured in thousands of tons to
builders and contractors. Many of the sales were consummated over
a round of golf. The good salesmen generally were good golfers, and
most of the company presidents had been good salesmen first.

One was Dale Mitchell, president of Martin Marietta Cement's
western division with plants in Tulsa, Oklahoma; Lyons, Colorado;
and Leamington, Utah. In an earlier career he had been a hard-
running, hard-hitting left fielder for the 1948 World Series–winning
American League Cleveland Indians. Mitchell had 1,244 hits over a
career of almost ten years for a formidable lifetime batting average of
.312. The year Cleveland beat the Boston Braves four games to two in
the series, Mitchell hit a home run and scored four times. He finished the season third among American League batters with a .336
average behind only Ted Williams and Lou Boudreau, the Indians'
shortstop and manager who batted .355. Mitchell had 204 hits that
year and was fourth in the league in stolen bases with thirteen.[2]

But for all the glory and exclusivity that goes with being a
lifetime .300 hitter, Mitchell laughed because, he said, he always
would be best remembered as the last man to face Yankee pitcher
Don Larsen in the 1956 World Series. That history-making baseball
event was Larsen's no-hit, no-run, no-man-reaches-base perfect game,
the only one ever pitched in series history. Then playing for the
Brooklyn Dodgers in the fifth game of the series, Mitchell went in as
a pinch hitter in the top of the ninth with two out. As *The New York
Times* reported, "One could have heard a dollar bill drop" in Yankee
Stadium as Larsen ran the count to one ball and two strikes. Mitchell
drove the next pitch foul into the stands and then took the game-
ending called third strike. It was a close call, disputed at the time, but
it went into the record books, and the Yankees went on to win the
series in seven games.

There were other colorful personalities who left their mark on
Martin Marietta during the two decades that aluminum, cement, and
chemicals represented a large slice of the commercial side of the
house. They included Delos Rentzel, a former undersecretary of
commerce who also had served as chairman of the Civil Aeronautics
Bureau and as administrator of the Civil Aeronautics Administration.
Another was John E. D. Grunow, the affable, ukelele-playing presi-

dent of cement operations who narrowly escaped a boating accident in the Potomac River one cold, Washington, winter evening. Grunow was a powerfully built former footballer who as a middle-aged executive kept in shape with a nightly row in his single-place scull off Georgetown, where college crews practiced regularly.

It was nearly dark that particular night in early December as John sculled up the river, his back to the direction he was moving. Suddenly he heard oars dipping the water close by and turned in time to see a large Georgetown University racing shell bearing down on him, its nine-member crew unaware of the small boat in its path. Grunow dived into the icy water just as the outrigger of the larger boat neatly sliced his craft in half. If the local newspapers had not reported the incident, John Grunow likely would never have mentioned it.

■

MARTIN MARIETTA CHEMICALS IN THOSE days included Southern Dyestuff Company, later to become the Sodyeco division; Sinclair & Valentine printing inks; Manlcy Sand, later the industrial sand division; and Master Builders, the world's leading producer of chemical additives and admixtures for improving the performance and appearance of concrete. The president of chemicals from 1964 to 1972 was Malcolm A. MacIntyre, an urbane Rhodes scholar, attorney, and former undersecretary of the Air Force. As successor to Eddie Rickenbacker, he had been president of Eastern Airlines before joining Martin Marietta and was best known as the father of the Eastern Shuttle, the on-the-hour commuter flights he inaugurated in the early sixties between Washington and New York, and Boston and New York.

MacIntyre was succeeded in the chemicals post by Dave LeVine, who became the most notable example of what George Bunker liked to call the "cross-pollination" of skills and talents in the corporation. At the time he made the move in 1971 to the commercial side, LeVine was a twenty-one-year veteran of aerospace project management, having grown up on the Titan programs, and was vice president of launch vehicles. He later became president of the cement company as well as chemicals and then was the corporation's senior vice president for all commercial operations for two years before retiring in 1982 after thirty-two years with the corporation.

Prior to the aluminum acquisition, cement produced a respectable one-fourth to one-third of the corporation's annual earnings.

The earnings percentage averaged only 12 percent for the next decade, then it dropped precipitously to 3 percent for each of the two years prior to the takeover attempt in 1982. By then, aluminum business was also off, contributing only 14 percent to the corporation's 1981 earnings.

Three years after acquiring the aluminum company, George Bunker stepped down as chief executive of Martin Marietta Corporation. At sixty-five, having reached the mandatory retirement age for officers, he relinquished the CEO position to Don Rauth, who by then was president of the corporation. Bunker continued as chairman of the board, but then in a corporate game of musical chairs, he also became chairman and president of the aluminum subsidiary, which had no mandatory retirement age.

In the aluminum post, Bunker was able to personally shepherd the continuing heavy investment that was beginning to pay off. By 1974, when the balance of the stock was purchased and the name was changed to Martin Marietta Aluminum, Inc., the subsidiary was paying handsome returns. Sales were $323 million, nearly double the 1969 level of $189 million. Aluminum that year was second only to aerospace as the major contributor to corporate sales. Aluminum earnings before interest and taxes were $77 million, more than triple any other element and a robust 45 percent of the corporation's total. By comparison that year, aerospace earnings were 13 percent, less than chemicals and about equal to aggregates. Only cement, at 10 percent, had lower earnings.

Although aluminum continued to contribute approximately one-fourth of Martin Marietta's sales and about one-third of its earnings for the next six years, a decline became evident by 1981. Favorable power rates had long since disappeared, making it difficult for Martin Marietta Aluminum to compete against the giant producers in a world badly glutted by cheaper foreign aluminum. The big four could weather price troughs by partial shutdowns of smelter capacity without interrupting other elements of their supply chain. Being much smaller, similar smelter cutbacks at Martin Marietta's aluminum smelters badly impacted other company units both on the raw material end and at the finishing mills.

George Maverick Bunker retired while aluminum was still consistently producing 25 percent of corporate sales and earnings. He retired from his aluminum posts and from the Martin Marietta board in the fall of 1977. Over a quarter of a century—all but the last five years of which he had been the chief executive—he had taken Martin Marietta, the corporation, from a single-factory airplane manufacturer on the brink of receivership to a widely diversified enterprise with 125 plants and sales of more than $1.4 billion. For the next eight years he lived quietly in retirement with his wife Natalie, dabbling for his own amusement in a retail hardware business he had established for a friend and former chauffeur.

Bunker succumbed to cancer in his Washington home on November 8, 1985, at age seventy-seven. At the memorial service in Washington National Cathedral's Bethlehem Chapel, several of Bunker's closest associates and friends eulogized him. Tom Pownall, chairman of the corporation, recalled him as an articulate, even eloquent, strong, and forceful man who "never raised his voice, never uttered a swear word." John E. Parker spoke of his long relationship with Bunker both as a friend and professionally as a longtime director of the corporation, and then Frank S. Lausche mounted the pulpit to say a word. The frail eighty-five-year-old former Ohio governor and U.S. senator had forgotten his glasses. The light was dim, so he spoke without referring to his notes. He said his friend Bunker was in the habit of calling him every morning just to check on him and see how he was, and Lausche spoke of Burning Tree, the exclusive suburban Washington golf club where he and Bunker were members. The club has a tradition of planting a tree in memory of a departed member, and in one of their last telephone conversations, Lausche said Bunker noted that neither of them was getting any younger. Bunker told him that he was sending a check to the club "to pay for the Lausche tree, just in the event I'm not around when it's time to plant it."

Several days after the service a Martin Marietta corporate jet carried Mrs. Bunker north for the burial of her husband's ashes in the soil of his native Canada. On the table in the cabin of the plane was a freshly opened, new bottle of ketchup.[3]

When about a year later Bunker's friend Frank Lausche died, his tree was planted within a nine-iron shot of the Bunker tree.

CHAPTER 32

Skylab—the First Space Station—and "ET"

■

With completion of the two-man Gemini program—NASA's middle step on the way to the Moon—in 1966, America's space program was in full bloom. And although the Apollo program would capture the biggest headlines, fulfilling John Kennedy's promise of a "man on the Moon . . . before this decade is out," there was much more going on, both with humans and without, in NASA's civilian realm as well as in the Defense Department's "blue-suited" and often classified arena of space.

Activation of Titan II in silos ready for launch as a strategic deterrent against threatened Soviet aggression was completed. Future Titans would be space launch vehicles, and Titan III had already been launched in the first of its many configurations by late summer of 1964. Designated Titan IIIA, it consisted of the basic two stages of Titan II plus a control module and a new upper stage called Transtage. Ten feet in diameter and as tall as a twenty-story building, its first launch was on September 1. It would be followed by Titan IIIB and Titan IIIC, the latter the workhorse of the Titan family. Consisting of the core stages plus two huge, strap-on solid rockets, each 10 feet in diameter, this goliath of a rocket stood 30 feet across the base and as high as 210 feet, depending on the upper stages that were added. Titan III made its debut on July 29, 1966.

One of those upper stages, aptly named Transtage, had been developed by Martin-Denver as the Air Force's maneuverable space truck. Carried into space on Titan III, Transtage then powered itself into higher orbits where it delivered its satellites. On June 13, 1968, a Transtage launched on a Titan IIIC executed six hours of intricate maneuvers to precisely place eight different satellites into eight separate geosynchronous orbits twenty thousand miles from Earth. It was the first global network ever established in space and the first multiple satellite placement by a single rocket, both additional "firsts" for Martin Marietta. By the close of the sixties, Transtage had placed thirty-three communications and research satellites into synchronous orbit, accounting for 80 percent of all such satellites in space up to that time.

In addition to Transtage, there were several manned space programs proposed by the Air Force with Martin Marietta competing to be the principal contractor. One was Dyna-Soar, a contraction for dynamic soaring, that was to have been a lifting body–type spacecraft, not unlike the Shuttle Orbiter, only smaller. It would have been launched atop an enlarged Titan. Although the Air Force spacecraft never materialized, the launch vehicle did, as Titan III. Next came the MOL, which stood for Manned Orbiting Laboratory, also an Air Force spacecraft that would have ridden into orbit on a Titan III. It, too, died aborning.

Meanwhile, the company had bid on and won from NASA in 1967 and 1968 a succession of space packages, including the Apollo Experiments Pallet, the Apollo Applications Program, and the gyroprocessor systems for the Apollo Telescope Mount. None saw hardware as individual programs but eventually all three, or parts of them, were combined on Skylab, the United States' first space station. Martin Marietta built major portions of both the Skylab structure itself and many of the experiments integral to it.

All these pioneering systems were also attempts by the Denver operation to build a business base. The end of Titan production was staring the division in the face, and there was literally nothing new "on the drawing boards," to borrow a phrase. Denver had been given the company space mantle, transferred from Baltimore, and was trying desperately to win new contracts. Employment was down to about 3,200 from a peak of around 18,000 during activation of the Titans when 14,500 employees were resident in Denver.

Bob Molloy called the period "the first of the valleys of death" the Denver operation would go through. Molloy was in manufacturing engineering at the time, and he was drafted for marketing. "We

Al Kullas, Al Varrieur, Hans Multhopp with Dyna Soar model

got so busy building things, and building them well, that we forgot you have to sell when you're at your peak. It was a serious mistake,'' he said. ''We forgot to sell. The Denver management group had been led to believe that if you do a good job on Titan, you don't have to worry; the customer will give you more work. I think that had been true up to then, but it sure wasn't anymore. ''It's hard to change cultures, and we definitely were not marketing-oriented at that time.''[1]

Molloy credited Tom Pownall, who came aboard in 1963 as vice president for marketing, with turning Denver around, although Pownall gave the credit to those who decided to move the company's charter for space business to Denver from Baltimore in 1964. In any case, Denver bid for and won a number of small space programs.

A few months after Pownall joined the company—hired by George Bunker from Fairbanks Morse after several years at General Dynamics—he was invited to appear before the board of directors with his assessment of Martin. As he recalled the occasion many years later, Pownall said, "I didn't know whether this was going to be the shortest-lived experience I ever had in my life or not, because I thought I had made a mistake joining the company. I thought it was on a bad course. It didn't have any business in Denver where the ICBMs were about to disappear, and it was in real trouble in Orlando. Baltimore was sort of a cipher. We had only two things: ICBMs and some tactical missile systems." So in his presentation to the board he compared Martin with every other company in the industry, and said it was deeply at the bottom in size.

"Then I took away all the things that we weren't. I peeled back a page and took away aircraft. Since we were not in aircraft, I took away aircraft from all the others—GD, Lockheed, Boeing, Grumann, and so on. Then I took away space because we had no space business. Now these other companies began to look very small. Then I took away all their 'black' [highly classified] business, which we had none of. By the time I had taken away all those other things, we were bigger than almost all our competitors. It was obvious to the board that we were not playing in the same game as the others and that we were never going to play with the big boys until we got in the same game," Pownall concluded.[2]

As a result, two initiatives were begun: to go after the classified business and to create a corporate task force to explore the company's options in space. Pownall said he favored keeping the effort in Baltimore because that's about all Baltimore had. But the task force thought it should be moved to Denver, and the Denver people, who were still relying on Titan business even though they believed it was about to end, finally "got aggressive and convinced headquarters to make an investment in new facilities geared to space." Pownall credited Don Rauth, who then headed the Denver operation, with leading that effort.

Denver had done fairly well winning small contracts in the area of advanced programs, a new effort that had been set up under Dr. Karl Kober, a German-born scientist with multiple doctorates. Among his fellow workers, Kober had a colorful reputation for being rather imperious and somewhat of a terror. Molloy described him as "one of the German paper clips . . . an enormously brilliant guy . . . absolutely fantastic. Once in a while he had to be reminded who had won the war, but aside from that he was superb."

Kober's office, which was next to Molloy's, had a huge kidney-shaped corner desk with a full return and credenza, surrounded by big plants. Molloy remembered one occasion when Kober was interviewing a rather senior applicant for a job. "There sat the imposing Kober, German accent and all, behind that enormous desk," Molloy said, "and he sends this Ph.D. to the blackboard and tells him to write all these mathematical equations. The poor guy nearly died. He probably hadn't used those equations in thirty years, since his college days, and of course the imperious Karl carved a *K* in the guy's chest with his verbal sword before the interview ended."

Molloy said Kober knew "everybody worth knowing in the technical community in the United States." His first job after immigrating to the United States was as chief scientist at the armament laboratory at Wright-Patterson Air Force Base. His commanding officer was a hard-bitten general who "had no use for Germans and never even spoke directly to the chief scientist," according to Molloy, who told a story that was part of the Kober legend. It was at the time Wright-Patterson was developing the radar system for the B-52 and was doing a lot of work with another lab in Whippany, New Jersey. The general flew his own personal B-29, and one morning, promptly at 0600, he took off with his staff for a meeting at Whippany. The plane was not plush, just a stripped-down bomber, and Karl was riding in what normally would be the radar operator's seat.

The weather was lousy, according to the story, everything socked in east of the Mississippi. About fifteen minutes out of Whippany, the general came on the intercom and said, "I'm starting to descend, Navigator, where are we?" The navigator replied, "I'm sorry, General, I'm lost." And without batting an eye or missing a beat, the general commanded, "Radar! Where are we?" On the B-29 there is a small window right by the radar operator's seat, so Kober looked out the window just in time to catch a hole in the overcast through which he saw a barn with an arrow and the words WHIPPANY 5 MILES, painted on its roof. Pressing the intercom button, Kober responded, "Five miles, sir!" and about that time the plane broke out of the clouds directly over the field. For the remainder of the day, on any question that came up, the general would ask, "Dr. Kober, what is your opinion?" Molloy swears it is a true story, which he had on good authority.

The Apollo Experiments Pallet was one of the programs Denver went after in that period. As the marketing expert, Molloy told company management he was confident that the program was real and worth pursuing. Molloy said his confidence was based on assurances by both the program director, General Davey Jones, and the associate administrator of NASA, Dr. Robert Seamans. On his word, Molloy said, company headquarters approved the expenditure of $5 million to build a large space chamber. "A week after we won the contract, the program was canceled, and I couldn't bear to look at that space chamber. It was my anchor, my albatross."

It wasn't until many years later, Molloy said, that the company learned the reason for the cancellation. "Here we had a superb technical experiment. NASA loved it. But we had put such good sensors on the AEP that had it been flown under NASA's mandate to make the data public, it would have blown the cover on some of the nation's most classified programs. NASA canceled the program. We weren't into the black stuff at that point and weren't smart enough to know," Molloy said.[3] The incident did bring the company and some of its extraordinary talents to the attention of that element of the defense community. It was also the beginning of a long and heavy involvement in classified programs, which ultimately accounted for approximately one-third of the Denver operation's sales.

Meanwhile, the team that had won the AEP program only to see it canceled was in disarray, Molloy said. George Smith, who had headed the effort, was anxious to put the team to work right away on something else before they were disbanded and badly demoralized. Molloy said Smith wanted to know if there was another request for proposal (RFP) in the house. There was—for a Planetary Entry Parachute Program (PEPP), but a decision had already been made not to bit it. It called for launching a planetary heat shield to an altitude of 120,000 feet where onboard rockets would fire to increase its velocity to that required for reentry through the thin atmosphere of Mars. The mission included measuring the effectiveness of various deceleration devices, including drag chutes and aerobrakes.

"Let's bid it!" Molloy quoted Smith. "And I told him, 'My god! George. We've only got ten days left to respond to the RFP.' 'Well, get a copy, and let's look at it,' he told me. So I did, and Kober, 'K' Hurtt, and I looked it over. Kober immediately said, 'We have to get the right parachute. I know exactly the man, Dr. So-and-so at the University of Minnesota. He's a national expert on parachutes.' Kober had him on the phone and on our team in less than an hour," Molloy said. "Karl was really incredible."

Skylab Multiple Docking Adapter

Just as the Apollo Applications Program and the Apollo Telescope Mount became part of Skylab, the Planetary Entry Parachute Program (PEPP) became part of the Viking Mars lander program. And the commitment to build a large space chamber, clean rooms, and other special space facilities that originally had been made to win the AEP program that was cancelled became key ingredients in Denver's win of both large space programs.

"K" Hurtt also remembered the hastily put-together PEPP proposal that won the program for the company. Hurtt had joined

Martin in the early days of the Denver organization, and he recalled that, just as Titan had been a real pioneering effort, so were Denver's early space efforts.

"We were doing things that just never, never had been done before," Hurtt said. "From a management talent point of view, there was not a lot of industry scar tissue. It really was a young person's business. There just were not many people with thirty years of experience building rockets or spacecraft." Hurtt also credited Pownall with the marketing smarts that enabled the company to go out and win major new programs in space, an arena in which it had not been previously active. Hurtt recalled Pownall's advice: "He was the one who really brought us an understanding of competitiveness in the broadest sense, of getting to know the customer and of working the customer at every level, from top to bottom. You just cannot tell people you're great, you have to convince them by building credibility with them. You also have to be creative across a whole range of parameters, including pricing and anticipating what your competitor is going to do."[4]

Skylab was a perfect example. The company had performed brilliantly for the same customer, NASA, on the Gemini-Titan II Launch Vehicle. It had demonstrated its talents again on the experiments pallet, on the gyros for the telescope mount, and on the planetary entry parachute. "We had established our credentials with that customer at every level, from the administrator and assistant administrators down through the program managers and the working NASA engineers and technicians," Hurtt said.

Skylab would become much more than the first space station; it would become a complete and complex orbiting home and scientific laboratory where nine astronauts lived and worked in shirt-sleeve comfort on three separate missions of three astronauts each. It would also become, in NASA's own post-mission words, "a program of unparalleled scientific scope which continues to yield highly valuable information about the universe and life within it . . . a comprehensive program of scientific experimentation that revealed heretofore unknown information about man's capability to withstand long periods of weightlessness, about the adaptability of other living creatures to the space environment and about life itself." In NASA's words, Skylab would also:

- produce a vast study of the Earth's crust
- permit a revealing study, unparalleled in scope and unmatched in results, of the great star Sun

- give an intimate look into the universe, a firsthand study of comets, meteors, the planets and stars
- include a factory where astronauts manufactured alloys, grew crystals, and learned to work in space
- severely test humans' capability to analyze, solve problems, and make innovative repairs in a hostile and unforgiving environment.[5]

The 118-foot-long structure that made up the Skylab space station consisted of four principal segments. The Orbital Workshop (OWS), the largest section, measuring 48 feet in length and 21½ feet in diameter, was provided by McDonnell Douglas. It was actually a fourth-stage tank of a Saturn launch vehicle outfitted to provide living and working space for the crew, along with scientific experiments, food preparation, clothing, and waste management devices sufficient for 140 days of habitation. Attached externally to the OWS were two winglike arrays of solar panels, each 27 feet by 31 feet, which were designed to supply a total of 10.5 kilowatts of electricity to the workshop. During the mission one of the solar wings failed to deploy, and after repeated attempts to free it, Skylab's power requirements were modified so that the space station could exist with only one solar panel.

Attached to the workshop was the Instrument Unit (IU), supplied by IBM Corporation, which contained the guidance, navigation, and control equipment for the launch vehicle on the way out from Earth. The IU acted as an interim control center for the space station until its own pointing and control system could take over. The third Skylab element, attached to the IU, was the Airlock Module (AM), also built by McDonnell Douglas, through which the astronauts could leave and enter for extravehicular activities without affecting the shirt-sleeve atmosphere inside Skylab.

Attached to the Airlock Module was the Multiple Docking Adapter (MDA), a multipurposed "garage" and entrance to Skylab and the front end of the entire cluster. This was Martin Marietta's responsibility. The MDA served as the laboratory from which the astronauts controlled all major experiments, and it became the hub of all Skylab experimentation and work. It contained two external ports, a primary one at the front end for docking the astronauts' shuttle spacecraft—the Apollo-like Command and Service Module (CSM)—and a second periphery port to provide primary and backup access to the cluster. The actual MDA structure, a NASA-supplied, ten-foot-diameter cylinder, seventeen feet in length, was assembled

29

P5M Marlin
sub chaser, 1951.

30

B-57 tactical bomber, 1951.

31

Bullpup
air-to-surface
missile, 1958.

Lacrosse guided artillery missile, 1958.

P6M SeaMaster, 1958.

Mace cruise missile, 1958.

35
Titan II ICBM in silo, 1964.

36
Pershing 2, 1981.

37
Transtage "space truck," 1964.

JFK views Pershing at White Sands, 1963.

X-24A under wing of B-52, 1969.

Charles de Gaulle visits Martin airshow display.

Gemini-Titan launch, 1964.

38

39

40

41

42

SNAP generator on offshore oil rig, 1965.

43

Skylab, first space station, 1973.

44

Solar-power mirror array, Barstow, California, 1975.

45
Astronaut in MMU retrieves satellite, 1984.

Space Shuttle rides
External Tank into space.

46

47

Viking Mars Lander, 1975, pre-launch.

48

Anti-ballistic Sprints at Kwajalein, 1972.

49

"Don't Tread on Me," 1982.

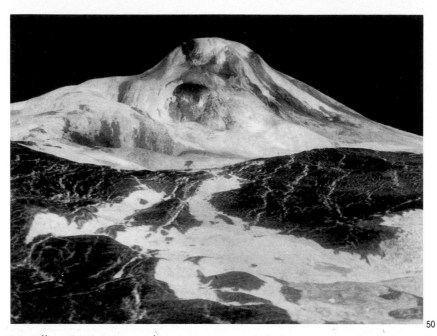

50

Magellan views Venus volcano Maat Mons, 1991.

Patriot over Tel Aviv, 1991.

51

and equipped by Martin Marietta engineers and technicians at Denver before mating and testing with the other Skylab elements. In preparation for three missions—of twenty-eight days, fifty-nine days, and eighty-four days in the space station—all nine Skylab astronauts spent many hours and days in the Denver plant. Martin Marietta people familiarized them with the layout, equipment, and the experiments they would operate in the Multiple Docking Adapter during their stay in Skylab.

The first crew, astronauts Charles "Pete" Conrad, Jr., Paul Weitz, and Joseph Kerwin, spent forty-nine minutes more than their planned twenty-eight days in Skylab, far longer than any space travelers before them. During their 404 orbits of the Earth, between May 25 and June 22, 1973, they took twenty-five thousand photographs of the Sun and nearly seven thousand five hundred pictures of Earth. In addition to collecting a wealth of scientific data, they demonstrated conclusively that astronauts could live and work effectively in the harsh environment called space. They not only performed their assigned duties but also repaired a stuck solar wing, deployed an awning to shield their craft from the excessive heat of the Sun, and improvised a variety of fixes that improved their home away from home.

The second Skylab mission lasted fifty-nine days, from July 28 to September 25, with astronauts Alan Bean, Jack Lousma, and Owen Garriott in the space station. Unlike their predecessors, who had had to overcome extreme heat, jammed solar arrays, and other difficulties, the second crew found their home and workshop clean and comfortable, ready for occupancy. But their mission was far from routine. All three suffered motion sickness during the first three days aboard Skylab but recovered completely.

Garriott and Lousma on August 6 set a world record six hours and thirty-one minutes for a spacewalk, erecting a new solar shield, loading film canisters in the solar observatory telescopes, installing panels to measure micrometeroid impacts, and doing other necessary maintenance and housekeeping chores. The second crew was accompanied on their mission by two spiders, Arabella and Anita, brought along as part of a study of space effects on other life forms. Although disoriented at first, both spiders ended up spinning perfectly normal Earth-like webs once they found their "space legs."

During the second mission, the astronauts spent more than three hundred hours in the Multiple Docking Adapter conducting astronomical observations. They obtained 77,600 telescopic images of the Sun's corona in the X-ray, ultraviolet, and visible-light portions of the spectrum, including observations of more than one hundred solar flares. They also "flew," within the confines of the Orbital Workshop, the M509 astronaut maneuvering unit designed and built by Martin Marietta and the forerunner of the Manned Maneuvering Unit (MMU) that would perform so spectacularly in space more than a decade later.

Encouraged by the accomplishments of the first two crews and particularly by the adaptability of Bean, Lousma, and Garriott to their nearly two months of weightlessness, NASA extended the third mission from the planned fifty-six days to eighty-four days. Rookie astronauts Gerald Carr, Bill Pogue, and Ed Gibson—none of whom had ever been in space—began their twelve-week mission on November 16, spending Thanksgiving, Christmas, and New Year's Eve in Skylab before returning to Earth on February 8, 1974. Their time in the Multiple Docking Adapter contributed significantly to the solar and earth resources data obtained by the two earlier crews. Carr and Pogue alternately operated the sensing devices that measured and photographed selected features on the Earth's surface. During their twelve weeks and 1,214 orbits of the Earth, according to the NASA publication, *Skylab: Our First Space Station,* the Mission 3 crew

> watched in fascination as vegetation changed colors with the seasons, as busy rivers froze and lay dormant in winter's icy grip, as puffy clouds floated away to reveal vast expanses of the planet they called home. One awed astronaut could only exclaim "Holy cow!" as he watched the lights of Acapulco, Guadalajara, and then Mexico City brilliantly greet them through the clear, cold December sky. Then, as they passed over the Texas coast, they could see clearly from Brownsville to Port Arthur, then New Orleans, and finally, the entire eastern United States, with lights aglow from the Great Lakes to the Gulf. "It's like a spider web with water droplets on it," Carr said.[6]

Using hand-held cameras, the third team of astronauts took about twenty thousand photographs through the special optical windows and recorded data on nineteen miles of magnetic tape. Their solar observations collected about seventy-five thousand additional telescopic images, including the first photographs of a solar flare at birth, an event impossible to predict. Scientist-astronaut Gibson watched the sun from his Multiple Docking Adaptor controls console for hours on end, day after day, until he eventually caught on film the actual birth of a Sun flare. Gibson and Carr scored another photographic first when, on an extravehicular space walk, they spotted the comet Kohoutek and captured it on the film of a hand-held camera while outside the Skylab.

In addition to the large hardware elements of Skylab furnished by the company, Martin Marietta designed and produced approximately 25 percent of Skylab experiment assemblies. The Denver division provided five complete experiment assemblies and supplied parts of nine others. It developed the control and display panel and the viewfinder/tracker system for the Earth Resources Experiments Package (EREP), and tested and installed its sensors. The division was also responsible for the Apollo Telescope Mount control and display console, which directed the solar observatory.

Stephanie Smith was one of the engineers who familiarized the Skylab astronauts with the Multiple Docking Adapter and all the controls and experiments they would operate while in space.

Astronaut Bill Pogue checks out MDA with Denver engineer Stephanie Smith

"ET," SPACE SHUTTLE'S EXTERNAL TANK

Hollywood's extraterrestrial, "ET," had nothing on Martin Marietta's ET, the External Tank that the company built to fuel the NASA Space Shuttle. The backbone of the entire Space Shuttle assembly at launch, the External Tank was so big that if turned on its side its 150-foot length and 30-foot diameter would have accommodated the distance and altitude of Glenn Martin's first aeroplane flight at Santa Ana in 1909. With the Orbiter and solid rockets attached, the External Tank resembled a giant whale with pilot fish clinging to its side.

The company's contract to build the ET was almost a fluke, Tom Pownall remembered. "We didn't have any large element of the Shuttle and had decided not to bid the External Tank because everyone felt the contract would be a lock for Chrysler or Boeing, who operated NASA's Michoud facility at New Orleans, where they had produced all the large tankage for Saturn. Our people figured we didn't have a prayer of breaking into that arrangement, and I said as much to Dr. [James] Fletcher, the administrator of NASA," Pownall said. "He, in effect, told me the tenure of NASA contractors

Space Shuttle External Tanks at Michoud

on earlier programs did not guarantee them anything, and then he said, 'You've been complaining about not being on the Shuttle program. The only piece still available is the big tank, so you'd better go after it.' I thanked him, and then I called Denver and told them, 'Get your team together. We're going to bid this dude!'" After a time, when he didn't think the proposal effort was going very well, Pownall said, "I got Bucky Merrill and some other guys from Baltimore and headquarters, and we went out to Denver and spent a couple of weeks ourselves finalizing the proposal and establishing a price we thought would win."[7]

The rest is history, of course. Martin Marietta won the contract to supply the External Tank and manage NASA's Michoud Facility at New Orleans in which to build it. Unlike other major elements of the Shuttle—the Orbiter and solid rocket motors are reusable—the External Tank is the only expendable component. After fueling the Shuttle all the way to orbit, the ET separates from the Orbiter, falls out of orbit, and is partially destroyed as it reenters the atmosphere and tumbles to a watery grave in the Indian Ocean.

In twenty years of production, the company produced sixty-five tanks, never missed a schedule, and consistently found ways to reduce costs. The monetary savings to the program and to NASA resulted in numerous awards to Martin Marietta's Michoud operation, including sharing in the monetary benefits as incentive awards. ET and the company's role in the Space Shuttle program garnered it a share in the Collier Trophy for 1981, the first flight year of the program; and each of the fifty-two Space Shuttle External Tanks flown since that first one also performed flawlessly.[8]

CHAPTER 33

Buck Rogers
and Vikings on Mars

■

Although many accomplishments in the long life of the corporation were momentous in either mission, timing, operational impact, business volume, or sheer size and lasting effect, perhaps none had the public's attention so riveted as two company programs conducted for NASA in the mid-1970s. One was the Manned Maneuvering Unit, promptly popularized by the press as the "Buck Rogers[1] Backpack," or the MMU, as Martin and NASA popularly called it. It permitted astronauts to fly independently in space without being tethered to their spacecraft. They literally operated as spacecraft themselves—human satellites circling their mother planet every ninety minutes at an orbital speed of 17,500 miles an hour.

The other spectacular was the Viking program, which landed two spacecraft on the surface of Mars. For years in excess of their designed lifetimes, the Viking landers transmitted to Earth more pictures and scientific data than mankind had ever before known about the red planet. Both were designed and built by Martin Marietta people at the corporation's Denver astronautics facilities, and both were outstanding examples of "mission success" in the ultimate meaning of that term.

■

THE MANNED MANEUVERING UNIT WAS one of many developments that grew out of the Skylab program. It began as M509, the backpack maneuvering unit that the Skylab astronauts flew inside the orbital workshop in 1973 and 1974 as an experiment to demonstrate and test the astronauts' ability to function in a zero-gravity environment without restraints tethering them to their spacecraft. Maneuvering in orbit is complicated by the fact that there is no stabilizing force where there is virtually no gravity. The lightest impulse or movement imparted to the astronaut causes motion that will not stop until an exactly equal but opposite impulse is applied.

As it evolved for use on the Space Shuttle missions in the 1980s, the MMU measured approximately four feet in height and two and a half feet in width. The backpack was slightly more than a foot in thickness, and its hand controllers extended thirty additional inches forward when raised to the operating position. The MMU weighed 338 pounds when loaded with 26 pounds of nitrogen propellant on Earth, but of course it was weightless in space. Twenty-four thrusters, each providing 1.7 pounds of thrust, were fired by the hand controllers. They provided direction and operational speed control, which ranged from one-third to one mile per hour up to a maximum of approximately forty miles per hour.

A special simulator at the Martin Marietta astronautics facility south of Denver provided five degrees of freedom and was so realistic that astronauts who later flew the MMU in space marveled that the experience virtually duplicated the laboratory simulation. In training the NASA astronauts spent extended sessions at the Denver plant "flying" the MMU attached to the simulator to rendezvous with full-scale mock-ups of orbiting satellites and other spacecraft. Identical MMU controls operated by the astronauts in the training sessions sent signals to a computer that moved the towering structure and simulated motions they could expect in actual space.

The first in-space flight of the Manned Maneuvering Unit came on February 7, 1984, on Space Shuttle mission 41B. Astronaut Bruce McCandless II, who had had a major role in its development, flew the MMU out of the Challenger cargo bay with the classic quip, "It may have been one small step for Neil, but it's a heck of a big leap for me." And with that reference to Neil Armstrong's first step on the

McCandless flies Manned Maneuvering Unit

Moon, McCandless became the first human to fly untethered in space. He put the MMU through its paces, checking out all systems. Then he flew first a distance of 150 feet from the Challenger and then more than 300 feet from the spacecraft, summarizing his performance with the comment, "We've sure got a nice flying machine here. . . . It's just like you are on that simulator in Denver."[2]

On the same Shuttle mission the next day, astronaut Robert L. Stewart remarked, "It's really easy to fly," as he also went MMUing the length of a football field from the Challenger. Both Stewart and McCandless spent more than five hours in two MMUs, practicing docking maneuvers that would be used on a later mission aimed at recapturing and repairing the disabled Solar Maximum Mission Observatory, a satellite better known as "Solar Max." In every respect during five hours and ten minutes of flight spread over two days, the MMUs performed flawlessly. The other three astronauts on the Shuttle 41B mission were Commander Vance D. Brand, Ronald E. McNair, and Robert L. Gibson.[3]

Ironically, the first human satellite originally planned to be a submariner. In his first two years at the United States Naval Academy, Midshipman McCandless had set his cap for the nuclear Navy, specifically submarines. But, he said, when the Soviets launched Sputnik in 1957, "suddenly the space age was upon us, so I took the aviation physical and, to my surprise, passed it." After graduation from Annapolis in 1958, he went to flight school, won his wings, and then flew F4 Phantoms from the carriers *Forrestal* and *Enterprise* for a few years. In the fall of 1965, after acquiring a master's degree from the Navy's postgraduate school at Stanford, McCandless said he was notified that he met the basic qualifications for the astronaut program—"nothing to get excited about . . . good health, fifteen hundred hours of first-pilot time. . . . Lots of people met those qualifications. . . . But I applied, and one thing led to another and again, somewhat to my surprise, I wound up in the astronaut program, in May 1966, in Houston."[4]

And the rest, as they say, is history, and abbreviated history at best, if you listen to the modest McCandless. After he had put on the MMU for his first flight, he said he simply released his feet from the foot restraints and jet-thrusted away from the Shuttle. "I honestly felt pretty comfortable. It was more of a relief than anything else to finally get going." Bruce said he thinks the most nervous person on the entire crew was the commander, Vance Brand. "Here was a guy who had to answer if . . . anything went wrong . . . like a thruster sticking in the 'on' position. I think it was weighing on his mind as I moved away from the spacecraft under my own power."

Was it possible McCandless could have gone too far, beyond the point where the Shuttle could have retrieved him? He admits there had been "some concerns" during planning for the untethered free flight. But the MMU was built with total redundancy, including a motor-operated shutoff valve at the thruster outlet. "So if you got the thruster stuck on," he explained, "once you recognized that it was stuck, you could command the appropriate system to close off completely and fly back on the remaining system." He said there was no time in his departure flight from the Shuttle when he couldn't get back on his own power or be retrieved "unless you really put your mind to powering aimlessly off into space."

Two months after McCandless's historic flight, the Shuttle Challenger once again was in Earth orbit with MMUs at the ready. This time, April 8, 1984, the principal objective was repair of the Solar Max satellite. Astronauts Robert L. Crippen, George D. Nelson, James D. van Hoften, Terry J. Hart, and Francis R. Scobee were the crew, decked out with logos as the "Ace Satellite Repair Co.," and Nelson was the mission specialist who flew the MMU. The Solar Max, a 2.75-ton satellite with two huge solar paddles, was spinning slowly in a useless orbit as the Challenger approached. Nelson's task, as he flew out of the cargo bay with a jaunty "one potato, two potato" quip, was to secure a device called a trunnion attachment to a protruding pin on the satellite. Then, using the MMU's thrusters, Nelson was to stop the disabled satellite's spin so that it could be taken aboard Challenger for repair. It would not be as simple as it sounded.

Slowly and skillfully, Nelson matched the satellite's spin rate, maneuvered between its delicate solar panels, and made contact. But the jaws on the trunnion device would not lock onto the protruding pin of the Solar Max. He tried again and again and again, unaware until later that an insulation fastener near the pin prevented the planned capture. Next, Nelson moved over to one of the solar panels and grabbed it with his gloved hands, hoping to stabilize the movement he had caused by the repeated bumping attempts to attach to the pin. Unsuccessful in this effort also, he finally was called back to the Challenger.

On a subsequent attempt three days later, Jim van Hoften, flying the MMU, was able to capture the Solar Max satellite and wrestle it into the cargo bay, where he and Nelson repaired it and relaunched it. It was the world's first capture and repair of an orbiting satellite and another first for a Martin Marietta–built flying machine. The MMU had proved it could carry astronauts safely to other objects in space and match their erratic twists and turns. Nelson and van Hoften were full of praise for its performance and ease of operation.

Two even more spectacular missions would be mounted with the MMU six months later to retrieve two satellites drifting aimlessly in improper orbits. As part of Space Shuttle 51A in November, astronaut Joseph Allen flew the MMU to the lame Palapa B-2. After carefully inserting a long "stinger" pole into a kick motor on the bottom of the satellite, he fired his MMU thrusters to stop the satellite's spin, then pushed it within the grasp of the Shuttle's manipulator arm. Two days later fellow astronaut Dale Gardner, also flying the MMU, caught the spinning Westar VI satellite and skillfully maneuvered it to the Shuttle. The two satellites, worth a total of $50 million, were returned to Earth for repair and relaunch on a later Shuttle mission.

The same year McCandless became an astronaut, 1966, Walter William Bollendonk joined Martin Marietta fresh out of Colorado University. His first job was as a technician on the original Titan program. He subsequently worked on Titan II and Titan III, on Centaur, Viking, Skylab, and MX—or Peacekeeper, as it came to be known. For the next quarter of a century he worked on just about every major program the company had in strategic defense and space, up through MMU and Tethered Satellite.

Bollendonk and McCandless met in 1982 when Bollendonk became program director on the MMU. McCandless actually became interested in an astronaut maneuvering unit much earlier, in 1967. At that time, he said, he teamed up with Charles Whitsett, an Air Force captain who had been involved with an earlier astronaut maneuvering unit built by another contractor for use on the Gemini program. It had problems, McCandless said, which prevented its use in space. Such devices then fell somewhat out of favor until McCandless and Whitsett persisted with Martin Marietta's help on development of first the prototype for Skylab and then the MMU.

"To keep the thing rolling," McCandless remembered, "it was supported by Martin Marietta dollars a lot more years than it was NASA dollars, and I remember working with Denver people like George Smith and "K" Hurtt." Finally, in September 1979, McCandless said, Shuttle managers at NASA gave the go-ahead to develop the MMU, provided Martin Marietta "could have the flight hardware on the dock at the Kennedy Center by the eleventh of July, which was like nine months from go-ahead." The date was to coincide with the scheduled first flight of the Space Shuttle, which did not fly until April 1981.

Meanwhile, MMU development "had a couple of up-and-down cycles, but it came along nicely to support the Solar Maximum rescue," McCandless said. Along the way, McCandless and Bollendonk both agreed, the working relationship on the program between NASA people and Martin Marietta was superlative.

"I think we mutually decided late in the program, prior to shipping the units to Kennedy, that if we wanted to prove to the highest level we could on Earth, we had to go through thermal vacuum testing," Bollendonk said.[5] The contract did not call for it, McCandless pointed out, and if Bollendonk as program manager had taken the position that the customer had not ordered it, quite possibly the thermal vacuum tests might not have taken place. It was another example, cited by McCandless who at the time was the customer, of the company going that extra mile to assure mission success.

In the case of the MMU, thermal vacuum testing uncovered "a few minor glitches and one major problem in the grounding system, which resulted in having to take apart the control electronics assemblies," McCandless said.

On reflection many years later, Bill Bollendonk said he thought McCandless made a valid point, and then he elaborated: "A contract is a vehicle by which we enter into a bilateral agreement, but it doesn't necessarily mean that it's the only way we do business. And when it's mutually beneficial for all parties to continue testing or to repeat something, it's clear that if we're going to have a manned flight to the highest level of hardware integrity, we've got to be able to stand up and say it's flightworthy to the absolute best of our knowledge. I think that's what we're always looking for."[6]

While the MMU was a high-profile program, McCandless and Bollendonk agreed it was not a big program in terms of its dollar value—less than $100 million. Their point was that the few people who made it happen, on both sides of the fence, were a working team whose members were always in communication, always willing to make whatever the sacrifice to get the hardware right, and then "get the hardware and the paper to look alike."

McCandless remained in the astronaut program for about twenty-five years, from the spring of 1966 until August 1991, when his thirty years of Navy/NASA service was up. He spent the next three months as a consultant to the Space Telescope Science Institute before joining Martin Marietta's astronautics group in Denver. He said he had offers from two other aerospace contractors and from NASA headquarters, but the decision to join Martin Marietta was easy. Besides the weather and the lower cost of living in Colorado, as opposed to the East Coast, "I knew and admired so many of the Martin Marietta people and the way they did business."

In recognition of the three extraordinary missions of the Manned Maneuvering Unit, NASA and Martin Marietta, and specifically Bruce McCandless, Bill Bollendonk, and NASA's Charles Whitsett, were awarded the Collier Trophy, emblematic of the nation's "greatest achievement in aviation for 1984." It was the seventh Collier Trophy honor for the company.[7]

VIKINGS (OF ANOTHER KIND) ON MARS

It was one of the most illustrious scientific teams ever put together— seventy scientists and researchers from government, academia, and corporate America, each a specialist in some field of study—biology, molecular analysis, imaging, inorganic chemistry, meteorology, entry science, seismology, thermal mapping, radio science, magnetics, and water vapor. Each was seeking, through study of the planet Mars, enlightenment in three areas that had been designated in 1965 by the Space Science Board of the National Academy of Sciences as goals for the nation's planetary exploration program: the origin and evolution of the solar system, the origin and evolution of life, and the dynamic processes that shape the terrestrial environment. Why Mars? Astronomers from the earliest time had guessed the red planet to be a second Earth because of the many similarities between the two planets. The considerable addition of more recent knowledge of the solar system only enhanced their belief that Mars was more Earth-like than any of the other planets. It is the fourth planet in order from the Sun; Earth is third. Both planets have a tilted axis, giving them variation in the length of their days. The axis of Mars tilts about 25 degrees, compared with 23.45 degrees for Earth's axis. Mars takes only a little more than forty minutes longer than an Earth day to rotate on its axis.

Our concept of Mars has been revolutionized over the ages with observations by telescope, spectroscope, and by satellite flyby, most notably Mariner spacecrafts 4, 6, and 7.

They were followed by the Martian orbiter, Mariner 9, which in 1971 and 1972 added significant new data on the atmospherics and surface characteristics of Mars, whetting scientific appetites for more information that could be obtained only from a spacecraft landing on the planet. Thus was the considerable field of Martian study that the Viking program would extend.[8]

NASA's Langley Research Center selected Martin Marietta in 1969 to be the principal industrial contractor for Project Viking. The $280 million contract called for the company to design and build two Mars lander spacecraft and the entry systems to place them gently on the planet. The company would also have responsibility for the integration, assembly, test, and checkout of the entire system, including all experiments and the Mars Orbiters, which would be supplied by NASA's Jet Propulsion Laboratory. Under a separate contract, Martin Marietta–built Titan IIIs would launch the Vikings, and the company received still a third contract to adapt the Centaur upper

Viking aeroshell and Denver vacuum chamber

stage to Titan III as the launch vehicle for the Viking mission and several others that would follow.

It was an awesome task and an equally awesome responsibility. The company's credentials with the National Aeronautics and Space Administration had been established on earlier programs such as Vanguard, Gemini, and the Planetary Entry Parachute Program. Skylab and the highly innovative Manned Maneuvering Unit had yet to fly. But the award of three Viking contracts to one company was truly unprecedented. In effect, it placed most of the space agency's Mars eggs in a single Martin Marietta basket. The company's role in the program had even greater scope. It would also manufacture the propulsion system for the Mars Orbiters and participate in the design and manufacture of instrumentation for several of the experiments.

At the time of the contract awards, the Viking landings were programmed for 1973. Subsequent budget cutbacks and other delays pushed the launch dates to 1975 and revised the landing schedules to 1976, by happy coincidence the bicentennial anniversary of the country's birth.

The two spacecraft that would perform this sophisticated mission were anything but sophisticated in appearance. George Alexander of the *Los Angeles Times*, in a guest article for Martin Marietta's quarterly magazine, *Today,* described the Lander: "Its form is perhaps as bizarre as any Martian machine ever conceived by a science-fiction writer." The six-sided structure was covered with all manner of oddly shaped funnels, covers, tanks, antennas, pedestals, and booms. "If the Viking had wheels instead of footpads," Alexander added, "it would resemble the overloaded car of some dust bowl family of the 1930s headed west." Packaged within the one thousand three hundred-pound Lander would be eight scientific experiments, two cameras, two nuclear power generators, a biology minilaboratory, two chemistry labs, a meteorology boom, a seismometer, plus an array of physical devices, including a shovel and sifter on the end of an extendable arm.

"A triumph of function over form," Alexander called it. He said Viking was designed "not as some streamlined space yacht but rather as a sturdy landing barge, a vessel that could beach itself safely upon the rugged Martian shores and, once there, carry out a wide range of scientific investigations."[9] He was right, of course, and that was exactly what it would do—probe, dig, smell, photograph, analyze, and communicate its findings back to Earth.

All of its exquisitely delicate instruments would have to survive

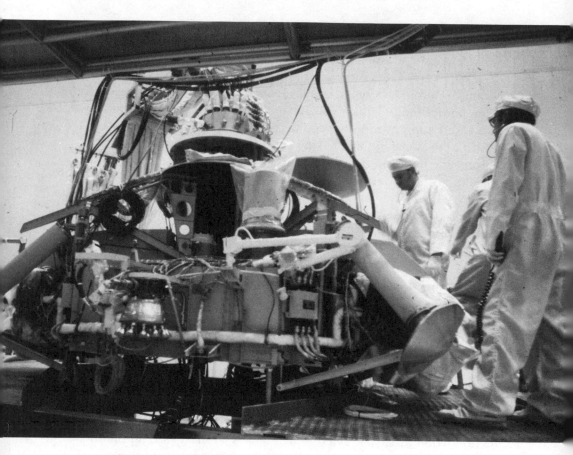

Viking Mars Lander

a cooking—the entire spacecraft inside an oven at 233 degrees Fahrenheit for two days—to make certain it carried no Earth bugs to the surface of Mars. And then it must survive the voyage, a staggering journey of 460 million miles that would take nearly a year to complete. Because of the distances involved, a complete radio transmission from Mars to Earth and back would require more than thirty-seven minutes. Therefore, the Viking landing sequence had to be totally automated. In fact, it would be the most highly automated space mission ever attempted. The schedule called for launching the two Vikings within a forty-day period but no closer than ten days. This would allow scientists and controllers back on Earth to use data from the first mission to make decisions about the second, including the choice of landing sites.

NASA mission planners at Langley organized the flight from

Earth liftoff to Mars touchdown into five phases: launch, cruise, orbit, entry, and landing. Martin Marietta planners divided the launch phase into four additional segments: liftoff and staging of the Titan III, initial burn and parking orbit of the Centaur upper stage, insertion into the trans-Mars trajectory, and acquisition of the space-craft by the Deep Space Network. Walter O. Lowrie drew the assignment to direct the hundreds of Martin Marietta people who would build the two spacecraft and integrate the subcontractor teams and scientific experimenters making up the Viking program.

In the wee hours of Tuesday, July 20, 1976, Walt Lowrie was one of the company people huddled over consoles and television monitors of the Jet Propulsion Laboratory in Pasadena, California, when that first Viking sought a place to land on Mars. Other Marietta "Martians" anxiously awaiting the entry and landing phases at JPL included John Goodlette, chief of engineering on the program; Dr. James D. Porter, the company's chief of mission planning for the Viking flight team; and J. Richard Cook, former Navy fighter pilot and former Titan flight test director, who manned one of the consoles as chief of Viking flight control.

John Adamoli, Cook's counterpart as spacecraft manager on Viking 2, was also there in preparation for his big moment, which would come a month and a half later. Ron Frank, who knew the Viking system inside out, was on the TV circuit. Rex Sjostrom, who had worked on the program since 1967, when it was known as Voyager, was head of the performance and analysis group, which gave him the privilege of announcing the status of the Lander during its descent. They were but a few of the 175 Martin Marietta people at JPL representing the thousands on the Viking team back in Denver and across the country who were watching by closed-circuit television.

Among those who had built Viking, assembled it, tested it, and lovingly nursed it toward this day was a twenty-year-veteran machinist with the company, Carl R. Stevens. He had cut the first chips of metal to form Viking on his boring mill and did the finishing machining as well. Another was a young planetary scientist at Martin Marietta, Dr. Benton C. Clark; he was anxiously waiting until the X-ray fluorescence spectrometer that he helped design and build would get a chance to analyze the first scoop of Martian soil.

The scene at JPL in those final hours of the first Viking's nearly yearlong flight—from the surface of Earth to the surface of Mars— was dramatically told by a trained reporter and writer who observed it. Here are excerpts from the drama Roy Calvin described in the company magazine, writing under the headline VIKING: INTELLECT AND INGENUITY TRIUMPHANT:[10]

July 20, 12:15 A.M., Pacific Daylight Time:
The day has come. The California night air is cool. The Jet Propulsion Laboratory is a cluster of brightly lighted buildings this midnight . . . a brilliant sight against the San Gabriel Mountains darkly outlined in the background. Every light in JPL must be burning. All hands are out tonight; there's nothing to hold back.

Outside Von Karman Hall, which is the press center, the TV vans have gathered in a busy swarm. Invited visitors, and there are hundreds of them, stroll the grounds of JPL. The voices in the night air are soft.

Inside on the closed-circuit television system, Dr. James D. Porter is holding forth with Dr. George Sands of NASA's Langley Research Center. Jim Porter is a Martin Marietta employee, Chief of Mission Planning. His youth seems accented by the slim beard that encircles his chin. Matter-of-factly, he is explaining in detail the sequence of events that must occur. He doesn't say must. He says will.

1:40 A.M.:
There is no audio on the TV monitors. Drs. Porter and Sands have finished their conversation, and there's a break. The monitors show the mission control room; in the half-light, a group of men peer intently at the green-lighted banks of monitors arrayed before them, following information being fed from the Viking Orbiter through the computers.

1:52 A.M.:
There's audio now. The "blue room," where the feed originates, sends a crackle that indicates sound is to follow. It does. "We have separation," George Sands says. "We have a check . . . separation is being confirmed all along the line." Jim Porter slips into a chair alongside George Sands and comes into view again on the TV monitors. He's smiling. (The event reported—separation of the Lander from the Viking Orbiter—actually took place nineteen minutes before, but the signal from Mars took that long to reach Earth.)

1:58 A.M.:

The TV monitors again show mission control. Beyond the controllers' desks and the consoles, through the glass walls of his office looking directly into the control room, looms the unmistakable figure of the man in charge of the entire project—NASA Langley's Jim Martin, a big man in a short-sleeved blue shirt. His iron-gray hair is clipped short. He bends over his desk, looking intently at something the TV camera from its distance doesn't pick up.

2:00 A.M.:

The blue room transmits the mission's "inside" voice network. The controllers are reporting, tersely and calmly. All the Lander systems are checking in "go." John Goodlette was right. That is some piece of machinery. One of the voices from the control console belongs to Martin Marietta's Dick Cook. He has pampered this Viking 1 Lander from its creation, through assembly and test at Denver, to the Kennedy Space Center, through all the preparations and checks that prepared it for launch from Canaveral. Now he's at his console in the control center. The Lander is falling more than 200 millions of miles away—a free fall at this moment, but that will change to a controlled fall soon.

3:00 A.M.:

Dr. Al Hibbs of JPL relieves George Sands as the principal commentator in the blue room. Dr. Hibbs was the voice of many an unmanned space exploit before; he has a marvelous sense of theater and peers over his granny-style half-glasses with great confidence to look head-on at the camera. The de-orbit burn for the Lander was smooth. We have the right velocity. Impishly, Al Hibbs adds, we also have the right direction. The Lander is going down toward its meeting with the Mars atmosphere.

4:00 A.M.:

From the blue room, fragments of the commentary: "Everything that is supposed to have happened has happened . . . and right on schedule. We are rapidly approaching the surface of Mars. We have about seven thousand miles to go." The landing impact, the commentator adds, "will be like walking fast into a wall."

435

4:43:08 A.M.:

Rounded off, the time to landing is twenty-eight minutes. Ron Frank of Martin Marietta is on the TV circuit with Al Hibbs and George Sands from the blue room. "We're going to talk it down," says Al Hibbs. "Viking is inexorably going to the surface . . . I think by now the Lander has felt the impact of the Mars Atmosphere, although we won't know about it for nineteen minutes."

Al Hibbs reminds that there's another Viking still streaking through the blackness of space toward Mars, and eight days from now it will have its course corrected for its encounter with the planet. Viking 2 is scheduled to go into Mars orbit on August 7.

The Lander falls, and the signals come back. Not an anomaly. Not a surprise. Not a hesitant second. It's all nominal.

4:53:14 A.M.:

"Viking should be on the surface of Mars by now, one way or another," says Al Hibbs. The answer won't come for nineteen minutes. The signals are flying over the millions of miles, one atop another. At the end is that touchdown signal. There is no way to extract it ahead of the signals being received, for the steady volume of 19-minute-old data keeps pouring in.

5:00 A.M.:

The project has devised a nominal descent curve, a single line in a gentle curve that measures the Lander's altitude against time, sweeping from left to right and ending at touchdown. The blue room puts it on the TV screens. Now the actuals, represented by large black dots, are being placed against the curve. A voice:

5:04:19 A.M.:

"Five hundred and sixty thousand feet."

5:04:35 A.M.:

"Five hundred thousand feet."

5:05 A.M.:

"Four hundred thousand feet . . . velocity fifteen thousand four hundred feet per second."

5:05:25 A.M.:

"Three hundred and fourteen thousand feet . . . fifteen thousand four hundred and eighty feet per second."

Every dot is falling on the nominal curve. Viking is going right down the pipe. Al Hibbs's voice breaks in, "It certainly is falling right down the curve . . . the G-load is down to 1.6 . . ."

5:09:34 A.M.:

". . . down to point-34G."

5:09:50 A.M.:

"Altitude seventy-four thousand feet . . . two thousand three hundred and twenty-seven feet per second."

The parachute has worked. The TV voice is constant now:

5:11:27 A.M.:

"Forty-eight hundred feet"

5:11:43 A.M.:

"Twenty-six hundred feet"

The blue room microphones have picked up a muted cheer from mission control.

5:12:07 A.M.:

"Touchdown! . . . We have several indications of touchdown."

The camera looks into mission control. Jim Martin stands up abruptly. The controllers, free of their consoles now, rush about, slapping each other on the back, embracing, shaking hands.

George Sands says, "The indicated landing time is evidently seventeen seconds later than the expected signal. Not bad," he adds, "when you're dealing with an automated spacecraft across two hundred and twenty-five million miles."

Not bad. . . . Not bad indeed.

Dick Cook, who less than three minutes before had looked impassive, is about to light a cigar.

Walt Lowrie, who had eaten, slept, and dreamed Viking as Martin Marietta's project director for the past several years, sweated the last minutes of the Lander's descent like everyone else. He had

Pownall (center) congratulates Viking's Jim Martin

watched from the mission director's conference area, a glass-walled room with a view into Jim Martin's office and the controllers' console area. Walt said later that his faith in the hardware was absolute, but he kept wondering whether the next voice on the network might introduce a surprise. When none came and Viking was down safely, he admitted to "just sheer exhilaration."

Rivaling the excitement and almost the suspense of the landing was transmission of the first picture from the surface of Mars, which came about forty-two minutes after the landing, with the scientists having taken over the JPL blue room from the engineers. Dr. Thomas A. "Tim" Mutch of Brown University, the leader of the Lander imaging team, had joined Al Hibbs on the monitors.

At 5:54 A.M., still the morning of Tuesday, July 20, the first narrow vertical strips began to fill the left side of the TV screen as computer signals from Mars were transformed into a television picture. It took approximately twenty-one almost-soundless minutes to complete the picture. Tim Mutch's "It's incredible" broke the silence as one of the Viking Lander footpads became visible resting on the rock-strewn Martian surface. In an instant that picture was gone and a second began to fill from the left side of the screen—a long panoramic view covering three hundred degrees and extending from the Lander to the horizon approximately 1.8 miles away. It truly was incredible. Viking had come down on a rolling, rocky sector of the Martian basin called Chryse Planita.

George Alexander, the *Los Angeles Times* science writer, noted that parts of the Lander intruding in the foreground of the panorama "gave a reassuringly familiar sense of scale and orientation to the image, as if the human viewer were actually gazing out on the scene from the windowed bridge of a ship." There would be more pictures, including the first in color confirming why Mars is called the "red planet." Alexander described that color scene as it unfolded on the TV screen:

> The fine-grained material had a reddish orange tint, more than a little reminiscent of the deserts in the southwestern United States and in North Africa. Some rocks were light gray while others were distinctly dark, with a greenish or even bluish cast to them. And the Martian sky, which at first had appeared to be a pale blue, was eventually determined to be a shade somewhere between a creamy orange and a faint salmon pink—the result of a large number of those super-fine particles of red dust suspended in the wispy Martian atmosphere.[11]

On completion of the second picture, President Ford telephoned from the White House to congratulate NASA administrator Dr. James Fletcher and Jim Martin. The president noted that the date was the seventh anniversary of the first American landing on the Moon.

NASA's Dr. Gerald A. Soffen, soft-spoken project scientist for the Viking flight team, who had worked toward this mission for sixteen years, said landing on Mars was like discovering a new continent. "We don't really know what lies ahead. As each day passes on the surface, we learn new questions to ask." On the eighth day, when the Viking's extended arm collected the first soil samples, "I came close to tears twice," Dr. Soffen said, "once when I saw the hole it dug in the surface, the second time when a young team member ran upstairs shouting, 'The PR lamp is on'—the light in the pyrolytic experiment telling us the biology instrument had received the soil and was incubating it."

A. Thomas Young from NASA Langley and Dr. Michael McElroy, Harvard scientist, felt that they "learned more about the atmosphere of Mars in half an hour from Viking than in fifty years of observations from Earth."

Young was NASA's mission director on Viking, reporting to Jim Martin and responsible for all the mission operations. He remembered that first picture transmission as being "the closest thing to exploring Mars for the first time . . . seeing something that nobody else has ever seen." And looking back on that day, the man who thirteen years later would become president of Martin Marietta said he didn't realize at the time just "how extraordinary it really was," the people, the program discipline, and the confidence that they would succeed. Once the Viking Lander was separated from the Orbiter, Young said, there was no control over it until the point of landing. After the command to separate had been sent, he went home for a few hours to sleep, and before returning to JPL, he remembered telling his wife Paige and their two children, "You need to understand one thing. This could fail. And the other thing you need to know is that we have done absolutely everything that we know to make it a success. So if something happens because of the unknowns or because of Mars, don't worry about it because we have done everything we can do."[12]

Young was one of the first NASA people assigned to studies for the Mars landing program at Langley in 1967. During the nine years he worked on it, he said his chief worry was not how much of his career he was spending on Viking but rather that "someone would come along and decide I should do something else. I mean if somebody had said to me while I was doing Viking, 'Do you want to be the administrator of NASA?' I would have said, 'Absolutely not.' I would have had no interest whatsoever." He said the same was true for the majority of people working on the program, which he believes was a major factor in the program's extraordinary success.

Young spent six more years with NASA after he left the Viking program, first as director of planetary programs at headquarters, then as deputy director of the Ames Research Center in California, and finally as director of the Goddard Space Flight Center in Maryland for two years before joining Martin Marietta in 1982 as vice president of aerospace research and engineering. "I had had no professional contact with Martin Marietta after Viking," he said, "but I knew the people—Larry Adams, Walt Lowrie, Norm Augustine— and the kind of people they were struck me as the kind of organization I'd be interested in working with if I ever left NASA." Young said he was very happy running Goddard and had not even considered a career change until one day he had a discussion with Adams. "We just kind of chatted, and he mentioned an opportunity existed. I interviewed with no other companies, talked to no other companies. I just knew Martin Marietta as an organization of high integrity, very similar to the parts of NASA I had known."

Martin Marietta team members at JPL had varying reactions to the stunning initial success of the spacecraft they had birthed over a period of more than eight years. Dick Cook marveled that there had never been a mission simulation as smooth as the actual landing. "It was happening almost too fast to comprehend," he said, "but when the communication rate changed from four thousand to sixteen thousand bits per second, I knew that baby was on the dance floor and the music was playing."[13]

John Goodlette had also noted that change in data rate. He was looking for three signals in the ten to sixteen seconds after touchdown, he said, and it was the final one, the switch from four thousand to sixteen thousand bits, that told him: "We're not only down but we have survived, and we'll get the payoff—data for the scientists." In a company career that had spanned more than half of his fifty-one years, John had seen many engineering triumphs. He put Viking at the very top of his list.

H. Edgar Craig, deputy program manager for spacecraft performance and flight path analysis, admitted to tightness in the bottom of his stomach during the landing. And he spoke of a succession of recurring nightmares in the weeks before the Viking landing. "I've dreamed that Lander down twenty times in the last month," he said, "and never once did I dream it down safely. I don't think I missed a single failure mode in those dreams."

B. Gentry Lee found the atmosphere at JPL "tentative, like pressure in a bottle longing to have the cap taken off but afraid to have it removed too soon. Toward the end it got awfully quiet as everyone listened to the announcements." As director of science analysis, Gentry decided to spend the moment of landing with the biology science team "because it seemed fitting to be with them." Nor was he alone in feeling emotions during the landing and subsequent watch as the first pictures took shape. "It was not a time to be coherent, not a time for philosophy," he said later. "It was a time for emotion, and I was very moved by the beauty of what we were seeing and what we had accomplished—the tears were most spontaneous."

Jennifer Asnin, Gentry Lee's secretary, said she was among the "crazies—hugging, kissing, crying" after the landing. Delighted with being part of the team, she said she "raced around during the descent watching these fabulous, brilliant people. We have two types," she said, "extroverted crazies like Gentry Lee and the quiets. But when we landed, they were all crazies . . . just the way it should have been."

Norman Greenwalt, the company's flight control chief, likened the experience to reading Shakespeare or listening to Beethoven: "It's like trying to explain the feeling of enhancement by reading Shakespeare's *Othello,* or . . . like Beethoven, who was deaf, being able to hear his last work after writing it. . . . It's hard to convey, but it is very satisfying."

Dr. James Gliozzi, geologist and assistant to the project scientist, will always remember the tenseness and asking himself, " 'Did we do everything we should have? What could I have overlooked?' Then I began to realize how fast the descent was and began to concentrate on each piece of the Lander as it was used . . . first the aeroshell, then I was amazed how short the time was on the 'chute.' " He was comfortable when the landing engines fired, and then touchdown brought "a feeling of elation, pride, overwhelming euphoria, a dramatic sense of accomplishment."

That accomplishment would continue for more than seven years, well beyond the Viking design life of ninety days, as experiments and cameras continued to relay scientific data and pictures from Mars to Earth. In a letter to Martin Marietta's eighty thousand shareowners, President J. Donald Rauth wrote: "The full dimension of accomplishment will be truly understood only with the passage of time and the scholarly assimilation and appreciation of the new fountain of knowledge that has now been opened."

The New York Times offered an editorial appreciation of Project Viking, which accompanied the news coverage by its Pulitzer Prize–winning science editor, John Noble Wilford:

> Time as well as space have in a sense been conjoined. The instrument that has performed this miracle is that inhuman little robot, sending out its signals, a mere creature of another miracle whose power is even more spectacular than that of all the Vikings and Mariners put together—the miracle of the human mind.[14]

The New York Times displayed the panoramic Marscape atop the full eight-column width of its front page the morning after the land-

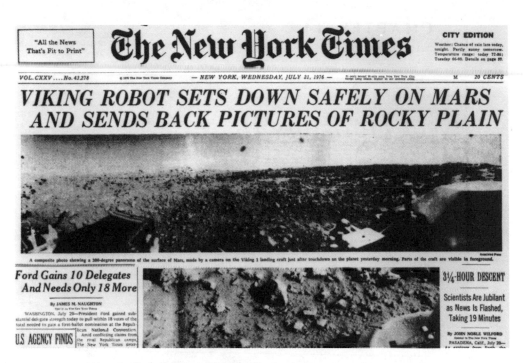

Historic first picture of Mars

ing. It was the first time ever that a news picture had been so displayed in the *Times*.

Viking Number 2 followed Number 1 from the same launch pad nineteen days later, well within the forty-day launch window established years earlier. Viking 2 reached the surface of Mars on September 3, performing its mission with equal success for seven years before NASA controllers turned it off. The marvel of those two Vikings working on the surface of Mars was recognized nationally in 1977 with the award of the Goddard Memorial Trophy to Martin Marietta and the entire Viking Project team. The trophy, given annually since 1958 by the National Space Club, is "for great achievement in advancing space flight programs contributing to United States leadership in astronautics." Generally awarded to an individual or a group of individuals, the 1977 Goddard Trophy was only the second in twenty years to honor an entire team of people and organizations for a remarkable technological triumph.[15]

CHAPTER 34

New Horizons in Electronics

■

"What I'd like to know," the irate Long Island businessman said as he reached into his desk drawer and pulled out a small pocket pager, "is why a company that can land something like Viking on Mars and send back those glorious pictures can't make a lousy hundred-dollar pager?" And with that he smashed the pager down on his desk, shattering it into pieces that flew into the startled faces of his two visitors from Martin Marietta.

"I'll never forget it," Robert J. Whalen said. "Here was the president of a company that our own people considered their best customer trashing our product. And he did it literally in the faces of the product director and the general manager of the company division that manufactured it."[1] It was Whalen's reintroduction to Martin Marietta Orlando after being named vice president and general manager of Florida's manufacturing operations in August 1976. It was a very clear message for the man whom most Martin Marietta people credit with being the inspiration for, if not the father of, Orlando's sophisticated business base of electronics and electro-optical systems in the second half of the century.

The personal pager business that Whalen and his colleague literally had thrown in their faces that day was one of the few consumer tangents on which the company's Orlando operation unsuccessfully strayed from an otherwise straight and highly successful pursuit of defense electronics contracts. The problem was not the $125 "HICAP" pager, it was that Martin Marietta knew nothing about the commercial marketplace, either as a marketer, distributor, or servicer. "When we sent salespeople out, they offered a pager, and if the potential customer didn't want a pager, our people left," Whalen said. "On the other hand, a Motorola representative would say, 'Well, if you don't want a pager today, how about a CB radio, or let me show you this telephone.' " The lesson was clear, Whalen said, and the pager business was sold before the end of the year to a competitor "who knew the consumer business."

"Big, bad, brilliant Bob Whalen," his colleagues called him. At six feet five and close to 250 pounds, Whalen was a bear of a man with the smile of a crocodile just after he's had you for dinner and the purr of a midway barker convincing you to try his show. Friend and competitor alike would attest to his analytical brilliance, his uncanny aptitude for developing a better mousetrap, and his larger-than-life presence when it came to selling his ideas to either management or a customer.

Whalen's introduction to Martin Marietta was on April Fool's Day, 1964, when as a ballistic missile expert for Space Technology Laboratory he was newly assigned to the Air Force's Titan III program. He was "volunteered" for the assignment by the head of STL, Dr. Ivan Getty. Whalen spent the next four years on Titan III, which turned into one of the most successful launch vehicles the U.S. Air Force and Martin Marietta ever produced. In 1968 he accepted a Martin Marietta job offer as director of advanced programs and marketing at Orlando, which at the time was essentially a manufacturer of tactical missiles, namely Bullpup, Lacrosse, Pershing, and Sprint. Production of Bullpup and Lacrosse had actually been phased out by that time, and Walleye and Shillelagh had just begun. Whalen said he did not know the first thing about tactical missiles, "and that's what intrigued me. At thirty-seven years of age, you think it's pretty exciting when you don't know anything about something, and you're just going to conquer it all."[2]

"So we looked around at who was doing well in what businesses . . . the Hughes, the Raytheons, and so on . . . all were doing well, and they had something in common: They built the missile seeker systems and the guidance. So we decided to get into seekers and guidance," Whalen continued. "We knew it would take a while, and we felt we would have to leapfrog everyone else if we wanted to be successful. We also figured people would want to see at night. We needed to get into night attack, and we also went after very accurate laser-guided systems and air-to-ground electro-optics." George Smith, who was Orlando general manager at the time, agreed with the strategy and supported it 100 percent.

Whalen said there were not many other companies or customer organizations focused on those areas. "Since lead times were so great and we were going for the long haul, we had to proceed on the basis of our own convictions and be steadfast in our belief," he said. "You couldn't have an admiral or a general wave you off here and there by telling you something else was the favorite of the moment. "We told ourselves that we were going to be smarter than anyone else in terms of requirements."

A systems analysis group was established under Bill Ammon with the sole purpose of finding out what was needed by the defense establishment without regard to existing product lines or funding. The U.S. withdrawal from Vietnam had already started, and increasing amounts of money were being diverted to the defense of Europe. They therefore decided to focus attention on Europe, and rather than the standard computer systems analysis, Whalen said, "we decided to go back in history and literally dissect what happened in World War II to see what lessons we could learn."

For six months to a year they visited historical societies, combed archives, and interviewed scores of Germans, mostly former generals and pilots. Much of the research focused on "Operation Barbarossa," the plan for Germany's attack on the Soviet Union, so code-named because of Adolph Hitler's fascination with Frederick Barbarossa, the twelfth-century King Frederick I of Germany. They studied six different plans that Hitler had written for his surprise invasion of the Soviet Union. Then they obtained data on the actual campaign, how many miles the Germans moved in a day, how many kills per sortie, and so on.

"The interesting thing," Whalen said, "was that our experience coming out of Vietnam was that you can't do better than destroy a tenth [.10] of a target per sortie, or less. Yet in the historical data, we went through one hundred thirty-eight thousand sorties— the Germans attacking us, us attacking the Germans, Soviets attacking Germans, the British attacking the Germans—and we found that on the average in World War II, .88 tactical targets were destroyed per sortie and approximately one tactical target was destroyed per ton of high explosive, with the exception of a tank which took 4.8 tons." Whalen said communicating such statistics to the Department of Defense was difficult because everybody said, "This is impossible . . . it can't happen." The prevailing view in the Pentagon at the time, he said, was that there would be thirty days' warning of a war that would last just ninety days. Stalin had three weeks' warning of the German invasion, Whalen said, but did not act on the information for fear of disrupting the diplomatic alliance he had with the Germans. "What we finally did was say, 'Look, if you take all the trucks on the Ho Chi Minh Trail and turn them loose all at one time, the vehicle density is more than a factor of twenty lower than the vehicle density of a U.S. division in defense of Europe. And that's why a war in Vietnam is so different from a war in Europe.' "[3]

The analysis took about a year and a half, but it took two more years, until 1973, to convince people that the systems necessary to defend European allies against surprise attack would be like the horse in *Twelfth Night*'s frequently misquoted line; they would be systems "of another color," not like those used in Vietnam.

The marketing strategy was to apply what they had learned from "Operation Barbarossa" to filter decisions on where to invest the company's research money. There was a second filter, which invariably saved time, effort, and money, and that was what Whalen called "the Jim Beveridge caution: 'Don't let the brilliance of a technical idea blind you to its marketing worthlessness,' or to say it another way, 'You can invent anything, but you've got to start with what will sell.' "

Applying those two screens to potential business proposals, Orlando decided to pursue systems using Forward-Looking InfraRed techniques, called FLIR. And they wanted to do that for a customer the company knew well. That had to be the Army, and the Army meant helicopter, they figured. Whalen credited Ron Schack with starting the company to work on something called SLOT, an acronym for Stabilized Line-of-Sight Tracker. At the same time, and mostly because of what Whalen described as "the relentless urging of marketing's George Lutz," Orlando went after and won an Army contract to manufacture FLIR common modules, a necessary ingredient for the company's better understanding of the business.[4]

"Now we had air-to-ground missiles, the air-to-ground pods, and FLIRs," Whalen said, "and we decided we also needed communications and electronics, an enormous business area that we weren't in. We didn't even talk the language . . . switches . . . control modal elements . . . that kind of stuff." To get that area going, Kerry Fox was brought on board from Collins Radio. Whalen said Fox was "indestructible," and he did what he was hired to do. But coming from a commercial electronics background as he did, Fox also urged the company to venture into the pocket pager business that literally broke up in Whalen's face a couple of years later.

One of the major growth programs for Orlando during this same period was Pershing II. Although not a new area of business, the improved Pershing came about because of the systems analysis screen being applied to the environment in which a nuclear-warhead Pershing was being deployed in Europe.

Bill Ammon's group determined that some areas could not be targeted because of the damage that would be caused to nearby civilians—once again the problem of everything being so close in Europe. What was needed was pinpoint accuracy that would permit the design of a still effective Pershing warhead but with greatly reduced yield. Whalen believes that if the focus had not been on the need, no one would have worked to achieve the breakthrough in guidance technology that enabled a longer-range Pershing II to play a pivotal role with the Soviets in the arms reduction process and the eventual democratization of Eastern Europe.

One of the first rewards of Orlando's revised market thrust was a program called Pave Penny, which Whalen said he did his best to talk Ron Schack out of. "Ron had really become involved in laser search techniques, and when the Air Force requested proposals on Pave Penny at twenty thousand to thirty thousand dollars per copy, I told him, 'This is ridiculous. What do you want to fool around with something like that for?' Ron persisted, and I finally told him, 'All right. As long as you don't spend more than a certain amount on the proposal, you can go ahead, and I'll call it Ron Schack's folly.' Well, Ron won it," Whalen said with a laugh, "and one hundred and twenty million dollars later in sales, we had earned a twelve percent fee. He really did well."

Pave Penny was a laser search and tracking system that provided precision weapon delivery capabilities for a variety of tactical aircraft. It was contained in a pod slung beneath the aircraft fuselage. The company built more than eight hundred pods and associated equipment for the U.S. Air Force and two international customers. It led to a similar laser spot tracker with a strike camera. Called LST/SCAM, the system enabled Navy and Marine Corps pilots of F/A18 aircraft to pinpoint and destroy camouflaged targets day or night, in all types of weather, and to photographically assess the damage during and after an attack. More than 250 systems were produced.

Joseph N. Kremonas remembers well the time and Whalen's arrival on the scene. Kremonas had been sent to Dayton, Ohio, by

Tom Pownall with an assignment to prepare a business analysis of the proper route the company should take to "break into laser-fire control." He said he and Pownall, the newly hired vice president, were the only two working in sales and requirements. "We figured precision guidance was the way to go," Kremonas said, "and that our laser smarts would help us get there."[5]

Another substantial new program won by Orlando in the 1970s—this one during Whalen's one-year sojourn at corporate headquarters—was a $50-million contract to produce a cannon-launched guided projectile (CLGP). Essentially a guided bullet, it was a laser-guided artillery shell fired from conventional 155-millimeter guns. The Army formally christened its new projectile "Copperhead," and it revolutionized field artillery firepower. Except for increases in range and yield of the shells, the concept of artillery fire had been virtually unchanged for five centuries. Prior to Copperhead, it was

Copperhead optic noses

not unusual to expend scores of shells, even hundreds, on a single target, firing some long, some short, until they bracketed and finally zeroed in on the target. With Copperhead, the Army compiled an 80 percent reliability record for taking out a target with a single round. The small gyros and computers that made Copperhead so accurate had to withstand firing from a cannon—a kick eight thousand times the force of gravity. It was not an easy task. The company produced more than twenty-eight thousand Copperhead rounds for the U.S. Army from 1973 through 1991.

When Whalen returned to Orlando as general manager in 1976, the division was in the midst of a major competition for an Army targeting and night-vision system for helicopters known as TADS-PNVS. The letters stood for Target Acquisition and Detection System, Pilot Night Vision Sight, familiarly referred to by project folk and customer alike as "TADS-PiN-ViS." Marty Coenson led the effort that resulted in Martin Marietta's being chosen as one of two contractors to compete in a fly-off, and it eventually won the contract to build TADS-PNVS. It would be one of the company's major programs well into the nineties. More important, the system turned night into day for helicopter pilots, dramatically increasing their operating envelope—the length of their operating day—and increasing as well the capability of the army's Apache attack helicopter to acquire and destroy targets.[6]

Almost simultaneously with the development of TADS-PNVS—the helicopter's eyes in the dark—Orlando was under contract to the Air Force at Wright Field on what was called SSNAP, Single Seat Night Attack Pod. Marty Schwartz, another of Orlando's advanced program whizzes, was working that area, and Whalen said Schwartz used the division's Surface Terrain Laboratory to help answer the question, "How would a pilot in a single seat cockpit fly at night?" The company had a great deal of experience seeing in the dark because of its TADS work. Nevertheless, it was caught by surprise and was unprepared when the Air Force "all of a sudden came out with something called LANTIRN," Whalen said.

One of the best of the service acronyms for painting a mental picture, LANTIRN stood for Low-Altitude Navigation and Targeting Infrared for Night and was intended to enable tactical fighter pilots to fly at night and in poor weather. The chief competitors for the program were PhilcoFord and Hughes.

Whelan called Mal Currie, then head of the missiles division at Hughes, and told him, "You know, Mal, I think we can really help you on this thing." Currie made a trip to Orlando, and the two

TADS/PNVS noses on Apaches

companies decided to team on the proposal, with Hughes as the prime and Martin Marietta as subcontractor. The Air Force Systems Command at that time was imposing contracts that mandated fixed-price development, the nemesis of defense contractors. Halfway through the proposal process, Whalen's presence was urgently requested at Hughes.

"They told me there'd been a little change in plan," Whalen recalled, "that the Hughes management wouldn't bid fixed-price development. 'So we'd like you to prime this job.' It was a hell of a time to tell me that, but apparently Hughes management was adamant. There it was . . . on the spot . . . boom. . . . So I said, 'Okay, we'll do it.' "[7] As it turned out, the program was to be bid at approximately $110 million, and with the change in roles, Martin Marietta's share jumped to nearly $100 million. Martin Marietta would be responsible for the FLIRs and the stabilization system; both companies were working on the automatic target recognition; and the laser would be subcontracted to International Laser Systems, Inc., a Martin Marietta spinoff company in which the corporation held no position at that time.

At that point in the competition, Whalen said, all of the Philco-

Ford low-altitude work on terrain following employed a carbon dioxide laser. Martin Marietta concluded, based on its experience and its conviction that the CO_2 laser was really not the answer—even though it was "almost spelled out in the RFP"—that it would go with a radar instead, and that the system should be contained in two pods—one for navigation, the other for targeting— rather than the one pod called for by the Air Force. The company's review group, the so-called blue team, as well as some members of management had problems with that decision, but it stood. Then, about that time, Whalen said, Currie called him and said Hughes wanted to do the missile boresight correlator, an element of the system that transfers the coordinates from the FLIR that acquired the target into the seeker, but he said Hughes could not bid it fixed-price.

It was somewhat late in the process, Whalen said, "but we wanted Hughes to do that work, so I told him, 'All right, Mal. Give me the other shoe.' " Currie responded that he wanted to bid the correlator at cost plus a fee. "How can I go to my management bidding a fixed-price contract with you bidding a portion cost-plus?" Whalen said he pleaded, to which Currie replied, "I give you my word that we will never overrun the job." Whalen said he thought about it for almost a full minute before telling the Hughes executive, "Well, Mal, you got us into this to begin with, and I have great respect for you . . . so okay."

Martin Marietta, with Hughes as subcontractor, won the contract to build LANTIRN. PhilcoFord protested that the winners' bid was not responsive to the Air Force RFP. The protest was overruled, and LANTIRN became one of the Air Force's most successful programs, turning night into day for fighter pilots on thousands of hours and millions of miles of training and combat flying. It was still going strong ten years and $4 billion after that first contract award. As for the lone cost-plus portion of the otherwise fixed-price contract, Whalen said Hughes performed its part of the job "on schedule and 100 percent perfect, with never an overrun."[8]

The Orlando division, which so dramatically reconfigured its business base in the 1970s and 1980s, grew into Martin Marietta Electronic and Missile Systems Group, with many other programs in electro-optics, millimeter wave radar, sensor fusion, image and signal processing, and observables technology in addition to information systems, ordnance, tactical missiles, launch systems, anti-submarine warfare, and undersea systems. Its growth was equally dramatic. From a structures and systems integration organization in 1976, with thirty-eight hundred people and $200 million of sales, primarily in tactical

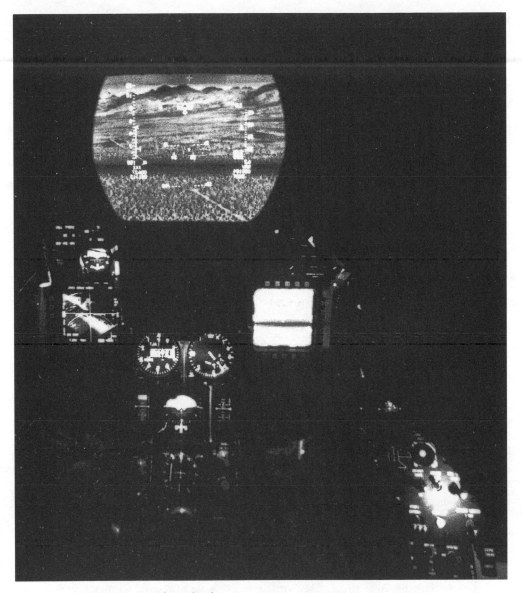

LANTIRN cockpit display

missiles, Orlando burgeoned to become in 1982 a robust, technology value-added electro-optics–oriented business, with ten thousand people, close to $900 million in sales, and the backlog to reach sales of $2 billion in the next five years.

Much of the credit for the company's success at winning new business in those fast-paced years at Orlando was given by Whalen to his colleagues, and many of the stories that colored his larger-than-life image came from them. At a senior staff offsite meeting a year or so before he left, Whalen said he took a moment to discuss the diverse personalities represented in the small group: "Going around the room, we had first of all 'Dr. No,' Phil Duke, head of finance, whose motto was, 'Don't do anything that'll cost money.' Next was Nick DePasquale, alias the 'Godfather,' who had a tough job in manufacturing and was always saying, 'No more new business. Let's just do what we've got.'

"There was Hugh Parks, a brilliant, brilliant engineer," Whalen said, "who absolutely lived on the edge and was fond of saying, 'A bid decision is an automatic cookie.' Winter Lantz, our personnel guy, was always analyzing us psychologically. And there was Len Wroten, 'Mr. Copperhead,' a tremendous guy and one of the greatest engineers I've ever met. Another great guy, a lovely man who was running engineering, Sy Zeiberg, we called our 'defense intellectual.' He was always giving us the Department of Defense viewpoint, and I used to plead with him: 'Come on Sy, I've got to make a buck. What are we going to do now that we're at this point?'

"Of course there was Bill Ammon, an economics major in college and our master analyst, who was continually pointing us in the right direction. And then finally there was one of the premier guys, Dean Warren, head of strategic planning. Dean was one of the brightest guys I've ever met, and he used to have marketing issues, business issues, and then what Dean called 'substantive issues.' And his substantive issues were facing up to the people issues. 'We don't have the right person here,' he was always saying, 'What are we going to do about it?' At our meetings, I'd be moving along just great, and Dean would say, 'You know, Bob, you haven't raised any of the substantive issues.' He was the proverbial nag who caused us to do what we should have done. Just a marvelous, marvelous guy."[9]

After he'd gone around the table, Whalen said he told the group, " 'Now think of it fellows. Think of the diversities and the personalities and the backgrounds here. You make us what we are, and we're the damndest team you ever saw, and I'm so proud to be a part of it.' And then I told them to remember 'I don't want yes-men,' and I told them one of the sayings that was a favorite of my wife's wonderful grandmother, 'When a fish smells, it smells from the head.' "

Six months later, in the midst of a string of tough problems that were costing the company money, Whalen said, "I was chewing out these guys at a staff meeting. I mean I just went after them. I didn't stop for fifteen minutes. . . . 'How in the world could this happen? . . . Now who was responsible for this?' There was a dead silence, and then Hugh Parks said, 'When a fish smells, it smells from the head.' And of course he was right. It turned out something I had done had put us in the soup. But to show Hugh I was as fast as he was, I paused for a moment and then said, 'Since when is my stupidity any reason for losing money for Martin Marietta?' And then I reminded them, 'Look, I told you I didn't want any yes-men, but can't any of you think of anything I've done right this year?' "[10]

Much attention was paid in those years to business plans, business strategy, and planning of all kinds, as is still the case throughout the corporation. But Whalen believes that running through the entire organization was a burning desire to win, a competitiveness and a tenacity that was incalculable in its positive effect on the end result. "They used to say"—he tells another story on himself—"if you overrun your budget and win, Bob will natter at you, but if you stay within your budget or underrun it and lose, he'll kill you." As for tenacity, he cited the case of the Hellfire laser seeker. The company had lost a competition to another contractor to build the Hellfire missile system, which was not just a "smart" system but a "brilliant" one in that it was capable of seeking out the correct target and destroying it without additional help from the pilot who had fired it. Whalen said Hugh Parks, who was in charge of advanced programs, refused to give up on the program.

"Hugh caused the Pentagon to take another look at what the winning contractor was doing and came away with a $10 million contract for something called LoCAL, which stood for Low-Cost Alternate Laser," Whalen said. "In a year's time we had built twelve of them and fired them so successfully that we beat the other contractor out of the Hellfire business on the next government buy." Martin Marietta would go on to produce close to eighteen thousand Hellfire missiles between 1986 and 1992, including many that performed with outstanding success in the Persian Gulf conflict.[11]

■

Bob Whalen left the company in 1982, admitting to some of the frustrations he faced as general manager of a large manufacturing operation—issues such as personnel, finance, and production. "Hey, this is not why I went to school," he said he told himself, or, as colleagues frequently heard him say, "I bring in the bears, I don't skin 'em." He departed Martin Marietta to become vice president and general manager of Global Analytics, a highly classified enterprise located in San Diego. It later became part of Alcoa Defense Systems, Inc.

Alcoa Defense Systems was acquired by McDonnell Douglas in 1989, but Whalen did not go with it. He returned instead to Martin Marietta. During the entire seven-year period he was away from Martin Marietta, he said Norman R. Augustine, who became president in 1986 and chairman in 1988, kept in touch by calling every few months "just to chat and see how I was." Whalen's return was to a specially created position as president of a new "skunk works"–type organization called Advanced Development & Technology Operations. As always happens in the aerospace industry, the name was immediately shortened to ADTO. In fact, many believe Whalen and Augustine worked out the acronym before settling on the name because they hoped it literally would "add to" the corporation's business base, perhaps even expand it into new areas of interest.[12]

Located in suburban San Diego, the Advanced Development operation is a highly unusual venture for a structured organization like Martin Marietta. Without restriction to present product lines or organizations, it was chartered to search out and develop new ideas and work them through prototyping. When ready for engineering development and production, a fledgling project is turned over to an existing operating element of the corporation. ADTO fits its entrepreneurial principal like a glove. It is free to pursue whatever potential product it desires without regard to any existing or potential customer organizations and without detailed approvals even from corporate headquarters. The sole criteria are Whalen favorites: "What and where is the need, and will it sell?"

Although without benefit of any archival "Barbarossas" this time, Advanced Development & Technology Operations does apply an analytical screen to its list of prospective products. Steering clear of specific technology that would compete with the corporation's existing businesses, it set its sights originally on efforts involving radar, antisubmarine warfare, millimeter wave, guided smart munitions, high-powered microwave devices, survivability, and torpedoes. And in the face of declining defense spending, if those technologies had a dual use in the commercial marketplace, so much the better.

ADTO's approach to the commercial world is not the oft-stated, oversimplified political preachment about beating "swords into plowshares," which historically has not been a practical conversion in the defense industry. Augustine would say such attempts have been "unblemished by success." The big difference is "we're attacking commercial markets in the same analytical way we did defense markets," Whalen said. "We start with what is needed and what will sell; to hell with technology! Then after we see what that is, we say, 'Okay, let's improve on that. What technologies or inventions do we have that will do it at the needed price?' Perhaps the most important thing is to recognize that we can't set up the sales and distribution, so we have to ally ourselves with people who already have those networks."

There is a written requirement that each new effort must meet three characteristics, each of them punctuated by a Whalen dictum:

1. It has to fit on one viewgraph: "If you can't describe on one viewgraph what you're doing, you don't know what you're talking about."
2. The idea must be totally unencumbered by technology: "After thirty-five years in the business, I'm tired of having technology tell me what I can't do."
3. There must be a need, and there has to be a target price up front. "It's got to cost this much, and I tell our people, 'Look, if you'll work on it, we'll pay you a salary. If not, hit the bricks.' "[13]

Starting with the market, the need, the price, and a strategy of alignment with an existing sales and distribution network, "you can come up with some very exciting things," he said. He was not prepared to discuss them publicly midway through the organization's third year of existence. The obvious reasons for his reticence: competition— "Industrial security is far more rigid than anything I've ever encountered in defense"—and premature commitment of the corporation to any given endeavor.

What is the ultimate goal of Advanced Development & Technology Operations? Keeping in mind that unlike other corporate elements it is not required to have a long-range plan, all it has to do is hit one home run to make the entire operation worthwhile.

PART VIII

Crisis and Opportunity

1982–89

■

CHAPTER 35

An Unwelcome Suitor and "PacMan"

■

On August 25, 1982, the Viking 2 spacecraft was still functioning well twenty-two days into the eleventh month of its fifth year on the surface of Mars when the telephone rang in Tom Pownall's Bethesda office. His secretary said it was William Agee, chairman of Bendix Corporation. It was shortly after 8:30 in the morning of what promised to be a heated Wednesday in more ways than being just another hot and humid summer day in the suburbs of the nation's capital. Pownall, Martin Marietta's president and chief executive officer, had been in his new position less than four months. He was out of his office, across the hall in a conference room, going over the long-range plan with Laurence J. Adams, executive vice president and chief operating officer. Eleanor Archer, Pownall's secretary, interrupted them.

"There's a Bill Agee on the line," she said. "He wants to talk to you immediately."

"Tell Mr. Agee this is an inopportune moment for me, that I am in a meeting away from my office and can't take the call. I will call him back," Pownall told his secretary. He walked across the hall and told Roy Calvin, vice president for public relations, to get the "strike team" together immediately, then proceeded down the broad executive wing corridor to Frank Menaker's office. At forty-two, Menaker had been general counsel only nine months.

"Bill Agee just called me," he told the general counsel. "I did not take the call." Within minutes, as Pownall and Menaker talked, Eleanor buzzed to say there was a messenger in the lobby with an envelope requiring a receipt.

"Please get it right away," Pownall said. He and Menaker walked back to the conference room where five of the other executives on the strike team were waiting. Opening the envelope, Pownall skimmed a six-paragraph letter and an attached three-page press release.

"Oh, hell, here we go!" Pownall said, and he read the letter aloud. It contained Agee's formal offer, in the name of the Bendix Corporation, to acquire Martin Marietta Corporation for $43 a share. At 10:15 A.M., the Dow Jones wire carried the news:

BENDIX ANNOUNCES $43-A-SHARE
OFFER FOR MARTIN MARIETTA

And there began thirty-three days of sheer hell and one of the strangest chapters in the history of corporate America.

The strike group, which for the duration would be known throughout the corporation as the "A-Team," had been put together some months before by J. Donald Rauth, the chairman. Including support staff and members of the board of directors, it would constitute the relatively small in-house group that literally waged Martin Marietta's war for the next month. Just how and where and with what, they were not then completely sure. But their actions would make daily headlines and evening television and became the stuff of three full-length books, the libretto for a comic opera, and the case study for several college courses on corporate take-overs.[1]

The company had known for almost a year that it might be an attractive target for takeover. Investment bankers Kidder, Peabody had knocked on the door nearly a year before to advise the company that it could be a target of a hostile takeover and to suggest some safeguarding steps. It was a prudent action for the corporation to take, Kidder's Martin A. Siegel told the company's senior management. He highlighted what they already knew: Martin Marietta's stock was depressed at $29 a share. It would have risen to only $33 by the time Agee struck. Cash reserves were minimal, and borrowing power was weak. Siegel had their attention when he told them they must be prepared to fight off those who would take their company away from them.

At thirty-three, Marty Siegel was head of Kidder, Peabody's mergers and acquisitions department. They called him the "Wunderkind of Wall Street." He reportedly earned a million dollars a year in salary and twice that much in special fees. He lived in a glass house on the Connecticut shore and occasionally helicoptered to Manhattan. He was trim, tanned, confident, and good-looking enough to be in the movies. Both men and women found him likable. On top of that, he was clever and a brilliant strategist. *Business Week* described him as "a kind of all-star middle linebacker" of the takeover game, "a canny virtuoso of defensive tactics with an enviable string of triumphs."

Both Marty Siegel's presence and his presentation won Kidder, Peabody a new client in Martin Marietta. In the following months, Siegel and his team submitted a long list of recommendations on what the company should do if attacked. In addition to retaining outside legal counsel, the recommendations had prepared the company for a rapid response. It was only the previous spring of 1982 that a *Newsweek* article summarizing Agee's investments in RCA and other companies speculated that in the future he could buy into Martin Marietta. That was March, so by mid-August, Martin Marietta people were more than a little tense when Bill Keough, director of investor relations, reported increased buying of Martin Marietta stock. Then Wayne Shaner, an assistant treasurer, received a call from a Wall Street trader who said "a reliable source" had told him Bendix was about to make a pass at Martin Marietta.

Robert W. Powell, Jr., the corporation's treasurer, telephoned Siegel in New York, then talked with Charles H. Leithauser, senior vice president and chief financial officer, and by long distance with Tom Pownall, whom he located at the Orlando plant. Agee had taken positions in the stocks of first RCA and then Gould, and had been successively rebuffed by both companies when he proposed merger. Powell wondered if Martin Marietta might be next, and in spite of Siegel's best guess that Agee was not currently focused on Martin Marietta, it was agreed that "maybe we should stop kicking the tires and start the engine," Powell said.

Even before the wire report, Pownall and Menaker had alerted the predesignated team. In addition to the CEO and general counsel, they were Leithauser, the chief financial officer; Powell, the treasurer; James D. Simpson, Menaker's predecessor as the corporation's general counsel for ten years before switching to an operating position as president of the chemicals division; Roy Calvin; and, of course, Don Rauth, the chairman who had given up the CEO responsibilities four months earlier in anticipation of retirement after forty-two years with Martin Marietta.

This was the so-called A-Team in place at least on paper, along with carefully selected outside professional counsel, when the Agee communication arrived. These seven, along with the corporation's dedicated and intimately involved board of directors, would carry the burden of the fight. Laurence J. Adams, who was left the task of running the company as the chief operating officer, was an eighth team member when needed. Critical day-to-day support would come from perhaps no more than three dozen immediate backups, most of them on the corporate staff at Bethesda. Behind them was a silent, unseen cheering section of 40,900 other Martin Marietta men and women who continued about their everyday work in an amazingly undistracted fashion. They would keep the company running and its customers supplied despite their personal concerns about their future. Nor would they have much firsthand knowledge of what was going on in the takeover attempt. They would have to depend on what was reported in the daily newspapers or nightly on network news shows. And in spite of a horde of executive recruiter headhunters who descended on a number of principals, not a single individual abandoned ship.

Outside team members, the so-called hired guns, in addition to Kidder, Peabody, included two prestigious law firms, Dewey Ballantine Bushby Palmer & Wood in New York and Miles & Stockbridge in Baltimore. The latter was a longtime Martin Marietta legal advisor. Dewey Ballantine, although not known as a major player in the hostile takeover world, was a skilled transaction law firm with a reputation for strong client loyalty. L. Robert Fullem and Leonard Larrabee were Dewey Ballantine principals. A third law firm, Wachtell, Lipton, Rosen & Katz, a specialty Manhattan law firm allied with Kidder and Siegel in a couple of previous takeover standoffs, was retained by Dewey Ballantine. Martin Lipton and Dick Katcher would see most of the action for them. One other firm enlisted to the Martin Marietta cause was Kekst & Co., a financial public relations house whose founder, Gershon Kekst, and senior partner, Lawrence Rand, were highly regarded on Wall Street for their "smarts" in this kind of fray.

Even with these preparations, to say that Martin Marietta was ready for the Agee attack would be overstatement. Tom Pownall had been chief executive officer only since the annual meeting in April. "I was just beginning to cope with my new responsibilities," Pownall said, "when this Bendix thing came along." He did not even know whether it would be his lead or the chairman's. It could have gone either way. "If Don had said, 'Look, my experience around here is much more extensive than yours, and we've got to keep the company moving and working. So I'll try to handle this affair while you keep the company going,' but he didn't." Instead, Rauth told him, "It's yours. You're the CEO. You've got the stick. I'm just a member of the board, and I'll try to keep the meetings under control if you need any help."

"That almost shattered me," Pownall said. "I mean I wasn't fighting it, but I thought, 'Holy Toledo. This is the league, and I've really not ever played in it.' Fortunately, we had some very common-sense people on the team."[2]

Although he would be the last to claim it, Pownall was a natural helmsman for the rough voyage on which the corporation was about to embark. By chance a native of Cumberland, Maryland—his mother was shopping there the day Tom chose to enter the world—he was a West Virginian through and through and proud of his "mountaineer" heritage. He had grown up milking cows on a farm outside Mooresville in West Virginia's eastern panhandle and from there had entered the U.S. Naval Academy by appointment from West Virginia's legendary congressman Jennings Randolph. Graduated an ensign in 1946, he served three years at sea aboard destroyers before resigning his commission in 1949 to enter business. He put on his uniform again as a reserve officer on a cruiser in the China Sea during the Korean War.

Square-cut and rugged in build, Pownall was prone to laughter and a good joke. He was a people person, and people generally liked him instantly. Although he tended toward informality and cordiality in speech and action, he wore his background proudly and could be as hard as nails when necessary. He was formal on one point: He hardly ever removed his suit coat when he was in the office, and his coat always displayed a tiny American flag pin in the lapel. Even without the flag, Pownall's piercing eyes and jutting chin made one think of the impressive Remington sculpture of an American bald eagle that dominated the credenza in his office. Pownall loved the business he was in and was unabashed in his admiration for his customers, the uniformed men and women in the military services who were responsible for the security of the nation. He frequently said the biggest mistake he had made in his life was getting out of uniform.

One of the "commonsense" people Pownall boasted about on the Martin Marietta team was the corporation's treasurer, Bob Powell, whose organization would be a significant key in the upcoming fight. On the day Bendix struck, Powell was with his son Steven on a long-weekend automobile tour of New England and upstate New York looking at prospective colleges. His secretary, Marcia Ortega, ran him down in the admissions office of Hobart and William Smith Colleges in Geneva, New York. Marty Siegel was in Memphis meeting with another client when Charlie Leithauser reached him by telephone. The company plane that was sent for Siegel and Powell picked up several directors as well for a meeting the next afternoon in Bethesda.

In that meeting Siegel first proposed the "countertender" as the best defense against Agee's tender offer for Martin Marietta's stock. It was a new term to most of the staff and the directors. One wag, making a bad pun, laughingly said he thought Siegel was talking about a "countertenor," a singer with a falsetto voice. The meeting was not a formal session of the board although most of the directors were there. Various options were outlined in addition to counter-tendering for Bendix's stock, but no vote was taken.

That strategy later would be labeled "PacMan," (an allusion to a popular video game of the day) by a merger specialist who defined it for the *Wall Street Journal*: "That's where my client eats your client before your client eats mine."[3]

"It was hard for me to digest as Siegel outlined it to us," Pownall said, "because I was familiar enough with our balance sheet to be bewildered by how the hell we were going to raise the necessary money. But we all agreed that if it was the best thing for us, we had better work it quickly, twenty-four hours a day for whatever days and weeks it took." A formal meeting of the board of directors was scheduled for Monday in New York to settle on Martin Marietta's response. The big determinant, Pownall felt, would be Siegel's idea of the countertender.

One thing Pownall knew for certain: Bendix did not have credentials to run Martin Marietta's aerospace business as a systems contractor. Bendix was a player in aerospace, but as a supplier of parts or at most a subcontractor for subsystems. "It's like saying two guys are both in the transportation business," Pownall said, "except that one of them drives a taxi and the other guy runs a railroad."[4]

The lawyers quickly determined that a countertender made sense if for no other reason than that it would enable them to overcome the time advantage Agee had. The laws of Maryland and Delaware—where Martin Marietta and Bendix were incorporated—gave Martin a calendar advantage to purchase control of Bendix and throw out its board before Bendix could call a meeting of Martin Marietta stockholders and oust its board. In Maryland, Martin's home state, the law required a minimum ten-day notice before a majority owner could call a meeting of stockholders. Delaware, the state of Bendix's incorporation, had no such waiting period. Control of a Delaware corporation could be assumed immediately upon majority control.

The calendar advantage, if Martin Marietta decided to counteroffer, looked like this:

August 25: Bendix attack formally registered with SEC, beginning what would amount to a twenty-three-day withdrawal period to acquire Martin Marietta stock.

August 30: Martin Marietta counterattacks and registers with SEC its tender offer for Bendix stock.

September 17: Bendix could buy all the tendered Martin Marietta stock but, under Maryland law, must wait a minimum of ten days after Bendix calls for a stockholder meeting to vote to displace Martin Marietta's board. Martin Marietta could gain a further advantage by delaying its stockholder meeting thirty, sixty, or even ninety days.

September 21: End of Martin Marietta withdrawal period. Martin Marietta, under Delaware law, could buy all Bendix stock tendered and immediately vote to take control of Bendix.

The calendar advantage thus appeared to be one of many key items Mr. Agee and his outside law firms, although aware of, ignored or dismissed. Perhaps even more important to the outcome was their misreading of the personalities and the resolve of Tom Pownall and other stalwarts on Martin Marietta's fourteen-member board of directors. A distinguished board, it was exceptional in the character, experience, and innate knowledge of its individual members. Only three were insiders—Pownall, Rauth, and Frank X. Bradley. The latter technically could be classified an outsider as president and CEO of an international bauxite mining consortium, but in effect he was an insider as a former longtime Martin Marietta employee and president of its aluminum company before he retired.

The eleven outside directors included two distinguished lawyers: Griffin B. Bell, former attorney general of the United States, and Eugene M. Zuckert, who had been secretary of the U.S. Air Force from 1961 to 1965 and a member of the Atomic Energy Com-

Takeover fight made headlines

mission before that. Others were Melvin R. Laird, former secretary of defense and nine-term congressman previously; John J. Byrne, the youngest member of the board at fifty who, as chairman of GEICO Corporation, had saved that huge insurance company from bankruptcy; and A. James Clark, self-made multimillionaire, generous benefactor of social and cultural causes, and hardworking chairman of a group of construction companies that had built—and was still building—much of metropolitan Washington. There was also James Lee Everett, III, down-to-earth bon vivant yet erudite chairman of Philadelphia Electric Company; Frank M. Ewing, chairman of the Maryland real estate development company that bore his name and also a millionaire many times over; Dr. William W. Hagerty, affable, respected president of Drexel University; John L. Hanigan, chairman of the apparel and footwear manufacturer and retailer Genesco Inc.; Charles E. Hugel, executive vice president of AT&T; and David C. Scott, chairman and CEO of Allis-Chalmers Corporation.

Pownall had asked the directors to assemble in Bethesda on Thursday, August 27, just to listen to some of the options being considered. Before the meeting ended, Jack Byrne took off his necktie and passed it with a note the length of the boardroom table to Tom Pownall. It was a red tie with a pattern of blue-and-white "Don't Give Up the Ship" naval pennants. The note from Byrne read:

This tie was given to me when all hell was breaking loose
at GEICO. I wore it until we turned the company around.
It might be useful to you in this crisis. I tender it to you.
    P.S. I need a tie. Will you pass yours down?

Pownall took off his tie and put on Byrne's. He would wear it
every day for the duration. Its first "public" showing immediately
followed the board meeting when he assembled all the employees of
corporate headquarters in the ground-floor lounge adjoining the
cafeteria.

"I cannot tell you what we're going to do," he told the assemblage, "but we are studying every angle. You can be sure that we are
going to do what is best for the company and its shareholders. Our
customers will be taken care of. I *can* tell you that we are in control."[5]

The brief message was taped, and cassettes were sent out that
night to all major company locations. It was one of the few personal
messages Martin Marietta employees received for the next month.
Although all press releases and formal notices were continuously
distributed to them nationwide, the feed was meager, restricted by
law to nothing but the formal documents. Anything and everything
that management did or said was "material" in the legal sense of the
word and could be used by the opposition, the courts, or the federal
regulators.

Before the board assembled in New York the following Monday
to formally decide on the company's reaction to the takeover threat,
much had to be accomplished, including raising close to a billion
dollars over the weekend. That task fell to Thomas H. Mendenhall,
assistant treasurer for cash management and banking. At thirty-three
he was a highly responsible, very likable young man whose rosy complexion and boyish bounce to his step belied his actual age; he could
have passed for twenty-three. Mendenhall's position made him the
chief contact with the corporation's banks, and he went about his
responsibilities in a very personal way. He was well known and liked
by his contemporaries in Martin Marietta's creditor world, where the
corporation's good name and reputation for sound and conservative
financial practices made his job easier. But the task before him was
formidable enough to further thin his already wispy brown hair.

■

WITHIN THE FIRST HOUR after the aggressor offer had reached Bethesda headquarters—even before his boss, Bob Powell, could return to town—Mendenhall was on the phone contacting the corporation's banks. The company's standing line of credit was $300 million. Mendenhall's target was an additional $400 million for a total of $700 million, a figure pulled out of the air, Charlie Leithauser admitted, because he guessed Bendix had that much cash. The target was raised to $800 million almost before Mendenhall had received the first commitment from Bank of America, which had been designated lead bank for the financing. The target amount quickly jumped to $900 million as the outside lawyers and investment bankers continued to massage the numbers, and it would approach a billion dollars before the weekend was out. Mendenhall had about sixty hours—mostly Saturday and Sunday nonbanking hours—to raise that princely sum.

Mendenhall's counterpart in the legal department was Doris M. Rush, a tall, slim, fifty-four-year-old assistant general counsel. Rush wore stylish suits or pants outfits, and with champagne-colored shoulder-length hair, always perfectly coiffed, her appearance was striking. Her specialty was Securities and Exchange Commission law, and she was a bulldog about financial law and SEC regulations, and their interpretation. Colleagues said Rush was born with a cigarette in her mouth and a telephone in her ear. She and Mendenhall worked closely each year on 10-K and other SEC-required financial filings of the corporation and had an easygoing professional relationship.

Closely associated with Rush was Sarah B. Barnett, an unflappable and indefatigable legal secretary. Pleasant and kind when there was time, she was all business under fire—efficient, quick, and not prone to waste time or mince words. With Rush and Mendenhall, she made a formidable team on more than one occasion before the takeover fight was concluded.

All day Friday and Saturday, Mendenhall talked by long-distance telephone to bankers, lining up informal commitments that he hoped would total $900 million by Sunday night. His instructions from Leithauser had been to line up the money "but don't sign for anything yet." The corporation did not want to pay a single penny of interest until it knew for certain that it was going to borrow the money. The banks, on the other hand, wanted to know how the money would be used. Mendenhall couldn't tell them. The bankers wanted to set conditions or otherwise restrict their commitments. He couldn't accept conditions or restrictions of any kind that might be challenged by the other side, the lawyers had told him. It was a high-stakes game he was playing, the most exciting of his young life.

He was also helping Doris Rush, who had been given the task of writing the financing agreement that would be filed with the SEC if Martin Marietta decided to make its own tender offer. Both of them had been warned that the document had to be "airtight" in that it promised the money unequivocally.[6]

By Sunday morning Mendenhall had verbal commitments in excess of $800 million. He had scheduled a meeting of all the bankers in New York City for 5 P.M when he would have them sign the banking agreement that Rush was preparing. The company plane was scheduled for "wheels up" at 1 P.M. from Dulles International Airport in Virginia, a forty-minute drive from Bethesda. On the small five-seat jet were Mendenhall, Bill Armistead, a Treasury Department staffer who had been working with Tom, and two Bank of America representatives. In Manhattan they took cabs to the 140 Broadway offices of Dewey Ballantine.

■

THE TREASURER'S OFFICE was not the only Martin Marietta function under fire. Every action and every reaction the corporation made was carefully orchestrated and restricted by the pertinent laws. Every utterance was skillfully crafted by batteries of lawyers, some almost to the point where they were incomprehensible to the lay public, including the press. The print and electronic media subjected everything to intense scrutiny, frequently with interpretations 180 degrees at variance, depending on the knowledge and interpretive skills of the reporter. So one of the first things Roy Calvin did as head of Martin Marietta's public relations was establish a single point for public announcements and press inquiries. As a corporate vice president and a member of the strike team, Calvin himself would be too close to the evolving strategies of the fight to handle the spokesperson task himself. There needed to be a single point of contact with the media, a spokesperson not always privy to all the corporate strategy who could talk to reporters, issue news releases, and monitor what the other side was telling the press. On many occasions it would be crucial that this representative of the company be able to say, "I do not know." Calvin's logical choice was his longtime associate and chief of staff, the corporation's director of public relations. He already was on a first-name basis with many of the nation's business editors and reporters, who knew him to be a credible source. Both he and Calvin earlier in their separate careers had been wire service reporters, albeit for competitor organizations. They knew the language and generally were able to speak for the corporation's benefit.[7]

"You need to drop everything you're doing and literally clear this room," Calvin said as he walked into his startled colleague's office. "From this moment on until this thing ends, one way or another, you're *it!* You will be Martin Marietta's only spokesman. I'll try to keep you fully informed, but most of the time you'll have only the legalese of our formal announcements composed by a committee of lawyers. You'll be mostly on your own, interpreting as best you can without committing us to more than we've said on paper. Do the best you can and keep me informed on who is asking what, and what, if anything, *they* know."

It was almost the only time the two men would meet face-to-face for the next month, although they would speak daily on the telephone, if only briefly. Each morning a complete list of the previous day's press contacts and subject matter was forwarded to Calvin. All other public relations functions unrelated to the takeover battle were handled expertly by Elliott H. Miller, director of PR special projects. He took over the day-to-day operation of Martin Marietta's corporate PR and with other members of the relatively small headquarters PR staff ran the department without missing a beat.

For the next thirty-three days the director of public relations, acting as Martin Marietta's "spokesperson," and Marianna Dickie, his longtime associate and secretary, would all but sleep in the office. Her pleasant greeting and professional manner were the first and often the only reception some of the anxious callers received for a time. In the pressure of constant deadlines and late-development breaks in the takeover fight, some of the callers were rude and some downright crude. But Marianna Dickie handled them all alike, with courtesy and aplomb, winning many admirers and friends among the press regulars.

It was a tough story to cover. Most developments occurred late in the day, preempting business pages with early evening deadlines and network evening newscasts. Only a handful of reporters were able to stay on top of the fast-breaking news. They included real pros like Tim Metz of *The Wall Street Journal,* the irascible Bob Cole of *The New York Times,* Mark Potts of *The Washington Post,* John Crudelle of Reuters, and Ted Shelsby of *The Sun* in Baltimore. Other regulars who called at least twice a day were Bernie Shellum of the *Detroit Free Press;* the *Detroit News* trio of Gene Ross, Dave McNaughton, and Gene Schabath, whose twenty-four-hour team coverage blanketed the readership in Bendix's home territory; Stacie Knable of *The*

Evening Sun and Dave Postal on the Baltimore crosstown rival *News American;* Larry Rasie of the *Hartford Courant,* and the ever-courteous Richard Lambert, New York correspondent of London's *Financial Times.* Aside from Washington and Baltimore, Martin Marietta's hometown newspapers in plant cities far from the action, such as Orlando, New Orleans, and Denver, had to depend on the wire services plus nightly phone summaries furnished by the spokesman from Bethesda.

Juggling three telephone lines, the office handled 1,115 first-call inquiries from the world's news media and returned seven hundred in addition. No inquiry went unanswered even if the response was only, "I can't elaborate. This is what we announced, and I can't go beyond that," or "I'll try to find out and get back to you."[8] To be sure there were the inevitable other "sources close to the company," but for the most part all interface with the public was through that office. Twelve- to sixteen-hour days were the norm, and many ran to twenty hours, most of it on the telephones. Meals were sent in. The rest rooms fortunately were just down the hall. Luckily for Mrs. Dickie—a widow with four grown children, two of them in college and one still at home—and her boss, they each lived within three miles of the office. The proximity enabled them to at least spend short nights in their homes.

■

A FEW MINUTES BEFORE FIVE O'CLOCK on Sunday afternoon, Mendenhall and Rush waited in the forty-second-floor conference room of 140 Broadway to greet the bankers invited to sign the financing agreement. Mendenhall was nervously pacing the floor and checking his watch. "Now remember, Doris," he kidded, "be nice to these people. We want them to give us a lot of money." The bankers and their lawyers began to arrive in groups of two or three: Citibank, Bankers Trust, Morgan, Chase Manhattan, Chemical Bank. Mendenhall knew most of them and greeted them warmly, mentally checking off the thirteen banks who were participants in Martin Marietta's credit agreement. Manufacturers Hanover, Mellon, Toronto Dominion, Maryland National, and Continental Illinois arrived. Only one bank was missing, Seattle First National. Its representative was ill, but the bank sent a telegram authorizing its commitment.[9]

Although all the bankers had come prepared to sign, this was their first opportunity to read the banking agreement, and its details—or lack thereof—raised questions and concerns. The Morgan representative wanted to know if there should be some sort of trigger that would release them from the agreement "if something crazy happened." Like what? Mendenhall asked. "Like borrowing the money if Bendix already owns you," the Morgan man replied. A Martin Marietta lawyer answered for Mendenhall. If there were outs in the agreement or if use of the money were burdened with conditions, he said, the company would have a difficult time convincing anyone that the banks were seriously committed. Most of those in the room appeared to understand that the banking agreement had to be airtight if it was to be used to finesse a way around Bendix. Then an even worse concern was voiced. "What about Regulation U?" one of them asked, referring to a rule that limits a loan to 50 percent of the value of the stock used to secure the loan.

That discussion waged for more than an hour while Mendenhall temporarily retired to the forty-fourth floor to confer with Bob Powell's and Dewey Ballantine's attorneys Fullem and Larrabee. All agreed it was a problem. Then Powell and Mendenhall, almost as one, came up with a solution: why not form a new subsidiary to purchase the Bendix stock and set it up so that it would be free of restrictions like Regulation U that applied to previously existing subsidiaries? That obstacle removed, the bankers began signing the agreement. Mendenhall knew he was still $30 million short of the $900 million goal, so he cornered the representatives of Bank of America and Citibank, each of whom agreed to up his bank's share by $15 million. Success in hand, Tom skipped the elevator and took the stairs up two floors, bursting in on Powell and some Miles & Stockbridge lawyers with his good news.

"We did it! We got the nine hundred million dollars," he fairly shouted. "That's fine," Bob Powell said, looking up with a smile. "But what we really need is nine hundred and thirty million." Stunned and frustrated, Mendenhall flushed bright red. Without saying a word he turned and left the office, walking slowly and dejectedly down the two flights of steps. His mind was working furiously, and when he reached the forty-second floor, he knew what he would do. Toronto Dominion Bank of Canada, unlike American banks, had no lending limit. He cornered Duncan Gibson and explained the need for $30 million more, a 60 percent increase over the $50 million already committed by his bank. Gibson thought it was doable but would have to get approval from Toronto, and he doubted he could raise his top people at that late hour Sunday night.

"I've got to get the commitment for the money tonight," Mendenhall told him.

"I can give you the highest assurance that you can get another thirty from us," Gibson said, "but I can't confirm it tonight."

"Cross your heart and hope to die, and I'll go upstairs and stop bargaining," Tom said.

"Go upstairs and stop bargaining," was the rejoinder.[10]

When he reentered the meeting upstairs, it was a very much subdued Tom Mendenhall who quietly announced, "You've got your nine hundred thirty million." This time it was Powell and the lawyers who were euphoric. Tom returned to the signing session in time to see the final signatures added to the agreement and to thank and say good night to the departing bankers.

It was one o'clock Monday morning, August 30, when he, Bob Powell, Doris Rush, and Bill Armistead joined Fullem and Larrabee to review the revised draft of the financing document that had to be filed with the SEC that day if Martin Marietta decided to go after the Bendix stock. The directors would meet later in the morning, and when they did, they would know the corporation had $930 million it could count on if needed.

Mendenhall's relief and satisfaction at having made possible the almost impossible was short-lived. The two lawyers were questioning the missing signatures: Ameritrust, Toronto Dominion, and Seattle First National. No problem, Tom told them. The Ameritrust and Toronto bankers had promised to return and sign as soon as their home offices opened in about eight hours, and he had a telegram authorizing the third commitment from Seattle.

The two lawyers didn't think the agreement looked good with a blank, and Powell agreed. "Yeah, this thing should be signed before the board meeting," he said. "We'll get the Seattle signature." And that's how Bill Armistead, the young treasury department assistant, became the sole passenger on a twelve-seat corporate jet for a forty-two-hundred-mile round-trip from New York to Seattle and back. The only thing that bothered him about making the trip, he laughingly recalled, was the suggestion that he take two copies of the agreement, get both signed, and mail one before leaving Seattle, just in case the plane crashed. Even with a 4 A.M. departure, Armistead was the only one of the group who had a good sleep that night, crisscrossing the United States at thirty thousand feet.[11]

When the board met later in the morning, not a single director thought Agee's $43 bid for Martin Marietta stock was a generous proposal. It was more like a gun to the head was the consensus. "ML" (the stockmarket's symbol for Martin Marietta) had traded on the New York exchange at $33 five days before on the eve of the tender offer. The stock was $40 when trading closed for the weekend on Friday.

Siegel pointed out to the board that the Agee offer was a premium of only 30 percent over the market price of the stock, compared to an average premium of 60 percent for control. What's more, he told the directors, the break-apart value of the company—that is, the value of the separate businesses added together—was equivalent to $75–$90 a share. Book value at cost is $71, he told them, and the stock had recently sold at a high of $51.

"Kidder doesn't think this is the time to sell," Siegel said. "But if you want to do that, the Bendix bid is inadequate."

Mel Laird asked what would happen to the morale of Martin Marietta's "outstanding group of people with some unusual defense programs." Don Rauth added that it was more than that. "Martin Marietta would be hurt if it was taken over by Bendix, which has no experience in big systems operations."

"I'm not sure we want someone with short-term goals to take over Martin Marietta. Our company has a long-term focus," another director added. Rauth asked for a vote.[12]

After listening to all the possible consequences, it took the directors just four hours to reject outright Agee's meager $43 offer. Then they recessed briefly before spending four more hours considering their other options. News of the Martin Marietta directors' unanimous agreement to go with Marty Siegel's bold PacMan strategy crossed the Dow Jones wire at 4:18 P.M., Eastern Daylight Time, on Monday, August 30:

MARTIN MARIETTA SETS $75
A SHARE OFFER FOR BENDIX

NY-DJ—Martin Marietta Corp. said its board authorized a cash tender offer for 11,900,000 shares of the Bendix Corp.'s common stock at $75 per share.

Following the offer, Martin Marietta said it expects to seek a merger or similar business combination in which remaining Bendix common shares would be converted into a combination of Martin Marietta preferred and/or common stock.

Thomas G. Pownall, president and chief executive of Martin Marietta, said, "Our board concluded that if these two corporations are going to be combined, the interests of shareholders will be best served by combining the two corporations on the terms contemplated by the Martin Marietta offer rather than the Bendix offer.

"We believe it would be harmful for Martin Marietta's aerospace business to pass into the hands of a management lacking deep experience and continuity in the major systems business. . . . Given Martin Marietta's past performance and future potential, the timing of the Bendix takeover proposal is an attempt to buy Martin Marietta stock at bargain prices."[13]

It was one of the clearest releases issued during the entire process. It was easy to read and understand. It was vintage Calvin or, as he was fond of saying, "Every word works or fights."

And fighting words they were to Bendix's Agee, whose legal minions had already moved in six states to have anti-takeover laws thrown out as unconsitutional. Those court actions effectively blocked any attempt by Martin Marietta to challenge the Bendix tender offer in those states. And so the battle raged day by day. It was out-and-out combat. Opposing attorneys dueled in the courts. The combatant companies squared off in the media—in paid newspaper solicitations of the other side's stockholder support as well as in printed editorial columns and on electronic newscasts. And the arbitrageurs swooped and gorged in the marketplace, buying low, driving the price up, then selling to the highest bidder without allegiance to anyone.

■

MEDIA INTERPRETATIONS OF WHO was doing what to whom at any given moment varied among pro and novice reporters alike as scores of newspapers and magazines, the financial dailies, the wire services, and the networks attempted to cover the story and "scoop" their competitors. Tom Pownall, who insists that he never read one word of the massive coverage, maintained many years later that the reason the media coverage was so great—the story was on the first business page and frequently on the very front page almost every day for a solid month—was that there was literally nothing else of interest going on in the world at the time.

"My recollection of this event," he said, "is not in keeping with almost anybody else's. It wasn't then, and it isn't now. The reason it got so much publicity was that it happened at a time when there was not one single, solitary event on the face of the Earth that had any activity associated with it. We were not two gigantic companies, even—fair-sized but not monstrous. We did our job, and we did it, we thought, pretty well. It was simply a very dull period. Very, very dull! And so this spiked everybody's imagination."[14] Pownall was known on occasion to oversimplify—if it served his purpose—just for effect or to modestly play down his own role.

For some of those embroiled in the battle, particularly the fraternity of judges, lawyers, clerks, and legal secretaries, Pownall's assessment was overly simple. At one time in the conflict, attorneys for Martin Marietta and Bendix argued points of law in eight different state courts and two federal appellate jurisdictions on the same day. Toward the end of the battle, Baltimore federal judge Joseph H. Young, who had ruled on more than one issue in the case and had attempted to gather all the actions into a single court, quoted Shakespeare in denying a Bendix move to halt Martin Marietta's eleventh-hour purchase of Bendix stock. "A pox on both your houses," he said.

In any case, business reporters thought it made "good copy," and editors, headline writers, and cartoonists had a field day, frequently at the participants' expense. It helped, from a parochial Martin Marietta view, that the aggressor was already thought of as wearing a black hat. Long before he made a move against Martin Marietta, Bill Agee had brought on himself the disdain, and in some instances the outright enmity, of the press and some of his peers in the business world. Two years prior, in September 1980, Agee, as chairman of the Bendix Corporation, announced to his headquarters personnel a massive restructuring following the sudden resignations of the president and vice president for strategic planning. Agee named to the vacant vice presidency his close associate Mary Cunningham, who had been with Bendix only fifteen months. She had joined the company as a twenty-seven-year-old straight out of Harvard Business School, beginning her meteoric rise as Agee's executive assistant.

With members of the press in attendance, Agee acknowledged rumors "buzzing around that her rise in this company has been unusual and that it has something to do with a relationship between us." If her rapid promotion was unusual, he told the Bendix people (and the world), it was because "she's a very unusual and talented individual." He acknowledged that they were "very close friends" and added, "She's a very close friend of my family." But that, he said, had nothing to do with the way he and others evaluated her performance in the company.

The nation's press had a field day with the Bendix chairman's "office romance." Mary Cunningham resigned within the month, and *Time* magazine noted that the story had gathered enough momentum "to eclipse national interest in who shot J.R." She took a similar strategic planning position with Joseph E. Seagram & Sons six months later, and a year after that she married Bill Agee following his divorce from his wife of many years and the mother of his three children. That was just two months before his move against Martin Marietta.

The episode made headlines again when RCA chairman Thornton Bradshaw, on the occasion of his rejecting an Agee-proposed merger with Bendix said: "Agee has not demonstrated the ability to manage his own affairs, let alone someone else's."[15] This, then, was the background tinting much of the press coverage of the Bendix–Martin Marietta takeover fight. The two newspapers in Detroit, *The Free Press* and *News*—essentially the Bendix hometown press because of corporate headquarters in suburban Southfield—were particularly aggressive. Larry Rand at Kekst & Co., the New York public relations advisers, wanted to exploit the Agee-Cunningham spectacle, but Martin Marietta executives did not think it would be proper and rejected the idea.

■

AS THE BATTLE SEESAWED, always waxing, never waning, the pages of the calendar flipped relentlessly toward the dates when Bendix could buy the Martin Marietta stock and vice versa, creating what the lawyers liked to call a "Mexican standoff." Meanwhile, it appeared to Wall Street professionals that Martin Marietta's counteroffer to acquire Bendix, bold as it was, did not have sufficient muscle. The corporation would have to strengthen its hand in some way if it hoped to line up a majority of Bendix shares by the necessary date.

Two of Pownall's fellow aerospace CEOs, both friends and admirers, offered to help. Paul Thayer, chairman of LTV Corporation, actually entered negotiations to purchase Martin Marietta's Baltimore operation. It was a legal tactic that would have altered Martin Marietta's corporate structure sufficiently to delay and perhaps cripple the Bendix stock purchase had it gone through. But those negotiations failed for lack of agreement on a selling price.

Then Harry Gray, the wily chairman of conglomerate United Technologies Corporation in Hartford, Connecticut, and also a good friend of Pownall's, offered to play the "white knight," a Wall Street

A cartoonist's view

term for a third corporation that comes to the rescue as a preferred merger partner of an intended takeover victim. But Gray put a twist on the scene: Quickly dubbed the "Gray Knight" by press pundits, he proposed, instead of a friendly merger with Martin Marietta to save it from Bendix, to make a $75-a-share not-so-friendly tender for control of Bendix. It duplicated the Martin Marietta price, paralleling Martin Marietta's offer, as *The Wall Street Journal* headlined:[16]

UNITED TECHNOLOGIES LAUNCHES BID
FOR BENDIX AS MARTIN MARIETTA ALLY

Offer is $75 a share for 50.3%;
Bendix Lifts Marietta Bid
By $5 a Share, to $48 Each

Agee reacted cautiously at first. He did sweeten the $43 offering price for Martin Marietta stock to $48 per share, thereby immediately strengthening Martin Marietta's financial image in the eyes of potential lenders, stockholders, and arbitrageurs, all of whom were trying to decide which way to jump. He also asked to meet separately with Pownall and Gray. The Agee letter to Pownall, which was released to the press as well, also stated:

> Martin Marietta's Board is distinguished and experienced. I am certain that they are well aware of their fiduciary responsibilities to all of your stockholders. . . . I think it important that you and I meet promptly to discuss our revised proposal. . . .[17]

Agee's letter, read to the Martin Marietta directors by Pownall on a telephone conference call, was something of a red flag.

"I don't need Bill Agee to tell me my fiduciary duties," former attorney general Griffin Bell interrupted. "What the hell is Agee up to?" another director wanted to know. "I don't understand the raise," Jack Byrne said. "Who is he competing with?" Marty Siegel, who also was on the telephone patch, said it was Kidder, Peabody's position that the price was inadequate at $48.

"Damn right it's inadequate," Bell said, sounding more irritated by the minute. "Why are we getting worked up about a five-dollar price increase? I don't think it's really worth considering." Byrne asked the chairman if he intended to meet with the Bendix chairman.

"Not with a gun to my head," Pownall answered. [18] The board voted unanimously to reject the $48 offer, and Pownall formally responded in a letter, also released to the press. It was just five brief sentences that pulled no punches:

> Our Board of Directors, who are well aware of their responsibilities, are indeed distinguished and experienced, as you correctly observed in your letter to me of this date. Upon consideration of your revised offer, that Board has voted unanimously tonight to reject it on grounds of inadequacy and as being contrary to the best interests of Martin Marietta shareholders.
>
> We also find it puzzling that Bendix is pursuing its attempt to alter its charter in order to prevent the Bendix shareholders from deciding for themselves what is in their best interests. . . . I can find no useful purpose to be served by a prompt meeting with you on the basis that you requested. . . .
>
> You should by now clearly understand that we intend

to achieve the objectives which we have established, either through our acquisition of Bendix or our agreement with United Technologies.[19]

Gray talked with Agee by phone and a meeting was scheduled, but then Agee backed out. Two days later Bendix formally rejected the UTC approach. At the same time, unknown to all but a few of his closest outside advisers, Agee had also opened talks with Allied Corporation chairman Edward J. Hennessy, Jr. Perhaps Allied would be interested in purchasing a piece of Bendix. If so, that would alter Bendix sufficiently to change the ground rules, thereby thwarting Martin Marietta even if it prevailed in its countertender.

Pownall later said he and Gray had worked through the Labor Day weekend on the details. "What we agreed would be helpful was that UTC tender for Bendix also. Their merger agreement would be very much like ours, somewhat different but generally along the same lines. And since they were much more powerful than we . . . a bigger corporation . . . their proposal would be regarded as more serious than ours."[20]

■

LABOR DAY WEEKEND traditionally marked the start of the week-long gathering of the Conquistadores del Cielo (Conquerors of the Sky), whose members have made significant contributions to aerospace. The chief executives of virtually all the major aerospace firms, including the airlines, were among the more than one hundred members. Normally fierce competitors, the twice-a-year gatherings afforded relaxed surroundings where they could hunt, shoot, ride horses, and "play cowboys." Pownall was president for 1982, and it was Martin Marietta's turn to be host at the A-Bar-A Ranch in Wyoming for the forty-sixth annual fall session. No Bendix people were Conquistadores.

Pownall and Gray normally would have been there from the start of the weekend, but their collaboration on UTC's companion tender offer delayed their arrival—Pownall a day later than Gray. Martin Marietta's director of corporate affairs, John T. de Visser, had made all the arrangements and as major domo was keeping things moving until his boss arrived. A jack-of-all-trades and master of most, John was the very essence of a continental right down to his slight accent. A native of Utica, New York, he had grown up in Belgium and spent World War II in underground intelligence where his language fluency and European ways served him well. Most of the aerospace leaders knew John for the fabulous Martin Marietta receptions he staged on alternate years at the Paris and Farnborough air shows.[21]

When Pownall finally arrived in Wyoming, the Conquistadores were at dinner in the ranch house. Gray spotted him entering and went to meet him. Arm in arm they entered the dining hall to prolonged applause from their standing peers. Nothing was said. Nothing had to be. It was a tribute to two of their own for the fight they were waging against an outsider.

All the while, the proration deadlines—the last chance for stockholders to tender their shares—had passed for both offers. The Bendix date by which Martin Marietta shareholders had to tender their stock to receive $43 per share was Saturday, September 4, three days before UTC formally entered the picture. Bendix claimed that a majority of Martin Marietta stock had been offered, as *The Wall Street Journal* reported on September 7, the Tuesday after Labor Day:

> BENDIX DRAWS 58% OF SHARES OF MARIETTA
> But Analysts Say Firm Still May Sweeten
> Its $43 Bid to Prevent Withdrawals[22]

That meant Bendix was well on the road to buying the Martin Marietta shares provided they were not withdrawn by the September 16 deadline. If they were not, Bendix could purchase them beginning on the 17th, but then would have to wait ten days under Maryland law to acquire control of Martin Marietta.

Meanwhile, Bendix shareowners had overwhelmingly offered their shares to Martin Marietta by September 9 in hopes of receiving $75 a share. If they left them in the pool past the withdrawal deadline, Martin Marietta could begin buying them on September 22 and take control of Bendix as soon as it had 51 percent of Bendix's stock. The headlines in *The New York Times* told that story:

> MARIETTA DRAWS 75% OF BENDIX
> But Takeover Fight
> Outcome Is Still Unclear

"It's now crystal clear," the *Times* quoted a source close to the struggle, "that each company will have more than 50 percent of the shares of the other. That brings us back to the question: 'Will each pull the trigger?'"[23]

A large block of 4.5 million Bendix shares in Martin Marietta's pool belonged to Bendix employees and was held in trust by Citibank of New York as part of their pension plan. It was called SESSOP, for Salaried Employees Incentive Savings and Stock Ownership Plan. Without that block, which represented 22.3 percent of all the outstanding Bendix stock, Martin Marietta would have fallen well short of its tender goal. How the shares came into play was one of the real cliff-hangers of the entire takeover fight.

Agee and the Bendix directors had instructed Citibank not to tender the SESSOP, but they had not reckoned on Martin Marietta's Doris Rush. Although a specialist in securities law, Rush had boned up on something called ERISA once she learned that the Bendix employee trust contained a significant percent of that company's outstanding stock. ERISA is an acronym for the Employee Retirement Income Security Act, a set of Labor Department regulations governing, among other things, SESSOPs like the one Citibank held for Bendix employees. ERISA permitted a trustee of such a retirement plan to follow the rules of the plan—in this case the Bendix management instruction not to tender—as long as the trustee also acted as a "prudent" investor.

Rush reasoned that to be a prudent investor, Citibank as trustee would have to tender the stock to Martin Marietta because the $75 offering price equated to a $100-million increase in value of the Bendix stock in the trust. Such was the difference between tendering for the $75 cash half of the Martin Marietta offer or waiting and having to take a lesser gain on the back end of the offer. Although the Rush logic was impeccable, outside counsel was not overly optimistic that she could prevail and offered little encouragement. "Bulldog" Rush was undaunted. It would not be the first time in her career that she had to go it alone.

A mathematics major in college, Rush was only one of three women hired as engineers by Sperry Corporation in the fifties. While working in the aerospace firm—essentially a man's domain in those days except for secretaries—she attended St. John's University Law School at night and was one of only a few women to receive her law degree in the class of 1958. She was hired at Martin Marietta in 1974 by Jim Simpson, then general counsel, and the two of them had joked about her "visibility."

"It's all right," she later recalled telling Simpson. "If Martin Marietta is a company that is future-oriented enough to put Viking on Mars, I think I can expect that they're the kind of people who accept the future."[24]

One of Rush's strong characteristics was that the less support she received, the more determined she became, particularly when she knew she was right. The deadline for tendering to the Martin Marietta offer was only thirty-six hours away when she picked up the telephone and called Arthur Sporn, a recognized authority on ERISA law at the firm of Barrett, Smith, Schapiro, Simon & Armstrong in New York. Identifying herself and Martin Marietta, she explained the Citibank situation, the rationale of its fiduciary responsibility as trustee for the Bendix employee shares, and her legal opinion that Citibank was compelled by ERISA law to tender them.

"Do you agree?" she asked, almost dropping her cigarette when Sporn said he did. He also agreed to write an opinion to that effect for delivery to Citibank, but he said it was not something he could do in twenty-four hours.

"Who said anything about twenty-four hours?" Doris Rush fairly shouted into the phone. "I'll be in your office in two hours, and I'll come prepared to help." The timing was perfect, if close, and the convenience of the corporation's jet made it possible. She had already agreed to be in New York for a second meeting that night set up by Tom Mendenhall for the bankers. He was putting together a second loan agreement for an additional $400 million. In New York, she spent more than five hours with Sporn in his offices at the tip of Manhattan, then caught a cab uptown for Mendenhall's buffet supper meeting with the bankers.[25]

Larry Adams had been recruited by Mendenhall to summarize the company's present position and additional financial requirements. If you were casting in Hollywood, you couldn't find a more convincing model of a corporate chief operating officer than the silver-haired, square-jawed Adams. His straight-arrow, deliberate approach conveyed the confidence the bankers were looking for; there obviously was a firm hand on the day-to-day control of Martin Marietta's businesses while other executives were embroiled in the takeover flight.

Doris Rush got a good night's sleep, her first in two weeks, then returned to Sporn's office to review the thirteen-page opinion. He had done an excellent job, and she spent the rest of the morning shepherding it through reviews by Frank Menaker and the Dewey Ballantine attorneys. About 2 P.M. it was hand-delivered to Citibank. To make certain it received prompt and proper attention—there being only ten hours left before the company's midnight deadline for receiving Bendix tenders—Rush made two other moves. Jim Simpson had a niece who worked for the Department of Labor, and Rush brought her up to date on Citibank and the Bendix employee trust.

Then she prevailed on Tom Mendenhall to call his contacts on the commercial side of Citibank. The bank not only was a participant in the Martin Marietta loan agreement, it was the depository for the tenders.

Rush told him that if the Sporn opinion did not work, Martin Marietta had lined up a Bendix employee and pension trust participant who was prepared to sue Citibank to force tender of the shares. Both he and Rush were aware of the so-called Chinese Wall, which separates the trust side from the commercial side of banks and brokerages. But they were leaving nothing to chance, either. Mendenhall got his point across by dropping a hint of the possible lawsuit and was assured by Citibank that the matter was receiving attention at the "highest levels" of the bank.

There was nothing left to do but wait. A check of the proration pool at 7 P.M. found it still struggling. Less than 10 percent, or about 2 million of the Bendix shares, had been tendered with only five hours to go. The goal was 50.3 percent, or 11.9 million shares. Spirits of the Martin Marietta people were sagging when most of them left to fly back to Bethesda. Only Rush remained in New York, confident that the Sporn opinion would work and Citibank would tender.

Nine million shares had been received by 10 P.M., and the pool had risen by a million more shares an hour later. That was still under 43 percent with less than an hour to go. At seven minutes before midnight, Citibank tendered all the shares in the employee trust, giving Martin Marietta a hefty majority of the Bendix stock, a total of 75 percent when all the tenders were counted.

"Congratulations, Doris, you've saved the company," Kidder, Peabody's Doug Brown called by phone from Citibank, where he had been monitoring the count. Lighting another cigarette, she inhaled deeply before dialing Tom Mendenhall's home. She called Frank Menaker, also waking him out of a sound sleep with the good news, and then she turned in herself.[26]

When she called the office in the morning, the mood was definitely up. Tom Mendenhall was convinced Martin Marietta would now prevail over Bendix, and he said his wife asked, "Who is this woman who made you do an Indian war dance in the middle of the night?"

■

"I UNDERSTAND I owe you a great deal of money," Menaker told Rush. "Doug Brown and the other Kidder people have been calling me, and they called Pownall, and they called Leithauser, and they are telling everybody that you literally saved the company! I was told that I owe you the biggest raise you have ever had in your life."

"I'll drink to that," she acknowledged, then told him what time she was coming back.

"We'll arrange for the limousine to pick you up at the airport," he said. "We really want to give you a hero's return."

As gratifying as the well-deserved approbation was, the Rush-engineered Citibank victory was but another battle at the midpoint of a war not yet won. It was only the sixteenth day since it all began. Even though the bulk of the Bendix pension shares would eventually be withdrawn, their tender had a tremendous psychological effect on the Agee camp. Bendix executives, Agee included, thought they had the Citibank shares locked up. Losing them to the Martin Marietta pool was a surprise. "It was unbelievable," Agee later admitted, "a serious, serious blow."[27]

By the time Doris returned to Bethesda, the early-morning euphoria at corporate headquarters had turned to grim concern. Bendix had scheduled a special meeting of stockholders for September 21 to approve two amendments to its charter. One was a so-called shark repellant aimed at crippling the Martin Marietta bid for Bendix by impeding Martin Marietta's ability to place its representatives on the Bendix board. The other would have prohibited "consent voting," thereby eliminating the time advantage still held by Martin Marietta.

As the deadlines approached for the two companies to purchase each other's stock, Martin Marietta again went on the offensive. It announced that it was dropping all conditions to its merger proposal but two. In a sort of double negative reverse, the complicated scenario boiled down to this: Martin Marietta said the only way it would *not* continue its pursuit of Bendix was if Bendix did not purchase Martin Marietta's stock on September 17 or if Bendix adopted the charter amendments at the special stockholders' meeting on September 21. The press immediately labeled the conditions the "doomsday" plan—or as one source close to the company was quoted: "What it does, in essence, is absolutely lock the switch, like the deadman's switch on the locomotive." He had no need to further paint the verbal picture of two trains, with throttles locked wide open, racing toward a head-on crash. Headlines in *The Wall Street Journal* and Baltimore's *The Evening Sun* carried the message on September 14:[28]

MARIETTA COMMITS ITSELF TO BUY CONTROL
IN BENDIX UNLESS FIRM DROPS TAKEOVER BID
and
MARTIN MARIETTA BOARD PUTS SQUEEZE ON BENDIX

Adding to the pressure, United Technologies upped its merger offer for Bendix from $75 to $85 per share, and Harry Gray in a letter to Agee stressed that the new offer was not just a revision of its previous tender offer for 11.9 million shares and controlling interest. Under the new plan, Gray said, UTC would seek full control of Bendix by an exchange of stock for the remaining 11.1 million shares.

Although by now the evidence of Agee misjudgments of Martin Marietta's resolve was crystal clear, he chose once again to ignore those signals. He rejected the UTC proposal, and on September 17, Bendix purchased 52.7 percent of Martin Marietta stock for $926.4 million, later expanding its holding to 70 percent. The purchase cocked one of the two triggers on Martin Marietta's double-barreled doomsday gun.

The only condition left that might avoid what now appeared to be the inevitable—Bendix owning Martin Marietta and Martin Marietta owning Bendix—was adoption of the Bendix "shark-repelling" charter amendments. The special stockholders' meeting scheduled for September 21 was postponed for twenty-four hours via a Bendix

Simpson (right) leads team from aborted Bendix meeting

press release. The reason, apparently, was insufficient votes to pass the amendments.

Martin Marietta's Jim Simpson, accompanied by Dewey Ballantine lawyers and representatives from Morrow & Company, the company's proxy solicitor, were among a crowd of about one hundred who reappeared for the meeting at Bendix headquarters the second day. Also present was UTC general counsel Irv Yoskowitz with a few of his associates. Security in the meeting room included a metal detector and color-coded badges issued to everyone. Bendix people wore blue badges, the color of the "Bendix blue banana" (a wave under the name in the company's logo). Martin Marietta's color was red, whether for courage or warning was not clear. Stockholders wore white, and the color of the UTC badges was appropriately gray.[29]

When the chairman of the meeting attempted to again postpone the meeting, Simpson was on his feet, interrupting. As a Bendix proxyholder, he called for a quorum vote. When the chairman persisted in adjourning the meeting and left the room, Simpson strode down the aisle and took over the microphone.

"My name is James Simpson. I am a proxyholder of Bendix Corporation stock, and I'm vice president of Martin Marietta Corporation. It is my belief that there is a quorum present and the proceeding should continue as originally scheduled. . . . Since the chairman has departed, I call for a vote on electing me chairman of this meeting. All in favor?" Simpson asked.[30]

"Aye!" came the response from the Martin Marietta and UTC delegations. When Simpson called for the negative vote, there was no response from the half-dozen Bendix people in the room, whereupon he declared himself chairman and called for discussion of the two management proposals to change the Bendix charter. Yoskowitz identified himself as vice president and general counsel of United Technologies, then said he believed the proposals were not in the best interest of shareholders and "we are going to vote against those amendments."

A Bendix lawyer standing in the back of the room challenged the proceeding, noting that the meeting had been adjourned. Simpson maintained it was not a proper adjournment but granted a recess, which turned into a heated argument between the opposing lawyers. When Simpson again took the microphone to announce the meeting would go on, the lights and sound system were turned off, plunging the huge room into darkness and confusion. As people milled about, stumbling over the boxes full of proxies, Simpson noted for the record that "this meeting is being interfered with," and then on a motion from Yoskowitz, he declared the meeting adjourned to the nearby Michigan Inn. He reconvened it there, and the amendments were defeated. The last condition to Martin Marietta's purchase of the Bendix stock had been removed.

During the one-day postponement of the meeting, Bendix had staged a series of "Unity Day" rallies for employees at plants throughout the country. There were bands, balloons, straw boaters, and open long-distance telephone lines free for the use of employees wanting to withdraw their SESSOP shares from the pension trust Citibank had tendered to Martin Marietta. The press and Martin Marietta received numerous phone calls from disgruntled Bendix employees who said they were being pressured, even threatened, into withdrawing their stock from the pool.

Meanwhile, back in the East, the pace was no less feverish. Attorneys thrust and parried with suits and countersuits in New York and Baltimore courtrooms while corporate executives agonized over their next moves in Morristown, Hartford, and Bethesda, as well as in Agee's suite at the Helmsley Palace, the Manhattan hotel that by this time had been firmly established as the Bendix command post.

On the day before the special stockholders' meeting was postponed, Agee flew to Maryland hoping to address the Martin Marietta directors who were meeting in Bethesda. He took with him his principal outside legal counsel, Arthur Fleischer, his principal investment banker, and his wife, Mary Cunningham. She had been one of her husband's closest advisers throughout, but only in the Bendix group's private deliberations. This would be her first appearance before outsiders.

Agee had met with Tom Pownall only once since the fight began. It was a brief, unreported session in an empty office on the fortieth floor of a Manhattan skyscraper shortly after Bendix had bought the Martin Marietta stock. Agee had tried to convince Pownall to end the donnybrook. He offered to make him vice chairman, "the second highest paid person in the combined company."

In recalling the meeting ten years later, Pownall said Agee was "trying to convey to me that he really liked me a lot, that one of the real reasons he was trying to buy the company was that he had such a high regard for me . . . and all that bull.

"I've got a job," Pownall said he told Agee. "I didn't come here to talk about me. You've offered to buy us, but we haven't offered to sell, and our stockholders haven't offered to sell. You're not even close to a price that would attract anybody who had any sense about what Martin Marietta is. Besides which," Pownall said, "a public tender offer is a contract to buy. . . . We just can't back away from that. If we were to do that, we'd be sued to death."[31]

At that point in their meeting, Pownall said Agee "picked up the telephone and called his attorney, who was sitting in a car down on the street." Fleischer joined the meeting and suggested the way around Pownall's concern would be for Bendix to indemnify the Martin Marietta directors against possible lawsuits. The suggestion was ludicrous to Pownall.

"I mean really pretty far out," Pownall said he told them. "Even with zero legal experience, common sense tells me you can't indemnify somebody in anticipation of their making an illegal act." The meeting broke up with Agee once again asking permission to address the Martin Marietta directors, who were going to meet in a couple of days. It was Agee's third request since the takeover attempt began.

" 'I can't give you permission,' I told him, 'but I will tell them you want to come. I don't know what their response will be.' "

A few days later, when the Martin Marietta directors met at Bethesda headquarters—it was not a formally convened meeting of the board—the Agee party was anxiously camped in a suite at the Marriott Pooks Hill, about five minutes away. Pownall reported on his meeting with Agee, who had followed up with a letter delivered to the board earlier in the day. It listed the "obvious benefits" of merging the two firms and the dangers to both if Martin Marietta proceeded with its announced plan to purchase the Bendix stock in slightly less than thirty-six hours. The letter also outlined the indemnification offer. As he had promised, Pownall told the directors of Agee's strong desire to meet with them.

"Have you asked to address the Bendix board of directors, Talm?" Griffin Bell asked, his heavy southern drawl that rhymed Pownall's first name with *balm*. "No," Pownall said. "Well, then, I don't see why we should meet him. What's he going to say?"

"I'll tell you what he's going to say," another director volunteered. "He's going to give us this silly, sophomoric pledge of allegiance like this last paragraph of his letter, as if we're the ones who started this damn thing."[32]

Pownall noted that Agee also wanted Arthur Fleischer, his outside attorney, to address them on the legal ramifications.

"We do not need his legal counsel to inform us of our responsibilities," Griffin Bell said indignantly. "We have our own counsel."

It was obvious that there was not much sentiment around the table in favor of inviting Agee to address them, and the discussion became fairly agitated as the directors debated the issues.

"What it comes down to is Agee wants us to renege on our commitment to pay the Bendix shareholders seventy-five dollars a share," said Gene Zuckert, the other prominent attorney on the board. "Tom, this is an ethical issue," Frank Bradley joined in. "We made a contract with these people. I don't see how we can put that aside." Two of the more financially grounded directors, Jack Byrne and Frank Ewing, wanted to know if there was some alternative to throwing the balance sheets of both firms into what Byrne called "such awful disaster."[33]

Bob Powell asked Bob Fullem of Dewey Ballantine to respond. Speaking slowly and deliberately, Fullem succinctly summarized the recent events and the choice to be made:

"Well, gentlemen, it seems to me we are looking at two issues: One, do we have an alternative to buying . . . do we have an out? And two, if we don't have an out, can we rely on this indemnification plan? When the board decided to waive its conditions," he continued, "the message was clear. We would buy—period—unless Bendix either dropped its bid, which it has not, or passed the charter amendments, which they have not. Our solicitors feel that since Bendix has postponed its meeting by twenty-four hours, they are having trouble coming up with the votes. On September thirteenth we made it perfectly clear to Agee that the choice was his. We were tying our decision to his decision. The board of directors, having made that decision and announced it to the public, is not culpable for the financial consequences.[34]

"Having said that—and we do not have an out to restrain us from buying the Bendix shares—the next question is: If the board decides in any event not to proceed with the plan to take down the shares, can we rely on Agee's indemnification plan?"

"Are we at risk if we accept the indemnification?" asked Mel Laird.

Once again choosing his words carefully, Fullem replied that he could not describe the risk as remote. Bell, Zuckert, and Laird continued to explore Fullem's assessment. Under each probe he would elaborate, always returning to his carefully chosen and skillfully worded position.

"The odds are," Fullem repeated, "that Agee's indemnification plan will work, but the risk is not remote that the indemnification plan will fail."

"That's it!" Zuckert said. "If our counsel says that is the risk, there is no sense debating it. Without counsel's assurance, we would be reckless to abandon our prearranged course."

Laird agreed. Then Griffin Bell added in his inimitable Deep South way: "You know, it's one thing for a board of directors to stand in front of a judge and say that they did what their counsel told them to do, but it is a very different thing to say that they went beyond what their counsel told them to do."

Resigned to their arguments, Byrne joined in: "Who am I to judge levels of risk," he said, "if Dewey Ballantine and the former attorney general of the United States and the former secretary of Defense say 'no go'?"

Lee Everett concurred: "I guess there is nothing left to talk about."

Finally, Frank Ewing, who had been leaning with Byrne toward indemnification, said to Pownall, "Before we do anything, Tom, you've got to sit down with Agee. Try something."

Pownall reminded his fellow directors that a final decision could still be received at a formal board meeting scheduled for the next evening, prior to the midnight target for buying the Bendix stock. "Tomorrow night we will review the facts," he said. He returned to his office and telephoned Agee, inviting him over for a talk.[35]

Disappointed when told the board would not hear him, Agee and his entourage climbed into two rented Martin Marietta limousines sent to pick them up. It was a short ride with an excellent view of the handsome yet unassuming four-story Martin Marietta headquarters. The building's tasteful concrete and exposed-aggregate exterior helped blend it with the green lawn and lush trees. A small pond mirrored the cars on the gently curving driveway until they dipped into a garage under the structure. An elevator took them directly from the garage to the executive wing where Pownall and several of his staff waited.

Pownall and Agee shook hands. Martin Marietta executives Frank Menaker, Larry Adams, Charlie Leithauser, and Roy Calvin shook hands with the Agee group. The atmosphere was cordial, if a bit stiff. Mary Cunningham shook a few hands before the group divided into parts, Agee joining Pownall in his office, the lawyers pairing off, and the bankers doing the same. Although Mary Cunningham was there, she took no part in meaningful discussions; however, the press made much of it the next day when it learned of her presence at the eleventh-hour talks. After all, the papers reported, she was not even a Bendix employee, she was an executive of Seagram's. Speculation that her presence was an "irritant" that may have influenced the discussions was quickly denied by Martin Marietta, which issued a statement that said in part:

> Most emphatically, Miss Cunningham's presence was not an irritant to Martin Marietta, and her presence, along-side her husband, Mr. Agee, the Bendix chairman, did not contribute in any manner to the failure of Bendix and Martin Marietta to reach agreement at that time or sub-sequently. . . . It was apparent that Mr. Agee took some comfort from his wife's presence.[36]

Some of the Martin Marietta group said later they may have been surprised or curious, even slightly amused, when she stepped out of the elevator, but they were otherwise unaffected by her presence. Pownall, in recalling the night, said he momentarily wondered if he "should go home and get Marilyn," his wife.[37]

Nothing did come of the discussions that night, either the private sessions between the two principals or the larger talks with their lawyers present. Martin Marietta's board declined to change the inevitable course that had been set when Bendix ignored the doomsday warning and bought the Martin stock. The longer the Bendix people stayed, the less time they had to arrange some other deal that could have delayed Martin Marietta's purchase of the Bendix stock.

The fact that the Agee party was in Bethesda and actually in the Martin Marietta headquarters building twice that day did leak out in spite of the heavy wraps everyone thought were in place. Even casual employee traffic through the executive wing had been cut off by John Ford and others in corporate security. Rumors were rife, however, and the press buzzed around for days, trying to crack the shield that Martin Marietta had erected around its team members and their movements. The reams of legal filings, newspaper advertising notices soliciting stockholder proxies, and official pronouncements released through the spokesperson's office were intended to be the only contacts with the outside world, including the press. Because the Bendix people were in the building, the spokesman deliberately left his office and the constantly ringing telephones. That way Marianna Dickie could say honestly that he was unavailable, and he did not have to answer the unwanted questions.

During one late-night absence from his office, he was conferring with his boss, Calvin, in an empty office in the executive wing. They had quietly turned off the light and left Calvin's office after Charlie Leithauser fell asleep on the couch. Everyone was tired. It was almost eleven o'clock, and the two PR men were slumped in their chairs, Calvin chain-smoking. Suddenly, into the room strode Mary Cunningham with a cheery "Hi there! I'm Mary Cunningham."

After introductions and handshakes, Calvin asked gently, "How's your guy doing?"

"He and Tom are still talking," she said. "I just wish they could be doing this by themselves without these batteries of lawyers and financial people. You know, Bill thinks the world of Tom, and I know Tom thinks the world of Bill." The two public relations men didn't trust themselves to look at each other. "They could get so much done if they didn't have all these people advising them to do this or do that," Mary Cunningham added. Then she asked Calvin, "What do you think is going to happen?"

"We are going to buy the stock," Roy replied.

"That is really a shame," she said. "You know, this whole thing has just been blown out of proportion. I think there have been many regrettable actions. Citibank's tendering of the employee stock really was quite outrageous, even Bill's and my SESSOP stock was tendered. Can you imagine any broker getting away with that without your permission? Some of our people were very angry," she added, referring to the Bendix-described Unity Day turnouts at Bendix plants throughout the country. "I think fifty thousand Bendix employees turning out for Unity Day was quite a show of support for Bill. It was a marvelous, spontaneous outpouring of loyalty and affection. Bill was touched by it."

At that moment the "Bill" of her monologue beckoned from the hallway. "Well, it was nice talking to you." She smiled in parting, and the two Agees and their associates stepped into the elevator and were gone.

Calvin and his colleague stared at each other in silence for a moment. It was as if they had been listening to a phonograph record that was impossible to interrupt. Both of them knew there had been dozens of phone calls the previous day from Bendix employees who said they were being paid time and a half to attend the Unity Day rallies and make toll-free long-distance calls withdrawing their SESSOP shares from the pool Citibank had tendered to Martin Marietta. Some of the Bendix people even asked for Martin Marietta

T-shirts, hats, or anything they could wear to show their defiance.

"Either she wrote that Unity Day press release," Calvin said, "or she memorized it."[38]

■

THERE WOULD STILL BE last-minute court rulings and appeals, but essentially it was nearly all over but the shouting. Agee had failed in his last-ditch attempt to change Martin Marietta's course. The next morning, determined not to be taken over by Martin Marietta, Agee threw himself and his entire company into the open arms of Allied Corporation and its chairman, Ed Hennessy. It was a wonderful deal for Allied. For $85 a share Allied would get the many Bendix businesses it desired plus, Hennessy thought, Martin Marietta because of the 70 percent stock Bendix already held in Martin Marietta. Not so, he would quickly discover in an introductory telephone call to Tom Pownall. Martin Marietta also intended to own a large chunk of Bendix. It was September 22, the much heralded date on which Martin Marietta could still buy control of Bendix.[39]

Because of a gap in securities laws, Martin Marietta had only a "magic minute" between midnight Wednesday, September 22, and 12:01 A.M. Thursday, September 23, to buy the Bendix stock, and buy it did! In the first few seconds of Thursday—as fast as the computer could spit them out—Bob Powell and Tom Mendenhall, who had been standing by at the Citibank depository, tendered and purchased 8,988,912 shares of Bendix Corporation common stock, approximately 44 percent, for $750 million. An open long-distance line conveyed the news to the home team—Tom Pownall, still wearing the "Don't Give Up the Ship" tie, waiting in the corner conference room of Bethesda headquarters with the directors and other members of the A-team. Corks popped, champagne poured, and there was lusty cheering, even by the "distinguished" members of the board.[40]

Waiting with them was a new player, Ed Hennessy of Allied. He and his advisers had flown in that afternoon. Hennessy had offered to buy the remainder of Martin Marietta's stock, but Pownall told him no deal. Instead, Martin Marietta would swap the Bendix stock it owned for an equal amount of Martin Marietta stock. An arrangement had been put together in anticipation of Martin Marietta's buying into Bendix. Allied would agree to a "standstill" concerning the remaining Martin Marietta stock it would hold, and Martin Marietta would have buy-back rights at predetermined prices. That had now happened and Hennessy joined in the celebration. Allied's previously agreed upon deal with Agee would have to be revised, as Agee would discover in the morning. He had been outmaneuvered.

Don Rauth carried a bottle of champagne down the hall to the public relations department and put it on the spokesman's desk. "Congratulations! You deserve a drink," he said, raising his glass to Marianna Dickie and others still in the office. "If anyone calls," Rauth said, "just tell them we're drinking champagne!"[41]

A BILLION IN DEBT AND A RETURN TO BASICS

When the lawyers and bankers had finished, Martin Marietta remained independent, although $1.3 billion in debt. Allied owned Bendix lock, stock, and barrel. Martin Marietta had made the Allied takeover possible by trading the majority block of Bendix stock Martin Marietta owned to Allied in exchange for an equal amount of Martin Marietta stock that Allied had acquired with its purchase of Bendix. The arrangement left about 38 percent of outstanding Martin Marietta stock in Allied's hands. As part of the settlement, a ten-year "standstill" agreement restricted Allied from voting or selling the stock, or from acquiring more. It also gave Martin Marietta the right to repurchase the stock on an escalating price scale over the ten-year period. The escalator was 14 percent per year, which dictated an early buy-back before the price became prohibitive. Allied would have two seats on the Martin Marietta board until the stock was recovered.

It was almost an untenable financial situation. The company's debt-to-total-capital ratio was a whopping 82 percent, a figure guaranteed to plunge Martin Marietta's ratings in the borrowing market. There was scant optimism within the company and in financial circles.

"There was no prospect we could ever buy back the stock if it got beyond the first year," Pownall said. "I mean, it would have been unbelievable."

"Sheer good fortune," in Pownall's words, walked in the door about that time. "The equity market opened up. Interest rates fell. The inflation rate fell. The Reagan defense buildup was catching hold, and business prospects were improving every day. All of a sudden going to the market to raise some equity money made sense. It stunned me, and it stunned Allied, too. It happened so swiftly that it caught everybody by surprise," Pownall said.[42] But in addition to good timing, Charles Leithauser received a large measure of credit as chief financial officer for managing the financial turnaround.

Three days before Christmas, and slightly less than three months after the "bloodiest" fight in the history of corporate take-over attempts up to that time, Martin Marietta went to the equity market to sell 2.3 million shares of preferred stock at $50 a share, or $115 million dollars. A week later the corporation raised $13 million more through the sale of some tax benefits. The recovery had begun.

More than $150 million additional was raised in the first four months of 1983. Of that, $86 million came in a second public offering of common stock in February, this time 2 million shares, as the price of the corporation's stock continued to climb on a generally improving market. Much of the balance was raised by the sale of stock to the Employee Retirement Trust and in an exchange of stock for debt securities of the aluminum subsidiary. Simultaneously, various assets from the commercial side of the house were being sold for cash—"monetized" was the vogue word on Wall Street a decade later. For the most part they were businesses the corporation had already at least mentally pigeonholed for later action because they had lost their bloom, so to speak. Cement was one that the corporation had tried to dispose of earlier. Several of the chemical specialty companies were also experiencing difficult times. Martin Marietta's aluminum business, a real winner when acquired in the late sixties because of favorable power contracts, had turned sour. The market was glutted with cheap aluminum while Martin Marietta metal prices were set by out-of-control energy costs. The aluminum company was losing $1 million a week going into 1982.

The first physical assets sold in March were two cement plants in Maine and Pennsylvania, followed by six more in May and a seventh in June. The three separate transactions totaled almost $240 million, and the last two of the corporation's nine cement plants were disposed of a year later for $65 million. Sales of other assets, including the textile dyestuff company, ten industrial sand plants, and a laser subsidiary, netted approximately $150 million, and various pieces of real estate were sold for $57 million.

The fact that the sale of the cement plants netted a profit of close to $30 million during a general depression in the cement industry earned Philip H. Sendel a reputation as a pretty shrewd horse trader. As vice president of the corporation and president of the cement group, Sendel led the successful negotiations that left him without a job, so the byword around Bethesda was "If you've got something to sell, give it to Sendel." He later moved to the aerospace side of the house and was president of the Aero & Naval Systems company at Baltimore for more than three years before retiring in 1988.

Wall Street was suitably impressed, as it should have been. All through the first half of 1983, while the orderly disposition of physical assets at reasonably good prices was taking place, the company continued to receive new and important contracts. The stock market reflected the excellent performance in the per-share price of Martin Marietta stock, which by June was $55, up nearly 24 percent from the $42 it had been trading at immediately after the Bendix affair. At that price the corporation once again in a public offering on June 2 sold 1.8 million additional common shares for $99 million. Added to the nearly $750 million raised from the sale of assets and the $150 million resulting from the various other cash conversions, the seven-month total was close to $1 billion, a remarkable achievement. Martin Marietta's recovery up to that point had been a heady combination of dedication, hard work, difficult decisions, prudent nail-biting, and a large measure of creative financial juggling. Mixed in with it all was that generous dollop of what Pownall had called "sheer good fortune," and it continued throughout the summer.

On August 25, exactly one year after the takeover attempt had started, Martin Marietta bought back 1.8 million shares, almost 28 percent, of the stock still held by Allied. The remaining 4.65 million shares were repurchased in October, completely eliminating Allied's holdings in Martin Marietta. By the end of the year the corporation's balance sheet was once more in reasonable condition. Short-term debt had been eliminated, and the long-term debt, which for a brief time immediately after the fight had been 82 percent of capitalization, was now reduced to a manageable 42 percent. Shareowners' equity had nearly doubled. The common stock had been split three shares for two and the dividend increased. Sales of nearly $4 billion were at a record level, and the corporation's net earnings of $141 million were up more than 50 percent. Allied's right to two board seats had been eliminated with the repurchase of the stock. Ed Hennessy's presence on the board was valued, however, so he was re-elected and still served with distinction a decade later.

The Martin Marietta that emerged from the takeover fight and the yearlong recovery had a different look. Cement was gone, and so were most of the chemical specialty companies and the industrial sand business. Aluminum remained but not for long. The only elements of the original American-Marietta were the construction aggregates operations and the magnesia chemicals operation. Aerospace was intact, of course, and was once again the primary focus. Martin Marietta had returned to its basics.

Tom Pownall's oft-repeated hindsight comment that "Bill Agee was the greatest thing that ever happened to Martin Marietta" was not entirely facetious. He truly believed the takeover attempt, or rather the recovery from it, caused the corporation to deal with some ailing businesses sooner rather than later. It simply stepped up the timetable. What was remarkable was that there were no fire sales. All divestitures were for book value or better, some of them for gains considerably in excess of book value. And even more remarkable was the fact that all the divested businesses were marketed and actively sold by the Martin Marietta people running them. They made up the team credited by their leader with active participation in the takeover fight. They served the corporation and themselves with distinction. The true difference in philosophies between Martin Marietta and Agee, Tom Pownall believed, was people.

"We treated Bendix as a team event," he said. "We felt everybody in Martin Marietta was a participant. The only person any of us ever saw from Bendix was Agee. I never saw a single, solitary lawyer, finance man, officer, or anybody. Even his chief aide . . . I mean his wife . . . worked for Seagrams. Agee was simply off on a sick moose all by himself," Pownall said.[43]

There was a sad footnote to the whole affair. Although three books on the subject and public perception will remember "Bendix versus Martin Marietta," it really was Agee versus Martin Marietta. He did gather monetary benefits for Bendix stockholders, including himself and the arbitrageurs. But Bendix, the respected industrial enterprise with 69,000 people and a long and proud heritage, never really was a participant, and after it was all over, Bendix simply did not exist anymore as a corporation.

CHAPTER 36

Windows of Opportunity

■

That first year of recovery, 1983, was an eye-opener for those paying attention to Martin Marietta's getting well quickly. The decade that followed the takeover attempt confirmed the rightness of the decision to fight to preserve the company, but it was not immediately clear what had been preserved and whether it could survive. There was little doubt that the corporation was once again primarily in the aerospace business. But what else? What other businesses remained after the sell-off? Could it compete? Could it restore its balance sheet after the overwhelming debt?

The picture was not clear, and the fuzziness extended to many of the corporation's publics—customer organizations, the media, subcontractors and suppliers, individual stockholders, institutional investors, and others on Wall Street. Included were many of the analysts who professed to follow the company closely. Just what was Martin Marietta now? Was it financially sound? What businesses did it still have? What future? Those were among the questions asked by respondents to a survey commissioned by the corporation (a blind survey in which the company was not identified as a sponsor but was listed among a half-dozen other corporations). Respondents were asked to compare the companies on a variety of issues, including name recognition, product lines, financial health, and management ability.

Except for name recognition, the consensus was confusion. Martin Marietta was known to most but for different reasons, some of them inaccurate. It was apparent that the company needed to turn up the volume on its traditionally low-key, even modest, pubic relations. If increased understanding was a key to acceptance and confidence, then Martin Marietta needed to sound its own horn more loudly, not just toot it.

Wall Street had taken technology to its heart, and the expression "high-tech" was very much in vogue if slightly overused. Nearly everything that Martin Marietta did involved technology, and its technological interests were diverse. What better theme could there be, the reasoning went, than to portray the corporation's strength in diverse technologies necessary to the country's future? An extensive new advertising program was begun under the banner MARTIN MARIETTA IS MASTERMINDING TECHNOLOGY. The repetitive double m in Martin Marietta and in Masterminding would act as a mnemonic device in assisting the reader or listener to remember the corporation's name. So argued the talented creative people at VanSant Dugdale, the Baltimore advertising agency retained for the ad campaign. They wanted to capitalize on the name recognition gained during the takeover fight, which the survey confirmed was there.[1]

It was good thinking that confirmed equally sound reasoning within the company. Only a few months before, after many of the commercial companies had been sold, there was a suggestion at a high management level to change the company's name back to simply "Martin." It was true that very little was left of the Marietta side of the house. But the suggestion overlooked the fact that "Martin Marietta" had received name recognition worth millions of dollars during the takeover battle, and it had been positive identification. Martin Marietta came across as the "white hat," establishing the corporation's name more firmly than ever. Furthermore, the name Martin Marietta had gained considerable respect among customers and others because of a long series of successes in space and defense programs. The task, therefore, was to capitalize on the name recognition by explaining just what the corporation was all about.

Two-page color spreads in the leading news and business magazines were accompanied by thirty-second story-line commercials on television. All stressed Martin Marietta's breadth and depth in technology. In a companion move, the corporation also became an underwriter for the long-running, award-winning entertainment series "Great Performances," produced by New York's WNET Channel 13 on public television. A follow-up survey taken fourteen months after the advertisements began showed impressive increases in recognition and knowledge of Martin Marietta among readers and viewers. There was an additional benefit: Employees throughout the corporation also identified with the ads and the Great Performances. The exposure became a source of pride with them and their families, solidifying the foundation of team and loyalty built during the takeover attack. Like any family beset by illness or other serious disruption, Martin Marietta people had been threatened. They had survived and now were even more closely bonded in the wake of the ordeal.

For those intimately involved in the takeover battle and its aftermath, the world seemed to stand still from August 1982 to August 1983. Not so for the vast majority of the corporation's forty thousand men and women who had steadfastly gone about their jobs, producing and delivering new systems and services and winning new business. There had been plenty of action in existing programs and in the competitive arena where the company was trying to win new contracts. Monday morning staff meetings at the corporate, group, company, and division levels focused at least weekly on status reports containing lists of "must win" programs, divided into A or B lists by size, desirability, or criticality to the "new business" forecast. Further subdivision defined the "likelies" and the "long shots." The procedure was less focused, perhaps, during the prime years of Martin Marietta's diversification when boom times in the commercial businesses tended to automatically balance the troughs in defense spending, but it took on added importance post-Bendix when aerospace once again became the largest element of the corporation. As a business tracking technique, it would be honed to a near art by late 1986, when Norm Augustine moved into the CEO's office and pointed his colleagues at several large "windows of opportunity."

■

FOR MARTIN MARIETTA HEADING INTO 1984, it was a "leaner, tougher" corporation, by its own admission in the annual report, "well positioned to capitalize on the opportunities in its future,"[2] whether those opportunities would be in traditional areas of defense and space or elsewhere. Expansion in the government sector was the broad objective. Two of the biggest prizes the company had in its sights—contracts with the Department of Energy and with the Federal Aviation Administration—were won in rapid succession as recovery year 1983 turned into 1984. The first, a decided long shot against formidable competition, was a management contract to operate the government's Oak Ridge nuclear operations for the Energy Department. It had taken a full-court press by a proposal team drawn from nearly every element of the corporation, but by the summer of 1983, the proposal had reached the semifinals, a three-company list from which the winner would be chosen.

Just twelve days before Christmas, the Department of Energy declared Martin Marietta its choice to be the management contractor at Oak Ridge and Paducah, Kentucky. The year-end euphoria of that "win" had hardly subsided when exactly one month into the new year the other "big one" was won. Martin Marietta was selected by the Federal Aviation Administration to be its principal contractor to manage the rebuilding of the nation's air traffic control, navigation, and communications system. It was another multihundred-million-dollar nondefense contract.

Tom Pownall had been right. The company was indeed a remarkable team of talented and dedicated people. The effect of winning those two competitions was like a tonic to the fifty-eight thousand (counting the nuclear people) Martin Marietta employees making up the team. It was positively therapeutic. Their company had recovered financially and now was aggressively expanding and moving forward.

Oak Ridge Joins the Corporate Family

The Oak Ridge award was particularly significant because the company had been the underdog in the proposal competition; it beat out the smart-money favorites, Westinghouse and Rockwell, two of the largest government contractors. Much of the credit for the successful Martin Marietta effort was given to Orlando's John Bright. He had spotted and brought to management's attention nearly two years earlier the small notice in *Commerce Business Daily* that Union Carbide would not seek to renew the contract under which it had managed the Oak Ridge operations for more than forty years. Bright immediately saw the potential for Martin Marietta to apply its expertise as a systems integrator to this important and highly sensitive national security work. He marshaled the people and the corporate support necessary to put together a proposal, then personally managed the effort until the contract was won.

Even before the Oak Ridge proposal, Bright had a reputation around the company for getting things done. His start was a bit out of the ordinary according to a well-worn tale, told in this instance by Tom Young. It seems that Bright, as a young man of twenty-one, was driving a front-end loader for the contractor who was building the Bay Hill golf course southwest of Orlando. The land in that area alternates between being sandy and solid and just plain muck. Floridians describe it as "halfway between dirt and peat moss and the closest thing to quicksand that exists." As Bright worked his shovel into a mucky thicket of palmetto scrub, he uncovered a nest of rattlesnakes that slithered and slid out of the shovel and all around the loader. John didn't like snakes, so the story goes, and it took him about two seconds to leap out of the cab of the loader and hit the ground running in the opposite direction. Unfortunately, he neglected to shut off the machine, which proceeded to move forward, into the muck until it simply sank out of sight. Needless to say, Bright's boss didn't take too kindly to that, and young John was quickly looking for new work. Walking eastward along Sand Lake Road, he came to another construction site where he applied and was given a job as a construction helper building a new aerospace plant for the Martin company. The plant was opened late in 1957, and John Bright was among the "local new hires" in 1958. Before retiring thirty-five years later, he had been vice president and general manager of the Ocala, Florida, plant.[3]

Oak Ridge, to those who work and live there and to those in the government responsible for what goes on there, is much more than an attractive community in eastern Tennessee's Anderson County. It is also a rather small, upscale, forward-thinking, enlightened home to nearly thirty thousand residents. It is a state of mind nurtured by its history as the site of the World War II Manhattan Project, which produced the atomic bomb. On the day Martin Marietta won the contract, the sprawling government nuclear reservation employed eighteen thousand people in three distinct facilities. About one-fourth of them were Ph.Ds or other advance-degreed scientists and engineers working in the complex known as Oak Ridge National Laboratory. They and their colleagues in the nuclear components manufacturing plant known as Y-12 and in two uranium enrichment facilities at Oak Ridge and at Paducah, Kentucky, immediately exchanged their Union Carbide badges for Martin Marietta identification and joined the payroll of Martin Marietta Energy Systems, Inc. Established as a wholly owned subsidiary, the energy systems company president reported directly to the president and chief operating officer of the corporation, Larry Adams. And to make the corporate commitment even stronger, Adams was also chairman of the energy systems subsidiary's board.

During the lengthy proposal process, Martin Marietta had wisely

Oak Ridge bioreactor researchers

targeted the community of Oak Ridge and its leaders for special emphasis. It was Tennessee-born John Bright's idea and a brilliant one. Although the community would not get to vote in the government's selection process, it was likely that community approval would be an extremely important consideration.

Martin Marietta took its turn preening and flaunting its corporate best before a luncheon meeting of the Oak Ridge Chamber of Commerce, as did each of the other companies bidding for the right to manage the Oak Ridge Nuclear Operation. Pownall, as chairman, carried the Martin Marietta banner, contributing his own personal luster earned as the tough captain who had saved his ship from a pirate takeover. The ground rules for the proposal allowed each of the competitors one private group event where it could woo the sixteen or so Carbide principals considered key to the Oak Ridge operation. Martin Marietta held a small reception and dinner where those key people and their spouses could mingle informally and converse with selected company principals and their spouses.

Martin Marietta also prepared a special four-page color insert, which was published as a paid advertisement in the *Oak Ridger,* the community's daily newspaper. Then the corporation did its competitors one better. A dozen of Oak Ridge's leading citizens, both civic and business leaders, were invited to spend a day as Martin Marietta's guests. They were flown as a group to Orlando, where each was paired with his or her counterpart—the mayor of Oak Ridge with the mayor of Orlando, the banker with a banker, the newspaper publisher, the chamber president, the attorney, the merchant—each in a one-on-one session. It was tremendously successful. Did it win the contract? Most people think not. Whether or not it influenced the government's proposal evaluators, it certainly made the Oak Ridgers feel a part of the process, and it established a mutually beneficial relationship between the community and the company that ultimately won the job.[4]

Clyde C. Hopkins, who was second in command of the Carbide unit operating Oak Ridge when Martin Marietta took over, had spent thirty years at Oak Ridge. He remained in that capacity until 1988 when he became president, succeeding Kenneth Jarmolow, Martin Marietta's first energy systems president. Hopkins believes the greatest benefit Martin Marietta brought to Oak Ridge was its "complete corporate involvement" in the enterprise.

"Previously we had been corporate stepchildren," Hopkins said. "You could almost say orphans. But Martin Marietta made us full members of its family, giving us not only support but the benefit of its expertise. Martin Marietta's focused, integrated approach to project management was very, very beneficial to Oak Ridge's day-to-day operations."[5]

One of the earliest innovations promised in Martin Marietta's proposal and high on the government's wish list was a technology transfer program. It provided a mechanism for licensing some of the inventions and new processes developed in the national laboratory for outside commercial exploitation. William Carpenter, one of the Orlando people originally involved with John Bright in winning the Oak Ridge contract, became the honcho for the technology transfer program, which he managed with distinction. Hopkins considered the program "outstanding" and said it became the model for all other government efforts to transfer technology to the private sector, both within the Department of Energy and across other federal agencies.

Technology transfer was not the only change Martin Marietta brought to Oak Ridge. The energy systems company became a model contractor to the U.S. Department of Energy, consistently scoring high in annual agency reviews that determine the company's management fee. A large part of the Department of Energy's confidence, apart from the corporate embrace extended to Oak Ridge employees, was the high level of corporate attention and support Martin Marietta gave the Oak Ridge operation by making it a full member of the corporation's structure.

Technology transfer and corporate involvement became equally important a decade later, in 1993, when the corporation competed for and won a Department of Energy contract to manage the Sandia National Laboratories, with close to 9,000 people, at Albuquerque, New Mexico, and in California, Nevada, and Hawaii.

AIR TRAFFIC CONTROL MODERNIZATION

The second half of the one-two competitive punch the corporation scored in late 1983 and early 1984 was the FAA contract to manage the modernization of the nation's air traffic control system. Here again it was the corporation's experience and strength in systems management and systems integration that the government recognized and wanted for a program of almost unprecedented size and scope. It would encompass a comprehensive modernization and restructuring of the nation's air traffic control, navigation, and communications system. The busiest and the safest in the world, the system had not been overhauled since the 1960s, the vintage of much of its equipment.

New computers, radars, microwave landing systems, automated weather data collection and forecasting capabilities, and automatic communications to link them together were under development and would have to be tested and installed. Martin Marietta would not develop or supply any of the hardware, but the company would have to assist the FAA to efficiently integrate and manage both the technology and the people necessary to produce the vital new systems and make them work as a unified whole. It would be the largest and most complex federal program since the Apollo Moon project.

A technical and managerial team out of the Denver aerospace operation had been tracking the FAA opportunity for three years. Frederic H. Hudoff was the leader of that team, and when the contract was won, he was named vice president of a new division of nearly one thousand people who formally became the air traffic control systems organization. Losing no time in tackling the monster they had won, an initial cadre of two hundred moved into leased

Air traffic control, Denver

space on School Street in downtown Washington, D.C., just a few blocks from FAA headquarters. They literally did what their new address implied: They went to school on their new assignment, learning as much as they could about their new customer and the National Airspace Plan in which they would play a key role for the next decade.

After three years, Fred Hudoff moved to new responsibilities as president of the data systems company and was succeeded at air traffic control systems by his deputy, Brian N. Etheridge. The biggest challenge facing the Martin Marietta people, Etheridge said, was getting to know the new customer and all the different viewpoints that existed in the FAA. "We were accustomed to an engineering-focused relationship more normal to building a spacecraft or an airplane but instead found a less structured environment," he said.[6]

Applying computer-based cost and schedule controls, the company was able to help enforce commonality and discipline among the disparate systems and processes, and eventually establish a baseline for the complex project. Etheridge likened the job to "overhauling the engine of a car while it is running full speed downhill." The trick was getting the "hardware out of the shops and on-line," he said. Nearly ten years later, as the scope of the company's original contract neared completion, Etheridge and the Martin Marietta team working with the FAA had a feeling of "enormous accomplishment." Nearing completion was a modern, state-of-the-art air traffic control, navigation, and communications system firmly rooted and expanding.

The initial $684 million FAA contract to Martin Marietta was extended by $300 million in 1988, and other additions and changes increased the value to more than $1 billion in its tenth and final year. The company's contract responsibilities also included integration of other contractors' services and equipment involving nearly $13 billion of additional FAA expenditures.

The National Airspace Plan is ongoing, of course, with the FAA committed to updating systems as advancing technologies permit. The company remains involved in several aspects of the continuing work even though there no longer is a single management contractor. The company provided similar systems integration and management for modernization of the U.S. Department of Defense air traffic control system, and a Canadian subsidiary, Martin Marietta Canada Ltd., led a team of companies that won a similar engineering and integration contract to modernize the system that controls Canada's air traffic.

DATA AND INFORMATION SYSTEMS

In still a third extension of talents and skills developed within the aerospace industry, the corporation established in mid-1984 a new operating group, Information & Communications Systems. Promptly taking on within the corporation the written abbreviation I&CS, which when spoken came out "INCS," the new organization recognized Martin Marietta's large and growing presence in the area known as C^3I: command, control, communications, and intelligence systems. With about $200 million of already established contracts broken out principally from Denver Aerospace, formation of I&CS placed additional emphasis on the design and integration of large, complex systems. The recently won FAA contract was such a system, and the air traffic control division became a part of I&CS.

Within two years the new organization had more than doubled its business base with sales of $421 million, about equal to Martin Marietta Data Systems, itself an earlier spinoff of in-house capability for computing services. Data systems had been accorded full company status in 1982 in recognition of an annual growth rate exceeding 25 percent. In addition to supporting the corporation's internal computing requirements, the Data Systems company had garnered an equivalent volume of sales supplying data management services to other companies and government agencies and had a growing segment of international business through a British subsidiary, Hoskyns Limited of London.

By 1986 the two companies were linked in a new corporate group called information systems. Combined sales of more than $888 million, close to one-fifth of the corporation's total that year, were derived from a broad base of contracts, ranging from air traffic control and battlefield communications to personnel administration and space operations. The group also managed large and complex computer facilities and developed advanced software for commercial and government customers.

Two contracts won by I&CS in Denver placed the corporation squarely in the forefront of Ronald Reagan's Strategic Defense Initiative, quickly dubbed "Star Wars" by the American media. Try as they would, neither the government nor its contractors could convince the media or critics of strategic defense to call it anything but Star Wars. As a defensive shield or protective umbrella, the system was anything but warlike, but Luke Skywalker and his Hollywood companions, R2D2 and C3PO, were the galactic heroes of the day, so the nickname was perhaps inevitable.

Lending credence to that inevitability was a unique national laboratory and test facility built by the company in 1986 and promptly named R2P2 for Rapid Retargeting, Precision Pointing. Its purpose was the testing of rapid retargeting systems for the Strategic Defense Initiative that required extremely accurate pointing capability, things such as space telescopes, space station instruments, and lasers. Its accuracy was equivalent to pinpointing an object as small as a football at a distance of three thousand miles.

There followed within the space of two years a $500-million contract for the design, installation, and operation of a National Test Bed that would be a primary element of SDI. The computer-driven facility, which quickly became the NTB in typical aerospace quick-speak, was built at Falcon Air Force Station in Colorado Springs. It represented a quantum leap in the field of computer simulation, enabling users to simulate, test, and evaluate strategic defense concepts, architectures, battle management, and hardware applications. Gerald A. Zionic, who had led the competitive design phase that attained the award, was given the responsibility of building the National Test Bed facility and getting it on line.

Twice during the 1980s, Martin Marietta's role in the Strategic Defense Initiative was the focus of presidential visits. The first by Ronald Reagan in 1987 unveiled Zenith Star, the space-based chemical laser system on which Martin Marietta had been working under deep security for several years. Arthur E. Koski, then public relations director for the astronautics group at Denver, drew the assignment of handling the multitude of national press who would descend on the plant, plus many of the myriad details that such a visit entails.

Notification that Denver was under consideration as a possible site for a major public update on the Strategic Defense Initiative came only ten days before the event was to be held. A White House advance man visited and toured the plant with Koski, Morris H. Thorson, Gene Horak, the factory manager, and Don Parson. What was needed, they were told, was a space big enough to hold about three thousand employees, up to one thousand invited community leaders, scores of reporters, television commentators and TV camera crews, plus telephone and other communications facilities, office space, and much more.

"Yes, we can," "Sure, we can do that," and "No problem" were Horak's stock responses to anything the White House man said was needed, Koski recalled.[7] Several days later, the word came back that Martin Marietta Denver had been selected. Since the Titan assembly area was the only place in the plant large enough to hold the people,

President Reagan with Zenith Star model

it meant moving some machines and equipment, even a couple of rockets in assembly. One entire bay of the plant was undergoing renovation at the time and was empty, so it was pressed into service and became space for the network television studios and an office for presidential press secretary Marlin Fitzwater.

When it became apparent that the president would announce and talk about the heretofore under-wraps Zenith Star program, a full-size mock-up was needed posthaste. None existed. So hundreds of square feet of plywood were crafted into a model about fifteen feet in diameter and sixty to eighty feet long, Koski said. The whole thing was wrapped in aluminum and gold foil to give it a metallic space-craft look. It was to be the backdrop for the stage on which the president would speak and a panel of technical dignitaries would sit. When the aluminum and gold foil was too reflective for the TV cameras, hours were spent with spray guns dulling the surface. Then the Secret Service discovered the huge model of Zenith Star was hollow, so nothing would do until a door had been cut in the back of it so agents could do a security check.

When the big day arrived, November 24, 1987, it went off without a hitch, Koski said. President Reagan toured the R2P2 facility and was briefed on various elements of SDI. Then he spoke of the "extraordinary effort each of you is making . . . of your mental prowess and creativity, and, yes, your hard work." He called SDI "not a weapon of war but an ensurer, a protector of the peace." He told the assembled employees, "You are laboring to develop a defensive system that will change history. Once you've completed your work, the world will never be the same. I suggest it will be a better and a safer world. And what better legacy can this generation leave than a safer world."

Less than a year later, when the White House sought a place for Vice President George Bush (also presidential candidate Bush) to make a major policy speech in the Rocky Mountain region, Martin Marietta's Denver astronautics plant immediately came to mind. "It was a piece of cake this time," Koski said. "We had all been there."

The other component of the Information Systems Group, Data Systems, would more than double its sales and earnings in the eighties. The more government agencies and corporate America turned to computers, the more many of them relied on outside specialists in data management. When they did, Martin Marietta Data Systems was there competing for their business. The company had been created as a business-getting component in 1970 out of the corporation's considerable in-house capabilities for managing its own computer and

Vice President Bush visits Denver plant

data processing needs. By 1982, when it was accorded company status and its financials were broken out for the first time as a business segment, the fledgling had sales of nearly $245 million. The company that year was supplying computer software systems and services to more than one thousand domestic and foreign customers in manufacturing, distribution, and government. The software portion of this business accounted for about half of the customers but less than a quarter of the data systems sales and eventually would be sold.

■

SHIRLEY FROCK WAS SOMETHING OF a rarity when she first joined Martin Marietta in 1964, in the early days of computerization. She was a woman in what had been mostly a male-dominated engineering environment. She also was exceptionally talented mathematically, knew how computers worked, and easily adapted to their use and programming. She had been teaching mathematics in the Philadelphia public school system and had a reputation as something of a "math whiz." During a sabbatical at her parents' home in Colorado, friends persuaded her to apply for a job at Martin Marietta's big aerospace plant.

Shirley took the employment examination under an assumed name, Shirley Blank, carefully avoiding the fact that her dad, Earl Frock, worked at the plant. She also declined a plant tour and carefully avoided entering company property or signing anything under her assumed name that might compromise later employment. She was determined to get the position on her own merit, not as Earl's daughter. Her perfect score on the math portion caused something of a stir among the employment people, who immediately offered her the position of trainee-computer programmer, with the job title of junior engineer. Quickly confessing to her real surname, she accepted the offer. Many years later she recalled that one of the first people she met when she reported for work in Denver was Dick Weber. As a youngster she had seen him pitch for the Martin Bombers when her father took her to the baseball games at Middle River. Weber was taken aback at the "new hire" who remembered his baseball days in Baltimore, until he learned she was Earl Frock's daughter.

Earl Frock, who had been in plant maintenance at Baltimore for fourteen years, was "lent" to Denver when that plant was built. It was to be a temporary assignment to help the new organization learn how to properly maintain a plant that was to be in use twenty-four hours a day. He never returned to his Baltimore job, retiring from Denver eleven years later, in 1967.

Young Shirley Frock stayed with the company four years, then tried her hand at a couple of private ventures in Denver before being wooed back in 1973 by Bob Bryan, data systems vice president for the western region. She had just changed her name—this time for real, to Mrs. Sam Prutch—when Bryan offered her a position as director of computer sharing services. It was the beginning of a multimillion-dollar business in which the corporation sold downtime on its central computers to a host of outside enterprises—other corporations, government agencies, retail businesses, schools, literally anyone needing the service and willing to pay for it.

Shirley Prutch held a variety of increasingly responsible positions as the data systems organization grew and stretched its reach in the frenetic world of data management and computer-driven information systems. She was in Bethesda in 1986, as vice president of the systems integration division, when she received a telephone call from Bob Choboy, head of Martin Marietta's office in Ankara, Turkey. The corporation at the time was trying to sell LANTIRN and other aerospace systems to NATO allies, including Turkey, but "everyone wanted to talk computers and information processing," Choboy told her. Could she please come to Ankara to speak with the minister of health, who was interested in computerizing the country's health care programs? Prutch had a trip scheduled to Kuwait, where Martin Marietta was working on an important contract, so she agreed to stop off in Ankara. Little did she know the part it would play in her future, including a fourth name.[8]

Turkey is a Muslim country, and although Ataturk had "lifted the veil" in 1934 and women had become active in the workplace and in the higher councils of Turkish government, Turks were not used to Western women in management positions. Prutch stood out first as an American in Ankara and second as a Martin Marietta executive dealing with the higher councils of government. She had one other distinction: blue eyes. Among the Turks, blue eyes are very special because they are "God's eyes." So the coincidental color of her eyes brought the likable Martin Marietta executive added attention. The Turks had trouble pronouncing *Prutch,* so she became Shirley "Hanna," which, translated freely, means Shirley My Dear, or Dear One. This familiar address, implying respect and admiration, was used throughout the two-plus years she visited and was stationed in Turkey for Martin Marietta. It was used by almost everyone she encountered, from President Torgot Ozal on down. Ozal was prime minister when Prutch first went to Turkey. The short, rotund Turkish leader never failed to single out the diminutive Shirley Hanna for special acknowledgment or greeting at state receptions and other public occasions.

One occasion was at the Turkish Mediterranean resort in Antayla. It was early spring and "colder than a son-of-a-gun," Prutch recalled. But Ozal ventured into the sea for a swim. Prutch had joined the gathering of government people and others watching Ozal from the shore. As he came out of the water, wrapping himself in a large towel and "looking every bit a bald, round Caesar emerging from the sea," he singled Prutch out and rushed to greet her with a loud exclamation, "Ah, Shirley Hanna, how good to see you!" Another time, during a visit to a technical meeting in Chicago, the Turkish prime minister was receiving a long line of guests at a reception when he spotted her. Again, he stopped what he was doing to generously greet and pay special attention to Shirley Hanna.[9]

Prutch maintained she was accorded such respect because "Martin Marietta was so well thought of in Turkey." That undoubtedly was true, but George H. Perlman, director of international business development for the corporation at the time, credits Shirley Prutch with "getting us started in Turkey"[10] and with being one of the reasons the Turks thought well of the corporation.

Martin Marietta later established with a Turkish construction and holding company, Gamma Industrie A.S., a joint venture called Martin Marietta Gamma Electronics, which became known as MMGE (a somewhat prophetic abbreviation for 1986). It was the conduit for the corporation's future business in that country. Ironically, it was not the business of computerized data management, which the Turks had been so interested in pursuing with the company in 1986. Other than a few studies, none of that business ever developed. Rather, the corporation would furnish LANTIRN and other aerospace systems to Turkey in the 1990s.

As the corporation grew in total sales and complexity, the percentage of data systems–type business diminished, and the data systems identity as such was split several ways. The same was true of the I&CS business, which eventually was commingled with related corporate elements. Together, however, what began relatively modestly in the seventies and eighties from homegrown, in-house capabilities blossomed handsomely. By the early nineties the information systems and data management businesses represented more than a billion dollars of the corporation's total sales.

Some other windows of opportunity that had been opened to the corporation in the eighties with major competitive "wins" were closed in the nineties as the U.S. defense budget turned down following the democratization of Eastern Europe, the breakup of the Soviet Union, and the end of the Cold War. Programs such as ADATS, the Air Defense/Anti-Tank System, developed with the Swiss firm Oerlikon-Buerhle, had a potential at one point of $10 billion as a system for the U.S. Army. But in spite of outstanding technical performance during the Army's fourth attempt in three decades to field such a capability, the ADATS program was canceled suddenly in 1992, one more victim of the relentless budget cutting under way at the Pentagon. A parallel program with the Canadians continued, however, with eventual sales projected at a billion dollars and possibly greater potential elsewhere internationally.

For the most part, the corporation had maximized the opportunities during the "window of the 1980s." Shareowners' equity, which had plunged to $436 million in 1982, was nearly $2 billion in 1992. The ratio of long-term debt to capitalization, which briefly stood at a whopping 82 percent immediately after the takeover attempt and was still an uncomfortable 74 percent entering 1983, was 20 percent a decade later. Backlog exceeded $12 billion. The price of Martin Marietta common stock is perhaps the best measure of the corporation's health and growth in the decade 1982 to 1992. The stock was selling at $33 a share on the New York Stock Exchange the evening before Agee's attack. On December 31, 1992, it was $69½ per share, the equivalent of $156⅝ a share had the price not been adjusted for two 3-for-2 stock splits that occurred in 1983 and 1985.[11]

CHAPTER 37

Titan Redux and Magellan

■

With the launch of the last Titan IIIC on March 6, 1982, one might have concluded it was the end of an era. Such had been the dreary but false conclusion more than a decade earlier when the last Titan II was slipped into its ICBM silo. Instead, it was just another beginning for the durable, adaptable, and continually growable family of Titans.

In seventeen years, going back to 1965, Titan IIIC had orbited eighty-two military and civilian satellites for a total of 111,000 spacecraft pounds placed in orbit around the Earth or sent into interplanetary space. Certainly it was a milestone, but one quickly to be surpassed. In the next decade extending into 1993, there would be twenty-eight more Titan IIIs in four different configurations, all but four of them national security missions. The four that were not were Commercial Titans. In addition, there were three Titan IIs—decommissioned ICBMs that had been refitted as space launch vehicles—plus six Titan IVs, the new generation, America's most powerful expendable launch vehicle.

In all, 325 operational Titans had been launched since the summer of 1960 when David S. LeVine sat on a bar stool in the Surf Restaurant at Cocoa Beach, Florida, and hazarded a guess on the future of the missile he was in charge of testing. The nation's other,

Titan II missiles refurbished as space boosters

older ICBM, Atlas, was beginning to put NASA payloads into space, and the conversation LeVine had with his colleagues concerned the likelihood of Titan's ever performing similar missions. The bet was that it would not. Atlas would get all the "glamour" jobs, and Titan would become primarily a military booster, the Air Force workhorse for defense and national security missions. It was still early in the flight testing of the original Titan as an intercontinental ballistic missile. No one had given a thought to a Titan II, much less a Gemini-Titan Launch Vehicle or a Titan III in a half-dozen configurations, including a fifth-generation Titan 34D, or the giant of them all, Titan IV.

More than thirty years later they had all flown, with an overall operational success rate of 95.8 percent. The program called "mission success" had been born on Titan and spread throughout Martin Marietta. Dave LeVine had been right: The majority of Titan missions had been Defense Department in origin. But he was wrong about all the glamour missions going to Atlas. Although Atlas was the darling of the NASA people at Cleveland, who were also planning a powerful upper stage called Centaur, there came a time when Atlas could no longer lift the weights being designed into spacecraft, and Titan came into its own. Titan II, with its storable propellants, had none of the cryogenic complexities of Atlas, was simpler to operate, and was more reliable. Helping to turn the tide was its selection as the launch vehicle for Gemini.

Ten Gemini-Titans carried twenty astronauts into orbit in 1965 and 1966 as the crucial middle step on the path to the Moon. Two Titan IIIEs boosted two Martin-built Viking spacecraft into space in 1975 to start separate 460-million-mile, year-long voyages to Mars. Two more Titan IIIs carried Voyager spacecraft into space in 1977 and firmly set them on paths through the planets.

■

FOR SUSPENSE AND SHEER WONDER, another Denver-built space program—this one named Magellan—rivaled the Viking mission to Mars. The Space Shuttle in 1989 carried the Martin-built Magellan spacecraft into Earth orbit and the start of a 143-million-mile trip to radar-map the hidden face of Venus. During a gestation period that extended more than a decade, the program came close to miscarriage on more than one occasion. It had been conceived in 1979 when the Jet Propulsion Laboratory, a contract offshoot of NASA, awarded a relatively modest $500,000 contract to Martin Marietta. It

Titan IV space launch vehicle

called for the design of a new spacecraft that could pierce the sulfuric acid veil hiding Venus and explore that atmosphere and, by means of radar mapping, the Venusian surface. Conceptually it was called VOIR, for Venus Orbiting Imaging Radar, and a second contract for a like amount was awarded to Hughes Space and Communications Group for the design of the radar.

It almost died aborning in 1980 for lack of budget support even within NASA, which was channeling most of its funds to manned space, primarily the Shuttle. Several more times in the early to mid-eighties the project appeared on the verge of extinction, even with a name change from VOIR to VRM, which stood for Venus Radar Mapper. Ultimately the project was saved through the ingenuity of the JPL and Martin Marietta and the persistence of the scientific community that pleaded the scientific value of a visit to the Earth's shrouded sister planet.

The ingenuity came about through the teaming of JPL and Martin Marietta scientists and engineers actively supported by other prominent scientists around the country who believed the Venus mission was a top priority. Existing designs and spare parts from other spacecraft programs that had already flown could be assembled into a spacecraft, they argued. Charlie Brown and Kenny Coughlin of Martin Marietta—Brown as project director and Coughlin as the chief marketer of the program—kept pushing the idea with NASA; it could cut program costs in half, they insisted. NASA agreed, and the Venus probe was on track again as a bargain basement spacecraft, later renamed again, this time for Ferdinand Magellan, the sixteenth-century Portuguese explorer.

J. Franklin McKinney, who became Martin Marietta's program manager when Charlie Brown retired in 1989 after thirteen years on the project, said the basic idea was to use off-the-shelf components, and "when we did need to build new hardware, to look at what technology was already available so we didn't have to develop from scratch." A spare high-gain antenna, twelve feet in diameter, was taken from Voyager leftovers. It would be used both for the radar mapping and for transmitting the data back to Earth. Voyager also contributed a bus—the basic framework or structure on which spacecraft electronics are mounted. The Ulysses spacecraft program contributed two radio telecommunications system amplifiers. The company's own Viking Mars project was the source of some unused thrusters. Some parts even came from exhibits in the National Air and Space Museum. It was little wonder that the Magellan spacecraft became known informally as "Secondhand Rose."

Magellan was finally scheduled to ride into Earth orbit aboard the Shuttle despite concern about the volatility of some of its propulsion components. Then the Challenger accident occurred early in 1986, and the Shuttle program was essentially shut down for nearly three years. The backlog of payloads awaiting rides on the Shuttle appeared to lessen Magellan's chances of flying. The delay caused the project to miss the most advantageous launch window when Earth and Venus were closest, and a black cloud—both figurative and literal—still hung over the program. A small electrical fire in the

Magellan clean room at Cape Canaveral left a fine black film over all the spacecraft's sensitive optic surfaces. It meant days of hand cleaning, but there was no permanent damage.

Launch day finally came on May 4, 1989. Magellan was carried to Earth orbit in the cargo bay of the Shuttle Discovery, where its

Magellan leaves Shuttle for Venus

crew started the spacecraft on its way to Venus, no short trip. The Magellan would have to travel unerringly for slightly more than fifteen months, on a 788-million-mile path that looped around the Sun before arriving at a specific point in space at a specific time when its target, Venus, would be there. A comparison of the accuracy involved in that rendezvous would be to fire a rifle from a revolving merry-go-round and have the bullet hit a target the size of a dime on another revolving merry-go-round seventy-five miles distant. Not only did it make the trip, its path through space was so accurate that a scheduled adjustment two days before Magellan was to enter orbit around Venus was not necessary.

On Wednesday, August 8, 1990—fifteen months and four days after leaving Canaveral—Martin Marietta engineers sitting at a bank of computers in the Denver astronautics facility transmitted a group of commands that would ultimately trigger computers aboard Magellan and initiate a chain of events that two days hence would place it in orbit around Venus. The forty thousand lines of programming sent from Denver were relayed through NASA's Jet Propulsion Laboratory in California to the Deep Space Network and on to Magellan. Because Venus and Earth are 143 million miles apart, the time required for a signal to reach that far is thirteen minutes, and it took that long again for Magellan's confirmation signal to be received on Earth by the anxious controllers at the company and at JPL.

James Vallela would later describe the tension-filled scene in *Martin Marietta Today* magazine. Among those at the company consoles in Colorado were engineers Chris Miller and Kenny Starnes, with Greg Privette and Rob Winslow, both members of Starnes's command and data subsystems group, hovering over them. It had been almost twenty-six minutes since the command was transmitted to Magellan, and Miller stared intently at the lower corner of his computer screen for a change in a single line of characters. The commands were critical and the tension was great. On the signals sent from Denver hung an automatic sequencing countdown and an eighty-three-second firing of a solid rocket motor on the spacecraft two days hence. If successful, it would slow Magellan from a speed of 24,000 miles per hour to 18,675 miles per hour, the Venus "capture" speed necessary for orbit around that planet.[1]

"There it is!" Miller suddenly exclaimed, the shift in the line of characters on the screen confirming the start of the sequence aboard Magellan. They would not be certain that the motor had fired for twenty-five minutes, the length of time communication is blacked out when the spacecraft is on the far side of Venus. But Miller and his colleagues knew the signal had been received and that Magellan would be rolling itself into position for Venus orbit entry and rotating its solar panels to the proper attitude. For the next fifty-one hours, they did nothing more than wait for confirmation that all the programmed events had taken place.

They were not idle hours. The Magellan engineers reviewed every step they had taken for the fifteen months since Magellan left Earth. Three floors below the Denver control room, senior staff engineer Michael J. Johnston watched over a set of computers that duplicated those aboard the spacecraft. They were running in parallel with the Magellan computers, processing the same data at the same time, so they didn't have to wait thirteen minutes to know if a problem arose.

Two days plus a few hours was a short time compared to the thirteen years since Frank McKinney first dreamed of sending a spacecraft to the far side of the Sun for a historic rendezvous with Venus, the second planet in the solar system. He was on the original team that structured the mission in 1977, and he credited "some very persistent scientists at NASA, JPL, and universities around the country for keeping the mission alive."

Friday, August 10, arrived soon enough. Now the pit of the stomach really tightened. Sure, the signals had been received, but would the bargain baby work properly? Had one too many corners been cut in the interest of cost? Early in the morning there was confirmation that the spacecraft solar panels had rotated into position for orbit insertion and that the two spacecraft recorders were running. At 10:28 A.M. Magellan slid behind Venus right on schedule, although telemetry didn't cease until 10:41 because of the thirteen-minute time lag.

"We won't know for sure that everything's okay until 11:06," Starnes pointed out. "If we get a signal too early—at 11:01—that means the rocket motor didn't fire, the spacecraft didn't slow down, and we aren't in orbit." When there was no signal one minute after eleven, the group visibly relaxed, and Starnes stopped gnawing on his knuckle. At 11:05 there was total concentration on the computer screen, watching again for a shift in the line of characters that would confirm VOI—Venus Orbit Insertion.

The clock read 11:06, and almost simultaneously the symbol on the screen changed and someone shouted, *"Signal!"* Cheers and applause exploded from the sixty or so Magellan people in the control room. Some unashamedly cried.[2]

The scene was almost duplicated at JPL, where NASA and Mar-

Jubilant Magellan team

tin Marietta people experienced the same feelings of relief, then satisfaction, then jubilation—and finally just plain joy. Charlie Brown, in the JPL control room as a guest of Frank McKinney, clasped his successor's hand. Both men had tears in their eyes.

"This is like watching one of your kids do something really special," Brown said softly. Two hours later, back in Denver, the control room was virtually empty; only a handful of engineers were watching the data stream in from Magellan in its elliptical orbit around Venus. It was not the end, of course, only another beginning. As the banner someone had hung on the wall suggested, LET'S MAKE A MAP!

For the next three years Magellan's radar pierced Venus's dense atmosphere and sent back the most extraordinary set of photographic strips. When pieced together they made an incredible picture-map of the Venuscape. The first so-called global maps of Venus were released by NASA on October 29, 1991, fourteen months after the radar imaging began. John Wilford wrote in *The New York Times*:

> New radar images from the Magellan spacecraft reveal that the planet Venus has apparently been completely resurfaced by volcanic eruptions and its second-highest mountain seems to be covered with fresh lava from an active volcano. . . .
>
> The first global maps of Venus, compiled from mosaics of radar images taken by the spacecraft as it orbits the planet . . . are already fueling a debate among scientists on the nature of Venusian volcanism—whether there was one long episode of catastrophic volcanic activity 800 million years ago or there has been a continuous history of eruptions that have steadily spread lava over the plains and transformed the surface over the last 800 million years.
>
> "We're still debating that question," said Dr. Stephen Saunders, the project's chief scientist. "We probably have a better global map of Venus now than we have of Earth because most of the ocean basins on Earth are so poorly mapped."[3]

Wilford went on to say that geologists were also fascinated by the mosaics showing "scatterings of large meteorite-impact craters; broad plains smoothed by fairly recent lava floods but occasionally etched by wide, sinuous channels that meander for scores of miles, and an equatorial belt thick with volcanic mountains and deep fracture zones."

Magellan project scientists also reported "erosion patterns suggesting the presence of high winds shifting sand and dust, but saw no evidence that liquid water could have existed on Venus any more recently than nearly 1 billion years ago," the story continued. Dr. John A. Wood, astrogeologist with the Smithsonian Astrophysical Observatory in Cambridge, Massachusetts, noted evidence of very recent volcanic activity, "perhaps less than ten years old," in the first sharp images of a towering mountain known as Maat Mons, the second highest Venus mountain, rising five miles above the surrounding plains. He noted that nearly all the Venusian mountain peaks, including Maxwell Montes with an elevation of more than six miles, appeared bright in the radar images, presumably because the soil had weathered and had been transformed into highly reflective materials like iron sulfide. Such was not the case with Maat Mons, the surface of which appeared dark, Dr. Woods was quoted as saying, which was evidence that it was "most likely fresh lava."[4]

He called Maat Mons "the best candidate we've seen for finding an active volcano on Venus," and Wilford noted that the only other places in the solar system known to have active volcanoes were Earth, Jupiter's satellite Io, and Neptune's Triton.

It its first seven months in orbit above a slowly rotating Venus, the Martin Marietta–built Magellan and its Hughes-built radar mapper produced photographlike images of about 80 percent of the cloud-shrouded surface. At the time of the NASA news conference seven months later, Magellan was more than midway through its second mapping cycle. The second time it was looking for changes in the surface as signs of volcanic activity and landslides, and was filling in strips in the mosaic missed the first time around. The spacecraft was in excellent condition and was scheduled to radar-survey the entire planet a second time, beginning in January 1992. As they said back on Earth, that's "mission success."

But the incredibly beautiful radar images did not just flow like magma from Venus. While its overall performance was merely magnificent, the spacecraft had developed a personality all its own, as Ken Leadbetter and three of his Martin Marietta team stationed at JPL could attest. Cynthia L. Haynie, a thirty-four-year-old electrical engineer with two master's degrees, one in computer science and the other in science and technology management, was a member of the "upload" team. She represented the company on the crew responsible for periodically updating Magellan and for sending it specific instructions to change its behavior.

A native of Dallas, Haynie had been with Martin Marietta for six years, starting out on the Peacekeeper ICBM program, then switching to Magellan about four years prior to the beginning of mapping. She took her bachelor's degree from Texas A&M and her first master's from Denver University. Her other advanced degree was earned at Pepperdine while working on the Magellan mission at JPL.

The other two company people more or less permanently assigned to JPL for the duration of the mission were Michael K. Bailey and James C. Neuman. An aerospace engineering graduate of the University of Arizona, thirty-two-year-old Bailey had spent all but three of his seven years with Martin Marietta working on Magellan. His specialty was computer sequence design, particularly for future mission extensions. Neuman, the "granddaddy" of the three at forty-two, had been with Martin Marietta since 1969. He first learned about the program in a carpool in 1982 and asked to transfer to it.

Neuman said he worked on manned, unmanned, and Earth-orbiting programs, but never on planetary ones. It intrigued him, he said, and his boss was good enough to allow him to transfer. "This was the scaled-down version from VOIR," he said. "The good news was, 'You've won the program.' The bad news was, 'We don't have any money.' So we had to rescope the program, and I was involved in the proposal for the new craft."[5] Neuman, Bailey, and Haynie worked for Leadbetter, who described them as a solid team linked even more closely by adversity. The visitor seeing only the impressive imagery coming from Venus would have had to ask, "What adversity?"

But it seemed the spacecraft was a bit flaky at times. Some on the project said it occasionally would "go to sleep." Neuman thought it was more a case of Magellan becoming "distracted," sometimes losing its focus on Venus and sometimes even on Mother Earth. Cynthia Haynie, who seemed to have more of a woman's intuition about the habits of an occasionally errant child, preferred to think of the spacecraft's lapses as "walkabouts." Mike Bailey agreed with her.[6] The term as they used it is derived from the movie *Crocodile Dundee*, where the characters were in the habit of taking a walk through the backcountry "to find themselves." It wasn't a matter of getting away from it all, she said, but rather just basically to find themselves.

The first time Magellan took a walkabout, the spacecraft was "gone" for seventeen hours, Neuman said, "and we worked around the clock to get it back. It scared the heck out of us, but when it came back, it found us. We didn't find it. Once we got it back, we knew we had an outstanding spacecraft and that it was doing what it was designed to do and doing it very well. We also knew that if it did it again, it would know how to get back." One headline writer pleaded, "Magellan, please call home." It finally did.

On another occasion, Neuman said, there was an indication the spacecraft had gone to sleep for a little while. Haynie called the short lapses "strollabouts." When they got it back that time, Neuman said, it was pointing incorrectly, "and we worked all night to get the pointing back. We could have gone home to sleep and come back the next day to correct the pointing, in which case we would have missed eight orbits of data, but instead we worked all night and missed only three-and-a-half orbits of data. The team spirit was pretty strong. We hated to lose even a minute of mapping data."

Cynthia Haynie remembered another time when the spacecraft was "coning," meaning it was scanning back and forth, searching for Earth, when it should have had a fixed focus. In telling the story, she frequently included Magellan in the personal pronoun *we*, almost as if she were up in space with it. "Normally, we know exactly where Earth is, but that time we didn't know. So we bang some commands up, hoping to get through, and when we finally stop the coning, the recovery procedure begins. Only the recovery really wasn't built at the time. . . . We kind of built it as we went. If you ever want to see a team work together, that was the time to see it. . . . There was a lot of anxiousness and a lot of people working twenty-four hours a day, seven days a week . . . but it really was a team effort."[7]

So much for the "anxieties" and the team and mission success. Well into its third year orbiting Earth's sister planet, Magellan had amassed an entire atlas of Venusian maps and had contributed more information about Venus than had been gathered in all prior planetary investigation. The radar images sent back by Magellan had resolution about ten times better than the best obtained previously by two Soviet Venera spacecraft. About midway through Magellan's first mapping cycle, *Science* magazine enthused in headline and story:

MAGELLAN PAINTS A PORTRAIT OF VENUS
The best images yet of Venus are providing unprecedented insights into the planet's geology—and whetting researchers' appetites for more.

Far exceeding NASA mission requirements, Magellan completed a third eight-month mapping cycle of the planet's surface and a subsequent eight-month gravity study to learn more about the planet's core. The original contract requirement was for two mapping cycles totaling sixteen months and covering 70 percent of the planet's surface. After three full cycles and thirty-one months of orbital activity, Magellan had mapped approximately 98 percent of the Venus surface. The picturelike radar images provided scientists with an unprecedented, highly detailed look at a world heretofore shrouded not only by distance but by permanent cloud cover.

When the radar finally stopped functioning with the completion of the third mapping cycle, the spacecraft continued to orbit the planet collecting gravity data. By analyzing subtle changes in the orbit, scientists on Earth were able to map the variations in the interior of the planet and compare them with surface features. For example, when Magellan passed over a dense region of the planet's interior, the spacecraft accelerated in its orbit, thereby identifying that region. When combined with surface imaging, the gravity observations provided an improved understanding of the forces of tectonics and volcanism that shape the planet. Unlike Earth, there is a strong correlation on Venus between internal concentrations of mass and surface topography.

On the anniversary of its third full year of operation, Magellan had completed 8,351 orbits of Venus and had traveled a total distance of more than 1 billion miles: 336 million miles in orbit plus the 788-million-mile trip from Earth three years before. Among several prestigious national honors awarded the Magellan team was the 1992 Goddard Memorial Trophy presented by the National Space Club. Others included the National Air and Space Museum Award, NASA Public Service and Group Achievement awards, and the 1992 Group Diploma of the Federation Aeronautique Internationale—the same group, incidentally, that issued Glenn L. Martin his pilot's certificate No. 2 more than eighty years before.[8]

PART IX

Desert Storm, the Proving Ground

1990–92

■

CHAPTER 38

Escape in the Desert

■

B ob Boddiford stopped his four-wheel-drive vehicle. In the predawn darkness, he could barely make out the shapes of two of the three cars that had been following him. They hadn't risked using headlights since leaving their residence compound outside Kuwait City. Roving patrols of the Iraqi invader were everywhere.

It hadn't been easy. Driving across the desert was difficult in the best of times. This morning was the worst. Twenty people, five of them children, had crowded into three vehicles. After packing food, water, and extra gasoline, they had been able to squeeze in only the barest of personal belongings plus one tiny terrier whose mistress, unable to leave her pet, had tucked the tiny dog into her pocketbook. They had been driving across the sand for two hours without benefit of roads, signposts, or landmarks—only three power lines that would, it was hoped, lead west toward the border with Saudi Arabia and safety. Their only other guides were a dime-sized compass in the handle of a Swiss army knife and a makeshift map hand-drawn from memory.[1]

Bob Boddiford could make out the dim profiles of only two vehicles where there had been three. He turned back, past the other four-wheel-drive vehicle, past a small Chevy front-wheel drive, until he came to the fourth car, also a front-wheeled Chevy, which had bogged down. Continued attempts to move forward spun the wheels deeper and deeper into the soft sand. They didn't like stopping after four hours of uninterrupted progress in the end-run they hoped they were making of the Iraqi forces.

Boddiford had not bargained on this Lawrence of Arabia role when he went to Kuwait in 1987 to head a Martin Marietta Data Systems program for the Kuwaiti air force. The program had grown from a small support staff to a good-sized group of people running a network of communications. Originally a contract to design and support, "the more we did, the more they wanted us to do," Boddiford recalled.

He and his wife Jan lived in an apartment complex right on the Persian Gulf, south of Kuwait City, where most of the Martin Marietta families lived, along with several dozen other contractor people from the States and elsewhere. It was a pleasant international community less than a block from the beach and only a twenty-minute drive to work at the Air Force base.

On the Thursday that Iraq invaded Kuwait, August 2, 1990, there were nine Martin Marietta Data Systems employees in Kuwait, plus five wives and five children. A green card British national and nine Filipino engineers made up the complement working on the Martin Marietta contract. With dependents, there were thirty-eight in all under Boddiford's charge on that fateful morning. Jan Boddiford had returned to the States for their son Doug's graduation from college in Orlando.

At six o'clock in the morning, Boddiford was getting ready for work when the telephone rang. The caller, an ex-Marine pilot who worked for the Kuwaiti air force, was Bob's regular contact in a "warden" network established by the U.S. Embassy to keep key U.S. nationals apprised of activities of interest. He spoke slowly and without emotion: "Bob, the Iraqis have come across the northern border, and we advise you not to go into the base today. Just stay put, and we'll get back to you." Then the telephone went dead.

That was the last phone contact the Boddiford group had with the embassy. Less than two hours later Iraqi tanks, trucks, and other armored vehicles rumbled down the highway, separating them from the beach. Kuwait is about the length of New Jersey, and that's all the time it took an armored column to make the trip. It was also the last Jan Boddiford heard from her husband for almost two weeks. It was three o'clock in the morning on August 3 when she got the word in

Orlando. Doug Boddiford had picked up a broadcast from CNN and awakened his mother to repeat the news bulletin:

KUWAIT HAS BEEN INVADED.

In Kuwait, all the Martin Marietta people lived in the same complex of apartment buildings. With telephones disrupted, Boddiford visited each individual or family to relay the scant information he had. Each was advised to stay within the compound wall. Telephone service did resume later in the day but was limited to about a mile in range. There was no way to contact the embassy twenty miles away in Kuwait City.

After a couple of days, Boddiford remembered a friend of his wife's who worked at the embassy as a secretary. She, too, lived nearby, so he called her: "Odessa, what are you hearing from the embassy?" She told him to come over. They had some hand-held radios with which to maintain contact with the embassy. That was how they stayed in contact with what was going on, Bob later recalled.

Tanks rumble into Kuwait City suburb

That was Saturday, day three of the Iraqi occupation. Basically, Boddiford said, the embassy was advising through the radio contact to stay put. "We're talking. We're arranging. We'll get everybody out."

"That was what we wanted to hear," Boddiford added. "Not only did we want to get out, but could we all go at the same time? They said they would get a plane in here. We were working for a U.S. contractor. We'd all go—Americans, Filipinos, Brits, whomever. That's basically what we were waiting to have happen."

There was very little harassment the first three or four days. The first troops that came were crack troops—the highly touted Republican Guard, presumably. There were roadblocks when the Americans went out scrounging for food. Panic buying had set in. They tried to buy whatever was available because they didn't know how long they would be there.

"They would stop us at the roadblocks, look at our paperwork, ask where we were going, check the trunk . . . that type of thing," Boddiford said. The first week there was a false sense of security. "I mean, the Iraqi were over there, so to speak, and we were over here, waiting, watching—everybody really hoping we'd get out the next day or the next day."

Almost every day someone tried to get to the border by simply driving down the highway. But the Iraqis had blocked all the exit points and sent them back. "We had one family that must have tried twice a day for two weeks, but they never made it," Boddiford said. For the most part, it was agreed that if they were going to get out, they wanted to go collectively. "We had eighteen people in eight families, including five kids under eight and five wives—one of them five months pregnant. So we all decided that we could support one another a little bit better if we tried to do things together rather than individually."

The Filipino engineers and their families had lived in another building about two miles away. Chris Bacud, their leader, and Boddiford decided early on to keep the Filipinos separate from the Americans. "According to what we were hearing on CNN and the Voice of America, the Iraqis were not threatening the Filipinos. Americans and Europeans, yes, but not Filipinos. So we decided we would try not to involve them in our possible plight," Boddiford added.

"Chris and I met every day. He drove over to my building, or I'd drive to his. There were soldiers everywhere. He updated me on what was going on in the Filipino community, and I did the same for him on the Americans. That's how we stayed in contact. If he had some extra food, he would say, 'Hey, I found this bag of rice.' If we had some extra, we'd give him some. We never knew how long we were going to be there," Boddiford said.

They didn't know what to expect but figured they had better make arrangements if there was to be a big sea assault. "We had located a big house rented by Americans who were on vacation. The house was about three miles inland from the coast, and we managed to get the key. Chris and I agreed that if anything really happened and we had to vacate, we'd put everybody into the cars and drive back to this house."

Boddiford said the perspective was different from the time of the Iran hostages, when "we would sit around listening to the radio wishing the United States would 'go get 'em.'

"We were sitting over there thinking, 'Maybe you guys shouldn't come so quick.' We watched CNN, and they threw a lot at you. We also listened to VOA and to the BBC, both of which were less emotional and fairly accurate.

"So if we heard something twice, we tended to believe it. And if we didn't hear it on BBC or VOA, we discounted CNN. . . . When they put on the pictures of the Kurds . . . when they gassed them . . . everybody really got upset. Everybody was nervous about the possibility of gas being used."

By the second week, Boddiford said, activity picked up on the beachfront. The Iraqis started setting up bases on the other side of the highway from the apartment compound. The whole beachfront was taken over—all the houses, villas, and boat clubs.

"More and more soldiers started drifting down in buses and trucks," Boddiford said. "They were more tattered and torn. They started stealing cars. There were incidents of break-ins and rapes. Soldiers started coming into our compound. They would sit down and have coffee and tea. They would come to the door looking for food."

Then they had another scare. The Iraqis began rounding up foreign nationals in a building just south of Boddiford's group.

"I happened to be with an embassy couple with a radio when they were advised to come in. Transportation was to be sent for them. That would have ended our communications with the embassy, so we kinda talked this embassy man into leaving his two radios with us. He wasn't supposed to do that. Even though we would not have an official 'call sign-on,' he did leave the radios for us, so at least we could listen. The senior embassy guy, who lived in our neighborhood, later came back down the coast and gave us official call signs. Now we became part of that embassy circuit and could call in once a day to find out what was what."

Boddiford kept one radio and gave the other to a fellow contractor representative. "He wasn't too receptive at first," Bob said, "because having a radio was not a good thing. The Iraqis had threatened to shoot anyone caught with one. So nobody wanted the damned radios. We carried them in gunnysacks. When they stopped our car, we'd kick them under the seat. But this fellow reluctantly took it and became part of our communications circle."

It wasn't long after, Boddiford said, that some drunken Iraqi soldiers came into the apartment compound one night. The Americans were in the habit of locking the gates and had set up a security system for the compound with patrols around the clock. About sixty men shared the watch, three hours on at a time, then off for six hours.

"There were three soldiers," Boddiford said. "Two of them were dead drunk. They climbed over the eight-foot wall and were spotted by two of our guys who had the night watch. One of our men, Don Nichol, confronted them. They pushed him around a bit and stole his watch. But he caused enough commotion by shouting challenges at them that he roused the rest of our group. We figured they couldn't shoot all of us, so we all went into the yard and just stood around them. They wanted cigarettes and more booze. One of the people living with us spoke Arabic, fortunately. He finally talked them into leaving by offering to get them both.

"That was around five-thirty at night. After they had left, everybody was kind of wired, and the women were really scared. So we decided we were going to move inland to that other apartment we had set up. By joining the twenty Americans already living there, we'd total about forty. That would make us more secure, we figured. About 10 o'clock, the phone rang. It was the contractor rep I'd given the radio to. He said he had to see me and wanted to come over. It was after curfew, and I told him we'd just had the incident with the drunken soldiers; perhaps he should wait until morning. 'No, Bob,' he said. 'I've got to see you tonight. I've got to give you something.' I thought he probably wanted to give me back the radio, so I told him, 'Okay, come on over.'

"He did give me the radio but then told me they were going to try to escape the next day. One of their guys had found an old route leading through the desert. There had been no activity on it for a couple of days. I got out this old map we had from the Holiday Inn and asked him to show me where they planned to go.

" 'We don't really know,' he told me. 'We're going to drive to this junkyard on the right and some sheds on the left, then get off the main road and see if we can find an old sand road that big trucks used to take to get access to the power lines that run into the desert. And when that runs out, we'll just head southwest.' "

Boddiford said he drew a small map, based on the meager directions. Kuwait is shaped like a crooked letter *L*. The bottom, or southeastern, arm of the *L* was literally covered with Iraqi troops, and all roads were blocked. Near the bottom of the upright leg of the *L*—to the northwest—was another blockage. So their plan was to drive north to avoid the troops in the eastern portion, then head southwest through the heel of the *L* and a hole they hoped existed between the two enemy forces.

"Eventually, if lucky," Boddiford said, "they'd just run into Saudi Arabia." Having worked there once, he knew there was a border road that connected Saudi towns, and he was able to find that road on the map.

The group planning the dawn escape had five cars and were to leave about 5:30 the next morning. A convoy of more cars was out of the question, they figured.

"Okay," Boddiford agreed. "If we decide to leave, we'll give you an hour's lead and then come behind you so we won't look like a crowd."

With that settled, Boddiford called all his people together. It was now eleven o'clock at night. They talked about the events of the day and how it was getting worse. Then he outlined the options: Move inland and continue to sweat things out or make a run for it.

"We talked for about an hour, until midnight," Boddiford said, "and I told them, 'Go talk to your wives and then come back.' So they came back. And to the man, except for one guy (a British national) who elected to stay, they said enough had happened that they were willing to try to get the hell out of there.

"Well, we spent that whole night, what was left of it, siphoning gasoline from one car to another. We couldn't take everything. We had eighteen people for four vehicles, only two of them with four-wheel drive. The other two were small Chevys. We had to put our Persian cat and another family's Doberman to sleep. That was rough, but we had no room for them and couldn't risk a possible alarm. One lady came to me with her little dog—a miniature terrier named

Winston Churchill. 'I'll put him in my pocketbook, and you'll never know he's there,' she told me. And she did just that and lowered the lid, and you couldn't tell the dog was there. She would have died if she had to leave that dog.

"So we took off right around five-thirty or six o'clock in the morning. We went north and found the sand road. We got lost several times. Finally, we just backtracked, and every road we found going southwest we took."

He said they actually saw signs of other activity in the area, signs that native people had gone that way. But they were never sure of their course. One of the other Martin Marietta men in the group was Issam Al Sharif (who later worked in Baltimore), a Syrian-born U.S. citizen who spoke Arabic. They had hoped to find a guide, someone who knew the desert, and eventually they did come upon a farm with sheep and camels and a lone shepherd.

"Issam spoke to him. He was a bedouin, and he knew the way through the desert. So we asked him to take us and offered to pay him in cash. His brother, on the next farm over, joined the negotiations," Boddiford said. It wasn't a yes-or-no deal. It was back and forth. The bedouins were worried that if they took the Americans and were caught, they would be shot, which was true. So they sat down and talked some more. Then they argued that even if they agreed to guide, how would they get back once the group reached Saudi Arabia? The negotiations were all in Arabic, and Issam came back each time and gave Boddiford the translation.

"Finally, I told Issam to tell them we'd give them one of the small cars to drive back to their farms. If he took us to the border, we'd give him a car to keep." With that condition plus the money, the bedouins agreed and squeezed into the cars. There were now twenty people in four cars.

They were just about halfway to the Saudi border, Boddiford said, when one of the Chevys got stuck in the sand, right down to its axle. "We worked for an hour trying to get it out," he said. "But we had to abandon it and shuffle the people around. So now we had twenty in three cars."

They drove for another half-hour, until they came to the base of a long sand dune where there must have been fifty or sixty cars, all stopped. Two of the cars were from the group that had preceded them that morning. They had actually been shot at by an Iraqi armored patrol that was now blocking the way at the top of the hill. The Iraqis were telling everybody to "go back to Kuwait, go back to Kuwait; we're not going to let you through.

"Some of the groups actually turned back," Boddiford continued, "but we had already invested too much time and emotion. I felt if we turned back, we'd never try it again. At that point our bedouin guides refused to go any farther because of the Iraqis. So I gave them the keys to the stuck car we had abandoned and we paid them, and they took off on foot, back the way we had come.

"Before leaving they did point the way we should go if we could get through. We guessed we were just about halfway, maybe a little more. We were about at that point where we had planned to turn southwest, straight for Saudi Arabia. Our spirits weren't too high. It must have been 120 degrees, and we were just standing around talking about what we could do. Maybe another fifteen minutes had passed when someone noticed that the Iraqi troops appeared to be climbing aboard their vehicles. Then their halftrack started up, then the trucks. And they just took off, heading east, as if they had received a call to go someplace else.

"That did it. The Martin Marietta people crowded into the two front-wheel-drive vehicles. Only a driver was left in the small Chevy so that it would be lighter and not get stuck in dunes. Once we saw it was clear ahead, we put our foot on the gas and just went . . . pretty much like "Rat Patrol" . . . just flying across the desert, actually leaving the ground on some bumps. The kids thought it was great.

"The Chevy was following me. I had one guy watching it and told him, 'If that little car stops, we'll go back and pick him up.' But nothing stopped us. We just drove as fast as we could for the border."

Actually, the people in the Boddiford car were so intent on the Chevy that they became separated from John Wood's car. He had started up the hill ahead of them to see which direction they should take.

"Wood thought I was going to wait for him," Boddiford said, "but I thought he was leaving. So I took off, and it must have been forty minutes of uninterrupted, full-power, uphill straightaway before we realized we were no longer together. When we finally leveled off and realized John Wood wasn't with us, there was considerable concern because there were wives in one car and husbands in the other. We waited for another ten minutes, but no John. We could see through binoculars a cloud of sand and dust some distance away to the west. We drove toward the dust, and sure enough, they were there with another group of vehicles that had been paralleling our path."

The Martin Marietta people had been separated for more than an hour, and Boddiford said there was quite a reunion on the spot.

The other group of cars had been following a Kuwaiti guide who had halted their convoy indefinitely to wait for some missing cars.

"There must have been fifty vehicles in all, spread out in a big fan," Boddiford said, "and it made me sort of nervous to be part of this mass just sitting there waiting. So John took out the compass, and we decided to strike out on our own, heading straight southwest, we hoped, for the border. As we drove off, we had to laugh when we heard some of the others shout: 'There go some people who know where they're going.' Once more we were racing across the desert, and you could see from the cloud of dust that others were following," Boddiford said. "It was like Oklahoma. We just kept going for maybe another forty-five minutes, until we saw some outbuildings ahead and to our right. They turned out to be a Saudi border post, and we came to a screeching halt right in the courtyard. A guard in a green uniform just stood there: no smile, no sign, no nothing.

"I jumped out of the car, ran up to him, and shouted, 'Saudi? Saudi? Saudi?' I said it three times, and finally the guy breaks into a big grin and answers me back:

" 'Yes! Yes! Yes! Welcome! Welcome! Welcome!' "

The date was August 12. Ten days since the invasion. Bob Bod-

Boddiford and friends, safe in Saudi Arabia

diford estimated his little band had been on the desert approximately nine hours since their predawn departure. It took them nine more hours to be processed through the Saudi border entry. The Saudis were ill-equipped to handle the hundreds of refugees streaming through, each requiring an entry visa.

The drive down the highway inside Saudi Arabia from their entry point to Riyadh took seven more hours. Boddiford said they were "a pretty motley crew" when they showed up at the hotel and told the desk clerk where they had come from. It was 6:30 in the morning, more than twenty-four hours from the start of their escape the previous day.

Boddiford's next move was to find a telephone and call his wife and sons in Orlando. It was the first time they knew he was safe. Then he called the company, and "they made arrangements to fly us out the next day—even met us at the airport in New York to make sure we all made connections home."

The Boddiford group's thrilling escape in the first days of the Middle East war was only one small vignette of Martin Marietta's participation in what turned out to be a five-month proving ground of people and their technology. The Boddifords had no way of knowing that Martin Marietta was already gearing up for involvement in Kuwait and Iraq that would rival any combat support it had done since World War II and Korea.

CHAPTER 39

"His Eyes and His Voice"

■

F ive months later, Desert Storm began. And fourteen Martin
Marietta systems—a dozen of them unclassified—and support people were in the front lines. Their involvement actually began August 5, three days after Saddam Hussein unleashed
his army on Kuwait. In a telephone call to Richard Howell, Martin
Marietta's Patriot program director at Orlando, the prime contractor, Raytheon Corporation, expressed an urgent need for the enhanced version with antiballistic missile capability.[1]

The original Patriot, the Army's mobile surface-to-air guided
missile for defense, was designed to defend against enemy aircraft, as
a replacement for all U.S. Nike Hercules and Improved Hawk air
defense systems worldwide. Patriot actually evolved from a development program that began in the mid-sixties. It was called SAM-D, an
acronym for Surface-to-Air Missile–Development. Full-scale development began in 1972.

In the Patriot system, the host-phased array radar and the computer control up to sixteen mobile launchers, each a firing unit of
eight Patriot missiles. The system allows simultaneous engagement of
multiple targets. The name PATRIOT is actually an acronym for
Phased Array Track Intercept of Target. But the system was so well
named and the acronym became so widely used that it seldom is
written in all capital letters anymore.

Patriot launch

At the time Dick Howell took that telephone call from his customer, there were only three Patriots in existence with first-
generation antiballistic missile capability. Designated as PAC-2
missiles, they were initial articles intended only for the PAC-2 development program.

"Our customer was asking, 'How fast can you rev up?' " Howell
said. "We were not scheduled to deliver the first PAC-2s until January. We had had twelve consecutive successes in test firings at White
Sands against a variety of targets, including the interception of another Patriot. So we knew we had a good system, but we hadn't
ramped up for production yet." The program was immediately put
on a crash basis, with two twelve-hour shifts. Each group of eight
missiles, packed in shipping containers that double as launch canisters in the field, was trucked with special security the sixty miles to
Patrick Air Force Base, just south of Cape Canaveral. By the end of
August, seventeen missiles were ready for delivery. In the next several
months Patriots were coming off the line at a rate of eighty to ninety
a month.

"We had four hundred and twenty-five missiles in Saudi Arabia by the first of January when the United States committed our forces over there," Howell said. It had all happened on the strength of that one phone call. Contract paperwork would not follow for some time. The response by Patriot project people was "unbelievable," in the eyes of Howell and other managers of Martin Marietta's Electronics, Information and Missiles Group. Within that organization the Missile Systems company was principal subcontractor to Raytheon for the Patriot missile and its launcher.

In that role, Martin Marietta actually manufactured 60 percent of the Patriot missile itself and 25 percent of the entire system. The company manufactured the aft section, assembled the entire missile, and installed the warhead. In addition, it manufactured the missile containers and the launcher vehicles. As the prime contractor to the Army, Raytheon supplied the guidance for the missile and manufactured the host-phased array radar that controls the system.

From the outset, the Patriot pipeline from factory to field was very direct: Orlando to Patrick to the Middle East. At Patrick, the Patriots were loaded on Air Force C5 or C141 cargo jets for direct flight to Saudi Arabia, most often to Dhahran but occasionally to Riyadh. On at least one occasion that was documented, missiles that left the Florida factory one day knocked Scuds out of the sky two days later. The motivational impact on the factory floor was unprecedented. The Martin Marietta men and women who had put them together saw actual Patriot intercepts of Scuds on television, either at home or on closed-circuit sets on the factory floor.

For the average engineer and factory worker, most of the military systems they produce prove themselves only in test programs. One never expects to see them actually used in combat and of course hopes there will never be that need. But if the systems are "fired in anger," they are expected to perform. Day after day, Desert Storm produced repeated stories of highly successful performance—mission success in capital letters—for the even-dozen systems fielded by Martin Marietta in the Middle East. Four of them—Patriot, LANTIRN, TADS, and Hellfire—are generally credited with strongly influencing the quick and successful conclusion of that one-hundred-day campaign.

Most visible, of course, were the "Scud-busting" Patriots. Dick Howell recalled later that General Carl Vouno, the Army chief of staff, had been quite skeptical at the start that the program would be able to deliver Patriots in a timely fashion. He had promised the program manager, Colonel Bruce Garrett, at the Army Missile Command in Huntsville, Alabama, that he would call less than a month later, on September 1, to check on its progress. As promised, the general called the colonel, and as Colonel Garrett later repeated to Howell: "I told General Vouno: 'Chief, we have sixteen Patriot PAC-2 missiles on a C5A at Patrick Air Force Base, ready to leave. They're all yours.' "[2]

"Then we really started turning them out," Howell said, "eighty to ninety a month until we had four hundred and twenty-five of them in the desert when the fighting broke out." When newspaper and television reporters discovered the missiles were actually built in Florida, not at Raytheon's Massachusetts plant, they beat a path to the Martin Marietta plant in Orlando.

Of course that fact had never been a secret in Orlando. Patriot-fever had been running high within the production team. All together there were thirty-three Patriot-firing batteries deployed in the Middle East—twenty in Saudi Arabia, six in Turkey, and seven in Israel. Patriots were deployed from Tel Aviv and Haifa in Israel and from Riyadh and Dhahran in Saudi Arabia. They were fired in a "shoot-shoot" mode. The doctrine was to fire two every time to make certain the incoming Scud was intercepted. After the first Scud attack and Patriot intercept at Dhahran on January 18, 1991, one U.S. soldier was quoted: "Up to that point, we hadn't felt personally threatened. Now we realized we were within range. Thank goodness the United States spent millions and billions of dollars on defense, and thank goodness they funded Patriot."

A total of 573 Patriot PAC-2 missiles were sent to the theater of operations. The exact boxscore for Patriot knockdowns of Iraqi Scuds was debated for months after Desert Storm. But quite apart from its tactical role, Patriot was the single most important political element in keeping the Israelis out of the war and thereby assuring full Arab participation in the successful allied coalition. Lieutenant General Charles A. Horner, commander of Coalition Air Forces, said it best on January 19, 1991, on a visit to the Orlando plant. "When the history of Desert Storm is written, the Patriot system will be singled out as the key. Patriot's success has ensured coalition solidarity."

President Bush, on a visit to Raytheon factory workers after the cease-fire, added his own view: "Thank God that when those Scuds came in, the people of Saudi Arabia and Israel and the brave forces of our coalition had more to protect their lives than some abstract theory of deterrence. Thank God for the Patriot missile."[3]

After that first Patriot intercept over Dhahran, red-white-and-blue "Scud-buster" T-shirts became the uniform practically over-

"Scud Buster" builders

night in the Orlando production plant. How the T-shirts came about is a sidebar story of employee fervor and team spirit. Lou Mazzonetto, Patriot procurement manager, had a ready-made, built-in source when Mel Schubert came to him and said, "We ought to have a T-shirt, Lou. Where can we get them?"[4] Schubert had drawn up some artwork, which Lou took home to his daughter Linda and her husband, Bill Galbreath, who operated a small shop making T-shirts for tourists.

"They made up the red, white, and blue color patterns and ran sixty of them," Lou said. "By the time we took delivery of the sixty, I had orders for nine hundred." Originally intended primarily for project employees, more than forty thousand shirts had been sold to employees and the public by the time the Middle East war ended. They became *the* collector's item. And there was still a modest demand for them eight months later.

■

MUCH HAS BEEN WRITTEN in the news columns as well as on the editorial pages about Patriot and its success. And Americans saw it succeed brilliantly and awesomely on their television sets practically

F-16s with LANTIRN pods

every evening, more often if they watched CNN throughout the day. Of equal or perhaps even greater value to the successful outcome of Desert Storm were two electro-optical systems built by Martin Marietta, also at Orlando. One was LANTIRN, an acronym for Low Altitude Navigation and Targeting Infrared System for Night. As its name suggests, the system has two functions: navigation and targeting. It enables fighter pilots to fly and destroy targets in total darkness or heavy overcast at altitudes as low as two hundred feet and at speeds in excess of five hundred miles per hour. Flying virtually on the deck, in any terrain, and at that speed makes them invisible to enemy radar.

LANTIRN has been one of the most dramatic advances in the history of modern air power. It opened the operating envelope of fighter aircraft from four or five hours of daylight, weather permitting, to around-the-clock operations. As with Patriot, Mission Success was at the heart of LANTIRN development. Prior to Desert Storm, the system had logged 8,138 hours of flight on 5,208 separate Air Force missions without a failure. Pilots, generals, chiefs of staff, and even a senator had flown it, some after only minimal training but all with high praise for its reliability and ease of operation.

When United States forces began Desert Storm in January 1991, their F15 and F16 fighter aircraft were equipped with only the LAN-TIRN navigation pod. Later missions included both navigation and targeting pods. Two of the pilots who flew over Iraq later visited Orlando and spoke to the Martin Marietta folks who built LANTIRN.

"The LANTIRN system to me was just absolutely unbelievable," said Captain Matt Riehl, an F15E pilot from Kansas City, who flew twenty-nine sorties during Desert Storm. "So simple to work, and it works so well. The first night of the war, when we went in, we were entirely comfortable that we were safe. I personally saw the best the Iraqis had, MIG-29s, up there. But with your NAV pod, we were able to fly down low, and they had absolutely no idea that we were there. Had we not had your NAV pod," he added, "I personally feel that we would have lost two or three airplanes . . . friends of mine that wouldn't have come home."[5]

Major Larry Widner, another F15E pilot who flew with both the navigation and targeting components of LANTIRN, thanked Martin Marietta employees for building such an excellent system. He said he had zero failures with the navigation pod and that he flew about twenty combat missions with the targeting pod, also without failures. "I personally took out a Scud that was parked underneath a bridge at three o'clock in the morning. A lot of good people did that," Major Widner added. "I feel that the LANTIRN system, especially the targeting pod, definitely shortened the war and saved lives. They could run, but they couldn't hide."

On another targeting pod mission that involved a downed air-craft, the pilot told the assembled LANTIRN workers: "I did not use the targeting pod to drop a bomb but rather to locate this downed airplane and consequently save the pilot who had ejected. So it was marvelous, and I thank you from the bottom of my heart and the bottom of my squadron's heart."

One of the truly amazing facts of the technological miracle demonstrated during Desert Storm was the user-friendliness of some of the systems deployed. The LANTIRN targeting pod was a prime example. They came off the Orlando production line about midway through the Middle East war. They went directly to Saudi Arabia and were hung on the F15Es.

"We sent everything we had," recalled Murray W. Garbrick, LANTIRN program vice president. "I mean, we stripped the factory of all the targeting pods, all the spares that we possibly could. We practically shut down the line."[6]

The only orientation received by U.S. pilots in Saudi Arabia was two hours of classroom instruction and one daytime orientation flight. They had flown LANTIRN's navigation pod but never the targeting component, so after a single familiarization flight in daylight, the fighter pilots went on combat missions that evening.

There were 136 LANTIRN navigation pods operating on fighter aircraft during Desert Storm, 100 of them on F16s and 36 on F15s. Nineteen F15s also carried targeting pods. In the thirty-six days between January 17 and February 21, 1991, F15E aircraft equipped with both pods of LANTIRN flew 406 combat sorties, more than 11 per day. During that time, less than 9 percent, or only thirty-four targeting pods, had to be replaced, half of them for focus and half for laser problems. That is a readiness factor of 91.6 percent, a remarkable level of reliability for a brand-new system straight off the factory floor.

■

EQUALLY REMARKABLE IN PERFORMANCE was another electro-optical system that acts as the eyes and nose of the Army's AH-64 Apache attack helicopter. Known as TADS/PNVS, and sometimes familiarly and phonetically called "Tads Pinvus" by project people, the letters stand for Target Acquisition Designation Sight/Pilot Night Vision Sensor. It was also designed and manufactured by the same group at Orlando, specifically by the Martin Marietta Electronic Systems company. It does for the Apache what LANTIRN does for fighter pilots: allows them to fly in complete darkness and obscuring weather at very low altitudes, while at the same time giving them the ability to locate, optically acquire, and destroy ground targets at standoff ranges beyond antiaircraft return fire.

It was the Apache, with its Hellfire missiles—also a Martin Marietta product—that destroyed Iraqi radars in the predawn darkness of Desert Storm's opening day. The TADS/PNVS system not only gave helicopter pilots eyes to see in the dark, it gave them the nose to optically sniff out the targets and then laser-spot, or designate, them for destruction by deadly effective Hellfire missiles.

The vital importance of systems such as LANTIRN and TADS to the quick and overwhelming success of Desert Storm was essentially overlooked by the ubiquitous American news media and was therefore essentially unknown to the layman back home. Unsatisfied with just the good news of winning the war, many in the American press writhed in endless postwar analysis and speculation on what might have been done better. Was the outcome really proof of technological superiority, of "high tech" proving itself, they asked, or was it a cooperative enemy that through either incompetence or lack of intestinal fortitude made our systems look so good?

"There is no doubt that we had a cooperative enemy," said Allan M. Norton, who was president of the Orlando manufacturing group that produced all of the Martin systems that performed so effectively in the Persian Gulf conflict, "but people have to understand how that cooperation came about. We took out the enemy's eyes and his voice the very first night . . . his ability to see us and his ability to communicate."[7]

Al Norton is a very large man and a very thoughtful person. He is soft-spoken and unflappable, and was best known to his fellow employees for his unfailing insistence on integrity and quality in the product, in its performance, and in the people who built it. His assessment of a "cooperative enemy" takes into account that Iraq had the fourth largest army in the world and the sixth largest air force.

"The Iraqi fighter pilots in their MIG-29s were very well trained people," Norton said, "but their entire CQ was destroyed in the opening engagement of the war. They could not communicate with one another, so there was a reason that we talk about a cooperative enemy. He didn't have any choice. We made him cooperate."

In Norton's opinion—a view shared by many of his customers—Martin Marietta–produced systems made a significant impact on the outcome of the war by providing precision weaponry and the most advanced night navigation and targeting systems in the world. As in every previous armed conflict in its long history, Martin Marietta supported its systems and its customers with technicians in the field. Many of these "field reps" were at the "front" or in what passed for quick-moving front lines, depending on the engagement. The only difference in Desert Storm was due to the miracle of modern-day communications: Martin Marietta's front-line field reps were in daily contact, sometimes hourly when necessary, with the stateside plant by means of cellular satellite telephones. And people at the manufacturing plant back home, including those with a critical need to know, had the added advantage of cable television, which, thanks to CNN coverage, complemented the telephoned reports and provided the bigger, overall picture virtually in real time.

CHAPTER 40

Mission Success

■

Martin Marietta had seventy-three technical representatives in the Middle East, all of whom volunteered to accompany units they had supported in the States. Like the Gene Fosters and Fuzz Furmans of fifty years ago, and hundreds of others, they are integral to the corporation's culture, to its belief in total customer support and ultimate "mission success."

Those who were part of Desert Storm "really made a difference," in the view of John E. Conn, director of product support at Orlando and himself a former field rep who saw action in Vietnam. "They really gave us a chance to show the customer that we do support our products," Conn said.[1] He illustrated with the story of just one, Tracy Cooper. Conn described him as typical—young, smart, loyal to the company, and dedicated to the product and the troops using it.

Cooper, at twenty-nine, had been with the company about eight years. He was hired after his discharge from the Army at Fort Hood, Texas, where he had been a technician trained on the TADS/PNVS program. Tracy was Martin Marietta's representative with the "Flying Tigers," the Fourth Battalion, 229th Attack Helicopter Regiment, part of the Seventh Corps, stationed at Illesheim, Germany.

When that battalion, with its eighteen Apache helicopters, was deployed to Saudi Arabia, Tracy went along. And when the Flying Tigers crossed the border into Iraq as part of Desert Storm's western flank, Tracy was with them to assist with maintenance and to make certain the Apache pilots and their electro-optical "eyes and nose" were ready to go. Earl Moody, another Martin Marietta field rep, recalled meeting Tracy Cooper, prior to the invasion, at Long Base Alpha, about thirty-five miles from the Iraq border. Moody headed a calibration team that periodically checked the TADS/PNVS equipment.

"We were there to do a cal [calibration] on three TADS systems, and since the unit or its aircraft were always on the move, we'd always locate our field rep first and he'd lead us to the systems," Moody said. "Tracy really knew his way around. He knew all the pilots and ground crews, and every piece of equipment. He lived in a storage room—no bed, just a sleeping bag. No shower or bathroom facilities. But it was a good sturdy building. It was the first time I'd met him," Moody said.[2]

The commanding officer of Tracy's helicopter regiment, Lieutenant Colonel Roger E. McCauley, knew him well, and on March 28, 1991, he wrote in a combat performance appraisal of Martin Marietta's field rep:

> From the time this battalion deployed to the desert, I counted Tracy Cooper as a combat multiplier of the first order. He knew no time clock, no weather constraints; he feared nothing except that an aircraft that he had the capability to fix would not be able to complete its combat mission. . . .
>
> On 26 Feb 1991 this battalion launched into Iraq, refueled, and conducted the army's first night Cross FLOT AH-64 attack against enemy armor forces in Kuwait. We reattacked the target early on the morning of 27 Feb 1991. Crews flew from six to eight plus hours of night system time during those two attacks, destroying 92 armored vehicles and trucks. The success of these attacks and the combat accomplishments of this battalion would have been significantly diminished without Tracy Cooper."[3]

As he wrote the performance appraisal on March 28, Colonel McCauley noted that his battalion had just been given the mission to "screen and secure VII Corps' western flank" and that they were the most westerly deployed U.S. soldiers in Iraq, a 496-kilometer drive

"Combat multiplier" Tracey Cooper in Iraq

away from their supply base in Saudi Arabia. The commendation continued:

> I have aircraft that need PNVS maintenance, and Tracy Cooper is here. Tracy Cooper is part of the reason Desert Storm was a success for this battalion. . . . All commanders were unanimous in recommending Tracy Cooper for the Bronze Star. Clearly this is a well-deserved honor for an American who supported this battalion in a manner above and beyond the call of duty.

■

IN ADDITION TO TADS/PNVS, LANTIRN, AND PATRIOT, the list of Martin Marietta systems in Desert Storm, and the accolades for their excellent performance, goes on and on:[4]

HELLFIRE missiles produced by Martin Marietta Missile Systems, scored bull's-eye hits, one on a target as previously noted, of Iraqi frontline radars and communications centers. More than two thousand nine hundred Hellfire missiles were fired, accounting for the destruction of 837 tanks or other tracked vehicles, 501 wheeled vehicles, ten helicopters on the ground, and fourteen fighter aircraft on the ground, plus 836 enemy troops captured in Apache-Hellfire engagements.

VERTICAL LAUNCHING SYSTEM More than half of the cruise missiles launched from ships in the Persian Gulf during Desert Storm were fired from the MK-41 Vertical Launching System manufactured by Martin Marietta Aero & Naval Systems at Baltimore. VLS, as it is called, is a modular system capable of storing a variety of missiles beneath armored hatches below a ship's deck. Operational on *Ticonderoga*-class cruisers and *Spruance*-class destroyers, it can launch its missiles singularly or in salvo at surface, air, or undersea targets. Included in its missile mix are Tomahawk antisurface missiles and Standard II anti-aircraft missiles that were used in Desert Storm.

Almost two years after the conflict's end, the United States, acting under United Nations resolutions, launched forty-five cruise missiles on January 17, 1993, against Iraqi targets that had violated the cease-fire. All but one of the Tomahawk missiles were fired from Martin Marietta–built Vertical Launching Systems on the decks of Aegis-class destroyers and cruisers in the Persian Gulf. Most of them were fired by the destroyer U.S.S. *Spruance.*

PAVE PENNY, a laser-target system used to identify targets by day or night, was operational in Desert Storm on A-10A, A-7D, A-7K, F-16, A-4M, and A-4S aircraft. Pave Penny had been operational since 1976.

LST/SCAM Laser Spot-Tracker/Strike Camera, better known as LST/SCAM, enabled F/A18 fighter pilots to pinpoint and destroy camouflaged targets on the first pass, day or night and in all types of weather. Its camera instantaneously assessed target damage, eliminating guesswork or the need for follow-up reconnaissance.

TACTAS, a Tactical Towed Array Sonar designated AN-SQR-19, was aboard three different classes of warships off Kuwait: *Ticonderoga*-class Aegis guided-missile cruisers, *Spruance*-class destroyers, and *Perry*-class guided-missile frigates. These firehose-like strings

VLS launches missile

Assembling towed sonar arrays

of sonar devices contained computer signal processing devices that determine the location of sound waves for identification and characterization of targets. They were the specialty product of the Ocean Systems Operation at Glen Burnie, Maryland, a division of Aero & Naval Systems.

CNCE, Command Nodal Control Element, was another participant in the Middle East. The Martin Marietta–designed and built CNCE managed the theater's tactical communications resources.

ASAS, the All Source Analysis System, is an automated tactical intelligence system that provided integrated information processing for battlefield commanders.

PAWS, portable ASAS weather station, is a ruggedized computer and video display of maps and personnel deployment transported in standard tactical vehicles and quickly set up or dismantled by military personnel.

COPPERHEAD, a laser-guided artillery projectile fired from conventional 155-millimeter howitzers, was also on duty during Desert Storm, although the need for artillery-range weapons was somewhat limited by the fast moving front. All three Copperheads fired in combat were direct hits. Twenty-eight of thirty fired in training by the Eighteenth ABN Corps Artillery during Operation Desert Shield were direct hits. The Seventh Corps Artillery had a less successful rate, only thirty-three hits out of fifty-seven, attributed by the Army to a lower state of training.

Desert Storm was military high technology at its best, and the American public watched it almost in real time from living rooms and office armchairs, thanks again to the miracle of modern communications. The technology displayed in Desert Storm was the ultimate proof of the creative intelligence of the men and women who designed, manufactured, and directed its use.

PART X

"A Merger of Marvelous Magnitude"[1]

1992 and Beyond

■

CHAPTER 41

Putting It Together

■

The late afternoon sun, all but gone, lingered in the brightness of the Bradford pear trees rimming the circular drive in front of corporate headquarters. Among the first to bloom in the spring, the trees also held the last blush of autumn. And on this November evening, just four days before Thanksgiving, their multihued leaves were reflected in a splash of raspberry and yellow on the soaring glass entrance of the gradually darkening building.

With the exception of one or two windows in the north wing, the headquarters building exhibited no life, its Sunday night quiet masking the flurry of activity by two teams of people working well into the night 210 miles to the north. There, on the fifty-third floor of a Manhattan skyscraper, a group of Martin Marietta financial and legal people were putting the finishing touches and their signatures on a super-secret agreement. When publicly announced the next morning, it caught the business world by surprise, fascinated the stock market, and changed forever the face of an already vibrant and historic enterprise.

At a Monday morning press conference in Washington on November 23, 1992, the chairman and CEO of Martin Marietta Corporation, Norman R. Augustine, and the chairman and CEO of General Electric Company, John F. Welch, Jr., gave corporate presence to a news release announcing:

> GE AEROSPACE TO MERGE
> INTO MARTIN MARIETTA
> TO CREATE BROADLY DIVERSIFIED
> GLOBAL TECHNOLOGY LEADER.

It was a $3.05 billion deal: $1.8 billion in cash and the remainder in Martin Marietta preferred stock. The resultant new Martin Marietta Corporation would represent sales approximating $11 billion ($5.9 billion from Martin Marietta and $5 billion from GE Aerospace), a business backlog of $19 billion, and nearly ninety thousand people, including twenty-seven thousand engineers and scientists. Tuesday's headlines reported the story:

> MARTIN MARIETTA TO ACQUIRE
> AEROSPACE DIVISION OF GE (*The Washington Post*)

> G.E. WILL SELL
> AEROSPACE UNIT
> FOR $3 BILLION (*The New York Times*)

> GE WILL SELL
> UNIT TO MARTIN
> MARIETTA CORP (*The Wall Street Journal*)

The headlines told the story but missed the significance. From the very outset leaders of both companies treated it as a merger, not an acquisition, and it truly was a "merger of marvelous magnitude," to borrow a line from the libretto for a comic opera of a decade earlier.[2] All the *i*'s and *t*'s were not dotted and crossed and the necessary federal antitrust approvals completed for close to four and a half months. But the deal was essentially done with its announcement, and from conception to signed agreement and public announcement had taken only twenty-seven days.

An amalgam of equals, the resultant enterprise became the largest aerospace electronics corporation in the world. It was also the fortieth largest corporation in America in terms of sales, with a backlog of more than $25 billion and operating centers in thirty-seven states and seventeen other countries. That it had come together so relatively easily was a result of two different but forward-looking managements that had arrived at the same conclusion independently of each other. It was an idea whose time had come.

THE ENCOUNTER

Jack Welch, the dynamic chairman of General Electric, and Norman Augustine, the energetic and peripatetic chairman of Martin Marietta, had known each other professionally for a couple of years as attendees at various business gatherings of their peers in corporate America. It would be an exaggeration to say they were personal friends, but they certainly were first-name business acquaintances who saw each other at meetings reasonably often.

The next time the two corporate leaders met was at a session of the Business Council at Hot Springs, Virginia, on October 8, 1992.

"We were standing by the front desk in the lobby of the Homestead," Augustine said, "and he said to me, 'You know, we ought to get together and talk about our aerospace businesses in these really rough times. It might be that between us we could put something together that would serve us both well.'

"That sounds like a very interesting idea," Augustine replied, "but you need to know that we at Martin Marietta cherish our independence."

"Oh, absolutely! I understand," Welch told Augustine. "That's not the idea, but would you care to talk about it?"

Augustine took the GE leader at his word. "I wouldn't have agreed to talk to a lot of people, but when he said, 'Absolutely! That's not the idea,' it was the respect and trust I had in him that made it possible for us to talk. He's a guy with a reputation worth gold, so I said, 'Fine!' But I didn't want to appear overly eager, and since he agreed there was no big hurry, I told him I would call him in a few weeks."[3]

Augustine said it was difficult to contain his excitement until he got back to the office and confided the Welch encounter to a few close advisers. He told Tom Young, Martin Marietta's president and chief operating officer, and Marcus C. Bennett, the chief financial officer, as well as John E. Montague, vice president for corporate development. The three of them knew immediately the significance of the Welch suggestion: They and Augustine had come up with the same idea two months earlier.

THE PREPARATION

Through the spring and summer of 1992, Norman Augustine had slipped away from the office one afternoon a week or so to meet at his Potomac home with three of his associates—Young, Bennett, and Montague—in a series of strategic reviews on where the corporation was and where it was going. It was the only uninterrupted time they could find. The sessions were freewheeling and thoughtful, occasionally continuing at corporate headquarters for presentations by one or two outsiders from the investment community. Tom Young said the sessions were the culmination of steps taken in the last half of the eighties to position Martin Marietta for possible growth opportunities. The "window of opportunity" through which Tom Pownall and Augustine had shepherded the corporation in the recovery years following the hostile takeover attempt by Bendix had paid off handsomely. Programs that Martin Marietta had bid and won were for the most part long-term in expected life and included the opportunity to earn a reasonable profit.

From 1983 on, the corporation won on the average more than 50 percent of the contracts for which it competed, an amazingly high percentage, particularly when compared to the industry average of 27 percent. Nearly as many programs were *not* bid as were won because the corporation refused to bid fixed-price contracts at prices it considered unreasonable, Young said. If the price considered low enough to win did not include a reasonable profit, the decision was not to bid it. At the same time, acquisition opportunities surfaced as the industry began to shrink. In the late 1980s when others were paying $1.50 per $1.00 of sales for defense companies, Martin Marietta sat out because it thought the asking prices were unattractive. Instead, cash was husbanded for better opportunities that management expected would appear in the mid-nineties.

The ratio of debt to capitalization had been reduced to 24 percent by the end of 1985 and was down to 20 percent in 1992. In one other area considered essential to future health, Young noted, the company began "right-sizing" before it had to in order to stay "lean and mean."[4] The Orlando operation, which Young headed from 1985 to 1989, prided itself on being the "lean machine," and that discipline spread through other operating units.

"We used to say," Augustine recalled, " 'we want to keep our powder dry; we want to have little leverage; we want to have a lot of cash; we want a healthy balance sheet so that when things turn down, we can be a buyer.' " If aerospace companies were too pricey, so were aggregates companies, but when the aggregates business nosed down, Martin Marietta began acquiring such firms. Between 1985 and 1992 the corporation purchased thirteen companies that added some 17 million tons of capacity and more than 1 billion tons of reserves to its aggregates business.

Late in August the "afternoon planners" put together what they called a "*strategic* strategic plan," which they presented to the board of directors. Strategic plans are the norm in Martin Marietta, but Augustine called this one "a layer above." This plan was zero-basing, asking the tough questions, the fundamentals of corporate life and death. In the chart presented to the directors, a number of options were dismissed, but the preferred option that surfaced was to join with other aerospace companies. At the top of that list was General Electric Aerospace. Its programs would fit like a glove with Martin Marietta's. There were no real areas of overlap, no obvious antitrust problems, and so many product areas that were obvious complements. In quite a few, the synergy offered potential for substantial efficiencies in operating costs as well as market penetration.

There was one serious drawback. How do you approach a $62 billion giant like General Electric about purchasing a one-twelfth or smaller slice of its pie without risking being swallowed yourself? "We were in the mode of trying to figure out how to deal with this," Augustine said, "because the last thing I wanted was to put Martin Marietta into play if the word got out that we were looking." The corporation had just emerged from a protracted bidding war for the aerospace assets of LTV Corporation, a package only a fraction the size of GE Aerospace. The competition for LTV included a company backed by a foreign government. Augustine opposed in principle such ownership for an American defense firm, and Martin Marietta dropped out rather than constantly escalate its bid.

"On the heels of the highly publicized LTV affair [which Loral eventually purchased in association with the Carlisle Investment Group] and having lived through the Bendix takeover attempt from a distance," Augustine said, "the question was how to raise this issue when the company of interest is ten times our size. . . . They could have squashed us like a bug if they had chosen to."[5] That was the dilemma facing Martin Marietta when Augustine encountered Jack Welch at the Homestead on October 8, 1992.

Welch's suggestion that the two companies meet and talk was warmly, if cautiously, welcomed, but the Martin Marietta executives had to wonder whether the GE giant was buying or selling. In view of Welch's assurance to Augustine that he understood that Martin Marietta cherished independence, their assessment was that GE probably was selling. After widening the closely held confidence to include general counsel Frank Menaker, it was agreed that the chairman should follow up and call Welch. For the time being, to assure secrecy and keep all options open, the circle of those in the know would be limited to Augustine, Young, and their three associates.

Unknown to them, GE had spent the summer doing pretty much the same analysis, and Martin Marietta was number one on its list. When Augustine called Welch to suggest he was ready for a get-together, Welch invited him to a late-evening dinner at GE's Fairfield, Connecticut, headquarters. Augustine requested that the meeting be very private. The dinner on October 27 ran for about three hours in a private dining room adjoining Welch's office. No one else was present except for those serving the food. Augustine would later laugh that he couldn't remember what was served for dinner, "but it was one of the more expensive meals I've ever eaten. We agreed from the outset that the merger of the two companies was a good idea, that it would be a whale of a fit, that it wouldn't have antitrust problems, and that it would be good for customers as well as employees and shareholders." Augustine said the GE chairman was very well prepared—so well, in fact, that he even used some Augustine charts to make his points. Augustine had made a presentation just a few days before to a meeting of New York security analysts, using data to show Martin Marietta's strategy for growth.

During their dinner Welch showed some charts, and the very first one was from Augustine's New York presentation. "He then used the information from my chart to price GE's aerospace business and used my own argument to show that it was worth much more," Augustine said. "It was really funny. He hadn't even gone to the trouble of reprinting them. He simply substituted the GE name for Martin Marietta's and put me in the awful spot of having to argue against my own charts."

Augustine said Welch also remembered and quoted him *verbatim* on Martin Marietta's desire to remain independent. "But we both agreed that if the two companies were to merge, it would be a merger of equals and that it would not be fruitful for each of us to take a hardover low price and a hardover high price and then fight for six months." Rather, they decided to deal candidly with each other, taking out what would normally be given away in negotiation and "just make our best offers."

Welch went through the basic structure of the deal he had in mind, and Augustine said, "He really had thought it through, including a rough structure for the debt . . . that is, how we would finance the merger. He gave me the number he thought it was worth, and I told him I thought that it was a bit high but not out of the ballpark. I told him I had to do some more homework because up until that time I did not know all that he was going to include. But it was clear that we were within range and that he was not posturing by starting out a factor or two high with the idea of negotiating down. I give him the preponderance of credit for making the deal happen."[6]

"FLINTSTONE" AND "30 ROCK"

The bottom line was that Jack Welch was willing to sell GE's aerospace company to Martin Marietta for a fair price provided GE would have some continuing interest in the merged companies. Augustine returned to Bethesda and filled in Tom Young and the others on his talk with Welch. They then went off to think it through and make some comparable studies on pricing in order to reach a figure Martin Marietta considered appropriate. Bennett, Montague, and Arnold Chiet, Martin Marietta vice president and general tax counsel, made two quick trips to New York, on October 30 and again on November 3, to confer with their GE counterparts. The circle was further enlarged on November 5 when Menaker, brought in Bob Fullem and Len Larrabee, principals in Dewey Ballantine, the New York law firm that had been Martin Marietta's outside legal counsel in the Bendix war. The company's investment banker, Goldman Sachs, also was brought into the picture. Meanwhile, Augustine updated members of the Martin Marietta board.

Further complicating matters for the handful of people involved at the start was Martin Marietta's annual long-range planning meeting of top executives, which took place on Captiva Island, Florida, Thursday and Friday, November 5 and 6. Augustine and Young were already there, and Bennett, Menaker, and Montague, who were in New York for preliminary meetings with General Electric people, were conspicuously absent. Bennett was scheduled to be on the Captiva agenda Friday and then was to accompany Augustine to Fairfield on Friday night for a meeting with Welch.

Along with three Goldman Sachs people, Bennett, Menaker, and Montague flew down to Captiva late Thursday. "We stashed the Goldman Sachs troops in separate quarters and put in an appearance late Thursday night," Bennett said. "Most of our people thought we had been off working an aggregates acquisition." Augustine took Stephen Zelnak, president of the materials group, aside and told him: "I don't want any disinformation, but you're going to hear a lot of rumors and I want you to know that we are not off buying a big aggregates business that you don't know about. However, if you'd offer a 'no comment,' it would be helpful." Zelnak then knew something was going on, but he did not know what.[7]

On November 6, after the Captiva meeting ended, Augustine, Bennett, Montague, and Menaker flew to Fairfield to meet with Welch and GE's senior vice president of finance, Dennis D. Dammerman. He and Bennett had been designated leaders of the respective financial teams. The Martin Marietta people took the corporate jet to Teterboro, New Jersey, where a GE helicopter picked them up for the night flight to Connecticut. On this occasion they met at the GE conference center at headquarters in two separate meetings. Menaker and Montague met with Benjamin W. Heineman, Jr., GE's senior vice president and general counsel, who conceptualized the deal for them. Augustine and Welch paired off, as did Bennett and Dammerman, in separate attempts to determine what the deal was worth from a value standpoint.

"We weren't too far apart on price," Augustine said after he and Welch had worked the issue alone for a while, "but we were having a hard time getting there. So we called in Mark and Dennis and together worked up several compromises on both sides. After a while we had each given something, and we finally got to a price that seemed reasonable." Augustine said it looked at that point like they might have a deal, "but we still had some more things to check, so I said, 'Now this is not yet a handshake,' and Jack Welch replied, 'Well, it's an eyeshake,' and Bennett concurring in that terminology said, 'Yes, that's what it is.' "[8]

When the lawyers rejoined the group, the seven people from the two companies stood around drinking Cokes and chatting. Jack Welch wrote his home telephone number down on a paper napkin for Augustine, and Augustine jotted down the rough numbers of their agreement on the same napkin. He still has the napkin but declined to produce it because "Jack's number is unlisted." On a third trip from Florida to New York City in as many nights—and one of those was to address a group of air traffic controllers—Augustine said, "We had a handshake." That handshake would hold without waiver throughout the negotiations.

Security surrounding the trips to Connecticut and New York and throughout the merger-making were extremely tight. As additional Martin Marietta people joined the team, including outside attorneys and bankers, each was asked to sign a pledge acknowledging the confidentiality of what they would be doing. Augustine even cautioned the Martin Marietta aircraft crew to forget everything they saw or heard on the various trips in and out of Teterboro, including the GE helicopter that frequently picked them up.

By November 10 the Martin Marietta team working the merger had expanded to include three more senior finance people: David Buchanan, vice president and controller; Janet McGregor, treasurer of the corporation, and Ray Niznik, director of employee benefits. On the legal side, three on Menaker's staff were added to the team: Jay Brozost, Steve Piper, and Marian Block, all assistant general counsels. Joining them a couple of days later were Phil Duke, vice president of finance and business development; Jerry Kircher, director of financial planning and analysis; and Dave Minnick, director of corporate development.

After the second meeting in Fairfield, all remaining sessions were at 30 Rockefeller Center in Manhattan. Most of the actual hammering out of details in structuring the merger was done on the fifty-third floor, just a few floors above the NBC offices, so references to 30 Rock added to the smokescreen. They could be interpreted, as interest in an aggregates business, further confusing the trail. Marc Bennett said the accommodations could not have been better. The fifty-third floor, reserved primarily for monthly meetings of the General Electric board, was sparsely populated, with only a scattering of secretarial staff. Catered food was sent in at breakfast, lunch, and dinner and for snacks late at night. Some of the merger sessions ran around the clock, and Bennett said he didn't know where the catered food came from, but it was "outstanding. Everyone on the team proceeded to gain weight."[9] Sometimes they ate all three meals there, leaving only for a few hours' sleep in a nearby hotel. Some of the group were away from Bethesda five or six days at a time, right through weekends. One night when they had spent only two hours in their respective rooms, Augustine jokingly accused Young of paying $75 an hour to sleep.

The Martin Marietta team had established by then an elaborate set of code names should their activities attract attention within the corporation or without. It was important that there be no leaks. Jack Welch had not yet told his people he was considering selling the aerospace unit, and Augustine did not want to create an auction atmosphere and set off a bidding war, as had been the case in the LTV sale. He likened the latter to the "cross-eyed discus thrower problem: He seldom wins any gold, but he sure keeps the crowd on its toes. Somebody starts lobbing crazy bids over the fence, and you don't know if they're for real or not. Often the least responsible bidders throw in the highest prices. . . . They usually can't produce the money anyway, so they just throw in a price. . . . It can really make a shambles of things," he said.[10]

For a time they used "Polaris" as a code name, on the theory that anyone hearing it would be thrown off the scent thinking of Lockheed, maker of the Polaris missile. In a further extension of the smoke-and-mirror game, they switched to "Gemini" for a while, which might suggest McDonnell-Douglas. *The Wall Street Journal* came out with a story that Martin Marietta was interested in buying some aggregates businesses, and General Dynamics announced that its materials services company was on the block and identified Martin Marietta as a potential buyer. With that piece of information out, the team changed its code name to Flintstone as a better screen for their activity. GE and GD sounded so much alike, it would help cover the real scenario, they reasoned.

"We didn't want to do anything dishonest," Augustine said, "but we were extremely sensitive about secrecy, about preventing any leaks that might lead to insider trading or otherwise influence the price of either company's stock."[11] It was also a particularly dicey situation for GE and Jack Welch. If it became known to more than one or two people that he was considering selling the aerospace business, then those working in GE aerospace as well as customers would wonder what was to become of them. If that happened, Welch had to worry that he could destroy the value of the business. So he had to approach it carefully. If he found the best fit for GE aerospace, he could convince the GE people that it was the best thing for them, for GE stockholders, and for the potential buyer—in this case, Martin Marietta. But he had to have a sure thing.

Another diversionary tactic was a flood of messages in the company's open-mail system, notes such as: "Please send me Lockheed's quarterly report" and "Have you seen General Dynamics' annual report?" If the sender put a small check in the bottom right-hand corner of the note, it meant the message was to be disregarded. In addition, Marc Bennett's secretary Beth A. Hwoschinsky, handled all the travel arrangements for the Bethesda people, further ensuring tight security.

Once Welch and Augustine agreed, shortly after the November 6 Fairfield meeting, on the $3,050,000,000 value of the merger, it was a matter of hammering out the details by the two teams working late hours, seven days a week, to bring it about in the remarkably short time of two weeks. Augustine and Welch stayed out of it unless called on. "People were off working contract issues, financing issues, benefits issues, SEC issues, pricing issues—you name it," Augustine said. "When something got to a crunch, then Jack and I would get on the phone and try to resolve it, and if we couldn't, at least we'd agree on the next step."

Simultaneously with working out all the financial details of the merger, Marc Bennett said Martin Marietta was conducting its "due diligence," the confirmation phase where the company needed to confirm everything GE had told it without having visited a single GE facility. Normally in such transactions a prospective buyer does on-site inspections of facilities, equipment, people, and programs. "Because of the need for secrecy, plant visits were out. We only talked to their key people," Bennett said.[12] "But the good news was that there were no investment bankers on their side trying to 'sell' us something, like an auction. We were able to look at their detailed material." Tom Young headed the due diligence phase, assisted by two operating people, Peter B. Teets, president of the Astronautics Group, and Joseph D. Antinucci, president of the Aero & Naval Systems company. The GE operating people included Eugene F. Murphy, president of GE Aerospace, and Robert W. Tieken, chief financial officer. Young would later credit Murphy with being "just outstanding in making it all come together."

While the finance people were "crunching the numbers" and Young and Murphy were analyzing the operating units and their programs, the lawyers were addressing scores of other issues. In preparing the contract under which the merger would take place, the lawyers encountered one very large sticking point: The seller, GE, wanted a contract that would give the buyer, Martin Marietta, no way out. The buyer, on the other hand, having done no hands-on due diligence, wanted a contract that provided all the "outs" in the world until closing. Again, the secrecy of the entire negotiation was setting the conditions. Frank Menaker explained: "The difference between the two approaches was that GE didn't want to ruin the value of its deal, but it could not allow due diligence without letting the world—and that included its own people—know what was going on. Martin Marietta, for its part, was willing to delay due diligence in exchange for outs until closing. So the big, big dilemma was how to write a contract that gave the buyer outs and the seller a conviction that the contract was going to close."[13] Menaker said that issue and the value of the preferred stock GE was to receive in the transaction were the biggest hurdles. GE wanted terms of the preferred stock to be as much like debt as they could get it, and Martin Marietta wanted the preferred stock to be as much like equity as it could get.

General Electric had taken the first crack at writing the contract and presented its proposal on Friday, November 13. Menaker, Piper, Block, and four Dewey Ballantine lawyers then proceeded to mark it up over the weekend and gave the rewritten contract back to GE on Monday, the 16th. Menaker said the rewrite was extensive. "In fact, we added riders to riders. Instead of just marking up the contract, we'd write an entire new paragraph and say, 'Delete this and add rider number so-and-so.'" For the balance of that week the two teams of lawyers reworked and rewrote the contract, the two teams of operating people did their due diligence exercise, and the two teams of finance people crunched the numbers—all of the teams working in parallel essentially around the clock on the fifty-third floor at 30 Rock.

"Every time we hit a bump in the road . . . if it was a large bump . . . Norm and Jack Welch would get us back on track," Bennett said. "So it worked surprisingly well." One session with Welch and Augustine, Dammerman and Bennett, Heineman and Menaker ran until three in the morning, with only a brief break to wish Welch a happy birthday. It was during the frantic final week, Augustine recalled. "Jack and I generally were able to resolve any problems simply by picking up the phone and talking to each other. This time I was at a Proctor and Gamble board meeting in Cincinnati when I received a call that sounded as if they were getting in hot water and things were coming apart. So Jack and I got on the phone and he said, 'Why don't you fly to New York, and I'll meet you there tonight.' And that's what we did. Jack was straight up," he said of Welch. "He was totally knowledgeable and interested in solving problems, not in arguing them. There are many times in such circumstances when you could get tired and annoyed with each other. We never did, and I give him the credit for it. He took the first move, and he also had the structure of the entire transaction put together in his mind. From the first moment our people sat down with their people in New York, the relationships were outstanding. Each group was off doing its job, helping each other and coordinating all the way for a superb team effort in total contrast with mergers one reads so much about."[14]

He laughed about many telephone calls he received at home from Jack Welch during the process. Augustine's wife Meg "obviously knew something was going on because I was hardly ever home," he said. "But she didn't know what, and after thirty-one years of marriage, she knew not to ask, that if I could tell her, I would." The Augustine telephone number for their Potomac, Maryland, home was unlisted but was known to close personal friends, one of whom happened to be an assistant secretary of the Air Force by the name of Jack Welch. The duplication in names produced some obvious assumptions, which further stretched the intrigue when GE's Welch called the Augustine home. "When he called my house, he would say, 'This is Jack Welch. Is Norm there?' And Meg, thinking it was the other Jack Welch, would answer, 'Oh, hi, Jack? How are you?' And he would say, 'I'm fine.' And Meg would say, 'How's Patty?' And he would say, 'Fine.' It wasn't until I had overheard this routine a couple of times from our end of the phone that I realized what was going on. Jack Welch was simply playing dumb, and Meg didn't know it wasn't the other Jack Welch." Augustine said he and Welch never discussed it. It wasn't until a month or so after the merger had been announced when Augustine was writing Welch a note on another matter that he added a postscript, "Incidentally, how *is* Patty?"[15]

Despite all the secrecy, there was one unfathomable event associated with the marathon discussions on the fifty-third floor of 30 Rockefeller Plaza. After one particularly late session in that final week, Dennis Dammerman, GE's chief financial officer, was leaving in the wee hours of the morning when a utility worker popped his head out of an open manhole in the sidewalk in front of 30 Rock and said, "Oh, the meeting up on fifty-three must be over. Good night, sir." To this day nobody knows who he was, what he was doing, or how he knew about the meetings on the fifty-third floor.[16]

November 19 was another late night at 30 Rockefeller Center. The next morning the completed package had to be presented to the Martin Marietta board. Friday was the first time Menaker and his team had sat down to review the rewritten contract from page one to the end. Legal considerations in such a merger are extensive, of course. In addition to the basic contract there was a merger agreement and a standstill agreement, the latter controlling GE's preferred stock position, which would be equivalent to 23 percent of the merged company's total ownership. "There were still some rump sessions—employee benefits and the tax people—going on in parallel," he said, "and we finally got it all together, except for taxes, Friday night."

Bennett and his finance team returned to Bethesda on Friday to prepare for the board meeting set for 8:30 A.M. Saturday at Martin Marietta headquarters. Bennett said, "Poor Frank had stayed in New York practically all night getting the contract finalized, then flew down Saturday morning in time for the meeting. He was on the agenda, and that's sailing it pretty close to the wind for a board meeting.'' Augustine had spoken to each board member individually by telephone several times prior to the formal meeting. The outside bankers and attorneys were there, and the entire merger was reviewed in detail, including the few items still open.

Menaker said Tom Young, who reviewed every single GE facility, was "positively brilliant. I have never seen anyone present so much data so well in all my life. He was so thorough. He gave the good points and the bad of every operation. He was unbelievable, and he acquired all that knowledge essentially in one week's time." The meeting lasted more than seven hours, breaking up about four o'clock Saturday afternoon. Prior to adjourning, the board formally and enthusiastically voted its approval of the merger of GE aerospace with Martin Marietta. The GE board had done similarly twenty-four hours earlier.

A DONE DEAL

Public disclosure was scheduled for the following Monday, November 22, but there was still much to do. Bennett and Menaker returned to New York following the board meeting. They still had to incorporate the tax provisions and a few other odds and ends into the contract and sign it. Augustine had given Bennett a written delegation of authority to formally execute the contract with a kidding jibe: "I told him since he signed all of his wife Ken's shopping bills, he was qualified to sign the three-billion-dollar contract."

It was almost nine o'clock on Sunday night before the documents were in final form for signatures. Marc Bennett's southern heritage is evident in his soft, somewhat husky, Georgia drawl, and he has been known to use his "country" charm to advantage. There are more than a few, however—including those who have faced him across a negotiating table and company managers who have had to defend financial statements—to whom he comes off somewhere between a wily fox and a hard-nosed CFO. Yet on more than one occasion during the tense proceedings with General Electric, Bennett felt a bit overwhelmed.

At one time, he said, his GE counterparts "accused me of trying to play the dumb wolf and the good ole country boy, but I had a document that listed three pages of transactions they had made in the last ten years or so—buying and selling things, and our page listed only two. So I told them, 'I don't want you people to think we're a little bit out of our element here.' I had to keep reminding them that they were a sixty-billion-dollar outfit and this negotiation was only one-tenth of that to them, but it was a make-or-break situation with us. I mean, we were dealing with the wizards of buying and selling, and Jack Welch had a reputation for buying things low and selling them high."

Welch, who later was highly complimentary of the roles Bennett and Dammerman played in the negotiation and of how well they got along, laughed at the characterization of Marc Bennett as a country boy. "That will be the day," he said. "That's the last thing we thought of him. We told him to park that country boy charm at the door." The GE chairman called Bennett "a first-class guy" and added, "There was never a lot of haggling over price. I mean, there was two hundred million dollars' worth of difference at the end, and they got it. We started at three billion five hundred million dollars and thought we'd settle at three billion two. They wanted three billion. In the end we settled for thirty-fifty [$3.05 billion] because strategically the deal was so right that we thought it more important than a couple of hundred million dollars."[17]

On Saturday night Dammerman and Bennett agreed the contract was sufficiently finalized that they could put their names on the signature pages and let the lawyers finish copyreading and assembling the pages. When they sat down to sign the agreement, Bennett admitted the magnitude of the $3 billion deal "sort of got to me." He recognized that once he put his name on the document, Martin Marietta would never be the same. "We were going into 1993 as the old Martin Marietta we had all known and would come out of 1993 as the new Martin Marietta that I hoped and expected would be a lot better. I was damn sure it would be a lot bigger."

The signature pages were put before Bennett. "The first one I signed on the GE line, and I told them, 'I hope you don't think I'm nervous or anything.' So they had to redo that page." It was nearly 8:30 P.M. when the signing was completed. He and Dammerman shook hands, and Bennett caught the airplane. Menaker and the lawyers stayed in New York to finish "flyspecking" the language and to make certain there were no typos. When he reached his Maryland home, Bennett telephoned Augustine to report "the eagle has landed." He said he was just crawling into bed when the telephone rang; it was Menaker from New York. They had hit a major snag having to do with a few changes in language that the lawyers had considered minor. But Ernst & Young, the independent auditing firm that had monitored the corporation's books since early airplane

Dammerman, Heineman, Menaker, and Bennett

days in Cleveland, needed more information on one area of the agreement. Bennett hung up and dialed David Buchanan. It was eleven o'clock, and Buchanan's sleepy wife reported him at the office. A quick call to the home of Robert W. Beddingfield, the senior Ernst & Young partner on the corporation's account, got an identical response. Beddingfield was also at Martin Marietta headquarters; they had both been there since sundown. Theirs were the two lights in the otherwise darkened headquarters building that Sunday night on the eve of announcing the largest corporate merger in recent aerospace history. A third phone call to the office caught Buchanan, who assured Bennett that he and Beddingfield were about to resolve the problem, "if you can hang on about fifteen minutes." Instead of going to sleep, Bennett fidgeted for fifteen minutes until Buchanan called back to say the potential "show stopper" had been resolved to the auditors' satisfaction.[18]

At eight-thirty Monday morning, November 22, 1992, the world learned of the General Electric Aerospace merger with Martin Marietta Corporation.

CHAPTER 42

A New Beginning

■

With all the clandestine maneuvering and diversionary tactics that kept the proposed merger a secret for a month and a half, the cat got at least its nose out of the bag literally at the eleventh hour. Late Sunday night, after GE had given confidential "heads-up" telephone notifications to several of its congressional contacts, *Washington Post* business writers Mark Potts and Steven Pearlstein were beneficiaries of a "leak." It was a real scoop, but good reporters that they are, it took them many "no comment" telephone calls and most of the night to satisfy themselves of its authenticity. And their front-page story, MARTIN MARIETTA PLANS DEAL FOR GE UNIT, missed all of the early–Monday morning home and out-of-town editions. In fact, it even missed downtown Washington street sales of the "final" edition, barely catching two truckloads of a replated final that went out to the suburbs. One of those trucks, coincidentally, dropped a bundle of papers at the corporation's Bethesda building and another bundle just happened to supply deliveries to suburban homes of Augustine, Young, and Bennett. Otherwise the story might have been missed altogether.

Even reporters occasionally have problems with management, and if Potts and Pearlstein were chagrined that the *Post* establishment didn't get their story on the street earlier, they were about to

Merger chairmen Augustine and Welch, 1992

at least get satisfaction. After the press conference announcing the merger, Jack Welch and Norm Augustine went over to *The Washington Post* for an interview session like the enlightened, media-conscious CEOs that they are.

Managing Editor Leonard Downie was impressed that the merger had been put together secretly in only a month, literally "under the noses" of two of his star reporters. The editor was good-naturedly needling Potts and Pearlstein for not tumbling to the story sooner since it involved a big firm right on their doorstep. Then he asked Augustine and Welch when they had first discussed the merger. When they told him that it was at the Homestead, Welch pointed at Potts, laughing, and said, "Right under *your* nose, Mark!" Potts had been at the Homestead covering sessions of the Business Council when Welch and Augustine made their initial contact.

Potts later said the tip he and Pearlstein received did not come from a congressional source, as everyone assumed. "It was an extremely indirect tip," he said. "If I told you what the tip was, you'd just die. It was one of those things where we added a few things together and figured out what was going on. It was a lucky guess on my part where I sat down and said, 'This can be one of three things,' and I got lucky on the first phone call. I think my wife gets credit for it. She's the one who figured out who it was." Potts said Pearlstein ultimately confirmed the lead from congressional sources, and the reason the story didn't make an earlier edition, Potts said, was that "we didn't get it nailed down until after midnight."[1]

It would take four and a half more months to complete all the legal work and secure Justice Department approval of the merger. But when it became official, April 2, 1993, the organization and early structure were already in place. Like the 1940s advertising jingle for a downtown Baltimore jewelry store that proclaimed: "Marriages are made in heaven, but engagements are made at S&N Katz," the new Martin Marietta appeared to be one of those heaven-made fits. It truly was a merger of marvelous magnitude that would be ready to spring into being within the month.

Both Welch and Augustine were unstinting in their praise of the transition process, of how effectively and speedily the two organizations became one. It was accomplished by a transition team made up of five members of each organization, including the co-chairs Tom Young and Gene Murphy. GE representatives were Lawrence R. Phillips, Robert W. Tieken, James B. Fellar, and Richard C. Abington, each a vice president in areas of human resources, finance, technical operations, and business development, respectively. Their Martin Marietta counterparts were vice presidents Bobby F. Leonard, Phil Duke, Robert J. Polutchko, and Richard G. Adamson. A newcomer, Stephen K. Conver, a former assistant secretary of the Army for research, development, and acquisition, was brought into the corporation to choreograph the integration. As vice president of operations integration, Conver reported to Young and Murphy.

There were also subcommittee teams looking at specific areas of integration, including benefits, international and commercial business, and operating practices. The only bias of the transitioners, Young said, was to ensure that the combined company—which automatically became the largest aerospace/electronics company in the world—would also be the best, "so that we can continue to excel, even in a declining marketplace." Both companies had been broadly diversified in aerospace and electronics. Each was a leader in a number of separate markets. The ultimate goal was to end up with the "best of the best" after careful elimination of any duplications, whether in plants, processes, or organizations.[2]

For a merger of its size—essentially the combining of two $5 billion corporations—there were very few antitrust concerns and a large degree of compatibility in systems produced for space, air, land, sea, and support. Complementing GE's leadership as a builder of commercial satellites was Martin Marietta's position as a developer and manufacturer of defense satellites and planetary explorer spacecraft as well as their launch systems. Martin Marietta's prowess as the developer of laser trackers and communications systems was nicely balanced by GE's position as a maker of flight and engine components as well as sensors. Aircraft navigation and targeting systems produced by Martin Marietta complemented GE's strengths in flight controls and gun systems. On the land, giant air defense radars developed by GE fit nicely with Martin Marietta's abilities in intelligence and battlefield communications. The matchups were equally good at sea, where GE's reputation as a maker of submarine combat systems, fire control, and guidance dovetailed with vertical launch systems and towed arrays produced by Martin Marietta. And Martin Marietta's strengths as a maker of support systems for integrated testing, automated logistics management, and facility management were complemented by GE's leadership in such support areas as simulation, image generation, and field support.

Space communications antenna

An indication of the synergy that could be expected of the new corporation was evident in the first months after the merger announcement. Even before the agreement had been consummated, close to $1.4 billion in new business contracts were won by the two companies. Included was $482 from NASA for science payload development, engineering, and operations services, $300 million from Raytheon for Patriot missiles and launchers for Saudi Arabia and Kuwait, $100 million from the government of Greece for LANTIRN night visions systems, $112 million from the U.S. Army for field artillery liquid propellant systems, $47 million from the U.S. Navy for advanced submarine towed sonar arrays, and $35 million from NASA for a propulsion subsystem on the Cassini spacecraft that would visit Saturn.

Of eight states where General Electric Aerospace had major operations, only Florida and California duplicated Martin Marietta's major operating locations. The merger of GE operating facilities in New York, New Jersey, Pennsylvania, Vermont, Massachusetts, and Virginia therefore extended Martin Marietta's already impressive geographic presence in Maryland, North Carolina, South Carolina, Georgia, Alabama, Tennessee, Louisiana, Kentucky, Ohio, Indiana, Illinois, Iowa, Kansas, Colorado, and New Mexico. The new corporation would also operate in fourteen other states, for a total of thirty-seven, as well as in seventeen other countries. Martin Marietta ranked first in research and development activities among Department of Defense contractors. GE Aerospace was second.[3]

But more important than physical size, numbers of employees, and dollar volume of sales, the two companies were amazingly alike in basic principle and corporate culture. Both were committed to excellence. Both placed high premium on quality products, performance, and customer service. Both were dedicated to high ethical standards and had been at the forefront of the "Defense Industry Initiative," a formal program in which leading firms voluntarily adopted a code of ethics and encouraged others to do so in the mid-eighties following the wave of fraud-waste-and-abuse charges— many of them baseless—that tarred the defense industry.

When it came time for the transition team to put together the new organization, heavy reliance was placed on the due diligence visits that had been made to every GE operation between the end of November 1992 and early April 1993, when the merger formally occurred. Tom Young, Peter Teets, Joe Antinucci, Leonard J. Wroten, Dick Adamson, and Charles A. Hall had visited every single GE Aerospace facility during the due diligence review. Young, with Au-

Trident II submarine systems

gustine, completed the loop a second time, meeting with employees and community groups. All employee concerns were addressed, not only in person by the two Martin Marietta executives but in a series of merger bulletins appropriately titled *TEAMING UPdate*. When the merger was finalized on April 2, the employee communication became *Better Together*.[4]

On May 1 the new organization went into effect. It consisted of six operating groups—space, electronics, information, materials, energy, and services. The four groups that combined elements of the merged companies were evenly divided, space and information headed by former Martin Marietta executives and electronics and services by former GE Aerospace principals. It had not been simply lip service when Augustine and Welch chose to treat the combination as a merger of equals rather than an acquisition. Probably the question most frequently on the minds of employees in both organizations, but particularly those in GE, was put to Augustine at a special meeting of Martin Marietta stockholders on March 25. At that meeting, where the merger was approved by 99 percent of the votes cast, an employee-stockholder asked what would be done by management to preserve Martin Marietta jobs from an influx of new employees from GE Aerospace. Augustine answered as he and others had throughout the process.

The combined companies would be far stronger than either could be individually in competing for business and providing jobs. But one of the givens of the merger, he said, would be efficiency of operation through elimination of duplicative facilities, functions, and people. Job security, he said right up front, would be determined solely on the basis of which position could best compete for business.

Initial reaction to news of the merger within the ranks of General Electric Aerospace was surprise if not outright shock, Welch said. But it was short-lived when it became apparent that Martin Marietta was dedicated not only to maintaining but growing its position in aerospace and electronics. Instead of being a very small piece of a $60-billion-plus giant that had much larger interests elsewhere, GE Aerospace could now be equal partners in an enterprise dedicated to more common interests.

GE chairman Jack Welch said later it was exactly such rationalization that led him to first speak to Augustine at the Homestead. At the General Electric annual strategic-planning review, held in July 1992, "we decided from our perspective that the growth rate in the [aerospace] industry was clearly not there," Welch said. "There were too many players chasing a declining pie, and our objective looked at combining the aerospace company with somebody. Then we went off for the summer and came back and had another look at it in September. That's when our people [John Rittenhouse, Gene Murphy, and Gary M. Reiner] came up with an analysis of Raytheon and Martin Marietta as the two," Welch said.[5]

"Raytheon was making noises of diversification. Norm Augustine was making noises of staying with his knitting. Both of these companies would have been good fits for GE Aerospace. One of our investment people had also seen a Martin Marietta presentation to security analysts, and everything Martin Marietta wanted to be we could make them be. So I took Norm's presentation and basically filled in the blanks. He wanted to be in the business and outlined a strategy that made sense. With our help his balance sheet could do it," the GE chairman added. "Raytheon had a lot of conflicting discussion. They wanted to be in defense one day, then they wanted to be in the appliance business, and then the next day the construction business. But Norm kept saying, 'This is my business.' So Raytheon finished second." Welch said General Electric would have approached Raytheon if Augustine had said "no dice."

So the decision was reached in September, and Welch broached the subject with Augustine in October. The GE chairman said he knew of Martin Marietta's fierce resistance to an earlier takeover attempt and of its defenses against such a move, so he wanted to make certain right from the start that Augustine "knew that I was amenable to all the options . . . that this was a friendly relationship . . . that I wasn't interested in any hostile behavior."

He said he had not known Augustine before he approached him at the Homestead except to say hello on occasional contact at business meetings. He described their initial encounter as "a very friendly opening" and said their mutual trust and enthusiasm for what he called "a chance to make this one hell of a company" pervaded their talks, the negotiations that followed, and the implementation of the merger.

"I found Norm, and Marc, too, to be the highest caliber guys you'd ever want to meet," the GE chairman added. "So we didn't have a momentary hitch. There was never anyone close to walking, no events or eruptions. . . . Everybody was trying to get it done," Welch said. He was particularly complimentary of David L. Calhoun, the head of GE's corporate audit staff, and Martin Marietta's John Montague. Their roles from announcement to closing were "extremely important," Welch said. "By taking care of the countless details involved in a multibillion-dollar merger, they literally closed the deal." The relationships at every level of the negotiation between GE and Martin Marietta people, in Welch's view, "couldn't have been better." And he believes those relationships, plus the obvious merits of the merger, helped ease most of the anxieties among employees once they got over the initial surprise and learned the facts.

"I think most people see it as a better chance. The attitudes in Syracuse and places like that were very positive. The logic made sense. The people we sold the business to, if we had to sell it, were the best," Welch said. There was some traditional reaction—"people liking GE a lot more after the sale than when they were with it. . . . There was some longing for GE that occurs when you lose something." But in general he thought the reaction "very positive." RCA people were, if anything, probably pleased to go on to a new life, Welch said, because they had a fairly unstressed life with RCA during the defense buildup. As soon as RCA merged with GE in 1986, defense started going down, and Welch said the RCA people "may have felt a little pressure in GE."[6]

If they did, they seemed to be unburdening themselves of that stress pretty quickly. At one GE installation that formerly had been an RCA facility, T-shirts appeared very soon after the announcement of the merger with Martin Marietta. Under the words "Martin Marietta" there was a cartoon depiction of the RCA Victor dog as a soccer player kicking a ball displaying the GE logo. A shirt was presented to some of the Martin Marietta people when they made the rounds of the plants.

"I think the selling of a business is a very traumatic event in someone's life," Welch said. "All of a sudden all of the relationships you have built up . . . what you have known . . . what counted . . . is changed. We've seen that many times, and no matter how hard you try to help people, trauma occurs. I would say from our standpoint this has been the most logical, the easiest, the smoothest, the best. It is really nice," he added, "if you have to sell something and deal with people's lives then sell it to Norm Augustine who you know will deal with people in the best possible sense. It's very real."[7]

There were other examples of GE employee affinity for their new teammates and vice versa. GE employees have long been in the habit of "dressing down" on Fridays—no ties or coats or dresses, just sweaters and slacks or other comfortable clothes. On the first inter-plant teleconference of the newly merged operations, according to Joseph Cleveland, manager of aerospace information technology at Philadelphia, GE participants at that location were casually dressed while their Martin Marietta counterparts appeared on the screen in suits and ties. So on the following week's teleconference, the Martin Marietta people appeared informally only to find their new Philadelphia colleagues in dresses, coats, and ties, which drew a good laugh all around.

■

DESPITE SLIGHT DIFFERENCES, IT WASN'T as if the two companies were strangers. Their paths had run in parallel through the years. They had collaborated on a host of programs, particularly in the last half-century following World War II, sometimes as joint principal contractors, sometimes as prime and subcontractor, or as sub and prime.

But there were even some significant GE–Martin Marietta ties that predated the existence of both GE Aerospace and Martin Marietta. One of the earliest was in the aggregates business, and it involved none other than Thomas Alva Edison. The "wizard of Menlo

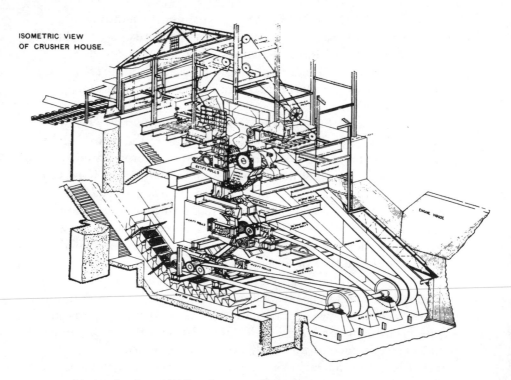

Isometric view of Edison's stone crusher

Park," whose incandescent light bulb was the raison d'être of today's General Electric Company, was thirty-nine years old when Glenn Martin was born. When Glenn built and flew his first airplane in 1909, Edison at sixty-two had scores of inventions to his credit, including a stone-crushing plant that was installed a year later in a limestone quarry at Tompkins Cove, New York. Martin Marietta owned and operated that quarry and another down the Hudson River at Haverstraw, New York, for twelve years, from 1966 until 1978, when they were sold. Instead of the old jaw crusher in use for many years in the industry, Mr. Edison's used giant studded rollers that turned at 180 revolutions per minute and were capable of breaking a twenty-ton slab of stone into seven-inch pieces in twenty seconds. Before installation of the Edison system, the quarry could produce an eight-hundred-ton barge load of stone every six hours. The new plant could do that much in an hour. The oldest stone quarry still operating in the United States, Tompkins Cove has been producing crushed stone, principally for construction of Manhattan skyscrapers, streets and subways, for more than 160 years. It still uses the same Edison-designed crusher and conveyor system, albeit all of its rollers, belts, and wheels have been replaced many times.[8]

Just a few years later, in 1919, a turbine-driven supercharger developed by GE gave added boost to the famous Liberty reciprocating engines that powered the first real Martin bomber, the MB-1. The early role of the turbosupercharger was limited primarily to high-altitude experimental aircraft. It would not become standard equipment until World War II, when oxygen requirements of aircraft radial engines increased as their operating altitudes increased. At altitudes where the conventional aircraft engine was beginning to be starved for lack of oxygen, the supercharger in effect created its own air by taking exhaust gases to drive a turbine that produced additional air for reintroduction into the original combustion process. After a proof mission in 1918 on the Liberty engine of a LePere Biplane, such superchargers became integral to the Liberty engines on Glenn Martin's MB-1 bomber. Dr. Sanford A. Moss, who pioneered GE's development of turbosuperchargers, visited the Martin aerocraft factory in Cleveland on more than one occasion during the building of the MB-1 and its successor, the MB-2 of Billy Mitchell and battleship-bombing fame.[9]

Arc-welding equipment produced by General Electric in 1930 changed forever the method of manufacturing aircraft, including Martin's famous China Clippers and renowned World War II planes. It was a GE team the government called on in the closing hours of

Martin MB-2 with GE turbocharger

World War II to go to Europe and identify and shepherd to the United States the Peenemünde rocket scientists who would be gathered at Fort Bliss and eventually at Huntsville, where they would staff development of the Redstone, Jupiter, and Pershing missiles and eventually Saturn and the Apollo Moon program.

Engineers and technicians from Martin Marietta and General Electric worked side-by-side on the early Viking high-altitude sounding rocket and on Vanguard. One of the reentry vehicles carried by Martin Marietta–built Titan ICBMs was designed and manufactured by GE. The radio guidance system that performed flawlessly on twelve flights of the Gemini-Titan Launch Vehicle was a GE product. Martin Marietta has been a major subcontractor to GE since 1969, supplying more than three thousand three hundred thrust reverser assemblies for several series of GE commercial jet engines. The programs on which the two companies have worked over the years are too numerous to list but have ranged across systems for all of the military services on land, sea, and in the air as well as for the National Aeronautics and Space Administration, both in Earth orbit and on interplanetary missions. On NASA's Mars Observer mission launched in the fall of 1992, GE built the spacecraft boosted into space by a Martin Marietta–produced Titan III. Martin Marietta also built the upper stage and the launch facility.[10]

The future appeared exceptionally bright for the combined

GE jet engine fan reverser

company, the "new Martin Marietta," which Jack Welch noted would have "a fraction of the overhead of the two companies that created it." Augustine saw it as "a win-win" for shareholders and customers and ultimately for employees. Wall Street seemed to share their enthusiasm. The price of Martin Marietta's stock jumped seventeen points in two-months' time. GE's stock increased fifteen points, about a third of which was attributed directly to the merger.[11]

Securities analyst Michael LaTronica then of Martin-Simpson & Co., called it a "superb fit from a strategic and tactical viewpoint," with synergy stemming from the "complementary technologies and markets the two companies address with little overlap." Peter Aseritis of First Boston said the merger would "substantially expand the new Martin Marietta's competitive position in space, telecommunications, defense electronics, information systems, technical services, materials, and energy" and would enable it to become "a more technically advanced, world-class supplier of defense and commercial high-technology products and processes." Lior Bregman of Oppenheimer & Co. found the combination "very promising" and predicted it would provide "improved efficiencies [through] resource utilization and economies of scale, stronger market position, and business prospects. . . ."[12]

LaTronica added that Martin Marietta "will become the gorilla rather than the chimpanzee in the markets it serves," a comparison Martin Marietta's chairman found to his liking. Augustine recalled that a few weeks before the merger was announced, a friend and chief executive of a competitor aerospace firm had shown a slide illustrating the weakness of the industry and its need to consolidate. The slide showed one gorilla, three chimpanzees, and six marmosets, one of which the friend jokingly had indicated to Augustine was Martin Marietta. After announcing the merger, Augustine called his competitor's office and left a message with the secretary: "Please tell him that one of the marmosets just took vitamins."[13]

■

THERE IS AN INTERESTING SIDELIGHT to the history of the two companies. In 1915, five years after the Edison crusher was installed in what eventually became a Martin Marietta aggregates operation and nearly eighty years before the merger of Martin Marietta and GE Aerospace, Thomas Alva Edison and Glenn L. Martin actually met and apparently had at least a nodding acquaintance. At the time, Edison was heading up an advisory panel to the secretary of the Navy,

Josephus Daniels, and he asked Martin to serve as a director of an adjunct advisory panel. The newly created group was identified as the American Society of Aeronautic Engineers, with headquarters at the Aero Club in New York City. Its original officers included vice presidents identified in the *Chicago Tribune* dispatch as "Orville Wright, inventor of the aeroplane; Glenn H. Curtiss, designer of the Curtiss aeroplane; W. Sterling Burgess, builder of the Burgess-Dunne aeroplane; Elmer A. Sperry, inventor of the gyroscopic aeroplane stabilizer; Peter Cooper Hewitt, inventor of the mercury vapor lamp and other electrical appliances; and John Jay Hammond, Jr., inventor of the secret of guiding vessels by wireless waves." The secretary was Lawrence B. Sperry, son of Elmer, and among the directors, in addition to Glenn Martin, were Emile Berliner, Edison F. Gallaudet, Grover C. Loening, F. A. Seiberling, and Joseph A. Steinmetz.[14] Many of these same people were also in the group that formed the Aircraft Manufacturers Association in 1917, a predecessor of the Aerospace Industries Association.[15]

Emile Berliner was, of course, the inventor of the Disk Gramophone and the man responsible for uniting in 1901 the painting of "Nipper," the attentive white fox terrier, with the Victor Talking Machine Company. The original had been painted in England by Francis Barraud, who sold it to the Gramophone Company Ltd. of London for its trademark. Berliner, a director of the English company, brought a copy of the trademark to America, where the U.S. Patent Office registered it as the "Trademark for Gramophones" in 1900. Berliner sold it to Victor the following year. That company's merger in 1929 with Radio Corporation of America created the famous RCA Victor trademark, "His Master's Voice," which is said to be the world's most recognized trademark in communications, electronics, and entertainment. When RCA merged with General Electric in 1986, the trademark became GE property, and that's where it still resides along with NBC. Much of the rest of RCA became GE Aerospace, which is now Martin Marietta.[16]

Epilogue

■

When the nearly one hundred thousand men and women of the new Martin Marietta Corporation and the thousands of existing retirees who preceded them observe their company's eighty-fifth birthday (1909–94), it will be with justifiable pride. Their contributions and the contributions of their forebears throughout the course of the twentieth century have made a significant mark on the security of their country and the peace of the world, and have expanded the frontiers of space as well as the technological prowess and economic progress of humankind.

Martin Marietta's anniversary year will also mark "Fifty Years of Freedom," the golden anniversary observance of "D-Day" and the Battle of Normandy, June 6, 1944, when Allied forces began the liberation of Europe. The role of Martin aircraft and Martin people in that turning point of world history helped win the peace. Equally notable were the contributions of Martin Marietta men and women to the world's security in the half-century since that conflict. Systems like Titan, Sprint, Pershing, LANTIRN, and TADS not only kept the peace but helped win the Cold War and provide conditions that continue to fuel fires of freedom around the globe.

This, then, is the heritage of many thousands upon thousands of men and women, including one who was once called "a merchant of death." It is the heritage of the company Glenn Martin built and of the people he hired and inspired and of those who have followed and are still following in their footsteps. Can there ever again be a comparable period of eighty-five years that will witness as much change technically, politically, or socially? Probably the answer would be "no" from most of those who lived through it. Undoubtedly "yes" would be the enthusiastic response of a new generation of visionaries, some of whom already are among the doers of today and the dreamers of tomorrow. Their challenges are as great as ever, the opportunities unlimited if not yet identified. The exciting potential is that today's budding geniuses—whether they be on the shop floor, in the laboratory, or in an executive office—might just blossom into a Bell, a Bunker, a Douglas, a Hermann, a Kindelberger, a Moss, a Steinmetz, or perhaps even an Edison, a Wright, or a Martin. Will there be places that nourish their growth? Will any of them be leaders who have the time to walk on the factory floor and call fellow employees by name? Will the new Martin Marietta be among the companies that—in laboratories, factories, and offices—tend the promising, tolerate and encourage differences, reward accomplishment, nurture genius, and fund the best?

There is no conclusion to this story. It is ongoing—the beginning of a new and larger enterprise about to enter another century, the patina of its illustrious heritage ever ready for the burnishment of new accomplishment.

APPENDIX 1

Production Chronology

■

D uring its first eighty years, an impressive number and variety of products were generated by Martin Marietta Corporation and its predecessor companies, namely The Martin Company and American-Marietta Company. In the first four decades, when aircraft were the only product, more than fifty distinctly different airplanes were built, some in ones and twos, others by hundreds and thousands.

By 1960, when the company formally exited production of aircraft to concentrate on missiles, rockets, spacecraft, and all manner of defense systems, Martin had produced 11,214 airplanes. With the merger of American-Marietta in 1961, the product line expanded to include a variety of commercial products ranging from construction aggregates and cement to paint, printing ink, textile dyestuff and other chemical products, and later aluminum.

In the following list of these products, *Time Frame* refers generally to the years of delivery or, in the case of some space systems, the year(s) of launch. In some instances for the earliest aircraft, exact dates and quantities are not well documented and can only be estimated.

Model	Type	Number	Time Frame
Model 1	First Martin aircraft	1	1909
TT	Army trainer	17	1913
Model 12[1]	Pusher biplane	1	1913
Great Lakes Tourer	First passenger aircraft	1	1913
TA	Hydro-aeroplane	1	1914
TA-2	Military hydro-aeroplane	1	1914
Model S	Passenger seaplane	1	1915
Model R	Army observation	1	1916
MB-1	Army twin-engine bomber	16	1919–20
MP	Mail-plane version of MB	6	1919
M12P	12-passenger version of MB	1	1919
MBT	Navy torpedo bomber	2	1919–20
MT	Army bomber	8	1920
MB-2	Army bomber	20	1920–21
M20-1	Navy observation	3	1923
N2M-1	Navy trainer seaplane	2	1923
MS-1	Navy submarine scout (all metal)	6	1923
NT-1	Navy trainer	1	1923
MO-1	Navy observation (battleship-based)	36	1923–24
MM-1	Night mail (Model 66)	3	1923
SC-1	Navy scout/torpedo bomber (submarine)	35	1924–25
SC-2	Navy scout/torpedo bomber	40	1925–26
T3M-1	Navy scout/torpedo bomber	24	1925–27
T3M-2	Navy scout/torpedo bomber	100	1925–27
T3M-4	Navy scout/torpedo bomber	1	1927–28
XT4M-1	Navy torpedo landplane	1	1927
T4M-1	Navy torpedo seaplane and landplane	102	1927–28
XT5M-1	Navy dive bomber	1	1927
PM-1	Navy patrol bomber	27	1929–30
PM-1B	Patrol bomber (Brazil)	3	1930
XT6M-1	Navy torpedo, carrier-based	1	1930
XP2M-1	Navy patrol (tri-motor)	1	1930
XP2M-1	Navy patrol (bi-motor)	1	1931
P3M-1	Navy PY-1 patrol	9	1930–31
P3M-2	Navy PY-1 patrol	9	1930–31
PM-2	Navy patrol	28	1930–31
X-BM-1	Navy dive bomber	1	1930–32
XB-907	Army high-speed bomber (B-10 forerunner)	1	1931–32
BM-1	Navy dive bomber	17	1931–32
BM-2	Navy dive bomber	17	1931–32
XB-10	Army bomber	1	1931
YB-10	Army bomber	14	1932–34
YB-10A	Army bomber	1	1933
YB-12	Army bomber	7	1933–34
YB-12A	Army bomber	25	1933–34
YB-14	Army bomber	1	1934
Model 130 Clipper[2]	Pan-Am flying boat	3	1934–35
Model 146	Army bomber	1	1935
B-10B	Army bomber	103	1935–36
139W	B-10B export (Argentina)	35	1936–38

Model	Type	Number	Time Frame
139W	B-10B export (Amtorg)	1	1936
139W	B-10B export (Siam)	6	1936–37
139W	B-10B export (Turkey)	30	1936–37
139W	B-10B export (China)	9	1936–37
139W	B-10B export (Dutch East Indies)	120	1936–39
139W	B-10B export (Russia)	1	1937
Model 162A[3]	Piloted scale model PBM-1	1	1937
Model 156	Clipper flying boat (Russia)	1	1938
Model 167 Maryland	Army attack bomber (XA-22)	1	1939
A-22 Maryland	Attack bomber (France)	310	1939–40
A-22 Maryland	Attack bomber (England)	185	1939–40
XPBM-1	Navy patrol bomber	1	1939
PBM-1 Mariner[4]	Navy patrol bomber	20	1940–41
B-26 Marauder	Army light bomber	5,266	1940–45
XPBM-2	Navy patrol bomber (catapult)	1	1941
XPB2M-1	Navy long-range patrol	1	1943
A-30 Baltimore	Recon bomber (England)	681	1942–43
PBM-3E[5]	Navy patrol bomber (radar)	1	1942
PBM-3R	Navy transport	50	1942–44
PBM-3C	Navy patrol bomber	274	1942–44
PBM-3S[6]	Navy antisub seaplane	94	1943–45
PBM-3D	Navy patrol bomber	300	1943–44
PBM-3B	Patrol (England, Australia)	32	1943–44
A-30A Baltimore	Recon bomber (England)	894	1943–44
B-29 Superfortress[7]	Army Air Corps heavy bomber	536	1943–45
XPBM-5	Navy patrol seaplane	2	1943
PBM-5[8]	Navy patrol seaplane	589	1944–45
XPBM-5A	Navy patrol amphibian	1	1945
JRM-1 Mars[9]	Navy long-range patrol/transport	5	1945–46
JRM-2 Mars	Navy long-range patrol/transport	1	1946
C-37 Conversion	USAF target-tow aircraft	200	1946–47
C-54 Conversion[10]	Commercial airliners	110	1946–47
2-0-2	Commercial airliners (NWA, LAN, LAV)	31	1946–50
AM-1 Mauler	Navy dive/torpedo bomber	131	1946–48
XP4M-1	Navy patrol landplane	2	1946
XBTM-1	Navy dive/torpedo bomber	3	1946
AM-1Q Mauler	Navy dive/torpedo bomber	18	1946–49
XB-48	USAF jet medium bomber	2	1947
Gorgon IV	Navy ram-jet test vehicle	1	1948
XP5M-1	Navy ASW seaplane	1	1948
PBM-5A	Navy patrol amphibian	40	1948–49
P4M-1 Mercator	Navy patrol landplane	19	1946–49
XB-51	USAF tactical bomber	1	1949
Viking	Navy high-altitude research rocket	15	1949–55
KDM-1	Navy ram-jet drone	28	1949
TM-61 Matador	USAF tactical missile	971	1949–57
2-0-2A	Airliner (TWA)	12	1950
4-0-4	Airliner (EAL, TWA)	101	1951–53
P5M-1 Marlin[11]	Navy ASW seaplane	121	1951–54
4-0-4	USCG transport	2	1952
Oriole	Navy air-air test missile	16	1952–54

Model	Type	Number	Time Frame
B-57A[12]	USAF light bomber	8	1951–55
RB-57A	USAF reconnaissance	67	1954–55
B-57B	USAF tactical bomber	202	1954–56
B-57C	USAF trainer	38	1955–56
B-57D	USAF high-altitude test bed	20	1955–56
B-57E	USAF target-tow	68	1956–57
P5M-2	Navy ASW seaplane	117	1953–60
XP6M-1 SeaMaster	Navy jet seaplane	2	1955
Shillelagh	Army tank-launched missile	12,500	1965–71
Walleye	Navy/AF TV-guided glide bomb	8,309	1965–71
TM-76 Mace	USAF tactical missile	295	1956–60
Vanguard	Navy/NASA satellite launch vehicle	15	1957–59
YP6M-1	Navy jet seaplane	6	1958
P6M-2 SeaMaster	Navy jet seaplane	8	1958
Bullpup[13]	USAF/Navy air-surface missile	39,611	1958–63
Lacrosse	Army field artillery missile	1,244	1958–64
Bold Orion (199B)	Air-launched ballistic missile	17	1959
SNAP 1[14]	Systems for Nuclear Auxiliary Power (research model)	1	1959
SNAP 3	3W prototype Radioisotopic Thermo-electric Generator (RTG)	1	1959
SNAP 3A	Navy 2.7W RTG, Transit 4 navigational satellite	2	1960
Missile Master	Army air-defense missile control	10	1960–61
Titan I	USAF Intercontinental Ballistic Missile	163	1960–62
BIRDiE	Army Battery Integration and Radar Display Equipment (air-defense missile control)	19	1960–62
Pershing[15]	Army tactical ballistic missile	754	1960–69
SNAP 1A	125W spacecraft RTG	1	1960
Titan II	USAF ICBM	102	1962–64
PM-1	USAF 1000kW nuclear power plant, Wyoming	1	1962
PM-3A	Navy 1000kW nuclear power plant, Antarctica	1	1962
SNAP 7A	USCG 100W RTG, sea buoy	1	1963
SNAP 7B	USCG 60W RTG, Baltimore lighthouse	1	1963
SNAP 7C	Navy 40W RTG, Antarctic weather buoy	1	1963
SNAP 7E	Navy 8W RTG, navigation beacon	1	1963
SNAP 9A	Navy 2.7W RTG, Transit 5 satellites	2	1963
SNAP 15	DoD 0.001W RTG, classified	1	1963
Titan III[16]	Space launch vehicle	150	1964–current
Gemini/Titan	Manned space launch vehicle	12	1964–66
SNAP 7D	Navy 60W RTG, Gulf of Mexico weather station	1	1964
SNAP 19	Navy 30W RTG, Nimbus weather satellite	3	1964
Transtage	Space maneuvering vehicle	47	1964–85
SNAP 7F	Navy 60W RTG, offshore oil platform	1	1965
SNAP 11	NASA 25W RTG, Surveyor moon probe	1	1965
PRIME	Precision Recovery Including Maneuvering Entry lifting body	3	1965–68
Sprint[17]	Army antiballistic missile	205	1965–75

Model	Type	Number	Time Frame
MH-1A (Sturgis)	Shipborne nuclear power station	1	1966
LCG	Navy Lightweight Commercial Generator	5	1966
X-24A	USAF manned reentry lifting body	1	1969
Fan Reversers	GE jet-engine assemblies	3,300	1969–current
Paveway	Laser bomb-guidance kit	16,000	1970–76
Monorail	Disney World monorail coaches	55	1970–75
LARS	Laser-Aided Rocket System	20	1970–72
Viking OPS	Mars Orbiter Propulsion System	2	1971–75
Lunar Drill	Astronaut zero-gravity tool	1	1971
Mariner Propulsion	Mariner 9 spacecraft subsystem	1	1971
Pave Penny	USAF laser designator (A-10)	793	1971–current
MARTRON	Martin Electronics airliner test set	51	1972–current
Skylab MDA	Multiple Docking Adapter	1	1973
X-24B	Manned reentry lifting body	1	1973
Viking Lander	Mars spacecraft	2	1974–75
CCMS	Checkout, Control and Monitor Subsystem for Shuttle launch control	5	1975–78
GSS	Ground Support System for Shuttle, Vandenberg Air Force Base	—	1976–85
Solar Power	NASA prototype photovoltaic concentrator	1	1975
Solar Power	DOE 10MW Solar One collector, Barstow, California	1	1975
Solar Power	DOE 1MW collector, Sandia Labs, Albuquerque, New Mexico	1	1976
ATLIS	Automatic Tracking, Laser Illumination System (France)	2	1976–78
ASALM	Advanced Strategic Air-Launched Missile	7	1977–80
Voyager[18]	Instrumentation for NASA planetary explorer	2	1977
SCATHA	Spacecraft Charging AT High Altitudes Research Satellite	1	1979
ADATS	Air-Defense/Anti-Tank System	10	1979–81
Assault Breaker	Army surface-to-surface missile	16	1979–81
Shuttle External Tank	Liquid-fuel tank for Space Shuttle	58	1979–current
Solar Power	500kW thermal collector subsystem (Spain)	1	1981
Solar Power	DOE 350kW photovoltaic system (Saudi Arabia)	1	1981
LANTIRN	Low-Altitude Navigation and Targeting, InfraRed for Night	313	1981–current
Copperhead	Army laser-guided artillery shell	28,223	1981–current
ASMPS	Army Staff Message Processing System	6	1981–82
Pershing II	Army tactical missile	276	1981–89
Solar Power	225kW photovoltaic system, Phoenix airport	1	1982
Hubble FOS	Faint-Object Spectrograph, Hubble Space Telescope	1	1982
AN/MSR-T4	USAF countermeasures training set	7	1982
Space Sextant	Satellite navigation system	1	1982
Patriot[19]	Army air-defense missile	3,839	1982–current
VLS	Navy Vertical Launching System	382	1983–current

Model	Type	Number	Time Frame
TADS/PNVS	Target Acquisition-Designation Sight/ Pilot Night-Vision Sensor	679	1983–current
B-1B Subassemblies	Horizontal/vertical stabilizers	100	1983–current
Peacekeeper[20]	USAF ICBM	68	1983–current
LST/SCAM	Navy Laser Spot Tracker/Strike CAMera	218	1983–current
NASP[21]	National Airspace System Plan	—	1984–current
MMU	Shuttle Manned Maneuvering Unit	2	1984
ASAS	Army All-Source Analysis System	111	1986–current
Deadeye	Navy laser-guided projectile	12	1986–89
CNCE	Army Communication Nodal Control Element	90	1986–89
Small ICBM	USAF next-generation ICBM	2	1986–current
Hellfire	Army laser-guided air-surface missile	17,828	1986–current
R2P2	Rapid Retargeting and Precision Pointing Simulator for Strategic Defense Initiative (SDI)	1	1986–current
AN/TYC-16	Army automatic message center	6	1986–90
ALV	Autonomous Land Vehicle, testbed for robotic research	1	1986
SLAT	Navy Supersonic Low-Altitude Target	13	1987–89
NTB	National Test Bed for SDI Simulation	—	1987–current
Titan IV	Space launch vehicle	4	1988–current
Zenith Star	SDI space-based laser experiment	—	1988–current
FAADS	Army Forward-Area Air-Defense System	75	1988–current
AADEOS	Army Advanced Air-Defense Electro-Optic System	16	1988–89
Titan II SLV	Space launch vehicle	2	1988–current
Towed Array	Navy antisub sonar system	440	1988–current
Magellan	Venus radar-mapping spacecraft	1	1989
Galileo Instrumentation[22]	Four systems on planetary explorer	1	1989
Commercial Titan	Commercial space launch vehicle	4	1989–current
Brilliant Pebbles	SDI space antimissile defense	—	1990
Mail Sorters	U.S. Postal Service bar-code processors	199	1990–current
Tethered Satellite	Hardware for deploying a towed satellite on a 78-mile tether from the Shuttle	1	1990
Brilliant Eyes	SDI small surveillance spacecraft	—	1991

NOTES TO APPENDIX I, PRODUCTION CHRONOLOGY

1. Exact numbers and configurations of all early aircraft are not well documented. Reference is made to selling planes—such as the "Beachey Special"—to "wealthy young bloods of the day." Model 12 indicates there were eleven previous models.
2. Three Clipper transpacific flying boats were built for Pan-American: the China Clipper, the Hawaii Clipper, and the Philippine Clipper. A fourth, larger version, the 156, was built for the U.S.S.R.
3. This piloted one-quarter scale model was an aviation first. Its performance so impressed the Navy that twenty full-size production models of the PBM-1 were built more than one year before a full-size prototype flew.
4. Beginning with the first PBM-1 (Patrol Bomber, Martin), this and all subsequent models through PBM-5 were named Mariner.
5. All PBM-3 aircraft were purpose-built and equipped for specific tasks. A total of 679 were built. Some were converted from one model to another; thus, quantities

shown for the various models total more than that figure. The 33R transport version could carry up to thirty-three passengers.

6. Twenty-seven 3S models were transferred to the U.S. Coast Guard in 1944.

7. Martin was a World War II second-source producer of the B-29, manufacturing 536 of the Boeing-designed heavy bombers in a government-owned Martin B-26 factory near Omaha, Nebraska, including the "Enola Gay" that dropped the atomic bomb on Hiroshima and "Bockscar," which dropped the second A-bomb on Nagasaki.

8. Forty-one PBM-5 aircraft were transferred to the U.S. Coast Guard in 1945 and designated PBM-5G.

9. Mars aircraft were named after Pacific Islands: Hawaii, Philippine, Marianas, Marshall, Hawaii II. JRM-2 was the Caroline Mars. The original order called for nineteen, but only five were built. Two were still flying as forest-fire tankers in 1993.

10. Declared surplus after World War II, the C-54 was available in large numbers at low prices. Martin converted 110 of the aircraft into DC-4 commercial airliners for various customers, including TWA, American, Northwest, Capital, Braniff, Northeast, Chicago & Southern, KLM, China National, and one South American airline.

11. Seven P5M-1G Marlins were transferred to USCG in 1954; these were later replaced by four P5M-2G models in 1961.

12. The B-57 Night Intruder was the U.S. Martin-built version of the British Canberra B.2. A total of 403 were built in a variety of models for different missions ranging from high-altitude bombing and reconnaissance to low-level night interdiction—more effective configurations than any other U.S. Air Force aircraft. Twenty-two B models were transferred to Pakistan in 1957. A number were later modified for use in Vietnam; the last was delivered in 1966.

13. Different models of Bullpup with a variety of payloads and guidance systems were produced. A number of NATO nations also built the missile under license from Martin.

14. The Atomic Energy Commission began the SNAP program in 1955 to develop nuclear auxiliary power systems for space applications. Martin Nuclear Division was contracted to develop radioisotope-fueled (odd-numbered) systems for various space and terrestrial uses.

15. Original Pershing launch equipment was replaced by an advanced system (Pershing Ia) in the field in the SWAP program in 1970. Tracked carriers were replaced with wheeled vehicles; the missile itself was unchanged. The entire system was upgraded in 1983 with the longer range, more accurate Pershing II.

16. Titan III, produced in a number of different models—A, B, C, D, E, and 34D—to fit a variety of satellite and planetary missions for the Air Force and NASA, also became the basis of Commercial Titan.

17. The hypersonic Sprint was one of two missiles in the U.S.-based Safeguard anti-ICBM defense system. Safeguard became operational in 1975 and was deactivated shortly thereafter as a condition of the START Treaty with the Soviet Union.

18. Martin Marietta was responsible for the radio astronomy receiver, hybrid microelectronic circuitry, composite structure, memory access modules, and propellant control units on Voyager.

19. Prior to the production decision in 1980, Patriot was known as SAM-D (Surface-to-Air Missile-Development). The total number shown includes 132 SAM-Ds. The company also built 698 launchers for the missile system.

20. Martin Marietta was U.S. Air Force associate contractor, responsible for assembly, test, and system support, transportation and handling of equipment and instrumentation and flight safety systems for eighteen developmental and fifty operational missiles.

21. Martin Marietta was selected in 1984 as the system engineering and integration contractor for the Federal Aviation Administration's comprehensive long-term modernization of air traffic control and airway facilities in the U.S. National Airspace System. Contracts to provide similar services were later negotiated with the U.S. Air Force, the Canadian government, and several European air traffic systems.

22. Launched toward Jupiter in 1989, Galileo carried four Martin Marietta instruments: nephelometer, atmosphere structure instrument, attitude and articulation control system, and net flux radiometer.

APPENDIX 2

Technological Firsts

■

In 1909, when Glenn L. Martin built his first airplane and taught himself to fly, and later, when he organized the country's first aircraft manufacturing facility, and even well into the 1940s and '50s, *technology* was a word seldom used. From its beginnings to the present, however, Martin Marietta has been at the forefront of technology, compiling a record of "firsts" and significant achievements that are perhaps unmatched. This heritage of technology has produced some of this century's most distinguished aircraft and today's most advanced aerospace systems as well as impacting other sophisticated products.

Although it would be difficult to recount all the important contributions of this technology, even a partial listing establishes a significant technological history.

- World record overocean flight (Model 12, 1912)
- First multipassenger airplane (Great Lakes Tourer, 1913)
- First army air bombardment (TT, 1913)
- First free-fall parachute (1913)
- First true dive-bomber (BM-1, 1919)
- First mail plane (Model 66, 1919)
- First sinking of a battleship by a bomber (BM-1, 1921)
- First all-metal U.S. airplane (MO-1, 1922)
- Record high-altitude flight (27,120 feet) and high-altitude parachute jump (24,206 feet) (MB-2, 1922)

- First dive-bomber to carry 1,000 pounds in terminal-velocity dive (XT-5M-1, 1928)
- First bomber to fly faster than contemporary pursuit planes (B-10, 1930)
- First scheduled transoceanic airplane (China Clipper, 1935)
- First power-operated aircraft gun turrets (1936)
- First self-sealing fuel cell (Mareng, 1940)
- Record long-range flights: 4,700 miles with 10 tons of cargo, Manila to Alameda, with 128 passengers (Mars flying boat, 1949)
- First U.S. missile built by assembly-line techniques (Matador, 1949)
- First jet aircraft with variable-incidence wings (XB-51, 1949)
- First T-tail jet bomber (XB-51, 1949)
- Developed honeycomb construction for aircraft and missiles (1953)
- First "smart bomb" (TV-guided Walleye, 1955)
- First jam-proof missile guidance system (Mace, 1956)
- First rocket to the fringe of space (U.S. Navy Viking, 158 miles altitude, 1958)
- First multistage launch vehicle (U.S. Navy–NASA Vanguard, 1958)
- First rocket use of hypergolic fuels (Vanguard, 1958)
- First development of gimbaled rocket engines (Viking, 1949)
- First use of gimbaled engines sensitive enough to eliminate stabilizing fins (Vanguard, 1958)
- First launch vehicle to navigate with self-contained airborne guidance (Vanguard, 1958)
- First air-launched multistage ballistic missile (Bold Orion, 1958)
- First field artillery missile (U.S. Army Lacrosse, 1959)
- First ICBM launch from an underground silo (U.S. Air Force Titan, 1959)
- First device to convert decay heat from radioisotopes into electrical energy on a practical level with no moving parts, (SNAP 3A, 1960)
- First development and proof of airbag restraint system for airline passengers and astronauts (1960s)
- First nuclear-powered unmanned weather station (SNAP 3A, 2.5 W, 1961)
- First nuclear power in space (U.S. Navy Transit satellite, 2.7 W, 1961)
- First pulsed-gas laser (1962)
- Developed Zero Defects, first major program to stress individual quality workmanship (1962). Program later adopted by government and copied by industry throughout the United States and abroad.
- First air-transportable nuclear power plant, a 1,000-kilowatt reactor installed at the U.S. Air Force radar station in Wyoming (PM-3A, 1962)
- First nuclear power plant in Antarctica, prime power source for U.S. scientific base at McMurdo Sound (PM-3A, 1,000 kilowatts, 1962)
- First undersea nuclear-powered navigational beacon (SNAP 7E, 7W, 1962)
- First nuclear power unit to wholly power a satellite (SNAP 19, 30W, 1964)
- First nuclear power plant on the Moon (SNAP 11, 25W, Surveyor Moon probe, 1965)
- First zero-reaction power tool (drill used by astronauts to take core samples from the Moon, Apollo 11, 1966)
- First large-scale industrial processing of strontium 90 as fuel for nuclear generators (LCG-25A, 1966)
- First barge-mounted nuclear power plant for emergency power supply (MH-1A, 10,000 kilowatts, U.S. Army Sturgis, 1966)
- First sequential placement of eight satellites in orbit by a single booster (Transtage, 1966)
- First automatic computer-based data system for patient control (Children's Hospital, Boston, 1966)
- First placement in the United States of a skid-resistant highly reflective artificial aggregate for highway paving (Synopal, 1967)
- First flight of U.S. Air Force X-24A manned lifting body, precursor to Space Shuttle (1969)
- First laser-aided rocket system (LARS, 1970)
- First surface exploration of Mars (Viking spacecraft, 1975–76)
- World's largest spacecraft fuel tank (154-foot Shuttle External Tank, 1978)

- First production laser-guided cannon projectiles (U.S. Army Copperhead, 1981)
- First operational night-vision targeting and navigation systems for fixed-wing aircraft (LANTIRN, 1981) and helicopters (TADS/PNVS, 1983)
- First untethered space flights by an astronaut for satellite repair and retrieval (Manned Maneuvering Unit, 1984)
- Development of a near-perfect, optical-black surface treatment for precision space-based optical systems (Martin Black, 1986)
- First radar mapping of planet Venus (Magellan, 1990)

Notes and Other Sources

■

INTRODUCTION

1. Rudyard Kipling, *Tommy*, stanza 5.

1. BEDSHEETS, BOX KITES, AND BIPLANES

1. Henry Still, *To Ride the Wind*. New York: Julian Messner, 1964, page 19. Copyright © 1964 by Henry Still. Reprinted by permission of Julian Messner, a division of Simon & Schuster, Inc.
2. Ibid., page 20.
3. Valleau C. Curtis, *History of Callicoon*, Sullivan County Library, Callicoon, New York.
4. Still, *To Ride the Wind*, page 31.
5. Ibid., page 43.

2. REALIZING THE DREAM

1. Vi Smith, *From Jennies to Jets: The Aviation History of Orange County*. Fullerton, California: Sultana Press, 1985, page 2.
2. Ibid.
3. Henry Still, *To Ride the Wind*. New York: Julian Messner, 1964, page 48.
4. Ibid., page 15.
5. Ibid., page 54.

3. PIONEERING DAYS

1. Quoted in *Box Kites to Bombers*, an undated publication of the Glenn L. Martin Company, page 68.
2. Henry Still, *To Ride the Wind*. New York: Julian Messner, 1964, page 70.
3. Ibid., quoted from *Flying Machines: Construction and Operation*.
4. Ibid., page 71, quoted from *Aero, America's Aviation Weekly*.
5. Ibid., page 72.
6. Ibid., page 74.

7. *Los Angeles Times* clipping in scrapbook, Glenn L. Martin papers, Library of Congress.
8. Vi Smith, *From Jennies to Jets: The Aviation History of Orange County*. Fullerton, California: Sultana Press, 1985, page 8.

4. FLEDGLING BUSINESSES

1. Grover M. Hermann, "Mr. Hermann's Own Account of His Family's History," *Sullivan County Democrat*, Callicoon, New York, May 10, 1979, page 9.
2. "Jimmy Ward, Famous Aviator, at Callicoon," *Sullivan County Democrat*, September 19, 1911, page 1.
3. Joseph Timmons, "Martin Wings His Way to Avalon and Return." *Los Angeles Examiner*, May 11, 1912, page 1.
4. "New Device Aids Martin Flying," *Santa Ana Blade*, July 6, 1912, clipping, Library of Congress.
5. "Martin Formed Company to Back Him," *Santa Ana Register*, August 16, 1912, clipping, Library of Congress.

5. BIRTH OF AN INDUSTRY

1. Estelle Lawton Lindsey, " 'Delightful,' Says Mrs. Martin, and Mr. Martin Calls Aerial Trip 'Immense,' " *Los Angeles Record*, November 29, 1913, clipping, Library of Congress.
2. There are published discrepancies on the relationship of Charles Broadwick to Tiny. Some say he was her husband, others her father. The best information available indicates he was her foster father.
3. The first parachute jump from a powered airplane is generally credited to Albert Berry on March 1, 1912, although other sources credit Grant Morton in 1911. It is not apparent that either used a packed "free-fall" chute like Tiny Broadwick's on June 20, 1913, for which Glenn Martin held a 1915 patent.
4. "Girl Leaps from Airplane; 1,000-ft Drop Fun, She Says," *Los Angeles Tribune*, June 21, 1913, page 1.
5. "Girl Drops a Thousand Feet Out of the Sky; Alights Unhurt," *Los Angeles Times*, January 10, 1914, clipping, Library of Congress.
6. Henry Still, *To Ride the Wind*. New York: Julian Messner, 1964, page 102.
7. "Skidding Tractor Injures Two Birdmen," *San Diego Union*, October 30, 1914, clipping, Library of Congress.
8. Differing accounts of the 1914 accident appeared in *Collier's*, June 3, 1933, page 49, and the *Saturday Evening Post*, August 31, 1937, page 30.

6. GRIM VISAGES OF AERIAL WARFARE

1. Didier Masson's exploits in Mexico were reported in: "Glenn Martin Witness in Anaya Case," *The Tucson Citizen*, February 2, 1914, and "Martin to Testify in Airship Probe," *Los Angeles Tribune*, May 13, 1913, clippings, Library of Congress.
2. "New Air Cruiser Faces Test Today," *Los Angeles Examiner*, June 23, 1913, clipping, Library of Congress.
3. "Aerial Man-o'-War Is Completed," *Los Angeles Sunday Tribune*, May 30, 1914, clipping, Library of Congress.
4. "Aeroplane Destroyer Built for War," *Los Angeles Express*, April 24, 1914, clipping, Library of Congress.
5. Glenn L. Martin, "Aviator Tells of New Terrors for Armies and Navies," *Los Angeles Evening Herald*, August 17, 1914, page 1, clipping, Library of Congress.
6. Henry Still, *To Ride the Wind*. New York: Julian Messner, 1964, page 111.
7. Ibid., page 109.

7. A WRIGHT MERGER THAT WAS WRONG

1. *Box Kites to Bombers*, an undated publication of the Glenn L. Martin Company, page 18.
2. Wayne Biddle, *Barons of the Sky*. New York: Simon & Schuster, 1991, page 86. (Copy-

right © 1991 by Wayne Biddle. Reprinted by permission of Simon & Schuster, Inc.) Donald Douglas quotation credited to 1959 oral history transcript, Oral History Research Office, Columbia University.

3. "Society Entertained at Aeroplane Party," *San Diego Union*, August 7, 1914, clipping, Library of Congress.

4. "Knight On Air Steed Takes Flowers to Maiden," *Los Angeles Tribune*, March 3, 1913, clipping, Library of Congress.

5. Henry Still, *To Ride the Wind*. New York: Julian Messner, 1964, page 114.

6. Biddle, *Barons of the Sky*, page 88.

7. See Chapter 8, page 92, for the evolution of Vought-named companies.

8. CLEVELAND AND THE FIRST GREAT BOMBER

1. Frank Kuznik, "Birdmen Come to Cleveland," *Air & Space/Smithsonian*, April-May 1992, pages 76–77. Fred Crawford became president of Thompson Products, 1933–53, and chairman, 1953–58.

2. Henry Still, *To Ride the Wind*. New York: Julian Messner, 1964, page 130.

3. Ibid., page 139.

4. *Box Kites to Bombers*, an undated publication of the Glenn L. Martin Company, page 18.

5. The chronology of Chance Vought's various affiliations was furnished by the Public Information Office of the LTV Aircraft Products Group, Dallas, Texas.

6. See centerfold, Genealogy of an Industry.

7. *Box Kites to Bombers*, page 20.

8. " 'All Aboard' the Air Flyer Is Coming Soon—Says Martin," *The Plain Dealer*, Cleveland, Ohio, February 2, 1919.

9. VINDICATION AND ESTABLISHMENT

1. Testimony of Brigadier General William "Billy" Mitchell before Appropriations Committee, U.S. House of Representatives, Washington, D.C., January 1921.

2. Lester Gardner letter to Glenn L. Martin, July, 14, 1921, Martin papers, Library of Congress.

3. General James H. Doolittle with Carroll V. Glines, *I Could Never Be So Lucky Again: An Autobiography*. New York: Bantam Books, a division of Bantam, Doubleday, Dell Publishing Group, Inc., 1991, page 69.

4. Wayne Biddle, *Barons of the Sky*. New York: Simon & Schuster, 1991, page 122, Memorandum of Brigadier General William "Billy" Mitchell.

5. Glenn L. Martin, "Marvels Wrought in Aviation in a Year; New Goals in Sight," *The Plain Dealer*, Cleveland, June 4, 1920, page 1, clipping, Library of Congress.

6. Farewell address, "Liberty Is at Stake," by Dwight D. Eisenhower, January 17, 1961. In *Vital Speeches of the Day*. Southold, New York: City News Publishing Co., vol. 27, February 1, 1961, page 229.

7. *Box Kites to Bombers*, an undated publication of the Glenn L. Martin Company, page 22. There is no record of Pond's full name.

8. Caldwell, rather contentious in his later years, became well known for his aviation writing and in 1958 was engaged by the company to write a history. The manuscript, described to this author at the time by the executive who had commissioned it as "too controversial to ever be published in the lifetimes of anyone mentioned in it," disappeared and never saw the light of day, much less publication.

10. THE PUBLIC TAKES FLIGHT

1. Henry Still, *To Ride the Wind*. New York: Julian Messner, 1964, page 150.

2. Ibid., pages 153, 155.

3. Author's interview with Don P. Herron, Easton, Maryland, May 24, 1991.

4. Author's interview with F. G. Foster and his wife Virginia, Orlando, Florida, September 20, 1990.

11. BALTIMORE, AS IN MIDDLE RIVER

1. Wayne Biddle, *Barons of the Sky*. New York: Simon & Schuster, 1991, page 163.
2. Author's interview with F. G. Foster and his wife Virginia, Orlando, Florida, September 20, 1990.
3. Author's interview with Philip H. Goebel, Winter Park, Florida, January 26, 1991.
4. Ibid.
5. Author's interview with Francis P. Vitek, Orlando, Florida, January 22, 1991.
6. Henry Still, *To Ride the Wind*. New York: Julian Messner, 1964, pages 175, 176.
7. Vitek interview.

12. A COLLIER TROPHY AND THE CHINA CLIPPER

1. Henry Still, *To Ride the Wind*. New York: Julian Messner, 1964, page 178.
2. Ibid., pages 180, 181.
3. Ibid., page 183.
4. Terry Gwynn-Jones, *Wings Across the Pacific*. New York: Orion Books, 1933, page 200.
5. Ibid.
6. Ibid., page 203.
7. Ibid., page 209.
8. Ronald W. Jackson, *China Clipper*. New York: Dodd, 1980, page 133. (Reprinted by permission of the author.)
9. Ibid., pages 188 and 191.

13. A "CENTURY OF PROGRESS" IN PAINT

1. World's Fair promotional brochure, *Progress in Industrial Color and Protection*, American Asphalt Paint Company, Chicago, 1933, page 16.
2. Lenox R. Lohr letter to Grover Hermann, 1933, Hermann papers, Mrs. Sally Hermann, Pebble Beach, California.
3. On the occasion of the fiftieth anniversary of The Marietta Paint & Color Company, by then a wholly owned subsidiary of American-Marietta Company, *The Marietta Times*, Marietta, Ohio, Saturday, June 5, 1948.
4. Author's interview with Irving H. Johnson, Monarch Beach, California, October 18, 1990.
5. Author's interview with Mrs. Sally Hermann, Pebble Beach, California, June 28, 1991.

14. BANKRUPTCY'S BRINK AND BASEBALL BATS

1. Author's interview with Francis P. Vitek, Orlando, Florida, January 22, 1991.
2. Henry Still, *To Ride the Wind*. New York: Julian Messner, 1964, page 189.
3. "Brief Financial History of Glenn L. Martin Company, 1929–35 Inclusive," Treasurer's Office, Martin Marietta Corporation.
4. Descriptive pamphlet, Crater of Diamonds State Park, Murfreesboro, Arkansas.
5. Author's interview with Joseph M. Ciekot, Orlando, Florida, January 19, 1991.
6. Author's interview with Franklin A. Gibson, Middle River, Maryland, June 21, 1991.
7. Author's interview with Marge Vance Katonka (Mrs. Frank), Lutherville, Maryland, March 10, 1993.
8. Author's interview with Genevieve Ciekot Jones (Mrs. Frank Jones), Orlando, Florida, April 29, 1992.
9. Gibson interview.
10. Author's interview with Richard E. Weber, Castle Rock, Colorado, June 6, 1991.
11. Author's interview with Harry George, Timonium, Maryland, March 10, 1992.
12. The two Cecil Tennant stories were told by Bobby F. Leonard, who started with the company in 1956 in security, became vice president of personnel in 1981, and was still going strong in 1993.

15. FOUR CORNERS OF THE WORLD

1. Author's interview with F. G. Foster and his wife Virginia, Orlando, Florida, September 20, 1990.

2. Author's interview with Francis O. Furman, Towson, Maryland, June 21, 1991.
3. Ibid.
4. Henry Still, *To Ride the Wind.* New York: Julian Messner, 1964, pages 195, 196.
5. Its testing complete, the flying model was suspended for years from the ceiling of A Building, until it was donated to the Smithsonian Institution in 1953. The Smithsonian in 1987 lent it to the Baltimore Museum of Industry, where a group of dedicated Martin Marietta retirees under the direction of Roy Shine set about a loving restoration of the "Little Mariner." Completed in 1992, it is displayed in the Baltimore museum.
6. Grant Hildebrand, *Designing for Industry: The Architecture of Albert Kahn.* Cambridge, Massachusetts: MIT Press, 1974.
7. After Glenn Martin's retirement in 1952 and his subsequent death in 1955, some of his personal furnishings at the plant were disposed of. Virginia Newton, a secretary to Jess Sweetser for many years, acquired Glenn's office bed, which she uses as an oversized couch or daybed on an enclosed porch at her Coral Gables, Florida, home. The author had the pleasure of sitting on this piece of Glenn Martin history during a 1991 interview, when Newton laughingly recalled the day the movers attempted to disassemble the bed and discovered it was one piece—a rugged, rigid, steel frame that had to be moved as it stood.
8. Still, *To Ride the Wind,* page 201.
9. William H. Jordy, *American Buildings and Their Architects: The Impact of European Modernism in the Mid-Twentieth Century,* Garden City, New York: Anchor Books, 1976.
10. Hildebrand, *Designing for Industry.*
11. "America's Oldest Builder of Bombing Planes Survives Near Bankruptcy to Find Its Factory Booked for the Duration of the War. Unfilled Orders: $66,500,000," *Fortune,* December 1939, pages 73–77, 128, 130.

16. WAR PRODUCTION

1. *The Avenue News,* independent Baltimore County weekly newspaper, vol. 17, no. 39, August 8, 1991.
2. Henry Still, *To Ride the Wind.* New York: Julian Messner, 1964, pages 196, 197.
3. The author was bombardier and the gunnery officer on B-24 and B-32 aircraft during World War II service, 1943 to 1945, and had hands-on experience with the Martin turret, a favorite with aerial gunners because of its ease of operation and reliability.
4. "Maryland Bombers: A Performance Report on Martin-built Ships in Middle East," *The Sunday Sun,* November 16, 1941.
5. Walter Boyne, "Martin's Mercenaries," *Airpower,* vol. 5, no. 1, January 1975, page 22. James S. McDonnell joined Martin at Baltimore in 1933 and left in 1938, shortly after his design effort on the 187, to form his own company in St. Louis, Missouri.
6. Ibid.
7. Release No. 1001, the Glenn L. Martin Company, Baltimore, 1945.
8. Boyne, *Airpower.*
9. Captain Richard C. Knott, U.S. Navy, *The American Flying Boat: An Illustrated History,* Naval Institute Press, Annapolis, Maryland, 1979.
10. Bob Smith, *PBM Mariner in Action,* Squadron/Signal Publications, 1986, page 33.
11. Ibid., page 49.
12. *FlyPast Magazine,* no. 101, December 1989, Key Publishing, Stamford, Lincolnshire, England, and *Water Bombers,* a publication of Forest Industries Flying Tankers, Port Alberni, British Columbia.
13. Ibid.

17. B-26 MARAUDER, THE STUFF OF LEGENDS

1. See Selected Bibliography, page 626.
2. President Franklin Delano Roosevelt toured the B-26 production lines at Middle River and at Omaha during World War II. It was at Omaha, on April 16, 1943, that FDR reportedly confided to plant manager G. T. Willey that the Martin-operated plant

had been selected as a second-source producer of the B-29 Superfortress, including special modifications for a super secret mission.

U.S. Senator Harry S. Truman, who became thirty-third president, later in 1943 chaired an official congressional inquiry into B-26 training accidents.

General Dwight David Eisenhower, who would become the thirty-fourth president, approved as supreme allied commander the recommendation of his air staff that the B-26 be given the pathfinder role on D-Day, 1944. As president, he also inspected the Titan ICBM at Denver.

Texas Congressman Lyndon Baines Johnson, a naval reservist who would become the thirty-sixth president, was sent by FDR that same spring on a fact-finding mission to the Pacific where he flew a combat sortie in the B-26 "Heckling Hare," a harrowing mission that won him the Distinguished Service Medal and became the subject of a book, *The Mission,* by Martin Caiden and Edward Hymoff (see Selected Bibliography).

Richard Milhous Nixon, a young Navy reservist who would become the thirty-seventh president, was stationed at the Middle River plant for a time after the war during government renegotiation of wartime contract profits, including the B-26.

3. Devon Francis, *Flak Bait: The Story of the Men Who Flew the Martin Marauders,* New York: Duell, Sloan and Pearce, 1948.
4. Author's interview with Harry George, Timonium, Maryland, March 10, 1992.
5. Author's interview with Ned I. Stephenson, Littleton, Colorado, June 25, 1991.
6. Author's interview with William L. Compton, Middle River, Maryland, January 30, 1993.
7. "Adolph Vlcek: Still Looking Ahead After 48 Years' Service," *Martin Marietta Today,* no. 3, 1978, pages 10 and 11.
8. Martin Caiden and Edward Hymoff, *The Mission.* Philadelphia, J. B. Lippincott, 1964, pages 122–68.
9. Author's interview with Francis O. Furman, Towson, Maryland, June 21, 1991.
10. J. K. Havener, *The Martin B-26 Marauder.* Blue Ridge Summit, Pennsylvania: Aero, Tab Books, 1988, page 36.
11. General James H. "Jimmy" Doolittle with Carroll V. Glines, *I Could Never Be So Lucky Again.* New York: Bantam Books, 1991, page 228.
12. Ibid., page 333, quoting Paul W. Tibbets with Clair Stebbins and Harry Franken, *The Tibbetts Story.* New York: Stein and Day, 1978, page 123.
13. Henry Still, *To Ride the Wind.* New York: Julian Messner, 1964, pages 213–15.
14. "Marauders Spearhead Invasion," *The Martin Star,* vol. 3, no. 6, July 1944, page 17.
15. Havener, *The Martin B-26 Marauder,* page 201 and cover illustration note on copyright page. Also author's interview with Emmett Lancaster, May 1, 1992. Lancaster's painting, *Lafayette, We Are Here! II,* is reproduced in this book with the permission of the artist. Havener himself was transitional training instructor in the B-26 as well as the pilot of fifty combat missions in the Marauder.
16. Quoted in John O. Moench, "Did the Soviets Receive Under Lend-Lease or Otherwise Any Martin B-26 Marauders?" a paper delivered to a conference of researchers, historians, and others at Colchester, England, April 30, 1992.
17. Havener, *The Martin B-26 Marauder,* pages 5–9.
18. John O. Moench, *Marauder Men: An Account of the Martin B-26 Marauder,* Longwood, Florida: Malia Enterprises, 1989, epilogue, page 419.

18. "ROSIE THE RIVETER" AND OTHER WARTIME PHENOMS

1. Technical Sergeant Ted Ryon, base historian, *History of Building 'D,'* publication of Historical Data and Properties, Offutt Air Force Base, Nebraska, April 15, 1988.
2. *Rosie the Riveter,* words and music by Redd Evans and John Jacob Lobb, Paramount Music Corp., 1944.
3. Henry Still, *To Ride the Wind.* New York: Julian Messner, 1964, page 208.
4. *Why Were You Hired as a Counselor?* personnel handbook, Glenn L. Martin Nebraska Company, 1941. Martin Marietta Museum, Orlando, Florida.

5. Author's interview with Delores Parker, Orlando, Florida, June 20, 1991.

6. Ryon, *History of Building "D."*

7. The term "mission success" dates to June 1966 and the early development of the Titan III, when Martin Marietta formally constituted the "Launch Vehicle Mission Success Organization" at Denver. Walter O. Lowrie was director of that program.

8. Author's interview with Earl R. Willhite, Timonium, Maryland, August 13, 1991.

9. Author's interview with Ira A. Ridenour, Orlando, Florida, January 25, 1991. The presidential confidence G. T. Willey shared was one of his proudest memories, one he kept to himself more than thirty years before mentioning it to Martin colleagues, including Ridenour, whose thirty-seven years of company service, 1939–76, coincided roughly with Willey's tenure.

10. Ryon, *History of Building "D."* Although records of the Martin Company indicate that 536 B-29s were built in the Omaha plant, the number was recorded as 531 in this Air Force publication.

11. Ibid.

12. Richard M. Keenan, "Last of the Superforts: A Story of How the B-29s Lived and Died," *Aerospace Historian*, vol. 17, no. 1, Spring 1970, pages 20–27.

13. Quoted in Russ Brinley, *The Missile Makers*, draft manuscript of a history of the Pershing system, page 15. Unpublished, Martin Marietta Archives.

14. Author's interview with J. Donald Rauth, Bethesda, Maryland, January 22, 1992. Over the years there have been a number of embellishments on the Rauth corn-drilling story, including one that an entire roomful of engineers had been assigned the task. Not so, says the man who was there. "The job was mine alone; I had the whole darn thing."

15. *The Martin Star*, employee magazine, vol. I, no. 1, February 1942, page 2.

16. Ibid., no. 8, September 1942, page 5.

17. Ibid., page 18.

18. Willhite interview.

19. *Air & Space*, August-September 1989, pages 71 and 72.

20. Ronald W. Jackson, *China Clipper*. New York: Dodd, 1980, epilogue, pages 205 and 206.

19. PEACE BUT NOT PROSPERITY

1. G. L. Martin to Frank Garbutt. G. L. Martin papers, container 23, Library of Congress.

2. "Russian Clipper," Glenn L. Martin Company news release #998, Baltimore, Maryland, October 16, 1945.

3. Author's interview with Francis O. Furman, Towson, Maryland, June 21, 1991.

4. Author's interview with C. E. Showalter, Orlando, Florida, June 25, 1991.

5. Author's interview with George W. Trimble, Carefree, Arizona, June 27, 1991.

6. Author's interview with George Rodney, Washington, D.C., March 4 and 19, 1992. The dorsal or top fin on an airplane is the structure that aerodynamically transitions the surface of the fuselage into the vertical stabilizer or tail. It was fairly large on the 2-0-2 but did give the plane a nice sweeping curve up the tail.

7. Author's interview with J. Donald Rauth, Bethesda, Maryland, January 22, 1992.

8. Rodney interview.

9. Ibid.

10. Rauth interview.

11. Rodney interview.

12. Sally Hermann, Grover's widow, was a gracious and generous contributor to this history, sharing pictures, clippings, and other memorabilia of her thirty-four years as Mrs. Grover Hermann.

13. Author's interview with Edwin G. Delcher, Lutherville, Maryland, August 13, 1992. Delcher, an employee of American-Marietta from 1945 to 1966, was controller for the last eight years.

14. Jonny Mop is a trademark of Empire Brushes, Inc.

15. "American-Marietta's Rule for Rapid Rise," *The Wall Street Journal*, Chicago edition, August 2, 1951, page 1. (Reprinted by permission Dow Jones Company, Inc.)

20. MISSILES AND ROCKETS AND AIRPLANES, TOO

1. Alfred Lord Tennyson, "Locksley Hall," line 119.
2. "You Won't Recognize This Airplane," Martin Aircraft advertisement, c. 1945.
3. Henry Still, *To Ride the Wind*. New York: Julian Messner, 1964, page 222.
4. "Many-Purpose Giant Stadium Is Advocated—Roof Held up by Air Pressure," *The Sun*, Baltimore, Maryland, May 2, 1945.
5. Albert W. Quinn, "Now It's June: Stadium Plans Set; Again? Ask Cynics," *The Sun*, June 6, 1948.
6. Kenneth W. Traut, his wife Dollie, and son Rick were the author's first Martin contacts when he joined the company at Canaveral in the winter of 1958 to "interpret" technical engineering jargon to the lay press. Reporters and broadcasters from all over the world converged on Canaveral in those days, hungering for nontechnical explanations of the newfangled missiles and rockets, which blew up as frequently as they worked.
7. Author's interview with William G. Purdy, Golden, Colorado, March 17, 1992.
8. Purdy's recollection of the Viking No. 10 near-disaster and Lieutenant Pitts's rifle-shooting role in the rescue was further amplified by Milton Rosen's own chronicle of that event in his lucid book, *The Viking Rocket Story*, New York: Harper & Brothers, 1955, pages 216 and 220.
9. Lloyd Mallan, *Peace Is a Three-Edged Sword*. Englewood Cliffs, New Jersey: Prentice-Hall, 1964, pages 161–63.
10. Author's interview with George Rodney, Washington, D.C., March 4 and 19, 1992.
11. Shades of Glenn Martin's original factory in Los Angeles when Donald Douglas joined the firm and complained that the only formal engineering stress work involved Glenn and several others jumping up and down on the wings.
12. Author's interview with William B. Johnson, Orlando, Florida, December 5, 1991.

21. RECEIVERSHIP: NEW PILOT AT THE CONTROLS

1. Henry Still, *To Ride the Wind*. New York: Julian Messner, 1964, page 236.
2. Glenn L. Martin, Wright Memorial Lecture, U.S. Chamber of Commerce Auditorium, Washington, D.C., December 17, 1953. Martin Marietta Archives.
3. Ibid.
4. Ibid.
5. Still, *To Ride the Wind*, pages 248 and 249.
6. Author's interview with William L. Compton, Middle River, Maryland, January 30, 1993. Piloting the 2-0-4 on Glenn's final flight were Willard Smith, chief of the corporate aircraft department at that time, and Karl Kruger, former P5M test pilot.
7. *Santa Ana Register*, December 9, 1955.
8. Details of the court settlement of claims on Glenn Martin's estate were given in the following publications: *The Sun:* January 10, 19, February 1, March 3, April 17, July 28, 1956.
   The Evening Sun: July 17, October 20, 1956.
9. Vi Smith, *From Jennies to Jets: The Aviation History of Orange County*. Fullerton, California: Sultana Press, 1985. Contains little-known facts about Della Martin's life after she inherited the bulk of her famous brother's estate, page 27.
10. Glenn L. Martin Papers, Manuscript Room, Library of Congress, James Madison Building, Washington, D.C.

22. ONWARD AND UPWARD AND ONE LAST AIRPLANE

1. William B. Bergen,"New Management Approach at Martin," *Aviation Age*, June 1954, pages 39–47.
2. William B. Harwood, "The SeaMaster—Half Bird, Half Fish," *Sunday Sun* Feature Section, July 27, 1958, page 1.
3. Author's interview with William L. Compton, Middle River, Maryland, January 30, 1993.
4. Author's interview with George Rodney, Washington, D.C., March 4 and 19, 1992.

5. Left to right, standing (all Martin engineers except where noted): Sandy Rosing, Lew Cooper, Kenny Coughlin, Jack Bitner, Bob Cox, Mark Nichols (NACA Langley), Charlie Koch, Jim Decker, Charlie Donlan (NACA), Jack Pearson, Ken Jarmolow, Mel Gough (NACA), Ed Uhl, Pete Clark, Ozzie Zahnow (NACA), George Trimble. Seated (all from Langley Research Center, NACA): Alex Mattson, John Stack, John Parkinson.
6. Richard Knott, "When Boats Flew," *Air & Space/Smithsonian,* June-July, 1986, pages 62–70.
7. James J. Haggerty, historian, Aerospace Industries Association, Washington, D.C., 1992.
8. Left to right: Drs. Kok, Louis Whitten, Joseph LaSalle; Ruth Aranow, Welcome Bender, Dr. Westwood.

23. VANGUARD: IN MORE THAN NAME

1. Roy Calvin, "On the Links and at Business, Jess Sweetser Had an Edge," *Martin Marietta Today,* Number Three, 1980, pages 14, 15.
2. Author's interview with William G. Purdy, Golden, Colorado, March 17, 1992.
3. *The Random House Dictionary of the English Language,* second edition, unabridged, 1987, also lists among definitions of the word *vanguard:* "4. (cap) *Rocketry.* a U.S. three-stage, satellite launching rocket, the first two stages powered by liquid-propellant engines and the third by a solid-propellant engine."
4. Kurt R. Stehling, *Project Vanguard.* Garden City, New York: Doubleday and Company, 1939.
5. Ibid.
6. Quoted in ibid.
7. Quoted in Constance McLaughlin Green and Milton Lomax, *Vanguard: A History.* Washington, D.C.: Smithsonian Institution Press, 1971, foreword.
8. Ibid., The second-stage rocket, developed by Aerojet-General Corporation, and the third-stage solid rocket, developed by Grand Central Rocket Company, subsequently became upper stages of the Air Force–Douglas Thor-Able launch vehicle, which compiled an impressive string of successful space launches extending throughout the second half of the century.
9. Green and Lomax, *Vanguard: A History.*
10. Stehling, *Project Vanguard,* pages 254–56.

24. TIME OF THE TITAN

1. Author's interview with William G. Purdy, Golden Colorado, March 17, 1992.
2. Ramo-Wooldridge's technical advisory task for the Air Force was spun off in 1957 as Space Technology Laboratory, which in 1960 evolved into the Aerospace Corporation. Meanwhile, R-W's merger with Thompson Products in 1958 created Thompson-Ramo-Wooldridge, which later became simply TRW, Inc.
3. Purdy interview.
4. Ibid.
5. Author's interview with Don P. Herron, Easton, Maryland, May 24, 1991. An employee from 1956 to 1968 and the first public relations director of the Denver operation, Herron credits Cal Snyder with a major role in Martin's locating in Colorado.
6. *30 Years of Progress,* Martin Marietta Denver Aerospace, July 1986, page 3.
7. Author's interview with Laurence J. Adams, Potomac, Maryland, February 3, 1992.
8. Ibid. Carnahan would go on to direct the entire Titan III program for a time, then manage California launch operations at Vandenberg Air Force Base, eventually chairing, as vice president, a corporation-wide Environmental Management Task Force.
9. Author's interview with David S. LeVine, Bethesda, Maryland, April 30, 1993.
10. Ibid. (Richard C. Lea, a company engineer, 1959–74, died in 1987.)
11. Martin was the first contractor to formalize the public relations function at Cape Canaveral primarily as press relations. References to Yates and the press are personal recollections of the author, that first young PR man.

12. LeVine interview.
13. Author's interview with Caleb B. Hurtt, Bethesda, Maryland, March 26, 1992.
14. Arthur C. Morrisey, *Martin Marietta Titan Launch History,* Denver, May 11, 1993.
15. Martin Caidin, *Rendezvous in Space.* New York: E. P. Dutton & Co., 1962. Caidin, a pilot, friend, and avid chronicler of the aerospace scene, also wrote *Mission,* with Edward Hymoff, a story of B-26s in the Pacific and of Lyndon Johnson as a young naval officer on a presidential fact-finding mission. *Cyborg,* published in 1972, among his more than 140 fiction and nonfiction books, probably created his largest audience; it became the basis for the long-running television series, *The Million Dollar Man.*
16. Laurence J. Adams, Fellow AIAA, "The Evolution of the Titan Rocket—Titan I to Titan II," paper delivered at the 41st Congress of the International Astronautical Federation, Dresden, Germany, October 6–12, 1990.
17. Herron interview.
18. Adams, "The Evolution of the Titan Rocket."
19. *30 Years of Progress,* page 8.
20. Author's interview with Vernon R. Rawlings, Towson, Maryland, January 12, 1991.
21. Purdy interview.
22. Author's interview with Robert Molloy, Bethesda, Maryland, June 11, 1991.
23. Robert W. Morra, "Mission Success," a paper prepared for a Martin Marietta Senior Management Meeting, Scottsdale, Arizona, March, 1991.
24. Walter O. Lowrie, untitled presentation, National Security Industrial Association, Washington, D.C., May, 1978.
25. Author interview with Arthur L. Welch, Bethesda, July 9, 1993. Welch, who would spend thirty-seven years with Martin Marietta, 1957–93, was a particular Martinphile having grown up in Liberal, Kansas, the scene of much of Glenn Martin's growing up.

25. PERSHING: A GAMBLE THAT PAID OFF

1. Russ Brinley, "The Missile Makers," an incomplete, unpublished manuscript history of the Pershing program. Martin Marietta Orlando Archives, chapter 4, page 35. Based on interviews with Medaris, Rudolph, Stark, and other program principals, 1984. A freelance writer, Brinley was a public relations representative at Orlando in the 1980s.
2. Linton Allen actually was the second banker the Martin people called on. The first had shown little interest.
3. Mark Andrews, "Flashback, Orange County History," *Orlando Sentinel,* December 6, 1992.
4. Author's interview with Philip H. Goebel, Winter Park, Florida, January 26, 1991.
5. Author's interview with Francis P. Vitek, Orlando, Florida, January 22, 1991.
6. Author's interview with C. E. Showalter, Orlando, Florida, June 25, 1991.
7. Ibid., Showalter remained as enthusiastic and dedicated even in retirement after forty-three years with the company. In 1987 he organized a team of approximately thirty retirees who painstakingly and with much love constructed a full-size replica of Glenn L. Martin's original aeroplane, later displayed in air shows as far distant as San Diego.
8. Brinley manuscript, chapter 3, pages 10 and 11.
9. Ibid.
10. Ibid., Dr. Arthur Rudolph spent more than forty years in the U.S. government's employ, contributing significantly not only to the Redstone, Jupiter, and Pershing programs but to the mighty Saturn launch vehicle that put Americans on the Moon and the Space Shuttle that followed. He was deported to Germany in the late 1980s after the Justice Department investigated charges that during World War II he had abused prisoners at the Mittelwerk underground V-2 rocket complex when he was technical director. The octogenarian German scientist was reported by Huntsville colleagues in 1992 to be very unhappy and desperately trying to return to his adopted home in the United States.
11. Ibid., chapter 3, page 14.

12. Ibid., page 16.
13. Ibid.
14. Author's interview with Edward J. Cottrell, Winter Park, Florida, March 20, 1993. Cottrell retired from the Army in 1960 after seventeen years to become director of public relations for Martin's Orlando division, a position from which he retired in 1983.
15. President George W. Bush, remarks, reported in *The Eagle*, Martin Marietta, Orlando, May 31, 1991.

26. MAKING GOOD ON THE PROMISE

1. Russ Brinley, "The Missile Makers," an incomplete, unpublished manuscript history of the Pershing program. Martin Marietta Orlando Archives, 1984, page 20.
2. Ibid., page 21.
3. Pershing II's accuracy was confirmed by David G. Harris, Public Affairs Officer, Army Missile Command, Huntsville, Alabama.
4. Brinley manuscript, page 16.

27. "ZERO DEFECTS" WAS INVENTED HERE

1. Author's interview with Joseph S. Taylor, Oneida, Florida, March 15, 1993. Taylor spent forty-six years with the company, most of it in quality control—first in Baltimore, then in Canaveral, again in Baltimore, and for his last twenty-plus years before retiring in 1986 in Orlando. Oldtimers in the company remember him as Joe Kraczyk; the name translated as "tailor" in the Polish heritage he prided. Kraczyk was frequently mispronounced and was hardly ever spelled correctly, and the family had the name legally changed to Taylor.
2. James Halpin, *Zero Defects—A New Dimension in Quality Assurance*, McGraw Hill, 1966. "Pershing's 25th Anniversary," *Martin Marietta News*, Orlando Aerospace Edition, December 3, 1982, page 15.
3. Crosby sold his quality consultancy, Phil Crosby Associates, to a British firm in 1992 and was living in semiretirement in Orlando.
4. Russ Brinley, "The Missile Makers," an incomplete, unpublished manuscript history of the Pershing program. Martin Marietta Orlando Archives, 1984, pages 17 and 18.
5. Ibid., page 14.
6. Taylor interview.

28. MARTIN MEETS MARIETTA

1. Author's interview with Mrs. Sally Hermann, Pebble Beach, California, June 28, 1991.
2. Clarence Miles, who died in 1977 at the age of eighty, was prominent in many city and state activities and was a major player in putting together the complicated merger that resulted in Martin Marietta Corporation. He perhaps is most popularly known as the man who brought major league baseball back to Baltimore in 1953 by organizing the group of investors, including George Bunker, that bought out the St. Louis Browns and moved the American League franchise east to become the Baltimore Orioles. Blakeford, the Miles home on the Eastern Shore, burned to the ground in 1970 and was replaced by White Banks, a lovely Georgian home where Eleanor Miles still resided at the time this book was written. She graciously supplied some of the details concerning the Donoho-Miles connection.
3. 1961 Annual Report, Martin Marietta Corporation.
4. Notes and memos, Harry L. Smith, associate general counsel of Martin Marietta Corporation, a thirty-three-year employee, 1958 to 1991.
5. 1968 Annual Report, Martin Marietta Corporation.
6. Charles J. V. Murphy, "The Millions Under Martin Marietta's Mattress," *Fortune*, November 1963, page 135.
7. Author's interview with W. Trent Ragland, Raleigh, North Carolina, December 8, 1992.

8. Ibid.
9. Ibid.
10. Ibid.
11. Trent Ragland became president of Superior Stone Company in 1954 after his father and uncle were shot to death by an escaped convict. A distinguished North Carolinian, active in the civic and political life of his city and state, he continued to run the company as an element of Martin Marietta until 1977, when he relinquished active control and took an advisory role as senior vice president.
12. Ragland interview.
13. Author's interview with Thomas G. Pownall, Washington, D.C., January 28, 1992.
14. Ragland interview.

29. GEMINI: TWO BY TWO INTO SPACE

1. Author's interview with Leonard Mitarotondo, Baltimore, Maryland, January 27, 1993.
2. Author's interview with Bastian B. Hello, Bethesda, Maryland, January 30, 1993.
3. *Gemini-Titan II Air Force Launch Vehicle Press Handbook*, Second Edition, Manned Flight, Final Revision, Martin Marietta Corporation Baltimore Division, February 2, 1967, page B-10.
4. Hello interview.
5. The $25,000 deducted from the maximum fee was on the GT-6 mission, but it was not for premature drop of the tail plug, which was properly sensed by the MDS, resulting in the engine cutoff. The penalty was for a red plastic dust cover, found on subsequent inspection, lodged in an opening of the gas generator. The dust cover, not readily visible, had been put in place properly during manufacture and assembly of the engine to ensure cleanliness of the generator during shipment and prelaunch testing. Less than half an inch in diameter, it escaped detection during subsequent checks not only by the engine maker's people but by Martin, Air Force, and NASA inspectors. Had the tail plug itself not caused the abort, engine shutdown still would have occurred automatically when the MDS detected the plugged opening.
6. "Florida Magazine" cover profile and interview with O. E. Pat Tibbs, *The Orlando Sentinel*, August 15, 1965.
7. Author's interview with Don P. Herron, Easton, Maryland, May 24, 1991.
8. Transcript of hearings, Committee on Aeronautical and Space Sciences, United States Senate, Washington, D.C., May 9, 1967, pages 508, 509.
9. Author's interview with George W. Trimble, Carefree, Arizona, June 27, 1991.

30. THE INNOVATORS: PRIME, SNAP, AND 199B

1. Author's interview with Joseph M. Verlander, Orlando, Florida, August 29, 1991.
2. Ibid.
3. Elliott H. Miller conversation with Dr. Jerome G. Morse, Denver, July 1, 1993.

31. A BALANCING ACT AND ADVENTURES IN ALUMINUM

1. Author's interview with John T. de Visser, Auteuil-le-Roi, France, April 11, 1992.
2. "Even Before Cement, Dale Mitchell Was a Star Performer," *Martin Marietta Today*, Number Three, 1978, page 14.
3. Author's conversation with Natalie Bunker Stoddard, Washington, D.C., April 6, 1993. The bottle of ketchup was a bit of nostalgia on the part of the crew, reflecting Bunker's first flight on the corporate airplane twenty-five years earlier. (See Chapter 28.)

32. SKYLAB—THE FIRST SPACE STATION AND "ET"

1. Author's interview with Robert Molloy, Bethesda, Maryland, June 11, 1991.
2. Author's interview with Thomas G. Pownall, Washington, D.C., January 28, 1992.
3. Molloy interview.
4. Author's interview with Caleb B. Hurtt, Bethesda, Maryland, March 26, 1992.

5. Leland F. Belew, *Skylab, Our First Space Station*. Washington, D.C.: George C. Marshall Space Flight Center, National Aeronautics and Space Administration, 1976, preface, page v.
6. Ibid., pages 134 and 135.
7. Pownall interview.
8. Through January 1993, fifty-three Space Shuttles had been flown.

33. BUCK ROGERS AND VIKINGS ON MARS

1. "Buck Rogers" was a hero of newspaper comic strips, comic books, radio, and early movie and television serials in the 1930s and '40s. He performed interplanetary feats that included self-propulsion packs not unlike the MMU. In 1993 the corporation's advertising agency, VanSant, Dugdale of Baltimore, obtained permission to use some of the old TV film in a commercial featuring the MMU as part of a corporate advertising series, "Masterminding Technology."
2. The picture of the MMU on the jacket of this book is of Bruce McCandless at his farthest point, approximately a football field in length, from the Shuttle Orbiter *Challenger* on that historic first flight on February 7, 1984.
3. Astronauts Ronald E. McNair and Francis R. Scobee died when the *Challenger* was destroyed during a launch accident on January 28, 1986.
4. Author's interview with Bruce McCandless II, Denver, Colorado, June 25, 1991.
5. Author's interview with Walter William Bollendonk, Denver, Colorado, June 25, 1991.
6. Ibid.
7. The 1932 Collier Trophy award to Glenn L. Martin for development of a high-speed, weight-carrying airplane, the B-10 Bomber, was the first time the company was so honored. The company also developed, or was a member of the developing team, for these subsequent Collier Trophy awards:

1936	Pan American Airways for "establishment of the transpacific airplane and the successful execution of extended overwater navigation in the regular operation thereof" (the Martin China Clipper)
1965	Gemini, all the program teams, represented by NASA's James Webb and Hugh Dryden (Martin Marietta for Gemini-Titan Launch Vehicle)
1973	Skylab (Martin Marietta for the Multiple Docking Adapter)
1976	B1 Bomber, U.S. Air Force/Rockwell and the industry team (Martin Marietta for vertical and horizontal stabilizers and forward vanes)
1981	Space Shuttle, NASA, Rockwell, Martin Marietta, Thiokol, and the entire government/industry team (External Tank)
1984	Manned Maneuvering Unit, NASA and Martin Marietta, astronaut Bruce McCandless II, program director Walter W. Bollendonk, and NASA's Charles E. Whitsett, Jr.

8. William R. Corliss, *The Viking Mission to Mars*. Washington, D.C.: National Aeronautics and Space Administration, SP-334, 1974.
9. George Alexander, "Viking Science: Tantalizing; Viking Scientists: Cautious," *Martin Marietta Today*, Number Three, 1976, pages 7–11. (At the time a science writer for the *Los Angeles Times*, Alexander was a longtime reporter of the space scene and later became the public affairs officer for the Jet Propulsion Laboratory at Pasadena, California.)
10. Roy Calvin, "Intellect and Ingenuity Triumphant," *Martin Marietta Today*, Number Three, 1976, pages 2–6. Roy Calvin, at the time the corporation's public relations vice president, was a former wire service and magazine writer. He retired in 1983.
11. Alexander, *Martin Marietta Today*, page 8.
12. Author's interview with A. Thomas Young, Bethesda, Maryland, May 7, 1993. Young, retired from NASA after twenty years of service, joined Martin Marietta in 1982 as vice president of research and engineering. He successively headed the Baltimore division, was president of the Missile and Electronic Systems Group at Orlando, and in 1989 became president and chief operating officer of the corporation. Other NASA members of the Viking team who also joined the company included Jim Martin, who was vice president and general manager of Baltimore operations until

his retirement in 1983, and Dr. Noel Hinners, NASA's associate administrator for space science, who joined the company in 1989 at Bethesda as vice president of strategic planning and later became chief scientist for astronautics at Denver.

13. "Super-outstanding Flight Team Is Key to Mars Mission, *Martin Marietta Today,* Number Three, 1976, page 18.

14. John Noble Wilford, editorial, *The New York Times,* July 21, 1975, page 1. Wilford, who has been covering the space beat since 1964 and won a Pulitzer Prize in 1984 for his scientific reporting, made his first trip to Canaveral in 1985 to cover the historic rendezvous mission of Gemini 7 and 6 (see Chapter 29). He has also written five books and collaborated on three others.

15. Martin Marietta shared Goddard Trophy honors four more times in the next fifteen years:

1977	Viking Project team
1980	As a member of the NASA/JPL Voyager Project team
1981	Again as a member of the Voyager Project team
1991	Norman R. Augustine, chairman of Martin Marietta Corporation
1992	Magellan Project team leaders including Charles D. Brown, the retired project manager, and J. Franklin McKinney, his successor as project manager.

34. NEW HORIZONS IN ELECTRONICS

1. Author's interview with Robert J. Whalen, La Jolla, California, March 4, 1993.
2. Ibid. The company built 39,611 Bullpup air-to-surface missiles, 1,244 Lacrosse surface-to-surface missiles, 8,309 Walleye, and 12,500 Shillelagh missiles.
3. Ibid.
4. Ibid.
5. Author's interview with Joseph N. Kremonas, Bethesda, June 4, 1993.
6. The operational success of TADS/PNVS in combat drew rave reviews from helicopter pilots and field commanders in Operation Desert Storm. See Chapters 39 and 40.
7. Whalen interview.
8. Air Force fighter pilots testified to LANTIRN's effectiveness in Operation Desert Storm. See Chapter 38.
9. Whalen interview.
10. Ibid.
11. See Chapter 38, "Desert Storm."
12. Augustine said the significance of the initials ADTO never occurred to him until he saw it in the manuscript of this book.
13. Whalen interview.

35. AN UNWELCOME SUITOR AND "PACMAN"

1. See Selected Bibliography.
2. Author's interview with Thomas G. Pownall, Washington, D.C., September 12, 1992.
3. Tim Metz and Virginia Inman, "Martin Marietta Spurns Bendix Offer as Inadequate, Countering with $75-a-Share Bid for Control of Suitor," *The Wall Street Journal,* August 31, 1982, page 3. (Reprinted by permission Dow Jones Company, Inc.)
4. Pownall interview.
5. Ibid.
6. Peter F. Hartz, *Merger: The Exclusive Inside Story of the Bendix–Martin Marietta Takeover War.* New York: William Morrow and Company, 1985, pages 32, 50, 51. (Copyright © 1985 by Peter F. Hartz, reprinted by permission of William Morrow and Company, Inc.)
7. The "spokesman" during the entire takeover battle was the author.
8. Author's conversation with Marianna Dickie, Bethesda, Maryland, December 12, 1992.
9. Hartz, *Merger,* pages 67–69.
10. Ibid., pages 70, 71.
11. Bob Powell, who retired from the corporation in 1992, vouched for the accuracy of

heroics attributed to Tom Mendenhall and Doris Rush and for the essence of the quotations used here, which were so skillfully woven into the narrative of, and are hereby credited to, Peter Hartz's gripping book *Merger*.

12. Hope Lampert, *Till Death Do Us Part: Bendix vs. Martin Marietta*. San Diego, California: Harcourt Brace Jovanovich, 1983, page 49. (Copyright © 1983 by Hope Lampert, reprinted by permission Harcourt, Brace & Company.)

13. "Martin Marietta Sets $75 a Share Offer for Bendix," Dow Jones News Wire, 4:18 P.M. Eastern Daylight Time, August 30, 1982.

14. Pownall interview.

15. Hartz, *Merger*, pages 13–15.

16. *The Wall Street Journal*, September 8, 1982.

17. Martin Marietta files, Bethesda, Maryland.

18. Hartz, *Merger*, pages 156, 157.

19. Martin Marietta files.

20. Pownall interview.

21. Interview with John T. de Visser, Auteuil-le-Roi, France, April 11, 1992.

22. *The Wall Street Journal*, September 27, 1982.

23. Sandra Salmans, *The New York Times*, September 11, 1993.

24. Hartz, *Merger*, page 165.

25. Ibid., page 183.

26. Ibid., page 185.

27. Allan Sloan, *Three Plus One Equals Billions*. New York: Arbor House, 1983, page 204. (Copyright © 1983 by Allan Sloan, reprinted by permission of William Morrow and Company, Inc.)

28. Tim Metz, *The Wall Street Journal*, September 14, 1982, and Stacie Knable, *The Evening Sun*, Baltimore, Maryland, September 14, 1982.

29. Hartz, *Merger*, pages 327, 328.

30. Author's interview with James D. Simpson, Washington, D.C., March 14, 1993.

31. Pownall interview.

32. Ibid.

33. Hartz, *Merger*, page 332.

34. Ibid., page 333.

35. Ibid., pages 336 and 337.

36. Martin Marietta files.

37. Pownall interview.

38. Author was present.

39. Ibid.

40. Pownall interview. The tie was returned to Jack Byrne after Pownall had it mounted in a glass case with a small metal hammer and the inscription *Break in case of emergency*. It hangs on the wall of Byrne's office.

41. Dickie interview.

42. Pownall interview.

43. Ibid.

36. WINDOWS OF OPPORTUNITY

1. VanSant Dugdale, the company's Baltimore advertising agency of record—in the post-takeover fight period, as it is today—conceived and executed all of Glenn Martin's advertising programs during World War II and postwar into the fifties.

2. 1983 Annual Report, Martin Marietta Corporation, Chairman's letter, page 12. The cover photograph of the 1983 annual report showed three flagpoles flying (from left to right) Old Glory, the flag of Maryland, and a third presented to the company after the fight—the Gadsden "Don't Tread On Me" flag depicting a coiled rattle-snake on a field of gold. (See photo.)

3. Author's interview with A. Thomas Young, Bethesda, Maryland, May 7, 1993.

4. Author's personal recollection.

5. Author's conversation with Clyde C. Hopkins, Oak Ridge, Tennessee, March 14, 1993.

6. Author's conversation with Brian N. Etheridge, Potomac, Maryland, March 20, 1993.

7. Author's interview with Arthur E. Koski, Denver, Colorado, March 2, 1993.
8. Author's interview with Shirley Frock Prutch, Taneytown, Maryland, March 20, 1993.
9. Ibid.
10. Author's conversation with George H. Perlman, Bethesda, Maryland, April 16, 1993.
11. Author's conversation with William D. Keough, investor relations director, Bethesda, Maryland, April 25, 1993.

37. TITAN REDUX AND MAGELLAN

1. James D. Vallela, "Cheers and Tears as Magellan Reaches Venus," *Martin Marietta Today*, Number Three, 1990, page 1.
2. Ibid., page 3.
3. John Noble Wilford, *The New York Times*, October 30, 1991.
4. Ibid.
5. Author's interview with James Neuman, Pasadena, California, March 18, 1991.
6. Author's interviews with Cynthia Haynie and Michael Bailey, Pasadena, California, March 18, 1991.
7. Ibid.
8. It was the fifth time that the company had been honored with the Goddard Trophy. (See Chapter 33, Note 15, for a complete list.)

38. ESCAPE IN THE DESERT

1. Author's interview with Robert L. Boddiford, Orlando, Florida, June 18, 1991. This interview also was the source of all other Boddiford quotations and dialogue in this section.

39. "HIS EYES AND HIS VOICE"

1. Author's interview with Richard A. Howell, Orlando, August 29, 1991.
2. Ibid.
3. Remarks of President George W. Bush on the occasion of a visit to the Raytheon Corporation, Lexington, Massachusetts, February 15, 1991.
4. Author's interview with Luciano Mazzonetto, Orlando, Florida, August 29, 1991.
5. Recorded comments of Air Force Captain Matt Riehl and Major Larry Widner, on a visit with Martin Marietta employees who built the LANTIRN system, Orlando, Florida, April 1991.
6. Author's interview with Murray W. Garbrick, Orlando, Florida, August 29, 1991.
7. Author's interview with Allan M. Norton, Orlando, Florida, August 29, 1991.

40. MISSION SUCCESS

1. Author's interview with John E. Conn, Orlando, Florida, August 29, 1991. Conn represented the company in Vietnam for Marine evaluation of a laser designator.
2. Author's interview with Earl Moody, Orlando, August 29, 1991.
3. Combat Appraisal of Tracy Cooper by Lieutenant Colonel Roger E. McCauley, commander of the 229th Helicopter Battalion, Saudi Arabia, March 28, 1991.
4. Performance statistics for each system by John E. Conn, Orlando, August 29, 1991.

41. PUTTING IT TOGETHER

1. The title of Part X is credited to Anne Croswell, author of *Sidekicks, or A Merger of Marvelous Magnitude: A Comic Opera of White Knights, Fair Maidens, and Golden Parachutes in the Manner of Gilbert and Sullivan* (New York: Workman Publishing, 1983). Although it doesn't claim to be, this work is a delightful spoof of the Martin Marietta–Bendix fight. It bears no resemblance to the Martin Marietta–GE Aerospace union, which truly was textbook in execution and marvelous in magnitude.
2. Croswell, *Sidekicks*.
3. Author's interview with Norman R. Augustine, Bethesda, Maryland, December 7, 1992.

4. Author's interview with A. Thomas Young, Bethesda, Maryland, May 7, 1993.
5. Augustine interview.
6. Ibid.
7. Author's interview with Marcus C. Bennett, Bethesda, Maryland, December 14, 1992.
8. Augustine interview.
9. Bennett interview.
10. Augustine interview.
11. Ibid.
12. Bennett interview.
13. Author's interview with Frank H. Menaker, Bethesda, Maryland, December 7, 1992.
14. Augustine interview.
15. Ibid.
16. Dammerman story told by Augustine, Bennett, and Welch.
17. Author's interview with John F. Welch, Jr., Fairfield, Connecticut, May 17, 1993.
18. Bennett interview.

42. A NEW BEGINNING

1. Author's interview with Mark Potts, Washington, D.C., May 24, 1993.
2. Author's interview with A. Thomas Young, Bethesda, Maryland, May 7, 1993.
3. *Introducing Our Partners: In the New Martin Marietta,* Martin Marietta Corporation, February 23, 1993.
4. Young interview.
5. Author's interview with John F. Welch, Jr., Fairfield, Connecticut, May 17, 1993.
6. Ibid.
7. Ibid.
8. *Engineering News Record,* vol. 63, no. 1, 1911, pages 8–11.
9. "They're Turbosupercharged," publication of General Electric, Schenectady, New York, November 1943.
10. The Mars Observer Titan III launch vehicle was the last of the "Commercial Titans." The upper stage was the Transfer Orbit Stage, TOS, built by Martin Marietta for Orbital Sciences Corporation.
11. Welch interview.
12. Various investment newsletters:
    Michael LaTronica, *Intra-Day Note,* Martin Simpson & Co., Inc., November 24, 1992. Peter Aseritis, *Equity Research,* First Boston, November 25, 1992. Lior Bergman, "Martin Marietta Promising Earning Power at a Discount," Oppenheimer & Co., Inc., January 27, 1993.
13. Augustine interview.
14. Leased wire dispatch, *Chicago Tribune,* July 23. Undated scrapbook collection of clippings, circa 1915, Glenn L. Martin Papers, Library of Congress.
15. James J. Haggerty, Aerospace Industries Association, Washington, D.C., 1993.
16. Frederick O. Barnum III, *His Master's Voice in America.* Camden, New Jersey: General Electric Company, 1991, pages 2, 3.

CENTERFOLD ILLUSTRATIONS

"Genealogy of an Industry," centerfold, created by Stead Design Associates, New Milford, Connecticut, is based on a Lockheed Georgia Company illustration, "Genealogy of Major American Aircraft Manufacturers," circa 1900, courtesy of Robert A. Fisette.

"Product Chronology," graphic history, centerfold reverse, designed and assembled by Clifford Stead and Serge Ghio, is based on graphic input and other information furnished by Thomas R. Gagnier of Orlando and Oak Ridge, Sanford A. Friedenthal of Orlando, and by Robert Murray and the Astronautics Graphics Group, Denver.

Selected Bibliography

■

Leland F. Belew, *Skylab, Our First Space Station*. Washington, D.C.: George C. Marshall Space
    Flight Center, National Aeronautics and Space Administration, 1976.
Wayne Biddle, *Barons of the Sky*. New York: Simon & Schuster, 1991.
Steven Birdsall, *B-26 Marauder in Action*. Squadron/Signal, 1981.
Martin Caidin, *Rendezvous in Space*. New York: E. P. Dutton & Co., 1962.
Martin Caidin and Edward Hymoff, *The Mission*. Philadelphia: J. B. Lippincott Company,
    1964.
William R. Corliss, *The Viking Mission to Mars*. Washington, D.C.: National Aeronautics and
    Space Administration, SP-334, 1974.
Anne Croswell, *Sidekicks, or A Merger of Marvelous Magnitude: A Comic Opera of White Knights,
    Fair Maidens, and Golden Parachutes in the Manner of Gilbert and Sullivan*. New York:
    Workman Publishing, 1983.
General James H. "Jimmy" Doolittle with Carroll V. Glines, *I Could Never Be So Lucky Again*.
    New York: Bantam Books, 1991.
Devon Francis, *Flak Bait: The Story of the Men Who Flew the Martin Marauders*. New York:
    Duell, Sloan and Pearce, 1948.
Roger A. Freeman, *B-26 Marauder at War*. New York: Charles Scribner & Sons, 1978.
Constance McLaughlin Green and Milton Lomax, *Vanguard: A History*. Washington, D.C.:
    Smithsonian Institution Press, 1971.
Terry Gwynn-Jones, *Wings Across the Pacific*. New York: Orion Books, 1933.
Peter F. Hartz, *Merger: The Exclusive Inside Story of the Bendix–Martin Marietta Takeover War*.
    New York: William Morrow and Company, 1985.
J. K. Havener, *The Martin B-26 Marauder*. Blue Ridge Summit, Pennsylvania: Aero, Tab
    Books, 1988.
Ronald W. Jackson, *China Clipper*. New York: Dodd, 1980.
Hope Lampert, *Till Death Do Us Part: Bendix vs. Martin Marietta*. New York: Harcourt Brace
    Jovanovich, 1983.
Lloyd Mallan, *Peace Is a Three-Edged Sword*. Englewood Cliffs, New Jersey: Prentice-Hall,
    1964.
Glenn L. Martin Company, *Box Kites to Bombers*, undated, c. 1950.
John O. Moench, *Marauder Men: An Account of the Martin B-26 Marauder*. Longwood,
    Florida: Malia Enterprises, 1989.

SELECTED BIBLIOGRAPHY

Milton Rosen, *The Viking Rocket Story*. New York: Harper & Brothers, 1955.

Allan Sloan, *Three Plus One Equals Billions: The Bendix–Martin Marietta War*. New York: Arbor House, 1983.

Bob Smith, *PBM Mariner in Action*. Squadron/Signal Publications, 1986.

Vi Smith, *From Jennies to Jets: The Aviation History of Orange County*. Fullerton, California: Sultana Press, 1985.

Kurt R. Stehling, *Project Vanguard*. Garden City, New York: Doubleday and Company, 1939.

Henry Still, *To Ride the Wind*. New York: Julian Messner, 1964./

Acknowledgments

■

In addition to those credited in the "Preface," the text, and the "Notes," the author is indebted to John D. Goodlette, Dr. Noel W. Hinners, and Joseph N. Kremonas for their thoughtful readings of the manuscript. The following people also made valued contributions to the preparation of this book:

■

At Martin Marietta: The late Jean Adams, Russell Arledge, Kevin Baker, William Barrett, Raymond V. Bartlett, Barbara Berger, Paul B. Blumhardt, Thomas L. Branigan, Tim Brenner, Peggy Carr, Audrey Carter, Rosalind Cheslock, Gay Chin, Charles Cignatti, Laura J. Cooper, Jacques H. Croom, Robert W. Drury, William Ewig, James Fink, Katie Finneran, Gareth D. Flora, Benjamin E. Franklin, Charles Glisson, Dr. David L. Goldheim, Carol A. Grametbauer, Scott Hazelwood, Janice K. Henry, C. Randy Huff, Roger A. Isabelle, J. Richard Jaeger, James Johnson, Cliff G. Kelley, Edward L. Knowles, Gerald R. Langheim, Saul R. Locke, Ronda Maisch, Gary P. Mann, Alex Melewski, Robert B. Morra, Barbara O'Brien, Helen Parton, William Peters, Pauline Reed, David Rhodes, Robert W. Riegel, James M. Ritter, Jean Ross, Jeremy Roth, Edward M. Schilling, Ruby C. Selby, Ann Smith, Donald R. Steffanus, James A. Sterhardt, Richard D. Tarallo, James Tierney, David Welch, Arthur L. Welch, Melissa Wilson, Charles O. Wingate. *At Callicoon:* Edith Curtis Craig, Florence Curtis, Mary Curtis, Robert Curtis, Howard Henry Hermann, Joel Wagner. *At the Library of Congress:* Fred Bowman, Charles Kelly, Mary Wolfskill.

At Simon & Schuster: Laureen A. Connelly, Suzanne Donahue, Leslie Ellen, Frederic W. Hills, Philip Metcalf, Eve Metz, Theodore Marcus.

Elsewhere: Ruth Bouldes, Larry Cohen, Robin Davenport-Patterson, Charles C. Dickson, Pearly Draughn, Rose Ann Ferrick, Michael Furman, Eric Falk, Carroll V. Glines, John Hartnett, William Herfeldt, Dave Hutchins, Julian R. Levine, Joseph Mizrahi, Linda Pajusi, Norman S. Portenoy, Dr. Edmund T. Rumble, Gary Still, Jeff Tomich, William Welling, Carolyn White, George O. Wiley, and a host of others.

INDEX

■

RAISE HEAVEN AND EARTH

Picture Credits

AP Wide World Photos: 314, 582
Airpower: 183
Army CW3 Dave Bouse: 557
Robert Boddiford: 537, 544
Mary Curtis: 24
Nancy Manship Davenport: insert, no. 27
© *The Detroit News,* 488
Engineering News Record: 590
First American Title Insurance Company: 35, 48, 54, 81
Gareth Flora: 129; insert, no. 15
Forest Industries Flying Tankers Ltd.: insert, no. 17
Francis O. Furman: 166
GE: 584, 586, 593
GE Engine Division: 592
Harry George: 267
Frank Gibson: 155
Mrs. Sally Hermann: 25, 59, 139, 140, 143
Don Herron: 306
Genevieve Ciekot Jones: 153
Emmett Lancaster: 210
Library of Congress: 69, 76, 82, 104
Los Angeles Times. 64
John Montague: 563, 580
NASA: 289, 290, 369, 380, 388, 391, 424, 524; insert, nos. 41, 43, 45, 46

NASA/JPL: 438; insert, no. 50
The New York Times Company, (© 1976/91, reprinted by permission): 443
Rockwell International: 88; insert, no. 11
George Rodney: 277 (below), 279
Leslie de Visser Rhody: 87
The San Diego Union Tribune: 80
Sipa Press/Bill Gentile: 451
Sullivan County Democrat: 51
©Fred Sutter: 533, 551
©Sygma: insert, no. 51
Time Warner Inc. (© 1939, reprinted by permission): 175
Tribune Media Services (reprinted by permission): 480
UPI/Bettmann: 97, left
U.S. Air Force: 203, 323, 325 (4 photos), 387, 522; insert, no. 39
U.S. Army: 297, 346, 547; insert, nos. 36, 38, 48
U.S. Department of Energy: 396, 506; insert, no. 42, 44
John T. de Visser: insert, no. 40
Charles "Bucky" Wingate: 147
Bob Witkowski: 274
©Brian Wolff: 559

ILLUSTRATIONS

"Genealogy of an Industry," barrelfold front, created by Stead Design Associates, New Milford, Connecticut, is based on a Lockheed Georgia Company illustration, "Genealogy of Major American Aircraft Manufacturers," circa 1900, courtesy of Robert A. Fisette.

"Product Chronology" graphic history, barrelfold back, designed and assembled by Clifford Stead and Serge Ghio, is based on graphic input and other information furnished by Thomas R. Gagnier of Orlando and Oak Ridge, Sanford A. Friedenthal of Orlando, and by Robert Murray and the Astronautics Graphics Group, Denver.